The
Perceptive I

The Perceptive I

A Personal Reader and Writer

EDMUND J. FARRELL
University of Texas at Austin

JAMES E. MILLER, JR.
University of Chicago

NTC Publishing Group
Lincolnwood, Illinois USA

Acknowledgments for literary selections begin on page 811, which is to be considered an extension of this copyright page.

ISBN 0-8442-5957-8 (student text)
ISBN 0-8442-5958-6 (instructor's edition)

Executive Editor: John T. Nolan
Sponsoring Editor: Marisa L. L'Heureux
Design management: Ophelia M. Chambliss
Cover and interior design: Megan Keane DeSantis
Production Manager: Rosemary Dolinski

Library of Congress Cataloging-in-Publication Data

Farrell, Edmund J.
    The perceptive I: a personal reader and writer / Edmund J.
  Farrell, James E. Miller, Jr.
        p.   cm.
    ISBN 0-8442-5957-8 (softbound)
      1. College readers.   2. English language—Rhetoric.
    3. Autobiography—Problems, exercises, etc.   I. Miller, James
Edwin.   II. Title.
PE1417.F37   1996
808'.0427—dc20   96-11829
                                                    CIP

"In most books, the I, or first person, is omitted; in this it will be retained; that, in respect to egotism, is the main difference. We commonly do not remember that it is, after all, always the first person that is speaking. I should not talk so much about myself if there were anybody else whom I knew as well. Unfortunately, I am confined to this theme by the narrowness of my experience. Moreover, I, on my side, require of every writer, first or last, a simple and sincere account of his own life, and not merely what he has heard of other men's lives; some such account as he would send to his kindred from a distant land; for if he has lived sincerely, it must have been in a distant land to me. Perhaps these pages are more particularly addressed to poor students. As for the rest of my readers, they will accept such portions as apply to them. I trust that none will stretch the seams in putting on the coat, for it may do good service to him whom it fits."

Henry David Thoreau, *Walden* (1854)

Contents

---

*Editor's title

---

*Editor's title

*Editor's title

---

*Editor's title

---

*Editor's title

---

*Editor's title

CLUSTER 14 ❧   SOUNDING FOR TRUTHS, REACHING FOR VERITIES   753

*Editor's title

Preface

The Perceptive I: A Personal Reader and Writer offers you a rich variety of essays selected for their ability, first, to arouse and hold your attention and, second, to serve as models for your own writing. Our writing inevitably carries our identity and stamps our words with our individuality—that elusive presence of our selves called "style." To enable you to find your own voice, your own individual style, we have conceived and shaped the book according to the following principles:

1. **The Basic Theory:** *The Perceptive I* is based on the theory that *all* writing is in some sense personal and that you should come to an understanding of the self's intricate involvement in any use of language in spoken or written form. On the one hand, you should learn that writing is not mere self-indulgence, a spreading of your ego on the page. But on the other hand, you should learn that the self is involved in what appears to be the most objective, seemingly depersonalized use of language—in essays that analyze, explain, argue, reason, describe, define, or compare and contrast. Even when the first-person pronoun "I" does not appear in an essay, it lurks in the text—an implicit "I think" or "I believe." The author's felt presence in the style of each sentence is an important factor in the essay's impact on readers.

2. **The Subjects of the Essays:** *The Perceptive I* has brought together a great number and variety of essays, dealing with every conceivable subject, to serve as models for writing. They are arranged and presented in such a way as to make you aware of the immense resources for writing you have stored in your own mind and memory. From this focus on self and memory at the beginning, the movement of the book is to greater and greater focus on the encounter of the self with the world over a lifetime of experience, whether it be separations and losses, triumphs or failures, roads taken or not taken, disruptions or disasters—or the search for values to live by or truths to affirm.

3. **The Language and Style of the Essays:** The essays in *The Perceptive I* are written in American English by American writers from the mid-nineteenth century to the present, with much greater emphasis

on the more recent period. Thus you will find in these essays your own language as it has been used to great effect by a multitude of people, ranging from the "illiterate" who are movingly eloquent in their own oral histories to the "learned" who in the written word continue their restless search for ever-deeper understanding of the mysteries of being and becoming.

4. **The Variety of the Voices of the Essays:** The voices heard in the essays in *The Perceptive I* represent the entire range of American voices of the past 150 years, male and female, young and old, and including all racial and ethnic groups. America has rightly been called a "nation of immigrants," and the book reflects this definition. But it is this very emphasis on both diversity and individuality that marks the essence of the "American voice"—fulfilling the meaning of the American motto that was chosen by the writers of the Declaration of Independence and that appears on all American coins, including the smallest—the penny: *E Pluribus Unum* (out of many, one).

5. **The Variety in the Forms of the Essays:** *The Perceptive I* contains all kinds of writing, or rhetorical strategies, usually introduced in a composition text—and more: narrating, describing, defining, comparing and contrasting, analyzing, arguing, reasoning, deducing, inferring, intuiting. In addition, it contains multiple examples of a wide range of forms, including diaries, journals, letters, memoirs, reminiscences, autobiographies, oral histories, personal and familiar essays. The guiding purpose of the book is to show that all writing is, indeed, personal, and even those essays written without the use of the first-person "I" embody in their style an individual, or personal, voice. The extent to which that voice is lively—or alive— will determine an essay's effect or influence on readers.

6. **The Impact of the Essays:** In selecting the essays for *The Perceptive I*, we placed great emphasis on their "readability." In short, the essays in this volume are meant to provide a good "read," first engaging you by the sheer pleasure of the reading experience. But the essays were also selected with an eye to inspiring in you the kind of reflection that leads to self-examination or even self-discovery— and the desire to explore this vital "inner material"—uniquely one's own—in language adequate to convey the ideas, emotions, or feelings inherent or implicit in it.

The Editorial Features

Each of the fourteen clusters of essays is introduced by a brief introduction setting forth the theme or subject that is—to some extent—the focus of all the five to ten essays in the cluster. The themes themselves were identified on the basis of their "connecting" with the lives of all individuals—in experiences you have already encountered in your own life or in those that lie ahead. The sequence of clusters embodies experiences roughly arranged in the order in which they are encountered in the living of a life, and thus the book begins with "Roots and Branches" and ends with "Sounding for Truths, Reaching for Verities."

Each essay is introduced by a headnote containing information useful for reading and understanding the essay that follows. The headnotes contain biographical information about the author and, when pertinent, the circumstances that gave rise to the writing of the essay. In the case of some oral biographies, there is little information about the author (or speaker) but more about the recorder or transcriber. On occasion, the headnote contains historical information useful for understanding people or incidents introduced in the essay.

After each essay appears a list of discussion questions; some point to factual matters, others to matters of opinion. You might use these questions to check your comprehension of the essay, or your instructor might use them for class or small-group discussion. Asterisks identify those questions that are suitable for use in small groups.

Also after each essay appears a list of writing topics, ranging from matters about the meaning or structure of the essay to questions of opinion on some stand the essay has taken. These topics are largely designed to elicit personal responses, springboards to the writing of essays in the first person.

Finally, at the end of each cluster appears a list of "Summary Writing Topics," touching on the theme and involving often two or more of the cluster's essays (or even on occasion essays in other clusters). These topics have been designed to extend your reach, encouraging you to map out a rigorous defense of a point of view in support of or in opposition to a position found in one or more essays or to conduct some in-depth research in the library to clarify a matter that has been obscured or distorted in one or another essay. The "Summary Writing Topics" will most often evoke writing in the third, rather than the first, person.

A Final Note on the Title

The first half of the title, *The Perceptive I*, contains in the last word an intended pun: "eye." The words are not at odds but complementary: the "I" sees with his or her own individual "eye" (two eyes act in unison as one). The vision affirmed here is not limited to the sense of sight, but extends to the faculty of comprehension—what is meant, for example, when someone says, realizing in a flash what had eluded understanding before: "Oh, I see!" Thus it is that the invisible, the intuitive, as well as the visible can be seen by a perceptive I: *sight* and *insight* become one.

And the word "personal" in the subtitle is not intended as restrictive but as all-embracing. All experiences, if really possessed, are deeply personal: individuals may think they have had an experience, but if it has not left an imprint on the imagination, the mind, or the emotions (personal faculties all), it has not in any true sense been "had." As T. S. Eliot said, "We had the experience but missed the meaning."

If the experience *has* left an imprint on one of these inner faculties, it has entered the private world of the self. Even when one of us goes to the library to do research to be used in an essay, it is that individual's distinctive personal faculties that motivate the critical choices of what to read and remember and what to select to use. In short, individuals are not microphones, cameras, or computers, recording and mechanically processing data; they are human beings with feelings, intellects, and imaginations, all individually shaped by a storehouse of memories (past experiences) that is theirs alone and no one else's. As these faculties have been shaped by past experiences, so they in turn perform *personally* the shaping of the new—and in the encounter, in a never-ending interaction, become subtly reshaped. The *self*, the *I*, is always in process of *becoming*.

Writing most often requires that single individuals, summoning all the strength of their individuality, retire to solitude (in spirit, if not in fact), and there speak with their own voice on paper. They may speak on any subject; they may select any method or form; and they may fulfill any purposes they choose. The one constant that runs through all the subjects possible, all the forms invented, and the purposes chosen is the writer's voice, the distinctive accent or "style" as it is transferred from interior depths to the blank sheet of paper.

Cluster

Roots and Branches

How did you acquire the sense that you are a distinct individual, unique in the universe, separate from all others, part of your immediate environment but not one with it?

Unquestionably that sense of uniqueness, of difference from all others, of I-ness, started in your infancy. Through verbal interactions with other human beings and physical interactions with your surroundings, you began as an infant to perceive differences, to make contrasts, to assert your dawning sense of selfhood: **I**, not you; **I**, not him or her; **I**, not it. These contrasts, fuzzy and hesitant at first, became clearer, more pronounced, as you grew.

As infant and child, you probably interacted first, most often, and most intensely with members of your immediate family—a parent or parents, perhaps a guardian, and, if you had them, brothers and sisters. By contrasting yourself to these individuals, you began to develop an ego, the Latin word for **I**. At the same time that you were establishing psychological differences from those nearest to you, you were nonetheless incorporating much from them that went beyond your genetic inheritance. Your present temperament, tastes, and values have roots in your childhood, in what you learned, consciously or unconsciously, from persons closely related to you during those formative years. Those from whom you probably learned most, your parents or guardians, once learned, in turn, from their parents, who had learned, in turn, from their parents. In short, the roots of who you are run deep, though you have undoubtedly branched from those roots, as did your predecessors, by expressing your individuality in diverse ways.

In the selections that follow, writers explore their relationships to either one or both of their parents. Sometimes it is a mother who appears to have had the stronger influence upon her offspring; sometimes it is a father. Occasionally, the two seem to have been equally influential. As you will discover, not all relationships between the generations were happy ones, though certainly some were. Others were sad or even deeply disturbing. Nevertheless, regardless of its particular emotional tone, each of these accounts subtly or overtly communicates this declaration by its narrator: "I am in good part who I am because of my parentage."

❧ . . . for a few hours I forgot that my father was an old man."

FATHER TIME

Christopher de Vinck

The recipient of the Ed.D. degree (1991) from Teachers College, Columbia University, Christopher de Vinck (b.1951) is the author of *The Power of the Powerless* (1988), *Only the Heart Knows How to Find a Precious Memory* (1991), *Augusta & Trab* (1992), *Songs of Innocence and Experience: Essays in Celebration of the Ordinary* (1994), and *Simple Wonders* (1995). A resident of Pompton Plains, New Jersey, de Vinck is the supervisor of language arts for the school district in East Orange, New Jersey. His short essay "Father Time" appeared in the June 17, 1994, issue of *The Wall Street Journal*.

1   The furnace in my parents' home was not working properly. Each time it was called upon for heat, it coughed up a miserable sound, then rumbled. After my mother phoned and explained the problem, I drove the 30 minutes to the house where I grew up. My father had, once again, forgotten to drain the furnace.

2   *My father is 82.*

3   When I pulled into the driveway I was overcome with a feeling of dread and depression. The trees in the yard seemed to droop. The house looked old and worn out. As I entered the foyer, I heard the television blaring in the living room. My father sat in his chair reading the closed captions on the bottom of the TV screen. His hearing-aid sat on the table. My mother explained that their cat, Misha, was dying, and that the vet thought it best that it be put to sleep the next day. The cat was 17 years old.

4   I walked down to the basement. It was cold and damp. As I reached for the string that was attached to the single lightbulb, I looked around the dim room: workbench, tool board, discarded wood. This was the basement where my father built a 12-foot sailboat, a fort for my plastic soldiers, and a weaving loom for my sister.

5   *My father was a lawyer.*

6   The tools in the basement were rusted; the workbench was covered with thick dust. I heard the loud television's muffled squawk through the floor above me.

7   After l opened a valve at the bottom of the furnace, I watched the brown sludge drain into a dry, empty bucket. Then I closed the first valve and opened the second, which filled the proper chamber with new water. The water level, which hadn't been checked in months, was precariously low.

8   *My father was a college professor.*

9   I turned out the basement light, walked up the creaking stairs, stepped into the kitchen, and helped myself to several grapes from the bowl of fruit that always seemed full. When I was a child, my father held my hand in the fruit market and asked me to help him select the best grapes.

10   My father tells the story about the day he was released from the prisoner-of-war camp in Belgium during World War II.

11   "I had a bit of money in my pocket, and the first thing I bought was a small bag of grapes. I'll never forget those grapes, so cold and sweet."

12   *My father was an editor.*

13   I walked into the living room with the grapes in my hand. My father leaned out of his chair and tried to adjust his reading glasses. My mother sat on the couch petting the thin, dying cat.

14   Just as I sat down beside her, my father turned and said, "Christopher, your mother and I took a walk yesterday afternoon through the park, around by the old swamp, and we saw the biggest turtle. Bring the children this weekend and we'll see if we can't find that turtle again." Then he turned to the television and adjusted the color quality.

15   *My father was a writer.*

16   After I kissed my mother goodbye, I left the house, slid into my car and drove off.

17   That following weekend my father led my wife, our three children and me on a grand turtle hunt. We walked single file between the dried bulrushes, jumped over streams, startled six geese, and climbed the park observation deck.

18   We returned to the house two hours later with pussy willows, apple blossoms, three types of wild violets, and three smiling grandchildren.

19   We didn't see a turtle that weekend. But for a few hours I forgot that my father was an old man. For a few hours I stepped along the outer edges of the swamp and tried to hear the turtle's laugh as I stood upon the spring afternoon with my father, expecting nothing more than our being together, and that was good.

❧

Discussion Questions

*1. What do you think is the intended effect of the italicized one-sentence paragraphs? Explain. Would the paragraphs be more effective if each were more fully developed? Why or why not?

*2. Find examples of adjectives, verbs, and nouns that de Vinck uses to establish a tone indicating that age has taken and continues to take its toll on his father.

*3. How would you describe the tone of the last third of the selection, beginning with paragraph 12? Explain.

*4. Would "The Turtle" serve as well as "Father Time" as a title for the selection? Why or why not? Would hunting a deer be as appropriate to the selection as hunting a turtle? Why or why not?

Writing Topics

1. Imagine yourself at age eighty-two. Assume that you keep a diary. Write entries for two consecutive days describing what you did and how you felt during this time.

2. In a brief essay, support through reasoning and examples either of the following thesis statements:

   a. The world is changing so rapidly that the elderly no longer have much to teach us.

   b. We still have much to learn from the elderly.

"I can only guess what she might have become.
There are clues in her moments of spirit and humor."

RUTH'S SONG
(BECAUSE SHE COULD NOT SING IT)

Gloria Steinem

Gloria Steinem (b. 1934) is a noted writer, editor, and lecturer. In 1968, she cofounded and became a contributing editor of *New York Magazine*, and in 1971, she cofounded *Ms. Magazine*, which she edited until 1987 and for which she is now consulting editor. Steinem has published widely on the rights of women and has served on numerous boards and committees dedicated to advancing feminist and liberal causes. Among works she has authored are *The Beach Book* (1963); *Outrageous Acts and Everyday Rebellions* (1983), from which "Ruth's Song" is excerpted; *Revolution from Within: A Book of Self-Esteem* (1992); and *Moving Beyond Words* (1993).

1   For many years I also couldn't imagine my mother any way other than the person she had become before I was born. She was just a fact of life when I was growing up; someone to be worried about and cared for; an invalid who lay in bed with eyes closed and lips moving in occasional response to voices only she could hear; a woman to whom I brought an endless stream of toast and coffee, bologna sandwiches and dime pies, in a child's version of what meals should be. She was a loving, intelligent, terrorized woman who tried hard to clean our littered house whenever she emerged from her private world, but who could rarely be counted on to finish one task. In many ways, our roles were reversed: I was the mother and she was the child. Yet that didn't help her either, for she still worried about me with all the intensity of a frightened mother, plus the special fears that came from her own world full of threats and hostile voices.

2   Even then, I suppose I must have known that years before she was thirty-five and I was born, she had been a spirited, adventurous young woman who struggled out of a working-class family and into college, who found work she loved and continued to do, even after she was married and my older sister was there to be cared for. Certainly, our immediate family and nearby relatives, of

whom I was by far the youngest, must have remembered her life as a whole and functioning person. She was thirty before she gave up her own career to help my father run the Michigan summer resort that was the most practical of his many dreams, and she worked hard there as everything from bookkeeper to bar manager. The family must have watched this energetic, fun-loving, book-loving woman turn into someone who was afraid to be alone, who could not hang on to reality long enough to hold a job, and who could rarely concentrate enough to read a book.

3   Yet I don't remember any family speculation about the mystery of my mother's transformation. To the kind ones and those who liked her, this new Ruth was simply a sad event, perhaps a mental case, a family problem to be accepted and cared for until some natural process made her better. To the less kind or those who resented her earlier independence, she was a willful failure, someone who lived in a filthy house, a woman who simply refused to pull herself together.

4   Unlike the story of my Uncle Ed, exterior events were never suggested as reason enough for her problems. Giving up her own career was never cited as her personal parallel of the Depression. (Nor was there discussion of the Depression itself, though my mother, like millions of others, had made potato soup for her family, and cut up blankets to make my sister's winter clothes.) Her real fears of dependency and poverty were no match for my uncle's possible political beliefs. The real hopes inspired by newspaper editors who praised her reporting were not taken as seriously as the possible influence of one radical professor.

5   Even the explanation of mental illness seemed to contain more personal fault when applied to my mother. She had suffered her first "nervous breakdown," as she and everyone else called it, before I was born, when my sister was about five. It followed years of trying to take care of a baby, be the wife of a kind but financially irresponsible man with show-business dreams, and still keep her much-loved job as reporter and newspaper editor. After many months in a sanatorium, she was pronounced recovered. That is, she was able to take care of my sister again, to move away from the city and the job she loved, and to work with my father at the isolated rural lake in Michigan he was trying to transform into a resort worthy of the big dance bands of the 1930s.

6   But she was never again completely without the spells of depression, anxiety, and visions into some other world that eventually were to turn her into the nonperson I remember. And she was never again without a bottle of dark, acrid-smelling liquid she called "Doc Howard's medicine," a solution of chloral hydrate that I later learned was the main ingredient of "Mickey Finns" or "knockout drops," and that probably made my mother and her doctor the pioneers of modern tranquilizers. Though friends and relatives saw this medicine as one more evidence of weakness and indulgence, to me it always seemed an embarrassing but necessary evil. It slurred her speech and slowed her

coordination, making our neighbors and my school friends believe she was a drunk. But without it, she would not sleep for days, even a week at a time, and her feverish eyes began to see only that private world in which wars and hostile voices threatened the people she loved.

7   Because my parents had divorced and my sister was working in a faraway city, my mother and I were alone together in these years, living off the meager fixed income that my mother got from leasing her share of the remaining land in Michigan. I remember a long Thanksgiving weekend spent hanging on to her with one hand and holding my eighth-grade assignment of *A Tale of Two Cities* in the other, because the war outside our house was so real to my mother that she had plunged her hand through a window, badly cutting her arm in an effort to help us escape. Only when she finally agreed to swallow the medicine could she sleep, and only then could I end the terrible calm that comes with crisis and admit to myself how afraid I had been.

8   No wonder that no relative in my memory challenged the doctor who prescribed this medicine, or asked if some of her suffering and hallucinating might be due to overdose or withdrawal, or even consulted another doctor about its use. It was our relief as well as hers.

9   But why was she never returned to that first sanatorium? Or to help that might have come from other doctors? It's hard to say. Partly, it was her own fear of returning to that pain. Partly, it was too little money, and a family's not-unusual assumption that mental illness is an inevitable part of someone's personality. Or perhaps other family members feared something like my experience when, one hot and desperate summer between the sixth and seventh grade, I finally persuaded her to let me take her to the only doctor from those sanatorium days whom she remembered without fear.

10   Yes, this brusque old man told me after talking to my abstracted, timid mother for twenty minutes: She definitely belongs in a state hospital. I should put her there right away. But even at that age, *LIFE* magazine and newspaper exposés had told me what horrors went on inside those hospitals. Assuming there to be no other alternative, I took her home and never tried again.

11   In retrospect, perhaps the biggest reason my mother was cared for but not helped for twenty years was the simplest: her functioning was not that necessary to the world. Like women alcoholics who drink in their kitchens while costly programs are constructed for male executives who drink, or like homemakers subdued with tranquilizers while male patients get therapy and personal attention instead, my mother was not an important worker. She was not even the caretaker of a very young child, as she had been when she was hospitalized the first time. My father had patiently brought home the groceries and kept our odd household going until I was eight or so and my sister went away to college. Two years later, when war-time gas rationing closed his summer resort and he had to travel to buy and sell in summer as well as winter, he said: How can I travel and take care of your mother? How can I make a

living? He was right. It was impossible to do both. I did not blame him for leaving once I was old enough to be the bringer of meals and answerer of my mother's questions. ("Has your sister been killed in a car crash?" "Are there German soldiers outside?") I replaced my father, my mother was left with one more way of maintaining a sad status quo, and the world went on undisturbed.

12   That's why our lives, my mother's from forty-six to fifty-three, and my own from ten to seventeen, were spent alone together. There was one sane winter in a house we rented to be near my sister's college in Massachusetts, then one bad summer spent house-sitting in suburbia while my mother hallucinated and my sister struggled to hold down a summer job in New York. But the rest of those years were lived in Toledo where both my mother and father had been born, and on whose city newspapers an earlier Ruth had worked.

13   First we moved into a basement apartment in a good neighborhood. In those rooms behind a furnace, I made one last stab at being a child. By pretending to be much sicker with a cold than I really was, I hoped my mother would suddenly turn into a sane and cheerful woman bringing me chicken soup à la Hollywood. Of course, she could not. It only made her feel worse that she could not. I stopped pretending. I almost never got sick again.

14   But for most of those years, we lived in the upstairs of the house my mother had grown up in and that her parents left her—a deteriorating farm house engulfed by the city, with poor but newer houses stacked against it and a major highway undermining its sagging front porch. For a while, we rented the two downstairs apartments to a newlywed factory worker and his wife, and a local butcher's family. Then the health department condemned our ancient furnace for the final time, sealing it so tight that even my resourceful Uncle Ed could not break it open to produce illegal heat.

15   In that house, I remember:

16   . . . lying in the bed my mother and I shared for warmth, listening to the early morning live radio broadcast of the royal wedding of Princess Elizabeth and Prince Philip, while we tried to ignore and thus protect each other from the unmistakable sounds of the factory worker downstairs beating up and locking out his pregnant wife.

17   . . . hanging paper drapes I had bought in the dime store; stacking books and papers in the shape of two armchairs and covering them with blankets; evolving my own dishwashing system (I waited until all the dishes were dirty, then put them in the bathtub); and listening to my mother's high praise for these housekeeping efforts to bring order from chaos, though in retrospect I think they probably depressed her further.

18   . . . coming back from one of the Eagles' Club shows where I and other veterans of a local tap-dancing school made ten dollars a night for two shows, and finding my mother waiting with a flashlight and no coat in the dark cold of the bus stop, worried about my safety walking home.

19   . . . in a good period, when my mother's native adventurousness came through, answering a classified ad together for an amateur acting troupe that performed Biblical dramas in churches, and doing several very corny performances of *Noah's Ark* while my proud mother shook metal sheets backstage to make thunder.

20   . . . on a hot summer night, being bitten by one of the rats that shared our house and its back alley. It was a terrifying night that turned into a touching one when my mother, summoning courage from some unknown reservoir of love, became a calm, comforting parent who took me to a hospital emergency room despite her terror at leaving home.

21   . . . coming home from a local library with the three books a week into which I regularly escaped, and discovering that for once there was no need to escape. My mother was calmly planting hollyhocks in the vacant lot next door.

22   But there were also times when she woke in the early winter dark, too frightened and disoriented to remember that I was at my usual afterschool job, and so called the police to find me. Humiliated in front of my friends by sirens and policemen, I would yell at her—and she would bow her head in fear and say, "I'm sorry, I'm sorry, I'm sorry," just as she had done so often when my otherwise-kindhearted father had yelled at her in frustration. Perhaps the worst thing about suffering is that it finally hardens the hearts of those around it.

23   And there were many, many times when I badgered her until her shaking hands had written a small check to cash at the corner grocery, and I could leave her alone while I escaped with my girlfriends to the comfort of well-heated dime stores that smelled of fresh doughnuts, or to air-conditioned Saturday-afternoon movies that were windows on a very different world.

24   But my ultimate protection was this: I was just passing through; I was a guest in the house; perhaps this wasn't my mother at all. Though I knew very well that I was her daughter, I sometimes imagined I had been adopted and that my real parents would find me, a fantasy I've since discovered is common. (If children wrote more and grown-ups less, perhaps being adopted might not be seen only as a fear, but also as a hope.) Certainly, I didn't mourn the wasted life of this woman who was scarcely older than I am now. I worried only about the times when she got worse.

25   Pity takes distance and a certainty of surviving. It was only after our house was bought for demolition by the church next door, and after my sister had performed the miracle of persuading my father to give me a carefree time before college by taking my mother with him to California for a year, that I could afford to think about the sadness of her life. Suddenly, I was far away in Washington, living with my sister who shared a house with several of her friends. While I finished high school and discovered to my surprise that my classmates felt sorry for me because my mother *wasn't* there, I also realized that

my sister, at least in her early childhood, had known a very different person who lived inside our mother, an earlier Ruth.

26   She was a woman I met for the first time in a mental hospital near Baltimore, a humane place with gardens and trees where I visited her each weekend of the summer after my first year away in college. Fortunately, my sister hadn't been able to work and be our mother's caretaker, too. After my father's year was up, my sister had carefully researched hospitals, and found the courage to break the family chain of simply tolerating our mother's condition.

27   At first, this Ruth was the same abstracted, frightened woman I lived with all those years, now all the sadder for being approached through long hospital corridors and many locked doors. But gradually she began to talk about her past life, and to confide memories that doctors there must have been awakening. I began to meet a Ruth I had never known:

28   . . . A tall, spirited, auburn-haired high-school girl who loved basketball and reading; who tried to drive her uncle's Stanley Steamer when it was the first car in the neighborhood; who had a gift for gardening and who sometimes wore her father's overalls in defiance of convention; a girl with the courage to go to dances even though her church told her that music itself was sinful, and whose sense of adventure almost made up for feeling gawky and unpretty next to her daintier, dark-haired sister.

29   . . . A very little girl, just learning to walk, discovering the places on her body where touching was pleasurable, and being punished by her mother who slapped her so hard she was pushed across the kitchen floor.

30   . . . A daughter of a handsome railroad engineer and a school-teacher who felt she had married "beneath her"; the mother who took her two daughters on Christmas trips to faraway New York on an engineer's free railroad pass, and showed them the restaurants and theaters they should aspire to — even though they could only afford to stand outside them in the snow.

31   . . . A good student at Oberlin College whose freethinking traditions she loved, where friends nicknamed her "Billy"; a student with a talent for both mathematics and poetry, who was not above putting an invisible film of Karo syrup on all the toilet seats in her dormitory the night of a big prom; a daughter who had to return to Toledo, live with her family, and go to a local university when her ambitious mother — who had scrimped and saved, ghostwritten a minister's sermons, and made her daughters' clothes in order to get them to college at all — ran out of money. At home, this Ruth became a part-time bookkeeper in a lingerie shop that catered to the very rich, commuting to classes and listening to her mother's harsh lectures on the security of becoming a teacher; but also a young woman who was still rebellious enough to fall in love with my father, the editor of their university newspaper, a funny and charming young man who was a terrible student, had no intention of graduating, put on all the campus dances, and was unacceptably Jewish.

32   I knew from family lore that my mother had married my father twice: once secretly, after he invited her to become the literary editor of the campus newspaper, and once a year later in a public ceremony, which some members of both families refused to attend because it was the "mixed marriage" of its day.

33   And l also knew that my mother had gone on to earn a teaching certificate. She had used it to scare away truant officers during the winters when, after my father closed the summer resort for the season, we lived in a house trailer and worked our way to Florida or California and back by buying and selling antiques.

34   But only during those increasingly adventurous weekend outings from the mental hospital in Baltimore—going shopping, to lunch, to the movies—did I realize that she had taught college calculus for a year in deference to her mother's insistence that she have teaching "to fall back on." And only then did I realize she had fallen in love with newspapers along with my father. After graduating from the university, she wrote a gossip column for a local tabloid, under the name "Duncan MacKenzie," since women weren't supposed to do such things. Soon after, she had earned a job as society reporter on one of Toledo's two big dailies. By the time my sister was four or so, she had worked her way up to the coveted position of Sunday editor.

35   It was a strange experience to look into those brown eyes I had seen so often and realize suddenly how much they were like my own. For the first time, I realized that she really was my mother.

36   I began to think about the many pressures that might have led up to her first nervous breakdown: leaving my sister whom she loved so much with a grandmother whose values my mother didn't share; trying to hold on to a job she loved but was being asked to leave by her husband; wanting very much to go with a woman friend to pursue their own dreams in New York but punishing herself for even the thought; falling in love with a co-worker at the newspaper who frightened her by being more sexually attractive, more supportive of her work than my father, and perhaps the man she should have married; and finally, nearly bleeding to death with a miscarriage because her own mother had little faith in doctors and refused to get help.

37   Did those months in the sanatorium brainwash her in some Freudian or very traditional way into making what were, for her, probably the wrong choices? I don't know. It almost doesn't matter. Without extraordinary support to the contrary, she was already convinced that divorce was unthinkable. A husband could not be left for another man, and certainly not for any reason as selfish as a career. A daughter could not be deprived of her father, and certainly not be uprooted and taken off to an uncertain future in New York. A bride was supposed to be virginal (not "shop-worn," as my euphemistic mother would

have said), and if your husband turned out to be kind, but innocent of the possibility of a woman's pleasure, then just be thankful for his kindness.

38   Of course, other women have torn themselves away from work and people they loved and still survived. But a story my mother told me years later has always symbolized for me the formidable forces arrayed against her.

> *It was early spring, nothing was open yet. There was nobody for miles around. We had stayed at the lake that winter, so I was alone a lot while your father took the car and traveled around on business. You were a baby. Your sister was in school, and there was no phone. The last straw was that the radio broke. Suddenly it seemed like forever since I'd been able to talk with anyone—or even hear the sound of another voice.*

> *I bundled you up, took the dog, and walked out to the Brooklyn road. I thought I'd walk the four or five miles to the grocery store, talk to some people, and find somebody to drive me back. I was walking along with Fritzie running up ahead in the empty road— when suddenly a car came out of nowhere and down the hill. It hit Fritzie head on and threw him over to the side of the road. I yelled and screamed at the driver, but he never slowed down. He never looked at us. He never even turned his head.*

> *Poor Fritzie was all broken and bleeding, but he was still alive. I carried him and sat down in the middle of the road, with his head cradled in my arms. I was going to make the next car stop and help.*

> *But no car ever came. I sat there for hours, I don't know how long, with you in my lap and holding Fritzie, who was whimpering and looking up at me for help. It was dark by the time he finally died. I pulled him over to the side of the road and walked back home with you and washed the blood out of my clothes.*

> *I don't know what it was about that one day—it was like a breaking point. When your father came home, I said: "From now on, I'm going with you. I won't bother you. I'll just sit in the car. But I can't bear to be alone again."*

39   I think she told me that story to show she had tried to save herself, or perhaps she wanted to exorcise a painful memory by saying it out loud. But hearing it made me understand what could have turned her into the woman I remember: a solitary figure sitting in the car, perspiring through the summer,

bundled up in winter, waiting for my father to come out of this or that antique shop, grateful just not to be alone. I came along, too, because I was too young to be left at home, and I loved helping my father wrap and unwrap the newspaper around the china and small objects he had bought at auctions and was selling to dealers. It made me feel necessary and grown-up. But sometimes it was hours before we came back to the car again, and to my mother who was always patiently, silently waiting.

40   At the hospital and in later years when Ruth told me stories of her past, I used to say, "But why didn't you leave? Why didn't you take the job? Why didn't you marry the other man?" She would always insist it didn't matter, she was lucky to have my sister and me. If I pressed hard enough, she would add, "If I'd left you never would have been born."

41   I always thought but never had the courage to say: *But you might have been born instead.*

42   I'd like to tell you that this story has a happy ending. The best I can do is one that is happier than its beginning.

43   After many months in that Baltimore hospital, my mother lived on her own in a small apartment for two years while I was in college and my sister married and lived nearby. When she felt the old terrors coming back, she returned to the hospital at her own request. She was approaching sixty by the time she emerged from there and from a Quaker farm that served as a halfway house, but she confounded her psychiatrists' predictions that she would be able to live outside for shorter and shorter periods. In fact, she never returned. She lived more than another twenty years. For six of them, she was well enough to stay in a rooming house that provided both privacy and company. Even after my sister and her husband moved to a larger house and generously made two basement rooms into an apartment for her, she continued to have some independent life and many friends. She worked part-time as a "salesgirl" in a china shop; went away with me on yearly vacations and took one trip to Europe with relatives; went to women's club meetings; found a multiracial church that she loved and attended most Sundays; took meditation courses; and enjoyed many books. She still could not bear to see a sad movie, to stay alone with any of her six grandchildren while they were young, to live without many tranquilizers, or to talk about those bad years in Toledo. The old terrors were still in the back of her mind, and each day was a fight to keep them down.

44   It was the length of her illness that had made doctors pessimistic. In fact, they could not identify any serious mental problem and diagnosed her only as having "an anxiety neurosis": low self-esteem, a fear of being dependent, a terror of being alone, a constant worry about money. She also had spells of what now would be called agoraphobia, a problem almost entirely confined to dependent women: fear of going outside the house, and incapacitating anxiety attacks in unfamiliar or public places.

45 Would you say, I asked one of her doctors, that her spirit had been broken? "I guess that's as good a diagnosis as any," he said. "And it's hard to mend anything that's been broken for twenty years."

46 But once out of the hospital for good, she continued to show flashes of a different woman inside; one with a wry kind of humor, a sense of adventure, and a love of learning. Books on math, physics, and mysticism occupied a lot of her time. ("Religion," she used to say firmly, "begins in the laboratory.") When she visited me in New York during her sixties and seventies, she always told taxi drivers that she was eighty years old ("so they will tell me how young I look"), and convinced theater ticket sellers that she had difficulty in hearing long before she really did ("so they'll give us seats in the front row"). She made friends easily, with the vulnerability and charm of a person who feels entirely dependent on the approval of others. After one of her visits, every shopkeeper within blocks of my apartment would say, "Oh yes, I know your mother!" At home, she complained that people her own age were too old and stodgy for her. Many of her friends were far younger than she. It was as if she were making up for her own lost years.

47 She was also overly appreciative of any presents given to her—and that made giving them irresistible. I loved to send her clothes, jewelry, exotic soaps, and additions to her collection of tarot cards. She loved receiving them, even though we both knew they would end up stored in boxes and drawers. She carried on a correspondence in German with our European relatives, and exchanged letters with many friends, all written in her painfully slow, shaky handwriting. She also loved giving gifts. Even as she worried about money, saved pennies, and took home sugar from restaurants, she would buy or make carefully chosen presents for grandchildren and friends.

48 Part of the price she paid for this much health was forgetting. A single reminder of those bad years in Toledo was enough to plunge her into days of depression. There were times when this fact created loneliness for me, too. Only two of us had lived most of my childhood. Now, only one of us remembered. But there were also times in later years when, no matter how much I pleaded with reporters *not* to interview our friends and neighbors in Toledo, *not* to say that my mother had been hospitalized, they published things that hurt her very much, and sent her into another downhill slide.

49 On the other hand, she was also her mother's daughter, and so had a certain amount of social pride and pretension. Some of her objections had less to do with depression than with false pride. She complained bitterly about one report that we had lived in a house trailer. She finally asked angrily: "Couldn't they at least say 'vacation mobile home'?" Divorce was still a shame to her. She might cheerfully tell friends, "I don't know *why* Gloria says her father and I were divorced—we never were." I think she justified this to herself with the idea that, having gone through two marriage ceremonies, one in secret and one

in public, they had been divorced only once. In fact, they were definitely divorced, and my father had briefly married someone else.

50   She was very proud of my being a published writer, and we generally shared the same values. After her death, I found a mother-daughter morals quiz I had written for a women's magazine. In her unmistakably shaky writing, she had recorded her own answers, her entirely accurate imagination of what my answers would be, and a score that concluded our differences were less than those "normal for women separated by twenty-odd years." Nonetheless, she was quite capable of putting a made-up name on her name tag when going to her conventional women's club where she feared our shared identity would bring controversy or even just questions. When I finally got up the nerve to tell her I was signing a 1972 petition of women who publicly said we had had abortions and demanded the repeal of laws that made them illegal and danger-ous, her only reply was sharp and aimed to hurt back. "Every starlet says she's had an abortion," she said. "It's just a way of getting publicity." I knew she agreed that abortion should be a legal choice, but I also knew she would never forgive me for embarrassing her in public.

51   In fact, her anger and a fairly imaginative ability to wound with words increased in her last years when she was most dependent, most focused on herself, and most likely to need the total attention of others. When my sister made a courageous decision to go to law school at the age of fifty, leaving my mother in a house that not only had many loving teenage grandchildren in it, but a kindly older woman as a paid companion, my mother reduced her to frequent tears by insisting that this was a family with no love in it, no home-cooked food in the refrigerator, and not a real family at all. Since arguments about home cooking wouldn't work on me, she devised a punishment that was creative and different. She was going to call up the *New York Times*, she said, and tell them that this was what feminism did: it left old sick women all alone.

52   Some of this bitterness brought on by failing faculties was eventually solved by a nursing home near my sister's house where my mother not only got the twenty-four hour help her weakening body demanded, but the attention of affectionate nurses besides. She charmed them, they loved her, and she could still get out for an occasional family wedding. If I ever had any doubts about the debt we owe to nurses, those last months laid them to rest.

53   When my mother died just before her eighty-second birthday in a hospital room where my sister and I were alternating the hours in which her heart wound slowly down to its last sounds, we were alone together for a few hours while my sister slept. My mother seemed bewildered by her surroundings, and by the tubes that invaded her body, but her consciousness cleared long enough for her to say: "I want to go home. Please take me home." Lying to her one last time, I said I would take her. "Okay, honey," she said. "I trust you." Those were her last understandable words.

54   The nurses let my sister and me stay in the room long after there was no more breath. My mother had asked us to do that. One of her many fears came from a story she had been told as a child about a man whose coma was mistaken for death, and who was nearly buried alive. She also had made out a living will requesting that no extraordinary measures be used to keep her alive, and that her ashes be sprinkled in the same stream as my father's.

55   Her memorial service was in the Episcopalian church that she loved because it fed the poor, let the homeless sleep in its pews, had members of almost every race, and had been sued by the Episcopalian hierarchy for having a woman priest. Most of all, she loved the affection with which its members had welcomed her, visited her at home, and driven her to services. I think she would have liked the Quaker-style informality with which people rose to tell their memories of her. I know she would have loved the presence of many friends. It was to this church that she had donated some of her remaining Michigan property in the hope that it could be used as a multiracial camp, thus getting even with those neighbors who had snubbed my father for being Jewish.

56   I think she also would have been pleased with her obituary. It emphasized her brief career as one of the early women journalists, and asked for donations to Oberlin's scholarship fund so others could go to this college she loved so much but had to leave.

57   I know I will spend the next years figuring out what her life has left in me.

58   I realize now why I've always been more touched by old people than by children. It's the talent and hopes locked up in a failing body and unsure mind that get to me—a poignant contrast that reminds me of my mother, even when she was strong.

59   I've always been drawn to any story of a mother and a daughter on their own in the world. I saw *A Taste of Honey* several times as both a play and a film, and never stopped feeling its sadness. Even *Gypsy* I saw over and over again, sneaking in backstage for the musical and going to the movie as well. I told myself that I was learning the tapdance routines, but actually my eyes were full of tears.

60   I once fell in love with a man only because we both belonged to that large and secret club of children who had "crazy mothers." We traded stories of the shameful houses to which we could never invite our friends. Before he was born, his mother had gone to jail for her pacifist convictions. Then she married the politically ambitious young lawyer who defended her, stayed home, raised many sons, and went slowly mad in a different kind of jail. I fell out of love when my friend wished I wouldn't smoke or swear, and hoped I wouldn't go on working. His mother's plight had taught him self-pity but nothing else.

61   For many years, I was obsessed with the fear that I would end up in a house like that one in Toledo. Now, I'm obsessed instead with the things I could

have done for my mother while she was alive, or the things I should have said to her.

62   I still don't understand why so many, many years passed before I saw my mother as a person, and before I understood that many of the forces in her life were patterns women share. Like a lot of daughters, I couldn't afford to admit that what had happened to my mother was not all personal or accidental. It would have meant admitting it could happen to me.

63   One mystery has finally cleared. I could never understand why my mother hadn't been helped by Pauline, her mother-in-law, a woman she seemed to love more than her own mother. This paternal grandmother had died when I was five, before my mother's worst problems began, but long after that "nervous breakdown." I knew Pauline was once a suffragist who addressed Congress, marched for the vote, and was the first woman elected to a school board in Ohio. She must have been a courageous and independent woman, yet I could find no evidence in my mother's reminiscences of her that Pauline had encouraged or helped my mother find a life of her own.

64   I finally realized that my grandmother had never changed the politics of her own life. She was a feminist who kept a neat house for a husband and four antifeminist sons, a vegetarian among five male meat eaters, and a woman who felt so strongly about the dangers of alcohol that she used only paste vanilla, yet she served both meat and wine to the men of the house. She made sure their lives and comforts continued undisturbed. After the vote was won, Pauline seemed to stop all feminist activity. My mother greatly admired the fact that her mother-in-law kept a spotless house, and prepared a week's meals at a time. Whatever her own internal torments, Pauline was to my mother a woman who seemed able to "do it all." "Whither thou goest, I shall go," my mother used to say to this much-loved mother-in-law, quoting the Ruth of the Bible. In the end, her mother-in-law may only have added to my mother's burden of guilt.

65   Like many later suffragists, my grandmother seems to have been a public feminist and a private isolationist. That may have been heroic in itself and the most she could be expected to do, but the vote and a legal right to work were not the only kind of support my mother needed.

66   So the world still missed a unique person named Ruth. Though she longed to live in New York and travel in Europe, she became a woman who was afraid to take a bus across town. Though she drove the first Stanley Steamer, she married a man who never let her drive at all.

67   I can only guess what she might have become. There are clues in her moments of spirit and humor.

68   After all the years of fear, she still came to Oberlin with me when I was giving a speech there. She remembered everything about its history as the first college to admit blacks as well as the first to admit women, and responded to

students with the dignity of a professor, the accuracy of a journalist, and the charm that was all her own.

69   When she could still make trips to Washington's wealth of libraries, she became an expert genealogist, delighting especially in finding the rogues and rebels in our family tree.

70   There was a story she told with great satisfaction. Before I was born, when she had cooked one more enormous meal for all the members of some famous dance band at my father's resort and they failed to clean their plates, she took a shotgun down from the kitchen wall and held it over their frightened heads until they had finished every last crumb of strawberry shortcake. Only then did she tell them the gun wasn't loaded.

71   Though sex was a subject she couldn't discuss directly, she had a great appreciation of sensuous men. When a friend I brought home tried to talk to her about cooking, she was furious. ("He came out in the kitchen and talked to me about *stew!*") But she forgave him when we went swimming. She whispered, "He has wonderful legs!"

72   On her seventy-fifth birthday, she played softball with her grandsons on the beach, and took pride in hitting home runs into the ocean.

73   Even in the last year of her life, when my sister took her to visit a neighbor's new and luxurious house, she looked at the vertical stripes of a very abstract painting in the hallway, and said tartly, "Is that the price code?"

74   She worried terribly about being socially acceptable herself, but she never withheld her own approval for superficial reasons. Poverty or style or lack of education couldn't stand between her and a new friend. Though she lived in a mostly white society and worried if I went out with a man of the "wrong" race, just as she had once married a man of the "wrong" religion, she always accepted each person as an individual.

75   "Is he *very* dark?" she once asked worriedly about a friend. But when she met this very dark person, she only said afterward, "What a kind and nice man!"

76   My father was the Jewish half of the family, yet it was my mother who taught me to have pride in this tradition. It was she who encouraged me to listen to a radio play about a concentration camp when I was little. "You should know that this can happen," she said. Yet she did it just enough to teach, never enough to frighten.

77   It was she who introduced me to books and a respect for them, to poetry that she knew by heart, and to the idea that you could never criticize someone unless you "walked miles in their shoes."

78   It was she who sold that Toledo house, the only home she had, with the determination that the money be used to start me in college. She gave both her daughters the encouragement to leave home for the four years of independence she herself had never had.

79　　After her death, my sister and I found a journal she had kept of her one cherished and belated trip to Europe. It was a trip she had described very little when she came home perhaps because she always deplored people who talked boringly about their personal travels and showed slides. Nonetheless, she had written a narrative essay called "Grandma Goes to Europe." After all those years, she still thought of herself as a writer. Yet she showed this long journal to no one.

80　　I miss her—but perhaps no more in death than I did in life. Dying seems less sad than having lived too little. But at least we're now asking questions about all the Ruths in all our family mysteries.

81　　If her song inspires that, I think she would be the first to say: It was worth the singing.

❧

Discussion Questions

　　*1. In the opening paragraph, Steinem describes her mother as "a loving, intelligent, terrorized woman." By paragraph numbers, locate in the selection evidence that Steinem presents to support each of the descriptive adjectives. Select three other adjectives that might have applied to Steinem's mother at various stages of her life. Support your choices by citing appropriate paragraph numbers.

　　2. By what stratagem did Steinem help preserve her own sanity during the years she cared for her mother? What "pressures" does Steinem later sense may have led to her mother's nervous breakdown?

　　3. Steinem states that her mother wasn't helped because "her functioning was not that necessary to the world" (paragraph 11). Have conditions for women sufficiently altered since Steinem's childhood so that the same assertion would not be made today? Explain.

　　4. In what ways is this selection about Steinem's mother "happier than its beginning"?

Writing Topics

　　1. Assume that Steinem's mother, Ruth, had the opportunity to write a one- to two-page obituary for herself. Write the obituary that you think she would have chosen to write.

　　2. Recall a relative or friend who seems to have, as did Steinem's mother, a number of contradictory qualities. In a biographical sketch, try to capture some of those qualities, presenting evidence for each.

&ᴀ. . . I cannot remember a time when
I was not in love with . . . books. . . ."

LISTENING

Eudora Welty

A native of Jackson, Mississippi, Eudora Welty (b. 1909) has been writing for over a half-century. Among her better-known works are *The Robber Bridegroom* (1942), *Delta Wedding* (1946), *The Ponder Heart* (1954), *The Optimist's Daughter* (winner of the Pulitzer Prize in 1973), *The Eye of the Story* (1978), and *One Writer's Beginnings* (1984), from which "Listening" was taken. For her contributions to American literature, Welty has received The National Institute of Arts and Letters Gold Medal (1972), The National Medal for Literature (1980), The Presidential Medal for Freedom (1980), and The National Medal of Arts (1987).

1   I learned from the age of two or three that any room in our house, at any time of day, was there to read in, or to be read to. My mother read to me. She'd read to me in the big bedroom in the mornings, when we were in her rocker together, which ticked in rhythm as we rocked, as though we had a cricket accompanying the story. She'd read to me in the diningroom on winter afternoons in front of the coal fire, with our cuckoo clock ending the story with "Cuckoo," and at night when I'd got in my own bed. I must have given her no peace. Sometimes she read to me in the kitchen while she sat churning, and the churning sobbed along with *any* story. It was my ambition to have her read to me while *I* churned; once she granted my wish, but she read off my story before I brought her butter. She was an expressive reader. When she was reading "Puss in Boots," for instance, it was impossible not to know that she distrusted *all* cats.

2   It had been startling and disappointing to me to find out that story books had been written by *people*, that books were not natural wonders, coming up of themselves like grass. Yet regardless of where they came from, I cannot remember a time when I was not in love with them—with the books themselves, cover and binding and the paper they were printed on, with their smell and their weight and with their possession in my arms, captured and carried off to myself. Still illiterate, I was ready for them, committed to all the reading I could give them.

3 Neither of my parents had come from homes that could afford to buy many books, but though it must have been something of a strain on his salary, as the youngest officer in a young insurance company, my father was all the while carefully selecting and ordering away for what he and Mother thought we children should grow up with. They bought first for the future.

4 Besides the bookcase in the livingroom, which was always called "the library," there were the encyclopedia tables and dictionary stand under windows in our diningroom. Here to help us grow up arguing around the diningroom table were the Unabridged Webster, the Columbia Encyclopedia, Compton's Pictured Encyclopedia, the Lincoln Library of Information, and later the Book of Knowledge. And the year we moved into our new house, there was room to celebrate it with the new 1925 edition of the Britannica, which my father, his face always deliberately turned toward the future, was of course disposed to think better than any previous edition.

5 In "the library," inside the mission-style bookcase with its three diamond-latticed glass doors, with my father's Morris chair and the glass-shaded lamp on its table beside it, were books I could soon begin on—and I did, reading them all alike and as they came, straight down their rows, top shelf to bottom. There was the set of Stoddard's Lectures, in all its late nineteenth-century vocabulary and vignettes of peasant life and quaint beliefs and customs, with matching halftone illustrations: Vesuvius erupting, Venice by moonlight, gypsies glimpsed by their campfires. I didn't know then the clue they were to my father's longing to see the rest of the world. I read straight through his other love-from-afar: the Victrola Book of the Opera, with opera after opera in synopsis, with portraits in costume of Melba, Caruso, Galli-Curci, and Geraldine Farrar, some of whose voices we could listen to on our Red Seal records.

6 My mother read secondarily for information; she sank as a hedonist into novels. She read Dickens in the spirit in which she would have eloped with him. The novels of her girlhood that had stayed on in her imagination, besides those of Dickens and Scott and Robert Louis Stevenson, were *Jane Eyre, Trilby, The Woman in White, Green Mansions, King Solomon's Mines.* Marie Corelli's name would crop up but I understood she had gone out of favor with my mother, who had only kept *Ardath* out of loyalty. In time she absorbed herself in Galsworthy, Edith Wharton, above all in Thomas Mann of the *Joseph* volumes.

7 *St. Elmo* was not in our house; I saw it often in other houses. This wildly popular Southern novel is where all the Edna Earles in our population started coming from. They're all named for the heroine, who succeeded in bringing a dissolute, sinning roué and atheist of a lover (St. Elmo) to his knees. My mother was able to forgo it. But she remembered the classic advice given to rose growers on how to water their bushes long enough: "Take a chair and *St. Elmo*.". . .

8 My mother had brought from West Virginia that set of Dickens; those books looked sad, too—they had been through fire and water before I was

born, she told me, and there they were, lined up—as I later realized, waiting for *me*.

9   I was presented, from as early as I can remember, with books of my own, which appeared on my birthday and Christmas morning. Indeed, my parents could not give me books enough. They must have sacrificed to give me on my sixth or seventh birthday—it was after I became a reader for myself—the ten-volume set of Our Wonder World. These were beautifully made, heavy books I would lie down with on the floor in front of the diningroom hearth, and more often than the rest volume 5, *Every Child's Story Book*, was under my eyes. There were the fairy tales—Grimm, Andersen, the English, the French, "Ali Baba and the Forty Thieves"; and there was Aesop and Reynard the Fox; there were the myths and legends, Robin Hood, King Arthur, and St. George and the Dragon, even the history of Joan of Arc; a whack of *Pilgrim's Progress* and a long piece of *Gulliver*. They all carried their classic illustrations. I located myself in these pages and could go straight to the stories and pictures I loved; very often "The Yellow Dwarf" was first choice, with Walter Crane's Yellow Dwarf in full color making his terrifying appearance flanked by turkeys. Now that volume is as worn and backless and hanging apart as my father's poor *Sanford and Merton*. The precious page with Edward Lear's "Jumblies" on it has been in danger of slipping out for all these years. One measure of my love for Our Wonder World was that for a long time I wondered if I would go through fire and water for it as my mother had done for Charles Dickens; and the only comfort was to think I could ask my mother to do it for me.

10   I believe I'm the only child I know of who grew up with this treasure in the house. I used to ask others, "Did you have Our Wonder World?" I'd have to tell them The Book of Knowledge could not hold a candle to it.

11   I live in gratitude to my parents for initiating me—and as early as I begged for it, without keeping me waiting—into knowledge of the word, into reading and spelling, by way of the alphabet. They taught it to me at home in time for me to begin to read before starting to school. I believe the alphabet is no longer considered an essential piece of equipment for traveling through life. In my day it was the keystone to knowledge. You learned the alphabet as you learned to count to ten, as you learned "Now I lay me" and the Lord's Prayer and your father's and mother's name and address and telephone number, all in case you were lost.

12   My love for the alphabet, which endures, grew out of reciting it but, before that, out of seeing the letters on the page. In my own story books, before I could read them for myself, I fell in love with various winding, enchanted-looking initials drawn by Walter Crane at the heads of fairy tales. In "Once upon a time," an "O" had a rabbit running it as a treadmill, his feet upon flowers. When the day came, years later, for me to see the Book of Kells, all the wizardry of letter, initial, and word swept over me a thousand times over, and the illumination, the gold, seemed a part of the world's beauty and holiness that had been there from the start. . . .

13   My mother always sang to her children. Her voice came out just a little bit in the minor key. "Wee Willie Winkie's" song was wonderfully sad when she sang the lullabies.

14   "Oh, but now there's a record. She could have her own record to listen to," my father would have said. For there came a Victrola record of "Bobby Shafftoe" and "Rock-a-Bye Baby," all of Mother's lullabies, which could be played to take her place. Soon I was able to play her my own lullabies all day long.

15   Our Victrola stood in the diningroom. I was allowed to climb onto the seat of a diningroom chair to wind it, start the record turning, and set the needle playing. In a second I'd jumped to the floor, to spin or march around the table as the music called for—now there were all the other records I could play too. I skinned back onto the chair just in time to lift the needle at the end, stop the record and turn it over, then change the needle. That brass receptacle with a hole in the lid gave off a metallic smell like human sweat, from all the hot needles that were fed it. Winding up, dancing, being cocked to start and stop the record, was of course all in one the act of *listening*—to "Overture to *Daughter of the Regiment*," "Selections from *The Fortune Teller*," "Kiss Me Again," "Gypsy Dance from *Carmen*," "Stars and Stripes Forever," "When the Midnight Choo-Choo Leaves for Alabam," or whatever came next. Movement must be at the very heart of listening.

16   Ever since I was first read to, then started reading to myself, there has never been a line read that I didn't *hear*. As my eyes followed the sentence, a voice was saying it silently to me. It isn't my mother's voice, or the voice of any person I can identify, certainly not my own. It is human, but inward, and it is inwardly that I listen to it. It is to me the voice of the story or the poem itself. The cadence, whatever it is that asks you to believe, the feeling that resides in the printed word, reaches me through the reader-voice. I have supposed, but never found out, that this is the case with all readers—to read as listeners—and with all writers, to write as listeners. It may be part of the desire to write. The sound of what falls on the page begins the process of testing it for truth, for me. Whether I am right to trust so far I don't know. By now I don't know whether I could do either one, reading or writing, without the other.

17   My own words, when I am at work on a story, I hear too as they go, in the same voice that I hear when I read in books. When I write and the sound of it comes back to my ears, then I act to make my changes. I have always trusted this voice. . . .

18   It was when my mother came out onto the sleeping porch to tell me goodnight that her trial came. The sudden silence in the double bed meant my younger brothers had both keeled over in sleep, and I in the single bed at my end of the porch would be lying electrified, waiting for this to be the night when she'd tell me what she'd promised for so long. Just as she bent to kiss me I grabbed her and asked: "Where do babies come from?"

19   My poor mother! But something saved her every time. Almost any night I put the baby question to her, suddenly, as if the whole outdoors exploded, Professor Holt would start to sing. The Holts lived next door; he taught penmanship (the Palmer Method), typing, bookkeeping and shorthand at the high school. His excitable voice traveled out of their dining-room windows across the two driveways between our houses, and up to our upstairs sleeping porch. His wife, usually so quiet and gentle, was his uncannily spirited accompanist at the piano. "High-ho! Come to the Fair!" he'd sing, unless he sang "Oho ye oho ye, who's bound for the ferry, the briar's in bud and the sun's going down!"

20   "Dear, this isn't a very good time for you to hear Mother, is it?"

21   She couldn't get started. As soon as she'd whisper something, Professor Holt galloped into the chorus, "And 'tis but a penny to Twickenham town!" "Isn't that enough?" she'd ask me. She'd told me that the mother and the father had to both *want* the baby. This couldn't be enough. I knew she was not trying to fib to me, for she never did fib, but also I could not help but know she was not really *telling* me. And more than that, I was afraid of what I was going to hear next. This was partly because she wanted to tell me in the dark. I thought *she* might be afraid. In something like childish hopelessness I thought she probably *couldn't* tell, just as she *couldn't* lie.

22   On the night we came the closest to having it over with, she started to tell me without being asked, and I ruined it by yelling, "Mother, look at the lightning bugs!"

23   In those days, the dark was dark. And all the dark out there was filled with the soft, near lights of lightning bugs. They were everywhere, flashing on the slow, horizontal move, on the upswings, rising and subsiding in the soundless dark. Lightning bugs signaled and answered back without a stop, from down below all the way to the top of our sycamore tree. My mother just gave me a businesslike kiss and went on back to Daddy in their room at the front of the house. Distracted by lightning bugs, I had missed my chance. The fact is she never did tell me.

24   I doubt that any child I knew ever was told by her mother any more than I was about babies. In fact, I doubt that her own mother ever told her any more than she told me, though there were five brothers who were born after Mother, one after the other, and she was taking care of babies all her childhood.

25   Not being able to bring herself to open that door to reveal its secret, one of those days, she opened another door.

26   In my mother's bottom bureau drawer in her bedroom she kept treasures of hers in boxes, and had given me permission to play with one of them—a switch of her own chestnut-colored hair, kept in a heavy bright braid that coiled around like a snake inside a cardboard box. I hung it from her doorknob and unplaited it; it fell in ripples nearly to the floor, and it satisfied the Rapunzel in me to comb it out. But one day I noticed in the same drawer a small white cardboard box such as her engraved calling cards came in from the

printing house. It was tightly closed, but I opened it, to find to my puzzlement and covetousness two polished buffalo nickels, embedded in white cotton. I rushed with this opened box to my mother and asked if I could run out and spend the nickels.

27   "No!" she exclaimed in a most passionate way. She seized the box into her own hands. I begged her; somehow I had started to cry. Then she sat down, drew me to her, and told me that I had had a little brother who had come before I did, and who had died as a baby before I was born. And these two nickels that I'd wanted to claim as my find were his. They had lain on his eyelids, for a purpose untold and unimaginable. "He was a fine little baby, my first baby, and he shouldn't have died. But he did. It was because your mother almost died at the same time," she told me. "In looking after me, they too nearly forgot about the little baby."

28   She'd told me the wrong secret—not how babies could come but how they could die, how they could be forgotten about.

29   I wondered in after years: how could my mother have kept those two coins? Yet how could someone like herself have disposed of them in any way at all? She suffered from a morbid streak which in all the life of the family reached out on occasions—the worst occasions—and touched us, clung around us, making it worse for her; her unbearable moments could find nowhere to go.

30   The future story writer in the child I was must have taken unconscious note and stored it away then: one secret is liable to be revealed in the place of another that is harder to tell, and the substitute secret when nakedly exposed is often the more appalling.

31   Perhaps telling me what she did was made easier for my mother by the two secrets, told and still not told, being connected in her deepest feeling, more intimately than anyone ever knew, perhaps even herself. So far as I remember now, this is the only time this baby was ever mentioned in my presence. So far as I can remember, and I've tried, he was never mentioned in the presence of my father, for whom he had been named. I am only certain that my father, who could never bear pain very well, would not have been able to bear it.

32   It was my father (my mother told me at some later date) who saved her own life, after that baby was born. She had in fact been given up by the doctor, as she had long been unable to take any nourishment. (That was the illness when they'd cut her hair, which formed the switch in the same bureau drawer.) What had struck her was septicemia, in those days nearly always fatal. What my father did was to try champagne.

33   I once wondered where he, who'd come not very long before from an Ohio farm, had ever heard of such a remedy, such a measure. Or perhaps as far as he was concerned he invented it, out of the strength of desperation. It would have been desperation augmented because champagne couldn't be bought in Jackson. But somehow he knew what to do about that too. He telephoned to Canton, forty miles north, to an Italian orchard grower, Mr. Trolio, told him

the necessity, and asked, begged, that he put a bottle of his wine on Number 3, which was due in a few minutes to stop in Canton to "take on water" (my father knew everything about train schedules). My father would be waiting to meet the train in Jackson. Mr. Trolio did—he sent the bottle in a bucket of ice and my father snatched it off the baggage car. He offered my mother a glass of chilled champagne and she drank it and kept it down. She was to live, after all.

34   Now, her hair was long again, it would reach in a braid down her back, and now I was her child. She hadn't died. And when I came, I hadn't died either. Would she ever? Would I ever? I couldn't face *ever*. I must have rushed into her lap, demanding her like a baby. And she had to put her first-born aside again, for me.

35   Of course it's easy to see why they both overprotected me, why my father, before I could wear a new pair of shoes for the first time, made me wait while he took out his thin silver pocket knife and with the point of the blade scored the polished soles all over, carefully, in a diamond pattern, to prevent me from sliding on the polished floor when I ran.

36   As I was to learn over and over again, my mother's mind was a mass of associations. Whatever happened would be forever paired for her with something that had happened before it, to one of us or to her. It became a private anniversary. Every time any possible harm came near me, she thought of how she lost her first child. When a Roman candle at Christmas backfired up my sleeve, she rushed to smother the blaze with the first thing she could grab, which was a dish towel hanging in the kitchen, and the burn on my arm became infected. I was nothing but proud of my sling, for I could wear it to school, and her repeated blaming of herself—for even my sling—puzzled and troubled me.

37   When my mother would tell me that she wanted me to have something because she as a child had never had it, I wanted, or I partly wanted, to give it back. All my life I continued to feel that bliss for me would have to imply my mother's deprivation or sacrifice. I don't think it would have occurred to her what a double emotion I felt, and indeed I know that it was being unfair to her, for what she said was simply the truth.

38   "I'm going to let you go to the Century Theatre with your father tonight on my ticket. I'd rather you saw *Blossom Time* than go myself."

39   In the Century first-row balcony, where their seats always were, I'd be sitting beside my father at this hour beyond my bedtime carried totally away by the performance, and then suddenly the thought of my mother staying home with my sleeping younger brothers, missing the spectacle at this moment before my eyes, and doing without all the excitement and wonder that filled my being, would arrest me and I could hardly bear my pleasure for my guilt.

40   Jackson's Carnegie Library was on the same street where our house was, on the other side of the State Capitol. "Through the Capitol" was the way to go

to the Library. You could glide through it on your bicycle or even coast through on roller skates, though without family permission.

41   I never knew anyone who'd grown up in Jackson without being afraid of Mrs. Calloway, our librarian. She ran the Library absolutely by herself, from the desk where she sat with her back to the books and facing the stairs, her dragon eye on the front door, where who knew what kind of person might come in from the public? SILENCE in big black letters was on signs tacked up everywhere. She herself spoke in her normally commanding voice; every word could be heard all over the Library above a steady seething sound coming from her electric fan; it was the only fan in the Library and stood on her desk, turned directly onto her streaming face.

42   As you came in from the bright outside, if you were a girl, she sent her strong eyes down the stairway to test you; if she could see through your skirt she sent you straight back home: you could just put on another petticoat if you wanted a book that badly from the public library. I was willing; I would do anything to read.

43   My mother was not afraid of Mrs. Calloway. She wished me to have my own library card to check out books for myself. She took me in to introduce me and I saw I had met a witch. "Eudora is nine years old and has my permission to read any book she wants from the shelves, children or adult," Mother said. "With the exception of *Elsie Dinsmore*," she added. Later she explained to me that she'd made this rule because Elsie the heroine, being made by her father to practice too long and hard at the piano, fainted and fell off the piano stool. "You're too impressionable, dear," she told me. "You'd read that and the very first thing you'd do, you'd fall off the piano stool." "Impressionable" was a new word. I never hear it yet without the image that comes with it of falling straight off the piano stool.

44   Mrs. Calloway made her own rules about books. You could not take back a book to the Library on the same day you'd taken it out; it made no difference to her that you'd read every word in it and needed another to start. You could take out two books at a time and two only; this applied as long as you were a child and also for the rest of your life, to my mother as severely as to me. So two by two, I read library books as fast as I could go, rushing them home in the basket of my bicycle. From the minute I reached our house, I started to read. Every book I seized on, from *Bunny Brown and His Sister Sue at Camp Rest-a-While* to *Twenty Thousand Leagues under the Sea*, stood for the devouring wish to read being instantly granted. I knew this was bliss, knew it at the time. Taste isn't nearly so important; it comes in its own time. I wanted to read *immediately*. The only fear was that of books coming to an end.

45   My mother was very sharing of this feeling of insatiability. Now, I think of her as reading so much of the time while doing something else. In my mind's eye *The Origin of Species* is lying on the shelf in the pantry under a light dusting of flour—my mother was a bread maker; she'd pick it up, sit by the kitchen

window and find her place, with one eye on the oven. I remember her picking up *The Man in Lower Ten* while my hair got dry enough to unroll from a load of kid curlers trying to make me like my idol, Mary Pickford. A generation later, when my brother Walter was away in the Navy and his two little girls often spent the day in our house, I remember Mother reading the new issue of *Time* magazine while taking the part of the Wolf in a game of "Little Red Riding Hood" with the children. She'd just look up at the right time, long enough to answer — in character — "The better to eat you with, my dear," and go back to her place in the war news. . . .

46   Even as we grew up, my mother could not help imposing herself between her children and whatever it was they might take it in mind to reach out for in the world. For she would get it for them, if it was good enough for them — she would have to be very sure — and give it to them, at whatever cost to herself: valiance was in her very fibre. She stood always prepared in herself to challenge the world in our place. She did indeed tend to make the world look dangerous, and so it had been to her. A way had to be found around her love sometimes, without challenging *that*, and at the same time cherishing it in its unassailable strength. Each of us children did, sooner or later, in part at least, solve this in a different, respectful, complicated way.

47   But I think she was relieved when I chose to be a writer of stories, for she thought writing was safe.

ε❧

Discussion Questions

1. Cite evidence from the selection that Welty's parents took a strong interest in their children's education.
2. Describe Welty's reading habits as a child.
3. In paragraphs 16–17, what relationship does Welty say exists for her between the act of hearing and the acts of reading and writing? Do you believe this relationship is important to anyone who writes? Why or why not?
4. Welty observes in paragraph 30 that "one secret is liable to be revealed in the place of another that is harder to tell, and the substitute secret when nakedly exposed is often the more appalling." How does this observation apply to her childhood?
*5. Which of the following adjectives seem to apply to one or both of Welty's parents, and which do not apply: generous; resourceful; uneducated; curious; arrogant; overprotective? Explain your choices.
*6. Was Welty's childhood one that you would have liked to have experienced? Why or why not?

Writing Topics

1.   Assume that you are a parent. Describe in a few paragraphs the things you would like to do to enhance your child's education, explaining why you believe each of these things to be important.
2.   Write a memoir of your own early experiences with reading. What favorable or unfavorable memories do you have with being read to, with learning to read by yourself, with particular books, and with libraries and librarians?

❧"I tell myself he drinks to ease an ache that gnaws at his belly, an ache I must have caused by disappointing him somehow. . . ."

UNDER THE INFLUENCE

Scott Russell Sanders

Scott Russell Sanders (b. 1945) grew up in Tennessee and Ohio. After completing his B.A. from Brown University in 1967, he won a Marshall Scholarship to attend Cambridge University, where he completed his Ph.D. in 1971. Sanders, who now teaches at the University of Indiana, is an accomplished personal essayist and nature writer whose work has appeared in Harper's, The Georgia Review, and other journals. His books include Stone Country (1983), Wilderness Plots (1988), In Limestone Country (1991), Secrets of the Universe (1992), The Paradise of Bombs (1993), Staying Put (1993), and, in 1995, Writing from the Center.

1   My father drank. He drank as a gut-punched boxer gasps for breath, as a starving dog gobbles food—compulsively, secretly, in pain and trembling. I use the past tense not because he ever quit drinking but because he quit living. That is how the story ends for my father, age sixty-four, heart bursting, body cooling and forsaken on the linoleum of my brother's trailer. The story continues for my brother, my sister, my mother, and me, and will continue so long as memory holds.

2   In the perennial present of memory, I slip into the garage or barn to see my father tipping back the flat green bottles of wine, the brown cylinders of whiskey, the cans of beer disguised in paper bags. His Adam's apple bobs, the liquid gurgles, he wipes the sandy-haired back of a hand over his lips, and then, his bloodshot gaze bumping into me, he stashes the bottle or can inside his jacket, under the workbench, between two bales of hay, and we both pretend the moment has not occurred.

3   "What's up, buddy?" he says, thick-tongued and edgy.

4   "Sky's up," I answer, playing along.

5   "And don't forget prices," he grumbles. "Prices are always up. And taxes."

6   In memory, his white 1951 Pontiac with the stripes down the hood and the Indian head on the snout jounces to a stop in the driveway; or it is the 1956 Ford station wagon, or the 1963 Rambler shaped like a toad, or the sleek 1969 Bonneville that will do 120 miles per hour on straightaways; or it is the robin's-egg blue pickup, new in 1980, battered in 1981, the year of his death. He climbs out, grinning dangerously, unsteady on his legs, and we children interrupt our game of catch, our building of snow forts, our picking of plums, to watch in silence as he weaves past into the house, where he slumps into his overstuffed chair and falls asleep. Shaking her head, our mother stubs out the cigarette he has left smoldering in the ashtray. All evening, until our bedtimes, we tiptoe past him, as past a snoring dragon. Then we curl in our fearful sheets, listening. Eventually he wakes with a grunt, Mother slings accusations at him, he snarls back, she yells, he growls, their voices clashing. Before long, she retreats to their bedroom, sobbing—not from the blows of fists, for he never strikes her, but from the force of words.

7   Left alone, our father prowls the house, thumping into furniture, rummaging in the kitchen, slamming doors, turning the pages of the newspaper with a savage crackle, muttering back at the late-night drivel from television. The roof might fly off, the walls might buckle from the pressure of his rage. Whatever my brother and sister and mother may be thinking on their own rumpled pillows, I lie there hating him, loving him, fearing him, knowing I have failed him. I tell myself he drinks to ease an ache that gnaws at his belly, an ache I must have caused by disappointing him somehow, a murderous ache I should be able to relieve by doing all my chores, earning A's in school, winning baseball games, fixing the broken washer and the burst pipes, bringing in money to fill his empty wallet. He would not hide the green bottles in his tool box, would not sneak off to the barn with a lump under his coat, would not fall asleep in the daylight, would not roar and fume, would not drink himself to death, if only I were perfect.

8   I am forty-two as I write these words, and I know full well now that my father was an alcoholic, a man consumed by disease rather than by disappointment. What had seemed to me a private grief is in fact a public scourge. In the United States alone some ten or fifteen million people share his ailment, and behind the doors they slam in fury or disgrace, countless other children tremble. I comfort myself with such knowledge, holding it against the throb of memory like an ice pack against a bruise. There are keener sources of grief: poverty, racism, rape, war. I do not wish to compete for a trophy in suffering. I am only trying to understand the corrosive mixture of helplessness, responsibility, and shame that I learned to feel as the son of an alcoholic. I realize now that I did not cause my father's illness, nor could I have cured it. Yet for all this grown-up knowledge, I am still ten years old, my own son's age, and as that boy I struggle in guilt and confusion to save my father from pain.

9   Consider a few of our synonyms for *drunk*: tipsy, tight, pickled, soused, and plowed; stoned and stewed, lubricated and inebriated, juiced and sluiced; three sheets to the wind, in your cups, out of your mind, under the table, lit up, tanked up, wiped out; besotted, blotto, bombed, and buzzed; plastered, polluted, putrified; loaded or looped, boozy, woozy, fuddled, or smashed; crocked and shit-faced, corked and pissed, snockered and sloshed.

10   It is a mostly humorous lexicon, as the lore that deals with drunks—in jokes and cartoons, in plays, films, and television skits—is largely comic. Aunt Matilda nips elderberry wine from the sideboard and burps politely during supper. Uncle Fred slouches to the table glassy-eyed, wearing a lamp shade for a hat and murmuring, "Candy is dandy but liquor is quicker." Inspired by cocktails, Mrs. Somebody recounts the events of her day in a fuzzy dialect, while Mr. Somebody nibbles her ear and croons a bawdy song. On the sofa with Boyfriend, Daughter giggles, licking gin from her lips, and loosens the bows in her hair. Junior knocks back some brews with his chums at the Leopard Lounge and stumbles home to the wrong house, wonders foggily why he cannot locate his pajamas, and crawls naked into bed with the ugliest girl in school. The family dog slurps from a neglected martini and wobbles to the nursery, where he vomits in Baby's shoe.

11   It is all great fun. But if in the audience you notice a few laughing faces turn grim when the drunk lurches on stage, don't be surprised, for these are the children of alcoholics. Over the grinning mask of Dionysus, the leering mask of Bacchus, these children cannot help seeing the bloated features of their own parents. Instead of laughing, they wince, they mourn. Instead of celebrating the drunk as one freed from constraints, they pity him as one enslaved. They refuse to believe *in vino veritas*, having seen their befuddled parents skid away from truth toward folly and oblivion. And so these children bite their lips until the lush staggers into the wings.

12   My father, when drunk, was neither funny nor honest; he was pathetic, frightening, deceitful. There seemed to be a leak in him somewhere, and he poured in booze to keep from draining dry. Like a torture victim who refuses to squeal, he would never admit that he had touched a drop, not even in his last year, when he seemed to be dissolving in alcohol before our very eyes. I never knew him to lie about anything, ever, except about this one ruinous fact. Drowsy, clumsy, unable to fix a bicycle tire, throw a baseball, balance a grocery sack, or walk across the room, he was stripped of his true self by drink. In a matter of minutes, the contents of a bottle could transform a brave man into a coward, a buddy into a bully, a gifted athlete and skilled carpenter and shrewd businessman into a bumbler. No dictionary of synonyms for *drunk* would soften the anguish of watching our prince turn into a frog.

13   Father's drinking became the family secret. While growing up, we children never breathed a word of it beyond the four walls of our house. To this day, my

brother and sister rarely mention it, and then only when I press them. I did not confess the ugly, bewildering fact to my wife until his wavering walk and slurred speech forced me to. Recently, on the seventh anniversary of my father's death, I asked my mother if she ever spoke of his drinking to friends. "No, no, never," she replied hastily. "I couldn't bear for anyone to know."

14   The secret bores under the skin, gets in the blood, into the bone, and stays there. Long after you have supposedly been cured of malaria, the fever can flare up, the tremors can shake you. So it is with the fevers of shame. You swallow the bitter quinine of knowledge, and you learn to feel pity and compassion toward the drinker. Yet the shame lingers in your marrow, and, because of the shame, anger.

15   For a long stretch of my childhood we lived on a military reservation in Ohio, an arsenal where bombs were stored underground in bunkers, vintage airplanes burst into flames, and unstable artillery shells boomed nightly at the dump. We had the feeling, as children, that we played in a mine field, where a heedless footfall could trigger an explosion. When Father was drinking, the house, too, became a mine field. The least bump could set off either parent.

16   The more he drank, the more obsessed Mother became with stopping him. She hunted for bottles, counted the cash in his wallet, sniffed at his breath. Without meaning to snoop, we children blundered left and right into damning evidence. On afternoons when he came home from work sober, we flung ourselves at him for hugs, and felt against our ribs the telltale lump in his coat. In the barn we tumbled on the hay and heard beneath our sneakers the crunch of buried glass. We tugged open a drawer in his workbench, looking for screwdrivers or crescent wrenches, and spied a gleaming six-pack among the tools. Playing tag, we darted around the house just in time to see him sway on the rear stoop and heave a finished bottle into the woods. In his good-night kiss we smelled the cloying sweetness of Clorets, the mints he chewed to camouflage his dragon's breath.

17   I can summon up that kiss right now by recalling Theodore Roethke's lines about his own father in "My Papa's Waltz":

> *The whiskey on your breath*
> *Could make a small boy dizzy;*
> *But I hung on like death:*
> *Such waltzing was not easy.*

Such waltzing was hard, terribly hard, for with a boy's scrawny arms I was trying to hold my tipsy father upright.

18   For years, the chief source of those incriminating bottles and cans was a grimy store a mile from us, a cinder block place called Sly's, with two gas pumps outside and a moth-eaten dog asleep in the window. A strip of flypaper,

speckled the year round with black bodies, coiled in the door-way. Inside, on rusty metal shelves or in wheezing coolers, you could find pop and Popsicles, cigarettes, potato chips, canned soup, raunchy postcards, fishing gear, Twinkies, wine, and beer. When Father drove anywhere on errands, Mother would send us kids along as guards, warning us not to let him out of our sight. And so with one or more of us on board, Father would cruise up to Sly's, pump a dollar's worth of gas or plump the tires with air, and then, telling us to wait in the car, he would head for that fly-spangled doorway.

19   Dutiful and panicky, we cried, "Let us go in with you!"

20   "No," he answered. "I'll be back in two shakes."

21   "Please!"

22   "No!" he roared. "Don't you budge, or I'll jerk a knot in your tails!"

23   So we stayed put, kicking the seats, while he ducked inside. Often, when he had parked the car at a careless angle, we gazed in through the window and saw Mr. Sly fetching down from a shelf behind the cash register two green pints of Gallo wine. Father swigged one of them right there at the counter, stuffed the other in his pocket, and then out he came, a bulge in his coat, a flustered look on his red face.

24   Because the Mom and Pop who ran the dump were neighbors of ours, living just down the tar-blistered road, I hated them all the more for poisoning my father. I wanted to sneak in their store and smash the bottles and set fire to the place. I also hated the Gallo brothers, Ernest and Julio, whose jovial faces shone from the labels of their wine, labels I would find, torn and curled, when I burned the trash. I noted the Gallo brothers' address, in California, and I studied the road atlas to see how far that was from Ohio, because I meant to go out there and tell Ernest and Julio what they were doing to my father, and then, if they showed no mercy, I would kill them.

25   While growing up on the back roads and in the country schools and cramped Methodist churches of Ohio and Tennessee, I never heard the word *alcoholism*, never happened across it in books or magazines. In the nearby towns, there were no addiction treatment programs, no community mental health centers, no Alcoholics Anonymous chapters, no therapists. Left alone with our grievous secret, we had no way of understanding Father's drinking except as an act of will, a deliberate folly or cruelty, a moral weakness, a sin. He drank because he chose to, pure and simple. Why our father, so playful and competent and kind when sober, would choose to ruin himself and punish his family, we could not fathom.

26   Our neighborhood was high on the Bible, and the Bible was hard on drunkards. "Woe to those who are heroes at drinking wine, and valiant men in mixing strong drink," wrote Isaiah. "The priest and the prophet reel with strong drink, they are confused with wine, they err in vision, they stumble in giving judgment. For all tables are full of vomit, no place is without filthiness."

We children had seen those fouled tables at the local truck stop where the notorious boozers hung out, our father occasionally among them. "Wine and new wine take away the understanding," declared the prophet Hosea. We had also seen evidence of that in our father, who could multiply seven-digit numbers in his head when sober, but when drunk could not help us with fourth-grade math. Proverbs warned: "Do not look at wine when it is red, when it sparkles in the cup and goes down smoothly. At the last it bites like a serpent, and stings like an adder. Your eyes will see strange things, and your mind utter perverse things." Woe, woe.

27   Dismayingly often, these biblical drunkards stirred up trouble for their own kids. Noah made fresh wine after the flood, drank too much of it, fell asleep without any clothes on, and was glimpsed in the buff by his son Ham, whom Noah promptly cursed. In one passage—it was so shocking we had to read it under our blankets with flashlights—the patriarch Lot fell down drunk and slept with his daughters. The sins of the fathers set their children's teeth on edge.

28   Our ministers were fond of quoting St. Paul's pronouncement that drunkards would not inherit the kingdom of God. These grave preachers assured us that the wine referred to during the Last Supper was in fact grape juice. Bible and sermons and hymns combined to give us the impression that Moses should have brought down from the mountain another stone tablet, bearing the Eleventh Commandment: Thou shalt not drink.

29   The scariest and most illuminating Bible story apropos of drunkards was the one about the lunatic and the swine. Matthew, Mark, and Luke each told a version of the tale. We knew it by heart: When Jesus climbed out of his boat one day, this lunatic came charging up from the graveyard, stark naked and filthy, frothing at the mouth, so violent that he broke the strongest chains. Nobody would go near him. Night and day for years this madman had been wailing among the tombs and bruising himself with stones. Jesus took one look at him and said, "Come out of the man, you unclean spirits!" for he could see that the lunatic was possessed by demons. Meanwhile, some hogs were conveniently rooting nearby. "If we have to come out," begged the demons, "at least let us go into those swine." Jesus agreed. The unclean spirits entered the hogs, and the hogs rushed straight off a cliff and plunged into a lake. Hearing the story in Sunday school, my friends thought mainly of the pigs. (How big a splash did they make? Who paid for the lost pork?) But I thought of the redeemed lunatic, who bathed himself and put on clothes and calmly sat at the feet of Jesus, restored—so the Bible said—to "his right mind."

30   When drunk, our father was clearly in his wrong mind. He became a stranger, as fearful to us as any graveyard lunatic, not quite frothing at the mouth but fierce enough, quick-tempered, explosive; or else he grew maudlin and weepy, which frightened us nearly as much. In my boyhood despair, I reasoned that maybe he wasn't to blame for turning into an ogre. Maybe, like

the lunatic, he was possessed by demons. I found support for my theory when I heard liquor referred to as "spirits," when the newspapers reported that somebody had been arrested for "driving under the influence," and when church ladies railed against that "demon drink."

31   If my father was indeed possessed, who would exorcise him? If he was a sinner, who would save him? If he was ill, who would cure him? If he suffered, who would ease his pain? Not ministers or doctors, for we could not bring ourselves to confide in them; not the neighbors, for we pretended they had never seen him drunk; not Mother, who fussed and pleaded but could not budge him; not my brother and sister, who were only kids. That left me. It did not matter that I, too, was only a child, and a bewildered one at that. I could not excuse myself.

?

32   On first reading a description of delirium tremens—in a book on alcoholism I smuggled from the library—I thought immediately of the frothing lunatic and the frenzied swine. When I read stories or watched films about grisly metamorphoses—Dr. Jekyll becoming Mr. Hyde, the mild husband changing into a werewolf, the kindly neighbor taken over by a brutal alien—I could not help seeing my own father's mutation from sober to drunk. Even today, knowing better, I am attracted by the demonic theory of drink, for when I recall my father's transformation, the emergence of his ugly second self, I find it easy to believe in possession by unclean spirits. We never knew which version of Father would come home from work, the true or the tainted, nor could we guess how far down the slope toward cruelty he would slide.

33   How far a man *could* slide we gauged by observing our back-road neighbors—the out-of-work miners who had dragged their families to our corner of Ohio from the desolate hollows of Appalachia, the tightfisted farmers, the surly mechanics, the balked and broken men. There was, for example, whiskey-soaked Mr. Jenkins, who beat his wife and kids so hard we could hear their screams from the road. There was Mr. Lavo the wino, who fell asleep smoking time and again, until one night his disgusted wife bundled up the children and went outside and left him in his easy chair to burn; he awoke on his own, staggered out coughing into the yard, and pounded her flat while the children looked on and the shack turned to ash. There was the truck driver, Mr. Sampson, who tripped over his son's tricycle one night while drunk and got so mad that he jumped into his semi and drove away, shifting through the dozen gears, and never came back. We saw the bruised children of these fathers clump onto our school bus, we saw the abandoned children huddle in the pews at church, we saw the stunned and battered mothers begging for help at our doors.

34   Our own father never beat us, and I don't think he ever beat Mother, but he threatened often. The Old Testament Yahweh was not more terrible in his wrath. Eyes blazing, voice booming, Father would pull out his belt and swear

to give us a whipping, but he never followed through, never needed to, because we could imagine it so vividly. He shoved us, pawed us with the back of his hand, as an irked bear might smack a cub, not to injure, just to clear a space. I can see him grabbing Mother by the hair as she cowers on a chair during a nightly quarrel. He twists her neck back until she gapes up at him, and then he lifts over her skull a glass quart bottle of milk, the milk running down his forearm, and he yells at her, "Say just one more word, one goddamn word, and I'll shut you up!" I fear she will prick him with her sharp tongue, but she is terrified into silence, and so am I, and the leaking bottle quivers in the air, and milk slithers through the red hair of my father's uplifted arm, and the entire scene is there to this moment, the head jerked back, the club raised.

35   When the drink made him weepy, Father would pack a bag and kiss each of us children on the head, and announce from the front door that he was moving out. "Where to?" we demanded, fearful each time that he would leave for good, as Mr. Sampson had roared away for good in his diesel truck. "Someplace where I won't get hounded every minute," Father would answer, his jaw quivering. He stabbed a look at Mother, who might say, "Don't run into the ditch before you get there," or, "Good riddance," and then he would slink away. Mother watched him go with arms crossed over her chest, her face closed like the lid on a box of snakes. We children bawled. Where could he go? To the truck stop, that den of iniquity? To one of those dark, ratty flophouses in town? Would he wind up sleeping under a railroad bridge or on a park bench or in a cardboard box, mummied in rags, like the bums we had seen on our trips to Cleveland and Chicago? We bawled and bawled, wondering if he would ever come back.

36   He always did come back, a day or a week later, but each time there was a sliver less of him.

37   In Kafka's *The Metamorphosis*, which opens famously with Gregor Samsa waking up from uneasy dreams to find himself transformed into an insect, Gregor's family keep reassuring themselves that things will be just fine again, "When he comes back to us." Each time alcohol transformed our father, we held out the same hope, that he would really and truly come back to us, our authentic father, the tender and playful and competent man, and then all things would be fine. We had grounds for such hope. After his weepy departures and chapfallen returns, he would sometimes go weeks, even months without drinking. Those were glad times. Joy banged inside my ribs. Every day without the furtive glint of bottles, every meal without a fight, every bedtime without sobs encouraged us to believe that such bliss might go on forever.

38   Mother was fooled by just such a hope all during the forty-odd years she knew this Greeley Ray Sanders. Soon after she met him in a Chicago delicatessen on the eve of World War II, and fell for his butter-melting Mississippi drawl and his wavy red hair, she learned that he drank heavily. But then so did

a lot of men. She would soon coax or scold him into breaking the nasty habit. She would point out to him how ugly and foolish it was, this bleary drinking, and then he would quit. He refused to quit during their engagement, however, still refused during the first years of marriage, refused until my sister came along. The shock of fatherhood sobered him, and he remained sober through my birth at the end of the war and right on through until we moved in 1951 to the Ohio arsenal, that paradise of bombs. Like all places that make a business of death, the arsenal had more than its share of alcoholics and drug addicts and other varieties of escape artists. There I turned six and started school and woke into a child's flickering awareness, just in time to see my father begin sneaking swigs in the garage.

39   He sobered up again for most of a year at the height of the Korean War, to celebrate the birth of my brother. But aside from that dry spell, his only breaks from drinking before I graduated from high school were just long enough to raise and then dash our hopes. Then during the fall of my senior year — the time of the Cuban missile crisis, when it seemed that the nightly explosions at the munitions dump and the nightly rages in our household might spread to engulf the globe — Father collapsed. His liver, kidneys, and heart all conked out. The doctors saved him, but only by a hair. He stayed in the hospital for weeks, going through a withdrawal so terrible that Mother would not let us visit him. If he wanted to kill himself, the doctors solemnly warned him, all he had to do was hit the bottle again. One binge would finish him.

40   Father must have believed them, for he stayed dry for the next fifteen years. It was an answer to prayer, Mother said, it was a miracle. I believe it was a reflex of fear, which he sustained over the years through courage and pride. He knew a man could die from drink, for his brother Roscoe had. We children never laid eyes on doomed Uncle Roscoe, but in the stories Mother told us he became a fairy-tale figure, like a boy who took the wrong turning in the woods and was gobbled up by the wolf.

41   The fifteen-year dry spell came to an end with Father's retirement in the spring of 1978. Like many men, he gave up his identity along with his job. One day he was a boss at the factory, with a brass plate on his door and a reputation to uphold; the next day he was a nobody at home. He and Mother were leaving Ontario, the last of the many places to which his job had carried them, and they were moving to a new house in Mississippi, his childhood stomping grounds. As a boy in Mississippi, Father sold Coca-Cola during dances while the moonshiners peddled their brew in the parking lot; as a young blade, he fought in bars and in the ring, seeking a state Golden Gloves championship; he gambled at poker, hunted pheasants, raced motorcycles and cars, played semiprofessional baseball, and, along with all his buddies — in the Black Cat Saloon, behind the cotton gin, in the woods — he drank. It was a perilous youth to dream of recovering.

42   After his final day of work, Mother drove on ahead with a car full of begonias and violets, while Father stayed behind to oversee the packing. When the van was loaded, the sweaty movers broke open a six-pack and offered him a beer.

43   "Let's drink to retirement!" they crowed. "Let's drink to freedom! to fishing! hunting! loafing! Let's drink to a guy who's going home!"

44   At least I imagine some such words, for that is all I can do, imagine, and I see Father's hand trembling in midair as he thinks about the fifteen sober years and about the doctors' warning, and he tells himself *God-damnit, I am a free man,* and *Why can't a free man drink one beer after a lifetime of hard work?* and I see his arm reaching, his fingers closing, the can tilting to his lips. I even supply a label for the beer, a swaggering brand that promises on television to deliver the essence of life. I watch the amber liquid pour down his throat, the alcohol steal into his blood, the key turn in his brain.

45   Soon after my parents moved back to Father's treacherous stomping ground, my wife and I visited them in Mississippi with our five-year-old daughter. Mother had been too distraught to warn me about the return of the demons. So when I climbed out of the car that bright July morning and saw my father napping in the hammock, I felt uneasy, for in all his sober years I had never known him to sleep in daylight. Then he lurched upright, blinked his blood-shot eyes, and greeted us in a syrupy voice. I was hurled back helpless into childhood.

46   "What's the matter with Papaw?" our daughter asked.

47   "Nothing," I said. "Nothing!"

48   Like a child again, I pretended not to see him in his stupor, and behind my phony smile I grieved. On that visit and on the few that remained before his death, once again I found bottles in the workbench, bottles in the woods. Again his hands shook too much for him to run a saw, to make his precious miniature furniture, to drive straight down back roads. Again he wound up in the ditch, in the hospital, in jail, in treatment centers. Again he shouted and wept. Again he lied. "I never touched a drop," he swore. "Your mother's making it up."

49   I no longer fancied I could reason with the men whose names I found on the bottles—Jim Beam, Jack Daniels—nor did I hope to save my father by burning down a store. I was able now to press the cold statistics about alcoholism against the ache of memory: ten million victims, fifteen million, twenty. And yet, in spite of my age, I reacted in the same blind way as I had in childhood, ignoring biology, forgetting numbers, vainly seeking to erase through my efforts whatever drove him to drink. I worked on their place twelve and sixteen hours a day, in the swelter of Mississippi summers, digging ditches, running electrical wires, planting trees, mowing grass, building sheds, as though what nagged at him was some list of chores, as though by taking his worries on my

shoulders I could redeem him. I was flung back into boyhood, acting as though my father would not drink himself to death if only I were perfect.

50   I failed of perfection; he succeeded in dying. To the end, he considered himself not sick but sinful. "Do you want to kill yourself?" I asked him. "Why not?" he answered. "Why the hell not? What's there to save?" To the end, he would not speak about his feelings, would not or could not give a name to the beast that was devouring him.

51   In silence, he went rushing off the cliff. Unlike the biblical swine, however, he left behind a few of the demons to haunt his children. Life with him and the loss of him twisted us into shapes that will be familiar to other sons and daughters of alcoholics. My brother became a rebel, my sister retreated into shyness, I played the stalwart and dutiful son who would hold the family together. If my father was unstable, I would be a rock. If he squandered money on drink, I would pinch every penny. If he wept when drunk—and only when drunk—I would not let myself weep at all. If he roared at the Little League umpire for calling my pitches balls, I would throw nothing but strikes. Watching him flounder and rage, I came to dread the loss of control. I would go through life without making anyone mad. I vowed never to put in my mouth or veins any chemical that would banish my everyday self. I would never make a scene, never lash out at the ones I loved, never hurt a soul. Through hard work, relentless work, I would achieve something dazzling—in the classroom, on the basketball floor, in the science lab, in the pages of books—and my achievement would distract the world's eyes from his humiliation. I would become a worthy sacrifice, and the smoke of my burning would please God.

52   It is far easier to recognize these twists in my character than to undo them. Work has become an addiction for me, as drink was an addiction for my father. Knowing this, my daughter gave me a placard for the wall: WORKAHOLIC. The labor is endless and futile, for I can no more redeem myself through work than I could redeem my father. I still panic in the face of other people's anger, because his drunken temper was so terrible. I shrink from causing sadness or disappointment even to strangers, as though I were still concealing the family shame. I still notice every twitch of emotion in the faces around me, having learned as a child to read the weather in faces, and I blame myself for their least pang of unhappiness or anger. In certain moods I blame myself for everything. Guilt burns like acid in my veins.

53   I am moved to write these pages now because my own son, at the age of ten, is taking on himself the griefs of the world, and in particular the griefs of his father. He tells me that when I am gripped by sadness he feels responsible; he feels there must be something he can do to spring me from depression, to fix my life. And that crushing sense of responsibility is exactly what I felt at the age of ten in the face of my father's drinking. My son wonders if I, too, am

possessed. I write, therefore, to drag into the light what eats at me—the fear, the guilt, the shame—so that my own children may be spared.

54   I still shy away from nightclubs, from bars, from parties where the solvent is alcohol. My friends puzzle over this, but it is no more peculiar than for a man to shy away from the lions' den after seeing his father torn apart. I took my own first drink at the age of twenty-one, half a glass of burgundy. I knew the odds of my becoming an alcoholic were four times higher than for the sons of nonalcoholic fathers. So I sipped warily.

55   I still do—once a week, perhaps, a glass of wine, a can of beer, nothing stronger, nothing more. I listen for the turning of a key in my brain.

🔊

Discussion Questions

1. What ruses does Sanders's father use to try to convince others that he has no problems with alcohol? How do others contribute to his game of pretense? Why?

*2. What adjectives seem most appropriate to describe Sanders's father when drunk? When sober? Support your choices by citing relevant paragraphs by number.

*3. The author writes in paragraph 7, ". . . I lie there hating him, loving him, fearing him, knowing I have failed him." What evidence does he present that would justify each of these feelings toward his father?

*4. Explain the significance that the following persons, places, events, or documents had for the author: Sly's, Ernest and Julio Gallo, the Bible, the birth of his sister and brother, the Ohio arsenal, the Cuban missile crisis, his father's retirement.

5. Describe the lasting effects his father's drinking had upon Sanders. How were other members of the immediate family affected? In what ways do Sanders's own children seem to have been affected, directly or indirectly, by their grandfather's drinking?

Writing Topics

1. Write a description of a personality change in someone you know. Choose some specific behaviors that best describe the person before and then after he or she seemed to change. Indicate how you outwardly and inwardly responded to the change in the individual.

2. Assume that you are Scott Sanders's mother and that you keep a journal. Write an entry in which you discuss your feelings about your husband's character.

❧She was an optimist who ignored trifles; for her, God was not in the details but in the intent."

THE SEAM OF THE SNAIL

Cynthia Ozick

Born in New York City in 1928, Cynthia Ozick is a novelist, short-story author, critic, poet, and playwright, one whose aesthetic and moral outlook has been strongly influenced by her identity as a Jew. A graduate of New York University (B.A., 1949) and of Ohio State University (M.A., 1950), Ozick has written numerous books, among them *The Pagan Rabbi and Other Stories* (1977), *Art & Ardor: Essays* (1983), *The Cannibal Galaxy* (1983), *The Messiah of Stockholm* (1987), *The Shawl* (1989), *Metaphor and Memory* (1989), and *Angel* (1993). A member of both The American Academy of Arts and Science and The American Academy of Arts and Letters, Ozick was the Phi Beta Kappa orator at Harvard University in 1985.

1   In my Depression childhood, whenever I had a new dress, my cousin Sarah would get suspicious. The nicer the dress was, and especially the more expensive it looked, the more suspicious she would get. Finally she would lift the hem and check the seams. This was to see if the dress had been bought or if my mother had sewed it. Sarah could always tell. My mother's sewing had elegant outsides, but there was something catch-as-catch-can about the insides. Sarah's sewing, by contrast, was as impeccably finished inside as out; not one stray thread dangled.

2   My uncle Jake built meticulous grandfather clocks out of rosewood; he was a perfectionist, and sent to England for the clockworks. My mother built serviceable radiator covers and a serviceable cabinet, with hinged doors, for the pantry. She built a pair of bookcases for the living room. Once, after I was grown and in a house of my own, she fixed the sewer pipe. She painted ceilings, and also landscapes; she reupholstered chairs. One summer she planted a whole yard of tall corn. She thought herself capable of doing anything, and did everything she imagined. But nothing was perfect. There was always some clear flaw, never visible head-on. You had to look underneath, where the seams were. The corn thrived, though not in rows. The stalks elbowed one another like gossips in a dense little village.

3   "Miss Brrrrooobaker," my mother used to mock, rolling her Russian *r*'s, whenever I crossed a *t* she had left uncrossed, or corrected a word she had misspelled, or became impatient with a *v* that had tangled itself up with a *w* in her speech. ("*Vw*entriloquist," I would say. "*Vw*entriloquist," she would obediently repeat. And the next time it would come out "wiolinist.") Miss Brubaker was my high school English teacher, and my mother invoked her name as an emblem of raging finical obsession. "Miss Brrrrooobaker," my mother's voice hoots at me down the years, as I go on casting and recasting sentences in a tiny handwriting on monomaniacally uniform paper. The loops of my mother's handwriting—it was the Palmer Method—were as big as soup bowls, spilling generous splashy ebullience. She could pull off, at five minutes' notice, a satisfying dinner for ten concocted out of nothing more than originality and panache. But the napkin would be folded a little off center, and the spoon might be on the wrong side of the knife. She was an optimist who ignored trifles; for her, God was not in the details but in the intent. And all these culinary and agricultural efflorescences were extracurricular, accomplished in the crevices and niches of a fourteen-hour business day. When she scribbled out her family memoirs, in heaps of dog-eared notebooks, or on the backs of old bills, or on the margins of last year's calendar, I would resist typing them; in the speed of the chase she often omitted words like "the," "and," "will." The same flashing and bountiful hand fashioned and fired ceramic pots, and painted brilliant autumn views and vases of imaginary flowers and ferns, and decorated ordinary Woolworth platters with lavish enameled gardens. But bits of the painted petals would chip away.

4   Lavish: my mother was as lavish as nature. She woke early and saturated the hours with work and inventiveness, and read late into the night. She was all profusion, abundance, fabrication. Angry at her children, she would run after us whirling the cord of the electric iron, like a lasso or a whip; but she never caught us. When, in seventh grade, I was afraid of failing the Music Appreciation final exam because I could not tell the difference between "To a Wild Rose" and "Barcarole," she got the idea of sending me to school with a gauze sling rigged up on my writing arm, and an explanatory note that was purest fiction. But the sling kept slipping off. My mother gave advice like mad—she boiled over with so much passion for the predicaments of strangers that they turned into permanent cronies. She told intimate stories about people I had never heard of.

5   Despite the gargantuan Palmer loops (or possibly because of them), I have always known that my mother's was a life of—intricately abashing word!—excellence: insofar as excellence means ripe generosity. She burgeoned, she proliferated; she was endlessly leafy and flowering. She wore red hats, and called herself a gypsy. In her girlhood she marched with the suffragettes and for Margaret Sanger and called herself a Red. She made me laugh, she was so varied: like a tree on which lemons, pomegranates, and prickly pears absurdly all hang together. She had the comedy of prodigality.

6   My own way is a thousand times more confined. I am a pinched perfectionist, the ultimate fruition of Miss Brubaker; I attend to crabbed minutiae and am self-trammeled through taking pains. I am a kind of human snail, locked in and condemned by my own nature. The ancients believed that the moist track left by the snail as it crept was the snail's own essence, depleting its body little by little; the farther the snail toiled, the smaller it became, until it finally rubbed itself out. That is how perfectionists are. Say to us Excellence, and we will show you how we use up our substance and wear ourselves away, while making scarcely any progress at all. The fact that I am an exacting perfectionist in a narrow strait only, and nowhere else, is hardly to the point, since nothing matters to me so much as a comely and muscular sentence. It is my narrow strait, this snail's road; the track of the sentence I am writing now; and when I have eked out the wet substance, ink or blood, that is its mark, I will begin the next sentence. Only in treading out sentences am I perfectionist; but then there is nothing else I know how to do, or take much interest in. I miter every pair of abutting sentences as scrupulously as Uncle Jake fitted one strip of rosewood against another. My mother's worldly and bountiful hand has escaped me. The sentence I am writing is my cabin and my shell, compact, self-sufficient. It is the burnished horizon—a merciless planet where flawlessness is the single standard, where even the inmost seams, however hidden from a laxer eye, must meet perfection. Here "excellence" is not strewn casually from a tipped cornucopia, here disorder does not account for charm, here trifles rule like tyrants.

7   I measure my life in sentences pressed out, line by line, like the lustrous ooze on the underside of the snail, the snail's secret open seam, its wound, leaking attar. My mother was too mettlesome to feel the force of a comma. She scorned minutiae. She measured her life according to what poured from the horn of plenty, which was her own seamless, ample, cascading, elastic, susceptible, inexact heart. My narrower heart rides between the tiny twin horns of the snail, dwindling as it goes.

8   And out of this thinnest thread, this ink-wet line of words, must rise a visionary fog, a mist, a smoke, forging cities, histories, sorrows, quagmires, entanglements, lives of sinners, even the life of my furnace-hearted mother: so much wilderness, waywardness, plenitude on the head of the precise and impeccable snail, between the horns. (Ah, if this could be!)

                  ʒ❧

Discussion Questions

*1.   What details reveal the breadth of abilities possessed by Ozick's mother? What details reveal her mother's imperfections?

2.   In the selection, what does Miss Brubaker, Ozick's high-school English teacher, represent for Ozick's mother? For Ozick herself?

*3. How would you summarize Ozick's attitude toward her mother? Select words, phrases, and sentences from the selection that support your assessment.

4. In paragraph 6, Ozick says she is "a kind of human snail." What evidence does she offer to justify the use of this metaphor?

5. Had Ozick compared herself to a turtle, also noted for its slow pace, would the metaphor have been equally effective? Why or why not?

6. Reread the last paragraph. What paradoxical tasks has "the human snail" taken upon itself?

Writing Topics

1. In a brief essay, support one of the following thesis statements with specific examples:
   a. Like Cynthia Ozick's mother, I am lavish by nature.
   b. Like Cynthia Ozick, I am a "pinched perfectionist."
   c. A hybrid of Cynthia Ozick and her mother, I share some traits of each.

2. Choose some living creature to which to compare yourself in a short paper. In your comparison, justify your choice by describing the traits that you believe you share with this creature.

"I wished that I could have grown up with him, that he could have been my best friend. . . ."

AN ANTHEM FOR MY FATHER

Gerald Early

Gerald Early (b. 1952), a native of Philadelphia, Pennsylvania, is a professor of English and African and Afro-American studies at Washington University in Saint Louis, Missouri. His works include *Tuxedo Junction: Essays on American Culture* (1990) and *The Culture of Bruising: Essays on Prizefighting, Literature, and Modern American Culture* (1991).

"An Anthem for My Father," excerpted from Early's *Daughters: On Family and Fatherhood* (1994), appeared in the September-October 1994 issue of *Modern Maturity.*

1   One afternoon [my daughters and I] were looking at a picture of me when I was a boy of about eight. It is the only picture they have seen of me as a boy (so few were taken, and most of those were lost). I am standing, with three other boys, in front of the altar of my church. We are all in our Sunday best, but I am the only one wearing a coat—a trench coat, buttoned to my throat. I remember the coat well and the day of the picture. It was an Easter Sunday. I am smiling to beat the band.

2   "You were a cute little boy," Linnet said.

3   "Yeah," said Rosalind, laughing, "big happy smile, big block head."

4   "I wish I could have known you when you were a boy," Linnet said, almost with a tone of poignant regret.

5   "Me, too" said Rosalind. "I bet you were a nice boy."

6   "You guys don't even like boys," I said grinning. "Besides, you wouldn't have liked me. I was a boring little boy. All I liked was baseball. It was all I thought about as a boy. It was all I wanted to play."

7   "Why did you like baseball so much, Daddy?" Linnet asked.

8   "You know," I said, casting my mind back a bit, "there would be these days, terribly hot summer days, and no one when I was a boy had air-conditioning except in the movie houses, a few corner grocery stores, and a couple of the Italian homeowners in the neighborhood. Well, on those days especially, there would be a group of us black boys who would get together to play baseball, softball, stickball, anything, somewhere in the heat. All day long that

is what we would do. And before each game, just as we saw done in the major-league games, we would sing the national anthem. Can you imagine that? A group of black boys out in some lot in the heat singing the national anthem. We didn't even like the song and most of us didn't like to sing but we did because that was how the professionals did it. Well, it was at those moments of singing the national anthem that I really loved baseball most of all because it made me feel like an American. I felt like I was part of the country."

9   They were silent for a time, I suppose more impressed by this response than they should have been.

10   "But," I said suddenly, "that's not all. I loved watching the pros play because I was a fatherless boy without brothers and so I could watch those young men and imagine one of them as an older brother or as my father. I loved baseball as a boy because . . ."

11   As I was saying this my thoughts drifted back to my father and how much I, when I was a boy, wished I could have known him, not as a man, but when he was a boy. I wished that I could have grown up with him, that he could have been my best friend, that we could have sung the national anthem together, and could have gone to games. My father and I would walk arm in arm, a fantasy so intense that I would sometimes see him before me, imagine him there, talk to him. So intense a fantasy was it that at times as a child I thought my make-believe was a sure sign that I was crazy. Whose little boy are you? For years, I lied to my childhood friends, telling them that my father wanted to name me after him, wanted to name me Henry.

12   "He wanted to," I would say proudly, "but my mom wouldn't let him." But I know that he hated his name, that he would never have given it to me. All children wish to know their parents as children, wish to know the origin of these people who rather spring upon them fully grown, fully developed, fully being what they are.

13   I finished my thought to my daughters: ". . . because it made me feel less lonely."

14   "Well," said Linnet, after a moment, "we still wish we could have known you as a boy. You were probably real nice. Not like the boys we know. I bet it would have been fun going to a baseball game with you."

15   "Yeah," said Rosalind, "going to a baseball game with that smiley little boy with the big block head. That would have been fun."

↾✿

Discussion Questions

1. What prompted the conversation between the father and his daughters? How well do they seem to relate to each other? Explain.

2. As a boy, on what occasions did Early sing "The Star-Spangled Banner"? How did he feel about the song? Why did he sing it?
3. When he was young, what longings and fantasies did Early have about baseball and about his father? Do you consider these fantasies to be normal or abnormal? Explain.

Writing Topics

1. At what moments have you been most proud to be a citizen of your nation? Try to recall at least two specific occasions on which you felt a surge of patriotism toward your country and describe them in detail—when, where, why, and how this feeling was evoked in you.
2. Assume that you are given the opportunity to spend a day with your father or mother when you are both young. In a short essay, describe what you would want the two of you to do—where you would like to go and what you would like to talk about, indicating why you would choose these particular places and topics.

𝒲y mother took care of him like he was a child, inspecting him carefully before he stepped out of the house. . . ."

NAFTALE

Gertrude Reiss

A writer since childhood and a former dancer, teacher of dance, and hospital administrative assistant, Gertrude Reiss (b. 1917) makes her home in Brooklyn. She reports, "I grew up during the Great Depression and, as a teenager, went to work in a coal company to help support my family. I earned twelve dollars a week, worked five-and-a-half days a week, and at night took the subway to New York, where I studied dance. . . ." After the last of her three children had completed his doctorate, Reiss, who notes, "I've been a student all my life," enrolled in Brooklyn College, which she continues to attend. Over the years, she has won numerous awards for her writing, much of it composed at night, when her children were asleep. "Naftale" appears in *Legacies* (1993), a collection of brief memoirs written by elderly contributors.

1   "Papa, I want to know about your life."

2   "So come, I'll tell you."

3   My father was a man of medium height, on the heavy side. He had always had a mustache. I think he must have been born with it. Day and night his head was covered by a skullcap; he never took it off, not even when he slept, in deference to his God. His pants never stayed up, and his shirttails never stayed tucked in. My mother took care of him like he was a child, inspecting him carefully before he stepped out of the house, constantly scolding him about his appearance. "Look at him, a grown man walking around with his pants falling down." He didn't seem to mind her nagging. It was an amusing game they both played.

4   My father was born, he told me, about November 4, 1880. He was not sure of the date, since no records were kept, but he knew he was born after the High Holy Days and before Hanukkah, so for him November 4 is his birthday.

5   He was the first of seven children. His mother, Leah, and his father, Hershel, were bakers. They lived in two rooms in Mahden, a shtetl in Galicia, then Austrian Poland. It was a poverty-stricken town; all the Jews, about three hundred families, lived from hand to mouth. Leah and Hershel baked bagels, zeml, and bread in their two little rooms. "Good bakers they were, too." My father bent his head back and closed his eyes. "What good smells! I can remember them still."

6   My father had more education than most of the children of his village. His schooling stopped after his bar mitzvah, at the age of thirteen, when he was sent to a neighboring town as an apprentice baker. "There I remained until I was eighteen. My father died of double pneumonia. He was forty-seven years old. Since I was the oldest, I had to leave my job and come home to help my mother support my brothers and sisters." Here he paused, took a deep breath, and went on.

7   "Now I come to the second and most important part of my story. I was betrothed to the most beloved and true girl, who is now my wife."

8   My mother, who was listening, blushed. "Go on, go on. You don't have to write that," she told me.

9   "I must say everything, just the way it was. Put it down. Just like that," said my father. "I was betrothed to the most beloved girl. I was twenty years old, and it was time I had a wife, so the shadchan ran around and tried to match me with this one and that one. None of the girls pleased me. I had my eye on your mother. Her father and my father were second cousins. My father, may his soul rest in peace, was very fond of your mother. She was a strong, industrious girl, with rosy cheeks and merry brown eyes. 'Hear now, Shmul,' my father said one day to your mother's father when we were both very young, 'my Naftale will be your Frumit's intended.'

10   "I loved your mother, and she was crazy about me." His eyes twinkled. My mother laughed. "After all, you mustn't forget, I was quite a catch. I was charming, handsome, and learned too! Your mother was an excellent cook. Everybody praised her. She was a virtuous girl, worked for a rabbi. So we fell in love and saw each other every day. What a scandal in the village! We weren't supposed to see each other until the wedding, but your mother couldn't stay away from me. Nu, we became engaged and exchanged presents. I gave your mother three rings."

11   "What kind of three rings!" exclaimed my mother. "You gave me a ring."

12   "Don't interfere. Who is telling the story? It's my life! Write exactly what I tell you. I gave her three rings, and she gave me fourteen gulden. It was supposed to be twenty-four gulden according to the agreement. You know, your mother still owes me ten gulden." He looked at my mother slyly.

13   "What are you talking about?" she said. "Didn't your son pay it back to you at our golden wedding? I don't owe you anymore."

14   "So we were married," my father continued. "We got a room for twenty gulden a year. We started with no money and no furniture, but we got flour and yeast on credit, so I baked bread and your mother baked cake. Little by little we were able to buy a few things. One child came and another. We managed to scratch a living for a few years. Then times got bad. What to do? Your mother and I put our heads together and made up our minds that I would go to America."

15   The crossing was rough, four weeks of traveling third-class. He could not eat the ship's food because his religion would not permit it. All the immigrants shared whatever food they had. "We lived on herring, challah, and cake."

16   In New York, a great-aunt who owned a little grocery store on the Lower East Side took him into her home. She had found him a job in a bakery for four dollars a week.

17   "Oy, was that a job. The boss wasn't of the best. Just because I was a greenhorn he thought he could pull the wool over my eyes. A greenhorn I was, but not a fool. Besides baking, he tried to make me lift heavy baskets of bread. 'Reb,' I complained, 'I'm a baker, not a donkey.' Nu, so what does that schlimazel do? He gave me such a smack in my face that I thought the heavens would open up. But I was clever. I raised such a cry that all the people came running. The entire block heard me. What a commotion! My boss got scared. After all, we were all greenhorns, and they took my part.

18   " 'Naftale,' said the boss, 'why should we fight? Jews shouldn't fight with each other. So I lost my head for a moment. Come, take twenty-five dollars and let's call the whole thing settled.' I took the money, but I swore I wouldn't work for him anymore. Besides, I was tired of being a baker. I wanted to learn a different trade. The money I sent home to my wife.

19   "My great-aunt lived on Ritt Street. On Saturdays men would congregate on the street outside the shul. I became friendly with one of them who was a garment worker. 'If you want to get into the garment trade, I can take you to a shop where they need a pants presser,' he told me. When I got there the boss said I was to work for three weeks without pay and on the fourth week he would give me two dollars. I agreed. What was my joy to see a landsman of mine in the shop! He worked there as a pants presser too. I could see everything was going to turn out well.

20   "During the week we were supposed to sleep in the shop. We made our beds on the worktables, using piles of pants as a mattress. That first night I didn't sleep so well. In the dark I heard someone moving near me, so I jumped off the table, and who do you think it was? My landsman! Imagine, he was going through my pants, trying to rob me. What a nerve! All I had to my name, four dollars, was in my pocket. I gave him such a laying-to that he would never lift his head up again.

21   "I climbed back on the table and had finally managed to close my eyes when someone shook me. 'Get up, Naftale. It's time to go to work.' All the men were stretching their tired bones, scratching their uncombed hair. A fire was started in the stove. We worked from three-thirty in the morning until seven, when we stopped, got out our phylacteries, and said our prayers. Then it was time to eat. 'Let Naftale go buy the food,' everyone agreed. 'The grocer will have pity on him and give him more because he's just off the boat a few days.'

22   "That's the way it was. I came back so laden with food and beer that the men let out a cheer. We dug into that tztzl bread, onions, and beer. The men urged me to go again, and without too much coaxing, off I went. Three times they sent me out for more beer. Before I knew it, I felt very merry and started to sing. I sang all the songs I knew in a good loud voice, and pretty soon everyone was singing with me. There was no more work that day."

23   Until I asked my father to tell me about his life, I never knew he was a happy man.

ৼ

Discussion Questions

*1.   Cite by appropriate paragraph numbers evidence that reveals the narrator's father to be each of the following: religious; careless about his appearance; loving; proud; humorous; industrious.

2.   What led Reiss's father in paragraphs 21-22 to buy food and beer for his fellow workers? What were the consequences?

3.   Judging from the last sentence of the selection, how do you think Reiss had perceived her father before he had talked about his life? From what the selection reveals about him, would you consider him to be a happy man? Why or why not?

Writing Topics

*1.   If you have ever misjudged a person's character, relate in an essay the circumstances that initially led you to make a faulty judgment, then those that encouraged you to change your mind. Conclude by revealing how you now view the individual's character.

2.   From the following four possible thesis statements, choose one, and in a brief essay support it with appropriate evidence:
    a.   My mother is a happy woman.
    b.   My mother is a sad woman.
    c.   My father is a happy man.
    d.   My father is a sad man.

Summary Writing Topics

*1. In recent years, several political leaders have referred to the American family as being "in crisis." Write an essay in which you both describe the nature of this crisis and cite its alleged causes and the recommendations being made to resolve it. In your conclusion, reveal which of these recommendations you believe would be most effective and your reasons for believing so.

2. If your family has been in the United States for a number of generations, trace its history from your great grandparents down to the present. Include in your chronicle information about these ancestors, such as their geographic locations, levels of education, kinds of employment, and apparent values.

3. If you or your parents migrated to the United States, write an essay that compares and contrasts life in this country to that in the country from which you or your parents migrated. Conclude your essay by indicating which nation you prefer and why.

*4. Write an investigative report on current U.S. policy on immigration. In your report, indicate whether you believe current policy should be changed. If so, point out toward whom and for what reasons it should be altered. If you believe present policy is sound, provide reasons for this belief.

*5. A number of court cases in the past decade have dealt with the rights of natural parents versus the rights of adoptive parents. Investigate one of these cases and write a report clarifying the issues involved and the basis on which the case was decided. Conclude by indicating both what your position would have been in reference to the case and your reasons for that position.

6. Assume that you had the opportunity to interview two authors of selections in "Roots and Branches." First indicate which authors you would interview, providing reasons for your choices; then compose at least five questions that you would like to ask each. After each question, explain why you would want to pose that question.

7. Choose the two parents from selections in "Roots and Branches" who you believe are most alike and the two who are least alike. In a short essay, justify your choices from evidence within the selections.

*8. Imagine that you are a foreigner with little information about American families. From what you have learned by reading the selections in "Roots and Branches," write a letter to a friend in which you report on the relationships between parents and children in the United States. Cite evidence from the selections to support your generalizations.

Cluster

2

Learning and Knowing

As a human being, you have maintained across time a core sense of self, thanks in good part to memory. Nevertheless, the **I** that is you is daily modified by what you experience, by what you are learning and coming to know. Five years ago, you were not the same person you are today; ten years hence, you will not be precisely the person you now are.

As you age, you steadily accumulate knowledge, some of it formally, some of it informally. Consider some of the things you know at present—about history, about people, about work, about etiquette, about science, about style. Then think about how you garnered that knowledge.

Chances are that some of it you acquired formally in school: what you know about the contribution of Ancient Greece to modern democracy, your understanding of photosynthesis or Euclidean geometry, your ability to differentiate satire from irony. Some things you may have learned through a combination of formal instruction, observation, and practice: how to work successfully in a group, how to wait on customers efficiently and courteously, how to apply brakes skillfully in traffic, how to cut food with a knife, what clothes to wear to the prom. And some knowledge you probably acquired almost exclusively from extended experience: what acquaintances to trust and not to trust, what writers or musicians appeal or do not appeal to you, what aptitudes you possess or lack for particular fields of study. All of what you have learned, have come to know, has contributed to the **I** that you currently are.

The selections you are about to read all have to do with learning and knowing as they transpire in school and out, formally and informally, on matters ranging from race to the teaching of literature. You will discover in reading them that what is being taught is not always what is being learned. You will also find that the writers' attitudes toward people and institutions vary from enthusiastic acceptance to ironic disdain. Regardless of attitudes held, the writers would likely concede that the experiences about which they write have in some way contributed to their view of themselves as unique individuals; in turn, as you read the selections, as you experience them, you will be subtly modifying the **I** that is you.

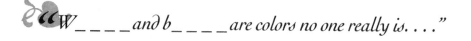

"W_ _ _ _ and b_ _ _ _ are colors no one really is. . . ."

COLORING LESSONS

David Updike

David Updike (b. 1957), a graduate of Harvard and Columbia Universities, teaches English at Roxbury Community College in Boston. He is the author of a collection of short stories, *Out on the Marsh* (1988), and of a number of works for juveniles, among them A *Winter Journey* (1985) and An *Autumn Tale* (1988). His interests include soccer and photography. "Coloring Lessons" appeared in *The New York Times Magazine* on Sunday, July 3, 1994.

1   It was the big annual fair at Shady Hill, a private school nestled away in one of our city's finer neighborhoods. Though October, it was warm and the ash gray clouds were giving way to soft, swelling shapes of blue. There were lots of kids already, their parents working the various concessions—apple bobbing and doughnut biting, water-balloon throwing at a heckling buffoon— all ploys to harvest money for the school's scholarship fund.

2   It seemed like the perfect event to bring an almost-4-year-old to, but my son, Wesley, was dragging on my arm, nervously surveying the scene. Getting tired of pulling him, disappointed that he was not having more fun, I stopped finally, kneeled down and asked him what was the matter.

3   He hesitated, looked around, chewing on his sleeve. "Too many pink people," he said softly. I laughed, but Wesley failed to see the humor of it and kept peering out through the thickening throng. "Too many pink people," he repeated. But along with my laugh came a twinge of nervousness—the parent's realization that our apprehensions are not entirely unfounded and that racial awareness comes even to 3-year-olds. I suspected, half wished, that his state of unhappiness had less to do with too many "pink" people than with too many people.

4   And we had taught him to use "pink" in the first place, in preference to the more common adjective used for people of my complexion. For my wife, we had opted for "brown" because that's the color she actually is: Wesley was learning his colors, after all, and it seemed silly and misleading to be describing people by colors they clearly are not.

5   The issue had arisen at his first day care—predominantly African-American—from which he had returned one day and asked whether he really

was "gray." We told him no, he wasn't gray, more brown, but a lighter, pinker shade than his mother.

6   A few months later he came home from his new day care, this time predominantly European-American, and asked, "Mommy, are we brown?"

7   "Yes," she said. "Why?"

8   "Melissa said we're b_ _ _ _."

9   "She did?"

10   "Yeah."

11   The whole question caused me to wonder what these two words, b_ _ _ _ and w_ _ _ _—so frequently used and so heavily laden with historical and social baggage—actually mean. I looked in a dictionary: the lighter of the two, I learned, is "the color of pure snow . . . reflecting nearly all the rays of sunlight, or a similar light. . . ."

12   The other means "lacking hue and brightness; absorbing light without reflecting any of the rays composing it . . . gloomy, pessimistic or dismal . . . without any moral light or goodness."

13   I am not the color of pure snow, and my wife and son reflect a good deal of light; they seem much closer in the spectrum to brown, "a dark shade with a yellowish or reddish hue." In any event, perhaps my problem with the two words is that they are, in the spectrum and in people's minds, absolutes and polar opposites, absorbing light or reflecting it but admitting no shades in between except gray—the pallor of the recently departed on the mortuary slab, blood drained from their earthly vessel.

14   All of which is likely to raise the hackles ("hairs on a dog's neck that bristle when the dog is ready to fight") of the anti-politically-correct thought police, who are fed up with all this precious talk about what we should call one another. They resist African-American—too many syllables, so hard to say— though they seem to be comfortable with Italian-American.

15   Let me enrage them further by suggesting that w_ _ _ _ may also have outlived its usefulness in describing people, and that we should take up European-American, instead, in keeping with the now-accepted Native, Asian- and African-American. Or maybe just plain "pink" will do, the color even the palest of us turn when push comes to shove and we reveal our humanity—when angry, say, or while laughing or having sex or lying in the sun, trying to turn brown.

16   W_ _ _ _ and b_ _ _ _ are colors no one really is, monolithic and redolent with historical innuendo and social shading, and the words encourage those of us who use them—everyone—to continue to think in binary terms, like computers. I am not suggesting the terms be abandoned, tossed onto the scrap heap of language with other discarded words—just that they are used too easily and often and should be traded in, occasionally, for words that admit that issues of race and ethnicity are more complicated than these monosyllables imply. Try not saying them, once or twice, and see how it feels. And if you are teaching a

child his or her colors, you might want to adopt a vocabulary that holds true for skin tones and for crayons.

17   But at the fair, things were improving slowly. I had, with misgivings, pointed out to Wesley that I am "pink," like some of his cousins and grandparents and uncles and aunts and school friends, and that it's not nice to say there are "too many" of us.

18   We walked around, mulling all this over, and I bought us a doughnut. We went into a gym and looked at old sports equipment, and I fought the temptation to buy something. We went outside again into the soft yellow sunlight and found happiness at a wading pool where, using fishing poles with magnets dangling from the lines, you could catch plastic fish with paper-clip noses. He caught a few and we traded them for prizes he then clutched tightly in his small, strong hands.

19   But he was still tired, and when I suggested we go home, he nodded and started to suck his thumb. I picked him up and carried him, and as we approached the gate he triumphantly called my attention to a "brown boy" with a baseball hat, who was just then coming in.

20   Again, his observation elicited in me a vague discomfort, and I wondered if we couldn't get away from all this altogether. But how?

21   "Wesley," I finally offered. "Do you have to call him 'brown boy'? Why don't you just say, 'That tall boy' or 'the boy with the blue hat' or 'the boy in the green sweatshirt'?" He mulled over my suggestion, but then rejected it.

22   "No," he said firmly. "He's brown."

❧

Discussion Questions

  1.   What was troubling Wesley at the outing shared with his father? For what reason might colors be particularly significant to Wesley?

  2.   Describe the ways in which Updike responds to Wesley's complaint. What "lessons" are taught in the selection, and what is learned by whom?

 *3.   Summarize Updike's arguments in paragraphs 11–16 regarding the dictionary definitions of race as they relate, first, to members of his family and, second, to groups of people. Do you consider his suggestion for a new description for "w_ _ _ _" to be a sound one? Explain.

 *4.   If you were asked to choose two adjectives to describe the emotional relationship between Updike and his son, what two would you choose? What evidence from the selection would support these choices?

*5. "Coloring Lessons" is a personal essay involving the author, his wife, and his son. Would the essay have been stronger if Updike had composed an impersonal third-person argument against current racial and ethnic classifications? Explain.

Writing Topics

*1. In an essay, describe an occasion when the issue of race was of importance to you. Consider where you were, when the event took place, who was involved, what happened, why and how it happened, how you felt at the time, and what you think you learned from the episode.

2. Write an account of your attempt to teach somebody something. Before beginning to write, consider these questions: What were you trying to teach? When? To whom? Why? How? With what success?

"I must stand up like a soldier, hold the book high in the air with both hands, and keep my feet still."

THE STUBBORN TWIG:
MY DOUBLE DOSE OF SCHOOLING

Monica Sone

Monica Sone (b. 1917), author of Nisei Daughter (1953), from which the following selection was taken, was a child in Seattle in the years immediately prior to World War II. There she lived near Skid Row in a hotel maintained by her Japanese-born father and mother. Considering herself a "Yankee," she resented her parents' forcing her to enroll in an afternoon Japanese school. Such schools, intended to teach the offspring of immigrants something of the language, history, and culture of their parents' native land, were common at the time. Some still exist today. During World War II, Sone and her family were sent to a relocation camp, Camp Minidoka, in Idaho. In 1943, she was released to work as a dental assistant in Chicago and later attended Wendell College in Indiana, where she majored in clinical psychology.

1　　The inevitable, dreaded first day at Nihon Gakko [Japanese school] arrived. Henry and I were dumped into a taxicab, screaming and kicking against the injustice of it all. When the cab stopped in front of a large, square gray-frame building, Mother pried us loose, though we clung to the cab door like barnacles. She half carried us up the hill. We kept up our horrendous shrieking and wailing, right to the school entrance. Then a man burst out of the door. His face seemed to have been carved out of granite and with turned-down mouth and nostrils flaring with disapproval, his black marble eyes crushed us into a quivering silence. This was Mr. Ohashi, the school principal, who had come out to investigate the abominable, un-Japanesey noise on the school premises.

2　　Mother bowed deeply and murmured, "I place them in your hands."

3　　He bowed stiffly to Mother, then fastened his eyes on Henry and me and again bowed slowly and deliberately. In our haste to return the bow, we nodded our heads. With icy disdain, he snapped, "That is not an *ojigi*." He bent forward with well-oiled precision. "Bow from the waist, like this."

4   I wondered, if Mr. Ohashi had the nerve to criticize us in front of Mother, what more he would do in her absence.

5   School was already in session and the hallway was empty and cold. Mr. Ohashi walked briskly ahead, opened a door, and Henry was whisked inside with Mother. I caught a glimpse of little boys and girls sitting erect, their books held upright on the desks.

6   As I waited alone out in the hall, I felt a tingling sensation. This was the moment for escape. I would run and run and run. I would be lost for days so that when Father and Mother finally found me, they would be too happy ever to force me back to Nihon Gakko. But Mr. Ohashi was too cunning for me. He must have read my thoughts, for the door suddenly opened, and he and Mother came out. He bowed formally again, "*Sah*, this way," and stalked off.

7   My will completely dissolved, I followed as in a terrible nightmare. Mother took my hand and smiled warmly, "Don't look so sad, Ka-chan. You'll find it a lot of fun when you get used to it."

8   I was ushered into a brightly lighted room which seemed ten times as brilliant with the dazzling battery of shining black eyes turned in my direction. I was introduced to Yasuda-sensei, a full-faced woman with a large, ballooning figure. She wore a long, shapeless cotton print smock with streaks of chalk powder down the front. She spoke kindly to me, but with a kindness that one usually reserves for a dull-witted child. She enunciated slowly and loudly, "What is your name?"

9   I whispered, "Kazuko," hoping she would lower her voice. I felt that our conversation should not be carried on in such a blatant manner.

10   "*Kazuko-san desuka?*" she repeated loudly. "You may sit over there." She pointed to an empty seat in the rear and I walked down an endless aisle between rows of piercing black eyes.

11   "Kazuko-san, why don't you remove your hat and coat and hang them up behind you?"

12   A wave of tittering broke out. With burning face, I rose from my seat and struggled out of my coat.

13   When Mother followed Mr. Ohashi out of the room, my throat began to tighten and tears flooded up again. I did not notice that Yasuda-sensei was standing beside me. Ignoring my snuffling, she handed me a book, opened to the first page. I saw a blurred drawing of one huge, staring eye. Right above it was a black squiggly mark, resembling the arabic figure one with a bar across the middle. Yasuda-sensei was up in front again, reading aloud, "*Meh!*" That was "eye." As we turned the pages, there were pictures of a long, austere nose, its print reading "*hana*," an ear was called "*mi-mi*," and a wide anemic-looking mouth, "*ku-chi*." Soon I was chanting at the top of my voice with the rest of the class, "*Meh! Hana! Mi-mi! Ku-chi!*"

14   Gradually I yielded to my double dose of schooling. Nihon Gakko was so different from grammar school I found myself switching my personality back

and forth daily like a chameleon. At Bailey Gatzert School I was a jumping, screaming, roustabout Yankee, but at the stroke of three when the school bell rang and doors burst open everywhere, spewing out pupils like jelly beans from a broken bag, I suddenly became a modest, faltering, earnest little Japanese girl with a small, timid voice. I trudged down a steep hill and climbed up another steep hill to Nihon Gakko with other black-haired boys and girls. On the playground, we behaved cautiously. Whenever we spied a teacher within bowing distance, we hissed at each other to stop the game, put our feet neatly together, slid our hands down to our knees and bowed slowly and sanctimoniously. In just the proper, moderate tone, putting in every ounce of respect, we chanted, *"Konichi-wa, sensei.* Good day."

15 For an hour and a half each day, we were put through our paces. At the beginning of each class hour, Yasuda-sensei punched a little bell on her desk. We stood up by our seats, at strict attention. Another "ping!" We all bowed to her in unison while she returned the bow solemnly. With the third "ping!" we sat down together.

16 There was *yomi-kata* time when individual students were called upon to read the day's lesson, clear and loud. The first time I recited I stood and read with swelling pride the lesson which I had prepared the night before. I mouthed each word carefully and paused for the proper length of time at the end of each sentence. Suddenly Yasuda-sensei stopped me.

17 "Kazuko-san!"

18 I looked up at her confused, wondering what mistakes I had made.

19 "You are holding your book in one hand,"she accused me. Indeed, I was. I did not see the need of using two hands to support a thin book which I could balance with two fingers.

20 "Use both hands!" she commanded me.

21 Then she peered at me. "And are you leaning against your desk?" Yes, I was slightly. "Stand up straight!"

22 *"Hai!* Yes, ma'am!"

23 I learned that I could stumble all around in my lessons without ruffling sensei's nerves, but it was a personal insult to her if I displayed sloppy posture. I must stand up like a soldier, hold the book high in the air with both hands, and keep my feet still.

24 We recited the Japanese alphabet aloud, fifty-one letters, over and over again. "Ah, ee, oo, eh, *OH!* Kah, kee, koo, key, *KOH!* Sah, shi, soo, seh, *SOH!"* We developed a catchy little rhythm, coming down hard on the last syllable of each line. We wound up the drill with an ear-shattering, triumphant, "Lah, lee, loo, leh, *Loh!* WAH, EE, OO, EH, OH! UN!"

25 Yasuda-sensei would look suspiciously at us. Our recital sounded a shade too hearty, a shade rhythmic. It lacked something . . . possibly restraint and respect.

26   During *kaki-kata* hour, I doubled up over my desk and painfully drew out the *kata-kanas*, simplified Japanese ideographs, similar to English block printing. With clenched teeth and perspiring hands, I accentuated and emphasized, delicately nuanced and tapered off lines and curves.

27   At five-thirty, Yasuda-sensei rang the bell on her desk again. "Ping!" We stood up. "Ping!" We bowed. "Ping!" We vanished from the room like magic, except for one row of students whose turn it was to do *otohban*, washing blackboards, sweeping the floor, and dusting the desks. Under sensei's vigilant eyes, the chore felt like a convict's hard labor.

28   As time went on, I began to suspect that there was much more to Nihon Gakko than learning the Japanese language. There was a driving spirit of strict discipline behind it all which reached out and weighed heavily upon each pupil's consciousness. That force emanated from the principal's office.

29   Before Mr. Ohashi came to America, he had been a zealous student of the Ogasawara Shiko Saho, a form of social conduct dreamed up by a Mr. Ogasawara. Mr. Ohashi himself had written a book on etiquette in Japan. He was the Oriental male counterpart of Emily Post. Thus Mr. Ohashi arrived in America with the perfect bow tucked under his waist and a facial expression cemented into perfect samurai control. He came with a smoldering ambition to pass on this knowledge to the tender Japanese saplings born on foreign soil. The school-teachers caught fire, too, and dedicated themselves to us with a vengeance. It was not enough to learn the language. We must talk and walk and sit and bow in the best Japanese tradition.

30   As far as I was concerned, Mr. Ohashi's superior standard boiled down to one thing. The model child is one with deep *rigor mortis* . . . no noise, no trouble, no back talk.

31   We understood too well what Mr. Ohashi wanted of us. He yearned and wished more than anything else that somehow he could mold all of us into Genji Yamadas. Genji was a classmate whom we detested thoroughly. He was born in Seattle, but his parents had sent him to Japan at an early age for a period of good, old-fashioned education. He returned home a stranger among us with stiff mannerisms and an arrogant attitude. Genji boasted that he could lick anyone, one husky fellow or ten little ones, and he did, time and time again. He was an expert at judo.

32   Genji was a handsome boy with huge, lustrous dark eyes, a noble patrician nose, jet crew-cut setting off a flawless, fair complexion, looking every bit the son of a samurai. He sat aloof at his desk and paid strict attention to sensei. He was the top student scholastically. He read fluently and perfectly. His handwriting was a beautiful picture of bold, masculine strokes and curves. What gnawed at us more than anything else was that he stood up as straight as a bamboo tree and never lost rigid control of his arms or legs. His bow was snappy and brisk and he always answered "*Hai!*" to everything that sensei said

to him, ringing crisp and clear with respect. Every time Mr. Ohashi came into our room for a surprise visit to see if we were under control, he would stop at Genji's desk for a brief chat. Mr. Ohashi's eyes betrayed a glow of pride as he spoke to Genji, who sat up erect, eyes staring respectfully ahead. All we could make out of the conversation was Genji's sharp staccato barks, "*Hai!* . . . *Hai!* . . . *Hai!*"

33   This was the response sublime to Mr. Ohashi. It was real man to man talk. Whenever Mr. Ohashi approached us, we froze in our seats. Instead of snapping into attention like Genji, we wilted and sagged. Mr. Ohashi said we were more like "*konyaku,*" a colorless, gelatinous Japanese food. If a boy fidgeted too nervously under Mr. Ohashi's stare, a vivid red stain rose from the back of Mr. Ohashi's neck until it reached his temple and then there was a sharp explosion like the crack of a whip. "*Keo-tsuke!* Attention!" It made us all leap in our seats, each one of us feeling terribly guilty for being such an inadequate Japanese.

34   I asked Mother, "Why is Mr. Ohashi so angry all the time? He always looks as if he had just bitten into a green persimmon. I've never seen him smile."

35   Mother said, "I guess Mr. Ohashi is the old-fashioned schoolmaster. I know he's strict, but he means well. Your father and I received harsher discipline than that in Japan . . . not only from schoolteachers, but from our own parents."

36   "Yes, I know, Mama." I leaned against her knees as she sat on the old leather davenport, mending our clothes. I thought Father and Mother were still wonderful, even if they had packed me off to Nihon Gakko. "Mrs. Matsui is so strict with her children, too. She thinks you spoil us." I giggled, and reassured her quickly, "But I don't think you spoil us at all."

37   Mrs. Matsui was ten years older than Mother, and had known Mother's father in Japan. Therefore she felt it was her duty to look after Mother's progress in this foreign country. Like a sharp-eyed hawk, she picked out Mother's weaknesses . . . It was impossible for us to remember the endless little things we must not do in front of Mrs. Matsui. We must not laugh out loud and show our teeth, or chatter in front of guests, or interrupt adult conversation, or cross our knees while seated, or ask for a piece of candy, or squirm in our seats. . . .

38   Mr. Ohashi and Mrs. Matsui thought they could work on me and gradually mold me into an ideal Japanese *ojoh-san,* a refined young maiden who is quiet, pure in thought, polite, serene, and self-controlled. They made little headway, for I was too much the child of Skidrow. As far as I was concerned, Nihon Gakko was a total loss. I could not use my Japanese on the people at the hotel. Bowing was practical only at Nihon Gakko. If I were to bow to the hotel patrons, they would have laughed in my face. Therefore promptly at five-thirty every day, I shed Nihon Gakko and returned with relief to an environment which was the only real one to me. Life was too urgent, too exciting, too colorful for me to be sitting quietly in the parlor and contemplating a spray of chrysanthemums in a bowl as a cousin of mine might be doing in Osaka.

ॐ

Discussion Questions

*1. Describe Sone's first impressions of Mr. Ohashi, the principal at Nihon Gakko; of Yasuda-sensei, her teacher; and of the other students.

2. What experiences in Mr. Ohashi's background influenced what took place in his school?

3. How did Sone's behavior at Nihon Gakko differ from her behavior at Bailey Gatzert, the American grammar school she attended? What was she learning at each school?

4. In what ways did Genji Yamadas differ from the other students? Compare Mr. Ohashi's response to Genji to the response of his fellow students.

5. Besides Mr. Ohashi, who else was trying to alter Sone's behavior and for what reason? Why was neither "teacher" successful?

Writing Topics

1. Consider a time when someone tried to change your behavior, either in school or out. Write an essay describing the situation in detail, indicating whether or not the attempts were successful and the reasons why.

*2. Choose one of the following thesis statements and write a thoughtful argument to support that position:
   a. American schools could benefit from Mr. Ohashi's methods of education.
   b. American schools could not benefit from Mr. Ohashi's methods of education.

*"As fast as my knowledge of English allowed,
they advanced me from grade to grade. . . ."*

INITIATION

Mary Antin

When she was in her early teens, Mary Antin (1881–1949) emigrated with her Jewish family from Polotzk, in eastern Russia, to Boston. Once in her new country, she shed her "despised immigrant clothing" and quickly replaced her prior identity as "Mashke" of Polotzk with plain "Mary Antin" of Boston. An excellent student, she attended the prestigious Girls' Latin School and, following her marriage to a biologist, Barnard College in New York. First serialized in *The Atlantic Monthly* in 1911, Antin's memoir *The Promised Land*, in which "Initiation" appears as Chapter 10, was published in 1912.

1   It is not worthwhile to refer to voluminous school statistics to see just how many "green" pupils entered school last September, not knowing the days of the week in English, who next February will be declaiming patriotic verses in honor of George Washington and Abraham Lincoln, with a foreign accent, indeed, but with plenty of enthusiasm. It is enough to know that this hundred-fold miracle is common to the schools in every part of the United States where immigrants are received. And if I was one of Chelsea's hundred in 1894, it was only to be expected, since I was one of the older of the "green" children, and had had a start in my irregular schooling in Russia, and was carried along by a tremendous desire to learn, and had my family to cheer me on.

2   I was not a bit too large for my little chair and desk in the baby class, but my mind, of course, was too mature by six or seven years for the work. So as soon as I could understand what the teacher said in class, I was advanced to the second grade. This was within a week after Miss Nixon took me in hand. But I do not mean to give my dear teacher all the credit for my rapid progress, nor even half the credit. I shall divide it with her on behalf of my race and my family. I was Jew enough to have an aptitude for language in general, and to bend my mind earnestly to my task; I was Antin enough to read each lesson with my heart, which gave me an inkling of what was coming next, and so carried me along by leaps and bounds. As for the teacher, she could best explain

what theory she followed in teaching us foreigners to read. I can only describe the method, which was so simple that I wish holiness could be taught in the same way.

3   There were about half a dozen of us beginners in English, in age from six to fifteen. Miss Nixon made a special class of us, and aided us so skilfully and earnestly in our endeavors to "see-a-cat," and "hear-a-dog-bark," and "look-at-the-hen," that we turned over page after page of the ravishing history, eager to find out how the common world looked, smelled, and tasted in the strange speech. The teacher knew just when to let us help each other out with a word in our own tongue, — it happened that we were all Jews, — and so, working all together, we actually covered more ground in a lesson than the native classes, composed entirely of the little tots.

4   But we stuck — stuck fast — at the definite article; and sometimes the lesson resolved itself into a species of lingual gymnastics, in which we all looked as if we meant to bite our tongues off. Miss Nixon was pretty, and she must have looked well with her white teeth showing in the act; but at the time I was too solemnly occupied to admire her looks. I did take great pleasure in her smile of approval, whenever I pronounced well; and her patience and perseverance in struggling with us over that thick little word are becoming to her even now, after fifteen years. It is not her fault if any of us to-day give a buzzing sound to the dreadful English *th*.

5   I shall never have a better opportunity to make public declaration of my love for the English language. I am glad that American history runs, chapter for chapter, the way it does; for thus America came to be the country I love so dearly. I am glad, most of all, that the Americans began by being Englishmen, for thus did I come to inherit this beautiful language in which I think. It seems to me that in any other language happiness is not so sweet, logic is not so clear. I am not sure that I could believe in my neighbors as I do if I thought about them in un-English words. I could almost say that my conviction of immortality is bound up with the English of its promise. And as I am attached to my prejudices, I must love the English language!

6   Whenever the teachers did anything special to help me over my private difficulties, my gratitude went out to them, silently. It meant so much to me that they halted the lesson to give me a lift, that I needs must love them for it. Dear Miss Carrol, of the second grade, would be amazed to hear what small things I remember, all because I was so impressed at the time with her readiness and sweetness in taking notice of my difficulties.

7   Says Miss Carrol, looking straight at me: —

8   "If Johnnie has three marbles, and Charlie has twice as many, how many marbles has Charlie?"

9   I raise my hand for permission to speak.

10   "Teacher, I don't know vhat is tvice."

11   Teacher beckons me to her, and whispers to me the meaning of the strange word, and I am able to write the sum correctly. It's all in the day's work with her; with me, it is a special act of kindness and efficiency.

12   She whom I found in the next grade became so dear a friend that I can hardly name her with the rest, though I mention none of them lightly. Her approval was always dear to me, first because she was "Teacher," and afterwards, as long as she lived, because she was my Miss Dillingham. Great was my grief, therefore, when, shortly after my admission to her class, I incurred discipline, the first, and next to the last, time in my school career.

13   The class was repeating in chorus the Lord's Prayer, heads bowed on desks. I was doing my best to keep up by the sound; my mind could not go beyond the word "hallowed," for which I had not found the meaning. In the middle of the prayer a Jewish boy across the aisle trod on my foot to get my attention. "You must not say that," he admonished in a solemn whisper; "it's Christian." I whispered back that it wasn't, and went on to the "Amen." I did not know but what he was right, but the name of Christ was not in the prayer, and I was bound to do everything that the class did. If I had any Jewish scruples, they were lagging away behind my interest in school affairs. How American this was: two pupils side by side in the schoolroom, each holding to his own opinion, but both submitting to the common law; for the boy at least bowed his head as the teacher ordered.

14   But all Miss Dillingham knew of it was that two of her pupils whispered during morning prayer, and she must discipline them. So I was degraded from the honor row to the lowest row, and it was many a day before I forgave that young missionary; it was not enough for my vengeance that he suffered punishment with me. Teacher, of course, heard us both defend ourselves, but there was a time and a place for religious arguments, and she meant to help us remember that point.

15   I remember to this day what a struggle we had over the word "water," Miss Dillingham and I. It seemed as if I could not give the sound of *w*; I said "vater" every time. Patiently my teacher worked with me, inventing mouth exercises for me, to get my stubborn lips to produce that *w*; and when at last I could say "village" and "water" in rapid alternation, without misplacing the two initials, that memorable word was sweet on my lips. For we had conquered, and Teacher was pleased.

16   Getting a language in this way, word by word, has a charm that may be set against the disadvantages. It is like gathering a posy blossom by blossom. Bring the bouquet into your chamber, and these nasturtiums stand for the whole flaming carnival of them tumbling over the fence out there; these yellow pansies recall the velvet crescent of color glowing under the bay window; this spray of honeysuckle smells like the wind-tossed masses of it on the porch, ripe and bee-laden; the whole garden in a glass tumbler. So it is with one who gathers words, loving them. Particular words remain associated with important occasions in

the learner's mind. I could thus write a history of my English vocabulary that should be at the same time an account of my comings and goings, my mistakes and my triumphs, during the years of my initiation.

17   If I was eager and diligent, my teachers did not sleep. As fast as my knowledge of English allowed, they advanced me from grade to grade, without reference to the usual schedule of promotions. My father was right, when he often said, in discussing my prospects, that ability would be promptly recognized in the public schools. Rapid as was my progress, on account of the advantages with which I started, some of the other "green" pupils were not far behind me; within a grade or two, by the end of the year. My brother, whose childhood had been one hideous nightmare, what with the stupid rebbe, the cruel whip, and the general repression of life in the Pale, surprised my father by the progress he made under intelligent, sympathetic guidance. Indeed, he soon had a reputation in the school that the American boys envied; and all through the school course he more than held his own with pupils of his age. So much for the right and wrong way of doing things.

18   There is a record of my early progress in English much better than my recollections, however accurate and definite these may be. I have several reasons for introducing it here. First, it shows what the Russian Jew can do with an adopted language; next, it proves that vigilance of our public-school teachers of which I spoke; and last, I am proud of it! That is an unnecessary confession, but I could not be satisfied to insert the record here, with my vanity unavowed.

19   This is the document, copied from an educational journal, a tattered copy of which lies in my lap as I write—treasured for fifteen years, you see, by my vanity.

     EDITOR "PRIMARY EDUCATION": —

         This is the uncorrected paper of a Russian child twelve years old, who had studied English only four months. She had never, until September, been to school even in her own country and has heard English spoken only at school. I shall be glad if the paper of my pupil and the above explanation may appear in your paper.

                                     M.S. DILLINGHAM.

     Chelsea, Mass.

SNOW

     Snow is frozen moisture which comes from the clouds.

     Now the snow is coming down in feather-flakes, which makes nice snow-balls. But there is still one kind of snow more. This kind of snow is called snow-crystals, for it comes down in little curly balls. These snow-crystals aren't quiet as good for snow-balls as feather-flakes, for they (the snow-crystals) are dry: so they can't keep together as feather-flakes do.

The snow is dear to some children for they like sleighing.

As I said at the top—the snow comes from the clouds.

Now the trees are bare, and no flowers are to see in the fields and gardens, (we all know why) and the whole world seems like asleep without the happy birds songs which left us till spring. But the snow which drove away all these pretty and happy things, try, (as I think) not to make us at all unhappy; they covered up the branches of the trees, the fields, the gardens and houses, and the whole world looks like dressed in a beautiful white—instead of green—dress, with the sky looking down on it with a pale face.

And so the people can find some joy in it, too, without the happy summer.

MARY ANTIN.

20   And now that it stands there, with *her* name over it, I am ashamed of my flippant talk about vanity. More to me than all the praise I could hope to win by the conquest of fifty languages is the association of this dear friend with my earliest efforts at writing; and it pleases me to remember that to her I owe my very first appearance in print. Vanity is the least part of it, when I remember how she called me to her desk, one day after school was out, and showed me my composition—my own words, that I had written out of my own head—printed out, clear black and white, with my name at the end! Nothing so wonderful had ever happened to me before. My whole consciousness was suddenly transformed. I suppose that was the moment when I became a writer. I always loved to write,—I wrote letters whenever I had an excuse,—yet it had never occurred to me to sit down and write my thoughts for no person in particular, merely to put the word on paper. But now, as I read my own words, in a delicious confusion, the idea was born. I stared at my name: MARY ANTIN. Was that really I? The printed characters composing it seemed strange to me all of a sudden. If that was my name, and those were the words out of my own head, what relation did it all have to *me*, who was alone there with Miss Dillingham, and the printed page between us? Why, it meant that I could write again, and see my writing printed for people to read! I could write many, many, many things: I could write a book! The idea was so huge, so bewildering, that my mind scarcely could accommodate it.

21   I do not know what my teacher said to me; probably very little. It was her way to say only a little, and look at me, and trust me to understand. Once she had occasion to lecture me about living a shut-up life; she wanted me to go outdoors. I had been repeatedly scolded and reproved on that score by other people, but I had only laughed, saying that I was too happy to change my ways. But when Miss Dillingham spoke to me, I saw that it was a serious matter; and yet she only said a few words, and looked at me with that smile of hers that was only half a smile, and the rest a meaning. Another time she had a great question

to ask me, touching my life to the quick. She merely put her question, and was silent; but I knew what answer she expected, and not being able to give it then, I went away sad and reproved. Years later I had my triumphant answer, but she was no longer there to receive it; and so her eyes look at me, from the picture on the mantel there, with a reproach I no longer merit.

22   I ought to go back and strike out all that talk about vanity. What reason have I to be vain, when I reflect how at every step I was petted, nursed, and encouraged? I did not even discover my own talent. It was discovered first by my father in Russia, and next by my friend in America. What did I ever do but write when they told me to write? I suppose my grandfather who drove a spavined horse through lonely country lanes sat in the shade of crisp-leaved oaks to refresh himself with a bit of black bread; and an acorn falling beside him, in the immense stillness, shook his heart with the echo, and left him wondering. I suppose my father stole away from the synagogue one long festival day, and stretched himself out in the sun-warmed grass, and lost himself in dreams that made the world of men unreal when he returned to them. And so what is there left for me to do, who do not have to drive a horse nor interpret ancient lore, but put my grandfather's question into words and set to music my father's dream? The tongue am I of those who lived before me, as those that are to come will be the voice of my unspoken thoughts. And so who shall be applauded if the song be sweet, if the prophecy be true?

23   I never heard of any one who was so watched and coaxed, so passed along from hand to helping hand, as was I. I always had friends. They sprang up everywhere, as if they had stood waiting for me to come. So here was my teacher, the moment she saw that I could give a good paraphrase of her talk on "Snow," bent on finding out what more I could do. One day she asked me if I had ever written poetry. I had not, but I went home and tried. I believe it was more snow, and I know it was wretched. I wish I could produce a copy of that early effusion; it would prove that my judgment is not severe. Wretched it was, —worse, a great deal, than reams of poetry that is written by children about whom there is no fuss made. But Miss Dillingham was not discouraged. She saw that I had no idea of metre, so she proceeded to teach me. We repeated miles of poetry together, smooth lines that sang themselves, mostly out of Longfellow. Then I would go home and write—oh, about the snow in our back yard!—but when Miss Dillingham came to read my verses, they limped and they lagged and they dragged, and there was no tune that would fit them.

24   At last came the moment of illumination: I saw where my trouble lay. I had supposed that my lines matched when they had an equal number of syllables, taking no account of accent. Now I knew better; now I could write poetry! The everlasting snow melted at last, and the mud puddles dried in the spring sun, and the grass on the common was green, and still I wrote poetry! Again I wish I had some example of my springtime rhapsodies, the veriest rubbish of the sort that ever a child perpetrated. Lizzie McDee, who had red hair and

freckles, and a Sunday-school manner on weekdays, and was below me in the class, did a great deal better. We used to compare verses; and while I do not remember that I ever had the grace to own that she was the better poet, I do know that I secretly wondered why the teachers did not invite her to stay after school and study poetry, while they took so much pains with me. But so it was always with me: somebody did something for me all the time.

25   Making fair allowance for my youth, retarded education, and strangeness to the language, it must still be admitted that I never wrote good verse. But I loved to read it. My half-hours with Miss Dillingham were full of delight for me, quite apart from my new-born ambition to become a writer. What, then, was my joy, when Miss Dillingham, just before locking up her desk one evening, presented me with a volume of Longfellow's poems! It was a thin volume of selections, but to me it was a bottomless treasure. I had never owned a book before. The sense of possession alone was a source of bliss, and this book I already knew and loved. And so Miss Dillingham, who was my first American friend, and who first put my name in print, was also the one to start my library. Deep is my regret when I consider that she was gone before I had given much of an account of all her gifts of love and service to me.

26   About the middle of the year I was promoted to the grammar school. Then it was that I walked on air. For I said to myself that I was a *student* now, in earnest, not merely a school-girl learning to spell and cipher. I was going to learn out-of-the-way things, things that had nothing to do with ordinary life — things to *know*. When I walked home afternoons, with the great big geography book under my arm, it seemed to me that the earth was conscious of my step. Sometimes I carried home half the books in my desk, not because I should need them, but because I loved to hold them; and also because I loved to be seen carrying books. It was a badge of scholarship, and I was proud of it. I remembered the days in Vitebsk when I used to watch my cousin Hirshel start for school in the morning, every thread of his student's uniform, every worn copybook in his satchel, glorified in my envious eyes. And now I was myself as he: aye, greater than he; for I knew English, and I could write poetry.

27   If my head was not turned at this time it was because I was so busy from morning till night. My father did his best to make me vain and silly. He made much of me to every chance caller, boasting of my progress at school, and of my exalted friends, the teachers. For a school-teacher was no ordinary mortal in his eyes; she was a superior being, set above the common run of men by her erudition and devotion to higher things. That a school-teacher could be shallow or petty, or greedy for pay, was a thing that he could not have been brought to believe, at this time. And he was right, if he could only have stuck to it in later years, when a new-born pessimism, fathered by his perception that in America, too, some things needed mending, threw him to the opposite extreme of opinion, crying that nothing in the American scheme of society or government was worth tinkering.

28   He surely was right in his first appraisal of the teacher. The mean sort of teachers are not teachers at all; they are self-seekers who take up teaching as a business, to support themselves and keep their hands white. These same persons, did they keep store or drive a milk wagon or wash babies for a living, would be respectable. As trespassers on a noble profession, they are worth no more than the books and slates and desks over which they preside; so much furniture, to be had by the gross. They do not love their work. They contribute nothing to the higher development of their pupils. They busy themselves, not with research into the science of teaching, but with organizing political demonstrations to advance the cause of selfish candidates for public office, who promise them rewards. The true teachers are of another strain. Apostles all of an ideal, they go to their work in a spirit of love and inquiry, seeking not comfort, not position, not old-age pensions, but truth that is the soul of wisdom, the joy of big-eyed children, the food of hungry youth.

29   They were true teachers who used to come to me on Arlington Street, so my father had reason to boast of the distinction brought upon his house. For the schoolteacher in her trim, unostentatious dress was an uncommon visitor in our neighborhood; and the talk that passed in the bare little "parlor" over the grocery store would not have been entirely comprehensible to our next-door neighbor.

30   In the grammar school I had as good teaching as I had had in the primary. It seems to me in retrospect that it was as good, on the whole, as the public school ideals of the time made possible. When I recall how I was taught geography, I see, indeed, that there was room for improvement occasionally both in the substance and in the method of instruction. But I know of at least one teacher of Chelsea who realized this; for I met her, eight years later, at a great metropolitan university that holds a summer session for the benefit of schoolteachers who want to keep up with the advance in their science. Very likely they no longer teach geography entirely within doors, and by rote, as I was taught. Fifteen years is plenty of time for progress.

31   When I joined the first grammar grade, the class had had a half-year's start of me, but it was not long before I found my place near the head. In all branches except geography it was genuine progress. I overtook the youngsters in their study of numbers, spelling, reading, and composition. In geography I merely made a bluff, but I did not know it. Neither did my teacher. I came up to such tests as she put me.

32   The lesson was on Chelsea, which was right: geography, like charity, should begin at home. Our text ran on for a paragraph or so on the location, boundaries, natural features, and industries of the town, with a bit of local history thrown in. We were to learn all these interesting facts, and be prepared to write them out from memory the next day. I went home and learned—learned every word of the text, every comma, every footnote. When the teacher had read my paper she marked it "EE." "E" was for "excellent," but my paper was

absolutely perfect, and must be put in a class by itself. The teacher exhibited my paper before the class, with some remarks about the diligence that could overtake in a week pupils who had had half a year's start. I took it all as modestly as I could, never doubting that I was indeed a very bright little girl, and getting to be very learned to boot. I was "perfect" in geography, a most erudite subject.

33   But what was the truth? The words that I repeated so accurately on my paper had about as much meaning to me as the words of the Psalms I used to chant in Hebrew. I got an idea that the city of Chelsea, and the world in general, was laid out flat, like the common, and shaved off at the ends, to allow the north, south, east, and west to snuggle up close, like the frame around a picture. If I looked at the map, I was utterly bewildered; I could find no correspondence between the picture and the verbal explanations. With words I was safe; I could learn any number of words by heart, and sometime or other they would pop out of the medley, clothed with meaning. Chelsea, I read, was bounded on all sides — "bounded" appealed to my imagination — by various things that I had never identified, much as I had roamed about the town. I immediately pictured these remote boundaries as a six-foot fence in a good state of preservation, with the Mystic River, the towns of Everett and Revere, and East Boston Creek, rejoicing, on the south, west, north, and east of it, respectively, that they had got inside; while the rest of the world peeped in enviously through a knot hole. In the middle of this cherished area piano factories — or was it shoe factories? — proudly reared their chimneys, while the population promenaded on a *rope walk*, saluted at every turn by the benevolent inmates of the Soldiers' Home on the top of Powderhorn Hill.

34   Perhaps the fault was partly mine, because I always would reduce everything to a picture. Partly it may have been because I had not had time to digest the general definitions and explanations at the beginning of the book. Still, I can take but little of the blame, when I consider how I fared through my geography, right to the end of the grammar-school course. I did in time disentangle the symbolism of the orange revolving on a knitting-needle from the astronomical facts in the case, but it took years of training under a master of the subject to rid me of my distrust of the map as a representation of the earth. To this day I sometimes blunder back to my early impression that any given portion of the earth's surface is constructed upon a skeleton consisting of two crossed bars, terminating in arrowheads which pin the cardinal points into place; and if I want to find any desired point of the compass, I am inclined to throw myself flat on my nose, my head due north, and my outstretched arms seeking the east and west respectively.

35   For in the schoolroom, as far as the study of the map went, we began with the symbol and stuck to the symbol. No teacher of geography I ever had, except the master I referred to, took the pains to ascertain whether I had any sense of the facts for which the symbols stood. Outside the study of maps, geography

consisted of statistics: tables of population, imports and exports, manufactures, and degrees of temperature; dimensions of rivers, mountains, and political states; with lists of minerals, plants, and plagues native to any given part of the globe. The only part of the whole subject that meant anything to me was the description of the aspect of foreign lands, and the manners and customs of their peoples. The relation of physiography to human history—what might be called the moral of geography—was not taught at all, or was touched upon in an unimpressive manner. The prevalence of this defect in the teaching of school geography is borne out by the surprise of the college freshman, who remarked to the professor of geology that it was curious to note how all the big rivers and harbors on the Atlantic coastal plain occurred in the neighborhood of large cities! A little instruction in the elements of chartography—a little practice in the use of the compass and the spirit level, a topographical map of the town common, an excursion with a road map—would have given me a fat round earth in place of my paper ghost; would have illumined the one dark alley in my school life.

❧

Discussion Questions

1. To whom or what does Mary Antin attribute her early educational success in America?
2. Would you agree with Antin's evaluation in paragraph 5 of the English language? Explain.
3. In what ways did each of Mary Antin's teachers—Miss Nixon, Miss Carrol, and Miss Dillingham—advance her education? To which of these teachers might Antin give the most credit for her commitment to writing? Why?
4. Do Antin's characteristics of "true teachers" cited in paragraphs 28-29 seem reasonable to you? Why or why not?
5. Would you support the criticism Antin makes in paragraphs 30-35 of the teaching of geography and her suggestion for improving it? Explain.
*6. By paragraph numbers, cite evidence in the selection that Antin was each of the following: proud; vain; generous; industrious; insightful.

Writing Topics

*1. Assume that you have a child. Write a description of the experiences, both in and out of the home, that you would like your child to have before he or she enters school, indicating why these experiences will enhance your child's education.

*2. Through appropriate reasons and examples, support in a short
essay one of the following thesis statements:
   a. Rote memorization has little educational value for students.
   b. Rote memorization plays an important role in students'
      education.

❧ . . . I, the reprobate, was heartened to discover that

even the good students were unhappy,

that they hated school no less than myself. . . ."

THE COLDNESS OF PUBLIC PLACES

Frank Conroy

Born in New York City in 1936, Frank Conroy attended schools in New York and Florida and was graduated in 1958 from Haverford College in Pennsylvania. When it was first published in 1967, Conroy's memoir *Stop-Time*, from which "The Coldness of Public Places" was taken, was immediately recognized as a masterful rendering of one contemporary American boy's journey from childhood to young adulthood. Other works by Conroy, who now directs the Writers' Workshop at the University of Iowa, are *Midair* (1984), a collection of short stories, and *Body & Soul* (1993), a novel.

The Street

1   I was already late, having completely missed home-room period, so there was no great harm in waiting a bit longer. I bought a hot dog and watched two boys from the morning session pitching pennies against the wall of Stuyvesant High School. The sun was high, filling half the street, and I moved out from under the vendor's striped umbrella to get its warmth. My heart was calm. Nothing could be done about my lateness and in the meantime there was the street, wonderfully quiet in the steady sunlight, the sharp taste of yellow mustard in my mouth, and the slow rhythms of the game to contemplate. For a few moments I was free, relieved of thought, temporarily released from the faint sickness inside me. Although I refused to admit it, I was getting sick. Delicate changes were going on—the subtle adjustments of a mind that feels itself threatened but cannot localize the threat, the hidden wariness toward all things and all people, a certain suspension of sensibility, like holding one's breath in a moment of crisis and finding when the danger passes there is no need of breath, that one can live without air.

2   "Get in there, you cocksucker," said one of the boys. Toeing the line, his body bent like a racer waiting for the gun, he launched his coin in a flat arch and smiled as it came to rest a half inch from the wall. "Wins."

3   "Can I shoot?"

4   They looked at me quickly. "Okay."

5   "He has to go first, though," the other boy said.

6   We threw coins for a while, unhurried, all of us relaxed and easy in the sun. The hot-dog vendor leaned against his cart, half asleep, his chin in his hands. I was about even when the two boys called a halt and set off toward First Avenue. They turned the corner arguing about a disputed play and I started up the steps, my shadow climbing crookedly ahead of me.

The First Floor

7   I could have sneaked in through one of the side exits, of course, but there wasn't much point since the new attendance taker in home room was above taking bribes and had doubtless included my name in the late list. Approaching the wide table at the head of the main corridor I felt a familiar gathering-of-self at the day's first encounter with the enemy, represented in this instance by the student serving as late monitor. He looked up from his books and gave me a smile. "Again, huh?"

8   "That's right." I was happy to see him instead of Mr. Schmidt, the teacher who sometimes served, because as fellow students we had a bond that transcended my sins. We shared the stoicism of the helpless, the dreamy *sangfroid* of the abused, playing out our respective roles with tongue in cheek as if to say there's more to me than meets the eye. As a good student he was glad to see me acting out his fantasies of rebellion, while I, the reprobate, was heartened to discover that even the good students were unhappy, that they hated school no less than myself, each in his own way.

9   "Three times this week and it's only Thursday."

10   "You have to stick with it to be champ." But my heart sank. I hadn't remembered, and three times in a single week was dangerous. The Dean might feel he should do something.

11   "Well, I hope you like Seward. That's where they'll send you."

12   He wasn't being superior, it was a flat statement of fact.

13   "I don't give a shit what they do."

14   He shrugged and pulled a pad of forms under his eyes, signed, and ripped off the sheet. "It's first period. You missed home room."

15   Two teachers came down the marble stairs (Staff Only) from the second floor and passed without a glance. I threw a fuck-you sign behind their backs.

16   The empty corridor ran the entire length of the building, one city block. The walls were green. Bare bulbs in wire cages glowed in a long line on the ceiling and the smell of disinfectant hung in the air. I walked down the exact center of the passageway, directly under the lights, whispering "fuck you, fuck you, fuck you" to the rhythm of my stride.

17   Pushing through a door I turned into the upper level of the gym. My chair was lying folded across the banked runway and I picked it up, opened it, and sat down next to the railing. Arms dangling, I watched the scene below. A hundred boys were doing calisthenics, jumping into the air and throwing up their arms in time to the instructor's whistle. Up, down, up, down—chasing the lost beat half-heartedly through the thunder of their heavy feet. The balcony trembled. Almost all of them were too fat, with huge womanly hips and flesh that jiggled under their T-shirts. I laughed aloud. It was too absurd. One knew from the movies what it was supposed to look like—football teams in early workouts, Hitler youth bouncing along smartly like so many machines—and for a moment the grotesque reality before my eyes seemed to reveal the truth so pointedly I wondered how the teacher could let it go on. The truth was, nobody cared. In the back rows they'd already given up, simply faking the gestures, some not even bothering to throw up their arms. Across the gym, on the opposite side of the track, I saw the other door monitor laughing in delight.

18   The instructor blew his whistle. "Left *face!* Right *face!* Mark *time!* One two, one two, one two. . . ." His voice was drowned in the chaotic roar. As if of one mind the boys made as much noise as possible, stamping their feet like angry infants.

19   The five-minute warning bell had rung. I sat with my ankles on the railing reading a novel about the Second World War. I should have used the time to do my homework, but the appeal of Nazis, French girls, K rations, and sunlight slanting through the forest while men attempted to kill one another was too great. I read four or five hours every night at home, but it was never quite as sweet as in school, when even a snatch read as I climbed the stairs seemed to protect me from my surroundings with an efficacy that bordered on the magical. And if the story dealt with questions of life and death, so much the better. How could I be seriously worried about having nothing to hand in at Math when I was pinned in a shallow foxhole, under a mortar barrage, a dead man across my back and an hysterical young lieutenant weeping for his mother by my side? I could not resist the *clarity of the world* in books, the incredibly satisfying way in which life became weighty and accessible. Books were reality. I hadn't made up my mind about my own life, a vague, dreamy affair, amorphous and dimly perceived, without beginning or end.

20   A boy pushed open the door and looked in. My function as monitor was to keep unauthorized people from going in and out, a responsibility I ignored, and when I turned my head it was with the pleasant anticipation of the law-breaker about to flout authority.

21   "Conroy?"

22   "Yes." Too bad. I could tell he was licit from his tone. Shouts drifted up from the gym floor.

23   He waved a slip of paper. "Two-oh-eight. Right away." I accepted the pass and began gathering my books.

24   How strange that when the summons came I always felt good. The blood would rush through my body, warming me with its cheerful, lively heat. If there was a slight dryness in my mouth there was also a comfortable tingling of the nerves, a sharpening of the reflexes, and a sense of heightened awareness. The call produced a mild euphoria, not out of any perverse desire to be punished but in anticipation of a meeting with fate, in expectation of plunging deeper into life. The Dean was less the Dean and more my dead father than either of us suspected at the time. I sustained a fantastic belief that the mechanical clichés of our disciplinary interviews were only the prelude to eventual mutual recognition. His threats seemed of no more importance than the how-do-you-dos and so-nice-to-meet-yous one mouthed to any new person, and in my eagerness to begin a real exchange I hardly heard them. I misread the boredom and irritation in his face, thinking it came from frustration at the slow pace of love, investing his dry soul with juices that had doubtless drained before I was born. The truth, that among the thousands of students I was no more than a number to him, that he was so overworked he couldn't possibly have remembered me from one time to the next without his records, that in fact everything between us was totally procedural—that truth was unthinkable.

The Second Floor

25   Three boys were on the bench. I sat down with them and watched the floor for a moment, not, as a naïve observer might have thought, to dramatize penitence, but simply to maintain my privacy in an important moment. Drawn close by their delinquency, the other boys whispered and passed notes, holding off fear with artificial camaraderie. I kept quiet, acclimating slowly to the electric air, knowing that where there was danger there might also be salvation.

26   I never rehearsed a defense. I must have thought the Dean preferred a boy who walked in and took his medicine to one who groveled, however cleverly. And of course when the moment of recognition came, when the barriers fell and we stood revealed, I didn't want to be in the midst of an elaborate lie. To hasten the emergence of love I could only be completely honest. Lies might make it difficult for him to reach me, and vice-versa.

27   I wanted to be won over by him, but not cheaply. If he won me cheaply he might betray me. The sense in which I knew this is hard to explain. It wasn't a principle I'd deduced from experience, it was knowledge without thought. Had someone asked me at the time what it meant to be betrayed by another person I couldn't have answered. Without being able to conceive betrayal I none the less protected myself against it, unconsciously, in my expectation of a commitment from the other person equal to my own. A perfectly valid stance between individuals but a tragic absurdity between a child and authority.

28   A side door I'd never noticed before opened and a student came out smiling. I caught a glimpse of a man at a desk, and for no reason at all I became convinced he was a policeman.

29   "Fischberg," the Dean's secretary called without looking up. The boy next to me left the bench and went through the side door. I heard the man inside tell him to close it.

30   The smiling student picked up a pass from the secretary and started out. As he passed I touched his arm. "Who's that in there?"

31   "I don't know. Some jerk asking if I had a happy home life."

32   "No talking there!"

33   A soft buzz sounded on the secretary's intercom. "Next," she said.

34   There was a momentary paralysis on the bench.

35   "Well, what are you waiting for?" She shuffled some papers on her desk. "Conroy? Is one of you Conroy?"

36   I walked to the Dean's door and went in.

37   "All right Conroy, step over here."

38   I crossed the carpet and stood in front of his desk. He took off his glasses, rubbed the bridge of his nose, and put them on again. After a moment he pushed against the edge of the desk and swiveled away to face the wall, leaning back with a sigh and then letting his chin come down slowly like a man dozing off.

39   "Why were you late?" he asked the wall.

40   "There was no reason, I guess."

41   "No reason?"

42   "I mean I don't have an excuse."

43   "You didn't miss your bus? You didn't forget your transit pass? The subways didn't break down?"

44   "No sir."

45   "I suppose not, since you've been late three times this week. You can't possibly have an excuse so you don't give one. Isn't that right?" He stared at the wall.

46   I didn't answer.

47   "Isn't that right?" he asked again in exactly the same flat tone.

48   "If you say so, sir."

49   He turned his head to look at me for a moment, his face expressionless, and then went back to watching the wall. "I don't have time for trouble-makers, Conroy. I get rid of them."

50   "I don't know why I'm late so often. I try to get here on time but somehow it just happens."

51   "Don't make a mystery out of it, Conroy. You're late because you're lazy and inattentive."

52   I could feel myself beginning to close down inside, as if my soul were one of those elaborate suitcases street peddlers use to display their wares, the kind that fold up from all directions at the approach of the law.

53   He lifted some papers from his desk. "You're nothing but trouble. Constantly late if you get here at all, inattentive in class, disrespectful to your teachers, twice reprimanded for gambling . . ."

54   "It was just pitching pennies, sir."

55   "I know what it was. Don't interrupt."

56   "Yes sir."

57   "At this moment you are failing three subjects."

58   "We haven't had any tests yet. I'm sure I'll pass the tests."

59   He looked up, his eyes narrowing in irritation. "You're failing three subjects. That leaves the decision up to me. You stay here or you get transferred to another school. You're in that category now."

60   I turned away, instinctively hiding the fear that might be on my face. Getting kicked out of Stuyvesant would be a catastrophe surpassing anything in my experience, perhaps because it seemed to eliminate the possibility of turning over a new leaf. I disbelieved in self-betterment. By turning a new leaf I meant no more than avoiding the more obvious forms of trouble.

61   Secretly, I did hope that things would get better. That I didn't know *how* they'd get better was balanced by my inability to understand why they were bad in the first place. It was a delicate world in which one had to move carefully, dealing with elements one understood vaguely if at all, knowing only that some elements seemed to sustain life and some to threaten it. Getting thrown out of school would disrupt things profoundly. I would no longer be able to experiment with those balanced elements, probing them gingerly here and there, adding some, taking away some, trying, in the least dangerous way, to find out what they were. In a trade school, my bridges burned behind me, I imagined myself in total isolation and darkness, unable to reorganize, unable to make the slightest adjustments in the course of my life, finally and irrevocably in the hands of a disinterested fate.

62   "What do you think I should do?" he asked.

63   "I want to stay. I can make it."

64   "What the hell is the matter with you, Conroy?"

65   I looked down at the edge of the desk. Something strange was happening. I seemed to be at two removes from reality, crouching behind my own body like a man manipulating a puppet through a curtain. "I don't know." My arms were reaching in through my back to make me talk. "That's the truth."

66   "If you don't," he said slowly, "you had better find out."

67   I climbed back into myself and nodded.

68   He opened the drawer of his desk and took out a small notebook. "Early report for two weeks. Get here fifteen minutes before the first bell and sign in with the hall monitor." He uncapped his pen and made a notation. "Leave plenty of time. Miss once and you're out. Understand?"

69   "Yes sir."

70   "That's all." He didn't look up.

71   I had my hand on the doorknob when he spoke again. "And see the man in the other room before you go back to class."

72   The bench had refilled and the boys turned as if to read their fates in my expression. I walked past and went up to the secretary. "He says I should see the man in there."

73   "Go on in, then. There's nobody with him."

74   I tapped the door lightly and entered.

75   "Come in. Sit down." He was standing over a desk. "You are . . . ah . . ." He looked down at his papers.

76   "Conroy."

77   "Oh yes, Conroy." He smiled nervously, poking one of the papers across the surface of the desk with his fingers. Hunched over, he coughed into his fist as he quickly read it. "Well now, Frank," he began. (It was a slight shock to be so addressed. My official name was Conroy, and neither teachers nor students called me anything else.) "I want to ask you some questions. Understand that I have nothing to do with the school or the Dean. I'm here simply as an observer, and to help if I can. You can answer freely without fear of . . ." he hesitated, searching for the right word.

78   "Repercussions?"

79   "Yes. That's right." He sat down. "Now let's see. You're fourteen years old. Any brothers or sisters?"

80   "An older sister," I said. "And oh yes, the baby. Jessica. She's only a few months old."

81   "I see. She would be your half-sister, I imagine, since I see here your father passed away some time ago."

82   "Yes." I began to pick at some lint on my trousers, feeling slightly uncomfortable.

83   "Do you get along with them all right?"

84   "What do you mean?" I understood him, but the question irritated me.

85   "Well, there are always little fights now and then. We all lose our tempers occasionally, I wondered if outside of that you got along with them all right."

86   "Of course I do."

87   "Okay." He paused, watching me indirectly. There was no more lint to pick from my leg so I began to brush out the cuff with a finger. "Do you have a job in the morning?"

88   "Yes. I work in a library."

89   "How do you like that?"

90   "It's okay."

91   "What do you do when you get home from school at night? Do you have any hobbies? Stamp collecting, that sort of thing?"

92   "No hobbies."

93   "Well, how do you pass the time?"

94   "I read a lot. Sometimes I play the piano."

95   "What kind of books?"

96   I hesitated, not sure how to answer. "All kinds, I guess."

97   "I suppose you don't like school very much."

98   "I don't think about it very much."

99   The bell rang, all over the building, and was followed instantly by the sound of thousands of students moving through the halls. I listened abstractedly, luxuriating in the knowledge that for the moment I'd escaped the routine. How can I explain the special pleasure of listening to the machine operating all around me while I myself was removed from it? I'd cut class and climb the stairs past the top floor to the deserted landing above. I'd sit with my back against the door to the roof listening to the bells, to the boys shouting on the stairs below, and to the long silences after the halls had emptied. The mood was quietly Olympian.

100   I hadn't realized how much the Dean had shaken me up, but now, as the bell I didn't have to answer rang again, I felt a tremor of release play over my body. Muscles everywhere began to relax and I threw back my head in an enormous involuntary yawn.

101   "What does your stepfather do for a living, Frank?"

102   Instantly I was alert. I knew the man was harmless, but my deepest rule, a rule so deep I maintained it without the slightest conscious effort, was never to reveal anything important about life at home. "He's a cab driver," I said slowly.

103   "Does your mother work too?"

104   I stared at the floor. "Sometimes." It occurred to me that my initial relief at getting away from the Dean might have made me careless with the man I now faced. He obviously had some image of me in his mind, some psychological cliché, and by answering carelessly I might unknowingly have supported it. I moved to the edge of my chair and sat up straight.

105   "Is there trouble at home?" he asked quietly.

106   My face flushed. A stupid question. An insulting question, as if I were a case to be dealt with by the book, as if he suspected some hidden deprivation or abnormality. "No, of course not. Nothing like that." I knew what he had in his mind. He held images of drunken fathers who beat their kids, slut mothers who roamed the house in old nightgowns, and long, screaming fights with crockery flying through the air. We weren't like that. I knew we were much better than that. I stood up. "Is that all?"

107   He fiddled with his papers for a moment, looking off into space. "Yes, I guess so," he said reluctantly. "If and when I come back to Stuyvesant I'd like to talk to you again."

108   I hiked my books high under my arm and went out the door. Standing motionless in the small room, I looked at the secretary and the four boys on the bench. The bell rang.

The Third Floor

109 Miss Tuts, a tiny red-haired woman, stood at the side of the room screaming at the boy in front of the blackboard. "No, no, no! Didn't you hear what I said? *Soixante-deux! Soixante-deux!* And write it out, don't just put the numbers."

110 The boy turned slowly to the board and raised the chalk. Hesitantly he began to write.

111 "Wrong," she yelled. "Sit down. You didn't prepare the lesson." Her figure was black against the big windows as she paced back and forth with quick little steps. "Bernstein! Put the vocabulary for today on the board. And don't forget the verbs."

112 Bernstein stood up, a perfect pear. "Just the French?"

113 "Yes," she cried irritably. "Do I have to explain every day?"

114 Someone laughed in the back.

115 "Quiet!"

116 Bernstein finished one column quickly and started on the next, writing the words in exactly the same order in which they'd appeared in the textbook. He could memorize effortlessly, and the pride with which he repeated the same trick day after day had not endeared him to his classmates.

117 "Bernstein sucks," the boy next to me said quietly.

118 "Did you say something, Aaronson?"

119 "No, Miss Tuts."

120 "Stand up and translate the first column."

121 "Le shawmbra, the room. Le lee, the bed . . ."

122 Someone hit Bernstein on the back with a ball of paper as he turned away from the board. Laughter from the rear of the room. Aaronson went on without skipping a beat. "Revay, to dream. Se lavay, to wash . . ."

123 "Who threw that?" Miss Tuts screamed, running to the front of the room. "Who threw that paper?"

124 Looking uncomfortable, Bernstein returned to his seat.

125 "Le shapoe, the hat. La . . ."

126 She slammed her hand on the desk. "Shut up! Sit down! Now, who threw that paper?"

127 Silence.

128 Plunk! Someone plucked the short-metal prong under the seat with his thumbnail. Plunk! Answers started coming in from different parts of the room. Plunk! Plunk!

129 "Stop it! Stop it this instant!"

130 Plunk! Plunk!

131 "I'll send you all to the Dean! The entire class!"

132 We laughed as she stalked out. Her threat was empty. It had been used too often.

The Fourth Floor

133   Dr. Casey was a big man, well over six feet tall with the build to go with it, but he was getting old. His square face was touched with the gray skin tone of age, and except for rare moments of anger his eyes had lost the flash of life. He stared out over his desk expressionlessly, his hands clasped before him. He talked from the first bell to the last, and no one interrupted him. As long as he talked we didn't have to work. We'd discovered there was no need to listen. We could catch up on homework for other classes, read, or do the crossword puzzle. He didn't care as long as we were quiet and looked busy. Perhaps he even thought we were taking notes.

134   "I put my sons through Harvard. Both of them. But they're gone now. Things change, that's what you people don't realize. When you're my age it becomes quite clear. Things change, things change constantly and the very things that seem most secure are actually changing very slowly, sometimes so slowly you can't see what's happening even though it's staring you in the face. You must stay alert at all times. Never believe the way things look. The garbage collectors believe everything is simple and that's why they're garbage collectors. You have to look behind the masks, you have to get behind the lies. Most of it is lies, you know. I am aware of that fact." He tapped the surface of the desk with his knuckles. "I can see through the lies because I've lived a full life. I didn't waste my time. In the First World War I was in graves registration. I saw things I can't tell you about. Things so horrible good taste prevents me from mentioning them. You people of course have no idea. That's why I'm here. That's why I'm here. That's why I'm sitting up here at this desk giving my life for your vicarious perusal." He stared out over the lowered heads of the boys and cleared his throat with a tremendous bellow. It was highly overdone, a self-conscious mannerism the boys had learned to ignore. Each day more and more phlegm was rolled more and more lovingly, as if he were testing our unconcern, as if, as the gesture became totally operatic, he were daring us to call his bluff. "My field was etymology. Where words came from. Words, after all, are the tools they use to break us down. I resist them because I know more about words than they do. Every educated man should know about words." He paused to let the thought sink in. "Then when they spew out their poison and their vomit I see it for what it is. Filth! Nothing more or less than that! And we are surrounded by it, gentlemen. The secretions of corrupted minds are the juices that nourish modern society, just as the blood of animals nourishes our bodies. Pus runs free over the body politic. Graft and corruption are everywhere. They've approached me many times, I assure you, whining and wheedling before me, making their filthy offers, trying to break me down. Well they can try for a thousand years and my answer will be the same. They can shove their special arrangements. They can shove their recommendations, gold watches and testimonial dinners. Let them eat their own swill." He spoke softly, as if withdrawn

into himself, as if the strength of his feelings had driven him back to a point where he was no more than an observer of his own actions. Leaning far back in his chair, his long legs extended straight out into the aisle, he peered through loosely clasped fingers, his entire body motionless as a corpse. "None of it surprises me. None of it. They show us one man riding another, riding him like a horse, like a beast of burden. That stuff gets through. They call it art. They spit on the nobility of the human body. They lower themselves to the level of animals. Below animals. A man riding a man is going too far. I call them dogs from the bottom of my soul."

135   The school day is over. A mood of manic hilarity fills every classroom as we wait for the final bell. The aisles are crowded with laughing, shouting boys. The teachers, already on their way home mentally, sit behind their desks with lowered heads and occupy themselves with small unnecessary tasks.

136   Despite the confusion we're ready to go at the signal. Our books are packed. Our jackets are on. We pour through the door and out into the hall with a collective sigh. We rush for the stairs, dodging in and out among the slower boys. The noise is terrific. On the stairs we really let loose. Screams and yells float up from the lower floors. Fists bang against the metal side panels in continuous thunder. Down, down, down, rushing past the painted numbers, swinging round like crack the whip at the landings, leaping steps when there's room, pushing the boy in front, being pushed from behind, all of us mad with freedom. Down, down. So easily, so effortlessly. The stream carries us safely past the third, the second, the first, and out into the immense throng streaming through the banks of open doors to the street. We flow over the sidewalk and between the parked cars onto the asphalt. In the darkness faces are indistinct. Matches flash for cigarettes. Around the corner the avenue gleams with neon. Most of us have already forgotten the five hours inside school because for most of us school is less than nothing. We spread like a liquid over the neighborhood and disappear into the subways.

❧

Discussion Questions

1. Describe Conroy's feelings about and attitude toward Stuyvesant High School as revealed in "The Street" and "The First Floor." By paragraph number, cite specific behaviors that reveal these feelings and attitude.

2. How and why did Conroy initially misread the Dean's motivation and behavior in "The First Floor" and "The Second Floor" (see paragraphs 24–71)? Explain why Conroy feared being expelled from Stuyvesant.

*3. Relate the biographical information that the selection provides about Conroy's age, family concerns, interests, and values. Is Conroy a person you would like to know? Why or Why not?

*4. What behaviors reveal each of the following people to be foolish in Conroy's eyes: the psychologist, Miss Tuts, Dr. Casey?

5. What changes does Conroy make in writing style (paragraphs 109–134) to reveal that Miss Tuts has little control of her classroom and that Dr. Casey is a blowhard?

*6. In a number of places in the selection, Conroy uses similes (comparisons that begin with *like* or *as*) to describe feelings or behavior. Choose one that you think is particularly effective or ineffective and explain why you find it so.

7. After a period of time, most people cannot recall past conversations word for word. Does Conroy's heavy use of dialogue in the selection weaken the credibility of what he has written? Why or why not?

Writing Topics

1. Reflect upon your own experiences in high school; then, in a short essay, use specific examples to support one of the following options for a thesis statement:

    a. In many ways, Stuyvesant High School seems quite similar to the high school I attended.

    b. In many ways, Stuyvesant High School seems quite different from the high school I attended.

2. From recollections of your high-school days, write a description of a class hour that remains particularly memorable for you. Include sufficient details about the subject, instructor, students, and sequence of events so that the class hour becomes memorable to your reader, as well.

*❧"Perhaps a year before the old man died,
I came to know two other white people for myself.
They were women."*

MY SOUL WAS WITH THE GODS

Zora Neale Hurston

The author of stories, novels, plays, and nonfiction books on folklore and African American culture, Zora Neale Hurston (1891–1960) was born in the all-black town of Eatonville, Florida, where her father, a Baptist minister, was a three-term mayor and where her mother, a seamstress, died when Hurston was nine years old. Educated in anthropology and folklore at Howard University and Barnard College, Hurston was part of the Harlem Renaissance in the 1920s, a group that included the writers Countee Cullen, Langston Hughes, Richard Wright, Claude McKay, Jean Toomer, and James Weldon Johnson. In recent years, Hurston's books, which had faded into obscurity, have regained popularity. Among them are *Mules and Men* (1935), a collection of folklore; *Their Eyes Were Watching God* (1937), a novel; and *Dust Tracks on a Road* (1942), her autobiography, in which "My Soul Was with the Gods" appears.

1   . . . I used to take a seat on top of the gate-post and watch the world go by. One way to Orlando ran past my house, so the carriages and cars would pass before me. The movement made me glad to see it. Often the white travelers would hail me, but more often I hailed them, and asked, "Don't you want me to go a piece of the way with you?"

2   They always did. I know now that I must have caused a great deal of amusement among them, but my self-assurance must have carried the point, for I was always invited to come along. I'd ride up the road for perhaps a half-mile, then walk back. I did not do this with the permission of my parents, nor with their foreknowledge. When they found out about it later, I usually got a whipping. My grandmother worried about my forward ways a great deal. She had known slavery and to her my brazenness was unthinkable.

3   "Git down offa dat gate-post! You li'l sow, you! Git down! Setting up dere looking dem white folks right in de face! They's gowine to lynch you, yet. And don't stand in dat doorway gazing out at 'em neither. Youse too brazen to live long."

4   Nevertheless, I kept right on gazing at them, and "going a piece of the way" whenever I could make it. The village seemed dull to me most of the time. If the village was singing a chorus, I must have missed the tune.

5   Perhaps a year before the old man died, I came to know two other white people for myself. They were women.

6   It came about this way. The whites who came down from the North were often brought by their friends to visit the village school. A Negro school was something strange to them, and while they were always sympathetic and kind, curiosity must have been present, also. They came and went, came and went. Always, the room was hurriedly put in order, and we were threatened with a prompt and bloody death if we cut one caper while the visitors were present. We always sang a spiritual, led by Mr. Calhoun himself. Mrs. Calhoun always stood in the back, with a palmetto switch in her hand as a squelcher. We were all little angels for the duration, because we'd better be. She would cut her eyes and give us a glare that meant trouble, then turn her face towards the visitors and beam as much as to say it was a great privilege and pleasure to teach lovely children like us. They couldn't see that palmetto hickory in her hand behind all those benches, but we knew where our angelic behavior was coming from.

7   Usually, the visitors gave warning a day ahead and we would be cautioned to put on shoes, comb our heads, and see to ears and fingernails. There was a close inspection of every one of us before we marched in that morning. Knotty heads, dirty ears and fingernails got hauled out of line, strapped and sent home to lick the calf over again.

8   This particular afternoon, the two young ladies just popped in. Mr. Calhoun was flustered, but he put on the best show he could. He dismissed the class that he was teaching up at the front of the room, then called the fifth grade in reading. That was my class.

9   So we took our readers and went up front. We stood up in the usual line, and opened to the lesson. It was the story of Pluto and Persephone. It was new and hard to the class in general, and Mr. Calhoun was very uncomfortable as the readers stumbled along, spelling out words with their lips, and in mumbling undertones before they exposed them experimentally to the teacher's ears.

10 Then it came to me. I was fifth or sixth down the line. The story was not new to me, because I had read my reader through from lid to lid, the first week that Papa had bought it for me.

11 That is how it was that my eyes were not in the book, working out the paragraph which I knew would be mine by counting the children ahead of me. I was observing our visitors, who held a book between them, following the lesson. They had shiny hair, mostly brownish. One had a looping gold chain

around her neck. The other one was dressed all over in black and white with a pretty finger ring on her left hand. But the thing that held my eyes were their fingers. They were long and thin, and very white, except up near the tips. There they were baby pink. I had never seen such hands. It was a fascinating discovery for me. I wondered how they felt. I would have given those hands more attention, but the child before me was almost through. My turn next, so I got on my mark, bringing my eyes back to the book and made sure of my place. Some of the stories I had reread several times, and this Greco-Roman myth was one of my favorites. I was exalted by it, and that is the way I read my paragraph.

12   "Yes, Jupiter had seen her (Persephone). He had seen the maiden picking flowers in the field. He had seen the chariot of the dark monarch pause by the maiden's side. He had seen him when he seized Persephone. He had seen the black horses leap down Mount Aetna's fiery throat. Persephone was now in Pluto's dark realm and he had made her his wife."

13   The two women looked at each other and then back to me. Mr. Calhoun broke out with a proud smile beneath his bristly moustache, and instead of the next child taking up where I had ended, he nodded to me to go on. So I read the story to the end, where flying Mercury, the messenger of the Gods, brought Persephone back to the sunlit earth and restored her to the arms of Dame Ceres, her mother, that the world might have springtime and summer flowers, autumn and harvest. But because she had bitten the pomegranate while in Pluto's kingdom, she must return to him for three months of each year, and be his queen. Then the world had winter, until she returned to earth.

14   The class was dismissed and the visitors smiled us away and went into a low-voiced conversation with Mr. Calhoun for a few minutes. They glanced my way once or twice and I began to worry. Not only was I barefooted, but my feet and legs were dusty. My hair was more uncombed than usual, and my nails were not shiny clean. Oh, I'm going to catch it now. Those ladies saw me, too. Mr. Calhoun is promising to 'tend to me. So I thought.

15   Then Mr. Calhoun called me. I went up thinking how awful it was to get a whipping before company. Furthermore, I heard a snicker run over the room. Hennie Clark and Stell Brazzle did it out loud, so I would be sure to hear them. The smart-aleck was going to get it. I slipped one hand behind me and switched my dress tail at them, indicating scorn.

16   "Come here, Zora Neale," Mr. Calhoun cooed as I reached the desk. He put his hand on my shoulder and gave me little pats. The ladies smiled and held out those flower-looking fingers towards me. I seized the opportunity for a good look.

17   "Shake hands with the ladies, Zora Neale," Mr. Calhoun prompted and they took my hand one after the other and smiled. They asked me if I loved school, and I lied that I did. There was *some* truth in it, because I liked geography and reading, and I liked to play at recess time. Whoever it was invented writing and arithmetic got no thanks from me. Neither did I like the arrangement where the teacher could sit up there with a palmetto stem and lick me

whenever he saw fit. I hated things I couldn't do anything about. But I knew better than to bring that up right there, so I said yes, I *loved* school.

18   "I can tell you do," Brown Taffeta gleamed. She patted my head, and was lucky enough not to get sandspurs in her hand. Children who roll and tumble in the grass in Florida, are apt to get sandspurs in their hair. They shook hands with me again and I went back to my seat.

19   When school let out at three o'clock, Mr. Calhoun told me to wait. When everybody had gone, he told me I was to go to the Park House, that was the hotel in Maitland, the next afternoon to call upon Mrs. Johnstone and Miss Hurd. I must tell Mama to see that I was clean and brushed from head to feet, and I must wear shoes and stockings. The ladies liked me, he said, and I must be on my best behavior.

20   The next day I was let out of school an hour early, and went home to be stood up in a tub of suds and be scrubbed and have my ears dug into. My sandy hair sported a red ribbon to match my red and white checked gingham dress, starched until it could stand alone. Mama saw to it that my shoes were on the right feet, since I was careless about left and right. Last thing, I was given a handkerchief to carry, warned again about my behavior, and sent off, with my big brother John to go as far as the hotel gate with me.

21   First thing, the ladies gave me strange things, like stuffed dates and preserved ginger, and encouraged me to eat all that I wanted. Then they showed me their Japanese dolls and just talked. I was then handed a copy of *Scribner's Magazine*, and asked to read a place that was pointed out to me. After a paragraph or two, I was told with smiles, that that would do.

22   I was led out on the grounds and they took my picture under a palm tree. They handed me what was to me then a heavy cylinder done up in fancy paper, tied with a ribbon, and they told me goodbye, asking me not to open it until I got home.

23   My brother was waiting for me down by the lake, and we hurried home, eager to see what was in the thing. It was too heavy to be candy or anything like that. John insisted on toting it for me.

24   My mother made John give it back to me and let me open it. Perhaps, I shall never experience such joy again. The nearest thing to that moment was the telegram accepting my first book. One hundred goldy-new pennies rolled out of the cylinder. Their gleam lit up the world. It was not avarice that moved me. It was the beauty of the thing. I stood on the mountain. Mama let me play with my pennies for a while, then put them away for me to keep.

25   That was only the beginning. The next day I received an Episcopal hymnbook bound in white leather with a golden cross stamped into the front cover, a copy of The Swiss Family Robinson, and a book of fairy tales.

26   I set about to commit the song words to memory. There was no music written there, just the words. But there was to my consciousness music in between them just the same. "When I survey the Wondrous Cross" seemed the

most beautiful to me, so I committed that to memory first of all. Some of them seemed dull and without life, and I pretended they were not there. If white people like trashy singing like that, there must be something funny about them that I had not noticed before. I stuck to the pretty ones where the words marched to a throb I could feel.

27   A month or so after the two young ladies returned to Minnesota, they sent me a huge box packed with clothes and books. The red coat with a wide circular collar and the red tam pleased me more than any of the other things. My chums pretended not to like anything that I had, but even then I knew that they were jealous. Old Smarty had gotten by them again. The clothes were not new, but they were very good. I shone like the morning sun.

28   But the books gave me more pleasure than the clothes. I had never been too keen on dressing up. It called for hard scrubbings with Octagon soap suds getting in my eyes, and none too gentle fingers scrubbing my neck and gouging in my ears.

29   In that box were Gulliver's Travels, Grimm's Fairy Tales, Dick Whittington, Greek and Roman Myths, and best of all, Norse Tales. Why did the Norse tales strike so deeply into my soul? I do not know, but they did. I seemed to remember seeing Thor swing his mighty short-handled hammer as he sped across the sky in rumbling thunder, lightning flashing from the tread of his steeds and the wheels of his chariot. The great and good Odin, who went down to the well of knowledge to drink, and was told that the price of a drink from that fountain was an eye. Odin drank deeply, then plucked out one eye without a murmur and handed it to the grizzly keeper, and walked away. That held majesty for me.

30   Of the Greeks, Hercules moved me most. I followed him eagerly on his tasks. The story of the choice of Hercules as a boy when he met. Pleasure and Duty, and put his hand in that of Duty and followed her steep way to the blue hills of fame and glory, which she pointed out at the end, moved me profoundly. I resolved to be like him. The tricks and turns of the other Gods and Goddesses left me cold. There were other thin books about this and that sweet and gentle little girl who gave up her heart to Christ and good works. Almost always they died from it, preaching as they passed. I was utterly indifferent to their deaths. In the first place I could not conceive of death, and in the next place they never had any funerals that amounted to a hill of beans, so I didn't care how soon they rolled up their big, soulful, blue eyes and kicked the bucket. They had no meat on their bones.

31   But I also meet Hans Andersen and Robert Louis Stevenson. They seemed to know what I wanted to hear and said it in a way that tingled me. Just a little below these friends was Rudyard Kipling in his Jungle Books. I loved his talking snakes as much as I did the hero.

32   I came to start reading the Bible through my mother. She gave me a licking one afternoon for repeating something I had overheard a neighbor telling her.

She locked me in her room after the whipping, and the Bible was the only thing in there for me to read. I happened to open to the place where David was doing some mighty smiting, and I got interested. David went here and he went there, and no matter where he went, he smote 'em hip and thigh. Then he sung songs to his harp awhile, and went out and smote some more. Not one time did David stop and preach about sins and things. All David wanted to know from God was who to kill and when. He took care of the other details himself. Never a quiet moment. I liked him a lot. So I read a great deal more in the Bible, hunting for some more active people like David. Except for the beautiful language of Luke and Paul, the New Testament still plays a poor second to the Old Testament for me. The Jews had a God who laid about Him when they needed Him. I could see no use waiting till Judgment Day to see a man who was just crying for a good killing, to be told to go and roast. My idea was to give him a good killing first, and then if he got roasted later on, so much the better.

33   In searching for more Davids, I came upon Leviticus. There were exciting things in there to a child eager to know the facts of life. I told Carrie Roberts about it, and we spent long afternoons reading what Moses told the Hebrews not to do in Leviticus. In that way I found out a number of things the old folks would not have told me. Not knowing what we were actually reading, we got a lot of praise from our elders for our devotion to the Bible.

34   Having finished that and scanned the Doctor Book, which my mother thought she had hidden securely from my eyes, I read all the things which children write on privy-house walls. Therefore, I lost my taste for pornographic literature. I think that the people who love it got cheated in the matter of privy houses when they were children.

35   In a way this early reading gave me great anguish through all my childhood and adolescence. My soul was with the gods and my body in the village. People just would not act like gods. Stew beef, fried fatback and morning grits were no ambrosia from Valhalla. Raking back yards and carrying out chamber-pots, were not the tasks of Thor. I wanted to be away from drabness and to stretch my limbs in some mighty struggle. I was only happy in the woods, and when the ecstatic Florida springtime came strolling from the sea, trance-glorifying the world with its aura. Then I hid out in the tall wild oats that waved like a glinty veil. I nibbled sweet oat stalks and listened to the wind soughing and sighing through the crowns of the lofty pines. I made particular friendship with one huge tree and always played about its roots. I named it "the loving pine," and my chums came to know it by that name. . . .

*

Discussion Questions

1. Describe the usual effect that the appearance of visitors had upon the staff and students of the school Hurston attended. How did Mr. Calhoun respond, and with what results, to the sudden appearance at the school of the young ladies?
2. With what gifts did Mrs. Johnstone and Miss Hurd reward Hurston for her ability and behavior? Which of these presents did Hurston most value? Why?
*3. Choose two or three adjectives to describe the ladies' attitude and behavior toward Hurston and justify each of your choices by citing relevant paragraph numbers.
*4. Relate what Hurston seemed to have learned from each of these persons or resources: her mother; Mrs. Calhoun; Mr. Calhoun; Mrs. Johnstone and Miss Hurd; mythology; privy-house walls.
*5. Cite evidence by paragraph numbers to indicate that Hurston was each of the following: brazen; bored; observant; proud; intelligent; imaginative; diplomatic; funny.

Writing Topics

1. Write an account of a time when you received an unanticipated gift or reward. What was it? What prompted its being given? Who was involved? How did you respond?
2. Hurston describes in some detail the books that held her interest when she was young. Select a book that had special appeal to you when you were a child. Write a brief description of its contents and relate why you felt toward the book as you did.

"It was plain that I had got to learn the shape of the river in all the different ways that could be thought of. . . ."

PERPLEXING LESSONS

Mark Twain

The author of such American classics as *Tom Sawyer*, *Huckleberry Finn*, *The Prince and the Pauper*, *A Connecticut Yankee in King Arthur's Court*, and *The Tragedy of Pudd'nhead Wilson*, Samuel Langhorne Clemens (1835–1910) early in his career adopted the pen name Mark Twain (signifying two fathoms deep) by which he is better known today. Born in Florida, Missouri, Twain was reared after the age of four in Hannibal, Missouri, where his family had settled. Following his father's death in 1847, Twain left school to become an apprentice printer and later a steamboat pilot, miner, journalist, short-story writer, essayist, novelist, and lecturer. In 1870, Twain married Olivia Langdon and settled in Hartford, Connecticut. "Perplexing Lessons" comes from *Life on the Mississippi*, Twain's account of his time as a riverboat pilot.

1   At the end of what seemed a tedious while, I had managed to pack my head full of islands, towns, bars, "points," and bends; and a curiously inanimate mass of lumber it was, too. However, inasmuch as I could shut my eyes and reel off a good long string of these names without leaving out more than ten miles of river in every fifty, I began to feel that I could take a boat down to New Orleans if I could make her skip those little gaps. But of course my complacency could hardly get start enough to lift my nose a trifle into the air, before Mr. Bixby would think of something to fetch it down again. One day he turned on me suddenly with this settler:

2   "What is the shape of Walnut Bend?"

3   He might as well have asked me my grandmother's opinion of protoplasm. I reflected respectfully, and then said I didn't know it had any particular shape. My gun-powdery chief went off with a bang, of course, and then went on loading and firing until he was out of adjectives.

4   I had learned long ago that he only carried just so many rounds of ammunition, and was sure to subside into a very placable and even remorseful old smoothbore as soon as they were all gone. That word "old" is merely affectionate; he was not more than thirty-four. I waited. By and by he said:

5   "My boy, you've got to know the *shape* of the river perfectly. It is all there is left to steer by on a very dark night. Everything else is blotted out and gone. But mind you, it hasn't the same shape in the night that it has in the daytime."

6   "How on earth am I ever going to learn it, then?"

7   "How do you follow a hall at home in the dark? Because you know the shape of it. You can't see it."

8   "Do you mean to say that I've got to know all the million trifling variations of shape in the banks of this interminable river as well as I know the shape of the front hall at home?"

9   "On my honor, you've got to know them *better* than any man ever did know the shapes of the halls in his own house."

10   "I wish I was dead!"

11   "Now I don't want to discourage you, but—"

12   "Well, pile it on me; I might as well have it now as another time."

13   "You see, this has got to be learned; there isn't any getting around it. A clear starlight night throws such heavy shadows that, if you didn't know the shape of a shore perfectly, you would claw away from every bunch of timber, because you would take the black shadow of it for a solid cape; and you see you would be getting scared to death every fifteen minutes by the watch. You would be fifty yards from shore all the time when you ought to be within fifty feet of it. You can't see a snag in one of those shadows, but you know exactly where it is, and the shape of the river tells you when you are coming to it. Then there's your pitch-dark night; the river is a very different shape on a pitch-dark night from what it is on a star-light night. All shores seem to be straight lines, then, and mighty dim ones, too; and you'd *run* them for straight lines, only you know better. You boldly drive your boat right into what seems to be a solid, straight wall (you knowing very well that in reality there is a curve there), and that wall falls back and makes way for you. Then there's your gray mist. You take a night when there's one of these grisly, drizzly, gray mists, and then there isn't *any* particular shape to a shore. A gray mist would tangle the head of the oldest man that ever lived. Well, then, different kinds of *moonlight* change the shape of the river in different ways. You see—"

14   "Oh, don't say any more, please! Have I got to learn the shape of the river according to all these five hundred thousand different ways? If I tried to carry all that cargo in my head it would make me stoop-shouldered."

15   "*No!* you only learn *the* shape of the river; and you learn it with such absolute certainty that you can always steer by the shape that's *in your head*, and never mind the one that's before your eyes."

16   "Very well, I'll try it; but, after I have learned it, can I depend on it? Will it keep the same form and not go fooling around?"

17   Before Mr. Bixby could answer, Mr. W. came in to take the watch, and he said:

18   "Bixby, you'll have to look out for President's Island, and all that country clear away up above the Old Hen and Chickens. The banks are caving and the shape of the shores changing like everything. Why, you wouldn't know the point above 40. You can go up inside the old sycamore snag, now."[1]

19   So that question was answered. Here were leagues of shore changing shape. My spirits were down in the mud again. Two things seemed pretty apparent to me. One was, that in order to be a pilot a man had got to learn more than any one man ought to be allowed to know; and the other was, that he must learn it all over again in a different way every twenty-four hours.

20   That night we had the watch until twelve. Now it was an ancient river custom for the two pilots to chat a bit when the watch changed. While the relieving pilot put on his gloves and lit his cigar, his partner, the retiring pilot, would say something like this:

21   "I judge the upper bar is making down a little at Hale's Point; had quarter twain with the lower lead and mark twain[2] with the other."

22   "Yes, I thought it was making down a little, last trip. Meet any boats?"

23   "Met one abreast the head of 21, but she was away over hugging the bar, and I couldn't make her out entirely. I took her for the *Sunny South*—hadn't any skylights forward of the chimneys."

24   And so on. And as the relieving pilot took the wheel his partner would mention that we were in such-and-such a bend, and say we were abreast of such-and-such a man's woodyard or plantation. This was courtesy; I supposed it was *necessity*. But Mr. W. came on watch full twelve minutes late on this particular night—a tremendous breach of etiquette; in fact, it is the unpardonable sin among pilots. So Mr. Bixby gave him no greeting whatever, but simply surrendered the wheel and marched out of the pilot-house without a word. I was appalled; it was a villainous night for blackness, we were in a particularly wide and blind part of the river, where there was no shape or substance to anything, and it seemed incredible that Mr. Bixby should have left that poor fellow to kill the boat, trying to find out where he was. But I resolved that I would stand by him anyway. He should find that he was not wholly friendless. So I stood around, and waited to be asked where we were. But Mr. W. plunged on serenely through the solid firmament of black cats that stood for an atmosphere, and never opened his mouth. "Here is a proud devil!" thought I; "here

---

[1] It may not be necessary, but still it can do no harm to explain that "inside" means between the snag and the shore. —M. T.

[2] Two fathoms. Quarter twain is $2\frac{1}{4}$ fathoms, $13\frac{1}{2}$ feet. Mark three is three fathoms.

is a limb of Satan that would rather send us all to destruction than put himself under obligations to me, because I am not yet one of the salt of the earth and privileged to snub captains and lord it over everything dead and alive in a steam-boat." I presently climbed up on the bench; I did not think it was safe to go to sleep while this lunatic was on watch.

25 However, I must have gone to sleep in the course of time, because the next thing I was aware of was the fact that day was breaking, Mr. W. gone, and Mr. Bixby at the wheel again. So it was four o'clock and all well—but me; I felt like a skinful of dry bones, and all of them trying to ache at once.

26 Mr. Bixby asked me what I had stayed up there for. I confessed that it was to do Mr. W. a benevolence—tell him where he was. It took five minutes for the entire preposterousness of the thing to filter into Mr. Bixby's system, and then I judge it filled him nearly up to the chin; because he paid me a compliment— and not much of a one either. He said:

27 "Well, taking you by and large, you do seem to be more different kinds of an ass than any creature I ever saw before. What did you suppose he wanted to know for?"

28 I said I thought it might be a convenience to him.

29 "Convenience! D—nation! Didn't I tell you that a man's got to know the river in the night the same as he'd know his own front hall?"

30 "Well, I can follow the front hall in the dark if I know it *is* the front hall; but suppose you set me down in the middle of it in the dark and not tell me which hall it is; how am *I* to know?"

31 "Well, you've *got* to, on the river!"

32 "All right. Then I'm glad I never said anything to Mr. W."

33 "I should say so! Why, he'd have slammed you through the window and utterly ruined a hundred dollars' worth of window-sash and stuff."

34 I was glad this damage had been saved, for it would have made me un-popular with the owners. They always hated anybody who had the name of being careless and injuring things.

35 I went to work now to learn the shape of the river; and of all the eluding and ungraspable objects that ever I tried to get mind or hands on, that was the chief. I would fasten my eyes upon a sharp, wooded point that projected far into the river some miles ahead of me, and go to laboriously photographing its shape upon my brain; and just as I was beginning to succeed to my satisfaction, we would draw up toward it and the exasperating thing would begin to melt away and fold back into the bank! If there had been a conspicuous dead tree standing upon the very point of the cape, I would find that tree inconspicuously merged into the general forest, and occupying the middle of a straight shore, when I got abreast of it! No prominent hill would stick to its shape long enough for me to make up my mind what its form really was, but it was as dissolving and changeful as if it had been a mountain of butter in the hottest corner of the tropics. Nothing ever had the same shape when I was coming down-stream

that it had borne when I went up. I mentioned these little difficulties to Mr. Bixby. He said:

36   "That's the very main virtue of the thing. If the shapes didn't change every three seconds they wouldn't be of any use. Take this place where we are now, for instance. As long as that hill over yonder is only one hill, I can boom right along the way I'm going; but the moment it splits at the top and forms a V, I know I've got to scratch to starboard in a hurry, or I'll bang this boat's brains out against a rock; and then the moment one of the prongs of the V swings behind the other, I've got to waltz to larboard again, or I'll have a misunderstanding with a snag that would snatch the keelson out of this steamboat as neatly as if it were a sliver in your hand. If that hill didn't change its shape on bad nights there would be an awful steamboat graveyard around here inside of a year."

37   It was plain that I had got to learn the shape of the river in all the different ways that could be thought of—upside down, wrong end first, inside out, fore-and-aft, and "thort-ships"—and then know what to do on gray nights when it hadn't any shape at all. So I set about it. In the course of time I began to get the best of this knotty lesson, and my self-complacency moved to the front once more. Mr. Bixby was all fixed, and ready to start it to the rear again. He opened on me after this fashion:

38   "How much water did we have in the middle crossing at Hole-in-the-Wall, trip before last?"

39   I considered this an outrage. I said:

40   "Every trip, down and up, the leadsmen are singing through that tangled place for three-quarters of an hour on a stretch. How do you reckon I can remember such a mess as that?"

41   "My boy, you've got to remember it. You've got to remember the exact spot and the exact marks the boat lay in when we had the shoalest water, in every one of the five hundred shoal places between St. Louis and New Orleans; and you mustn't get the shoal soundings and marks of one trip mixed up with the shoal soundings and marks of another, either, for they're not often twice alike. You must keep them separate."

42   When I came to myself again, I said:

43   "When I get so that I can do that, I'll be able to raise the dead, and then I won't have to pilot a steamboat to make a living. I want to retire from this business. I want a slush-bucket and a brush; I'm only fit for a roustabout. I haven't got brains enough to be a pilot; and if I had I wouldn't have strength enough to carry them around, unless I went on crutches."

44   "Now drop that! When I say I'll learn a man the river, I mean it. And you can depend on it, I'll learn him or kill him."

45   A pilot must have a memory; but there are two higher qualities which he must also have. He must have good and quick judgment and decision, and a cool, calm courage that no peril can shake. Give a man the merest trifle of pluck to start with, and by the time he has become a pilot he cannot be unmanned by

any danger a steamboat can get into: but one cannot quite say the same for judgment. Judgment is a matter of brains, and a man must *start* with a good stock of that article or he will never succeed as a pilot.

46   The growth of courage in the pilot-house is steady all the time but it does not reach a high and satisfactory condition until some time after the young pilot has been "standing his own watch" alone and under the staggering weight of all the responsibilities connected with the position. When the apprentice has become pretty thoroughly acquainted with the river, he goes clattering along so fearlessly with his steamboat, night or day, that he presently begins to imagine that it is *his* courage that animates him; but the first time the pilot steps out and leaves him to his own devices he finds out it was the other man's. He discovers that the article has been left out of his own cargo altogether. The whole river is bristling with exigencies in a moment; he is not prepared for them; he does not know how to meet them; all his knowledge forsakes him; and within fifteen minutes he is as white as a sheet and scared almost to death. Therefore pilots wisely train these cubs by various strategic tricks to look danger in the face a little more calmly. A favorite way of theirs is to play a friendly swindle upon the candidate.

47   Mr. Bixby served me in this fashion once, and for years afterward I used to blush, even in my sleep, when I thought of it. I had become a good steersman; so good, indeed, that I had all the work to do on our watch, night and day. Mr. Bixby seldom made a suggestion to me; all he ever did was to take the wheel on particularly bad nights or in particularly bad crossings, land the boat when she needed to be landed, play gentleman of leisure nine-tenths of the watch, and collect the wages. The lower river was about bank-full, and if anybody had questioned my ability to run any crossing between Cairo and New Orleans without help or instruction, I should have felt irreparably hurt. The idea of being afraid of any crossing in the lot, in the *daytime*, was a thing too preposterous for contemplation. Well, one matchless summer's day I was bowling down the bend above Island 66, brimful of self-conceit and carrying my nose as high as a giraffe's, when Mr. Bixby said:

48   "I am going below awhile. I suppose you know the next crossing?"

49   This was almost an affront. It was about the plainest and simplest crossing in the whole river. One couldn't come to any harm, whether he ran it right or not; and as for depth, there never had been any bottom there. I knew all this, perfectly well.

50   "Know how to *run* it? Why, I can run it with my eyes shut."

51   "How much water is there in it?"

52   "Well, that is an odd question. I couldn't get bottom there with a church steeple."

53   "You think so, do you?"

54   The very tone of the question shook my confidence. That was what Mr. Bixby was expecting. He left, without saying anything more. I began to imagine all sorts of things. Mr. Bixby, unknown to me, of course, sent somebody

down to the forecastle with some mysterious instructions to the leadsmen, another messenger was sent to whisper among the officers, and then Mr. Bixby went into hiding behind a smoke-stack where he could observe results. Presently the captain stepped out on the hurricane-deck; next the chief mate appeared; then a clerk. Every moment or two a straggler was added to my audience; and before I got to the head of the island I had fifteen or twenty people assembled down there under my nose. I began to wonder what the trouble was. As I started across, the captain glanced aloft at me and said, with a sham uneasiness in his voice:

55 "Where is Mr. Bixby?"

56 "Gone below, sir."

57 But that did the business for me. My imagination began to construct dangers out of nothing, and they multiplied faster than I could keep the run of them. All at once I imagined I saw shoal water ahead! The wave of coward agony that surged through me then came near dislocating every joint in me. All my confidence in that crossing vanished. I seized the bell-rope; dropped it, ashamed; seized it again; dropped it once more; clutched it tremblingly once again, and pulled it so feebly that I could hardly hear the stroke myself. Captain and mate sang out instantly, and both together:

58 "Starboard lead there! and quick about it!"

59 This was another shock. I began to climb the wheel like a squirrel; but I would hardly get the boat started to port before I would see new dangers on that side, and away I would spin to the other; only to find perils accumulating to starboard, and be crazy to get to port again. Then came the leadsman's sepulchral cry:

60 "D-e-e-p four!"

61 Deep four in a bottomless crossing! The terror of it took my breath away.

62 "M-a-r-k three! M-a-r-k three! Quarter-less-three! Half twain!"

63 This was frightful! I seized the bell-ropes and stopped the engines.

64 "Quarter twain! Quarter twain! Mark twain!"

65 I was helpless. I did not know what in the world to do. I was quaking from head to foot, and I could have hung my hat on my eyes, they stuck out so far.

66 "Quarter-*less*-twain! Nine-and-a-*half!*"

67 We were *drawing* nine! My hands were in a nerveless flutter. I could not ring a bell intelligibly with them. I flew to the speaking-tube and shouted to the engineer:

68 "Oh, Ben, if you love me, *back* her! Quick, Ben! Oh, back the immortal *soul* out of her!"

69 I heard the door close gently. I looked around, and there stood Mr. Bixby, smiling a bland, sweet smile. Then the audience on the hurricane-deck sent up a thundergust of humiliating laughter. I saw it all, now, and I felt meaner than the meanest man in human history. I laid in the lead, set the boat in her marks, came ahead on the engines, and said:

70   "It was a fine trick to play on an orphan, *wasn't* it? I suppose I'll never hear the last of how I was ass enough to heave the lead at the head of 66."

71   "Well, no, you won't, maybe. In fact I hope you won't; for I want you to learn something by that experience. Didn't you *know* there was no bottom in that crossing?"

72   "Yes, sir, I did."

73   "Very well, then. You shouldn't have allowed me or anybody else to shake your confidence in that knowledge. Try to remember that. And another thing: when you get into a dangerous place, don't turn coward. That isn't going to help matters any."

74   It was a good enough lesson, but pretty hardly learned. Yet about the hardest part of it was that for months I so often had to hear a phrase which I had conceived a particular distaste for. It was, "Oh, Ben, if you love me, back her!"

❧

Discussion Questions

   1.   Explain why the "lessons" Mr. Bixby was trying to teach Twain were so difficult to learn.
   2.   Relate some of the detailed information Twain had to possess before he could say he knew "the shape of the river." How did that information differ from what students normally learn in school about the Mississippi?
   3.   Describe the erroneous assumption that Twain makes with regard to Mr. W., the pilot who relieved Mr. Bixby. How does Mr. Bixby respond to Twain's misapprehension?
   4.   What two qualities for a pilot does Twain declare in paragraph 45 to be more important than memory? Explain how, and with what result, Mr. Bixby tests both those qualities in Twain.
  *5.   Choose two adjectives to describe Mr. Bixby as a teacher and two to describe Twain as a learner. Justify your choices by citing relevant paragraphs by number.

Writing Topics

   1.   Write a description of a job you once had to learn, including the responsibilities you were assigned and the way you acquired the knowledge and skills needed to fulfill those responsibilities. Reveal your feelings about the position you held and the work you performed.
   2.   Assume that a friend of yours has decided to drop out of college, declaring that on-the-job training is more important than a formal education. Write your friend a letter in which you present arguments intended to persuade him or her to finish school.

&.. . *the high schools would do well to return to their proper business of preparing foundations."*

THE TOTAL EFFECT AND THE EIGHTH GRADE

Flannery O'Connor

A native of Georgia, [Mary] Flannery O'Connor (1925–1964) set most of her fiction in the South, a setting that allowed her to give full play to her sharp ear for dialect and irreverent sense of humor. A devout Catholic herself, O'Connor frequently created as characters backwood religious fanatics whose bizarre acts of violence were attempts to prove God's existence. Before dying of lupus, a degenerative disease, O'Connor wrote two novels, *Wise Blood* (1952) and *The Violent Bear It Away* (1960); two collections of short stories, *A Good Man Is Hard to Find* (1955) and *Everything That Rises Must Converge* (1965); and a miscellaneous collection of prose, *Mystery and Manners: Occasional Prose* (1961). *The Habit of Being*, a collection of her letters, was published in 1978.

1   In two recent instances in Georgia, parents have objected to their eighth- and ninth-grade children's reading assignments in modern fiction. This seems to happen with some regularity in cases throughout the country. The unwitting parent picks up his child's book, glances through it, comes upon passages of erotic detail or profanity, and takes off at once to complain to the school board. Sometimes, as in one of the Georgia cases, the teacher is dismissed and hackles rise in liberal circles everywhere.

2   The two cases in Georgia, which involved Steinbeck's *East of Eden* and John Hersey's *A Bell for Adano*, provoked considerable newspaper comment. One columnist, in commending the enterprise of the teachers, announced that students do not like to read the fusty works of the nineteenth century, that their attention can best be held by novels dealing with the realities of our own time, and that the Bible, too, is full of racy stories.

3   Mr. Hersey himself addressed a letter to the State School Superintendent in behalf of the teacher who had been dismissed. He pointed out that his book is not scandalous, that it attempts to convey an earnest message about the nature of democracy, and that it falls well within the limits of the principle of "total

effect," that principle followed in legal cases by which a book is judged not for isolated parts but by the final effect of the whole book upon the general reader.

4   I do not want to comment on the merits of these particular cases. What concerns me is what novels ought to be assigned in the eighth and ninth grades as a matter of course, for if these cases indicate anything, they indicate the haphazard way in which fiction is approached in our high schools. Presumably there is a state reading list which contains "safe" books for teachers to assign; after that it is up to the teacher.

5   English teachers come in Good, Bad, and Indifferent, but too frequently in high schools anyone who can speak English is allowed to teach it. Since several novels can't easily be gathered into one textbook the fiction that students are assigned depends upon their teacher's knowledge, ability, and taste: variable factors at best. More often than not, the teacher assigns what he thinks will hold the attention and interest of the students. Modern fiction will certainly hold it.

6   Ours is the first age in history which has asked the child what he would tolerate learning, but that is a part of the problem with which I am not equipped to deal. The devil of Educationism that possesses us is the kind that can be "cast out only by prayer and fasting." No one has yet come along strong enough to do it. In other ages the attention of children was held by Homer and Virgil, among others, but, by the reverse evolutionary process, that is no longer possible; our children are too stupid now to enter the past imaginatively. No one asks the student if algebra pleases him or if he finds it satisfactory that some French verbs are irregular, but if he prefers Hersey to Hawthorne, his taste must prevail.

7   I would like to put forward the proposition, repugnant to most English teachers, that fiction, if it is going to be taught in the high schools, should be taught as a subject and as a subject with a history. The total effect of a novel depends not only on its innate impact, but upon the experience, literary and otherwise, with which it is approached. No child needs to be assigned Hersey or Steinbeck until he is familiar with a certain amount of the best work of Cooper, Hawthorne, Melville, the early James, and Crane, and he does not need to be assigned these until he has been introduced to some of the better English novelists of the eighteenth and nineteenth centuries.

8   The fact that these works do not present him with the realities of his own time is all to the good. He is surrounded by the realities of his own time, and he has no perspective whatever from which to view them. Like the college student who wrote in her paper on Lincoln that he went to the movies and got shot, many students go to college unaware that the world was not made yesterday; their studies began with the present and dipped backward occasionally when it seemed necessary or unavoidable.

9   There is much to be enjoyed in the great British novels of the nineteenth century, much that a good teacher can open up in them for the young student.

There is no reason why these novels should be either too simple or too difficult for the eighth grade. For the simple, they offer simple pleasures; for the more precocious, they can be made to yield subtler ones if the teacher is up to it. Let the student discover, after reading the nineteenth-century British novel, that the nineteenth-century American novel is quite different as to its literary characteristics, and he will thereby learn something not only about these individual works but about the sea-change which a new historical situation can effect in a literary form. Let him come to modern fiction with this experience behind him, and he will be better able to see and to deal with the more complicated demands of the best twentieth-century fiction.

10   Modern fiction often looks simpler than the fiction that preceded it, but in reality is more complex. A natural evolution has taken place. The author has for the most part absented himself from direct participation in the work and has left the reader to make his own way amid experiences dramatically rendered and symbolically ordered. The modern novelist merges the reader in experience; he tends to raise the passions he touches upon. If he is a good novelist, he raises them to effect by their order and clarity a new experience — the total effect — which is not in itself sensuous or simply of the moment. Unless the child has had some literary experience before, he is not going to be able to resolve the immediate passions the book arouses into any true, total picture.

11   It is here the moral problem will arise. It is one thing for a child to read about adultery in the Bible or in *Anna Karenina*, and quite another for him to read about it in most modern fiction. This is not only because in both the former instances adultery is considered a sin, and in the latter, at most, an inconvenience, but because modern writing involves the reader in the action with a new degree of intensity, and literary mores now permit him to be involved in any action a human being can perform.

12   In our fractured culture, we cannot agree on morals; we cannot even agree that moral matters should come before literary ones when there is a conflict between them. All this is another reason why the high schools would do well to return to their proper business of preparing foundations. Whether in the senior year students should be assigned modern novelists should depend both on their parents' consent and on what they have already read and understood.

13   The high-school English teacher will be fulfilling his responsibility if he furnishes the student a guided opportunity, through the best writing of the past, to come, in time, to an understanding of the best writing of the present. He will teach literature, not social studies or little lessons in democracy or the customs of many lands.

14   And if the student finds that this is not to his taste? Well, that is regrettable. Most regrettable. His taste should not be consulted; it is being formed.

Discussion Questions

1. Cite the "recent instances in Georgia" that seem to have motivated O'Connor to write her brief essay. What underlying issue most concerns her?

*2. Is O'Connor's analogy in paragraph 6 between learning algebra or irregular French verbs and the reading of literature an acceptable one? Why or why not?

*3. In paragraph 7, O'Connor proposes that students not be assigned contemporary fiction or even American literature of the nineteenth century until they have read widely in English literature of both the eighteenth and nineteenth centuries. Explain why you agree or disagree with her reasoning.

4. On what grounds does O'Connor support her assertion, found in paragraph 10, that "modern fiction often looks simpler than the fiction that preceded it, but in reality is more complex"? How does the principle of "total effect" enter into her argument?

*5. O'Connor uses the first-person pronoun I sparingly in "The Total Effect and the Eighth Grade." Would the selection be just as effective without its use? Explain.

Writing Topics

1. Assume that you have a friend who is an avid reader of eighteenth- and nineteenth-century novels. Write a letter in which you try to persuade your friend that one can "enter the past imaginatively" by viewing films. Use specific examples.

2. Assume that you have a friend who is an avid film viewer. Write a persuasive letter arguing that novels can provide experiences that films cannot. Support your argument with examples.

Summary Writing Topics

*1. Research current methods of teaching English in American schools to nonnative students. Then write an essay citing these methods and identify the strengths and deficiencies of each.

*2. In an essay, present the arguments both for and against making English the official language of the United States. Relate which arguments you find most persuasive and why.

*3. Read at least two major reports written during the past decade on ways to improve American secondary education. Write an essay exploring which recommendations given in the reports seem most sound and which seem least sound. Provide support for your views.

*4. Imagine that you are the superintendent of a new school district and are interested in hiring teachers. Write a letter to prospective candidates in which you relate the specific characteristics you are looking for in those applying for both elementary and secondary teaching positions. In your letter, explain why you believe each of these characteristics to be important.

5. Interview at least three people who are in a profession or trade that appeals to you. In a written report, describe each person, the qualifications he or she had to meet to fill the position, and what each person regards as the positive as well as negative aspects of the job. Conclude by revealing whether or not you are still interested in pursuing that vocation.

6. Analyze differences in writing style between Mary Antin in "Initiation" and Frank Conroy in "The Coldness of Public Places." In your analysis, consider such matters as the length of sentences and paragraphs; ratio of monosyllabic to polysyllabic words; the frequency of dialogue; the use of figures of speech, including simile and metaphor; and the tone or implied attitude of the author toward his or her audience and material. Conclude by indicating which style you prefer and why.

*7. Write a report on intuition in which you define the term, explain how it is formed, describe its uses in creativity and daily life, and evaluate its reliability and worth as a way of knowing.

8. Of the authors who contributed to "Learning and Knowing," select the three who you believe exhibited the keenest senses of humor. Write an analysis in which you cite evidence from the selections to support your choices.

9. Assume that you have been asked to edit a revised edition of *The Perceptive* I. You need to retain three selections of those appearing in Cluster 2, "Learning and Knowing." Write a report indicating which selections you would retain and why.

Cluster

Encounters:
Strangers/Acquaintances/Friends

Most of us crave solitude from time to time, some respite from the usual hurly-burly of our daily lives. Yet few of us would elect to become hermits, living out our days reclusively in deep woods, far removed from other human beings.

Like the great majority of our fellow creatures, we normally choose to live in communities in which other persons can help satisfy our material wants. Rather than attempt to be entirely self-sufficient, we rely upon grocers to supply us with food, mechanics and plumbers to fix our cars and pipes, dry cleaners to remove stains from our garments, firefighters and police to safeguard our property, doctors to keep us in good health.

We are usually dependent upon others for far more, though, than just the satisfaction of our physical needs. Our psychological identity and sense of well-being are determined in good part by the nature of our encounters, both infrequent and frequent, with people in our communities—by how we react to strangers, establish acquaintanceships, cultivate and sustain friendships. Self-consciously we watch for clues to how our appearance, our ideas, our values are being received by those with whom we communicate, often modifying our tastes and beliefs in light of our audience's response. Moreover, we often incorporate into our psyches the thoughts, convictions, and ideals of those with whom we interact. In short, through our associations with others, we are constantly, and most often subtly, altering our concept of our self, of the **I** that, although in flux, seems to define us.

The selections you are about to read have to do with their writers' encounters with other people. Some of these encounters were short-lived—that of an afternoon, a year of schooling, or a period of childhood. Others were more sustained, nurtured across decades. Some of the relationships established through these encounters never moved beyond being that of one stranger to another to becoming that of acquaintances. Some, however, evolved through stages to emerge as strong friendships, with one even progressing beyond friendship to love and marriage.

Whether brief or lengthy, the encounters all affected human lives, altering slightly or considerably each writer's concept of herself or himself. As you read, you will find that some selections stimulate reveries of your own encounters with various individuals. Accumulatively, the selections, regardless of how different their content from your own experiences, should enrich your sense of self and should have some influence on the quality of your future interactions with those who cross your path.

"When you go to prison,' Aunt Ruthie counseled him, 'take out some books. Learn a different profession.'"

AUNT RUTHIE SHOWS THE WAY

Patricia Volk

Patricia Volk (b. 1943), a native of New York City and a graduate of Syracuse University, served as art director for *Seventeen* magazine and *Harper's Bazaar* before becoming senior vice president for an advertising firm. Since 1988, she has been a full-time writer. Among her publications are two collections of short stories, *The Yellow Banana* (1988) and *All It Takes* (1990), as well as a novel, *White Light* (1987). "Aunt Ruthie Shows the Way" appeared in the November 20, 1994, issue of *The New York Times Magazine*.

1   "Your Uncle Al and I had a whirlpool romance," Aunt Ruthie tells me. Then she pauses. "Is that the word I mean?" We're having lunch to celebrate her 89th birthday. She dabs a little applesauce on her blintzes.

2   "I make the best applesauce," she says. "You want to know the secret? I put in the pits."

3   "You leave them *in?*"

4   "There's taste in the pits," she explains. "You quarter the apples, cook them in water, then you put them through a . . . through a. . . ." The word is gone.

5   There are 159,260 women over 80 in New York City. You'll see them taking tai chi at the Y. You'll see them at Fairway, elbowing toward the Florida grapefruits or examining the string beans one by one. (How a woman selects string beans tells a lot about her life.) They're on the bus after 10 a.m. and before 3. In winter, they wear woollies.

6   You used to see them at the Woman's Exchange and Mary Elizabeth's tearoom. Or at Schrafft's, having tuna on toasted cheese bread and butterscotch sundaes with coffee ice cream. New York's oldest women have outlived their hangouts. Most have outlived their husbands. Few are as lucky as Brooke Astor and Kitty Carlisle Hart and my mother's friend's mother, who, at 97, stands on her dining room table twice a year to clean the chandelier.

7   "If I live to be 100 I won't finish these blintzes," Aunt Ruthie says. "Take one, darling."

8   "You really leave the pits in?"

9   "And the skin."

10   Maybe you've heard about my Aunt Ruthie. She was the woman taken hostage in her Bronx apartment four years ago. An ex-paratrooper, Jose Cruz, climbed in through a window and held Aunt Ruthie at gunpoint for five hours before the police exchanged her for two cigarettes. "When you go to prison," Aunt Ruthie counseled him, "take out some books. Learn a different profession. It's important in life to get hold of yourself."

11   Aunt Ruthie got hold of herself young. In 1923, after graduating from Morris High School in the Bronx, she got a clerical job at Pathé Exchange on West 45th Street. Aunt Ruthie couldn't help noticing that the office supervisor, a Miss Maloubier, took lunch from 12 to 4. Six months later, Aunt Ruthie had Miss Maloubier's job. She worked her way up to $50 a week, which she gave to her mother, who gave her an allowance. "That's the way it was then, darling. I didn't think anything else."

12   A woman who looks like George Burns sits at the table next to us. She knows Aunt Ruthie from the building and starts complaining. When we finally disengage, Aunt Ruthie blinks at me in an exaggerated way. First one eye, then the other, then both, then one again. I think she is sending a code that she doesn't like the woman, so I nod to show I get it. Then Aunt Ruthie tells me she can't see out of her left eye.

13   "You accept these things," she shrugs. "No pain, thank goodness."

14   Aunt Ruthie can remember the taste of her mother's egg sandwiches and recite "All the world's a stage." But she's puzzled that she has "lost" Latin. In 1930, when she married Uncle Al, her mother-in-law insisted she retire.

15   "But you'd worked there five years. You loved that job. Didn't you mind?"

16   "She was against it. So against it. At that time, there weren't many married women working."

17   Aunt Ruthie's not tough, but she's resilient. She's Old New York genteel. I worry that when she dies, her syntax will disappear from the universe. There should be a place that preserves the way women of her generation spoke, the way YIVO preserves Yiddish. For instance, when you agree with Aunt Ruthie, she prolongs the agreement with "Am I right?" as in:

18   Aunt Ruthie: "So help me, that woman looks just like George Burns."

19   Me: "You're right. She looks just like George Burns."

20   Aunt Ruthie: "Am I right?"

21   "I'll be jiggered," she likes to say. "Out of this world," "Isn't it something?" "May I be struck with lightning," "As I live and breathe," "She's not my cup of tea," "You should only never know," "always the lady," "I won't hear of it," "Frigidaire" and "down below" or "*there*." She calls everybody "darling." I ask her about a word my grandmother—her sister—used.

22   "*Umbashrign*. It's like 'God bless you.' On that order."

23   Aunt Ruthie lives by herself; she's not half of the New York Odd Couple, a widow and her live-in companion. You see these women on sunny days,

walking with care or getting pushed. Aunt Ruthie does just fine, even though she was hit by a stolen van in front of Key Food two years ago and wound up with a broken hip and shoulder. Now, when she leaves the apartment, she uses a shopping cart. She weights it with the Yellow Pages, for balance.

24　　"I make out I'm going shopping," she laughs. In her black tight skirt, black sweater and black oxford heels with toecaps, Aunt Ruthie looks stylish even with the cart. A friend stops by our table and admires her red jacket.

25　　"Trying to get noticed, Ruth?"

26　　"Well, what do you think?" Aunt Ruthie jokes back.

27　　Then she whispers to me: "The Blair catalog. $39."

28　　Every week, Aunt Ruthie gets together with the girls. These are new girls. The old girls, her four best friends, are dead. And every week, Aunt Ruthie gets her pageboy done. It's still got a lot of black.

29　　"Is that your real color?"

30　　"I swear to you as my name is Ruth. But people don't believe me, so I tell them I use shoe polish."

31　　Back at the apartment, Aunt Ruthie asks if I could use her mah-jongg set. When I admire a needlepoint pillow, she says, "Take it home."

32　　I dreamed last night that I took Aunt Ruthie to the Metropolitan Museum. "Leave your shopping cart at home," I told her. "We'll slide." We did the Great Hall exactly like ice skaters, gliding over the stone floors in flat shoes.

33　　After dinner I call my mother, "What's the thing you push food through that gets out the pits?" I ask.

34　　"A Foley food mill," Mom says. So I dial the Bronx.

35　　"Of course," Aunt Ruthie gasps. "The letters are right there on the side! Darling, would you tell something, please? I want to know. How on earth could I forget that?"

36　　Beats me.

ع&

Discussion Questions

1. The author comments in paragraph 17 that "Aunt Ruthie's not tough, but she's resilient." Point out some examples of Aunt Ruthie's resiliency.

2. The author further comments in paragraph 17, "I worry that when she [Aunt Ruthie] dies, her syntax will disappear from the universe." What is unusual about her aunt's speech?

3. What evidence is there that Aunt Ruthie is mentally alert; gregarious; careful about her appearance; generous; resourceful?

4. Do you consider Aunt Ruthie to be unusual for someone her age? Why or why not?

Writing Topics

1. Write a character sketch of an elderly person you know. In your sketch, include details about this person's appearance, habits, past experiences, attitudes—whatever would help make him or her distinctive for your reader.
2. Imagine that you are eighty years old and have been asked by a young relative to describe the highlights of your life. Compose a written response that would satisfy both your relative's curiosity and your sense of what has been significant to your existence.

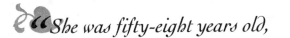

She was fifty-eight years old,

she had abandoned the opera, and she was not any age.

She was robed in who she was. . . ."

L' APRÈS-MIDI DE MARY GARDEN

Paul Horgan

Paul Horgan (1903-1995), a highly versatile author, wrote short stories, novels, histories, biographies, plays, poems, essays, and children's books. Much of his work was set in the Southwest, particularly New Mexico. Horgan's history of the cultures that flourished along the Rio Grande, *Great River* (1954), received a Pulitzer Prize, as did his biography of Father Jean Baptiste Lamy, *Lamy of Santa Fe* (1975). Among his many novels are *The Fault of Angels* (1933), *No Quarter Given* (1935), *Main Line West* (1936), *The Common Heart* (1942), *Give Me Possession* (1957), *A Distant Drummer* (1960), *Everything to Live For* (1968), *Whitewater* (1970), *Mexico Bay* (1982), and *The Richard Trilogy* (1990).

1   On Tuesday morning, 29 January 1935, in New York, I awoke to a state of alarm mixed with elation. It was the publication day of *No Quarter Given*, my second novel, and Harper and Brothers were giving an all-out cocktail party for the occasion. In those days, the literary cocktail party was more of an event than it is now. All of New York's literary *gratin* turned out. Faces famous in caricature, minds tautly competitive, common charity disdained, the guests came to be seen and reported. The guest of honor was often said to be the least of the attractions. I had read all this in New Mexico, where I lived. Now about to be thrown in the thick of it, I thought how comfortable it would be simply to bolt. The dreadful day yawned ahead of me. How to get through it until five o'clock, when I must appear? Whenever the thought of the coming ordeal struck me, I felt the classic symptoms of stage fright—a tightening of the scalp, a thump at the solar plexus.

2   At breakfast, a sudden refuge in distraction faced me in the *New York Times*. There I found an item announcing that Mary Garden, the lustrous opera singer and actress, would present a lecture-recital in the Plaza Hotel ballroom at three o'clock that day. Her subject was Claude Debussy. Tickets could be had at a

box office in the hotel. All my life — I was thirty-two — I had wanted to see and hear this amazing artist.

3   To mention Caruso, Melba, Farrar, Chaliapin, or, for today, Maria Callas, is to suggest the like position of Mary Garden in the international operatic world of her time. Much of her lore was known to me. I knew her voice through recordings. While still a vocal student in Paris she had won instant fame by brilliantly taking over the lead role in Charpentier's *Louise* when the artist singing the part became ill. On that night, Garden was established for life. She was twenty-six. Two years later Debussy chose her to create the role of Mélisande. Another triumph. As Massenet's Thaïs she inflamed her artistic success with her erotic enactment of the courtesan — a performance which gave the public its stubborn opinion, however mistaken, about how "daring" her private life must be. For one year she was general manager of the great Chicago Opera, grandly bankrupting the company by the beauty and extravagance of her productions. James Gibbons Huneker and Carl Van Vechten had written paeans to her which I had read. Here was my chance to attend this great artist, and also take my mind off my trouble for a good part of the afternoon.

4   But it would help to be with friends. One came happily to mind — Natalie Hall, the operatic soprano. She and her mezzo-soprano sister Bettina were known for starring in a long-running Broadway operetta. I telephoned Natalie. To hear, to see Garden? Wildly grateful. Could she bring Bettina, whom I'd never met? We would meet, all three, at two forty-five in the Plaza Palm Court. I telephoned for reservations and was asked to take up the tickets by half past two — the ballroom was selling out. My day began to look up.

5   In good time I arrived at the Plaza, already somewhat insulated against my nervous state — but not for long. In the lobby was a portentous reminder — a large-lettered display announcing the day's events in the hotel:

MISS MARY GARDEN, LECTURE-RECITAL
3 P.M., Grand Ballroom
Second Floor South

And below that, ominously:

RECEPTION FOR MR. PAUL HORGAN
Harper & Brothers
5 to 7, White and Gold Suite
Second Floor North

There seemed to be no escape. At the box office I asked for my tickets. The young woman clerk shuffled them out and I was about to pay for them when behind her a tall, glossy, youngish man wearing a gardenia in his buttonhole snapped up the tickets, palmed my money aside, and said, "No, n'no, Mr. Horgan: with our compliments," and handed the three tickets to me.

6 "But why? Thank you, but I don't understand."

7 "I am Mr. Piza, Madame's manager. I have seen notice of your reception. My congratulations." Swarthy and elegant, he bowed like a South American. "We are delighted. Allow me."

8 Confused but elevated, l thanked him again and went to the Palm Court. There they were, the two beauties, one for each arm. Embraces. We made our way to the elevator.

9 "Garden: how exciting," said Natalie, the classic brunette, and Bettina, the glowing blonde, said, "Fabulous."

10 The ballroom was filling fast. We found our spindly gold chairs in a box on the right side of the room with a fine view of the small formal stage where a concert grand piano waited.

11 Suddenly the stage bloomed with light. There was a bated pause, and with a sudden step, Mary Garden appeared from stage right, halted, raised her arm to rest her hand on the proscenium, and held her pose. (A fleeting reminder of Toulouse-Lautrec's Yvette Guilbert.) Everyone stood. She let them, and then, with all standing, she made a wide gesture, showing the insides of her wrists, and leaned forward slowly in a bow that was not at all the grateful player's humble thanks, but a grant of permission to attend. She then went to the bend of the piano, poised in command, as the house settled. Already there was a sense of great occasion—how great, we did not then know, for it was her final appearance in public as a singer.

12 Small and delicate as she was, she had an affinity of countenance with the great cats, here refined exquisitely to retain the tiger's high cheeks above the fixed, meaningless smile; intent gaze; alert focus on all environs; thoughtless confidence of power; all supported by the gift of seeming beautiful at will. So, too, her movement, lithe, exact, gracile, was of the feline order. She was fifty-eight years old, she had abandoned the opera, and she was not any age. She was robed in who she was, which was enough to give the world.

13 Otherwise, her costume suggested both theater and salon, as best I can recall this—and all that follows.

14 She wore a close-fitting hat of black silk with a mesh of veil that came down just past her eyes—her eyes gleamed with a tigerish light in a little blue cave of shadow that put the years at a distance, and yet conveyed the vivid present. Her hair was a tawny gold. A floor-length fall of pale yellow satin, her gown was so tight over her straight hips that you wondered how she could step. A short-sleeved torero jacket in black sparkling stuff met long white gloves that reached above the elbows. A necklace of big pearls was looped once about her throat, with the rest of it swaying almost to her knees. How tall was she? A few inches over five feet, it was recorded somewhere; but she was a figure so commanding that illusion created height. By her valiant posture she seemed to tell us not to be nervous—all would be well, indeed brilliant.

15 And it was.

16   She went right to work, saying something like, "Claude Debussy. The most fascinating yet mysterious public person I have ever met."

17   She then went on to speak for perhaps thirty minutes, in an international accent. Her tone was conversational, emphatic when proper, beguiling when memory was tender; always correct as to the language, though when she needed French, the pronunciation made no pretense to sound native.

18   In particles, then: Debussy was "a very strange man," as she wrote fifteen years later in her autobiography. (Much that she wrote and much that she said in her lecture are merged in my memory.) She said he was not tall, rather stocky. Quite extraordinarily, he had *two* foreheads — yes, two, one bulging on top over which he brushed his dark hair, the other showing in the clear above his black brows. His eyes, dark, sometimes quite expressionless, were fascinating. You never quite knew what he was thinking. Things he said were original, quite. He was mad about women, though one didn't know if he ever loved anyone, really. People always wondered, of course, some even asked, if he and she had ever been lovers. The idea was preposterous — not that he did not make the attempt one day on a railroad platform in Versailles, but no, there was nothing to it. A perfect artistic understanding, that was all, and it was enough. They rehearsed *Pelléas et Mélisande* for four months. Debussy attended, Messager conducted, they had forty orchestra rehearsals, unheard of. But when the opening came, Debussy was not there, and in fact he never attended a public performance. Some were offended. Not she. She understood when he said that for ten years the opera had been his life, and as he knew it best in that way, no other way was as real to him. When the role of Mélisande became hers at his desire, the author of the play, Maeterlinck, made a scandal, tried to have her removed in favor of his mistress, Mme Georgette Leblanc, but no, Debussy held fast, he never gave in, Mélisande remained hers, then, and for as long as she, and *she herself*, chose, in whatever opera company she was singing. Debussy had a devoted first wife, Lily, who adored him; she overlooked much, but never expected what happened, when he left her quite abruptly for a rich woman. Lily tried to kill herself, and at that he seemed concerned, but in the hospital when she assured him that she would now live, he shrugged and simply went away, and that was all of that. A very strange man, but yes, fascinating, a great pianist, though a poor singer when he sang the part to everyone in a first reading — his voice was small and husky. He adored Mélisande's voice (he always used that name instead of "Mary Garden") and he loved her voice so much that he composed and dedicated to her a whole group of songs, the *Ariettes*. . . .

19   And I remembered this when years afterward I read in his letters that Debussy wrote of her: "Le succès de 'notre Garden' ne m'étonne pas; il faudrait autrement avoir des oreilles bouchées à l'émeri pour résister au charme de sa voix. Pour ma part, je ne puis concevoir un timbre plus doucement insinuant. Cela ressemble même à de la tyrannie, tant il est impossible de l'oublier." (I am not amazed at the success of "our Garden"; you'd have to have your ears

plugged by a ground-glass stopper to resist the spell of her voice. I can't imagine a timbre more softly persuasive. It's like a tyranny, impossible to put out of mind.)

20   And she remembered what he said of her to Carré, the director of the Opéra Comique, at a rehearsal of *Pelléas et Mélisande* while she was creating the character: *Je n'ai rien à lui dire* — he could suggest nothing to enhance her realization of the role. But that was how it always was with her work — she never *studied* how to do a part — she always simply *knew*, it came from nowhere, and it was always the truth. At the end of that particular rehearsal she heard him say to Carré, "What a strange person, this child." Then in his baffling, remote way, he picked up his hat and walked off — he was always doing that, suddenly walking out. . . .

21   In the Plaza Hotel Grand Ballroom, she was up to her old tricks — casting a spell, as she had done in countless opera performances. With her random notes on Claude Debussy, she brought him before us and we believed. When she finished speaking, she allowed a long thoughtful pause; and then, with peremptory grace, she turned toward the wings, extending her hand to bring forth her accompanist, Jean Dansereau, and a self-effacing youth who would turn pages. Now they would give us songs by Debussy, fourteen of them, including, according to the next day's *Times*, the air of *Lia* from *L'Enfant prodigue*, the third of the *Ariettes*, *Je tremble en voyant ton image*, *Green*, *La Chevelure*, and *Mandoline*. M. Dansereau, a small, wiry Frenchman, played the piano texts with a tonal intelligence equal to hers — by turns scintillant, brooding, declamatory.

22   How to be exact in describing a performance made of sound, that medium as fugitive as time? Her voice was without luster — she was past the age of brilliant tone. Perfect in pitch, it had at moments almost a *parlando* quality, in a timbre reminiscent of dried leaves stirred by air. But what expression, now smoky with passion, again rueful for life's shadows! What musicality; and what sense of meaning — the texts of Guignand, Bourget, Pierre Louÿs, Verlaine, Baudelaire came forth in all the beauty and power of Debussy's description: "the spell of her voice . . . so softly persuasive." We were persuaded. Did any artist more fully know who, and what, she was? Was this the first attribute of the interpretive genius?

23   For two hours I forgot my coming trial, and when the concert ended, my companions and I were in lingering thrall. I said we must try to go backstage to pay our respects, and as singers, the Misses Hall agreed with stars in their eyes.

24   At the hidden entrance to the stage, then, I presented us to Mr. Piza, who was on guard there. Could we say one word to Miss Garden of our perfect fulfillment?

25   "Ah, thank you, I'm afraid not. You see, Madame never receives after a performance. But I will tell her. Thank you."

26   "No, it is our thanks," I said. And then, in a leap beyond the bounds of the plausible, I added, "But you so kindly invited me to your occasion, perhaps you

would let me invite Madame and yourself to my own party," and I mentioned the reception for my new book, already under way at well after five.

27   "Yes, I know, of course. But again—" Mr. Piza was extremely polite in excusing Madame from unscheduled and, in fact, unexamined events.

28   We sighed and turned away. 1 began to feel the familiar stress under my necktie again. Natalie looked at me and said, "You'll be all right."

29   By her concern she drove home my dread. I nodded. Compelled to a brave show, I took the sisters to the lobby where I bought flowers for us all—violets for them to hold, a dark red carnation for my buttonhole.

30   "Let's go up, then," I said, viewing the elevator with its brass lace as a tumbril. But the Hall sisters had to leave me: they must have an early supper to be ready for their evening show. With a gaunt smile I embraced them and saw them go; and then I ascended to the White and Gold Suite on the second floor, to be discharged upon a waste of polished parquet. Three lofty rooms facing the park were thrown into one, which at first glance seemed almost empty.

31   Where was the party, that clamorous huddle of people at cocktails, shouting each other down with a high decibel count thermally stimulated by their massed body heat? But as I looked about I saw that there were guests present— perhaps sixty or so—who were ranged tightly on little gold chairs lining the walls. A few were talking to others beside them, others sat silent, holding drinks. In the center of the floor was a Harper group of three persons, waiting for me impassively. I advanced upon Mr. Cass Canfield, the publisher, Mr. Eugene Saxton, my first great editor, and Miss Ramona Herdman, the charming publicity chief.

32   "You're late," said Mr. Canfield dryly.

33   "Not fatally," said Mr. Saxton with his perpetually amused smile.

34   The wallside chairs became aware and glanced in my direction, but no moves were made. The party seemed enclosed in ice. A waiter came our way and I acquired a martini.

35   Finally, "Shouldn't you meet people?" asked Miss Herdman.

36   She took me to the wall and walked me along to shake hands as we went. The guests looked briefly at me and returned to their self-absorptions. I had a sense that every known Van Doren was present, and I recognized other glittering names, for none of which, of course, was mine a match. The gathering, meant to be festive, was lost to the lifeless inane. Something had to be done if Harper and Brothers were not to endure a total waste. The case was so poor— a young writer from the far provinces facing his first New York public event— that nothing was at risk, even to my making a fool of myself. If nobody would talk to me, I would invade them in another persona. To play the host, I became a waiter. I took a tray of canapés and began to go down the rows of gilt chairs offering a bite here, another there, which were accepted as intrusions or declined as interruptions.

37   And then: there should have been a fanfare for tympani and cymbals. Glancing along the wall in my duty I had a sudden shock of peripheral vision which made me turn sharply for a direct view.

38   There in the central doorway of the party rooms stood Mary Garden, in her pose of permitting herself to the public. As there was no one to announce her, she was waiting to be received. Behind her were the members of her *cuadrilla*, extending the symbol of her torero jacket: Mr. Piza; M. Jean Dansereau; the female secretary, Miss Croucher (or some such name) in tweeds; a maid holding two fur coats and three large handbags; and, hugging his music briefcase, the remote young man who turned pages. The great world was there for me.

39   I managed to set my tray down on a vacant chair and go to the doorway. Euphoria gave me character. Reaching the presence, I bowed like a Renaissance courtier and declared, I think ringingly, "Madame! You pay us an enchanting honor!"

40   With a piercing gleam out of her veiled cave, Mary Garden raised her right hand in a torchlike gesture and briskly demanded of her manager behind her shoulder, "Piza-who-is-this?"

41   "It is your host, Madame, Mr. Paul Horgan, for whom the reception is held."

42   "So it is. *Allons.*"

43   And so it was that I led her procession into the room, while all around us the murmur arose, *Look, look, it's Mary Garden!* which she acknowledged only by a slight lift of her shoulders. I heard Mr. Canfield inquire flatly, "Was she invited?" and Miss Herdman reply, "No, I made the list," and I, feeling like someone else, said, "*I* invited her" and escorted Madame to the precise middle of the room, where in her habit of center stage she elected to take up her position. The *cuadrilla* ranged itself behind her. The gilt chairs were emptying fast as guests came about us to form a dense circle, though instinctively at a respectful distance. I was aloft in the translation of character which came to my rescue. As Harper and Brothers loomed a little nearer, politeness required that I say:

44   "Madame, may I introduce—"

45   "No-no," she interrupted in an elevated voice, "I will speak only to you," adding a smile worthy of Thaïs. An audience-hush fell over the company. There I was, trapped with glory and fame. What could I, must I, say further?

46   "May I offer you a drink, Madame?"

47   She excused the banality with a crosswise wave of her forefinger.

48   "A cigarette?"

49   "*Jamais—ma voix.*"

50   With the genius of desperation I knew I must play above my form. I said, "This has been an historic afternoon for the centuries, Miss Garden!"

51   "You attended my *seance musicale?*"

52   "Yes, Madame, the event of a lifetime of musical events."

53   "Lifetime?" She made a smile of devastating wistfulness. "A lifetime: how old are you?"

54   "Thirty-two. But—"

55   "How perfect—neither an ending nor a beginning! But my afternoon—"

56   "Yes, the superb lecture. You hardly seemed to speak, Madame. You created pictures in the air."

57   "Pictures in the air. How lovely."

58   "Your text was astonishing. You spoke, not in phrases, not in sentences, but in paragraphs!"

59   "I did?" She commanded the *cuadrilla*. "Piza? Did you hear? Miss Croucher, write that down, make a note, so valuable, we must keep this."

60   She knew I was talking nonsense, but she felt the extremity that compelled it, and together we wrote our scene out of thin air in the ping-pong of drawing-room comedy.

61   "Yes," I said, "and the songs: never such musical line, never such penetration beyond what the poet meant!"

62   "Yes," she said, "poetry alone has never touched me, except to make me restless and nervous."

63   "Yes, good poetry is all nerves. When poetry is bracing, it is all bad."

64   "But then Debussy's music was always the right music for the words. Think of it: until we parted, but not as friends, he always said he was going to write an opera of Romeo and Juliet for me."

65   She spoke fast and imperiously, her voice a little edgy; and she made little steps in place, a miniature dance, to animate the scene and hold attention. Juliet invoked hazy romance. She measured me down and up with her veiled rays. I was only an underweight specimen at best, but . . .

66   "Piza, look at him!" she declaimed. "Did you ever see a figure more *soigné?*" She danced a little near me and reached out her white-gloved hands and molded my flanks, waist, and hips, and cried, "Don't, you must promise me, don't you ever gain a single pound!"

67   From the always-growing throng of onlookers came a wordless murmur that meant, *Really!*

68   "Tell me," she said, "what do you write? I hope novels. I adore novels. When I want the truth I go to fiction."

69   "Yes, a novel, *No Quarter Given.*"

70   "No quarter: I never gave quarter. What is it about?"

71   "It's enormous. It's about—"

72   "What a novel I could write! Perhaps one day I shall. Though perhaps I have already lived my novel. One should never repeat. I shall never forget what someone said to me—was it Paul Bourget or Jacques-Emile Blanche? I forget—one should never repeat except in love. You will write many more books. I must have them all, I am an excellent critic."

73 And so on, and so on, as the minutes flew. Questions like sparks that died away, with hardly a pause for an answer; and *le tout New York* craned and stared for every word and gesture. I did what l could to keep the ball in the air, and I broke the law only twice — once when my sister Rosemary (to whom my novel was dedicated) arrived, and I introduced her to Madame. Again, when I saw an old friend appear despite a state of mourning for her husband's recent death — Mrs. Isabel Ames of New Mexico. I was touched that under the circumstances she came to my party and I broke ranks to go to greet her. In the piercing voice of an elderly lady used to coping with deafness in the family, Mrs. Ames said:

74 "They tell me that you are talking to someone named Mary Garden. Is she anything to the real one?"

75 "It *is* the real one," I murmured, trying to hush my friend.

76 "My God," cried Mrs. Ames, a lifetime of laughter in her endearing old face, "I thought she was dead years ago!"

77 Madame's management of this cheerful affront was masterly. Everyone had heard it. All leaned to see what she would do about it. She simply grew tall, raised her gaze well above everyone present, and defied comment. The effect of vitality was immense. In an instant I was back in her service. Finger on lip, she brooded a moment, and then:

78 "I want to ask you something — you *will* do it, won't you: I want you to do it: you are the one to do it: I can tell, I can *always* tell, you are the one to do it."

79 "But anything, Miss Garden, of course."

80 "Then I want you to write a play for me — a delicious three-act comedy of manners, very high style, *gaie comme les hirondelles*, witty, blazing with epigrams, don't you know, yet with an undertone of sadness — not *sad*, don't you know, but *triste*, like a lovely day in autumn and full of love — *amusing* love, don't you know, nobody throwing themselves about, but so touching. And please: Mr. Horgan: give me just one little song to sing? the second act? perhaps, yes, I think, just before the curtain, so the *meaning* of the song will come to us in the *last* act! Do you think?"

81 With becoming extravagance I agreed to write the play. A book news reporter or two made notes. Mr. Canfield loomed open-mouthed. Mr. Saxton beamed indulgently. The comedy was running down. Mr. Piza leaned across Madame's shoulder and showed her his watch, made murmur about waiting obligations; and, facing me — "Ah!" — the white-gloved hand rose to the brow deploring the second-rate demands made upon the numinous.

82 "I must go. Send me your novel, Hotel Pierre. I will read it. I will write you instantly about it. You have been gallant. We must meet soon again. Do not neglect my play."

83 She made a sweeping turn toward the exit, creating a parabola of knee-length pearls, and I escorted her away with the *cuadrilla* in tow. As I bent to kiss her hand, I caught a glimpse of the smile with which she made an open

secret of the farce in our scene; and then she dutifully held a farewell pose in the elevator gates. The gates clanged shut. Behind me, the crowd had shifted to observe insatiably, someone started to clap, the ovation grew, and to farewell applause, Mary Garden's car descended with the effect of a great sigh of release.

84   I returned to the party. It was exploding in a clamor of talk. Everyone had the same thing to talk about. The ice was not only broken, it was shattered. I was besieged with questions—what else had she said; did she mean it all; had I known her before; where; would I really write her a play; tell about your novel; do you often come East from New Mexico. Suddenly in the New York way, I had many ten-minute friends. Briefly I was a hero. Nobody left before nine o'clock.

85   On the following morning I went to Brentano's where I inscribed a copy of *No Quarter Given* to Mary Garden and asked that it be sent to her at the Pierre Hotel. In hopes of a rapturous reply, I included my hotel address. Nothing came from her, about either the novel or our future collaboration. After some days of growing realism, I telephoned the Pierre Hotel. Mary Garden had checked out days ago.

86   Any forwarding address?

87   "Of course not," replied the Pierre Hotel coldly, in defense of the vanishing point of celebrity.

❧

Discussion Questions

1.   For what reasons did Horgan awake on the morning of January 29, 1935, "to a state of alarm mixed with elation"?
2.   What announced event in the *New York Times* did Horgan think would help him get through the day? What made the event particularly significant?
3.   Describe Mary Garden's physical appearance and cite reasons for her renown.
4.   When Garden talks about Debussy in paragraph 18, how does Horgan create a conversational tone in his sentence structures?
5.   How and why did Garden's manager, Mr. Piza, behave generously to Horgan? How did Horgan attempt to repay this generosity?
6.   Describe the reception given for Horgan prior to Mary Garden's appearance. In what ways did her appearance affect the gathering?
7.   Cite evidence from paragraphs 38–85 that reveals Mary Garden at the reception to be vain; charming; sensitive; insincere.

Writing Topics

1. Recall a time when you felt some form of fear, such as stage fright. Write an essay in which you reveal what caused your fright, what you did under the circumstances, and what, if anything, the experience taught you about yourself and perhaps about others.

2. Write a description of a time when you were saved from a potentially embarrassing situation by the intervention of an acquaintance or friend. Describe the situation in detail, including how the friend or acquaintance rescued you.

"I never talk to Maris about the black people I knew in my childhood and girlhood. . . ."

THE WAY IT WAS

Virginia Bell Dabney

Virginia Bell Dabney, born in 1919 in Chicago, spent much of her adult life writing materials for a voluntary health agency in Virginia, one concerned with respiratory diseases. She was over seventy years old when her memoir, *Once There Was a Farm: A Country Childhood Remembered* (1990), was published to laudatory reviews, with one critic commenting, "A good deal more than an affectionate tribute, it is an elegy; it moves with the natural dignity of longing and regret. . . ." "The Way It Was" appears in this memoir. The mother of three daughters, Dabney now lives and writes in the Allegheny Mountains of Virginia.

1   Maris is at my door at four in the afternoon saying, "I'm dying for a cup of coffee. I've been trying to get a patient into the hospital all afternoon."

2   Maris is a registered nurse in the home-health-care team at a community hospital. She comes in and throws her coat on a chair as I move the kettle over the hottest part of the wood stove.

3   "Who this time?" I say.

4   "Old Mrs. Hughes. Her daughter hit her in the stomach yesterday with a telephone book and is refusing to admit that her mother needs to go to the hospital. Of course she needed to go earlier, but now she says she just wants to die."

5   I know Mrs. Hughes. For a while I worked under Maris's direction as a home-health aide, and the situation is as bad as she says at the Hughes house. Mrs. Hughes's only daughter, Geneva, visits rarely, and sometimes Geneva's husband holds the old woman's arms behind her so she can be struck by the daughter. This is punishment for her complaints about their neglect. When eighty-one-year-old Birdie Hughes told me this while I fixed her lunch one day I was indignant. "You don't have to stand for that," I said. "I'll call Social Services and they'll send someone out to talk to your daughter."

6   But Mrs. Hughes said in her thin old voice out of her old bowed frame, "No, honey, I don't want you to do that. I wouldn't a told you if I'd thought

you'd report it. Geneva's my only child; I can't bear to have the law after her."
She made me promise never to speak of it outside of her house. But here is
Maris and she knows. I fix her coffee and get cookies and we both enjoy our
caffeine.

7   I tell her some of my stories of Mrs. Hughes—for example, how she likes
to write her name over and over on pieces of paper that she then tears up.

8   "Why do you do that?" I wanted to know.

9   "Oh, honey, I've seen them people at the dump goin' through them trash
bags. They're not goin' to find Birdie Hughes's name in there."

10   Bent, white-haired and not strong, Birdie was no longer able to drive the
truck she kept at a local garage. "I go down and visit it sometime," she said.
"You kin take me down there someday." She was confined to the house and
yard but she managed to see much of the little that went on around her. I
arrived one day when the street in front of her small house was being repaired,
and after she had with difficulty unlocked three locks to let me in, she said,
"Come here, honey, and look at this." She led me to the window overlooking a
ditch being dug in the street and pointed. "I never seen the like," she said. "That
man diggin' has titties."

11   I leaned over her bent back and saw a person in a hard hat tossing shovels
full of dirt out of the ditch with a hefty swing. I studied the figure and said to
Birdie, "Mrs. Hughes, that's a woman."

12   "What? A woman? Now I never seen a woman on a road crew. You sure?"
She stared hard with old blue eyes intent. "Well, if that don't beat all. I thought
sure that—"

13   "She has 'em all right," I said, "but on her they're normal."

14   Mrs. Hughes had mourned for her husband for twenty years. Because her
greatest need, more than food or health care, was for someone to talk to, I asked
her about her wedding.

15   "Jake was sixteen years older'n me," she said. "I was just fifteen—or was
it fourteen?—when he told my daddy he wanted to marry me. He had to wait,
you know, because my daddy wanted me to finish school, and I did too.

16   "The Christmas I was sixteen we was settin' around talkin'—Jake came
over to sit with me every Sunday and holiday—and he said, 'When we goin' to
git married?' And a notion just took me. I said, 'We kin go to the church right
now and the preacher'll marry us.'

17   "So I told my sister Orleen to put on a sweater so she could stand up with
me, and we didn't tell anyone else. We just walked up to the church—it was
open for Christmas, you know—and the preacher married us.

18   "Then we come back and Jake went on to his house and I stayed at home.
I was terrible shy, you know, and he didn't press me. It was three months
before we slept together, and even then he stayed on his side of the bed and I
stayed on mine. It was a long time before we got any closer."

19   Maris shakes her head now and laughs, then puts down her empty coffee cup. "I wish you'd come back to work," she says.

20   "I'm working on this book . . ." I say.

21   "You gonna put all those poor patients in it?"

22   "No," I tell her, "but I might put you in it."

23   "Well, say I finally got that pitiful old woman into Adventist Hospital in spite of her bitchy daughter."

24   Maris drops by my house occasionally without announcement. She is the only black woman I really know in this western part of Virginia, where there are few blacks. Only among her poor white patients is Maris called a "nigger." She is a deep cream color, with a dusting of freckles. She can speak black English or she can sound like a professor of nursing, which she was at one point in her career. She is old enough to have watched the Selma march on television, to have been proud of Martin Luther King, even to have cheered for the integration of Little Rock.

25   "What was it like for you when you went to school? Were you made to feel second class?" I ask her.

26   "No," she says in a slightly surprised voice. "I went to school in Verona, and I did what everybody else did. I went to pajama parties and proms just like my classmates. It was just different there. I was never called 'nigger' in my life until I took this job." Her hometown is about fifty miles away, in the Shenandoah Valley.

27   When Maris leaves we hug on the promise that she will come back soon. She is careful to go before sundown; once she stayed until dark and had to call her husband to explain why she was late. That time she made a wrong turn at the end of my road and drove for miles into the mountains. Her husband phoned to ask about her and said angrily, "I wish she'd never started working with you mountain people," lumping me with Mrs. Hughes who, with other poor stricken ones, feels shame when a black nurse comes to the door.

28   I never talk to Maris about the black people I knew in my childhood and girlhood, but I do tell her that my mother never let us use the word *nigger*. "It is disrespectful to the colored people we know," she said. "Besides it's a common, vulgar term. Don't let me hear you use it."

29   As far as I know, that's about as far as my mother's early sensitivity about black and white relationships went. When she moved to Virginia there were many black families near our farm. Some of the restless younger ones left home for the excitement of Philadelphia and Washington and found jobs there, but back home there were mothers and aunts, older brothers and fathers, who did not want to leave. If it had not been for this labor pool, my mother could not have managed a farm, raised a family, sold cookware, done fine sewing, and for a time developed and printed her own photographs.

30   I think the way we lived is sometimes called "the simple life." It was certainly uncomplicated by labor-saving devices. Water was pumped by hand

from a well. Washing was done by scrubbing clothes on a washboard, in big round tubs requiring two people to empty, then filled again with rinsing water. Clothes were wrung out by hand.

31   I used to play at the feet of the woman who ironed all the dampened cotton clothes, table linens and sheets for our family of four females. "You move now," she would say. "I might drop this iron on you head." Three irons were kept heating on the hot wood stove, and she picked up one with a wooden handle that clamped on. She would use it until it became too cool to *ssst* when she touched it with a licked finger. Then she set it back on the stove, unclamped the handle and moved it to another, hotter iron. There was an art to using these instruments without leaving scorch marks on clothes. Each one weighed five pounds or more, and they smoothed garments with weight as well as heat. After a day's ironing a woman was as tired as if she had been digging potatoes or hoeing.

32   "You mama the first lady I ever knew don't want to tear up the house for spring cleaning," Susan said once. Her tone was one of approval. "When I worked for Mrs. Oberman, she got to wash every strip of cloth in the house and git the dirt out between the planks in the floor before Easter."

33   My mother did not believe our house needed to be spotless. She considered preoccupation with cleaning and polishing a waste of time; "Life's too short," she said. Perhaps a little at Christmas, or when a visitor from Chicago was coming, but even for a wedding in the living room I doubt that my mother would have dusted the spiders from behind the tall bookcase in the corner. The necessary work of each day just to keep the farm going required all her strength and more. Though her kitchen was occupied half a day by a black woman, Mother was the one who shivered into the kitchen before dawn in winter to start a fire in the big cookstove. When temperatures dropped into the low figures she often had to break the ice in the kitchen bucket to get water for her coffee and for the breakfast cereal.

34   For these early chores she wore a bathrobe of heavy blanket cloth, totally utilitarian, the only kind of heavy bathrobe shown in the catalogs of the time. It was a dark garment with a shadowy print, a shawl collar outlined in silvery cord, and tied with a matching heavy tasseled cord. As sharply as when I was five I can recall today how that robe smelled comfortingly of her nighttime warmth, woodsmoke and coffee.

35   Mother started another fire in the living room for us to dress by and tended the one there and in her bedroom in between sewing our clothes, keeping the farm accounts and cooking. Any unused room stayed unheated; before the dining room was built we studied in the kitchen on cold winter nights. A small fire was lit in the stove in Allison's room when her studying was done, just big enough to warm a space around it so she could undress. The sheets were icy cold, and if I was sleeping with her I had to get in first because I slept next to the wall. The wall was cold too.

36 "Come on," I would say, "I'm freezing."

37 "Don't think you can put your cold feet on me," she would warn, which of course was what I'd had in mind.

38 Then Mother would come upstairs with two hot irons wrapped in towels for our feet, or a flat soapstone heated and wrapped in newspapers to slide under the sheets. Even so, when we curled up under the covers there was a period of shivering before our bodies finally warmed an envelope of air around us. These were the only times that Allison and I snuggled together; we had to in order to warm that bed. In our sleep we moved apart, and we hardly ever slept together in summer.

39 Winter began in November, never mind what the calendar said. It was then that my mother talked to Solomon about our hogs. It was time to put up the year's supply of pork. When frost lay white over the fields and the ground was frozen hard underfoot, a neighbor was summoned to help Solomon kill the pigs and scrape them so free of hair that their skins shone in the cold.

40 I was not allowed to go outside during hog-killing hours, nor did my mother. The pigpen was so far from the house that it was mostly a quiet affair, at least where we were. I was allowed out only after the pigs were cleaned and hung by their feet, stiff and pink in the frigid morning. By afternoon Mother was cutting them up on the kitchen table, using great knives and a cleaver. This was before *Charlotte's Web*, so I was able to view the pigs' carcasses with interest as food, not as animals I had known. The day had a certain festive air. Parts from the two pigs were given to Solomon, his helper and the woman assisting in the kitchen, and their pleasure was contagious. The liver, feet, some of the side meat, the brains and some of the fat went to them. The whitest fat my mother rendered into lard over the lowest heat on the stove. She used it for biscuits, yeast bread and even for cakes. Lard is an animal fat much out of favor today, but it lent a subtle flavor to breads that cannot be obtained any other way.

41 Any skin that was cut off went to our helpers, who could make it delectable. Out in the yard the men cleaned the intestines with many washings; afterward these were divided among them and they took them home to roast into chitter-lings. It was a fairly stinking process that ended in crisp, delicious bits of pork.

42 Susan salvaged all the tiny bits of fat. "What do you do with those?" I asked.

43 "You ain't had cracklins? I make cracklin bread and bring you some."

44 "That bread's much too fat," my mother interposed. "She can't digest it."

45 "It's mighty good . . ." Susan said, but my mother had spoken, so I had to wait until my twenty-third year for my mother-in-law to give me cracklin bread that she had made. I ate it without a qualm. Bits of fat fried until they were crisp were incorporated in thick corn bread and baked on a greased black pan. They were eaten hot on a cold day, preferably with turnip greens boiled with thick bacon or fatback. It was food that stuck to the ribs, and

probably to my in-laws' older arteries, but it tasted good and remains one of the dishes that southerners still remember when they talk of "down-home cooking."

46   For days after hog-killing time my mother rendered lard in pots on the wood stove. She ground meat for sausage, cooked and canned it. Pork loins that we could not eat immediately she canned in jars set deep in boiling water for hours. The house smelled chokingly of hot fat, and my mother's face was red with heat. Susan washed up the mountain of pots and pans and sometimes sang under her breath.

47   Outside Solomon was stringing up hams and squares of bacon in a smoker. The smoker was made of a large bottomless barrel suspended within a teepee of poles over a very low hickory fire; we must have used green wood to produce so much smoke and so little fire. The meat was dangled from the crossed poles and hung inside the barrel. The process went on for days.

48   A few years later my mother discovered a mixture called Hickory Smoked Salt, and after that simply buried the ham and bacon in tubs of the stuff. It contained nitrates to hasten the drying of the meat, but we did not know these might not be good for us; the cured meat tasted as though it had been smoked for days.

49   The first black woman I remember in our house day after day was Aunt Alice Winslow. She introduced herself this way, pronouncing the title "Ant." Her husband was white-haired Uncle Peter, born into slavery seventy years before. Aunt- and uncledom was conferred on aging slaves by white folks, and the custom persisted for several generations after they were free.

50   Aunt Alice wore many petticoats, baked a cherry roll that could bring angels to earth and told wonderful stories. The ones I loved were about a rabbit belonging to the Philadelphia family she had worked for. This animal had some of the cunning of Br'er Rabbit and was constantly in mischief. I asked for these stories over and over, and each time I was bent, curled, speechless with laughter.

51   As she grew older, Aunt Alice could go no farther than to the nearest white family to work, but when she was dying it was my mother who took her food and sometimes medicine. By then Aunt Alice had almost nothing but a house and a tiny amount of money sent her by her nephew in Philadelphia. A great-nephew stayed with her, but he was hardly more than a child, and it troubled my mother that he was trying to care for a dying woman. She went to see if Aunt Maggie Woods, who lived half a mile from Aunt Alice, could help. Aunt Maggie was the midwife she had brought to Daphne. She had a reputation as a conjure woman, and she listened impassively to my mother, her black eyes darting sharp points of light from her copper-colored face. After a pause she took her pipe out of her mouth and said, "I kin make a charm to ease her some. One dollar all it cost."

52   My mother said, "I don't think charms can help her now. But your kindness will help her know that somebody is looking after her." She offered Aunt

Maggie payment if she would bathe Aunt Alice and do what she could for her several days a week.

53   There was another pause. I stood behind my mother watching the smoke from Aunt Maggie's pipe seem to curl up through her straw hat. We stood there for so long that chickens were beginning to peck around our feet. Finally she said, "I reckon I kin take my stick and go over to Mrs. Winslow's. But," and she smiled a toothless smile, "I make her a charm anyway. Won't cost you nothin'."

54   When we got home my mother wrote to Aunt Alice's nephew in Philadelphia telling him the sick woman needed whatever help he could send—the boy staying with her, Mother said, could not care for such a sick woman. And until Aunt Alice died, her nephew Albert sent my mother one or two dollars every week to ease the old woman's last hours. With that my mother paid the doctor for the strongest pain-killer he would prescribe. She herself gave the first dose to Aunt Alice, and then explained to the boy living with her exactly how and when to give more.

55   "Do you think you can remember this?" Mother asked him. He nodded. "It's important," she said.

56   He nodded again. "I know," he said, so low that she could barely hear him. "I do it so she won't moan so bad."

57   After Aunt Alice, Susan came to our household. She was a gaunt woman with shining dark skin marked by smallpox and an enjoyment of life that bubbled under the surface of her workday self. She allowed Allison and me to see it, but I don't think she ever gave way to it in front of my mother. Once when she carried some eggs for my mother's customers out to the car and did not know where to put them because a neighbor was in the passenger side, she just stood there holding them.

58   "Where must I put these?" she asked, peering around the armful of boxes.

59   The neighbor reached up and told her, "Put all them boxes in my lap; this here dress is old as Adam anyways."

60   "So I put 'em in her lap," Susan told us, "and I guess she was right—she sho' had on Eve's shoes," and she doubled over with laughter that we joined. She told this story frequently, but I don't think she ever repeated it to my mother.

61   Allison and I both loved Susan, but I was the one who followed her when she went to the barn to talk with Solomon as he milked, who trailed her back to the house and who then accompanied her home when she left for the day. I didn't stay; I went along as a friendly puppy would because I liked trotting along with her and racing back at top speed.

62   Susan's room in our house was the kitchen. Though I would try to entice her into the living room to sit, and later into our new dining room, she would only come in, look at what I had called her to see and then return to the kitchen.

63   "Why don't you stay in here with me?" I asked her.

64   "It ain't right. You come out here with me in the kitchen. I has to watch the fire."

65   I knew that neither Susan nor Solomon ever entered the front door, and that they never went beyond the kitchen except when work demanded it. When I asked Mother about this, she gave a characteristic answer: "It just isn't done," she said. That told me nothing except that the subject was closed: no more questions.

66   So it was because of Susan that I also spent most of my house time in the kitchen; Allison was often there too. I don't remember that we did anything except listen to Susan. She would read to us out of *Grit*, a small newspaper that she subscribed to. She slowly read us the jokes, the stories of strange people and of amazing happenings something like those in tabloids now featured on grocery checkout lines.

67   "Do you really think that's so?" we would ask.

68   "Yas, it's so," she would say, a little offended. "They wouldn't put it in the paper if it won't so."

69   We saved the comic pages for Susan from the *Chicago Tribune*, which arrived two or three days late at our house. Allison and I read them first, but looking at them again with Susan made them freshly funny. She read them aloud, panel by panel, telling us what was happening: "Maggie's gettin' madder and madder at Jiggs—look, she got one eye closed and her mouth turned down, she gone hit him in a minute—there she go! She done bounced that rollin' pin offa his head!" She was especially fond of Rachel, the black housekeeper who was once a character in *Gasoline Alley*. That Rachel was exaggerated and unrealistically thick-lipped did not occur to her, or to any of us at the time. She was just a comfortable mammy sort who delighted Susan by talking about her "pillow-slip teef." Susan knew exactly what she meant: Front teeth were indispensable when holding a pillow slip so that a pillow could be stuffed into it with both hands. She also liked Mushmouth, the black man in *Moon Mullins*. To her and to us all the characters in comics were celebrities; it pleased her that some of her own race were represented. Barney Google and his mule, Mutt of *Mutt and Jeff*, Andy Gump and the squat, bowlegged Jiggs were all caricatures. I don't believe she felt demeaned by Rachel or Mushmouth, any more than Allison or I were by Maggie with her rolling pin. Our social consciousness had not been raised.

70   Those were the years when my mother was away from home four or five hours a day selling Wearever pots and pans. On such days Susan was with us until late afternoon, and I hung around listening to her talk with Solomon when he brought the horse to drink at the well trough, when he came in to get the milk buckets and wash his hands, or when, on April days, they both sat outdoors on the ground on empty feed sacks cutting up potatoes to plant.

71   They talked a great deal about two churches, Ebenezer and Rising Sun, perhaps six or seven miles apart, where the social life of the black community

centered. In August, both churches held revival services (as did many white churches) and there were baptisms of all the people who "came to Jesus" during revival. Listening to Solomon and Susan I had the feeling that the August revival season was a joyful and extended festival, for them more exciting than Christmas or any other holiday. They talked of the people who had left to work up north; all these, they said, would be coming back to the churches where they grew up. It would be a time of reunion with children, brothers, sisters, uncles and cousins. Many of them would be riding together in big cars, with American flags fluttering from their radiator caps, and they would stream back home from Philadelphia, New York and the District of Columbia.

72   Both Susan and Solomon had time off from work for those weeks in August, as did workers on other farms around. We were affected by the festivities in another way: Our sale of frying chickens increased noticeably as church members prepared feasts for eating on the grounds after services.

73   As that time drew near, Susan sang hymns that I hadn't heard before, along with old ones she sang every day. She had a plangent, bluesy voice, and the twists and turns she gave each line of music were strange to me and sometimes sad. I tried singing the ones I could remember, but I could never imitate the intricate modulation. I didn't know then about soul music, and I realized later, when it became well known, that Susan was an early and accomplished singer of soul.

74   Susan usually did not swear, and Solomon never did. At moments of mild surprise Susan said, "Dah Jesus!" but in times of real tension she said, "Shit!" This was three generations before the word came in from barnyards and outhouses to join casual conversation. I didn't know its meaning, but it spat nicely between the teeth when something went wrong.

75   One Saturday night we were all at dinner; Rob was there with Daphne, and Daphne's friend Winnie was seated next to her fiancé. I was between my mother and Allison. There was laughter and talk, my mother's dinner was delicious, and I, struggling with a chicken drumstick I was supposed to eat with a knife and fork, sent it slithering into my lap. It was the appropriate moment for me to say, "Oh, shit!" Loudly, the way Susan said it.

76   The talk stopped. I saw my mother's astonished face and was paralyzed by the sight. "Where," she said coldly, "did you get that word?"

77   "Susan says it all the time," I offered, my voice thin and small.

78   "You are not to use it again, ever, understand?"

79   I nodded. The meal was ruined for me; I could not touch the drumstick, which was now back on my plate. Talk resumed among the adults, and Allison looked hard into her plate trying not to laugh. I could not even eat dessert. When the others rose from the table, Rob came over to me and said softly, "Why don't you come along and show me the new calf?" I just shook my head. As soon as my mother was talking in the kitchen I slipped out the door into the summer twilight and went behind an old haystack to cry. I thought of staying

there forever until they grew frightened and sent someone out to look for me, but when my mother called me twice I went slowly back to face her.

80 She met me outside the door, wiped my face with her apron and said, "You understand, don't you honey, that you mustn't use that word anymore?" I barely got out a yes, snuffling. "You come on in and eat your dessert and we'll forget all about it."

81 Before she forgot, though, she evidently talked to Susan about the word the next day, for Susan mended her ways. From then on her burnt finger, a smashed cup, the rip in her dress, brought from her, "Shit! I mean shucks."

82 During the worst of the Depression, Susan worked two days for us and two days for another family. In between, Mary Marshall came to wash dishes and do general cleaning so that her family would not starve.

83 Mary's husband, John, had recently died of appendicitis because he refused to go to the doctor or the hospital until the pain in his side changed to a raging tiger in his belly. When he reached the surgeon fifty miles away it was already too late. His death left Mary in despair over bringing up five boys and a girl. We were her nearest neighbors, and after she had used up her tears crying on Mother's shoulder we did not see her for a while. She and big John Marshall had "scuffled," she said, all their married life, and had a home, a cow and pigs, a few chickens and a garden.

84 John had been a trusted sawmill hand who managed to work most of the time. One winter day a chimney fire had ignited their roof and the house burned down. John and Mary hastily built another, and then it too was engulfed in the forest fire that burned our house, along with their cow shed, chicken house and store of hay. Once more, as soon as lumber was delivered from Hensley's Cross Corners mill, John and his older boys had put up yet another house. He never seemed to rest; late at night and early in the morning he was nailing boards, building a chimney, putting on a roof. Then in the fall, when he was digging potatoes, his painful appendix, poulticed by Mary and dosed with strong laxatives by John, finally ruptured.

85 When Mary appeared at our door on a cool October day, John had been in his grave a month. She looked thinner and very tired, though she smiled — or tried to.

86 "I'm so glad you came over," my mother said. "The pullets are beginning to lay, and I have a lot of eggs too small to sell. Why don't you take them back with you to fill up those big boys?"

87 Mary thanked her with dignity, but then had to wipe her eyes with her apron. "I come to see if you . . . if you could let me have a little milk today."

88 "Of course," my mother said.

89 "I can't pay you right away," Mary said, her voice unsteady. "I thought I might could help you out some in the house."

90   Getting out a milk pan, Mother evidently heard more in Mary's words than I did. She said, "You don't have to pay for milk . . . are you folks going hungry over there?"

91   Mary hesitated. "We still has a little cornmeal," she said. "And some turnip greens."

92   "Is that all?"

93   "Yes ma'am."

94   "Was John able to leave you anything, Mary?"

95   "Just six children and four walls. You know he didn't never mean to leave us like this, Mrs. Bell."

96   When Mary left she carried eggs, milk, cornmeal and flour. My mother added a jar of bacon fat for flavoring the turnip greens. The next morning Mary was at our door by eight o'clock wearing a fresh white apron, and she went right to work cleaning up the kitchen. It was not a small job. There were always dishes from the night before and from breakfast. Before she could get to the dishes, she had to take soaking pots out of the sink and find a place for them on the end of the stove or even on the floor. My mother was usually there skimming cream from milk and putting it in the churn. If the milk was "turning" it was dumped into buckets for the chickens and pig. Then the milk pans had to be carefully washed and scalded so that no trace of sour milk remained.

97   Mary was more equal to that kitchen than anyone else, though she must have quailed at the door whenever my mother said cheerfully, "There are quite a few dishes this morning." But her face never lost its look of bright expectancy, even when she looked at the sticky aftermath of Mother's jam making, which overflowed all available surfaces. When she finished and all the pots and pans were put away, the kitchen was neat and clean beyond anything my mother and I were able to accomplish. Mother always became bored halfway through a big dishwashing job and left the hard things to soak. I liked to do more, but she would tell me, "That's enough now; you don't have to stay in here all morning. Let the rest go for now." In her eyes the time spent in cleaning for what she considered appearance's sake was a terrible waste. But when Mary did it, singing, Mother would say, "You make this kitchen a pleasure to work in."

98   Mary Marshall became my mother's only close friend nearby; I was too young for her to confide in and Daphne and Allison could not be talked to except through the laborious route of letters. It may have been her quiet, listening look, her way of folding her hands in her lap and being still. Whatever it was, only Mary could come into the house, walk through the dining room, saying to me, "I goin' tip upstairs to see you mother," and call on the stairs, "I'm comin' up," prompting my mother's answer, "Fine. Come right up." She would walk into my mother's room softly, saying, "How you this mawnin'?" and sit down to talk, knowing she was wanted. In any stage of undress (though she never emerged from the washroom in less than her slip) Mother welcomed her, and they would talk for an hour or so. Only to Mary did she confide her fears

about Daphne having more children than she should, or talk of Rob's short-comings as a son-in-law. In turn Mary treated her to slightly jealous gossip about Susan (she could never quite accept Susan's still working for us), and told her something of her own troubles with her boys since John's death. Her daughter, always called Sister, was a good girl, she said, but hadn't ought to have just boys around.

99   My mother talked of Allison and how long she'd been away from home because she couldn't manage train fare home. "I wanted to send her money, but she's got this idea that . . . Well, she just flatly said she wouldn't take anything from me. You know she used to say when she left that she was never coming back, and I think it's her pride."

100   Mary answered the pain she recognized under the words, saying soothingly, "She git over that, you just wait."

101   By coming silently to the bottom of the steps I heard my mother talking to Mary about my father. "He retires in two years," she said. "I don't know what he will do here: he's a city man."

102   "I reckon he will res'," Mary said. "He been workin' a long time."

103   "I'm afraid . . ." my mother said. Mary made a sound of sympathy. "I'm afraid he may have a hard time learning to live like we do," Mother finished.

104   Mary sighed. "We just has to do the bes' we can," she said. "And hope."

105   "And hope," my mother echoed. But she never mentioned these fears to me.

106   For her work and friendship, Mary received the standard pay for black women, but it was barely enough pay to keep her family in cornmeal, molasses and fatback. If her few chickens refused to lay, she could get eggs from us free. When she had to sell her cow, my mother had milk to spare. She did have a garden, but how she managed to clothe six children I do not know. When her daughter was ready for high school, a way had to be found for her to live in the county seat, which was near the only available high school for blacks. Black schoolchildren were not provided school buses then, and Sister would have to walk. She told Mary, and Mary told my mother, that her daughter didn't care what she had to do to go to high school, but she was determined to get her diploma. Sister had her eyes set on a future different from her mother's.

107   Mother found a family in that town who would give Sister a basement room and meals in exchange for her help with cooking and housekeeping, and Sister became a live-in servant whose time at school was part of her pay. My mother told me, "You don't know how lucky you are. You just have to get up, eat your breakfast, dress and ride the bus each morning. Sister will have to cook breakfast for Mr. and Mrs. Crizer, wash the dishes, clean up the kitchen, sweep the walk, fix her lunch and then walk to school."

108   I did not dwell on the inequality of our circumstances. At the time I was struggling with the perils of adolescence and a growing awareness that some of my classmates also suffered from unequal opportunity. There were girls who rose every morning to help their mothers with other children before they came

to school, and who went home to do half a day's work on the farm before finally opening their books and wearily trying to study. Writing assignments terrified them, and one or two would catch up with me between classes and ask, "What can I write? I don't even know how to begin." Sometimes I could provide skeleton outlines for filling in—general titles like "My Family and Our Farm" and "What I Have to Do on the Farm"—and once primed they could produce a page of material, even when they made lists instead of paragraphs. But what I liked best were the short essays I wrote for them, trying to make them sound like something they might write. The fun was in changing my mind's gears to think as they thought and choosing words they would have used. I don't know if I could do it now, but it seemed easy then. Our English teacher was an exceptionally good one for such a small school and I grew smug thinking that he never suspected my under-the-desk writing service.

109   I think now of one girl in particular. Quiet Janie was the oldest girl in a family of ten children. By the time she reached high school she was already cooking meals and sewing for the younger ones. When she stepped from the school bus at the road to her house, she faced ironing, cooking, attending to younger children if her mother was ill (as she often was) and cleaning up the supper dishes before studying—all this without benefit of electricity or indoor plumbing. The other children helped, but Janie was older and steadier. When she finished school with little distinction in any subject except math and home economics, I believed she would never escape the family.

110   But Janie, taking herself in hand, had other ideas. In the summer after graduation she got a job at a local cannery, but one week of hard, mind-dulling work there was enough. She left, and with her week's wages in hand journeyed to Richmond and signed herself over to the Medical College of Virginia as a nurse probationer. In those days first-year nursing students were required to perform the most menial tasks about the hospital for their board and tuition, but Janie, released from a life of constant work, had more time to herself than ever before—time, as it turned out, to be young for the first time since childhood. She finished nursing school just before World War II, was recruited into the army and ended the war years as a captain in the United States Air Force, caring for badly wounded men flown in from the battlefields.

111   Mary Marshall's daughter, Sister, grown sturdy on corn bread and greens, more beautiful than her mother had ever been, finished high school with ease and went to the same nursing school as Janie, in a "separate but equal" class with other black students. After she was graduated and capped, she was called "Nurse Marshall" rather than "Miss Marshall" by her white supervisors in medicine. Though she may have outperformed or equaled white students in her profession, custom decreed that no black woman could be addressed by the same title as her white colleagues. Sister lived long enough to be called Miss or Mrs. by white physicians, supervisors and patients, but her mother, Mary, died before this honor could astonish her old age.

112   I do not talk of all this when Maris comes, throwing her blue, soft-lined coat across the couch, putting her feet to warm in the oven of my wood cookstove. The stove is partly for old times' sake, though it is airtight and Amish-made and its grave simplicity could have been designed by Shakers. Its eight-inch-wide stovepipe soars straight through the cathedral roof fifteen feet above, a lovely black column against the stairs and the shelves behind it.

113   It is as much Susan, Aunt Alice, Mary or Sister as I who greet Maris, and who listen to her quick words and high-pitched laughter. She talks about her youngest son; she is disturbed because at eleven years of age he keeps to himself, is interested in nothing but taking radios and televisions apart and putting them back together, or in reading everything he can find on electronics. "I decided he needed a birthday party," Maris says, "and I invited a lot of kids, even though he said he didn't want a party. I said, 'You gonna have this party and you're gonna have a good time.'

114   "Well, we had it, and about an hour after the cake and presents he came into the kitchen and said, 'I want you to know I hate this party and I'm not having a good time and I wish they'd all go home.' Can you beat that?"

115   "And?" I say.

116   "Well, all the kids were having a great time except him, so I took a deep breath and told him, 'If you'll go back in there and be polite for another forty-five minutes I'll never give you another party, okay?' And he said okay. After they'd gone, he dusted off his hands and said, 'Well, that's that. What a waste of time.' "

117   "Are you sure he's only eleven?"

118   "My husband says he hasn't been a child since he learned to read directions for putting toys together. He didn't want to play with them; he just wanted to know how they worked."

119   We're having coffee and cinnamon buns. She says, "I'm gonna miss this. I came to tell you I'm quitting this job. Moving back to Georgia." I am not surprised and say I thought the stress of her work would get her down.

120   "Not job stress. Husband stress. My husband says he's tired of cold winters. He says that Virginia ain't south like the rest of the South, and besides I come home too tired and too bitchy when I travel all day."

121   Our good-byes at the car are restrained; in our minds we have already parted. She tells me to visit them in Brunswick and I say she must come back to this house whenever she is in Virginia, but neither of us expects to see the other again.

122   I watch her car disappear over the hill and know that sometimes I will remember her laughter and the laughter of Susan, though in different rooms.

❧

Discussion Questions

1. What is the connection between Birdie Hughes, Dabney, and Maris? How would you describe Birdie's personality to someone who knew nothing about her?

2. How would you describe Dabney and Maris's relationship in the selection—that of strangers, acquaintances, or friends? Explain.

*3. By relevant paragraph numbers, cite evidence that reveals Dabney's mother to be resourceful; messy; firm; generous.

*4. Would you classify each of the following persons as a stranger, an acquaintance, or a friend in their relationship to Dabney's mother and to Dabney herself: Solomon; Aunt Alice Winslow; Aunt Maggie Woods; Susan; Mary Marshall? Be sure to explain your choices.

5. Would you consider Dabney's mother to be prejudiced, unprejudiced, or both? Explain.

6. What do you think Dabney means by each of the following sentences: "It is as much Susan, Aunt Alice, Mary or Sister as I who greet Maris . . ." (paragraph 113); "I . . . know that sometimes I will remember her [Maris's] laughter and the laughter of Susan, though in different rooms" (paragraph 122).

7. The movement in this memoir is from present to past to present again. Cite by paragraph number where the transitions in chronology occur and describe what Dabney does to make these shifts in time seem smooth.

Writing Topics

1. If you have an acquaintance or a friend whose race or ethnicity is different from your own, write an essay describing your relationship to this person. You might consider including such matters as these: how you met, what interests you share, what differences exist between you, and what obstacles, if any, you have had to deal with in order to preserve your relationship.

2. Most people who have or have had prejudices against another group have encountered an individual from the group who did not fit their preconceived notions. If you have had an experience such as this, describe in a short essay what your prejudices were, how the individual you met differed from your expectations, and whether as a consequence of your encounter you have changed in any significant way.

℮❝What we learned from the Molinas was how to have fun, and what we taught them was how to fight."

BEING MEAN

Gary Soto

Gary Soto (b. 1952), a native of Fresno, California, attended California State University, Fresno (B.A., 1974) and the University of California, Irvine (M.F.A., 1976). A frequently anthologized Mexican-American writer, Soto is the author of seven collections of poetry, including *Canto Familiar* (1995) and *New and Selected Poems* (1995), and six collections of prose, among them *A Summer Life* (1991), *Pacific Crossing* (1992), and *Crazy Weekend* (1994). His prose collection *Living Up the Street* (1992), in which "Being Mean" appears, won an American Book Award from the Before Columbus Foundation. Soto, who has also produced three films for Mexican-American children, lives with his family in Berkeley, California.

1   We were terrible kids, I think. My brother, sister, and I felt a general meanness begin to surface from our tiny souls while living on Braly Street, which was in the middle of industrial Fresno. Across the street was Coleman Pickles, while on the right of us was a junkyard that dealt in metals—aluminum, iron, sheet metal, and copper stripped from refrigerators. Down the street was Sun-Maid Raisin, where a concrete tower rose above the scraggly sycamores that lined Braly Street. Many of our family worked at Sun-Maid: Grandfather and Grandmother, Father, three uncles, an aunt, and even a dog, whose job was to accompany my grandfather, a security guard, on patrol. Then there was Challenge Milk, a printing shop, and the 7-Up Company, where we stole sodas. Down the alley was a broom factory and Western Book Distributor, a place where our future stepfather worked at packing books into cardboard boxes, something he would do for fifteen years before the company left town for Oregon.

2   This was 1957. My brother Rick was six, I was five, and Debra was four. Although we looked healthy, clean in the morning, and polite as only Mexicans can be polite, we had a streak of orneriness that we imagined to be normal play. That summer—and the summer previous—we played with the Molinas, who

lived down the alley from us right across from the broom factory and its brutal *whack* of straw being tied into brooms. There were eight children on the block that year, ranging from twelve down to one, so there was much to do: wrestle, eat raw bacon, jump from the couch, sword fight with rolled-up newspapers, steal from neighbors, kick chickens, throw rocks at passing cars. While we played in the house, Mother Molina just watched us run around, a baby in her arms crying like a small piece of machinery turning at great speed. Now and then she would warn us with a smile, "Now you kids, you're going to hurt yourselves." We ignored her and went on pushing one another from an open window, yelling wildly when we hit the ground because we imagined that there was a school of sharks ready to snack on our skinny legs.

3   What we learned from the Molinas was how to have fun, and what we taught them was how to fight. It seemed that the Sotos were inherently violent. I remember, for instance, watching my aunts going at one another in my grandmother's backyard while the men looked on with beers in their hands and mumbled to one another, perhaps noting the beauty of a jab or a roundhouse punch. Another time the police arrived late at night in search of our Uncle Leonard, who had gotten into a fight at a neighborhood bar. Shortly thereafter, I recall driving with my mother to see him at what she said was a "soldiers' camp." She had a sack of goods with her, and after speaking softly to a uniformed man, we were permitted to enter. It was lunchtime and he sat on a felled log, laughing with other men. When he saw us coming, he laughed even harder.

4   In turn, I was edged with a meanness, and more often than not the object of my attacks was Rick. If upset, I chased him with rocks, pans, a hammer, whatever lay around in the yard. Once, when he kicked over a row of beans I had planted in the yard, I chased him down the alley with a bottle until, in range, I hurled it at him. The bottle hit him in the thigh and, to my surprise, showered open with blood. Screaming, his mouth open wide enough to saucer a hat inside, he hobbled home while I stood there, only slightly worried at his wound and the spanking that would follow, shouting that he had better never do that again. And he didn't.

5   I was also hurt by others who were equally as mean, and I am thinking particularly of an Okie kid who yelled that we were dirty Mexicans. Perhaps so, but why bring it up? I looked at my feet and was embarrassed, then mad. With a bottle I approached him slowly in spite of my brother's warnings that the kid was bigger and older. When I threw the bottle and missed, he swung his stick and my nose exploded blood for several feet. Frightened, though not crying, I ran home with Rick and Debra chasing me, and dabbed at my face and T-shirt, poked Mercurochrome at the tear that bubbled, and then lay on the couch, swallowing blood as I slowly grew faint and sleepy. Rick and Debra looked at me for a while, then got up to go outside to play.

6   Rick and I and the Molinas all enjoyed looking for trouble and often went to extremes to try to get into fights. One day we found ourselves staring at some

new kids on the street—three of them about our age—and when they looked over their picket fence to see who we were, I thought one of them had sneered at us, so I called him a name. They called back at us, and that provocation was enough to send Rick to beat on one of them. Rick entered their yard and was punched in the ear, then in the back when he tried to hunch over to protect himself. Furious as a bee, I ran to fight the kid who had humbled Rick, but was punched in the stomach, which knocked the breath out of me so I couldn't tell anyone how much it had hurt. The Molinas grew scared and ran home, while Rick and I, slightly roughed up but sure that we had the guts to give them a good working over, walked slowly home trying to figure out how to do it. A small flame lit my brain, and I suggested that we stuff a couple of cats into potato sacks and beat the kids with them. An even smaller light flared in my brother's brain. "Yeah, that'll get them," he said, happy that we were going to get even. We called to our cat, Boots, and found another unfortunate cat that was strolling nonchalantly down our alley in search of prime garbage. I called to it and it came, purring. I carried it back to our yard, where Rick had already stuffed Boots into a sack, which was bumping about on the ground. Seeing this, the cat stiffened in my arms and I had trouble working the cat into the sack, for it had spread its feet and opened its claws. But once inside, the cat grew calm, resigning itself to fate, and meowed only once or twice. For good measure I threw a bottle into my sack, and the two of us—or, to be fair, the four of us—went down the alley in search of the new kids.

7   We looked for them, even calling them names at their back porch, but they failed to show themselves. Rick and I believed that they were scared, so in a way we were victors. Being mean, we kicked over their garbage cans and ran home, where we fought one another with the sacks, the cats all along whining and screaming to get out.

8   Perhaps the most enjoyable summer day was when Rick, Debra, and I decided to burn down our house. Earlier in the summer we had watched a television program on fire prevention at our grandmother's house, only three houses down from us on Sarah Street. The three of us sat transfixed in front of the gray light of the family's first TV. We sat on the couch with a bowl of grapes, and when the program ended the bowl was still in Rick's lap, untouched. TV was that powerful.

9   Just after that program Rick and I set fire to our first shoe box, in which we imagined were many people scurrying to get out. We hovered over the fire, and our eyes grew wild. Later, we got very good at burning shoe boxes. We crayoned windows, cut doors on the sides, and dropped ants into the boxes, imagining they were people wanting very badly to live. Once the fire got going, I wailed like a siren and Rick flicked water from a coffee can at the building leaping with flames. More often than not, it burned to ash and the ants shriveled to nothing—though a few would limp away, wiser by vision of death.

10   But we grew bored with the shoe boxes. We wanted something more exciting and daring, so Rick suggested that we brighten our lives with a house fire. "Yeah," Debra and I cried, leaping into the air, and proceeded to toss crumpled newspapers behind the doors, under the table, and in the middle of the living room. Rick struck a match, and we stood back laughing as the flames jumped wildly about and the newspaper collapsed into ash that floated to the ceiling. Once the fire got started we dragged in the garden hose and sprayed the house, the three of us laughing for the love of good times. We were in a frenzy to build fires and put them out with the hose. I looked at Rick and his eyes were wide with pleasure, his crazed laughter like the mad scientists of the movies we would see in the coming years. Debra was jumping up and down on the couch, a toy baby in her arms, and she was smiling her tiny teeth at the fire. I ran outside flapping my arms because I wanted to also burn the chinaberry that stood near our bedroom window. Just as I was ready to set a match to a balled newspaper I intended to hurl into the branches, our grandmother came walking slowly down the alley to check on us. (It was her responsibility to watch us during the day, because our father was working at Sun-Maid Raisin and our mother was peeling potatoes at Reddi-Spud.) Grandma stopped at the gate and stared at me as if she knew what we were up to, and I stared back so I could make a quick break if she should lunge at me. Finally she asked, "How are you, honey?" I stared at my dirty legs, then up to her. "Okay. I'm just playing." With the balled newspaper in my hand, I pointed to the house and told her that Rick and Debra were inside coloring. Hearing this, she said to behave myself, gave me a piece of gum, and returned to her house.

11   When I went back inside, Rick and Debra were playing war with cherry tomatoes. Debra was behind the table on which the telephone rested, while Rick crouched behind a chair making the sounds of bombs falling.

12   "Rick," I called, because I wanted to tell him that Grandma had come to see how we were doing, but he threw a tomato and it splashed my T-shirt like a bullet wound. I feigned being shot and fell to the floor. He rolled from behind the chair to hide behind a door. "Are you dead?" he asked. I lifted my head and responded: "Only a little bit."

13   Laughing, we hurled tomatoes at one another, and some of them hit their mark—an ear, a shoulder, a grinning face—while others skidded across the floor or became pasted to the wall. "You Jap," Debra screamed as she cocked her hand to throw, to which I screamed, "You damn German." We fought, laughing, until the tomatoes were gone. Breathing hard, we looked at the mess we had created, and then at each other, slightly concerned at what it might mean. Rick and I tried to clean up with a broom while Debra lay exhausted on the couch, thumb in her mouth and making a smacking sound. I can't recall falling asleep but that's what happened, because I awoke to Rick crying in the kitchen. Our mother had come home to an ash-darkened living room, a puddled kitchen, and tomato-stained walls. She yelled and spanked Rick, after which

she dragged him to the stove where she heated a fork over a burner and threatened to burn his wrists. "Now are you going to play with fire?" she screamed. I peeked into the kitchen and her mouth was puckered into a dried fruit as Rick cried that she was hurting him, that he was sorry, that he would never do it again. Tears leaped from his face as he tried to wiggle free. She threw the fork into the sink, then let him go. She turned to me and yelled: "And you too, Chango!" She started after me, but I ran out the front door into the alley, where I hid behind a stack of boards. I stayed there until my breathing calmed and my fear disappeared like an ash picked up by the wind. I got up and, knowing that I couldn't return home immediately, I went to the Molinas. Just as I turned into their yard I caught sight of two of them climbing, hand over hand, on the telephone wires that stretched from above the back porch to the pole itself. A few of the younger Molinas looked on from an open window, readying for their turn, as the radio blared behind them. I threw a rock at the two hanging from the wires, and they laughed that I missed. The other kids laughed. Their mother, with a baby in her arms, came out to the back porch, laughed, and told us to behave ourselves.

❧

Discussion Questions

1. What special interests did Soto, his brother Rick, and his sister Debra share with the Molina children? Do you think these interests would be sufficient to sustain a lasting friendship? Explain.
2. What made a particular summer day "most enjoyable" for Soto and his siblings? How did each child respond to the events taking place? What or who put an end to the festivities?
3. Compare Mrs. Soto to Mrs. Molina. Who, in your judgment, is the better mother? Why?
4. Support with reasons one of the following choices:
   a. Given the ages of the Soto children—six, five, and four—I find their described behavior to be far-fetched.
   b. Given the ages of the Soto children—six, five, and four—I do not find their described behavior to be far-fetched.

Writing Topics

1. Write an essay using one of the following thesis statements, which are patterned after Gary Soto's opening sentence for his selection. Support your thesis with convincing reasons:
   a. I was a terrible kid, I think.
   b. I was a pretty good kid, I think.

2. Recall from your childhood a friendship that no longer exists. Write an essay in which you describe the relationship, providing details about the other person, how you became acquainted, and what you shared together. Conclude by relating how the friendship came to an end.

❧. . . by the end of his career,

students were complaining to administrators

about his pungent rhetoric."

THE GRAMMARIAN WHO LOST
A WAR OF WORDS

James S. Hirsch

James S. Hirsch, born in St. Louis in 1962, received his undergraduate degree in journalism (1984) from the University of Missouri at Columbia and his master's degree (1986) from the LBJ School of Public Policy at The University of Texas at Austin. Following receipt of his graduate degree, Hirsch worked for three years as a reporter for *The New York Times* before joining the staff of *The Wall Street Journal* in 1989. "The Grammarian Who Lost a War of Words" appeared in the December 29, 1994, issue of the *Journal*. Hirsch reports that Russell Hogan, the subject of his article and his English teacher during his junior and senior years of high school, profoundly influenced his career as a writer.

1   As a high school grammar teacher, Russell Hogan preached that the verb "to be" lacked punch, so he banned it from our writing assignments. When a parent complained, Mr. Hogan said of his students: "Give them an inch, and they take a mile."

2   Last year Mr. Hogan gave in himself. He took early retirement from Clayton High School in St. Louis, ending a 35-year teaching career, disillusioned and frustrated. Over time, assaults on the language had become increasingly common, but he quit in large part because of a different kind of assault on him and his controversial teaching style.

3   Mr. Hogan, now 61, animated his classes with playful mockery and occasional "classy insults" directed at students. "Your mind is so low," he would say, "that even the hand of God could not reach down into the mire and lift you to the depths of degradation."

4   For scores of students, including me, his sometimes acidic wit enlivened class and conveyed his passion for the subject. But it intimidated others. Yet even his detractors conceded that Mr. Hogan was a successful one-man army

fighting the good fight against ambiguous antecedents, superfluous commas and creeping colloquialisms.

5 "He was on a mission," says an admiring former student, Robert Kerr, now a lawyer. "He broke down the language and made you feel as if you were studying it for the first time."

6 Toward the end of his career, however, Mr. Hogan found himself in a bind. At a time when high school students were less interested in linguistics, they were much pricklier about language itself—and highly critical of Mr. Hogan's acerbic flourishes.

7 "The world was changing on me, and I had to make adjustments," he says, from his brick house in a quiet tree-lined neighborhood of this St. Louis suburb. "I didn't really feel free to be myself."

8 His living room is arranged like a well-written sentence, functional, free of clutter and with just enough detail, such as an antique teapot from China, to make it interesting. The most noticeable change in him since he was my teacher 14 years ago is a chronic smoker's cough, but his sly humor hasn't changed.

9 Mr. Hogan taught literature as well as language composition, or grammar, at well-regarded high schools in Illinois and then in Clayton, Mo. In many ways, he spent his career swimming against cultural tides. Grammar has been devalued at teachers' colleges and de-emphasized in the schools. Fewer students seem to care about it, and television and movies have quickened the pace at which nonstandard English becomes standard.

10 "I once heard a girl being described as 'really stud,' and I thought, 'Well, we've totally lost that word,' " Mr. Hogan says.

11 Still, he did what he could, valiantly. He proscribed students from using "none" with a plural verb; the pronoun means "not one," he argues, and should always be singular. And heaven help the student who passes off "presently" for "currently." "Presently" means "soon."

12 As head of Clayton's English department, Mr. Hogan was also tough on other instructors. He once told a teacher to learn more grammar. She objected, so Mr. Hogan wrote out a sentence—"I like him singing to me"—and asked the teacher if it was correct. She said, "Yes." Wrong again. It should be "I like *his* singing to me," because "singing" is a gerund, a verbal noun, and pronouns attached to gerunds are in the possessive case, just as they would be with other nouns: his hat. The teacher agreed to learn more grammar.

13 Despite his insisting on such fine points, Mr. Hogan does not believe grammar rules are immutable. Rather, they envolve as "professional users" of language accept different guidelines. He taught for years that a pronoun following a form of the verb "to be" should be in the nominative case, not the objective. "It is I," not "It is me." But several years ago, Mr. Hogan threw in the towel. "Even I was saying 'It's me.' "

14 At one time, Mr. Hogan's willingness to talk to students outside class about movies, music and pop culture made him popular, but by the end of his career,

students were complaining to administrators about his pungent rhetoric. Mr. Hogan says he believes his satirical stilettos — "In the bloodstream of life, you are a clot" — were effective because "these were the brighter kids I was teaching, and they saw the humor." But, he acknowledges, "My style was risky."

15   And then some. Two school years ago, when a student was caught filching a $3 textbook, a female classmate said in class, "Big deal, it's only $3."

16   Mr. Hogan turned to her and responded, "Would you go to bed with me for $50,000?" Before he could deliver the next line — "It's not how much, it's whether or not it's moral" — the girl ran out of class, crying. He later apologized to her but was reprimanded by the principal.

17   "I was insulted," he says. "I was told she couldn't process [my comment], and I thought, 'I am really out of touch.'" He retired at the end of the school year.

18   Mr. Hogan may have crossed the line at times, but his retirement strikes me as a loss. I recall one day when I made an error in class, he muttered, "I'll kill him." I knew it was Mr. Hogan's unorthodox way of saying he loved the language, and only because he cared about his students with equal fervor did he make such remarks. I felt oddly comforted and never made the mistake again.

19   Mr. Hogan still teaches summer school at Clayton, and a good thing, too, as raids against the language continue unabated. Call Clayton High School after hours these days, and a recorded voice says: "The office is presently closed."

❧

Discussion Questions

1. What support does Hirsch offer for each of the following references to Hogan's teaching style: "his sometimes acidic wit" (paragraph 4); "a successful one-man army fighting the good fight against ambiguous antecedents, superfluous commas and creeping colloquialisms" (paragraph 4); "spent his career swimming against cultural tides" (paragraph 9)?

2. A former student says in paragraph 5 that Hogan "was on a mission." What was that mission, and how successful do you think Hogan was in accomplishing it? Explain.

3. What changes in students and what specific incident led to Hogan's decision to take early retirement? How does Hirsch feel about his former teacher's retirement? Why?

4. Cite indications from the selection that Hogan's interests extended beyond the classroom. Would you have wanted him as a teacher? Why or why not?

5. Do you think Hirsch regards Hogan as an acquaintance, a friend, or something in-between? Explain.

Writing Topics

1. Assume that you are the principal of Clayton High School, where Russell Hogan teaches. Write a letter to Hogan, either accepting or declining his request for early retirement. Provide clear reasons for your decision.
2. Assume that you are a student of Hogan. Write a letter to him in which you support with persuasive reasoning either of the following opening sentences:
    a. It is time you resigned.
    b. Now is not the time to resign.

"Phad never heard about marked cards until he told me about them and showed me his."

DOC MARLOWE

James Thurber

After a short career as a journalist, James Thurber (1894-1961) joined the staff of The New Yorker in 1927. There he helped set the tone for the new magazine and established a reputation as brilliant essayist, short-story writer, and artist, one who examined with humorously sardonic insight the follies of men and women. Among Thurber's books are Is Sex Necessary? (1929, written with E. B. White), The Seal in the Bedroom and Other Predicaments (1932), The Middle-Aged Man on the Flying Trapeze (1935), Let Your Mind Alone (1937), The Male Animal (1940, a play written with Eliot Nugent), Fables for Our Time (1940), The Thurber Carnival (1945), The Thirteen Clocks (1950), Alarms and Diversions (1957), and Lanterns and Lances (1961), the last written after Thurber had lost his long struggle against blindness.

1   I was too young to be other than awed and puzzled by Doc Marlowe when I knew him. I was only sixteen when he died. He was sixty-seven. There was that vast difference in our ages and there was a vaster difference in our backgrounds. Doc Marlowe was a medicine-show man. He had been a lot of other things, too: a circus man, the proprietor of a concession at Coney Island, a saloon-keeper; but in his fifties he had traveled around with a tent-show troupe made up of a Mexican named Chickalilli, who threw knives, and a man called Professor Jones, who played the banjo. Doc Marlowe would come out after the entertainment and harangue the crowd and sell bottles of medicine for all kinds of ailments. I found out all this about him gradually, toward the last, and after he died. When I first knew him, he represented the Wild West to me, and there was nobody I admired so much.

2   I met Doc Marlowe at old Mrs. Willoughby's rooming house. She had been a nurse in our family, and I used to go and visit her over week-ends sometimes, for I was very fond of her. I was about eleven years old then. Doc Marlowe wore scarred leather leggings, a bright-colored bead vest that he said he got from the Indians, and a ten-gallon hat with kitchen matches stuck in

the band, all the way around. He was about six feet four inches tall, with big shoulders, and a long, drooping mustache. He let his hair grow long, like General Custer's. He had a wonderful collection of Indian relics and six-shooters, and he used to tell me stories of his adventures in the Far West. His favorite expressions were "Hay, boy!" and "Hay, boy-gie!," which he used the way some people now use "Hot dog!" or "Doggone!" He told me once that he had killed an Indian chief named Yellow Hand in a tomahawk duel on horse-back. I thought he was the greatest man I had ever seen. It wasn't until he died and his son came on from New Jersey for the funeral that I found out he had never been in the Far West in his life. He had been born in Brooklyn.

3   Doc Marlowe had given up the road when I knew him, but he still dealt in what he called "medicines." His stock in trade was a liniment that he had called Snake Oil when he traveled around. He changed the name to Blackhawk Liniment when he settled in Columbus. Doc didn't always sell enough of it to pay for his bed and board, and old Mrs. Willoughby would sometimes have to "trust" him for weeks at a time. She didn't mind, because his liniment had taken a bad kink out of her right limb that had bothered her for thirty years. I used to see people whom Doc had massaged with Blackhawk Liniment move arms and legs that they hadn't been able to move before he "treated" them. His patients were day laborers, wives of streetcar conductors, and people like that. Sometimes they would shout and weep after Doc had massaged them, and several got up and walked around who hadn't been able to walk before. One man hadn't turned his head to either side for seven years before Doc soused him with Blackhawk. In half in hour he could move his head as easily as I could move mine. "Glory be to God!" he shouted. "It's the secret qualities in the ointment, my friend," Doc Marlowe told him, suavely. He always called the liniment ointment.

4   News of his miracles got around by word of mouth among the poorer classes of town — he was not able to reach the better people (the "tony folks," he called them) — but there was never a big enough sale to give Doc a steady income. For one thing, people thought there was more magic in Doc's touch than in his liniment, and, for another, the ingredients of Blackhawk cost so much that his profits were not very great. I know, because I used to go to the wholesale chemical company once in a while for him and buy his supplies. Everything that went into the liniment was standard and expensive (and well-known, not secret). A man at the company told me he didn't see how Doc could make much money on it at thirty-five cents a bottle. But even when he was very low in funds Doc never cut out any of the ingredients or substituted cheaper ones. Mrs. Willoughby had suggested it to him once, she told me, when she was helping him "put up a batch," and he had got mad. "He puts a heap of store by that liniment being right up to the mark," she said.

5   Doc added to his small earnings, I discovered, by money he made gambling. He used to win quite a few dollars on Saturday nights at Freck's saloon, playing poker with the marketmen and the railroaders who dropped in there.

It wasn't for several years that I found out Doc cheated. I had never heard about marked cards until he told me about them and showed me his. It was one rainy afternoon, after he had played seven-up with Mrs. Willoughby and old Mr. Peiffer, another roomer of hers. They had played for small stakes (Doc wouldn't play cards unless there was some money up, and Mrs. Willoughby wouldn't play if very much was up). Only twenty or thirty cents had changed hands in the end. Doc had won it all. I remember my astonishment and indignation when it dawned on me that Doc had used the marked cards in playing the old lady and the old man. "You didn't cheat *them*, did you?" I asked him. "Jimmy, my boy," he told me, "the man that calls the turn wins the money." His eyes twinkled and he seemed to enjoy my anger. I was outraged, but I was helpless. I knew I could never tell Mrs. Willoughby about how Doc had cheated her at seven-up. I liked her, but I liked him, too. Once he had given me a whole dollar to buy fireworks with on the Fourth of July.

6   I remember once, when I was staying at Mrs. Willoughby's, Doc Marlowe was roused out of bed in the middle of the night by a poor woman who was frantic because her little girl was sick. This woman had had the sciatica driven out of her by his liniment, she reminded Doc. He placed her then. She had never been able to pay him a cent for his liniment or his "treatments," and he had given her a great many. He got up and dressed, and went over to her house. The child had colic, I suppose. Doc couldn't have had any idea what was the matter, but he sopped on liniment; he sopped on a whole bottle. When he came back home, two hours later, he said he had "relieved the distress." The little girl had gone to sleep and was all right the next day, whether on account of Doc Marlowe or in spite of him I don't know. "I want to thank you, Doctor," said the mother, tremulously, when she called on him that afternoon. He gave her another bottle of liniment, and he didn't charge her for it or for his "professional call." He used to massage, and give liniment to, a lot of sufferers who were too poor to pay. Mrs. Willoughby told him once that he was too generous and too easily taken in. Doc laughed—and winked at me, with the twinkle in his eye that he had had when he told me how he had cheated the old lady at cards.

7   Once I went for a walk with him out Town Street on a Saturday afternoon. It was a warm day, and after a while I said I wanted a soda. Well, he said, he didn't care if he took something himself. We went into a drugstore, and I ordered a chocolate soda and he had a lemon phosphate. When we had finished, he said, "Jimmy, my son, I'll match you to see who pays for the drinks." He handed me a quarter and he told me to toss the quarter and he would call the turn. He called heads and won. I paid for the drinks. It left me with a dime.

8   I was fifteen when Doc got out his pamphlets, as he called them. He had eased the misery of the wife of a small-time printer and the grateful man had given him a special price on two thousand advertising pamphlets. There was very little in them about Blackhawk Liniment. They were mostly about Doc himself and his "Life in the Far West." He had gone out to Franklin Park one day with a photographer—another of his numerous friends—and there the

photographer took dozens of pictures of Doc, a lariat in one hand, a six-shooter in the other. I had gone along. When the pamphlets came out, there were the pictures of Doc, peering around trees, crouching behind bushes, whirling the lariat, aiming the gun. "Dr. H. M. Marlowe Hunting Indians" was one of the captions. "Dr. H. M. Marlowe after Hoss-Thieves" was another one. He was very proud of the pamphlets and always had a sheaf with him. He would pass them out to people on the street.

9   Two years before he died Doc got hold of an ancient, wheezy Cadillac somewhere. He aimed to start traveling around again, he said, but he never did, because the old automobile was so worn out it wouldn't hold up for more that a mile or so. It was about this time that a man named Hardman and his wife came to stay at Mrs. Willoughby's. They were farm people from around Lancaster who had sold their place. They got to like Doc because he was so jolly, they said, and they enjoyed his stories. He treated Mrs. Hardman for an old complaint in the small of her back and wouldn't take any money for it. They thought he was a fine gentleman. Then there came a day when they announced that they were going to St. Louis, where they had a son. They talked some of settling in St. Louis. Doc Marlowe told them they ought to buy a nice auto cheap and drive out, instead of going by train—it wouldn't cost much and they could see the country, give themselves a treat. Now, he knew where they could pick up just such a car.

10   Of course, he finally sold them the decrepit Cadillac—it had been stored away somewhere in the back of a garage whose owner kept it there for nothing because Doc had relieved his mother of a distress in the groins, as Doc explained it. I don't know just how the garage man doctored up the car, but he did. It actually chugged along pretty steadily when Doc took the Hardmans out for a trial spin. He told them he hated to part with it, but he finally let them have it for a hundred dollars. I knew, of course, and so did Doc, that it couldn't last many miles.

11   Doc got a letter from the Hardmans in St. Louis ten days later. They had had to abandon the old junk pile in West Jefferson, some fifteen miles out of Columbus. Doc read the letter aloud to me, peering over his glasses, his eyes twinkling, every now and then punctuating the lines with "Hay, boy!" and "Hay, boy-gie!" "I just want you to know, Dr. Marlowe," he read, "what I think of low-life swindlers like you [Hay, boy!] and that it will be a long day before I put my trust in a two-faced lyer and imposture again [Hay, boy-gie!]. The garrage man in W. Jefferson told us your old rattle-trap had been doctored up just to fool us. It was a low down dirty trick as no swine would play on a white man [Hay, boy!]." Far from being disturbed by the letter, Doc Marlowe was plainly amused. He took off his glasses, after he finished it and laughed, his hand to his brow and his eyes closed. I was pretty mad, because I had liked the Hardmans, and because they had liked him. Doc Marlowe put the letter carefully back into its envelope and tucked it away in his inside coat pocket, as if it were something precious. Then he picked up a pack of cards and began to lay

out a solitaire hand. "Want to set in a little seven-up game, Jimmy?" he asked me. I was furious. "Not with a cheater like you!" I shouted, and stamped out of the room, slamming the door. I could hear him chuckling to himself behind me.

12   The last time I saw Doc Marlowe was just a few days before he died. I didn't know anything about death, but I knew that he was dying when I saw him. His voice was very faint and his face was drawn; they told me he had a lot of pain. When I got ready to leave the room, he asked me to bring him a tin box that was on his bureau. I got it and handed it to him. He poked around in it for a while with unsteady fingers and finally found what he wanted. He handed it to me. It was a quarter, or rather it looked like a quarter, but it had heads on both sides. "Never let the other fella call the turn, Jimmy, my boy," said Doc, with a shadow of his old twinkle and the echo of his old chuckle. I still have the two-headed quarter. For a long time I didn't like to think about it, or about Doc Marlowe, but I do now.

❧

Discussion Questions

1. Describe Doc Marlowe's physical appearance and his personality when Thurber first encountered him. Why might Thurber, as a young boy, have thought Marlowe to be "the greatest man" he had ever seen?

2. Cite evidence that Doc's Blackhawk Liniment was a worthwhile product. What prevented Doc from making a living from its sales? By what means did he usually supplement his income?

3. Describe Doc's dealings with Mr. and Mrs. Hardman in paragraphs 9–11. How does he respond to the Hardmans' complaints about his behavior?

4. Cite by number the paragraphs that show Doc Marlowe to be each of the following: a liar; a generous and caring individual; a cheat; a vain man; a person of integrity.

Writing Topics

1. Think of an acquaintance or friend you know or have known who stands out in your memory for some reason—perhaps a command-ing physical appearance, unusual personal traits, or a magnetic personality. Write a character sketch in which you try to convince the reader that the individual you have depicted is indeed memorable.

2. Write a description of a time in your life when you felt cheated. Before writing, consider these questions: What was the situation? Who was involved? What took place? What did you learn from the experience?

"She was (and is) the natural teacher I've never been."

TEACHER
John Barth

John Barth (b. 1930) is a writer noted for blurring the distinction between illusion and reality, for manipulating fictional forms, for playing complex word games, and for featuring nihilistic antiheroes. Among his works are *The Floating Opera* (1956; rev. 1967), *The End of the Road* (1958; rev. 1967), *The Sot-Weed Factor* (1960), *Giles Goat-Boy* (1966), *Lost in the Funhouse* (1968), *Chimera* (1972, winner of the National Book Award), *Letters* (1979), *Sabbatical* (1982), and *The Last Voyage of Somebody the Sailor* (1991). A Professor Emeritus of Creative Writing at Johns Hopkins University, Barth makes his home in Baltimore, Maryland.

1   In the featureless, low-rise, glass-and-aluminum box in which, back in the early 1960s, I taught Humanities 1 (Truth, Goodness, and Beauty) at Pennsylvania State University, her hand was always up—usually first among those of the thirty undergraduates enrolled in my section. Many were seniors from the colleges of education, home economics, engineering, even agriculture, fulfilling their "non-tech elec"; Hum 1 was not a course particularly designed for liberal-arts majors, who would presumably pick up enough T G & B in their regular curriculum. But Miss Rosenberg of the bright brown eyes and high-voltage smile and upraised hand, very much a major in the liberal arts, was there (1) because it was her policy to study with as many members as possible of that university's huge faculty—almost regardless of their subject—who she had reason to believe were of particular interest or effectiveness; (2) because other of her English professors had given me O.K. notices; and (3) because the rest of my teaching load in those days was freshman composition (a requirement from which she'd easily been absolved) and the writing of fiction (an art for which she felt no vocation).

2   Hum 1, then:

3   What is Aristotle's distinction between involuntary and *non*-voluntary acts, and what are the moral implications of that distinction? Miss Rosenberg?

4   What does David Hume mean by the remark that the rules of art come not from reason but from experience? Anybody? Miss Rosenberg.

5   What are all those *bridges* for in *Crime and Punishment?* Let's hear from somebody besides Miss Rosenberg this time. (No hands.) Think of it this way: What are the three main things a novelist can do with a character on a bridge? (No hands. Sigh.) Miss Rosenberg?

6   Her responses were sound, thoughtful, based unfailingly upon thorough preparation of the assigned material; and she was always ready. If she was not the most brilliant student I'd ever taught — I was already by then a dozen years into the profession, with more than a thousand students behind me — she was the best. Which is not to say that Miss R. (the sixties weren't yet in high gear; in central Pennsylvania, at least, most of us still lectured in jackets, white shirts, and neckties and called our students Miss and Mr., as they called us Professor) was docile: if she didn't understand a passage of Lucretius or Machiavelli or Turgenev, she interrogated it and me until either she understood it or I understood that I didn't understand it either. Her combination of academic and moral seriousness, her industry, energy, and animation — solid A, back when A meant A.

7   The young woman was physically attractive, too: her skirt-and-sweatered body trim and fit (from basketball, softball, soccer, tennis, fencing), her brown hair neatly brushed, her aforecited eyes and smile. Ten years out of my all-male alma pater, I still found it mildly exciting — diverting, anyhow — to have girls, as we yet thought of them, in my classroom. But never mind that: as a student, for better or worse, I was never personally close to my teachers; as a teacher, I've never been personally close to my students. And on the matter of *physical* intimacies between teacher and taught, I've always agreed with Bernard Shaw's Henry Higgins: "What! That thing! Sacred, I assure you. . . . Teaching would be impossible unless pupils were sacred."

8   Now: What is the first rung on Plato's "ladder of love"? Nobody remembers? Miss Rosenberg.

9   All the same, it interested me to hear, from a friend and senior colleague who knew her better, that my (and his) star student was not immune to "crushes" on her favorite teachers, who were to her as were the Beatles to many of her classmates: crushes more or less innocent, I presumed, depending upon their object. This same distinguished colleague I understood to be currently one such object. She frequented his office between classes; would bicycle across the town to drop in at his suburban house. I idly wondered . . . but did not ask him, much less her. Sacred, and none of my business.

10   I did however learn a few things further. That our Miss R. was from Philadelphia, strictly brought up, an overachiever (silly pejorative; let's say superachiever) who might well graduate first in her four-thousand-member class. That she was by temperament and/or upbringing thirsty for attention and praise, easily bruised, traumatically strung out by the term papers and examinations on which she scored so triumphantly. That her emotional budget

was high on both sides of the ledger: she expended her feelings munificently; she demanded—at least expected, anyhow hoped for—reciprocal munificence from her friends and, presumably, from her crushees.

11   Mm hm. And the second rung, anybody? (No hands, except of course . . .) Miss Rosenberg.

12   En route to her A in Hum 1 we had a couple of office conferences, but when she completed her baccalaureate (with, in fact, the highest academic average in Penn State's hundred-year history, for which superachievement she was officially designated the university's one hundred thousandth graduate at its centennial commencement exercises), I was still Mr. Barth; she was still Miss Rosenberg. She would have prospered at the best colleges in our republic; circumstances, I was told, had constrained her to her state university. What circumstances? I didn't ask. Now (so my by-this-time-ex-crushee colleague reported) she had several graduate fellowships to choose from; he believed she was inclining to the University of Chicago.

13   I too, as it happened, was in the process of changing universities. I neither saw, nor heard from or about, nor to my recollection thought of excellent Miss Rosenberg for the next four years.

14   There is chalk dust on the sleeve of my soul. In the half century since my kindergarten days, I have never been away from classrooms for longer than a few months. I am as at home among blackboards, desks, lecterns, and seminar tables as among the furniture of my writing room; both are the furniture of my head. I believe I know my strengths and limitations as a teacher the way I know them as a writer: doubtful of my accomplishments in both métiers, I am not doubtful at all that they *are* my métiers, for good or ill.

15   Having learned by undergraduate trial and error that I was going to devote my adult life to writing fiction, I entered the teaching profession through a side door: by impassioned default, out of heartfelt lack of alternatives. I'd had everything to learn; the university had taught me some of it, and I guessed that teaching might teach me more. I needed time to clear my literary throat, but I was already a family man; college teaching (I scarcely cared where or what; I would improvise, invent if necessary) might pay landlord and grocer, if barely, and leave my faculties less abused and exhausted than would manual labor or routine office work, of both of which I'd had a taste. Teaching assistantships in graduate school at Johns Hopkins had taught me that while I was not a "natural" teacher, I was not an unnatural one, either. Some of my undergraduate students knew more about literature, even about the rules of grammar, syntax, and punctuation, than I did. I pushed to catch up. I accepted gratefully a $3,000-a-year instructorship in English composition at Penn State, where I taught four sections of freshman comp—six teaching days a week, twenty-five students per section, one composition per student per week, all papers to be corrected and graded by a rigorous system of symbols, rules, standards. That's

three thousand freshman compositions a year, at a dollar per. It drove one of my predecessors, the poet Theodore Roethke, to drink. But there were occasional half days free, some evenings, the long academic holidays and summers. I stayed on there a dozen years, moving duly through the ranks and up the modest salary scale; got novels written and children raised; learned a great deal about English usage and abusage. And I had a number of quite good students among all those hundreds in my roll book . . . even a few superb ones.

16   My academic job changes happened to coincide with and correspond to major changes in society. As America moved into the High Sixties, I moved from Penn State's bucolic sprawl—still very 1950ish in 1965, with its big-time football, its pompommed cheerleaders, its more than half a hundred social fraternities, its fewer than that number of long-haired, pot-smoking counterculturals among the fifteen-thousand-plus undergraduates, its vast experimental farms and tidy livestock barns, through which I used to stroll with my three small children when not writing sentences or professing Truth, Goodness, and Beauty—moved to the State University of New York's edgy-urban new operation in Buffalo. The Berkeley of the East, its disruptivist students proudly called the place. The Ellis Island of Academe, we new-immigrant faculty called it, also with some pride; so many of us were intellectual heretics, refugees from constrained professional or domestic circumstances, academic fortune hunters in Governor Nelson Rockefeller's promising land.

17   Those next four years were eventful, in U.S. history and mine. Jetting once a month to guest-lecture at other universities, I literally saw the smoke rise from America's burning urban ghettos. More than once I returned from some tear-gassed campus to find my own "trashed," on strike, or cordoned off by gasmasked National Guardsmen. It was a jim-dandy place, SUNY/Buffalo, to work out the decade. My marriage came unglued; I finished *Giles Goat-Boy*, experimented with hashish and adultery, wrote *Lost in the Funhouse* and "The Literature of Exhaustion," began *Chimera*. Education, said Alfred North Whitehead, is the process of catching up with one's generation. The tuition can be considerable.

18   One afternoon in the sixties' final winter I took off from Buffalo in a snowstorm for my monthly off-campus lecture, this one at Boston College. The flight was late in arriving. My Jesuit host, who was to have taken me to a prelecture dinner, had his hands full just getting us across the snowed-in city to the BC campus, where most of my audience was kindly waiting. Promising dinner later, he hustled me onstage to do my number and then off to the obligatory reception (invited guests only) in a room above the auditorium. Since we were running late, we skipped the usual postlecture question period. Even so, as happens, people came forward to say hello, get their books signed, ask things.

19   Such as (her head cocked slightly, bright eyes, bright smile, nifty orange wool miniskirted dress, beige boots—but my host was virtually tugging at my sleeve; we'd agreed to cut short this ritual and get upstairs to that reception as quickly as courtesy allowed): "Remember me?"

20   For a superachiever in the U.S.A., public-school teaching is a curious choice of profession. Salaries are low. The criteria for employment in most districts are not notably high; neither is the schoolteacher's prestige in the community, especially in urban neighborhoods and among members of the other professions. The workload, on the other hand, is heavy, in particular for conscientious English teachers who demand a fair amount of writing as well as reading from the hundred or more students they meet five days a week. In most other professions, superior ability and dedication are rewarded with the five P's: promotion, power, prestige, perks, and pay. Assistant professors become associate professors, full professors, endowed-chair professors, emeritus professors. Junior law partners become senior law partners; middle managers become executives in chief; doctors get rich and are held in exalted regard by our society. Even able and ambitious priests may become monsignors, bishops, cardinals. But the best schoolteacher in the land, if she has no administrative ambitions (that is, no ambition to get out of the classroom), enters the profession with the rank of teacher and retires from it decades later with the rank of teacher, not remarkably better paid and perked than when she met her maiden class. Fine orchestral players and repertory actors may be union-scaled and virtually anonymous, but at least they get, as a group, public applause. Painters, sculptors, poets may labor in poverty and obscurity, but as Milton acknowledged, "Fame is the spur." The condition of the true artisan, perhaps, is most nearly akin to the gifted schoolteacher's: an all but anonymous calling that allows for mastery, even for a sort of genius, but rarely for fame, applause, or wealth; whose chief reward must be the mere superlative doing of the thing. The maker of stained glass or fine jewelry, however, works only with platinum, gemstones, gold, not with young minds and spirits.

21   Sure, I remembered her, that snowy night: Penn State, Hum 1, hand raised. After a moment I even recalled her name, a feat I'm poor at in company. My sleeve was being tugged: the reception. So what was she doing there? She'd seen notice of my reading in the newspaper and hauled through the snow from Brookline to catch her old teacher's act. No, I meant in Boston: Ph.D. work, I supposed, somewhere along the River Chuck, that cerebral cortex of America. Or maybe she'd finished her doctorate—I couldn't remember her specialty— and was already assistant professoring in the neighborhood? No: it was a long story, Ms. R. allowed, and there were others standing about, and my sleeve was being tugged. Well, then: Obliging of you to trek through the drifts to say hello to your old teach. Too bad we can't chat a bit more, catch up; but there's this reception I have to go to now, upstairs. You're looking fine indeed.

22   She was: not a coed now, but a city-looking smart young woman. Where was it she'd been going to go after Penn State? What interesting things had her ex-crushees among my ex-colleagues told me about her? Couldn't remember: only the hand invariably raised (sometimes before I'd reached my question mark) in Truth, Goodness, and Beauty, the lit-up smile, and maybe one serious

office conference in her senior year. Was there a wedding ring on that hand now? Before I could think to look, I was Jesuited off to an elevator already filled with the invited.

23   As its doors closed, she caught them, caused them to reopen, and lightly asked, "May I come along?" Surprised, delighted, I answered for my host: former star student, haven't seen her in years, we did her out of her Q & A, of course she may come along.

24   No wedding ring. But at the reception, too, I was rightly preempted by the Boston Collegians whose guest I was. Ms. Rosenberg and I (but it was Shelly now, and please call me Jack) had time only to register a few former mutual acquaintances and the circumstance of my being in Buffalo these days (she'd read that) and of her having left Chicago (a long story, Jack) to teach in Boston. Aha. At Boston U? Tufts? Northeastern?

25   The incandescent smile. Nope: in the public schools. First at Quincy Junior High, then at Weston Junior High, currently at Wayland High. She was a public-school teacher of English. A schoolteacher is what she'd wanted to be from the beginning.

26   We supposed I ought to mingle with the invited. But as she'd already taken two initiatives — the first merely cordial, the second a touch audacious — I took the next four. My host, the kindly priest, meant to dine me informally after the reception, at some restaurant convenient to my motel, into which I'd not yet been checked. I urged her to join us, so that we could finish our catching up off company time. She agreed, the priest likewise. As she had her car with her and the weather was deep, they conferred upon likeliest roads and restaurants (one with oysters and champagne, the guest of honor suggested) and decided upon Tollino's on Route 9, not far from the Charterhouse Motel, where I was billeted. She'd meet us there.

27   My duty by the invited done, she did. Tollino's came through with half-shell Blue Points and bubbly; the priest had eaten, but he encouraged us to take our time (though the hour was late now) and to help ourselves. He even shared a glass with us. We tried politely to keep the conversation three-way; it was clear to all hands, however, that our patient host was ready to end his evening. Initiative two: The Charterhouse was just a few doors down the road; Ms. Rosenberg had her car. If she was agreeable . . .

28   Quite. The good father was excused; he would fetch me to the airport in the morning. Another round of oysters then, another glass of champagne to toast our reacquaintance. Here's to Penn State, to old mutual friends and ex-crushees, to Truth, to Goodness, to Beauty. Here's to lively Boston, bumptious Buffalo, and — where was it? Chicago, right. A long story, you said. On with it: long stories are my long suit.

29   A schoolteacher is what she'd wanted to be from the beginning. Though she'd used to weep at her difficulties with higher math, and was unnerved even back

then by the prospect of examinations and term papers, she'd loved her Philadelphia public-school days. At the Pennypacker Elementary School and especially at the fast-track Philadelphia High School for Girls, Penn State's future academic superstar had regarded herself as no more than a well-above-average performer. But she'd relished each new school day; had spent the long summer breaks enthusiastically camp-counseling, the next-best thing to school.

30   Her resolution to "teach school" never wavered. At the urging of her professors at Penn State she'd gone on to graduate study in literature and art history in the University of Chicago's Division of the Humanities; she'd done excellent work there with Edward Wasiolek, Elder Olson, Edward Rosenheim. She'd even charmed her way into one of Saul Bellow's courses, to check that famous fellow out. But she had no ambition for a doctorate: her objective was *schoolteaching!* (she said it always with exclamation mark and megawatt smile), and she wanted to get to it as soon as possible. On the other hand, she'd had no truck with "education" courses: Mickey Mouse stuff, in her opinion, except for the history and philosophy of education, which she'd found engrossing. Her baccalaureate was in English, her M.A. was to have been in the humanities. Neither had she been a teaching assistant; hers was a no-strings fellowship.

31   I pricked up my ears. *Was to have been?*

32   Yes: she'd left Chicago abruptly after a year and a half, for nonacademic reasons, without completing the degree. This irregularity, together with the absence of education courses on her transcripts, had made it necessary for her first employer, in Quincy, to diddle benignly with her credentials for certification to teach in the commonwealth's public schools, especially as she'd come to Boston in midacademic year. She was hired and was being paid as "M.A. equivalent," which she certainly was.

33   Abruptly, you said? For nonacademic reasons?

34   Yup. A love trauma, only recently recovered from. Long story, Jack.

35   Tollino's was closing. Initiative three: I supposed there was a bar of some sort in or near my motel, where we could have a nightcap and go on with our stories (I too had one to tell). Should we go check me into the Charterhouse and have a look?

36   Sure. We made the short change of *mise-en-scènes* down the snowplowed highway in her silver-blue Impala convertible, behind the wheel whereof my grown-up and, it would seem, now seasoned former student looked quite terrific in those beige boots and that orange miniskirted dress under that winter coat. And in the motel's all-but-empty lounge I was told at last the long story and some shorter ones, and I told mine and some shorter ones, and presently I took Initiative four.

37   Plato has Socrates teach in *The Symposium* that the apprehension of Very Beauty, as distinct from any beautiful thing or class of things, is arrived at by commencing with the love of, even the lust for, some particular beautiful object

or person. Thence one may proceed to loving beautiful objects and persons in general, the shared quality that transcends their individual differences — may learn even to admire that shared quality without lusting after it: "Platonic love." Thereby one may learn to love the beauty of nonmaterial things as well: beautiful actions, beautiful ideas (a philosopher colleague back at Penn State, remarking to me that he could not read without tears the beautiful scene near the end of Turgenev's *Fathers and Children* where Bazarov's old parents visit their nihilist son's grave, added, "But I weep at the Pythagorean theorem, too"). Whence the initiate, the elect, the platonically invited, may take the ultimate elevator to Beauty Bare: the quality abstracted even from beautiful abstractions. This is the celebrated "ladder of love," as I understood and taught it in Humanities 1 at Penn State, Miss Rosenberg's hand raised at every rung. Our relationship began at the top of that ladder, with those lofty abstractions: Truth, Goodness, Beauty. Now my (former) student taught her (former) teacher that that process is reversible, anyhow coaxial; that ladder a two-way street; that ultimate elevator — May I come along? — a not-bad place to begin.

38   She was (and is) the natural teacher I've never been. Distraught by the termination of her first adult love affair, she'd abruptly left Chicago and her almost completed graduate degree and found asylum in Boston with a Girls' High classmate, now a Harvard doctoral candidate. In the midst of this turmoil — and in midyear — she entered the profession she'd known since first grade to be her calling; and with no prior training or direct experience, from day one on the chair side of the teacher's desk she was as entirely in her element as she'd known she would be. M.A. or no M.A., she was a master of the art; personal crisis or no personal crisis, she improvised for the Quincy Junior High fast-trackers, later for the whiz kids at Weston and Wayland, a course in literature and art history as high-powered and high-spirited as its teacher. She flourished under the staggering workload of a brand-new full-time super-conscientious public-school English teacher. She throve in the life of her new city: new friends, apartment mates, parties, sports, explorations, dates, liaisons — all worked in between the long hours of preparing lesson plans and study questions, assembling films and organizing projector slides, critiquing papers, grading quizzes and exams, and teaching, teaching, teaching her enthusiastic students, who knew a winner when they learned from one.

39   In subsequent Boston visits (No need to fetch me to the airport this morning, Father; I have a ride, thanks) I would meet various of her colleagues — most of them likewise energetic, dedicated, and attractive young men and women — and a few of her students, bound for advanced placement in the Ivy League. I would come to see just how good "good" public schooling can be, how mediocre mine was, how barely better had been my children's. Alas, I was unable to witness my former student's teacherly performances as she'd witnessed a semester's worth of mine. Public schools are not open to the public; anyhow, my presence would have been intrusive. By all accounts they were

superlative, virtuoso. From what I knew of her as a student, I could not imagine otherwise.

40 Yet she came truly into her professional own when, after our marriage, we moved to Buffalo—returned to Buffalo in my case, from a honeymoon year as a visiting professor at Boston University—and, beginning to feel the burden of full-time public-school teaching, she took with misgivings a half-time job in a private girls' high school, the old Buffalo Seminary. Its noncoed aspect gave her no trouble; much as she'd enjoyed her male students in Boston, she'd enjoyed even more the atmosphere of the Philadelphia High School for Girls. But the notion of private schools—"independent schools," they call themselves— ran counter to her liberal-democratic principles. Buff Sem's exclusiveness was not academic, as had been that of Girls' High and the Wayland fast track; she feared it would be social, perhaps racist: a finishing school for the daughters of well-to-do Buffalonians who didn't want their kids in the racially and economically integrated city system.

41 Her apprehensions were not foundationless. Despite generous scholarship programs and sincere attempts at "balance," good U.S. private schools are far more homogeneous—racially, economically, socially, academically—than our public schools are, especially our urban public schools. But her misgivings evaporated within a week in the sunny company of her new charges. The girls as a group were no brighter than those at Quincy, Weston, Wayland; *less* bright, as a group, than her fast-trackers in those public schools or her own high school classmates back in Philadelphia. But they were entirely likable, not at all snobbish, and wondrously educable. There are next to no disciplinary problems in a good private girls' school, at least not in the classroom. And with only twelve or so students per class, and with only two classes, and without the powerfully distracting sexual voltage of coeducation at the high school level— what teaching could get done!

42 We stayed for only one academic year. But more than a dozen years later she is still remembered with respect and affection by her seminary headmaster and by her students from that *Wunderjahr*. She had become Mrs. Barth in two respects: It pleased her to append her husband's last name to her own (to be called Mrs. *John* Barth, however, rightly rankles her; she is herself, not Mrs. Me), and she had become the pedagogical phenomenon her students refer to among themselves as "Barth." One does not speak of taking "Mrs. Barth's course" in myth and fantasy, or in the short story, or in the nineteenth-century Russian novel, or in the literature of alienation; one speaks of "taking Barth." For along with large infusions of the curricular subject matter, what one gets from "taking Barth" is a massive (but always high-spirited, high-energy) education in moral-intellectual responsibility: responsibility to the text, to the author, to the language, to the muses of Truth, Goodness, and Beauty . . . and, along the way, responsibility to the school, to one's teachers and classmates, to oneself.

43   Very little of this came via her husband. I don't doubt that "Barth" learned a few things from her undergraduate professor about the texts in Hum 1 — texts on which, however, I was no authority. No doubt too her daily life with a working novelist and writing coach sharpened her understanding of how fiction is put together, how it manages its effects. But she is a closer reader than I, both of literary texts and of student essays, and a vastly more painstaking critic of the latter, upon which she frequently spends more time than their authors. The Barth who writes this sentence involves himself not at all with the extracurricular lives and extraliterary values of the apprentice writers in his charge. My concern is with their dramaturgy, not with the drama of their personal lives, and seriously as I take my academic commitments, they unquestionably rank second to my commitments to the muse. The Barth "taken" by the girls at the Buffalo Seminary, and thereafter (since 1973, when we moved from Buffalo to Baltimore) at Saint Timothy's School, gives them 100 percent of her professional attention: an attention that drives her to work time and a half at her "half-time" job, and that is directed at her charges' characters and values as well as at their thought processes, their written articulateness, and their literary perceptivity. I'm at my best with the best of my students, the ones en route to joining our next literary generation, and am at my weakest with the weakest. She works her wonders broadcast; the testimonial letters — I should get such reviews! — pile in from her C and D students as well as from the high achievers, and from their parents. Often those letters come from college (wimpy, the girls complain, compared to taking Barth; we thought college would be *serious!*); sometimes they come years later, from the strong young urban professionals many of those students have become: You opened my eyes. You changed my life.

44   This she has done for more than a dozen years now at Saint Tim's, a fairly aristocratic, Episcopal-flavored boarding school in the horse-and-mansion country north of Baltimore. It has proved a virtually ideal place for the exercise of her gifts. She has her complaints about it (as I do about my dear once-deadly-serious Johns Hopkins). She worries about grade inflation, about the risk of softening performance standards, about the unquestioning conservatism of many of her students. She freely admires, however, the general fineness of the girls themselves, who wear their privileges lightly and who strive so, once their eyes have been opened, to measure up to her elevated standards, to deserve her praise. (I have met numbers of the best of these girls and am every time reminded of Anton Chekhov's remark to his brother: "What the aristocrats take for granted, we paid for with our youth." Encircled by a garland of them at a party at our house, Donald Barthelme once asked my wife, "Can't I take a few of them home in my briefcase?")

45   She hopes to go on with this wonder working . . . oh, for a while yet. She doubts she has the metabolism for a full-length career, sometimes wonders

whether she has it for a full-length life. As her habits of relentless self-criticism and superpreparation have required a half-time situation on which to expend more than full-time energy, so—like some poets and fictionists—she will accomplish, perhaps must accomplish, a full professional life in fewer than the usual number of years. We feel similarly, with the same mix of emotions, about our late-started marriage, consoling ourselves with the reflection that, as two teachers who do most of our work at home, we are together more in one year than most working couples are in two. At the front end of her forties, unlike some other high-energy schoolteachers, she has no interest in "moving up" or moving on to some other aspect of education. For her there is only the crucible of the classroom—those astonishing fifty-minute bursts for which, like a human satellite transmitter, she spends hours and hours preparing—and the long, patient, hugely therapeutic individual conferences with her girls, and the hours and hours more of annotating their essays: word by word, sentence by sentence, idea by idea, value by value, with a professional attention that puts to shame any doctor's or lawyer's I've known. How I wish my children had had such a high school teacher. How I wish *I* had!

46   So: for a while yet. A few years from now, if all goes well, I myself mean to retire from teaching, which I'll have been at for four decades, and—not without some trepidation—we'll see. An unfortunate side effect of the single-mindedness behind my best former student's teaching is that, like many another inspired workaholic, she's short on extraprofessional interests and satisfactions. And both of us are socially impaired persons, so enwrapped in our work and each other that our life is a kind of solipsism *à deux*. We'll see.

47   My university's loss will easily be made up. Talented apprentice writers doubtless learn things from the sympathetic and knowledgeable coach in a well-run writing program; I surely did. But they acquire their art mainly as writers always have done: from reading, from practice, from aesthetic argument with their impassioned peers, from experience of the world and of themselves. Where the talent in the room is abundant, it scarcely matters who sits at the head of the seminar table, though it matters some. The Johns Hopkins Writing Seminarians will readily find another coach.

48   But if when I go she goes too—from schooling her girls in art and life, nudging them through the stage of romance, as Whitehead calls it, toward the stage of precision—*there's* a loss can nowise be made good. Writers publish; scholars, critics publish. In a few cases, what they publish outlives them, by much or little. But a first-rate teacher's immortality is neither more nor less than the words (spoken even decades later by her former students to their own students, spouses, children, friends): "Mrs. Barth used to tell us . . ."

49   I like to imagine one of hers meeting one of mine, some sufficient distance down the road. *He* has become (as I'd long predicted) one of the established writers of his generation; *she* is a hotshot young whatever, who's nevertheless

still much interested in literature, so exciting did her old high school English teacher make that subject. They're in an elevator somewhere, upward bound to a reception for the invited, and they're quickly discovering, indeed busily seeking, additional common ground. Somehow the city of Baltimore gets mentioned: Hey, they both went to school there! Later, over oysters and champagne, they circle back to that subject. She'd been in high school, he in graduate school: Saint Timothy's, Johns Hopkins. Hopkins, did he say, in the mid-eighties? She supposes then (knowledgeably, indeed, for a young international banker) that he must have worked with her old English teacher's husband, the novelist . . .

50 Sure, we all had Barth.

51 What a smile she smiles! You think *you* had Barth, she declares (it's late; the place is closing; they bet there's a nightcappery somewhere near his motel). Never mind *that* one: Out at Saint Timothy's, we had *Barth!* Talk about teachers!

52 Let's.

❧

Discussion Questions

1. Under what circumstances did Barth first encounter Ms. Rosenberg? What were his initial impressions of her?

2. How does Barth's writing style convey Ms. Rosenberg's eagerness as a student for attention and excellence?

3. Compare and contrast Barth's and Ms. Rosenberg's motivation to teach and their practices as teachers. Would you have wanted either or both as your teacher? Explain.

4. Under what circumstances did Barth and Ms. Rosenberg meet again? What in the intervening four years had happened in each of their lives? After their reunion, what happened to each of them over time?

5. What reasons does Barth provide to support his assertion in paragraph 20 that "the condition of the true artisan, perhaps, is most nearly akin to the gifted schoolteacher's . . ."? How do these roles differ in your opinion? Do you consider one role to be more important than the other? Explain.

*6. By listing relevant paragraph numbers, cite evidence from the selection that showed Ms. Rosenberg to be, at various times, each of the following: curious; industrious; immature; caring; sociable; unsure of herself; proud.

7. Do you think "My Wife" would have been equally or even more appropriate as the title of Barth's essay? Why or why not?

Writing Topics

1. Think of a close relationship you have with another person. In an essay, describe your initial encounter with this individual, including your first impressions of him or her. Then indicate how the relationship has developed over time and where it seems to be at present.

2. Clearly, Barth is proud of his wife. Think of a person you know who is doing or has done something that makes you feel proud. Describe this person and what he or she does or has done that has prompted you to feel as you do.

Summary Writing Topics

*1. Assume that you edit a magazine and are interested in publishing John Barth's essay "Teacher." Because of limitations of space, you need to shorten the essay by 15 percent. Write to Barth explaining your problem and informing him of the cuts you propose to make, cuts that you believe will do least damage to the selection.

2. Assume that from the selections you have just read you must choose two individuals to remain strangers to you, two to become acquaintances, and two to become friends. Write an essay in which you reveal your choices for each category, providing clear reasons for your selections.

*3. In "The Way It Was," Virginia Bell Dabney describes the discriminatory nursing education received by Mary Marshall's daughter, Sister. Research the ways in which court-ordered equal rights in education have affected American colleges and universities since the U.S. Supreme Court decision of 1954, *Brown vs. the Board of Education, Topeka, Kansas.* Then, write an essay describing your major findings.

4. Assume that you are the book editor for a metropolitan newspaper. Write a review of a new book that deals with ways to make friends and increase one's popularity. In the review, evaluate both the author's writing style and the advice he or she offers.

5. Write a critique for a school publication of the friendship between major characters in a recent film or novel. Describe how the friendship started and summarize the ways in which the friendship developed. Finally, tell why you did, or did not, find the relationship to be credible.

*6. Read at least eight other essays by James Thurber. Then, on the basis of your increased knowledge of Thurber's writing style and subject matter, compose an essay for which the thesis statement would be one of the following options:
  a. "Doc Marlowe" is typical of the essays Thurber usually writes.
  b. "Doc Marlowe" is not typical of the essays Thurber usually writes.

7. Assume that you are Ms. Rosenberg. After dating John Barth a while, you decide to write a close friend in San Francisco a letter describing your future husband, whom your friend has not met. From what you have learned and can infer about Barth from having read "Teacher," describe him in your letter, as Ms. Rosenberg might.

*8. Interview three people middle-aged or older about a strong friendship each has maintained for at least twenty years. In an essay intended for your classmates, briefly describe the people you interviewed and the friendship each person related. Conclude by summarizing what you believe are the major factors that hold a friendship together for a long time.

Cluster

Separations and Losses

Separations and losses hurt, particularly if the separation is one from environs and individuals we care about, if the loss is that of a person we love. Anyone who has moved from one community to another knows the pain that accompanies departure from familiar sites and good-byes to old friends. Anyone who has attended the funeral of someone dear is acquainted with the penetrating sadness that attends final earthly farewells.

Separations drive us back into ourselves, isolating us from people and places. Once we become separated from established community and friends, we are forced to redefine who we are within the orbit of an unfamiliar environment and in relationship to individuals who are strangers to us. Until our new surroundings become as familiar as an old neighborhood, and until the strangers become our acquaintances and friends, we most often feel alone and lonely, cut off from the communal ties that heretofore had helped provide us our identity, our **I**-dentity.

As disquieting to our psychological equilibrium as a separation from known haunts and companions may be, even more traumatic to our sense of well-being is the death of someone close. With the passing of a loved one, we are left with feelings of desolation and often of desertion, along with a startling realization of the impermanence of all human relationships. Moreover, we frequently become ensnared in a self-spun web of psychically disturbing questions, ones that have perplexed others for untold centuries: "What is the significance of human life?" "What is the meaning of my own existence?" "Why am I alive and the person I loved no longer breathing?" "What does 'death' mean, and what may succeed its arrival?"

The selections that follow all have to do with separation and loss: separation from one's home, one's family, even one's native land; loss of one's friends and family members, ranging from the sudden death of a sensitive nurse's patient to the sudden death of a father's cherished son. As you read, you may find yourself emotionally moved by the forced geographical transitions of various writers and by the deaths of people related to them, individuals you will have come to know at least briefly—mothers, fathers, sons, brothers, husbands, and wives. Through vicarious participation in the sorrow accompanying the passing of these people, you will likely arrive at a heightened sensitivity of the fragility of all human life and, thereby, a deeper appreciation of the preciousness of your own existence.

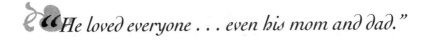

"He loved everyone . . . even his mom and dad."

MY SON, A GENTLE GIANT, DIES

Michael Gartner

The present editor and co-owner of the *Ames Daily Tribune*, Ames, Iowa, Michael Gartner (b. 1938) has also been an editor for *The Wall Street Journal*, the *Des Moines Register and Tribune*, and the *Courier Journal and Louisville Times*. From 1988–1993, he served as president of NBC News. Gartner is a syndicated columnist on language as well as a columnist for **USA TODAY**, in which "My Son, a Gentle Giant, Dies" appeared on July 6, 1994.

1   Bear with me, if you will, for a personal column.

2   It's about my son Christopher. He turned 17 last November. He died on Thursday, June 30. He was a healthy, robust boy on Tuesday. He got sick on Wednesday. And he died on Thursday.

3   You would have liked him. Everyone did.

4   He was a gentle giant, everyone's best friend, and the world's leading expert. On everything. He was always cheerful. He was, says the foreman at the farm where he worked this summer, simply "magical."

5   He was adopted. I say this with relish and love because adoption usually is mentioned only in stories about bad kids. In newspaper stories, serial murderers are adopted. Nobel Prize winners aren't. It's sort of a newspaper's code for saying, "Don't blame the parents. It's not their fault he killed the neighbors." But in this case, it's not my fault he was such a great kid.

6   So we looked not alike at all, and he thought that was funny. I'm 5 feet 8 inches and weigh about 160. He was close to 6-4, I imagine, and weighed around 300. He looked like a cement block with a grin. Once, a year or so ago, he introduced me to a friend. "This is my dad," he said proudly. The friend looked at me, looked at Chris, and then looked confused. "You should see my mother," Chris said with a straight face.

7   I mentioned him in a column last Nov. 29—that was his 17th birthday. I wrote about the death of Finnegan, our old floppy-eared hound, and I told how when Christopher was 6 he and I had taken a trip. I asked him about our two dogs, Finnegan and a clipped-ear Bouvier named Mandy. "Who do you like best," I asked, "Finnegan or Mandy?" "Finnegan," he quickly replied, "because his ears are so big you can wipe your tears on them."

8   He read the column that evening. "Did you get paid for writing that?" he asked. Yes, I said, I did. How much? he asked. I told him. "You know," he said, "that column wouldn't have been anything without that quote from me. I think I should get half."

9   That's the kind of kid he was. He always had an angle.

10   He was loving.

11   He loved everyone, especially his grandparents, but even his mom and dad. "I love you, Dad," he'd say with meaning and without embarrassment. He knew that was unusual. The summer before last, he and my wife and I played golf one Saturday—he could hit a golf ball a mile, though you never knew whether it would be a mile east or a mile west—and he asked what we were doing for dinner later. "Mom and I are going out," I said. "Do you want to go with us?" "Nah," he said, "I think I'll do something with Joey." I pushed him to join us. Finally, he said, "Look, Dad, you don't understand. At my age you're not even supposed to *like* your parents."

12   He was funny.

13   "Dad," he said a couple of months ago, "I know what I'd like for my next birthday—a handicap parking sticker. You know, there are a lot more places than there are people who use them." I explained that it was unlikely they'd give a robust kid a handicap parking sticker. So Christopher, who didn't much care for studying, changed his tack: "You know, if I had one I could leave for everywhere I go 10 minutes later—and I could use that time for studying."

14   As a parent, you live in fear your child will die in a car wreck, and in his year and a half of driving Christopher did manage to wreck all four of our family cars. He hit a tree the day he got his license. ("It wasn't my fault, Dad." "Well, Christopher," I said, "it was yours or the tree's." He knew that, he said, and then argued, almost persuasively, how the tree was to blame.) And last spring he backed one of my cars into another of my cars, which must be a record of sorts. He announced his other accident to me over the phone by beginning, "Dad, you know those air bags stink when they go off."

15   But it was a sudden, initial attack of juvenile diabetes that killed him, that killed him despite medical heroics and fervid prayers. It is awful and horrible and sad, and no words can comfort his four grandparents, his brother and sister, his friends or his parents.

16   Yet his friend, Tim Russert of NBC, called Friday, devastated as we all are, and said the only thing that has helped.

17   "If God had come to you 17 years ago and said, 'I'll make you a bargain. I'll give you a beautiful kid for 17 years, and then I'll take him away,'" Tim said. "You would have made that deal in a second."

18   And that was the deal.

19   We just didn't know the terms.

                                        ❧

Discussion Questions

1. Gartner refers to his son Christopher as "a gentle giant." Does the description seem appropriate? Explain.
2. In what ways was the relationship between Gartner and his son unusual?
3. Describe the time sequence and cause of Christopher's death. What helped console Gartner over his loss? Would you have been willing to make the same deal? Why or why not?
4. Cite evidence by paragraph numbers that Christopher was cheerful; humorous; reckless; loving.
5. Describe how Gartner's short paragraphs (3, 9, 10, 12, 18, and 19) affect the tone of the selection. Would you have preferred that the tribute to Christopher be longer? Why or why not?

Writing Topics

1. If you have ever had an acquaintance, friend, or relative die unexpectedly, write a short essay describing the circumstances of the person's death, how the news affected you at the time, and what means of consolation you found—for example, in the friendship or words of others, your memories of the individual, your religious faith, or a combination of sources.
2. Before you die, what are some of the future experiences—educational, vocational, familial, travel, whatever—that you most want to have? In an essay, indicate two or three specific experiences that hold great appeal for you, why they do, and how you hope to achieve them one day.

That hour began my wanderings.
Not so much in geography, but in time.
Then not so much in time as in spirit."

WANDERING

Zora Neale Hurston

After her mother's died, nine-year-old Zora Neale Hurston had to move from the friendly, familiar surroundings of the small, all-black town of Eatonville, Florida, to Jacksonville to attend school. She reports that it was Jacksonville that made her know she was "a little colored girl." Hurston went on to study anthropology and folklore at Howard University and Barnard College before becoming an eminent part of the literary movement of the Harlem Renaissance. For more biographical information on Hurston, see the headnote on page 89.

1   I knew that Mama was sick. She kept getting thinner and thinner and her chest cold never got any better. Finally, she took to bed.

2   She had come home from Alabama that way. She had gone back to her old home to be with her sister during her sister's last illness. Aunt Dinky had lasted on for two months after Mama got there, and so Mama had stayed on till the last.

3   It seems that there had been other things there that worried her. Down underneath, it appeared that Grandma had never quite forgiven her for the move she had made twenty-one years before in marrying Papa. So that when Mama suggested that the old Potts place be sold so that she could bring her share back with her to Florida, her mother, urged on by Uncle Bud, Mama's oldest brother, refused. Not until Grandma's head was cold, was an acre of the place to be sold. She had long since quit living on it, and it was pretty well run down, but she wouldn't, that was all. Mama could just go on back to that yaller rascal she had married like she came. I do not think that the money part worried Mama as much as the injustice and spitefulness of the thing.

4   Then Cousin Jimmie's death seemed to come back on Mama during her visit. How he came to his death is an unsolved mystery. He went to a party and started home. The next morning his headless body was found beside the railroad track. There was no blood, so the train couldn't have killed him. This had

happened before I was born. He was said to have been a very handsome young man, and very popular with the girls. He was my mother's favorite nephew and she took it hard. She had probably numbed over her misery, but going back there seemed to freshen up her grief. Some said that he had been waylaid by three other young fellows and killed in a jealous rage. But nothing could be proved. It was whispered that he had been shot in the head by a white man unintentionally, and then beheaded to hide the wound. He had been shot from ambush, because his assailant mistook him for a certain white man. It was night. The attacker expected the white man to pass that way, but not Jimmie. When he found out his mistake, he had forced a certain Negro to help him move the body to the railroad track without the head, so that it would look as if he had been run over by the train. Anyway, that is what the Negro wrote back after he had moved to Texas years later. There was never any move to prove the charge, for obvious reasons. Mama took the whole thing very hard.

5   It was not long after Mama came home that she began to be less active. Then she took to bed. I knew she was ailing, but she was always frail, so I did not take it too much to heart. I was nine years old, and even though she had talked to me very earnestly one night, I could not conceive of Mama actually dying. She had talked of it many times.

6   That day, September 18th, she had called me and given me certain instructions. I was not to let them take the pillow from under her head until she was dead. The clock was not to be covered, nor the looking-glass. She trusted me to see to it that these things were not done. I promised her as solemnly as nine years could do, that I would see to it.

7   What years of agony that promise gave me! In the first place, I had no idea that it would be soon. But that same day near sundown I was called upon to set my will against my father, the village dames and village custom. I know now that I could not have succeeded.

8   I had left Mama and was playing outside for a little while when I noted a number of women going inside Mama's room and staying. It looked strange. So I went on in. Papa was standing at the foot of the bed looking down on my mother, who was breathing hard. As I crowded in, they lifted up the bed and turned it around so that Mama's eyes would face the east. I thought that she looked to me as the head of the bed was reversed. Her mouth was slightly open, but her breathing took up so much of her strength that she could not talk. But she looked at me, or so I felt, to speak for her. She depended on me for a voice.

9   The Master-Maker in His making had made Old Death. Made him with big, soft feet and square toes. Made him with a face that reflects the face of all things, but neither changes itself, nor is mirrored anywhere. Made the body of Death out of infinite hunger. Made a weapon for his hand to satisfy his needs. This was the morning of the day of the beginning of things.

10   But Death had no home and he knew it at once.

11   "And where shall I dwell in my dwelling?" Old Death asked, for he was already old when he was made.

12   "You shall build you a place close to the living, yet far out of the sight of eyes. Wherever there is a building, there you have your platform that comprehends the four roads of the winds. For your hunger, I give you the first and last taste of all things."

13   We had been born, so Death had had his first taste of us. We had built things, so he had his platform in our yard.

14   And now, Death stirred from his platform in his secret place in our yard, and came inside the house.

15   Somebody reached for the clock, while Mrs. Mattie Clarke put her hand to the pillow to take it away.

16   "Don't!" I cried out. "Don't take the pillow from under Mama's head! She said she didn't want it moved!"

17   I made to stop Mrs. Mattie, but Papa pulled me away. Others were trying to silence me. I could see the huge drop of sweat collected in the hollow at Mama's elbow and it hurt me so. They were covering the clock and the mirror.

18   "Don't cover up that clock! Leave that looking-glass like it is! Lemme put Mama's pillow back where it was!"

19   But Papa held me tight and the others frowned me down. Mama was still rasping out the last morsel of her life. I think she was trying to say something, and I think she was trying to speak to me. What was she trying to tell me? What wouldn't I give to know! Perhaps she was telling me that it was better for the pillow to be moved so that she could die easy, as they said. Perhaps she was accusing me of weakness and failure in carrying out her last wish. I do not know. I shall never know.

20   Just then, Death finished his prowling through the house on his padded feet and entered the room. He bowed to Mama in his way, and she made her manners and left us to act out our ceremonies over unimportant things.

21   I was to agonize over that moment for years to come. In the midst of play, in wakeful moments after midnight, on the way home from parties, and even in the classroom during lectures. My thoughts would escape occasionally from their confines and stare me down.

22   Now, I know that I could not have had my way against the world. The world we lived in required those acts. Anything else would have been sacrilege, and no nine-year-old voice was going to thwart them. My father was with the mores. He had restrained me physically from outraging the ceremonies established for the dying. If there is any consciousness after death, I hope that Mama knows that I did my best. She must know how I have suffered for my failure.

23   But life picked me up from the foot of Mama's bed, grief, self-despisement and all, and set my feet in strange ways. That moment was the end of a phase in my life. I was old before my time with grief of loss, of failure, and of remorse. No matter what the others did, my mother had put her trust in me. She had felt

that I could and would carry out her wishes, and I had not. And then in that sunset time, I failed her. It seemed as she died that the sun went down on purpose to flee away from me.

24   That hour began my wanderings. Not so much in geography, but in time. Then not so much in time as in spirit.

25   Mama died at sundown and changed a world. That is, the world which had been built out of her body and her heart. Even the physical aspects fell apart with a suddenness that was startling.

26   My oldest brother was up in Jacksonville in school, and he arrived home after Mama had passed. By then, she had been washed and dressed and laid out on the ironing-board in the parlor.

27   Practically all of the village was in the front yard and on the porch, talking in low tones and waiting. They were not especially waiting for my brother Bob. They were doing that kind of waiting that people do around death. It is a kind of sipping up the drama of the thing. However, if they were asked, they would say it was the sadness of the occasion which drew them. In reality it is a kind of feast of the Passover.

28   Bob's grief was awful when he realized that he was too late. He could not conceive at first that nothing could be done to straighten things out. There was no ear for his excuse nor explanation—no way to ease what was in him. Finally it must have come to him that what he had inside, he must take with him wherever he went. Mama was there on the cooling board with the sheet draped over her blowing gently in the wind. Nothing there seemed to hear him at all.

29   There was my sister Sarah in the kitchen crying and trying to quiet Everett, who was just past two years old. She was crying and trying to make him hush at the same time. He was crying because he sensed the grief around him. And then, Sarah, who was fifteen, had been his nurse and he would respond to her mood, whatever it was. We were all grubby bales of misery, huddled about lamps.

30   I have often wished I had been old enough at the time to look into Papa's heart that night. If I could know what that moment meant to him, I could have set my compass towards him and been sure. I know that I did love him in a way, and that I admired many things about him. He had a poetry about him that I loved. That had made him a successful preacher. He could hit ninety-seven out of a hundred with a gun. He could swim Lake Maitland from Maitland to Winter Park, and no man in the village could put my father's shoulders to the ground. We were so certain of Papa's invincibility in combat that when a village woman scolded Everett for some misdemeanor, and told him that God would punish him, Everett, just two years old, reared back and told her, "He better not bother me. Papa will shoot Him down." He found out better later on, but that goes to show you how big our Papa looked to us. We had seen him bring down bears and panthers with his gun, and chin the bar more times than any man in competing distance. He had to our knowledge licked two men who Mama told him had to be licked. All that part was just fine with me. But I was

Mama's child. I knew that she had not always been happy, and I wanted to know just how sad he was that night.

31   I have repeatedly called up that picture and questioned it. Papa cried some too, as he moved in his awkward way about the place. From the kitchen to the front porch and back again. He kept saying, "Poor thing! She suffered so much." I do not know what he meant by that. It could have been love and pity for her suffering ending at last. It could have been remorse mixed with relief. The hard-driving force was no longer opposed to his easy-going pace. He could put his potentialities to sleep and be happy in the laugh of the day. He could do next year or never, what Mama would have insisted must be done today. Rome, the eternal city, meant two different things to my parents. To Mama, it meant, you must build it today so it could last through eternity. To Papa, it meant that you could plan to lay some bricks today and you have the rest of eternity to finish it. With all time, why hurry? God had made more time than anything else, anyway. Why act so stingy about it?

32   Then too, I used to notice how Mama used to snatch Papa. That is, he would start to put up an argument that would have been terrific on the store porch, but Mama would pitch in with a single word or a sentence and mess it all up. You could tell he was mad as fire with no words to blow it out with. He would sit over in the corner and cut his eyes at her real hard. He was used to being a hero on the store porch and in church affairs, and I can see how he must have felt to be always outdone around home. I know now that that is a griping thing to a man—not to be able to whip his woman mentally. Some women know how to give their man that conquesting feeling. My mother took her over-the-creek man and bareknuckled him from brogans to broadcloth, and I am certain that he was proud of the change, in public. But in the house, he might have always felt over-the-creek, and because that was not the statue he had made for himself to look at, he resented it. But then, you cannot blame my mother too much if she did not see him as his entranced congregations did. The one who makes the idols never worships them, however tenderly he might have molded the clay. You cannot have knowledge and worship at the same time. Mystery is the essence of divinity. Gods must keep their distances from men.

33   Anyway, the next day, Sam Moseley's span of fine horses, hitched to our wagon, carried my mother to Macedonia Baptist Church for the last time. The finality of the thing came to me fully when the earth began to thud on the coffin.

34   That night, all of Mama's children were assembled together for the last time on earth. The next day, Bob and Sarah went back to Jacksonville to school. Papa was away from home a great deal, so two weeks later I was on my way to Jacksonville, too. I was under age, but the school had agreed to take me in under the circumstances. My sister was to look after me, in a way.

35   The midnight train had to be waved down at Maitland for me. That would put me into Jacksonville in the daytime.

36   As my brother Dick drove the mile with me that night, we approached the curve in the road that skirts Lake Catherine, and suddenly I saw the first picture of my visions. I had seen myself upon that curve at night leaving the village home, bowed down with grief that was more than common. As it all flashed back to me, I started violently for a minute, then I moved closer beside Dick as if he could shield me from those others that were to come. He asked me what was the matter, and I said I thought I heard something moving down by the lake. He laughed at that, and we rode on, the lantern showing the roadway, and me keeping as close to Dick as I could. A little, humped-up, shabby-backed trunk was behind us in the buckboard. I was on my way from the village, never to return to it as a real part of the town.

37   Jacksonville made me know that I was a little colored girl. Things were all about the town to point this out to me. Streetcars and stores and then talk I heard around the school. I was no longer among the white people whose homes I could barge into with a sure sense of welcome. These white people had funny ways. I could tell that even from a distance. I didn't get a piece of candy or a bag of crackers just for going into a store in Jacksonville as I did when I went into Galloway's or Hill's at Maitland, or Joe Clarke's in Eatonville.

38   Around the school I was an awful bother. The girls complained that they couldn't get a chance to talk without me turning up somewhere to be in the way. I broke up many good "He said" conferences just by showing up. It was not my intention to do so. What I wanted was for it to go full steam ahead and let me listen. But that didn't seem to please. I was not in the "he said" class, and they wished I would kindly please stay out of the way. My underskirt was hanging, for instance. Why didn't I go some place and fix it? My head looked like a hoo-raw's nest. Why didn't I go comb it? If I took time enough to match my stockings, I wouldn't have time to be trying to listen in on grown folk's business. These venerable old ladies were anywhere from fifteen to eighteen.

39   In the classroom I got along splendidly. The only difficulty was that I was rated as sassy. I just had to talk back at established authority and that established authority hated backtalk worse than barbed-wire pie. My brother was asked to speak to me in addition to a licking or two. But on the whole, things went along all right. My immediate teachers were enthusiastic about me. It was the guardians of study-hour and prayer meetings who felt that their burden was extra hard to bear.

40   School in Jacksonville was one of those twilight things. It was not dark, but it lacked the bold sunlight that I craved. I worshipped two of my teachers and loved gingersnaps with cheese, and sour pickles. But I was deprived of the loving pine, the lakes, the wild violets in the woods and the animals I used to know. No more holding down first base on the team with my brothers and their friends. Just a jagged hole where my home used to be.

41   At times, the girls of the school were lined up two and two and taken for a walk. On one of these occasions, I had an experience that set my heart to fluttering. I saw a woman sitting on a porch who looked at a distance like Mama. Maybe it *was* Mama! Maybe she was not dead at all. They had made some mistake. Mama had gone off to Jacksonville and they thought that she was dead. The woman was sitting in a rocking-chair just like Mama always did. It must be Mama! But before I came abreast of the porch in my rigid place in line, the woman got up and went inside. I wanted to stop and go in. But I didn't even breathe my hope to anyone. I made up my mind to run away someday and find the house and let Mama know where I was. But before I did, the hope that the woman really was my mother passed. I accepted my bereavement.

ें.

Discussion Questions

1.   What deaths and worries apparently affected the health of Hurston's mother?
2.   What death-bed instructions did the mother give her nine-year-old daughter in paragraph 6? For what reasons did Hurston fail to carry out these instructions? In what ways did this failure affect the young girl?
3.   Cite by number the paragraphs in which Hurston weaves folklore into her narration. Do you believe that the folklore adds to or detracts from the selection? Explain.
4.   How did Hurston's mother and father regard each other? For what reasons? How did Hurston seem to regard each of them?
5.   How did the treatment Hurston received in Jacksonville differ from that which she had experienced in Eatonville? What did the young girl particularly miss about her former surroundings?
6.   Do you believe that Hurston adequately prepares the reader of "Wandering" for the concluding sentence, "I accepted my bereavement"? Explain.

Writing Topics

1.   In "Wandering," Hurston suffered a double loss: that of her mother and that of familiar surroundings. If you have ever moved from one geographic location to another, describe in an essay what prompted the move, how you felt about it at the time, what adjustments you had to make to your new surroundings, and how you now feel about the entire experience.

2. As a student, you most likely have had the experience of moving from one school to another, of one educational level to another, possibly within the same town. Write a detailed account of one of these transitions, such as your completion of junior high school and commencement of high school. How did you feel about what lay ahead—excited? anxious? fearful? optimistic? sorrowful? relieved? How would you now evaluate the experience?

"My love . . . seems to bind me with mighty cables that nothing but Omnipotence can break."

SULLIVAN BALLOU TO SARAH BALLOU

Sullivan Ballou

During the Civil War, in which three million Americans fought and in which more died (600,000) than in World War II, tens of thousands of letters were exchanged between soldiers and loved ones back home. Sullivan Ballou, a major in the Second Rhode Island Volunteers, wrote the following letter to his wife, Sarah, one week before he was killed in Virginia during the first major battle of the war—the first battle of Bull Run, also known as the first battle of Manassas. In a televised interview, Ken Burns reported that during the five-and-a-half years he spent making *The Civil War*, his acclaimed television series broadcast on PBS, he carried Ballou's letter with him to remind him of what the conflict was all about.

July 14, 1861
Camp Clark, Washington, D.C.

My very dear Sarah,

1   The indications are very strong that we shall move in a few days, perhaps tomorrow. And lest I should not be able to write you again, I feel impelled to write a few lines that may fall under your eyes when I am no more.

2   I have no misgivings about or lack of confidence in the cause in which I am engaged and my courage does not halt or falter. I know how American Civilization now leans on the triumph of the Government and how great a debt we owe to those who went before us through the blood and suffering of the Revolution. And I am willing, perfectly willing, to lay down all my joys in this life to help maintain this government and to pay that debt.

3   Sarah, my love for you is deathless. It seems to bind me with mighty cables that nothing but Omnipotence can break. And yet my love of Country comes over me like a strong wind and bears me irresistibly, with all these chains, to the battlefield.

4   The memories of all the blissful moments I have enjoyed with you come creeping over me, and I feel most deeply grateful to God and you that I have

enjoyed them so long. And hard it is for me to give them up and burn to ashes the hopes of future years when, God willing, we might still have lived and loved together and seen our boys grown up to honorable manhood around us. I have, I know, but few and small claims upon Divine Providence, but something whispers to me — perhaps it is the wafted prayer of my little Edgar, that I shall return to my loved ones unharmed.

5   If I do not return, my dear Sarah, never forget how much I loved you, nor that when my last breath escapes me on the battlefield, it will whisper your name. Forgive my many faults and the many pains I have caused you. How thoughtless, how foolish I have sometimes been! How gladly would I wash out with my tears every little spot upon our happiness.

6   But, O Sarah! If the dead can come back to this earth and flit unseen around those they loved, I shall always be near you in the gladdest days and in the darkest nights . . . *always* always, and if there be a soft breeze upon your cheek, it shall be my breath, as the cool air fans your throbbing temple, it shall be my spirit passing by. Sarah, do not mourn me dead; Think I am gone and wait for thee, for we shall meet again. . . .

ॐ

Discussion Questions

1. What prompted Sullivan Ballou to write to his wife? What assertions in his letter did Ballou make to Sarah about his love for her? How did he account for his being on the battlefield?
2. By paragraph number, cite evidence from the letter that shows Ballou to be patriotic; religious; fatherly; hopeful; contrite; faithful.
3. If Sullivan Ballou were writing to Sarah from a battlefield today, how would the letter differ in writing style from that of 1861? Would you consider these stylistic changes to be improvements or not? Explain.

Writing Topics

1. Assume that you are Sarah Ballou, have received Sullivan's letter of July 14, and have heard no news of his death. You decide to write Sullivan a letter in return. What will you say to him?
2. Imagine that you are Sullivan Ballou and that you did return safely from the war. The year is now 1900, and you are in Washington, D.C., for a reunion of the Second Rhode Island Volunteers. You take out some hotel stationery and begin a letter to Sarah. What will you say to her?

The robbery changed everything. Gone was the coziness, the softness in her life; gone was the safety."

I NEVER THOUGHT
IT WOULD HAPPEN TO ME

Irvin D. Yalom

Irvin D. Yalom (b. 1931), a professor of psychiatry at the Stanford University School of Medicine, was educated at George Washington University (B.A., 1952) and Boston University School of Medicine (M.D., 1956). He is the author of The Theory and Practice of Group Psychotherapy (1970), Existential Psychotherapy (1980), Inpatient Group Psychotherapy (1983), Love's Executioner (1990), in which " 'I Never Thought It Would Happen to Me' " appears, and When Nietzche Wept: A Novel of Obsession (1992). In addition, Yalom has coauthored Encounter Groups: First Facts (1973), Every Day Gets a Little Closer: A Twice-Told Therapy (1974), and Concise Guide to Group Psychotherapy (1989).

1   I greeted Elva in my waiting room, and together we walked the short distance to my office. Something had happened. She was different today, her gait labored, discouraged, dispirited. For the last few weeks there had been a bounce in her steps, but today she once again resembled the forlorn, plodding woman I had first met eight months ago. I remember her first words then: "I think I need help. Life doesn't seem worth living. My husband's been dead for a year now, but things aren't getting any better. Maybe I'm a slow learner."

2   But she hadn't proved to be a slow learner. In fact, therapy had progressed remarkably well—maybe it had been going too easily. What could have set her back like this?

3   Sitting down, Elva sighed and said, "I never thought it would happen to me."

4   She had been robbed. From her description it seemed an ordinary purse snatching. The thief, no doubt, spotted her in a Monterey seaside restaurant and saw her pay the check in cash for three friends—elderly widows all. He must have followed her into the parking lot and, his footsteps muffled by the roaring of the waves, sprinted up and, without breaking stride, ripped her purse away and leaped into his nearby car.

5   Elva, despite her swollen legs, hustled back into the restaurant to call for help, but of course it was too late. A few hours later, the police found her empty purse dangling on a roadside bush.

6   Three hundred dollars meant a lot to her, and for a few days Elva was preoccupied by the money she had lost. That concern gradually evaporated and in its place was left a bitter residue—a residue expressed by the phrase "I never thought it would happen to me." Along with her purse and her three hundred dollars, an illusion was snatched away from Elva—the illusion of personal specialness. She had always lived in the privileged circle, outside the unpleasantness, the nasty inconveniences visited on ordinary people—those swarming masses of the tabloids and newscasts who are forever being robbed or maimed.

7   The robbery changed everything. Gone was the coziness, the softness in her life; gone was the safety. Her home had always beckoned her with its cushions, gardens, comforters, and deep carpets. Now she saw locks, doors, burglar alarms, and telephones. She had always walked her dog every morning at six. The morning stillness now seemed menacing. She and her dog stopped and listened for danger.

8   None of this is remarkable. Elva had been traumatized and now suffered from commonplace post-traumatic stress. After an accident or an assault, most people tend to feel unsafe, to have a reduced startle threshold, and to be hypervigilant. Eventually time erodes the memory of the event, and victims gradually return to their prior, trusting state.

9   But for Elva it was more than a simple assault. Her world view was fractured. She had often claimed, "As long as a person has eyes, ears, and a mouth, I can cultivate their friendship." But no longer. She had lost her belief in benevolence, in her personal invulnerability. She felt stripped, ordinary, unprotected. The true impact of that robbery was to shatter illusion and to confirm, in brutal fashion, her husband's death.

10   Of course, she knew that Albert was dead. Dead and in his grave for over a year and a half. She had taken the ritualized widow walk—through the cancer diagnosis; the awful, retching, temporizing chemotherapy; their last visit together to Carmel; their last drive down El Camino Real; the hospital bed at home; the funeral; the paperwork; the ever-dwindling dinner invitations; the widow and widower's clubs; the long, lonely nights. The whole necrotic catastrophe.

11   Yet, despite all this, Elva had retained her feeling of Albert's continued existence and thereby of her persisting safety and specialness. She had continued to live "as if," as if the world were safe, as if Albert were there, back in the workshop next to the garage.

12   Mind you, I do not speak of delusion. Rationally, Elva knew Albert was gone, but still she lived her routine, everyday life behind a veil of illusion which numbed the pain and softened the glare of the knowing. Over forty years ago,

she had made a contract with life whose explicit genesis and terms had been eroded by time but whose basic nature was clear: Albert would take care of Elva forever. Upon this unconscious premise, Elva had built her entire assumptive world—a world featuring safety and benevolent paternalism.

13   Albert was a fixer. He had been a roofer, an auto mechanic, a general handyman, a contractor; he could fix anything. Attracted by a newspaper or magazine photograph of a piece of furniture or some gadget, he would proceed to replicate it in his workshop. I, who have always been hopelessly inept in a workshop, listened in fascination. Forty-one years of living with a fixer is powerfully comforting. It was not hard to understand why Elva clung to the feeling that Albert was still there, out back in the workshop looking out for her, fixing things. How could she give it up? Why should she? That memory, rein-forced by forty-one years of experience, had spun a cocoon around Elva that shielded her from reality—that is, until her purse was snatched.

14   Upon first meeting Elva eight months before, I could find little to love in her. She was a stubby, unattractive woman, part gnome, part sprite, part toad, and each of those parts ill tempered. I was transfixed by her facial plasti-city: she winked, grimaced, and popped her eyes either singly or in duet. Her brow seemed alive with great washboard furrows. Her tongue, always visible, changed radically in size as it darted in and out or circled her moist, rubbery, pulsating lips. I remember amusing myself, almost laughing aloud, by imagining introducing her to patients on long-term tranquilizer medication who had de-veloped tardive dyskinesia (a drug-induced abnormality of facial musculature). The patients would, within seconds, become deeply offended because they would believe Elva to be mocking them.

15   But what I really disliked about Elva was her anger. She dripped with rage and, in our first few hours together, had something vicious to say about everyone she knew—save, of course, Albert. She hated the friends who no longer invited her. She hated those who did not put her at ease. Inclusion or exclusion, it was all the same to her: she found something to hate in everyone. She hated the doctors who had told her that Albert was doomed. She hated even more those who offered false hope.

16   Those hours were hard for me. I had spent too many hours in my youth silently hating my mother's vicious tongue. I remember the games of imagina-tion I played as a child trying to invent the existence of someone she did not hate: A kindly aunt? A grandfather who told her stories? An older playmate who defended her? But I never found anyone. Save, of course, my father, and he was really part of her, her mouthpiece, her animus, her creation who (according to Asimov's first law of robotics) could not turn against his maker— despite my prayers that he would once—just once, please, Dad—pop her.

17   All I could do with Elva was to hold on, hear her out, somehow endure the hour, and use all my ingenuity to find something supportive to say—usually some vapid comment about how hard it must be for her to carry around that

much anger. At times I, almost mischievously, inquired about others of her family circle. Surely there must be someone who warranted respect. But no one was spared. Her son? She said his elevator "didn't go to the top floor." He was "absent": even when he was there, he was "absent." And her daughter-in-law? In Elva's words, "a GAP"—gentile American princess. When driving home, her son would call his wife on his automobile telephone to say he wanted dinner right away. No problem. She could do it. Nine minutes, Elva reminded me, was all the time required for the GAP to cook dinner—to "nuke" a slim gourmet TV dinner in the microwave.

18   Everyone had a nickname. Her granddaughter, "Sleeping Beauty" (she whispered with an enormous wink and a nod), had two bathrooms—two, mind you. Her housekeeper, whom she had hired to attenuate her loneliness, was "Looney Tunes," and so dumb that she tried to hide her smoking by exhaling the smoke down the flushing toilet. Her pretentious bridge partner was "Dame May Whitey" (and Dame May Whitey was spry-minded compared with the rest, with all the Alzheimer zombies and burned-out drunks who, according to Elva, constituted the bridge-playing population of San Francisco).

19   But somehow, despite her rancor and my dislike of her and the evocation of my mother, we got through these sessions. I endured my irritation, got a little closer, resolved my countertransference by disentangling my mother from Elva, and slowly, very slowly, began to warm to her.

20   I think the turning point came one day when she plopped herself in my chair with a "Whew! I'm tired." In response to my raised eyebrows, she explained she had just played eighteen holes of golf with her twenty-year-old nephew. (Elva was sixty, four foot eleven, and at least one hundred sixty pounds.)

21   "How'd you do?" I inquired cheerily, keeping up my side of the conversation.

22   Elva bent forward, holding her hand to her mouth as though to exclude someone in the room, showed me a remarkable number of enormous teeth, and said, "I whomped the shit out of him!"

23   It struck me as wonderfully funny and I started to laugh, and laughed until my eyes filled with tears. Elva liked my laughing. She told me later it was the first spontaneous act from Herr Doctor Professor (so that was *my* nickname!), and she laughed with me. After that we got along famously. I began to appreciate Elva—her marvelous sense of humor, her intelligence, her drollness. She had led a rich, eventful life. We were similar in many ways. Like me, she had made the big generational jump. My parents arrived in the United States in their twenties, penniless immigrants from Russia. Her parents had been poor Irish immigrants, and she had straddled the gap between the Irish tenements of South Boston and the duplicate bridge tournaments of Nob Hill in San Francisco.

24 At the beginning of therapy, an hour with Elva meant hard work. I trudged when I went to fetch her from the waiting room. But after a couple of months, all that changed. I looked forward to our time together. None of our hours passed without a good laugh. My secretary said she always could tell by my smile that I had seen Elva that day.

25 We met weekly for several months, and therapy proceeded well, as it usually does when therapist and patient enjoy each other. We talked about her widowhood, her changed social role, her fear of being alone, her sadness at never being physically touched. But, above all, we talked about her anger — about how it had driven away her family and her friends. Gradually she let it go; she grew softer and more gentle. Her tales of Looney Tunes, Sleeping Beauty, Dame May Whitey, and the Alzheimer bridge brigade grew less bitter. Rapprochements occurred; as her anger receded, family and friends reappeared in her life. She had been doing so well that, just before the time of the purse snatching, I had been considering raising the question of termination.

26 But when she was robbed, she felt as though she were starting all over again. Most of all, the robbery illuminated her ordinariness, her "I never thought it would happen to me" reflecting the loss of belief in her personal specialness. Of course, she was still special in that she had special qualities and gifts, that she had a unique life history, that no one who had ever lived was just like her. That's the rational side of specialness. But we (some more than others) also have an irrational sense of specialness. It is one of our chief methods of denying death, and the part of our mind whose task it is to mollify death terror generates the irrational belief that we are invulnerable — that unpleasant things like aging and death may be the lot of others but not our lot, that we exist beyond law, beyond human and biological destiny.

27 Although Elva responded to the purse snatching in ways that *seemed* irrational (for example, proclaiming that she wasn't fit to live on earth, being afraid to leave her house), it was clear that she was *really* suffering from the stripping away of irrationality. That sense of specialness, of being charmed, of being the exception, of being eternally protected — all those self-deceptions that had served her so well suddenly lost their persuasiveness. She saw through her own illusions, and what illusion had shielded now lay before her, bare and terrible.

28 Her grief wound was now fully exposed. This was the time, I thought, to open it wide, to debride it, and to allow it to heal straight and true.

29 "When you say you never thought it would happen to you, I know just what you mean," I said. "It's so hard for me, too, to accept that all these afflictions — aging, loss, death — are going to happen to me, too."

30 Elva nodded, her tightened brow showing that she was surprised at my saying anything personal about myself.

31 "You must feel that if Albert were alive, this would never have happened to you." I ignored her flip response that if Albert were alive she wouldn't have

been taking those three old hens to lunch. "So the robbery brings home the fact that he's really gone."

32   Her eyes filled with tears, but I felt I had the right, the mandate, to continue. "You knew that before, I know. But part of you didn't. Now you really know that he's dead. He's not in the yard. He's not out back in the workshop. He's not anywhere. Except in your memories."

33   Elva was really crying now, and her stubby frame heaved with sobs for several minutes. She had never done that before with me. I sat there and wondered, *"Now* what do I do?" But my instincts luckily led me to what proved to be an inspired gambit. My eyes lit upon her purse—that same ripped-off, much-abused purse; and I said, "Bad luck is one thing, but aren't you asking for it carrying around something that large?" Elva, plucky as ever, did not fail to call attention to my overstuffed pockets and the clutter on the table next to my chair. She pronounced the purse "medium-sized."

34   "Any larger," I responded, "and you'd need a luggage carrier to move it around."

35   "Besides," she said, ignoring my jibe, "I need everything in it."

36   "You've got to be joking! Let's see!"

37   Getting into the spirit of it, Elva hoisted her purse onto my table, opened its jaws wide, and began to empty it. The first items fetched forth were three empty doggie bags.

38   "Need two extra ones in case of an emergency?" I asked.

39   Elva chuckled and continued to disembowel the purse. Together we inspected and discussed each item. Elva conceded that three packets of Kleenex and twelve pens (plus three pencil stubs) were indeed superfluous, but held firm about two bottles of cologne and three hairbrushes, and dismissed, with an imperious flick of her hand, my challenge to her large flashlight, bulky notepads, and huge sheaf of photographs.

40   We quarreled over everything. The roll of fifty dimes. Three bags of candies (low-calorie, of course). She giggled at my question: "Do you believe, Elva, that the more of these you eat, the thinner you will become?" A plastic sack of old orange peels ("You never know, Elva, when these will come in handy"). A bunch of knitting needles ("Six needles in search of a sweater," I thought). A bag of sourdough starter. Half of a paperback Stephen King novel (Elva threw away sections of pages as she read them: "They weren't worth keeping," she explained). A small stapler ("Elva, this is crazy!"). Three pairs of sunglasses. And, tucked away into the innermost corners, assorted coins, paper clips, nail clippers, pieces of emery board, and some substance that looked suspiciously like lint.

41   When the great bag had finally yielded all, Elva and I stared in wonderment at the contents set out in rows on my table. We were sorry the bag was empty and that the emptying was over. She turned and smiled, and we looked

tenderly at each other. It was an extraordinarily intimate moment. In a way no patient had ever done before, she showed me everything. And I had accepted everything and asked for even more. I followed her into her every nook and crevice, awed that one old woman's purse could serve as a vehicle for both isolation and intimacy: the absolute isolation that is integral to existence and the intimacy that dispels the dread, if not the fact, of isolation.

42   That was a transforming hour. Our time of intimacy—call it love, call it love making—was redemptive. In that one hour, Elva moved from a position of forsakenness to one of trust. She came alive and was persuaded, once more, of her capacity for intimacy.

43   I think it was the best hour of therapy I ever gave.

❧

Discussion Questions

1. What event prompted Elva to comment, "I never thought it would happen to me"? Describe the immediate effects of the event upon her life.
2. In what ways had Albert, Elva's deceased husband, been employed during his lifetime? Describe the role Albert played for Elva during their lengthy marriage.
3. Why did Yalom comment in paragraph 14 that initially he could "find little to love" in Elva? After what point in therapy—and why— did doctor and patient begin to get along well together?
4. How did Yalom's own background affect his responses to Elva, both early on and later in therapy?
5. In an important session, how did Yalom bring Elva to understand what she really meant in saying, "I never thought it would happen to me"?
6. Describe the "inspired gambit" on Yalom's part that enabled that same session of therapy to be "a transforming hour."
7. Summarize the various separations and losses, as well as the gains, that Elva experienced during her time of therapy.

Writing Topics

1. Imagine that you have found Elva's purse and that you know nothing about the woman. On the basis of what the purse contained when it was emptied in Yalom's office, write a character description of its owner. In your essay, indicate why certain objects in the purse have led you to make particular assumptions about the person who possessed them.

2. Yalom at first found little to love about Elva but over time grew to care deeply about her. Write a description of a relationship you have had with someone whom you initially disliked but grew to like, or even to love. Indicate what you originally found distasteful about this person and what led you to change your mind about him or her.

ᴥ. . . I realized I had mined a new intensity,
full of terror and,
though I didn't know it then, of love."

A DEATH IN THE FAMILY

Kenneth A. McClane

Kenneth A. McClane (b. 1951) holds undergraduate and graduate degrees from Cornell University, where he is now a professor of English and former director of the creative writing program. He is the author of numerous books of poetry and of a collection of essays, Walls: Essays 1985–90. "A Death in the Family," first published in The Antioch Review, Spring 1985, was mentioned as a notable essay in The Best American Essays of 1986.

He was a kid of about the same age as Rufus, from some insane place like Jersey City or Syracuse, but somewhere along the line he had discovered that he could say it with a saxophone. He had a lot to say. He stood there, wide-legged, humping the air, filling his barrel chest, shivering in the rags of his twenty-odd years, and screaming through the horn Do you love me? Do you love me? Do you love me? *And, again,* Do you love me? Do you love me? Do you love me?

James Baldwin, Another Country

I recall how difficult it was for me to realize that my brother loved me. He was always in the streets, doing this and that, proverbially in trouble, in a place, Harlem, where trouble indeed was great. At times we would even come to blows, when, for example, drunk as he could be, he wished to borrow my car and I had visions of his entrails splayed over the city. I remember one incident as if it were yesterday: Paul, my younger brother, physically larger than me, his hand holding a screw driver, poised to stab me, his anger so great that his brother, the college professor, wouldn't let him drive his "lady" home, even though he could barely walk. I can still see him chiding me about how I had always done the right thing, how I was not his father, how I was just a poor excuse for a white man, the last statement jeweled with venom. And from his place, this was certainly true: I had done what I was expected to do; and the world, in its dubious logic, had paid me well. I was a college teacher; I had published a few collections of poems; I had a wonderful girlfriend; and what suffering I bore, at least to my brother's eyes, centered around my inability to leave him alone. Luckily, this confrontation ended when my father rushed in on us, our distress exceeded only by the distress in his eyes. Later, my brother would forget the events of that evening, but not the fact that I had not lent him the car. For my part I would never forget how we were both so angry, so hate-filled. I, too, that night, might have killed my brother.

2   As children we were often at each other's throats. The difference in our ages, just two years, was probably a greater bridge than either of us welcomed. And so we often went for each other's pressure points: the greater discomfort enacted, the more skillful our thrust. But this was child's play, in a child's world. On that November night when my brother and I confronted each other with hate and murder in our eyes, I realized I had mined a new intensity, full of terror and, though I didn't know it then, of love.

3   Though he was incredibly angry (bitter some might say), I always admired my brother's honesty and self-love. It seemed that everything he thrust into his body was a denial of self—alcohol, smoke, cocaine—yet his mind and his quick tongue demanded that he be heard. In a world full of weakness, he was outspoken, never letting anyone diminish him. When he was at the wheel in that torturous abandon euphemistically called "city driving," he invariably would maneuver abreast of a driver who had somehow slighted him, and tell him, in no uncertain language, where he could go and with utmost dispatch. Paul never cared how big, crazy, or dangerous this other driver might be. When I cautioned him, reliving again and again the thousand headlines of *Maniac Kills Two Over Words*, he would just shrug. "He's a bastard, needs to know it." I remember how scared I became when he would roll down the window—scared and yet proud.

4   My brother was unable to ride within the subway, moving immediately to the small catwalk between the cars, where the air might reach him. He complained that he was always too hot, that the people were too close; indeed, as soon as he entered the train, sweat began to cascade off him, as if he had just completed a marathon. Later this image would remain with me: my brother, feet apart, sweat pouring from his body, trying to keep his delicate balance between the two radically shifting platforms, while always maintaining that he was fine. "Bro, I'm just hot." I would later learn that these manifestations were the effects of acute alcoholism; I would later learn much about my brother.

5   Like the day's punctuation, Paul would make his numerous runs to the *bodega*, bringing in his small brown paper bags, then quickly returning to his room, where he would remain for hours. Some days you would barely see him; my father could never coax him out. Paul saw my father as the establishment, "fat man" he would call him, though this too was somewhat playful. With Paul play and truth were so intermeshed that they leased the same root. One had to

be forever careful of traveling with a joke only to find that no joke was intended. Or, just as often, finding sympathy with something Paul said, one was startled to see him break out in the most wondrous smile, amusement everywhere. In this spectacle, one thing was enormously clear: Paul was a difficult dancer. And like all artists, his mastery was also, for the rest of us, cause for contempt. We enjoyed his flights; but we also sensed, and poignantly, that they were had at our expense. Clearly we had failed as listeners, for Paul had not sought to befuddle us; but we, as the majority, were in the position of power and could always depend on it as our last defense. And power, arguments to the contrary, is rarely generous.

6   My brother would stay in his room for hours, watching the box, playing his drums, talking to his endless friends who, until he was just about to die, came to sit and talk and smoke. Paul inevitably would be holding court: he knew where the parties were, could get anyone near anything, had entrée with the most beautiful girls, who sensed something in his eyes that would not betray them. Many of his friends would later become doctors, a few entertainers, all of them by the most incomprehensible and tortuous of routes. The black middle class — if it can really be termed that — is a class made up of those who are either just too doggedly persistent or too stupid to realize that, like Fitzgerald's America, their long sought-after future remains forever beckoning and end-lessly retreating. And Paul's friends, who sensed his demise well before we did, as only the doomed or the near-doomed can, were as oddly grafted to class — or even the promise of respectability — as it is humanly possible to imagine. Like Paul, they sat waiting for the warden, knowing only that the walls exist, that the sentence is real. Indeed, if the crime were lack of understandable passion, they were guilty a hundredfold. But it is not understanding, alas, that the world is interested in. And the world — they rightfully sensed — was certainly not interested in them.

7   Paul was no saint. Like most of us, he exhibited the confusions and the possibilities that intermittently set us on our knees or loose with joy. He wasn't political in the established way; his body, in its remoteness, was political. It said that the state of the world was nothing he cared to be involved with. Fuck it, he'd say.

8   In the language of the street, Paul was a "lover." And like all lovers he believed that the pounding of the bed frame testified to something that "his woman" best understood. And in the logic of his bed and of those who shared it, women's lib to the contrary, there seemed to be no complaints. Often I wondered about his use of the term "my woman," the possessiveness of it, the language that brought to mind the auction block and a brutal history that had profited neither of us. But Paul's woman was like his life: if I had my job and my poems, he had his woman. Feminists might complain of this uneasy pairing — I certainly share their concern — but within the brutal reward struc-ture of the ghetto, where one's life is often one's only triumph, such a notion is

understandable. My brother's woman was his only bouquet, the one thing that testified that he was not only a man, but a man whom someone wanted. Arguments notwithstanding, no manner of philosophy or word play can alter the truth. My brother loved his "woman" in the most profound sense of the word, since his love centered on the greatest offering he could give, the sharing of himself. And I do not mean to be coy here. For when you are, in Gwendolyn Brooks's terms, "all your value and all your art," the gift of yourself is an unprecedented one.

9   But this is a brother's testimony; it is a way of a brother living with a brother dead. It doesn't have the violence of unknowing—the great violence that kept me for so long feeling guilty, which still makes the early morning the most difficult time. I remember how Paul volunteered to watch our cats when Rochelle and I, living for a three-month exile in Hartsdale, New York, had to be away. Max, the large white one, hell-bent on intercourse with the hardly possible, hid within the wall and Paul went nearly crazy, looking here and there, wondering if he should call, afraid that disaster had no shores. Strange how I recall this; it certainly isn't important. But Paul was scared—scared more so because he loved animals, saw in their pain more than he saw in ours, in his.

10   In July, my father called to say that I had best come to New York. Paul was ill. Very ill. He would probably die. The whole thing was incredible. My father has the nagging desire to protect those he loves from the worrisome. What this tends to create, however, is the strangest presentiment: when he does finally communicate something, it is always at the most dire stage, and the onlooker can barely understand how something has become so involved, so horrible, so quickly; or is thrown, similarly, into the uncomfortable position of confronting the possibility that one failed to acknowledge something so momentous occurring. In either case, one is completely unprepared for revelation, and no matter what my father's heroic designs (and they were that), one's horror at not being allowed to participate in the inexorable, outdistances any possible feeling of gratitude. Although pain cannot be prepared for, neither can it be denied. But on this day, my father's voice was that of cold disbelief—the doctor without any possible placebo. And I was in the air in a few hours.

11   At that time I was involved in teaching summer school, and the day before one of my students had suggested that we read Baldwin's "Sonny's Blues." I had read the story some years before and had been favorably impressed, though I couldn't remember any of its particulars. Well, at 6:15 I got on the airplane, armed with a few clothes and Baldwin. Little did I know that that story would save my life, or at least make it possible to live with it.

12   "Sonny's Blues" is about an older brother's relationship with his younger brother, Sonny, who happens to be a wonderful jazz pianist and a heroin addict. The story, obviously, is about much more: it involves love, denial, and the interesting paradox by which those of us who persist in the world may in fact

survive not because we understand anything, but because we consciously exclude things. Sonny's older brother teaches algebra in a Harlem high school, where algebra is certainly not the only education the students are receiving. There are drugs, dangers, people as hell-bent on living as they are fervent on dying. But most importantly, "Sonny's Blues" is about the ways in which we all fail; the truth that love itself cannot save someone; the realization that there are unreconcilable crises in the world; and, most importantly, the verity that there are people amongst us, loved ones, who, no matter what one may do, will perish.

13   Now, I read this story on the plane, conscious, as one is only when truly present at one's distress, of the millions of things going on about me. The plane was headed to Rochester, a course only capitalism can explain, for Rochester is west of Ithaca; and New York, my destination, is east of Ithaca, my place of origin. Clearly this makes no sense, but neither does serving gin and tonic at 6:15 a.m. And I was thankful for that.

14   The hospital was located in central Manhattan, some five blocks from my father's newly acquired office. My father had just moved from his long-held office at 145th Street, because he had routinely been robbed; the most recent robbery had taken on a particularly brutal nature, when the intruders placed a huge, eight-hundred-pound EKG machine atop him to pin him to the floor. Robberies in this neighborhood were not unusual: my father had been robbed some eight times within the previous four years. But with the escalation of the dope traffic, and the sense that every doctor must have a wonderful stash, doctors, whether, like my father, they had no narcotics at all, became prime targets. My father loved his office; he had been there since he first came to New York in 1941. Although he could have made much more money in midtown, he remained by choice in Harlem. As a child I could not understand this. I wanted him to be amongst the skyscrapers, with the Ben Caseys. Little did I know then that his forsaking of these things was the highest act of selflessness. As he once quietly stated, probably after a bout of my pestering, "Black people need good doctors, too." I imagine my father would have remained in his office until a bullet found his head had not my mother finally put her foot down and declared, "Honey, I know thirty-five years is a long time, but you've got to move."

15   I walked past my father's new office and headed into the Intensive Care Unit of Roosevelt Hospital. There I met my father and the attending physician—two doctors, one with a son—and listened to the prognosis. Medicine, as you know, has wonderful nomenclature for things: the most horrible things and something as slight as hiccups have names that imply the morgue. But the litany of my brother—septicemia, pneumonia—had the weight, rehearsed in my father's face, of the irreconcilable. My brother was *going* to die. The doctor said my brother was *going to die*. They would try like hell, but the parameters (the word parameters had never before been so important to me) left little in the way of hope.

16   It is difficult enough to be a parent and have a thirty-one-year-old child dying of alcoholism, his gut enlarged, his eyes red, lying in a coma. It is even more difficult, however, when you are a parent and also a doctor. For you have a dual obligation, one to a profession, a way of seeing, and one to nature, a rite of loving. As a doctor, my father knew what was medically possible—as surely as did any well-trained specialist—in my brother's precarious situation; he certainly knew what the parameters dictated. But as a parent, hoping like any parent that his child might live, he knew nothing, hope being a flight from what is known to the fanciful. And so these two extremes placed my father in a country rarely encountered, a predicament where I could sense, even then, his distress, but a place from which no one could save him.

17   In the two weeks that would follow, my mother, in grief, would ask my father what were Paul's chances. And he—doctor, parent, and husband—would be placed in that country again and again. As a parent every slight twitching of Paul, a slight movement of the lips, a small spasm of the hand, would move him to joy, to speculation—was that an attempt at words, was Paul reaching out? But as a doctor, he knew the terrible weight of parameters—how a word, no matter how strange its sound or source, does involve meaning. So, often he was placed in the terrible paradox of stating what he least wanted to hear. That yes, it was possible that Paul was reaching for us; but the parameters, the this test and the that test, suggested that Paul was still critical, very critical. And we never pressed him further, probably sensing that he would have to announce that these small skirmishes with the inevitable, like water pools just before turning to ice, could not remove the fact, no matter how much we or he would wish it so, that Paul was going to die. Moreover, for us, this dalliance with hope was a temporary waystation so that we could harden our own tools for the coming onslaught. My father did not have this privilege; he was, like all the greatest heroes, the angel without the hope of heaven.

18   In many ways the third factor in my father's difficult situation now came most into play, that of husband. My mother, like all of us, clung to hope; but more, she clung to her son. There is no way to detail the sense of a mother's love. In substance, a mother protects her son from the world, which, she rightly senses, is unceasingly bent on his destruction. Yet in my house, since Paul was an artist, so remote, my mother, in a sense, defended a phantom, defending him in much the way one supports the constitutional right of due process. For my mother, Paul was to be protected in theory: he was an artist; he was sensitive; he was silent. This identification with him and with those of his facets the world was bound not to respect—and indeed never did—made her involvement with Paul all the more intense, for he was not only the issue of her womb but the wellspring of her imagination.

19   My father certainly understood some of this, yet his way of reacting to any ostensible conundrum was conditioned by his medical school training. If there is a problem, he maintained, it can be reasonably addressed. And so he hoped

that Paul would descend from his room and tell him what the problem was, why he wasn't finishing college, why he continued to drink so heavily, what, in God's name, did he do up in that room? And as it became obvious that the Socratic method demanded an interchange between two consenting mentors, my father became increasingly concerned and distressed. (The problem with any axiom is that it is valuable only as long as it works: my father's belief in reason had served him happily heretofore; yet now he was encountering an unforeseen circumstance. And he, like all of us when confronting Paul, had little in the bank.)

20 　In any event, my father, in the hospital, was forced continually to grapple with three very difficult responsibilities all somehow connected. My mother, as Paul, miraculously, showed slight signs of rallying (the doctors had originally stated that he had a 10 percent chance of surviving), continued to find reasons, as all of us did, for hope. I recall how my wife and I visited one day and Paul actually extended his wobbling hand—and I, relating this later to my father, actually did press him, asking him if he thought Paul could possibly make it. My father, caught between a brother's hope and the sense that miracles do happen, and possibly even to him, said: "Yes, I think he could; but the parameters (*again that word*) are inconclusive." (Now I know that he didn't believe that Paul could live—the doctor in him didn't believe it, that is.)

21 　But the most difficult moments for my father came, I think, when he had to explain to my mother, his wife, what he saw, trying always to remember that she was a grieving mother and a hopeful one; and no matter what was happening, might happen, he had to remain a source of strength for her, as she had so often been for him. In this difficult barter, my father also had to worry about my mother's natural inclination to believe the impossible, for hope would make us all immortal, while at the same time protecting that part of her which would permit her to bear this thing, no matter what the outcome. My father continued to caution my mother about the dire state of my brother. The word *parameter* became as palpable to my family as my brother's breath. And the boundaries, no matter what my brother's outward appearance, remained the same. It was enough to drive one crazy. With the weather, when the sun rises and the skin feels warm, the thermometer registers one's sense of new heat. Yet with my brother it seemed that our senses were at war with the medical reality. What, then, in this place, were cause and effect?

22 　During the last week of my brother's life, my mother became increasingly angry with my father, blurting out, "You sound as if you want your son to die." Clearly this was an outburst culled out of anguish, frustration, and grief. And yet it adequately gave language to my father's paradox. Never have I seen the mind and the heart so irrefutably at odds.

23 　My brother died after five coronaries at two a.m. thirteen nights after he was admitted to intensive care. His funeral took place some 250 miles from New York, on lovely Martha's Vineyard, where Paul and the family had spent

our happiest years. The funeral was a thrown-together affair: 90 percent grief and the rest dogged persistence that something had to be done. The service was a plain one, with an Episcopal minister reading from the dreary *Book of Common Prayer*. My mother had hoped that someone could better eulogize my brother, someone who might get beyond the ashes-to-ashes bit and talk about the stuff of him, possibly so that we, his family, might finally get to know the person who had slowly drained away from us. The one reverend who knew my brother begged off, with the excuse that Paul had traveled a great distance from when he knew him. And that, to say the least, was the profoundest ministry that man had ever preached.

24   Although the funeral was a hasty affair, with little notice — and though we hardly knew many of Paul's friends — somehow a large contingent gathered, coming from Vermont, New York, and elsewhere, many of them for the first time at a funeral of one of their peers. I can't adequately describe the motley assemblage. Suffice it to say that these were the Lord's children, the ones who had tasted the bread of this world and waited, still, for manna. One young woman said a few words, choked them out, and then the sobbing began.

25   I think this meditation aptly ends with his friends, for they knew him and loved him as we did. In Baldwin's *Another Country*, one of the characters, Vivaldo, is described as feeling that "love is a country he knew nothing about." With the death of my brother, I learned about love: my love for him; my love for my parents; their love for one another; my love for those thin-shelled children who gathered on that small hillside to pay witness to one of theirs who didn't make it, who evidenced in his falling that death indeed is a possibility, no matter how young one is or how vigorous. I can't say that I know who my brother was, but I know that I miss him, more now than ever. And love, yes, is a country I know something about.

🐾

Discussion Questions

1.   Describe some of the major differences between McClane and his brother Paul. What qualities did McClane admire about his sibling?

2.   Explain what you think McClane meant in paragraph 5 by the statement ". . . Paul was a difficult dancer."

3.   What did McClane learn from James Baldwin's "Sonny's Blues" that helped him deal with Paul's death?

4.   Explain what conflicts there were for Dr. McClane in his triple role of doctor, father, and husband.

5.   Cite by paragraph numbers evidence from the selection that reveals Paul to have been hot-tempered; alcoholic; musical; trustworthy; sociable; sensitive and caring.

6. In light of McClane's explanation in paragraph 8, did you find Paul's attitude toward "his woman" to be acceptable?
7. With the death of his brother, what in the final paragraph does McClane declare to have learned about love? Do you find sufficient evidence in the essay to justify these claims? Explain.

Writing Topics

1. In a brief essay, describe your relationship to a brother or sister, if you have one. After exploring the traits you have in common and the major differences that exist between you, conclude by summarizing your feelings toward your sibling.
2. McClane writes, "I can't say that I know who my brother was. . . ." Depict in a short essay a person with whom you are acquainted, perhaps closely, but whom you can't claim to understand fully. Recount your relationship to this person and what it is you find puzzling about him or her.

"To this day I miss my mother. . . . I never wanted my daughter to be as close to me as I was to her."

NO DESIRE TO GO BACK

Kathrine O'Hara

(as told to Joan Morrison and Charlotte Fox Zabusky)

Joan Morrison and Charlotte Fox Zabusky compiled the oral history *American Mosaic: The Immigrant Experience in the Words of Those Who Lived It* (1980). For the volume, they interviewed 140 immigrants from approximately fifty countries, among them Katherine O'Hara from Ireland, who, at the time of the book's publication, was living by herself in a small New England town and still cleaning people's houses several times a week. Joan Morrison graduated from the University of Chicago in 1944. An adjunct professor since 1987 at the New School for Social Research in New York City, Morrison has written widely on the social sciences for such publications as *Mademoiselle*, *The New York Times*, *Better Homes and Gardens*, and *McCall's*. Charlotte Fox Zabusky, who formerly directed an immigration program, is a teacher of English as a second language.

1   I wanted my mother to be happy. I used to say to her as a little girl, "You don't have to worry now, because when I grow big, I'm going to America and I'm going to make plenty of money and I'm going to send it home to you. You're going to have everything, mamma." It seems so strange that it came to pass.

2   It was during the time that there was all those bills coming in, due to the fact of my mother's illness; because there was so much to be done—hospitals and taking care of her. She was ill a long time, and it was very, very sad. You'd see the automobile come rushing down the street, and you'd see that it was the sheriff in there. I knew what was coming. The sheriff was coming to the house, and the bailiffs was coming all the time, and he would have to be telling the boys to go and get whatever remaining cattle was on the farm, because they would seize them for the money that was owed. And we needed those. We needed to eat. I think it more or less left me scared to death, seeing it, you know. And I'd always think, "I'm really going to go to America and I'm going to make a lot of money and I'm going to send it home."

3   Then we had a foot-and-mouth disease and all the stock died. We had a lot of land and we had a lot of horses and a lot of sheep, and I used to go horseback riding to count them. And one day I went over and they were all dead, the cattle. I can still see them. They were lying down, and they had gotten near the brook, and as soon as they tasted the water, they had died. It was a very severe loss. My mother was living at the time. It was a big blow to us. Hard luck came in more ways than one.

4   There were seven of us, and we were all home when my mother passed away in 1926 at the age of thirty-nine. She left all of us very young. My sister was very young, I was young. I had one brother older than me. I was very, very sad, because I was crazy about my mother. She was so young and she was so good. I mean I idolized her, and I just couldn't take it. I used to pray every day for her to live and not to die. To this day I miss my mother. I always claimed I never wanted my daughter to be as close to me as I was to her. I prayed when I was carrying my daughter that she would never have the feeling for me that I had for my mother. I'd never let myself get that close to my daughter, and I never was. It hurt—don't think it didn't. But when I'm gone, I don't want her to feel the way I did about my mother. [*Cries.*]

5   My father really should have been a priest. He wasn't happy with a family and a farm or a business. He wasn't meant for that type of life. He never adjusted, being a farmer. He had been a well-educated man. He was educated for nine years in the seminary. He was about to become a priest, and the last six months there was a change of mind. He never told anyone why. That was a secret he carried to his grave. And then he started business after that. He had a grocery store and a liquor store combined. That's where he married my mother, and then after that they moved out to the country, to the farm. He had a farm, a nice estate, but he was a man that was never cut out for farming. He struggled along as best he could, and then he got into a lot of debt when we had a depression, and everything went down. And then there was my mother's illness. When she passed away, I was around fifteen.

6   Then, when I was eighteen, my father decided I'd have to come to America—I had an aunt out here—to work, help out with money that was owed, so he wouldn't lose the home. I was thrilled. I didn't want any more of the sheriffs.

7   I arrived in Boston on May 8, 1930. My aunt was not at the pier to meet me. The immigration authorities took over. They were very kind. They asked me how much money I had to pay for a taxi, and I told them—I had learned the money on board the ship coming over. They took me to Commonwealth Avenue, where my aunt worked as a cook for a millionaire family. When we got there, the caretaker said that my aunt had moved on to the summer residence, but she had arranged for me to stay in a rooming house.

8   The next week I went into an employment agency, by the name of Mrs. Benson, on Berkeley Street in Boston, and I got a job with a society lady in

Brookline. There was nine on the staff, and I was a parlor maid. I waited on table. It was a very nice job and a lovely lady. She gave me twelve dollars a week, but it wasn't enough for the demands my father had put on me. In September I left. When I was leaving her, she gave me a five-dollar gold piece for good luck.

9   I went back to Mrs. Benson's office. A lady by the name of Mrs. Elliot had interviewed four girls for a position, and I saw the lady and I liked her from the start. Mrs. Elliot and I sat down, we discussed everything, and she hired me right there for sixteen dollars a week. She had a big house in Westwood and she had a cook. And there was another girl there, a laundress. I took care of the children. I bathed them, gave them their breakfast, got them ready for the school, and the lady took them to school—drove them by car. It was the time of the Lindbergh kidnapping, you may remember.

10   In my own heart, I didn't like being a servant, but I never showed it. As far as working, as far as wages, everything was what I expected. But as far as my own life and my own feeling, no. I resented the fact that I had to work the way I did under somebody else. I always felt the jobs I had was inferior to what I had home. But I expected to be able to pay off all my father's debts. That was all I was interested in. As far as myself was concerned, I didn't care.

11   For two solid years I sent money home. I never bought a stitch of clothes. I used what I had when I came over. I bought nothing.

12   My father wrote to me when I was five years in America. He told me that now everything was paid and everything was fine and I was to return home. He had a man over there, and he would like me to settle down and get married. I refused to go. I said I was not going home. I had no desire to go back. My mother was gone, and I certainly wasn't going to go to my father to pick out someone for me. I had common sense enough for that. He never wrote to me for two years, my father. After a couple of years, he softened up and he wrote to me.

13   Then I met my husband. He was French-Canadian—very tall, dark, handsome—and I fell in love with him, or thought I did. Well, he was an unfortunate man. His parents, his family, always liked liquor, and he was trying so hard to keep away from it. It didn't work. I stayed married to him for eleven years, and I got very ill over it. We were living in Boston proper. I did everything to keep that marriage, but when my little girl was six years old, I went to the German church, to Father Kugler, and he told me to go ahead and get a divorce. He says there was only one drawback: If I ever met someone, I might want to remarry again, I could not be married in the Catholic Church, which I understood. So I went ahead and got the divorce. There was no alternative.

14   I didn't have any problems with the Church. I went to Mass, I received Communion, although I was divorced, because I was not remarried. But then after that I met a very nice man and I remarried. Then I did not go to church, and I did not receive Communion. I only went Christmas or something. I missed

my church. I always knew I would, but even though I missed it, I always knew I wasn't doing anyone harm. My daughter was brought up a Catholic. And then I went back to the Church. When my second husband died, I went back. . . .

15   I went back to Ireland three years ago, for the first time. I went down to County Wicklow, where the old homestead was. That was a sad entrance for me. I found it very severe to go in there. That's where my mother died. My brother is still living there. I felt sorry to see my brother on the farm. I thought it was severe, cold, hard work. It was not an easy life. They don't feel that same way, but I was writing a letter to my niece the other day, and I was saying, "I'm so glad because one of my brother's children is going on to be accepted in Dublin for some kind of a good position." I said to her, "I'm so happy, because I feel the farm is so severe." I don't know why.

ಹ

Discussion Questions

1.   Why, as a child, had O'Hara wanted to come to the United States? What eventually led to her being here?
2.   Describe the conditions of O'Hara's life in Ireland and the nature of her work in Boston.
3.   Why did O'Hara claim (paragraph 4) that she never wanted her daughter to be as close to her as she had been to her mother?
4.   For what reasons did O'Hara refuse her father's request that she return to Ireland?
5.   What caused complications in O'Hara's relationship to the Catholic Church? How was the problem eventually resolved?
6.   Describe O'Hara's feelings upon her return visit to Ireland.

Writing Topics

1.   Assume that you are O'Hara and that you have done what your father wished—returned to Ireland and married the man your father has chosen. Ten years after the wedding, you decide to write to a friend in Boston to describe what has happened in your life since the marriage. Write the letter that you believe O'Hara might have written.
2.   Many people have had the experience of leaving a familiar place (e.g., a house, a school, a neighborhood, a town) and of revisiting it years later. If you have had this experience, describe in an essay the place as you originally knew it, including your feelings toward it. Then tell how it appeared to you upon your return and how you felt about any changes that had occurred.

*"Then the door opened, and there was Mother,
all strangely dressed in black. . . ."*

WHERE IS MY EVERYTHING?

Elizabeth B. Cowles

Born in Boston, Massachusetts in 1903, Elizabeth B. Cowles, the mother of two daughters, now lives in Santa Barbara, California. She reports that writing has been her interest since she was fifteen and that her instructors in adult education courses and in extension courses offered by the University of California have encouraged that interest. "Where Is My Everything?" appears in *Legacies* (1993), edited by Maury Leibovitz and Linda Solomon.

1   I was the little nine-year-old in a long summer nightie standing at the upper windows of my grandmother's old Victorian house. I was watching a small group of my mother's friends walk up Grandmother's street. What were they doing here in Stillwater so early in the morning? They belonged in Winona, where we lived, in the rectory next to the church.

2   I thought of my father, who was across the ocean visiting old friends in London. It frightened me that he was so far away. *He* would know why these people were here.

3   I turned from the window and went down the hall to my mother's room. She was asleep. I tugged at her arm. "Mother," I asked anxiously, "what are those people from Winona doing here?" She was instantly awake. Flinging off her covers, she stood listening to the low voices on the porch below, the voices of her friends, who were ringing the bell hesitantly.

4   "I'll let them in," I said, and dashed down the stairway, happy to see them. But they did not speak to me or even smile as they crowded inside. Aunt Jennie started up the stairs to Mother's room, and I followed closely. Mother was just standing there. I heard Aunt Jennie say, "Eva, there's been an . . . an accident. Edward . . ." I watched my mother sink slowly to the floor.

5   Frightened, I ran into my older brothers' room, shaking them awake. "Father's had an accident!" I cried. I sat on their bed. Alice, twelve, joined us. We all talked of accidents—broken arms, broken legs. It might take Father weeks to return by boat, but by then he'd be all right. My brothers pushed me out so they could get dressed, and I went back to question Mother. But now

she would not let me in. When I pulled on the door, Aunt Jennie opened it a peep. "Run along," she whispered. "You mustn't disturb your mother!"

6   Quickly I dressed and went downstairs. Everything was confusing. I heard whispered words. "So sudden . . . heart . . . dead." The words infuriated me. They couldn't be talking about my father. *He'd* had an *accident!* In the kitchen I stared at Annie, our cook, who had come with us from Winona. Her face was red and blotched with tears. She raised mournful blue eyes to me. "The poor dear," she said softly. "Right in the middle of his sermon he was . . . he just slipped away to God." Who was she talking about? Angrily I grabbed a raisin muffin from the oven pan. Annie did not snap at me to "put it back!"

7   I wandered through rooms. What was the matter with everyone? No one was explaining about the accident. Upstairs, in my little sisters' room, someone was hastily packing their clothes. Why? Then there was a taxi at the door taking the two little ones and Aunt Jennie away. Why didn't Aunt Jennie take me too?

8   Alice was lying on the big double bed where she and I slept, her face in the pillow, crying in great gulps. Pressing against the bed, I whispered, "Alice, did Father break his arm? Was it his leg? What happened to him?"

9   "He's dead," she sobbed.

10   "Alice! You're lying! I heard Aunt Jennie tell Mother he'd had an *accident!*"

11   There was no answer.

12   I remember sitting on the top step of the stairway. I could hear muffled voices in Mother's room. Then the door opened, and there was Mother, all strangely dressed in black, a short black veil over her face. As she passed me, starting down the steps, I clung to her long black skirt, crying, "Mother . . . where are you going?" Someone released the material from my tight fingers. From the stairs I saw the front door open. I saw another taxi, saw friends help Mother in, and then they were gone.

13   The house was so quiet. Were they all going to go and leave me? I did not want to stay here alone with my grandmother.

14   It was many weeks before I got back to Winona, and then I wasn't allowed to go home or see my mother. I stayed with a maiden aunt two blocks from the rectory. I was told Mother was ill and I was not to disturb her. The rest of the children were scattered among friends. I didn't see them either.

15   One day Aunt Nellie came out on the front porch, where I was playing jacks. "I have to run over to the rectory for a few minutes," she said. "I'll be right back." When I begged to go with her, she hesitated, then said, "All right." Did she know I was beginning to be afraid to be alone anywhere?

16   We walked down the tree-shaded street. As we drew near, I could see that our big house was newly painted. "Father will like that," I thought happily as I hurried up our sidewalk. Aunt Nellie opened the front door and dashed down the hall to intercept a departing painter. I stood in the doorway frozen with terror.

17   Everything was gone! The large, empty rooms and halls glistened with fresh paint. The windows were curtainless, the waxed floors bare.

18   Where was my mother! Where did I live? Where was our *everything?*

19   Aunt Nellie returned, smiling, and took my hand. "Doesn't everything look nice and fresh?" she said. "The new minister and his family are moving in tomorrow."

20   For many days I pretended it wasn't true, but when we children were together again in a small, strange house, still tiptoeing around so we wouldn't disturb Mother, I knew that Father would never come back. . . . I would never see my father again.

❧

Discussion Questions

1. How old was Cowles and where was she when the selection begins? How did she learn of her father's "accident"?
2. Cite the people, factors, and misunderstandings that either shielded or prevented Cowles from comprehending that her father was dead. What events and conditions caused her to begin "to be afraid to be alone anywhere"?
3. What circumstances finally persuaded Cowles that her father "would never come back"?
4. Point out how Cowles's use of diction, length of sentences, and end punctuation marks help communicate her confusion as a child over her father's death.
5. Would "Where Is My Father?" be a more effective title for the selection? Explain.

Writing Topics

1. Like Cowles, most young children have difficulty understanding the reality of death. Describe in a brief essay the first time that death affected you personally. How old were you? Who or what had died, and under what circumstances? How did you respond emotionally to the event? How did others treat you? What lasting effects, if any, did the experience have upon you?
2. Develop an essay supporting one of the following thesis statements, using your own experience, wherever appropriate, to help bolster your stance:
   a. We should tell children the truth about any topic or event that directly affects their lives.
   b. We should not tell children the truth about some topics or events that directly affect their lives.

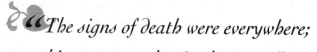

The signs of death were everywhere;
his name was hot in the street."

THE CORONER'S PHOTOGRAPHS

Brent Staples

Brent Staples (b. 1951) grew up in Chester, Pennsylvania, the oldest son among nine children. Scholarships enabled him to attend Widener College in Chester and graduate school at the University of Chicago, where he wrote his Ph.D. dissertation on the mathematics of decision making. Following graduation, he became a science writer for the *Chicago Sun-Times* before joining the staff of *The New York Times*, for which he is an editorial writer. "The Coroner's Photographs" appears in *Parallel Time: Growing Up in Black and White* (1994), a highly acclaimed memoir in which Staples explores the complexities of his past, including his relationship to his family and his journeys between the worlds of black and white people.

1 My brother's body lies dead and naked on a stainless steel slab. At his head stands a tall arched spigot that, with tap handles mimicking wings, easily suggests a swan in mourning. His head is squarish and overlarge. (This, when he was a toddler, made him seem top-heavy and unsteady on his feet.) His widow's peak is common among the men in my family, though this one is more dramatic than most. An inverted pyramid, it begins high above the temples and falls steeply to an apex in the boxy forehead, over the heart-shaped face. A triangle into a box over a heart. His eyes (closed here) were big and dark and glittery; they drew you into his sadness when he cried. The lips are ajar as always, but the picture is taken from such an angle that it misses a crucial detail: the left front tooth tucked partly beyond the right one. I need this detail to see my brother full. I paint it in from memory.

2 A horrendous wound runs the length of the abdomen, from the sternum all the way to the pubic mound. The wound resembles a mouth whose lips are pouting and bloody. Massive staplelike clamps are gouged into these lips at regular intervals along the abdomen. This is a surgeon's incision. The surgeon was presented with a patient shot six times with a large-caliber handgun. Sensing the carnage that lay within, he achieved the largest possible opening and

worked frantically trying to save my brother's life. He tied off shattered vessels, resectioned the small intestine, repaired a bullet track on the liver, then backed out. The closing would have required two pairs of hands. An assistant would have gripped the two sides of the wound and drawn them together while a second person put in the clamps. The pulling together has made my brother's skin into a corset that crushes in on the abdomen from all sides. The pelvic bones jut up through the skin. The back is abnormally arched from the tension. The wound strains at the clamps, threatening to rip itself open. The surgeon worked all night and emerged from surgery gaunt, his greens darkened with sweat. "I tied off everything I could," he said, and then he wept at the savagery and the waste.

3   This is the body of Blake Melvin Staples, the seventh of my family's nine children, the third of my four brothers, born ten years after me. I know his contours well. I bathed and diapered him when he was a baby and studied his features as he grew. He is the smallest of the brothers, but is built in the same manner: short torso but long arms and legs; a more than ample behind set high on the back; knocking knees; big feet that tend to flat. The second toe is also a signature. It curls softly in an extended arc and rises above the others in a way that's unique to us. His feelings are mine as well. Cold: The sensation moves from my eyes to my shoulder blades to my bare ass as I feel him naked on the steel. I envision the reflex that would run through his body, hear the sharp breath he would draw when the steel met his skin. Below the familiar feet a drain awaits the blood that will flow from this autopsy.

4   The medical examiner took this picture and several others on February 13, 1984, at 9:45 a.m. The camera's flash is visible everywhere: on the pale-green tiles of the surrounding walls, on the gleaming neck of the spigot, on the stainless steel of the slab, on the bloody lips of the wound.

5   The coroner's report begins with a terse narrative summary: "The deceased, twenty-two-year-old Negro male, was allegedly shot by another person on the premises of a night club as a result of a 'long standing quarrel.' He sustained multiple gunshot wounds of the abdomen and legs and expired during surgery."

6   Blake was a drug dealer; he was known for carrying guns and for using them. His killer, Mark McGeorge, was a former customer and cocaine addict. At the trial Mark's lawyer described the shooting as a gunfight in which Blake was beaten to the draw. This was doubtful. Blake was shot six times: three times in the back. No weapon was found on or near his body. Blake's gunbearer testified that my brother was unarmed when Mark ambushed and gunned him down. But a gunbearer is not a plausible witness. A drug dealer known for shooting a rival in plain public view gets no sympathy from a jury. The jury turned back the prosecution's request for a conviction of murder in the first degree. Mark

was found guilty of second-degree murder and sentenced to seven years in jail. Five years for the murder. Two years for using the gun.

7   Blake is said to have cried out for his life as he lay on the ground. "Please don't shoot me no more. I don't want to die." *"Please don't shoot me no more. I don't want to die."* His voice had a touch of that dullness one hears from the deaf, a result of ear infections he suffered as a child. The ear openings had narrowed to the size of pinholes. He tilted his head woefully from side to side trying to pour out the pain. His vowels were locked high in his throat, behind his nose. This voice kept him a baby to me. This is the voice in which he would have pleaded for his life.

8   The coroner dissects the body, organ by organ:

HEART: 300 grams. No valve or chamber lesions. Coronary arteries show no pathologic changes.

LUNGS: 900 grams combined. Moderate congestion. Tracheobronchial and arterial systems are not remarkable.

LIVER: 1950 grams. There is a sutured bullet track at the interlobar sulcus and anterior portion of the right hepatic lobe. There has been moderate subcapsular and intraparenchymal hemorrhage.

SPLEEN: 150 grams. No pathologic changes.

KIDNEYS: 300 grams combined. No pathologic changes.

ADRENALS: No pathologic changes.

PANCREAS: No pathologic changes.

GI TRACT: The stomach is empty. Portions of the small bowel have been resected, along with portions of the omentum. The bowel surface is dusky reddish-brown, but does not appear gangrenous.

URINARY BLADDER: Empty.

NECK ORGANS: Intact. No airway obstructions.

BRAIN: 1490 grams. Sagittal and serial coronal sections show no discrete lesions or evidence of injury.

SKULL: Intact.

VERTEBRAE: Intact.

RIBS: Intact.

PELVIS: There is a chip fracture of the left pubic ramus, and there is also fracturing of the right pubic ramus. There is extensive fracturing of the left femur, and there is a through-and-through bullet wound of the right femur just below the hip joint.

9   The coroner describes the wounds in detail. The surgical incision and its grisly clamps are dismissed in a single sentence. The six bullet holes receive one full paragraph each. The coroner records the angle that each bullet traveled through the body, the organs it passed through along the way, and where it finally came to rest. With all this to occupy him, the coroner fails to note the scar on Blake's left hand. The scar lies in the webbing between the thumb and index finger and is the result of a gun accident. A shotgun recoiled when Blake fired it and drove the hammer deep into the web, opening a wound that took several stitches to close.

10   I saw the wound when it was fresh, six weeks before Blake was murdered. I was visiting Roanoke from Chicago, where I then lived. I sought Blake out to tell him that it was time to get out of the business and leave Roanoke. The signs of death were everywhere; his name was hot in the street. Blake and I were making small talk when we slapped each other five. Blake clutched his hand at the wrist and cried out in pain. Then he showed me the stitches. This ended the small talk. I told him that he was in danger of being killed if he didn't leave town.

11   Staples men have been monolinguists for generations. We love our own voices too much. Blake responded to my alarm by telling me stories. He told me about the awesome power of the shotgun that had injured him. He told me about making asses of the police when they raided his apartment looking for drugs. The door of his apartment was steel, he said; they'd sent for a tow truck to pull it from its frame. Inside they found him twiddling his thumbs in the bathroom. He'd flushed the cocaine down the toilet. The night he told me these stories was the last time I saw him alive.

12   Six weeks later my brother Bruce called me with the news. "Brent, Blake is dead," he said. "Some guy pulled up in a car and emptied out on him with a magnum. Blake is dead." I told myself to feel nothing. I had already mourned Blake and buried him and was determined not to suffer his death a second time. I skipped the funeral and avoided Roanoke for the next three years. The next time I visited my family I went to see the Roanoke Commonwealth Attorney and questioned him about the case. He was polite but impatient. For him, everything about the killing had been said. This, after all, had been an ordinary death.

13   I asked to see the files. A secretary brought a manila pouch and handed it to the Commonwealth Attorney, who handed it to me and excused himself from the room. The pouch contained a summary of the trial, the medical examiner's report, and a separate inner pouch wrapped in twine and shaped like photographs. I opened the pouch; there was Blake dead and on the slab, photographed from several angles. The floor gave way, and I fell down and down for miles.

❊   ❊   ❊

14   As a child I was never where I was. Part of me raced ahead looking for a foothold in the future. Part of me was somewhere behind rushing to catch up. At thirteen I was obsessed with the idea that moments I'd lived were slipping away and becoming lost to me one by one. I would seize onto something I'd just seen or thought and ask myself if I'd remember that thing five minutes, five hours, or five days from now. The answer was always no.

15   Things weren't hanging together. Even dramatic things floated briefly in memory, then drifted away. Perhaps I had lost a whole lifetime this way. Perhaps my family wasn't my family at all but a counterfeit group with whom I'd fallen in after forgetting who I was. Thoughts like this overran my obsessions with flying and fire and knives.

16   The fear of losing memories struck keenly when I was happy. An example of this was the day I discovered a trail of crumpled dollar bills on the sidewalk in front of my house. The first bill was a few feet from the front step; the second a few feet behind that one; the third—a five!—lay in the gutter at the corner. There was no one to contest me for the money. It was Sunday morning and the streets were blessedly vacant. The bills had doubtless been dropped by a drunk who'd come reeling out of the speakeasy a few doors away. The money meant games and games of pinball and endless Coca-Colas. It was at rapturous heights like these that I asked myself how long I'd remember this. Not the money itself, but the joy of finding it. The answer was: not long. Giddiness faded. Even a fist full of dollars couldn't sustain it.

17   Writers have said that children live in an endless present with little thought for what has passed or what will be. Mine was a different childhood. I paid endless dues for sorrows that were yet to come. I was also morbidly vigilant about the past. Not the past of a year ago or even the previous day, but the past of the last few seconds. I handled memories over and over again, hoping to give them permanence.

18   This vigilance came on me in seizures that could strike me anywhere: while I lay in the grass making out figures in the clouds, as I pushed a shopping cart down the supermarket aisles, and especially while I stood at the crosswalk waiting for the light to change. I clung to every detail of the hot rod that had just roared by: the glint of the sun flowing over its body, the thunder of the engine, the twin puffs of smoke from its dual exhausts. I included the backdrop, too: the steepled church across the street, the sign out front that described the

sermon and gave the minister's name; the wrought-iron fence around them. This took concentration; it excluded everything except drawing breath. The sign changed from DON'T WALK to WALK to DON'T WALK again. Someone called out "Hey, you, wake up!" and I did. To them I was a silly boy asleep at the crosswalk. For me this was serious business: I had saved a part of my life that would otherwise have been lost.

❖   ❖   ❖

19   I suspected mental illness. My eighth-grade science teacher relieved me of this burden with a movie about the physics of time. The movie was a cartoon. It began with a rocket sitting on the launch pad, ready for takeoff. At the launch site were a perky set of twins, Bill and Bob, accompanied by cheerleaders and a roaring crowd. The twins were fresh from high school, sporting identical pompadours and identical varsity sweaters. Bill climbed into the rocket and blasted off into space at the speed of light. Bob stayed behind with the crowd and waved. What the narrator said next made me sit up and take notice. He said that time passed more slowly for the traveling twin than for the one who stayed at home. Light speed slowed the clock and the beating of the heart. Bill returned from space as perky and erect as the day he left. His brother, Bob, was old and withered and confined to a wheelchair.

20   The movie was a saving bolt from the blue. I wasn't mentally ill. In fact, I'd gotten it exactly right: Time was sneaky and elastic, not at all what it was cracked up to be. That science had studied the problem brought me an enormous sense of relief.

21   This fixation had come from the way my family lived. We moved all the time. We went on and on like bedouins with couches, tables, and mattresses jumbled in the backs of pickup trucks. We moved as the family grew. We moved when my parents were separated and again when they reconciled. We moved when we fell behind in the rent. We moved when the sheriffs put our furniture on the sidewalk. We moved after the family had pounded a house to pieces. We'd had seven different addresses by the time I reached the eighth grade. That's why I was never where I was. The move was out there lurking, just off the mental shore. Best to be ready when it came.

22   My mother went house hunting when we were about to be evicted. The places were chosen swiftly, and we moved without preparation. The household dissolved into a river of stuff and children that flowed through the door in spasms, keyed to the coming and going of the truck.

23   The chaos of these nights exhausted even the deepest goodwill. The friends and relatives who helped us drove up in their trucks to find us dashing through the house, hurling things into boxes. First they grumbled under their breaths. Then they withdrew into sullen reveries. We raced to move the heavy things before these helpers quit. This meant triage with the furniture, abandoning bedsteads and couches where they stood. If the new house was close enough,

we carried the small things by hand. We became a caravan of children, with lamps and end tables in hand, strung out like bedouins down the street.

24   The chaos swallowed things that would never be seen again. Family portraits. Volumes from the set of encyclopedias. Legal documents of every sort, including birth certificates, leaving some of us uncertain of when we were born.

25   Each new house was a change of skin. New creaking in the floors, new traffic noises, new voices passing beneath the windows. Some sidewalks were cement and some were brick. On cement, high heels clicked solidly by like the ticking of a clock. Brick sidewalks were ancient, their surfaces powdery and uneven. When high heels slipped in the powder, the sound was like the wrong-way screech of the chalk on a blackboard. *Skwitch, skwatch, skwawtch* was a woman walking.

26   In bed, I was shocked awake by groaning timbers or by voices that seemed to be in the room but were actually passing on the street below. The room would seem foreign at first. The shafts of moonlight would be wrong, as though the windows had suddenly changed walls. Then I would notice Brian and Bruce sleeping heavily on either side of me, and catch sight of Blake and Brad in the daybed across the room. I returned to sleep but woke up several times before dawn. Each time my brothers lay differently twisted in sheets, a new frieze cut from the dance of sleep.

27   At college I woke up alone in a room, for the first time that I could remember. I never slept with my brothers again. Months and then years went by without my even seeing them. When we met, I was often stunned by changes in them that seemed to have come overnight and were now irrevocable. What had been set in motion I was powerless to undo.

28   The moving left its mark. Grown and out on my own, I was phobically wary of possessions, of anything that would trouble me when it was time to go. My first apartment was an enormous five-room flat, with a dining room, a kitchen, and a walk-in pantry big enough to sleep one. I lived in that flat for six years with the walls barren of pictures and without a table of any kind. I ate from the seats of folding chairs or from beer crates while sitting on the floor. The move may have been years away, but when it came, couches and tables and bookshelves would be what they'd always been — encumbrances that had to be hoisted and dragged away. Time and time again I lived five years at a stretch without unpacking. The need to be poised for flight governed matters trivial and profound. I avoided magazine subscriptions; in them was the presumption that I'd stay put for an entire year. I disposed of friends and lovers without a thought.

29   I envisioned Blake's murder a year and a half before it happened. The image came from a letter he wrote me just after he'd ambushed Mark at a disco. Blake was on the run and in need of money. He denied having done the shooting and claimed that the police had fingered him for no reason at all. This was

an obvious lie. I read the letter as an admission of guilt and understood that revenge was on the way. The first image of Blake dead on the ground came to me on its own. Later I summoned it up deliberately, trying to build a tolerance to the idea. There is no way to say this without its sounding callous and premeditated. In truth it was an act of reflex, no more thought out than pulling back from fire.

30   When Blake turned twenty-two years old he had three months to live. He and Mark were tearing at each other like warring dogs bound by the same leash. Blake reached for his pistol whenever Mark came into view. This gesture was often a bluff. It had to be. The police knew Blake as a drug dealer and shooter. He couldn't have carried a gun everywhere. Downtown, near the police station or the courthouse, he could have been stopped and frisked at any time. It was at these naked times that he would have reached for his gun with the most conviction.

31   As Blake's fear increased, his guns got bigger and more numerous. No longer content with pistols, he acquired the double-barreled shotgun and the gunbearer who carried it. I envision him wandering through the streets of Roanoke, thrusting a trembling hand into his gunbearer's bag. All around him are the means of escape, the buses, the trains, and planes that could take him anywhere. I whisper, "Leave this place." He never does. He never even hears me.

❧

Discussion Questions

1. Describe briefly Blake's physical and emotional characteristics. How and why was he slain?
2. How did Staples respond to news of his brother's death? What accounted for his behavior?
3. Would you consider the relationship between Staples and his brother to have been emotionally close? Explain.
4. Cite support that Staples offers for his assertion, "Mine was a different childhood" (paragraph 17). How does Staples account for his peculiar behavior as a youngster? What event convinced him that he wasn't mentally ill?
5. How does Staples's behavior as an adult reveal that he was strongly influenced by childhood experiences? Might Blake's failure to heed his brother's advice have grown out of childhood experiences as well?
6. In paragraph 3, Staples says of his brother, "His feelings are mine as well. Cold:. . ." Is this statement supported by Staples's style of writing in "The Coroner's Photographs"? Explain.

Writing Topics

1. Recount in an essay a childhood experience that has influenced your behavior as an adult. Provide details about the experience, the context in which it occurred, how you responded at the time, and how the event affects your behavior today.

2. In an essay, describe in what ways you considered yourself as a child to be different from other children. How did these assumed differences affect you emotionally? Are you still affected by them? If so, in what ways? If not, how did you come to accept them?

🍃 *"When you start talking about the patients,*

that's where the hurt begins."

DEALING WITH VIETNAM

Mary Stout

(as told to Kathryn Marshall)

Mary Stout was born in 1944 in Columbus, Ohio, where she grew up and where she enlisted in the Army in 1964, during her last year at the Mount Carmel School of Nursing. After volunteering for Vietnam in 1966, Stout was first assigned to the Second Surgical Hospital in An Khe, a hospital later moved to Chu Lai. In 1977, she received a B.A. in Social Welfare from Ohio Dominican College in Columbus and from 1987 to l991 was president of the Vietnam Veterans of America. Married to Carl Stout, she is the mother of three grown daughters and works as a program analyst for the Department of Veterans Affairs in Washington, D.C. Kathryn Marshall was born in Memphis, Tennessee, in 1951. After studying ballet in New York City, she decided at age seventeen to become a writer. A graduate of the University of Texas at Austin (B.A., 1973) and the University of California, Irvine (M.F.A., 1975), Marshall has authored two novels, *My Sister Gone* (1977) and *Desert Places* (1977), and has contributed numerous articles to magazines. During her school years, she became interested in the role women were playing in the Vietnam War, an interest that eventually led to *In the Combat Zone* (1987), her collection of the personal recollections of twenty women who had served in Vietnam during battle.

1   My father wasn't too hot about me joining the Army. What finally brought him around was I offered to have the nurse recruiter come talk to him. I thought that if anyone could convince my father, she could. Because the first thing that struck me when she came to talk to our class was that she was a perfect lady.

2   Which is what I was brought up to be. You know, we had the nuns. When I was in high school we even had to curtsy to them. So being a lady was, you know, very serious. And I think seeing the nurse recruiter really changed my father's idea.

3 It was 1964 when I signed up and 1965 when I graduated. At that time, there wasn't really much news about Vietnam. I didn't know what was going on there. And I had no idea that Vietnam was going to be a major part of my life.

4 In basic training I realized that everyone was a little bit bitten by the war bug. We spent a few days in a field-type hospital with mock casualties and all that kind of thing. You started to get the idea that this was the kind of nursing you were supposed to be doing. So a lot of people volunteered right out of basic training.

5 With me, what happened was that at Fort Ord, my first duty assignment, I met Carl Stout, who is my husband now. I knew we were going to get married, so when he got orders to go to Vietnam, I volunteered to go. I thought it would be important for us, for our life together, that I had that experience, too. It just seemed like Vietnam was going to be a real important experience in his life, and I didn't want to be cut off from it. I remember when my orders came through and I told my parents, my father asked me point-blank if I had volunteered.

6 Carl didn't get to Vietnam until the middle of December because he had to go to jungle school in Panama. I got there the first of November. The Second Surgical was in An Khe then, which is up in the highlands. An Khe was the base camp of the First Cav., but they were at that time pulling away. The area was pretty secure and there wasn't a lot of action there. So we were working eight-hour days, five days a week, and doing a lot of surgery on civilians. Then, in May, the hospital was moved to Chu Lai.

7 The Army was defending Chu Lai then because they were moving the Marines north, more toward the DMZ. Chu Lai was getting hot about the time we got there. Almost immediately we started twelve-hour days, six days a week. At first I was on the post-op wards, but after two or three weeks I went to the chief nurse and said I really wanted to work in intensive care. I guess I just felt I was ready to take on that challenge.

8 I learned pretty fast that you had to separate yourself emotionally from your patients in intensive care. Still, you remember particular people. Like this one guy who had been in an APC [armored personnel carrier] and they hit a mine and the gasoline exploded. He was the only one who came out of it alive. But he had terrible burns. We just expected him to die, waited for him to die. He was right across from my desk—we always kept the worst ones near the nurses' desk—and just looking at him I felt so helpless. I knew we couldn't evac him because he'd go into shock, and I knew I couldn't talk to him because there was nothing I could say. And he was conscious. I felt so guilty. Even after I got back I felt guilty about that guy.

9 I never could face death. Whenever we had patients die, I'd have to leave the ward or at least make sure I was at the other end when they came with the body bags. Because if I didn't have to look at the body bag, it seemed that person wasn't really dead. I just never could deal with the death part of it. And I'm not sure, you know, how I reconciled that.

10   Like I said, I tried to separate myself emotionally. But I remember faces; I even remember names. There was one guy named Johnny Darling—I remember him because he was in Carl's unit. A lot of times Carl's unit was in the Chu Lai area. Whenever I was off duty and the choppers would come in, I'd go straight to the emergency room and see what unit they were. I always had this fear that one day Carl would come in. I mean, I had a lot of confidence that he would take care of himself and that everything would be all right. But still, I always had to go and make sure he wasn't there.

11   Johnny Darling had stepped on a mine and lost both of his feet. The night he came in I walked over and started asking the units if anything had happened to Carl's company. And I remember this big black sergeant saying, "Oh, you're Lieutenant Reis. Don't worry about Lieutenant Stout. We're taking real good care of him." But, you know, I was always scared that something would happen to Carl.

12   We had a lot of people come in with missing arms, legs, hands: you name it, it was gone. We had one sergeant—I think he lost both legs at the hip, plus a hand and an arm. And he was blind, had a head injury and lots of internal injuries. I guess it was a mine of some kind—that's the kind of damage a mine does. That guy we did surgery on—even with all those things wrong, he was still alive. It was absolutely amazing.

13   So I think we did wonderful, wonderful work. I can't even imagine anything else I could have done where it would have felt more satisfying. In Vietnam I worked harder than I ever have, and I did more good. Thinking back, it sometimes amazes me.

14   There was one time, though, that I just got so overwhelmed I thought I couldn't take it anymore. It all had to do with this one patient named Steve.

15   Steve had a lot of internal injuries, but he had been through surgery and was doing really well—I didn't separate myself from him because I didn't think he was going to die. Also, I liked talking to him. He was fun to be around. I don't remember what we found in common now, but he was just one of those people I felt especially close to. Anyway, I came to work at seven o'clock one night and his breathing was pretty bad. I talked to the nurse who was on duty, asked her what the doctor had said. Now Steve's particular doctor was the only one we didn't have much faith in—maybe that's one of the reasons I got so close to Steve, because I was worried about his surgery. The corpsmen called this doctor the Butcher. And believe me, he deserved that name.

16   So the other nurse said the Butcher had been in to see Steve and had said he was just fine. Said we were supposed to just suction him—Steve had, among other things, a chest full of real rusty phlegm. So we keep suctioning him and suctioning him and he isn't totally feeling well, so I call the Butcher, who says he's just been up to see him and asks if his breathing has changed since I came on. I tell him no, it's really about the same but it's not too good. And then the head of the hospital walks onto the ward.

17   The head of the hospital—we were always real paranoid about him coming on the ward, because every time he came, someone went into cardiac arrest. I mean, this wasn't a joke. This was a kind of frightening thing. Anyway, he came on the ward and walked up to Steve and said something to me about his breathing. And Steve was talking to this doctor. And all of a sudden this doctor, the head of the hospital, says, "He's going into cardiac arrest." And he died, just like that.

18   We were on him right away—suctioning, bagging him. We put in a trachea tube, did everything we could, but we couldn't bring Steve back. And so finally the doctor turned to me and said, "This is all your fault. He should have had a trach, you should have known that—" Well, I had never had to make a decision about someone having a trach. That was one of the things we relied on the doctors for.

19   They came to take Steve off, like they did everyone else. I left the ward. But I had to work through the rest of the night. All I know is, I did it in a kind of fog. Because when I was walking off the ward before they brought the body bag, I was saying to myself, "Never again will I become close to anybody."

20   At seven o'clock the next morning I went straight to my room. I had a bottle of Black Label that I had bought to take to Carl. So I sit there contemplating it, saying, "If you drink that whole bottle right now, you'll probably die." And just then Carl's battery commander, who I had never met, knocks on the door. "I just stopped by," he says, "to introduce myself and tell you that anytime you want to come to the battery, we would love to have you." I asked him when he was going back, and he was going back right that minute. So I grabbed my steel pot and left. I didn't sign out or anything; I just got in that helicopter and went to spend the day with Carl.

21   When I got back that night, I went down to the club. That was something I did real often. At night, when I couldn't sleep, I'd go and throw down a couple of boilermakers. Anyhow, that night I went down and was sitting at the bar—just sitting there by myself, not talking to anybody—when the hospital commander comes up and sits down next to me. "Well," he says, "I'm glad you can be here at the club having a good time when you just killed somebody." And I get up and walk fast out the door.

22   The officers' club sat up on a cliff. There was a road that went down to the beach. I walked down the road and walked into the ocean, just kept on walking out. And then somebody—to this day I do not know who, or where he came from, or how he saw me—grabbed hold of me, picked me up, and carried me back to the beach. He just sat there and held me. God knows how long I cried. I just cried and cried and told him about Steve. I don't remember this person saying anything except "It's going to be OK."

23   For a long time he held me. Then he walked me back up the hill. And, you know, I don't think I even looked at him; I don't think I could even have seen him in the dark through all my tears. But I do believe it wasn't anybody that I knew.

24 Steve is something that never left me.

25 Because once I got back from Vietnam, I could not take criticism at all. Carl would come home and say something about the house, or the meal wasn't right, or just everyday kinds of little things —not that I didn't take the criticism, but it was like a lance. It was very, very painful. And I would have this image of Steve.

26 I would, well, not so much see Steve as feel him. Feel his actual physical presence. It was like Steve was there and things were the way they were when he died. It was the same feeling, the same feeling l had when he died —a feeling of helplessness and absolute uselessness. I'd think, "You didn't do this right, you didn't do that right, you didn't do right for Steve." So I was living with these terrible, terrible feelings of guilt. In my mind, I was seeing Steve all the time.

27 It wasn't just Steve I couldn't put into any perspective. It was Vietnam, the whole experience. When Carl and I first got home, nobody asked about Vietnam. Or if they asked, they asked the political kinds of questions. Of course, this was sixty-seven and the antiwar protests were starting and everything was becoming negative about Vietnam.

28 I got out of the Army when Carl and I got married. The Army wasn't too good about assigning people together then, so it seemed like the best thing. It was strange for me, though. There were times when I felt very insignificant. Like, for the first couple of years after Carl and I got back, we would go to parties and the guys would tell war stories. Once, in Long Beach, the Petroleum Club had a big party for Vietnam veterans, but they were only honoring the men. Carl always told people, at parties and things, that I was a Vietnam veteran, too. And they would say, "Oh, you are?" And I'd say, "Yes." And that would be the end of it.

29 About three years after I got back I became aware that something was going on with me. Carl and I were in Wichita, Kansas, then. He was going to school at Wichita State. I was feeling very dead, because I wasn't doing anything with my mind except taking care of babies, so I decided to go to school, too. But I was feeling lots of pressure and lots of stress and seeing Steve all the time, and after a while it got to the point where I was almost immobilized.

30 I was taking this psychology course and really liked the instructor. One day I told him about how I couldn't take criticism —Carl was, you know, getting upset about having to take care of the kids when I was trying to study or go to school. So I told the instructor this, and I told him about Steve. Steve was with me all the time then; everything was the way it was when he died.

31 So, with this instructor's help, I started to deal with the guilt. In lots of ways, I got over it. But the memories are still there —the memories of the guilt and pain. And the memory of the loss. Everybody who was in Vietnam —particularly the nurses, but the guys, too, and even people who didn't serve —has one name on the memorial that epitomizes the tragedy of Vietnam. And for me that name is Steve. I can't find his name, and I can't remember his last name.

For a while there I struggled real hard to remember it. But the most important thing is that Steve would never have wanted me to feel guilty about his death.

32   Three or four years ago Carl went to Korea and I was on my own for the first time. That was when I really started dealing with all my Vietnam stuff, because suddenly I had all the responsibility. I was always wondering if I was doing the right thing, if Carl would approve, if he would be angry — there was a lot of pressure and a lot of responsibility that I had never faced by myself before. That's when Vietnam was on my mind constantly. I'd be trying to concentrate on something, and suddenly I was thinking about Vietnam. So I decided to see if I could get in contact with some other veterans.

33   The first time I ever met another Army nurse was through the VVA. The chapter called me up and said this woman was coming down to the office and would I come talk to her. Well, I didn't want to talk to this woman — I was doing fine talking to the guys. Because my feeling was that I didn't want someone to open up all those places. I didn't have to deal with my things with the guys. They don't understand a woman's feelings. They don't understand about losing patients, about taking care of people and then having to see them die — the medics, maybe, and the corpsmen. But talking to another nurse, I knew, was going to open up some things. So I hemmed and hawed and finally went down and met her.

34   Well, we kind of skirted around. We talked about the rats, you know, and about the living conditions. But we weren't really, either of us, talking about the patients. When you start talking about the patients, that's where the hurt begins.

35   So I was driving her home. And I remember her saying something about a patient, mentioning someone's name. And I said, "Who was that?" Then she really opened up and I pulled the car to the side of the road. "My God," I said, "you've got one, too. The name of my patient was Steve." And we sat for a long time and talked.

36   That's how I started putting a lot of pieces together. I'd remember an incident and what hospital it happened at, whether we were in An Khe or Chu Lai, what the weather was like. For a while it seemed like I wanted to remember every minute, because I had spent so much time blocking all the memories out. Now I'm real content knowing the memories are coming back and that, when they come, I'm able to deal with them.

37   I don't want there to be another Vietnam.

38   Still, if my kids want to go into the military, I'll encourage them. Because I think the military is a good opportunity, especially for women. It's one of the few places women are treated equally. And if my kids want to volunteer to go to a war, I'll encourage them to do that. But it better be a war. I don't want any of these conflicts.

39   That was the problem with Vietnam — we didn't declare war, so we didn't get the country behind it. I don't know, if we'd declared war, whether we could have won or not. But declaring war would have changed the whole perspective

of the country about the people who served there. Because the most damaging thing to us wasn't the war experience. It was our perception of that experience after we came home.

40   I have to tell you I was more frightened in this country after we came back than I ever was in Vietnam, even when we had mortar attacks and rockets were going off. Just before Carl and I were going to Wichita so he could go to Wichita State, we heard about a ROTC instructor in Syracuse whose house had been fire-bombed. I told Carl, "Grow your hair long, wear a moustache. Don't tell anyone you're in the military," because I was frightened of the anti-war protesters. I was frightened for my children.

41   It wasn't safe here. This was supposed to be home, and if you'd gone and served your country, it wasn't safe.

42   I believe the war was wrong, wrong from the concept of we'd been warned it was a war we shouldn't get into. High government officials made decisions against the best advice of the military. The military knew it was a war we were going to have a hard time winning, and the government just didn't listen.

43   I've always blamed the government. When I was over in Vietnam I thought we were right to do what we could to keep them from becoming a communist country. Now I think it was inevitable that Vietnam would go communist. And if we hadn't interfered, Vietnam would be in a lot better shape than it is.

44   But I still think service to your country is service of the highest order. I've never been ashamed of having volunteered.

❧

Discussion Questions

1. What sequence of events led to Stout's serving in Vietnam? Describe how her duties in Chu Lai differed from those in An Khe.
2. How did Stout usually deal with death? Why was the loss of Steve's life particularly painful for her?
3. Describe Stout's immediate and long-term emotional responses to Steve's death. How did an unknown man, a college instructor, and an Army nurse who had served in Vietnam help Stout deal with her guilt?
4. Explain the circumstances that motivated Stout to make each of the following statements: ". . . I think we did wonderful, wonderful work" (paragraph 11); "There were times when I felt very insignificant" (paragraph 26); ". . . I didn't want to talk to this woman—I was doing fine talking to the guys" (paragraph 31); ". . . I was more frightened in this country after we came back than I ever was in Vietnam . . ." (paragraph 38).
5. Point out characteristics of the style of this selection that indicate that it is an oral history rather than a formally written essay.

Writing Topics

1. If you, like Stout, have ever been led to feel guilty about something for which you were not responsible, describe the experience in a brief essay. Include details about your age at the time, the situation, the people involved, and both your immediate and long-range feelings about what occurred.

2. Choose one of the following thesis statements for development in an essay. Support your chosen statement with clear reasons and appropriate examples:
   a. Feelings of guilt do far more harm than good to individuals.
   b. Without guilt, evil would predominate in society.
   c. Feelings of guilt are appropriate in some situations but inappropriate in others.

Summary Writing Topics

1. Assume that you are a staff writer for a magazine investigating the deaths of young black males. Write an article comparing and contrasting the background and personality of Paul McClane ("A Death in the Family") to those of Blake Staples ("The Coroner's Photographs").

2. Assume that you are a free-lance reporter. Write an article on the life and death of Blake Staples ("The Coroner's Photographs") as it might be written for a tabloid newspaper, such as *The National Enquirer* or *Star*.

3. Assume that a classmate remarks to you that the selections by Gartner and Cowles are too simple for a college textbook. Respond to this criticism in an essay that defends the inclusion of the two selections in *The Perceptive* I. Using evidence from the selections, point out to your classmate qualities of "My Son, a Gentle Giant, Dies" and "Where Is My Everything?" that she or he may have overlooked.

*4. Critics of the mortuary business have alleged that burial in the United States is too expensive. Write an investigative report, intended for your local newspaper, on the costs of being buried in your community. Include in your report the costs for funeral arrangements for what would be regarded as a modest, an average, and an elaborate funeral. Based on what you have learned about burials in your community, conclude by indicating whether the allegations of critics of the mortuary business are justified.

*5. After completing relevant background reading, including "Dealing with Vietnam," write an essay in which you support with persuasive reasons one of the following thesis statements:
    a. During the Vietnam War, moving to Canada to avoid being drafted was morally justifiable.
    b. During the Vietnam War, moving to Canada to avoid being drafted was not morally justifiable.

*6. In an essay intended for classmates, present the issues involved in the present controversy over the issuance to and use of handguns by civilians. Conclude by revealing where you stand and why on these issues.

7. In an essay intended for classmates, support with sound reasoning and appropriate evidence from the selections one of the following thesis statements:
    a. Oral histories such as "No Desire to Go Back" and "Dealing with Vietnam" are more reliable and believable than are such written accounts as "Wandering" and " 'I Never Thought It Would Happen to Me.' "

    b. Oral histories such as "No Desire to Go Back" and "Dealing with Vietnam" are not more reliable and believable than are such written accounts as "Wandering" and " 'I Never Thought It Would Happen to Me.' "

8. Using evidence from selections in "Separations and Losses" and from your own experience, support in an essay the idea that separation from one's home, family, or nation can be just as psychologically painful as the loss of a loved one through death.

Cluster

Helpers and Shapers

Consider what you are now wearing. Think about what you have eaten during the last twenty-four hours. Reflect on the structure and furnishings of the place where you currently live. Recall the mode of transportation you use to get from your residence to class.

No one of us is entirely self-reliant, able to make all our own clothes, grow all our own food, construct and supply our own dwellings, build our own bikes or cars. If we do carpentry, chances are that we do not make our own hammers, saws, and nails; if we do plumbing, quite likely we do not build our own pipes and connectors; if we do gardening, we probably do not fashion our own hoses, rakes, and hoes. For our physical well-being, we depend upon the competencies of many different people, most of them strangers to us: farmers, grocers, mechanics, seamstresses, tailors, electricians, masons, carpenters, truck drivers, factory workers, doctors, nurses, dentists—the list could go on and on.

Now consider the person who you are. Think about your attitudes, tastes, talents, and ethics—core elements of your personhood. Had you lived in relative isolation since birth, you would not be today the person you sense yourself to be, even though a mirror might not be able to discriminate between a you reared in the wilderness and a you reared in society. Just as others, principally unknown to you, have been largely responsible for determining the state of your physical well-being, others, more familiar to you, have been largely responsible for determining the condition of your psychic health. Through exercising influence upon you, these latter individuals have contributed to the formation of your present intellectual, moral, and psychological traits.

The particular influence of another person upon you may have been short-lived, or it may have been enduring; it may have emanated from the love of a parent or friend or from the enmity of a rival; it may have been represented by the perceptive advice of a counselor or employer or by the barbed criticism of a teacher or guardian. Whatever the particular case, you have undoubtedly been molded in some way, for good or ill, by others.

What follows is a cluster of selections in which writers relate how others have affected their development and produced critical effects upon their lives. The "helpers" and "shapers" include a mother, a distant cousin, a slave owner, and a number of teachers, all of whom differ in temperament and approach toward their "students." Together, the selections should remind you of the influence that *he*, *she*, and *they* can have upon the composition of an **I**.

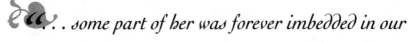

. . . some part of her was forever imbedded in our

psyches, and we were not the worst for it."

MY MOTHER, RACHEL WEST

Dorothy West

Dorothy West (b. 1907) was reared in an upper-middle class black family in Boston, where her father was a successful dealer of wholesale produce. Although an only child, West was surrounded by a household of relatives, including numerous cousins, all controlled by her mother. While attending the Columbia School of Journalism, West became the youngest member of the Harlem Renaissance, the group of writers that included Langston Hughes, Countee Cullen, Richard Wright, and Zora Neale Hurston. West published her first novel, *The Living Is Easy*, in 1948 and her second, *The Wedding*, in 1995, a year that also saw the publication of *The Richer, the Poorer*, a collection of her stories, sketches, and reminiscences. Between novels, West made her living working for the *Vineyard Gazette*, the weekly newspaper on Martha's Vineyard, Massachusetts, where she has made her home since the 1940s.

1   When my mother died, we who had sparred with her over the years of our growth and maturity said with relief, well, we won't have her intruding herself in our lives again. Our saying it may have been a kind of swaggering, or maybe we were in shock, trying to hide what was really inside us.

2   My mother had often made the declaration that she was never going to die. She knew what was here, she would say with a laugh, but she didn't know what was there. Heaven was a long way from home. She was staying right here.

3   So we just accepted it as fact that she would be the death of us instead. When her own death came first, we didn't know what to make of it. There was a thinness in the air. There was silence where there had been sound and fury. There was no longer that beautiful and compelling voice bending us to her will against our own.

4   The house that I grew up in was four-storied, but we were an extended family, continuously adding new members, and the perpetual joke was, if we lived in the Boston Museum, we'd still need one more room. Surrounded by all

these different personalities, each one wanting to be first among equals, I knew I wanted to be a writer. Living with them was like living inside a story.

5 My mother was the dominant figure by the force of her vitality, and by the indisputable fact that she had the right to rule the roof that my father provided. She was a beautiful woman, and there was that day when I was grown, eighteen or so, ready to go off on my own, sure that I knew everything, that I said to her, "Well, your beauty was certainly wasted on you. All you did with it was raise children and run your sisters' lives."

6 My mother had done what she felt she had to do, knowing the risks, knowing there would be no rewards, but determined to build a foundation for the generations unborn. She had gathered us together so that the weakness of one would be balanced by her strength, and the loneliness of another eased by her laughter, and someone else's fears tempered by her fierce bravado, and the children treated alike, no matter what their degree of lovability, and her eye riveting mine if I tried to draw a distinction between myself and them.

7 We who had been the children under her command, and then the adults, still subject to her meddling in our intimate affairs, were finally bereaved, free of the departed, and in a rush to divorce ourselves from any resemblance to her influence.

8 When one of us said something that Mother might have said, and an outraged chorus shouted, "You sound just like her," the speaker, stung with shame and close to tears, shouted back, "I do not!"

9 Then as time passed, whoever forgot to watch her language and echoed some sentiment culled from my mother responded to the catcalls with a cool, "So what?"

10 As time increased its pace, although there were diehards who would never relent, there were more of us shifting positions, examining our ambivalent feelings, wondering if the life force that had so overwhelmed our exercise of free will, and now no longer had to be reckoned with, was a greater loss than a relief.

11 When a newborn disciple recited my mother's sayings as if they were gospel, the chiding came from a scattered chorus of uninspired voices.

12 Then there was the day when someone said with wonder, "Have you noticed that those of us who sound just like her are the ones who laugh a lot, love children a lot, don't have any hangups about race or color, and never give up without trying?"

13 "Yes, I've noticed," one of us answered, with the rest of us adding softly, "Me, too."

14 I suppose that was the day and the hour of our acknowledgment that some part of her was forever imbedded in our psyches, and we were not the worst for it.

15 But I still cannot put my finger on the why of her. What had she wanted, this beautiful woman? Did she get it? I would look at her face when it was shut away, and I would long to offer her a penny for her thoughts. But I knew she

would laugh and say, "I was just thinking it's time to start dinner," or something equally far from her yearning heart.

16   I don't think she ever realized how often she made the remark, "Speech was given man to hide his thoughts." At such times I would say to myself, she will die with her secrets. I had guessed a few, but they had been only surface deep, easy to flush out. I know that the rest went with her on her flight to heaven.

ᶻ⋆

Discussion Questions

1. Describe the household in which West was reared and the responsibilities in it that her mother had assumed.
2. Why, in paragraph 3, does West comment about her mother, "When her own death came first, we didn't know what to make of it"?
3. Relate how those "ruled" by Mrs. West initially responded to her death and to the accusation, "You sound just like her." What realization did Mrs. West's charges eventually come to about those who sounded "just like" the author's mother?
4. Do you find West's comment and question in paragraph 15, "But I still cannot put my finger on the why of her. What had she wanted, this beautiful woman?" to be consistent with what she writes about her mother in paragraph 6? Explain.
5. West uses the words *beauty* and *beautiful* to describe her mother. What other nouns and adjectives does she use to depict her mother's appearance and personality? After reading the selection, do you feel you sufficiently know Mrs. West from the information provided? Explain.
6. Would you agree that Mrs. West was primarily a helper in, rather than a shaper of, her children's lives? Why or why not?

Writing Topics

1. West quotes her mother as having frequently said, "Speech was given man to hide his thoughts." In a short essay, describe an occasion when your words belied what you were truly thinking. Relate the circumstances, the people involved, the reasons you said what you did, and what it was you were actually thinking.
2. Assume that you are Mrs. West and that you keep a journal. Write an entry on the evening after your eighteen-year-old daughter had said to you, "Well, your beauty was certainly wasted on you. All you did with it was raise children and run your sisters' lives."

❧ *"For someone who claimed he didn't love to teach,*
he made a great deal of difference to a
great many students."

RAYMOND CARVER, MENTOR

Jay McInerney

Jay McInerney was born in 1955 in Hartford, Connecticut. Following his graduation from Williams College (B.A., 1976), he held various positions—editor for Time-Life, Inc., fact-checker for The New Yorker, teacher at Syracuse University—before becoming a full-time writer in 1983. McInerney is the author of Bright Lights, Big City (1984), Ransom (1985), Story of My Life (1988), and Brightness Falls (1992). McInerney, a former student of writer Raymond Carver at Syracuse University in the 1980s, claims that Carver had a major impact on his life, especially on his writing. By the time of his death from cancer, Raymond Carver (1938–1988) had established himself as a masterful and highly influential practitioner of the American short story. His stories, many of them centered on the lives of lonely and troubled members of the working class, appear most notably in the collections Will You Please Be Quiet, Please? (1976), What We Talk About When We Talk About Love (1981), Cathedral (1983), and Where I'm Calling From (1988).

1   A year after his death, the recurring image I associate with Raymond Carver is one of people leaning toward him, working very hard at the act of listening. He mumbled. T. S. Eliot once described Ezra Pound, qua mentor, as "a man trying to convey to a very deaf person the fact that the house is on fire." Raymond Carver had precisely the opposite manner. The smoke could be filling the room, flames streaking across the carpet, before Carver would ask, "Is it, uh, getting a little hot in here, maybe?" And you would be sitting in your chair, bent achingly forward at the waist, saying, "Beg pardon, Ray?" Never insisting, rarely asserting, he was an unlikely teacher.

2   I once sat in and listened while Carver was interviewed for two and a half hours. The writer conducting the interview moved the tape recorder closer

and closer and finally asked if Carver would put it in his lap. A few days later the interviewer called up, near despair: Ray's voice on the tapes was nearly inaudible. The word "soft-spoken" hardly begins to do justice to his speech; this condition was aggravated whenever he was pressed into the regions of generality or prescription.

3   As I say, he mumbled, and if it once seemed merely a physical tic, akin to cracking knuckles or the drumming of a foot, I now think it was a function of a deep humility and a respect for the language bordering on awe, a reflection of his sense that words should be handled very, very gingerly. As if it might be almost impossible to say what you wanted to say. As if it might be dangerous, even. Listening to him talking about writing in the classroom or in the living room of the big Victorian house he shared with Tess Gallagher in Syracuse, you sensed a writer who loved the words of the masters who had handed the language down to him, and who was concerned that he might not be worthy to pick up the instrument. You feel this respect for the language—humility bordering on dread—in every sentence of his work.

4   Encountering Carver's fiction early in the 1970s was a transforming experience for many writers of my generation, an experience perhaps comparable to discovering Hemingway's sentences in the twenties. In fact, Carver's language was unmistakably like Hemingway's—the simplicity and clarity, the repetitions, the nearly conversational rhythms, the precision of physical description. But Carver completely dispensed with the romantic egoism that made the Hemingway idiom such an awkward model for other writers in the late twentieth century. The cafés and *pensions* and battlefields of Europe were replaced by trailer parks and apartment complexes, the glamorous occupations by dead-end jobs. The trout in Carver's streams were apt to be pollution-deformed mutants. The good *vin du pays* was replaced by cheap gin, the romance of drinking by the dull grind of full-time alcoholism. Some commentators found his work depressing for these reasons. For many young writers it was terribly liberating.

5   One aspect of what Carver seemed to say to us—even someone who had never been inside a lumber mill or a trailer park—was that literature could be fashioned out of strict observation of real life, wherever and however it was lived, even if it was lived with a bottle of Heinz ketchup on the table and the television set droning. This was news at a time when academic metafiction was the regnant mode. His example reinvigorated realism as well as the short story form.

6   Though he was a teacher for much of his life, Carver never consciously gathered a band of disciples around himself. But when I was knocking around between graduate schools and the New York publishing world in the late seventies and early eighties, no other writer was as much discussed and mimicked by

the writers one met at readings and writers' conferences. Probably not since Donald Barthelme began publishing in the 1960s had a story writer generated such a buzz in the literary world.

7   Having fallen under Carver's spell on reading his first collection, *Will You Please Be Quiet, Please?*, a book I would have bought on the basis of the title alone, I was lucky enough to meet him a few years later and eventually to become his student at Syracuse University in the early eighties. Despite the existence of several thousand creative writing programs around the country, there is probably no good answer to the question of whether writing can be taught. Saying that Faulkner and Fitzgerald never got M.F.A.s is beside the point. Novelists and short story writers like to eat as much as anyone else, and tend to sniff out subsidies while they pursue their creative work. For writers in the twenties, the exchange rate was favorable in Paris, and in the thirties there was the WPA, and a gold rush of sorts in Hollywood. The universities have become the creative writers' WPA in recent years.

8   Carver was himself a product of the new system, having studied writing at the University of Iowa Writers' Workshop and at Stanford, and later earned a living teaching. It was something he did out of necessity, a role he was un-comfortable with. He did it to make a living, because it was easier than the other jobs he'd had—working at a sawmill and a hospital, working as a service station attendant, a janitor, a delivery boy, a textbook editor. Though grateful for genteel employment, he didn't really see why people who had a gift for writing should necessarily be able to teach. And he was very shy. The idea of facing a class made him nervous every time. On the days he had to teach he would get agitated, as if he himself were a student on the day of the final exam.

9   Like many writers in residence at universities, Ray was required to teach English courses in addition to creative writing courses. One was called Form and Theory of the Short Story, a title Ray inherited from the graduate English catalogue. The method in these classes was to assign a book of stories he liked each week, including contemporary and nineteenth-century authors as well as works in translation. We would read the books and discuss them for two hours. Flannery O'Connor, Chekhov, Ann Beattie, Maupassant, Frank O'Connor, John Cheever, Mary Robison, Turgenev, and more Chekhov. (He loved all the nineteenth-century Russians.) Class would begin with Ray saying something like, "Well, guys, how'd you like Eudora Welty?" He preferred listening to lecturing, but he would read his favorite passages, talk about what he loved in the book he had chosen. He dealt in specifics, stayed close to the text, and eventually there would come a moment when the nervousness would lift off of him as he spoke about writing that moved him.

10   One semester, a very earnest Ph.D. candidate found his way into this class, composed mainly of writers. At that time, the English department, like many around the country, had become a battleground between theorists and humanists, and post-structuralism lay heavy upon the campus. After a few weeks of Carver's free-ranging and impressionistic approach to literature, the

young theorist registered a strong protest: "This class is called Form and Theory of the Short Story but all we do is sit around and talk about the books. Where's the form and the theory?"

11   Ray looked distressed. He nodded and pulled extra hard on his cigarette. "Well, that's a good question," he said. After a long pause, he said, "I guess I'd say that the point here is that we read good books and discuss them. . . . And then you *form* your own *theory*." Then he smiled.

12   As a teacher of creative writing, too, Carver had a light touch. He did not consider it his job to discourage anyone. He said that there was enough discouragement out there for anyone trying against all odds to be a writer, and he clearly spoke from experience. Criticism, like fiction, was an act of empathy for Ray, putting yourself in the other guy's shoes. He couldn't understand writers who wrote negative reviews and once chided me for doing so. He believed fiction and poetry were fraternal enterprises. Among the very few people that Ray vocally disliked were a poet who had refused to lend him $50 when his car broke down in Salt Lake City, two critics who had attacked his own work, and writers who had attacked any of his friends.

13   For a shy man, his gregarious generosity of spirit was remarkable. He kept up a correspondence with dozens of other writers, students, and fans. He wrote letters of recommendation and encouragement, helped people get jobs and grants, editors and agents, accompanied friends in need to their first AA meetings.

14   One day when I berated him for going easy on a student I thought was turning out poor work, he told me a story: he had recently been a judge in a prestigious fiction contest. The unanimous winner, whose work has since drawn much praise, turned out to be a former student of his, probably the worst, least promising student he'd had in twenty years. "What if I had discouraged her?" he said.

15   His harshest critical formula was: "I think it's good you got that story behind you." Meaning, I guess, that one has to drive through some ugly country on the way to Parnassus. If Carver had had his way, classes and workshops would have been conducted entirely by students, but his approval was too highly valued for him to remain mute.

16   Once he sat through the reading of a long, strange story in his graduate writing workshop: as I recall, the story fleshed out two disparate characters, brought them together, followed their courtship and eventual marriage. After a series of false starts they decided to open a restaurant together, the preparations for which were described in great detail. On the day it opened a band of submachine-gun-toting terrorists burst in and killed everyone in the restaurant. End of story. After nearly everyone in the smoky seminar room had expressed dissatisfaction with this plot, we all turned to Ray. He was clearly at a loss. Finally he said softly, "Well, sometimes a story needs a submachine gun." This answer seemed to satisfy the author no less than those who felt the story in question had been efficiently put out of its misery.

17   My first semester, Ray somehow forgot to enter my grade for workshop. I pointed this out to him, and we went together to the English office to rectify the situation. "You did some real good work," he said, informing me that I would get an A. I was very pleased with myself, but perhaps a little less so when Ray opened the grade book and wrote an A next to my name underneath a solid column of identical grades. Everybody did good work, apparently. In workshop he approached every story with respect—treating each as if it were a living entity, a little sick, possibly, or lame, but something that could be nursed and trained to health.

18   Though Ray was always encouraging, he could be rigorous if he knew criticism was welcome. Fortunate students had their stories subjected to the same process he employed on his own numerous drafts. Manuscripts came back thoroughly ventilated with Carver deletions, substitutions, question marks, and chicken-scratch queries. I took one story back to him seven times; he must have spent fifteen or twenty hours on it. He was a meticulous, obsessive line editor. One on one, in his office, he almost became a tough guy, his voice gradually swelling with conviction.

19   Once we spent some ten or fifteen minutes debating my use of the word "earth." Carver felt it had to be "ground," and he felt it was worth the trouble of talking it through. That one exchange was invaluable; I think of it constantly when I'm working. Carver himself used the same example later in an essay he wrote that year, in discussing the influence of his mentor, John Gardner.[1] "Ground is ground, he'd say, it means *ground*, dirt, that kind of stuff. But if you say 'earth,' that's something else, that word has other ramifications."

20   John Gardner, the novelist, was Ray's first writing teacher. They met at Chico State College in California in the 1960s. Ray said that all of his writing life he had felt Gardner looking over his shoulder when he wrote, approving or disapproving of certain words, phrases, and strategies. Calling fouls. He said a good writing teacher is something like a literary conscience, a friendly critical voice in your ear. I know what he meant. (I have one; it mumbles.)

21   After almost twenty years Carver had a reunion with his old teacher, who was living and teaching less than a hundred miles from Syracuse, in Binghamton, New York, and Gardner's approval of his work had meant a great deal to him. In the spring of 1982, I happened to stop by Ray's house a few minutes after he heard that Gardner had died in a motorcycle crash. Distraught, he couldn't sit still. We walked around the house and the back yard as he talked about Gardner.

---

[1] **John Gardner:** Medievalist, novelist, short-story writer, and critic (1933–1982), among whose works are *Grendel, The Sunlight Dialogues, October Light, On Moral Fiction,* and *The Life and Times of Chaucer.*

22   "Back then I didn't even know what a writer looked like," Ray said. "John looked like a writer. He had that hair, and he used to wear this thing that was like a cape. I tried to copy the way he walked. He used to let me work in his office because I didn't have a quiet place to work. I'd go through his files and steal the titles of his stories, use them on my stories."

23   So he must have understood when we all shamelessly cribbed from him, we students at Syracuse, and Iowa and Stanford and all the other writing workshops in the country where almost everyone seemed to be writing and publishing stories with Raymond Carver titles like "Do You Mind If I Smoke?" or "How About This, Honey?" He certainly didn't want clones. But he knew that imitation was part of finding your own voice.

24   I encountered Carver near the beginning of what he liked to call his "second life," after he had quit drinking. I heard stories about the bad old Ray, stories he liked to tell on himself. When I met him I thought of writers as luminous madmen who drank too much and drove too fast and scattered brilliant pages along their doomed trajectories. Maybe at one time he did, too. In his essay "Fires," he says, "I understood writers to be people who didn't spend their Saturdays at the laundromat." Would Hemingway be caught dead doing laundry? No, but William Carlos Williams[2] would. Ditto Carver's beloved Chekhov. In the classroom and on the page, Carver somehow delivered the tonic news that there was laundry in the kingdom of letters.

25   Not that, by this time, Ray was spending much time at the laundromat, life having been good to him toward the end in a way for which he seemed constantly to be grateful. But hearing the typewriter of one of the masters of American prose clacking just up the street, while a neighbor raked leaves and some kids threw a Frisbee as the dogs went on with their doggy life—this was a lesson in itself for me. Whatever dark mysteries lurk at the heart of the writing process, he insisted on a single trade secret: that you had to survive, find some quiet, and work hard every day. And seeing him for coffee, or watching a ball game or a dumb movie with him, put into perspective certain dangerous myths about the writing life that he preferred not to lecture on—although he sometimes would, if he thought it might help. When we first became acquainted, in New York, he felt obliged to advise me, in a series of wonderful letters, and a year later I moved upstate to become his student.

26   Reading the dialogues of Plato, one eventually realizes that Socrates' self-deprecation is something of a ploy. Ray's humility, however, was profound and unself-conscious and one of the most astonishing things about him. When he asked a student, "What do you think?" he clearly wanted to know. This seemed a rare and inspiring didactic stance. His own opinions were expressed with such caution that you knew how carefully they had been measured.

---

[2] **William Carlos Williams:** Much-admired American poet and physician (1883–1963) whose poems are rooted in the commonplace detail of ordinary life.

27   For someone who claimed he didn't love to teach, he made a great deal of difference to a great many students. He certainly changed my life irrevocably and I have heard others say the same thing.

28   I'm still leaning forward with my head cocked to one side, straining to hear his voice.

❧

Discussion Questions

1. To what reasons or causes does McInerney attribute Carver's soft-spokenness and habit of mumbling? What personality trait made the role of teacher a difficult one for Carver?

2. In what respects, according to McInerney, was Carver's language "unmistakably like Hemingway's" (paragraph 4)? In what ways did Hemingway and Carver differ in personality and choice of subject matter?

3. What was Carver's academic background? His work experiences? What writer had strongly influenced Carver's own career? How?

4. Describe Carver's methods of teaching short stories and creative writing. Would you consider him to have been a good teacher? Why or why not?

5. What was Carver's own definition of a good writing teacher? In McInerney's view, did Carver qualify by this definition?

*6. Explain what you think McInerney means by the following sentences: "He believed fiction and poetry were fraternal enterprises" (paragraph 12); "But he knew that imitation was part of finding your own voice" (paragraph 23); "In the classroom and on the page, Carver somehow delivered the tonic news that there was laundry in the kingdom of letters" (paragraph 24).

*7. By paragraph number, cite two or three anecdotes McInerney employs to illustrate points about Carver's personality. Could McInerney have written an effective essay on Carver without such anecdotes?

Writing Topics

1. If you, like McInerney and Carver, have at some time consciously imitated the actions or personal characteristics of another person, write a short essay about the experience. What was it you were trying to imitate? Why? Under what circumstances? With what results?

2. As McInerney notes, Carver tried to convert commonplace experiences into art. Write a vivid description of a commonplace experience you have had recently: doing the laundry, eating lunch, getting dressed, brushing your teeth, cooking dinner, whatever. Try to include in the description specific relevant details—colors, textures, smells, brand names, spatial arrangements, and so on.

. . . here was a man who turned on indifference,

neglect, carelessness with bitter and

caustic contempt. . . ."

A COEDUCATIONAL COLLEGE
OF THE EIGHTIES

Ida M. Tarbell

In her day, Ida M. Tarbell (1857–1944) was one of the leading muckrakers, American reformers whose writings alerted the public to corruption in politics and business and to the need to address social ills. Although she wrote biographies of Napoleon, Lincoln, and others, Tarbell is best known for her exposés in *McClure's Magazine* (1894–1906) and for her two-volume *History of the Standard Oil Company* (1904), a study of corporate monopoly. "A Coeducational College of the Eighties" appears in her autobiography *All in the Day's Work* (1939).

1   When I entered Allegheny College in the fall of 1876 I made my first contact with the past. I had been born and reared a pioneer; I knew only the beginning of things, the making of a home in a wilderness, the making of an industry from the ground up. I had seen the hardships of beginnings, the joy of realization, the attacks that success must expect; but of things with a past, things that had made themselves permanent, I knew nothing. It struck me full in the face now, for this was an old college as things west of the Alleghenies were reckoned—an old college in an old town. Here was history, and I had never met it before to recognize it.

2   The town lay in the valley of a tributary of the Allegheny River—French Creek. Its oldest tradition after the tales of Indians was that George Washington once drank from a spring on the edge of the campus. Certainly he passed that way in 1753 when he came up the river valley from Fort Duquesne (Pittsburgh), following the route which led to Fort Le Bœuf near Lake Erie. He comments in his diary, published the year after his trip, on the extensive rich meadows through which he had passed, one of which "I believe was nearly four miles in length and considerable wider in some places." To this particular "rich meadow" a few years later came one David Mead and laid out a town and

sold land. Here soon after came the representative of the Holland Land Company, colonizers of first quality. Good men came, distinguished names in Pennsylvania's history, and they wanted a college. The answer to their wish came in 1815 when one of the most scholarly men of that day, Timothy Alden of Massachusetts, heard their call and, picking up all his worldly possessions, made the two months' trip by coach and boat to the settlement called Meadville.

3   Timothy Alden, like many of his fellows, was fired by a deep belief that through Christian democracy alone could men arrive at the better world towards which he, scholar that he was, knew they had been groping from their earliest beginnings. But men could only come to an understanding of their individual and collective responsibilities to democracy through education. Therefore, as men spread westward he and others like him must follow them with education.

4   But once in Meadville how little he found with which to carry out his project—a log courthouse for a schoolhouse, and little or no money, though of what they had men gave freely. Now Timothy Alden knew that throughout the East were men of scholarly traditions convinced as was he that democracy would work only if men were trained to understanding and sacrifice. He believed that they would help his Western venture. In 1816 he went East to find out. He was not wrong in thinking there would be sympathy for the young college. Out of their meager store men gave—this one, fifty cents; that one, five dollars; few, more—and men gave books, one, two, five. The list of donors now in the college archives shows many of the best known names of the day— Lowell, Adams, Tucker, Parkman, Channing in Boston and twenty-nine fine New York names. Friends were made for Allegheny in every town and city where its brave story was told. Timothy Alden came back with $361 in money and with books, more needed than money, estimated to be worth $1,642.26.

5   From that time he kept the undertaking steadily before the East, promoted it by every method known to the times. A great response to his passionate effort came in 1819 when the college world of the East was shocked by learning that William Bentley of Salem, Massachusetts, had left his famous collection of "classical and theological books, dictionaries, lexicons and Bibles" to a college in the wilderness of northwestern Pennsylvania, a college without a home, still doing its work in a log courthouse. That gift, long a bitter drop in the cup of Harvard, it is said, made a home of its own necessity for Allegheny, and in 1820 the corner stone of Bentley Hall, named for the donor, was laid. It took many years to complete it; but, when done on the lines Timothy Alden had himself laid down, it was one of the most beautiful buildings in the country. Today it easily stands after Independence Hall as the most perfect piece of Colonial architecture in the state of Pennsylvania. For me Bentley Hall was an extraordinary experience. It was the first really beautiful building I had seen, a revelation, something I had never dreamed of.

6   Fifty-six years had passed since the corner stone of Bentley Hall was laid, and not one of them without disappointments and sacrifices. More than once it had seemed as if the brave attempt must fail. Two buildings only had been added in these years: Culver Hall, a frame boarding house for men; Ruter Hall, a grim uncompromising three-story rectangular brick structure, fifty by ninety feet in size, a perfect reflection of the straitened period to which it belonged. The "Factory" was our slighting name for Ruter Hall, but in this stern structure I was to find a second deep satisfaction—the library; in a room on the top floor, ninety feet long and at least sixteen in height was housed not only the splendid Bentley collection, but one even more valuable, that of Judge James Winthrop of Cambridge, Massachusetts, rare volumes from the great presses of Europe, three tons of books brought overland in wagons by Boston teamsters in 1822. They lined the great unbroken inside wall, as well as every space between openings. From the window seats one looked out on the town in the valley, its roofs and towers half hidden by a wealth of trees, and beyond to a circle of round-breasted hills. Before I left Allegheny I had found a very precious thing in that severe room—the companionship there is in the silent presence of books.

7   Allegheny did not of course admit women at the start; but the ferment caused by the passing of the Fourteenth Amendment making it clear that only men were to be regarded as citizens stirred the Allegheny constituents mightily. Its chief patron, as I have said, was the Methodist Church. Now the Methodist Church was a militant reformer. The greatest of its bishops, Matthew Simpson, had backed Mrs. Stanton and Miss Anthony and their colleagues at every step. Leaders among Methodist women had been abolitionists, aggressive temperance advocates, and now they became militant suffragists. Their influence began to tell. In 1870, with misgivings in not a few minds the admission of women was voted. This was the same year that the University of Michigan opened its doors to women, and two years before Cornell. In the six years before I entered ten women had graduated. When I came there were but two seniors, two juniors, no sophomores. I was a lone freshman in a class of forty hostile or indifferent boys. The friendly and facetious professor charged with the care of the "young ladies" put it that I was "Lost in the Wilderness of Boy."

8   From the first I was dimly conscious that I was an invader, that there was abroad a spirit of masculinity challenging my right to be there, and there were taboos not to be disregarded. My first experience was that of which Virginia Woolf speaks so bitterly in "A Room of One's Own"—the closing of the college green to her at Oxbridge. Nearly fifty years before her book was written I was having at Allegheny the same experience.

9   The sloping green of the campus below Bentley Hall was inviting. Between classes I made my way one day to a seat under a tree only to hear a horrified call from the walk above, "Come back, come back quick." An imperative summons from an upperclass woman. "You mustn't go on that side of the walk, only men go there."

10   It was not so simple to find a spot where you could go and be comfortable. If Bentley Hall, where all the classes were held, was a beautiful piece of architecture, its interior could hardly have been more severe. The rooms were heated with potbellied cast-iron stoves, seated with the hardest wooden chairs, lighted by kerosene lamps. In winter (and the winters were long) the snow tracked in kept the floors wet and cold. Often one wore a muffler in chapel. But of all that I was unheeding. My pioneer childhood served me well. Moreover, I realized at the start that I had found what I had come to college for, direction in the only field in which I was interested—science. I found it in a way that I doubt if Cornell could have given me at the moment, shy and immature as I was: the warming and contagious enthusiasm of a great natural teacher, one who had an ardent passion for those things which had stirred me and a wide knowledge which he fed by constant study and travel—Jeremiah Tingley, the head of Allegheny's department of natural science.

11   Professor Tingley was then a man of fifty, sparkling, alive, informal. Three years before, he had been one of the fifty chosen from many hundred applicants to spend the summer with Louis Agassiz[1] on the island of Penikese in Buzzards Bay. Agassiz had planned with enthusiasm for the Penikese Summer School, and for those privileged to enter who could understand and appreciate it was an unforgettable experience; certainly it was for Jeremiah Tingley. He carried there Agassiz's faith in observation and classification, as well as his reverence for Nature and all her ways. For both men the material world was but the cover of the spirit. Professor Tingley would quote Agassiz sometimes: "Nature always brings us back to absolute truth whenever we wander."

12   This fervent faith had a profound and quieting effect on my religious tumult. I learned a new word: Pantheism. Being still in that early stage of development where there must be a definite word by which to classify oneself, I began to call myself a pantheist—and I had a creed which I repeated more often than the creed I had learned in childhood:

> *Flower in the crannied wall,*
> *I pluck you out of the crannies,*
> *I hold you here, root and all, in my hand*
> *Little flower—but if I could understand*
> *What you are, root and all, and all in all,*
> *I should know what God and man is.*

It reassured me; I was on the right track, for was I not going to find out with the microscope what God and man are?

---

[1] **Louis Agassiz:** Swiss-born naturalist, teacher, and author (1807–1873), who became a well-known professor at Harvard and founder of the Marine Biological Laboratory at Woods Hole, Massachusetts.

13   Professor Tingley's method for those he found really interested in scientific study was to encourage them to look outside the book. There was where I had already found my joy; but I suspected it was the willful way, that the true way was to know first what was in the books. Here in Professor Tingley's classes you were ordered to go and see for yourself. He used to tell us a story of his first experience at Penikese. A stone was put before him, a round water-washed stone, on which he was to report. He looked at the stone, turned it over. There was nothing to report. "It is not the outside, it is the inside of things that matters," said Agassiz. And in the laboratory that became our watchword: Look inside.

14   Discovering my interest in the microscope, I was not only allowed, I was urged to use the magnificent binocular belonging to the college, was given the free run of the laboratory along with a few as crazy as myself. Here my most exciting adventure apart from what I found under the microscope came from actually having my hands on a "missing link." Evolution, to which I was clinging determinedly, could only be established, I realized, by discovering the links. There was one peculiar to the waters in our valley, the *Memopomo Alleghaniensis*, a creature twelve to fifteen inches long with gills and one lung, able to live in the water or mud as circumstances required. The mud puppy, as it was appropriately called, was slimy, loathsome, but I worked over it with awe. Was I not being admitted into the very workshop of Nature herself—seeing how she did it?

15   Professor Tingley took his little group of laboratory devotees into his home circle. He and Mrs. Tingley were housed in a wing of Bentley Hall—big rooms built for classrooms. They had no children, and in the years of their study and travel they had gathered about them things of beauty and interest. The atmosphere of those rooms was something quite new and wonderful to me. It was my first look into the intimate social life possible to people interested above all in ideas, beauty, music, and glad to work hard and live simply to devote themselves to their cultivation.

16   And such good talks! Much of it was concerned with fresh scientific thought, the inventions and discoveries which were stirring the world. An omnivorous reader of the scientific publications of Europe and America, Professor Tingley kept us excited, not only by what had been done but what it might mean. There was the telephone. I had been in college but a few weeks when my father asked me to go with him and my brother to the Centennial Exposition of 1876. President Bugbee, who had made me his special care for a time—Mrs. Bugbee even taking me into their home until an appropriate boarding place could be found—was heartily in favor of my going. I went, and when I returned Professor Tingley's first question was, "Did you see the telephone?" I hadn't even heard of it. Two exhibits only of that exposition made a deep enough impression on me to last until today—my first Corot and the Corliss engine. Professor Tingley was greatly disappointed, and I did not understand why until a few weeks later he called the student body together to explain and illustrate

the telephone by a homemade instrument. "You'll talk to your homes from these rooms one day," he told us. "New York will talk to Boston." He didn't suggest Chicago. "Dreamer," the boys said. "Dreamer," my father and his Titusville friends said a little later when an agent of the Bell Associates, the first company to attempt putting the new invention within reach of everybody, came to town selling stock. How often I heard it said later, "If I'd bought that telephone stock!"

17 Years later I told Alexander Graham Bell of my introduction to the telephone. "Nobody," he said, "can estimate what the teachers of science in colleges and high schools were doing in those days not only to spread knowledge of the telephone but to stir youth to tackle the possibilities in electricity."

18 What I best remember is not the telephone but Professor Tingley's amazing enthusiasm for the telephone. This revelation of enthusiasm, its power to warm and illuminate was one of the finest and most lasting of my college experiences. The people I had known, teachers, preachers, doctors, business men, all went through their day's work either with a stubborn, often sullen determination to do their whole duty, or with an undercurrent of uneasiness, if they found pleasure in duty. They seemed to me to feel that they were not really working if they were not demonstrating the Puritan teaching that labor is a curse. It had never seemed so to me, but I did not dare gloat over it. And here was a teacher who did gloat over his job in all its ramifications. Moreover, he did his best to stir you to share his joy.

19 But while I looked on what I was learning in the laboratory as what I had come to college for, while each term stiffened my ambition to go deeper and deeper into the search for the original atom, science was not all that interested me. The faculty, if small, was made up largely of seasoned men with a perspective on life. There was not only deep seriousness but humor and tolerance, and since we were so small a college the student was close enough to discover them, to find out what each man as an individual had to offer him. As I learned the power of enthusiasm from Jeremiah Tingley, I learned from another man of that faculty the value of contempt. Holding the chair of Latin was one of the few able teachers I have known, George Haskins, father of that sound scholar of international repute, the late Charles Homer Haskins, at the time of his death Professor Emeritus of Medieval History at Harvard University. What deep satisfaction his career gave his father, himself a man of many disappointments!

20 George Haskins labored, usually in vain, to arouse us to the choiceness of Latinity, the meaning of Rome's rise and fall, the quality of her men, the relation of that life to ours. Professor Haskins' contempt for our lack of understanding, for our slack preparation, was something utterly new to me in human intercourse. The people I knew with rare exceptions spared one another's feelings. I had come to consider that a superior grace; you must be kind if you lied for it. But here was a man who turned on indifference, neglect, carelessness with bitter and caustic contempt, left his victim seared. The sufferers lived to say, some of them at least: "I deserved it. He was never unjust, never inappreciative of effort."

21   "Cherish your contempts," Henry James advised me once when he had drawn from me a confession of the conflict between my natural dislike of saying anything unpleasant about anybody and the necessity of being cruel, even brutal, if the work I had undertaken was to be truthful in fact and logic. "Cherish your contempts," said Mr. James, "and strength to your elbow." If it had not been for George Haskins I doubt if I should have known what he meant; nor should I ever have become the steady, rather dogged worker I am. The contempt for shiftlessness which he inspired in me aroused a determination to be a good worker. I began to train my mind to go at its task regularly, keep hours, study whether I liked a thing or not. I forced myself not to waste time, not to loaf, not to give up before I finished. If I failed at any point in this discipline I suffered a certain mental and spiritual malaise, a dissatisfaction with myself hard to live with.

22   In spite of my painful efforts to make a regular worker out of myself, life at college was lightened by my discovery of the Boy. Incredible as it seems to me now, I had come to college at eighteen without ever having dared to look fully into the face of any boy of my age. To be sure, I had from childhood nourished secret passions for a succession of older individuals whom I never saw except at a distance, and with whom I never exchanged a word. My brother and his friends, my father and his friends—these I had always hobnobbed with; but those who naturally should have been my companions, I shunned. I was unable to take part in those things that brought the young people of the day together. I did not dance—the Methodist discipline forbade it. I was incredibly stupid and uninterested in games—still am. I had no easy companionable ways, was too shy to attempt them. I had my delights; the hills which I ran, the long drives behind our little white horse, the family doings, the reading of French regularly with my splendid friend Annette Grumbine, still living, still as she was then a vitalizing influence in the town and state for all that makes for a higher social life—these things and my precious evening walks, the full length of Titusville's main street, alone or with some girl friend while we talked of things deepest in our minds.

23   But in all this there was no boy. I was not long in discovering him when I reached Allegheny, for the taboos I encountered at the start soon yielded under the increased number of women, women in college, in special courses, in the Preparatory Department. They swept masculine prohibitions out of the way— took possession, made a different kind of institution of it, less scholastic, gayer, easier-going. The daily association in the classrooms, the contacts and appraisements, the mutual interests and intimacies, the continual procession of college doings which in the nature of things required that you should have a masculine attendant, soon put me at my ease. I was learning, learning fast, but the learning carried its pains. I still had a stiff-necked determination to be free. To avoid entangling alliances of all kinds had become an obsession with me. I was slow in laying it aside when I began to take part in the social life of the college, and

because of it I was guilty of one performance which was properly enough a scandal to the young men.

24   There were several men's fraternities in the college; most of the boys belonged to one or another. It was an ambition of the fraternities to put their pins on acceptable town and college girls. You were a Delta girl, or a Gamma girl or a Phi Psi girl. I resented this effort to tag me. Why should I not have friends in all the fraternities? And I had; I accumulated four pins and then, one disastrous morning, went into chapel with the four pins on my coat. There were a few months after that when, if it had not been for two or three non-Frat friends, I should have been a social outcast.

25   I spent four years in Allegheny College. Measured by what I got instead of by what I did not get and was obliged to learn later, I regard them as among the most profitable of my life. I find often that men and women accuse the college of not opening their minds to life as it is in the world. For a mind sufficiently developed to see "life as it is" I cannot conceive a more fruitful field than the classics. If I had been sufficiently mature I could have learned from George Haskins' teachings of Cicero and Tacitus and Livy more than I know today about the ways of men in their personal and their national relations, more of the causes of war, of the weaknesses of governments. But I was not ready for it. Life is the great teacher, and she leads us step by step. It is not the fault of the human teacher that his pupil must learn to climb by climbing.

26   It was in the spring of 1880 that I graduated. I still carried the same baggage with which I had entered—a little heavier to be sure, a little better packed, a little better adapted to the "Purpose." The only difference which threatened disturbance was that I had added an item which I had refused to bring with me in 1876. Then I was not willing to believe I would ever marry—now I thought possibly some day I might; but the item was not heavy, not heavy enough at least to prevent my rejoicing over the fact that I was graduating with a job. I had signed a contract with an institution of which I had never heard until the negotiations leading to it opened. After frequent communications with the faculty a representative of the Poland Union Seminary of Poland, Ohio, with some misgivings had employed me to serve as its Preceptress—$500 a year "and board yourself." I was jubilant. It meant economic independence—the first plank in my platform. I would use my leisure to work with the microscope; I would save my money; I would one day go abroad and study with some great biologist. I would never abandon my search for the beginning of life, the point where I expected to find God.

27   It was then with entire confidence in the future that I started out in August of 1880 for the town of Poland on the Western Reserve of Ohio, to begin what women were then talking of in more or less awed tones as a Career.

❧

Discussion Questions

*1. Describe Tarbell's background prior to her entering Allegheny College in 1876. Summarize what she had learned about fields of study, about other people, and about herself by the time of her graduation in 1880.

2. What led to the admission of women into Allegheny College, once an all-male institution? Describe the atmosphere that Tarbell initially encountered because of her gender.

*3. How did increased enrollment of women permanently alter Allegheny College, according to Tarbell? If the college had once been an all-female institution, what effect do you think that the enrollment of numerous men would have had on the institution? Explain.

4. Relate the various ways in the classroom and out by which Jeremiah Tingley encouraged students who were truly interested in scientific study. Why might he be considered to have been a visionary?

*5. Explain what you think Louis Agassiz meant by each of the following statements: "Nature always brings us back to absolute truth whenever we wander" (paragraph 11); "It is not the outside, it is the inside of things that matters" (paragraph 13).

*6. In what ways did the interests and the teaching style of George Haskins differ from those of Jeremiah Tingley? Describe the influence that each professor had on Tarbell's interests, habits, and career.

7. Would you consider either Haskins or Tingley to have been a better teacher than the other? Explain.

Writing Topics

1. If you have ever encountered a person like George Haskins, one who at first seemed hypercritical of your endeavors but whose criticism, in time, you came to respect, recount the experience in a brief essay. Reveal your relationship to your critic—perhaps child to parent, student to teacher, or employee to employer—what you did that elicited the criticism, what the criticism was, how you felt about the experience then, and how you feel about it now.

2. Assume that you are Tarbell's editor and that you would like her to enliven "A Coeducational College of the Eighties" with some dialogue, which you notice is absent. Write Tarbell a letter in which you suggest two or three places in the selection that you think would benefit from dialogue, indicating why you chose these particular places as being appropriate and furnishing her with a brief sample of what you have in mind.

"It's fruitcake weather! Fetch our buggy.
Help me find my hat."

A CHRISTMAS MEMORY

Truman Capote

Truman Capote (1924–1984) was born in Monroeville, Alabama. Following his parents' separation, he spent much of his childhood with various relatives. By age twenty-four, he had become a resident of New York City and the author of an impressive novel, *Other Voices, Other Rooms.* That work was quickly followed by a collection of short stories, A *Tree of Night* (1949); novels, *The Grass Harp* (1951) and B*reakfast at Tiffany's* (1958); profiles and travel pieces, *Local Color* (1950) and *The Muses Are Heard* (1956); and eventually collections of essays, reportage, and biographical sketches, *The Dogs Bark* (1973) and *Music for Chameleons* (1983). However, Capote's most successful book remains I*n Cold Blood* (1966), an account of the grotesque murder of a Kansas family by two men, a book that Capote called a "nonfiction novel" and that he considered his finest work.

1   Imagine a morning in late November. A coming of winter morning more than twenty years ago. Consider the kitchen of a spreading old house in a country town. A great black stove is its main feature; but there is also a big round table and a fireplace with two rocking chairs placed in front of it. Just today the fireplace commenced its seasonal roar.

2   A woman with shorn white hair is standing at the kitchen window. She is wearing tennis shoes and a shapeless gray sweater over a summery calico dress. She is small and sprightly, like a bantam hen; but, due to a long youthful illness, her shoulders are pitifully hunched. Her face is remarkable—craggy and tinted by sun and wind; but it is delicate too, finely boned, and her eyes are sherry-colored and timid. "Oh, my," she exclaims, her breath smoking the windowpane, "it's fruitcake weather!"

3   The person to whom she is speaking is myself. I am seven; she is sixty-something. We are cousins, very distant ones, and we have lived together as long as I can remember. Other people inhabit the house, relatives; and though they have power over us, and frequently make us cry, we are not, on the whole,

too much aware of them. We are each other's best friend. She calls me Buddy, in memory of a boy who was formerly her best friend. The other Buddy died when she was still a child. She is still a child.

4   "I knew it before I got out of bed," she says, turning away from the window with a purposeful excitement in her eyes. "The courthouse bell sounded so cold and clear. And there were no birds singing; they've gone to warmer country. Oh, Buddy, stop stuffing biscuit and fetch our buggy. Help me find my hat. We've thirty cakes to bake."

5   It's always the same: a morning arrives in November, and my friend, as though officially inaugurating the Christmas time of year that exhilarates her imagination and fuels the blaze of heart, announces: "It's fruitcake weather! Fetch our buggy. Help me find my hat."

6   The hat is found, a straw cartwheel corsaged with velvet roses out-of-doors has faded: it once belonged to a more fashionable relative. Together, we guide our buggy, a dilapidated baby carriage, out to the garden and into a grove of pecan trees. The buggy is mine; that is, it was bought for me when I was born. It is made of wicker, rather unraveled, and the wheels wobble like a drunkard's legs. But it is a faithful object; springtimes, we take it to the woods and fill it with flowers, herbs, wild fern for our porch; in the summer, we pile it with picnic paraphernalia and sugar-cane fishing poles and roll it down to the edge of a creek; it has its winter uses, too: as a truck for hauling firewood from the yard to the kitchen, as a warm bed for Queenie, our tough little orange and white rat-terrier who has survived distemper and two rattlesnake bites. Queenie is trotting beside it now.

7   Three hours later we are back in the kitchen hulling a buggy-load of wind-fall pecans. Our backs hurt from gathering them: how hard they were to find (the main crop having been shaken off the trees and sold by the orchard's owners) among the concealing leaves, the frosted, deceiving grass. Caarackle! A cheery crunch, scraps of miniature thunder sound as the shells collapse and the golden mound of sweet oily ivory meat mounts in a milk glass bowl. Queenie begs to taste, and now and again my friend sneaks her a mite, though insisting we deprive ourselves. "We mustn't, Buddy. If we start, we won't stop. And there's scarcely enough as there is. For thirty cakes." The kitchen is growing dark. Dusk turns the window into a mirror: our reflections mingle with the rising moon as we work by the fireside in the firelight. At last, when the moon is quite high, we toss the final hull into the fire, with joined sighs, watch it catch flame. The buggy is empty, the bowl is brimful.

8   We eat our supper (cold biscuits, bacon, blackberry jam) and discuss tomorrow. Tomorrow the kind of work I like best begins: buying. Cherries and citron, ginger and vanilla, canned pineapple, raisins and walnuts and whisky and oh, so much flour, butter, many eggs, spices: we'll need a pony to pull the buggy home.

9   But before these purchases can be made, there is the question of money. Neither of us has any. Except for skinflint sums persons in the house occasionally provide (a dime is considered very big money); or what we earn ourselves from various activities: holding rummage sales, selling buckets of hand-picked blackberries, jars of homemade jam and apple jelly and peach preserves, rounding up flowers for funerals and weddings. Once we won seventy-ninth prize, five dollars, in a national football contest. Not that we know a fool-thing about football. It's just that we enter any contest we hear about: at the moment our hopes are on the fifty-thousand dollar Grand Prize being offered to name a new brand of coffee. (we suggested "A.M."; and, after some hesitation, formy friend thought it perhaps sacrilegious, the slogan "A.M.! Amen!"). To tell the truth, our only *really* profitable enterprise was the Fun and Freak Museum we conducted in a back-yard woodshed two summers ago. The Fun was a stereopticon with slide views of Washington and New York lent us by a relative who had been to those places (she was furious when she discovered why we'd borrowed it); the Freak was a three-legged biddy-chicken hatched by one of our own hens. Everybody hereabouts wanted to see that biddy: we charged grownups a nickel, kids two cents. And took in a good twenty dollars before the museum shut down due to the decease of the main attraction.

10   But one way and another we do each year accumulate Christmas savings, a Fruitcake Fund. These moneys we keep hidden in an ancient bead purse under a loose board under the floor under my friend's bed. The purse is seldom removed from this safe location except to make a deposit, or, as happens every Saturday, a withdrawal; for on Saturdays I am allowed ten cents to go to the picture show. My friend has never been to a picture show, nor does she intend to: "I'd rather hear you tell the story, Buddy. That way I can imagine it more. Besides, a person my age shouldn't squander their eyes. When the Lord comes, let me see him clear." In addition to never having seen a movie, she has never: eaten in a restaurant, traveled more than five miles from home, received or sent a telegram, read anything except funny papers and the Bible, worn cosmetics, cursed, wished someone harm, told a lie on purpose, let a hungry dog go hungry. Here are a few things she has done and does do: killed with a hoe the biggest rattlesnake ever seen in this country (sixteen rattles), dip snuff (secretly), tame hummingbirds (just try it) till they balance on her finger, tell ghost stories (we both believe in ghosts) so tingling they chill you in July, talk to herself, take walks in the rain, grow the prettiest japonicas in town, know the recipe for every sort of old-time Indian cure, including a magical wart-remover.

11   Now, with supper finished, we retire to the room in a faraway part of the house where my friend sleeps in a scrap-quilt-covered iron bed painted rose pink, her favorite color. Silently, wallowing in the pleasures of conspiracy, we take the bead purse from its secret place and spill the contents on the scrap quilt. Dollar bills, tightly rolled and green as May Buds. Somber fifty-cent pieces, heavy enough to weight a dead man's eyes. Lovely dimes, the liveliest coin, the one that really jingles. Nickels and quarters, worn smooth as creek pebbles.

But mostly a hateful heap of bitter-odored pennies. Last summer others in the house contracted to pay us a penny for every twenty-five flies we killed.

12   Oh, the carnage of August: the flies that flew to heaven! Yet it was not work in which we took pride. And, as we sit counting pennies, it is as though we were back tabulating dead flies. Neither of us has a head for figures; we count slowly, lose track, start again. According to her calculations, we have $12.73. According to mine, exactly $13. "I do hope you're wrong, Buddy. We can't mess around with thirteen. The cakes will fall. Or put somebody in the cemetery. Why I wouldn't dream of getting out of bed on the thirteenth." This is true: she always spends thirteens in bed. So, to be on the safe side, we subtract a penny and toss it out the window.

13   Of the ingredients that go into our fruitcakes, whisky is the most expensive, as well as the hardest to obtain: State laws (at that time) forbid its sale. But everybody knows you can buy a bottle from Mr. Haha Jones. And the next day, having completed our more prosaic shopping, we set out for Mr. Haha's business address, a "sinful" (to quote public opinion) fish-fry and dancing café down by the river. We've been there before, and on the same errand; but in previous years our dealings have been with Haha's wife, an iodine-dark Indian woman with brassy peroxide hair and a dead-tired disposition. Actually, we've never laid eyes on her husband, though we've heard that he's an Indian too. A giant with razor scars across his cheeks. They call him Haha because he's so gloomy, a man who never laughs. As we approach his café (a large log cabin festooned inside and out with chains of garish-gay naked light bulbs and standing by the river's muddy edge under the shade of river trees where moss drifts through the branches like gray mist) our steps slow down. Even Queenie stops prancing and sticks close by. People have been murdered in Haha's café. Cut up. Hit on the head. There's a case coming up in court next month. Naturally these goings-on happen at night when the colored lights cast crazy patterns and the victrola wails. In the daytime Haha's is shabby and deserted. I knock at the door, Queenie barks, my friend calls: "Mrs. Haha, ma'am? Anyone to home?"

14   Footsteps. The door opens. Our hearts overturn. It's Mr. Haha Jones himself! And he *is* a giant; he *does* have scars; he *doesn't* smile. No, he glowers at us through Satan-tilted eyes and demands to know: "What you want with Haha?"

15   For a moment we are too paralyzed to tell. Presently my friend half-finds her voice, a whispery voice at best: "If you please, Mr. Haha, we'd like a quart of your finest whisky."

16   His eyes tilt more. Would you believe it? Haha is smiling! Laughing, too. "Which one of you is a drinkin' man?"

17   "It's for making fruitcakes, Mr. Haha. Cooking."

18   This sobers him. He frowns. "That's no way to waste good whisky." Nevertheless, he retreats into the shadowed café and seconds later appears

carrying a bottle of daisy yellow unlabeled liquor. He demonstrates its sparkle in the sunlight and says: "Two dollars."

19   We pay him with nickels and dimes and pennies. Suddenly, jangling the coins in his hand like a fistful of dice, his face softens. "'Tell you what," he proposes, pouring the money back into our bead purse, "just send me one of them fruitcakes instead."

20   "Well," my friend remarks on our way home, "there's a lovely man. We'll put an extra cup of raisins in *his* cake."

21   The black stove, stoked with coal and firewood, glows like a lighted pumpkin. Eggbeaters whirl, spoons spin round in bowls of butter and sugar, vanilla sweetens the air, ginger spices it; melting, nose-tingling odors saturate the kitchen, suffuse the house, drift out to the world on puffs of chimney smoke. In four days our work is done. Thirty-one cakes, dampened with whisky, bask on window sills and shelves.

22   Who are they for?

23   Friends. Not necessarily neighbor friends: indeed, the larger share are intended for persons we've met maybe once, perhaps not at all. People who've struck our fancy. Like President Roosevelt. Like the Reverend and Mrs. J. C. Lucey, Baptist missionaries to Borneo who lectured here last winter. Or the little knife grinder who comes through town twice a year. Or Abner Packer, the driver of the six o'clock bus from Mobile, who exchanges waves with us every day as he passes in a dust-cloud whoosh. Or the young Wistons, a California couple whose car one afternoon broke down outside the house and who spent a pleasant hour chatting with us on the porch (young Mr. Wiston snapped our picture, the only we've ever had taken). Is it because my friend is shy with everyone *except* strangers that these strangers, and merest acquaintances, seem to us our truest friends? I think yes. Also, the scrapbooks we keep of thank-you's on White House stationery, time to time communications from California and Borneo, the knife grinder's penny post cards, make us feel connected to eventful worlds beyond the kitchen with its view of a sky that stops.

24   Now a nude December fig branch grates against the window. The kitchen is empty, the cakes are gone; yesterday we carted the last of them to the post office, where the cost of stamps turned our purse inside out. We're broke. That rather depresses me, but my friend insists on celebrating—with two inches of whisky left in Haha's bottle. Queenie has a spoonful in a bowl of coffee (she likes her coffee chicory-flavored and strong). The rest we divide between a pair of jelly glasses. We're both quite awed at the prospect of drinking straight whisky; the taste of it brings screwed-up expressions and sour shudders. But by-and-by we begin to sing, the two of us singing different songs simultaneously. I don't know the words to mine, just: *Come on along, come on along, to the darktown strutters' ball.* But I can dance: that's what I mean to be, a tap dancer in the movies. My dancing shadow rollicks on the walls; our voices rock the chinaware; we giggle: as if unseen hands were tickling us. Queenie rolls on her back,

her paws plow the air, something like a grin stretches her black lips. Inside myself, I feel warm and sparky as those crumbling logs, carefree as the wind in the chimney. My friend waltzes round the stove, the hem of her poor calico skirt pinched between her fingers as though it were a party dress: *Show me the way to go home*, she sings, her tennis shoes squeaking on the floor, *Show me the way to go home*.

25   Enter: two relatives. Very angry. Potent with eyes that scold, tongues that scald. Listen to what they have to say, the words tumbling together into a wrathful tune: "A child of seven! whisky on his breath! are you out of your mind? must be loony! road to ruination! remember Cousin Kate? Uncle Charlie? Uncle Charlie's brother-in-law? shame! scandal! humiliation! kneel, pray, beg the Lord!"

26   Queenie sneaks under the stove. My friend gazes at her shoes, her chin quivers, she lifts her skirt and blows her nose and runs to her room. Long after the town has gone to sleep and the house is silent except for the chimings of clocks and the sputter of fading fires, she is weeping into a pillow already as wet as a widow's handkerchief.

27   "Don't cry," I say, sitting at the bottom of her bed and shivering despite my flannel nightgown that smells of last winter's cough sirup. "Don't cry," I beg, teasing her toes, tickling her feet, "you're too old for that."

28   "It's because," she hiccups, "I *am* too old. Old and funny."

29   "Not funny. Fun. More fun than anybody. Listen. If you don't stop crying you'll be so tired tomorrow we can't go cut a tree."

30   She straightens up. Queenie jumps on the bed (where Queenie is not allowed) to lick her cheeks. "I know where we'll find real pretty trees, Buddy. And holly, too. With berries big as your eyes. It's way off in the woods. Farther than we've ever been. Papa used to bring us Christmas trees from there: carry them on his shoulder. That's fifty years ago. Well, now: I can't wait for morning."

31   Morning. Rime lusters the grass; the sun, round as an orange and orange as hot-weather moons, balances on the horizon, burnishes the silvered winter woods. A wild turkey calls. A renegade hog grunts in the undergrowth. Soon, by the edge of knee-deep, rapid-running water, we have to abandon the buggy. Queenie wades the stream first, paddles across, barking complaints at the swiftness of the current, the pneumonia-making coldness of it. We follow, holding our shoes and equipment (a hatchet, a burlap sack) above our heads. A mile more: of chastising thorns, burrs and briars that catch at our clothes; of rusty pine needles brilliant with gaudy fungus and molted feathers. Here, there, a flash, a flutter, an ecstasy of shrillings remind us that not all the birds have flown south. Always, the path unwinds through lemony sun pools and pitch vine tunnels. Another creek to cross: a disturbed armada of speckled trout froths the water round us, and frogs the size of plates practice belly flops; beaver workmen are building a dam. On the farther shore, Queenie shakes herself and trembles. My friend shivers, too: not with cold but enthusiasm. One of her

hat's ragged roses sheds a petal as she lifts her head and inhales the pine-heavy air. "We're almost there; can you smell it, Buddy?" she says, as though we were approaching an ocean.

32   And, indeed, it is a kind of ocean. Scented acres of holiday trees, prickly-leafed holly. Red berries shiny as Chinese bells: black crows swoop upon them screaming. Having stuffed our burlap sack with enough greenery and crimson to garland a dozen windows, we set about choosing a tree. "It should be," muses my friend, "twice as tall as a boy. So a boy can't steal the star." The one we pick is twice as tall as me. A brave, handsome brute that survives thirty hatchet strokes before it keels with a creaking, rending cry. Lugging it like a kill, we commence the long trek out. Every few yards we abandon the struggle, sit down and pant. But we have the strength of triumphant huntsmen; that and the tree's virile, icy perfume revive us, goad us on. Many compliments accompany our sunset return along the red clay road to town; but my friend is sly and noncommittal when passersby praise the treasure perched in our buggy: what a fine tree and where did it come from? "Yonderways," she murmurs vaguely. Once a car stops and the rich mill owner's lazy wife leans out and whines: "Giveya two-bits cash for that ol tree." Ordinarily my friend is afraid of saying no; but on this occasion she promptly shakes her head: "We wouldn't take a dollar." The mill owner's wife persists. "A dollar, my foot! Fifty cents. That's my last offer. Goodness, woman, you can get another one." In answer, my friend gently reflects: "I doubt it. There's never two of anything."

33   Home: Queenie slumps by the fire and sleeps till tomorrow, snoring loud as a human.

34   A trunk in the attic contains: a shoe box of ermine tails (off the opera cape of a curious lady who once rented a room in the house), coils of frazzled tinsel gone gold with age, one silver star, a brief rope of dilapidated, undoubtedly dangerous candy-like light bulbs. Excellent decorations, as far as they go, which isn't far enough: my friend wants our tree to blaze "like a Baptist window," droop with weighty snows of ornament. But we can't afford the made-in-Japan splendors at the five-and-dime. So we do what we've always done: sit for days at the kitchen table with scissors and crayons and stacks of colored paper. I make sketches and my friend cuts them out: lots of cats, fish too (because they're easy to draw), some apples, some watermelons, a few winged angels devised from saved-up sheets of Hershey-bar tin foil. We use safety pins to attach these creations to the tree; as a final touch, we sprinkle the branches with shredded cotton (picked in August for this purpose). My friend, surveying the effect, clasps her hands together. "Now honest, Buddy. Doesn't it look good enough to eat?" Queenie tries to eat an angel.

35   After weaving and ribboning holly wreaths for all the front windows, our next project is the fashioning of family gifts. Tie-dye scarves for the ladies, for the men a home-brewed lemon and licorice and aspirin syrup to be taken "at

the first Symptoms of a Cold and after Hunting." But when it comes time for making each other's gift, my friend and I separate to work secretly. I would like to buy her a pearl-handled knife, a radio, a whole pound of chocolate-covered cherries (we tasted some once, and she always claims, "I could live on them, Buddy, Lord yes I could—and that's not taking His name in vain"). Instead, I am building her a kite. She would like to give me a bicycle (she's said so on several million occasions: "If only I could, Buddy. It's bad enough in life to do without something *you* want: but confound it, what gets my goat is not being able to give somebody something you want *them* to have. Only one of these days, I will, Buddy. Locate you a bike. Don't ask how. Steal it, maybe"). Instead, I'm fairly certain that she is building me a kite—the same as last year, and the year before: the year before that we exchanged slingshots. All of which is fine by me. For we are champion kite-fliers who study the wind like sailors; my friend, more accomplished than I, can get a kite aloft when there isn't enough breeze to carry clouds.

36   Christmas Eve afternoon we scrape together a nickel and go to the butcher's to buy Queenie's traditional gift, a good, gnawable beef bone. The bone, wrapped in funny paper, is placed high in the tree near the silver star. Queenie knows it's there. She squats at the foot of the tree staring up in a trance of greed: when bedtime arrives she refuses to budge. Her excitement is equaled by my own. I kick the covers and turn my pillow as though it were a scorching summer's night. Somewhere a rooster crows falsely, for the sun is still on the other side of the world.

37   "Buddy, are you awake?" It is my friend, calling from her room, which is next to mine; and an instant later she is sitting on my bed holding a candle. "Well, I can't sleep a hoot," she declares. "My mind's jumping like a jack rabbit. Buddy, do you think Mrs. Roosevelt will serve our cake at dinner?" We huddle in the bed, and she squeezes my hand I-love-you. "Seems like your hand used to be so much smaller. I guess I hate to see you grow up. When you're grown up, will we still be friends?" I say always. "But I feel so bad, Buddy. I wanted so bad to give you a bike. I tried to sell my cameo Papa gave me. Buddy"—she hesitates, as though embarrassed "—I made you another kite." Then I confess that I made her one, too; and we laugh. The candle burns too short to hold. Out it goes, exposing the starlight, the stars spinning at the window like a visible caroling that slowly, slowly daybreak silences. Possibly we doze; but the beginnings of dawn splash us like cold water: we're up, wide-eyed and wandering while we wait for others to waken. Quite deliberately my friend drops a kettle on the kitchen floor. I tap-dance in front of closed doors. One by one the household emerges, looking as though they'd like to kill us both; but it's Christmas, so they can't. First, a gorgeous breakfast: just everything you can imagine— from flapjacks and fried squirrel to hominy grits and honey-in-the-comb. Which puts everyone in a good humor except my friend and I. Frankly, we're so impatient to get at the presents we can't eat a mouthful.

38   Well, I'm disappointed. Who wouldn't be? With socks, a Sunday school shirt, some handkerchiefs, a hand-me-down sweater and a year's subscription to a religious magazine for children. *The Little Shepherd*. It makes me boil. It really does.

39   My friend has a better haul. A sack of Satsumas, that's her best present. She is proudest, however, of a white wool shawl knitted by her married sister. But she *says* her favorite gift is the kite I built. And it *is* very beautiful; though not as beautiful as the one she made me, which is blue and scattered with gold and green Good Conduct stars; moreover, my name is painted on it, "Buddy."

40   "Buddy, the wind is blowing."

41   The wind is blowing, and nothing will do till we've run to a pasture below the house where Queenie has scooted to bury her bone (and where, a winter hence, Queenie will be buried, too). There, plunging through the healthy waist-high grass, we unreel our kites, feel them twitching at the string like sky fish as they swim into the wind. Satisfied, sun-warmed, we sprawl in the grass and peel Satsumas and watch our kites cavort. Soon I forget the socks and hand-me-down sweater. I'm as happy as if we'd already won the fifty-thousand-dollar Grand Prize in that coffee-naming contest.

42   "My, how foolish I am!" my friend cries, suddenly alert, like a woman remembering too late she has biscuits in the oven. "You know what I've always thought?" she asks in a tone of discovery, and not smiling at me but a point beyond. "I've always thought a body would have to be sick and dying before they saw the Lord. And I imagined that when he came it would be like looking at the Baptist window: pretty as colored glass with the sun pouring through, such a shine you don't know it's getting dark. And it's been a comfort: to think of that shine taking away all the spooky feeling. But I'll wager it never happens. I'll wager at the very end a body realizes the Lord has already shown himself. That things as they are"—her hand circles in a gesture that gathers clouds and kites and grass and Queenie pawing earth over her bone—"just what they've always been, was seeing Him. As for me, I could leave the world with today in my eyes."

43   This is our last Christmas together.

44   Life separates us. Those who Know Best decide that I belong in a military school. And so follows a miserable succession of bugle-blowing prisons, grim, reveille-ridden summer camps. I have a new home, too. But it doesn't count. Home is where my friend is, and there I never go.

45   And there she remains, puttering around the kitchen. Alone with Queenie. Then alone. ("Buddy," she writes in her wild, hard-to-read script, "yesterday Jim Macy's horse kicked Queenie bad. Be thankful she didn't feel much. I wrapped her in a Fine Linen sheet and rode her in the buggy down to Simpson's pasture where she can be with all her Bones. . . .") For a few Novembers she

continues to bake her fruitcakes singlehanded; not as many, but some: and, of course, she always sends me "the best of the batch." Also, in every letter she encloses a dime wadded in toilet paper: "See a picture show and write me the story." But gradually in her letters she tends to confuse me with her other friend, the Buddy who died in the 1880s more and more, thirteenths are not the only days she stays in bed: a morning arrives in November, a leafless, birdless coming of winter morning, when she cannot rouse herself to exclaim: "Oh, my, it's fruitcake weather!"

46   And when that happens, I know it. A message saying so merely confirms a piece of news some secret vein had already received, severing from me an irreplaceable part of myself, letting it loose like a kite on a broken string. That is why, walking across a school campus on this particular December morning, I keep searching the sky. As if I expected to see, rather like hearts, a lost pair of kites hurrying toward heaven.

⁊

Discussion Questions

*1.   Relate anything you found unusual about the relationship between Buddy and his cousin. Would you consider the relationship to have been a healthy one? Why or why not?

2.   Recount step-by-step the preparation that went into the making of the fruitcakes. By what various means did Buddy and his cousin earn money to purchase ingredients for the cakes?

3.   Describe the process by which Buddy and his cousin obtained a tree for Christmas. How did they manage to decorate it?

*4.   Cite by paragraph number indications that Buddy's cousin was each of the following: generous; sensitive; courageous; secretive; superstitious; patient; and limited in experience.

*5.   Relate the role that each of the following played in the selection: Queenie, Haha Jones, a three-legged biddy-chicken, the knife grinder, two angry relatives, kites, and a military school.

6.   From the selection, cite at least three clues indicating that the events recounted took place sometime between 1930 and 1940.

*7.   Reread paragraphs 1, 11, 23, and 34. Relate what effects the mix of fragmentary and complete sentences has upon these paragraphs.

8.   Sentiment suggests "refined or tender feeling"; sentimentality suggests "false, excessive, or exaggerated feeling." At what point or points in the selection does Capote risk being accused of sentimentality? Would such an accusation be justified? Explain.

Writing Topics

1. In paragraph 31, Buddy assures his cousin that she is "fun" rather than "funny." Assume that a foreign exchange student who is a classmate writes you a note asking you to explain the distinction that Buddy is making. Write your classmate a note describing the difference between a person who is fun and one who is funny. In your note, be sure to explain the connotations of the word *funny* as applied to a person.

2. Buddy and his cousin engage in a variety of activities to earn money to finance their fruitcakes. If you have ever taken on work to earn money for a particular item or activity, relate the experience in a brief essay. Include information about the object of your labor: why you wanted it, what you did to achieve it, and whether, in retrospect, it was worth the effort.

"How much of my delight in all beautiful things is innate, and how much is due to her influence, I can never tell."

MY TEACHER'S GENIUS

Helen Keller

Disease left Helen Keller (1880–1968) deaf and blind when she was only nineteen months old. Cut off from all communication, she was put in the care of Anne Sullivan Macy (1866–1936), who remained her teacher and companion until Macy's death. By the age of ten, Keller had learned to speak, and by the age of twenty-four, she had graduated *cum laude* from Radcliffe College. During the remainder of her life, she received numerous honorary degrees from universities throughout the world. Among Keller's books are The Story of My Life (1903), from which "My Teacher's Genius" is taken, The World I Live In (1908), Out of the Dark (1913), My Religion (1927), and Teacher, Anne Sullivan Macy (1955).

1   The most important day I remember in all my life is the one on which my teacher, Anne Mansfield Sullivan, came to me. I am filled with wonder when I consider the immeasurable contrasts between the two lives which it connects. It was the third of March, 1887, three months before I was seven years old.

2   On the afternoon of that eventful day, I stood on the porch, dumb, expectant. I guessed vaguely from my mother's signs and from the hurrying to and fro in the house that something unusual was about to happen, so I went to the door and waited on the steps. The afternoon sun penetrated the mass of honeysuckle that covered the porch, and fell on my upturned face. My fingers lingered almost unconsciously on the familiar leaves and blossoms which had just come forth to greet the sweet southern spring. I did not know what the future held of marvel or surprise for me. Anger and bitterness had preyed upon me continually for weeks and a deep languor had succeeded this passionate struggle.

3   Have you ever been at sea in a dense fog, when it seemed as if a tangible white darkness shut you in, and the great ship, tense and anxious, groped her way toward the shore with plummet and sounding-line, and you waited with beating heart for something to happen? I was like that ship before my education

began, only I was without compass or sounding-line, and had no way of know-ing how near the harbour was. "Light! give me light!" was the wordless cry of my soul, and the light of love shone on me in that very hour.

4   I felt approaching footsteps. I stretched out my hand as I supposed to my mother. Some one took it, and I was caught up and held close in the arms of her who had come to reveal all things to me, and, more than all things else, to love me.

5   The morning after my teacher came she led me into her room and gave me a doll. The little blind children at the Perkins Institution had sent it and Laura Bridgman had dressed it; but I did not know this until afterward. When I had played with it a little while, Miss Sullivan slowly spelled into my hand the word "d-o-l-l." I was at once interested in this finger play and tried to imitate it. When I finally succeeded in making the letters correctly I was flushed with childish pleasure and pride. Running downstairs to my mother I held up my hand and made the letters for doll. I did not know that I was spelling a word or even that words existed; I was simply making my fingers go in monkey-like imitation. In the days that followed I learned to spell in this uncomprehending way a great many words, among them *pin*, *hat*, *cup* and a few verbs like *sit*, *stand* and *walk*. But my teacher had been with me several weeks before I understood that everything has a name.

6   One day, while I was playing with my new doll, Miss Sullivan put my big rag doll into my lap also, spelled "d-o-l-l" and tried to make me understand that "d-o-l-l" applied to both. Earlier in the day we had had a tussle over the words "m-u-g" and "w-a-t-e-r." Miss Sullivan had tried to impress it upon me that "m-u-g" is *mug* and that "w-a-t-e-r" is *water*, but I persisted in confounding the two. In despair she had dropped the subject for the time, only to renew it at the first opportunity. I became impatient at her repeated attempts and, seizing the new doll, I dashed it upon the floor. I was keenly delighted when I felt the fragments of the broken doll at my feet. Neither sorrow nor regret followed my passionate out-burst. I had not loved the doll. In the still, dark world in which I lived there was no strong sentiment of tenderness. I felt my teacher sweep the fragments to one side of the hearth, and I had a sense of satisfaction that the cause of my discomfort was removed. She brought me my hat, and I knew I was going out into the warm sunshine. This thought, if a wordless sensation may be called a thought, made me hop and skip with pleasure.

7   We walked down the path to the well-house, attracted by the fragrance of the honeysuckle with which it was covered. Some one was drawing water and my teacher placed my hand under the spout. As the cool stream gushed over one hand she spelled into the other the word *water*, first slowly, then rapidly. I stood still, my whole attention fixed upon the motions of her fingers. Suddenly I felt a misty consciousness as of something forgotten—a thrill of returning thought; and somehow the mystery of language was revealed to me. I knew then that "w-a-t-e-r" meant the wonderful cool something that was flowing

over my hand. That living word awakened my soul, gave it light, hope, joy, set it free! There were barriers still, it is true, but barriers that could in time be swept away.

8   I left the well-house eager to learn. Everything had a name, and each name gave birth to a new thought. As we returned to the house every object which I touched seemed to quiver with life. That was because I saw everything with the strange, new sight that had come to me. On entering the door I remembered the doll I had broken. I felt my way to the hearth and picked up the pieces. I tried vainly to put them together. Then my eyes filled with tears; for I realized what I had done, and for the first time I felt repentance and sorrow.

9   I learned a great many new words that day. I do not remember what they all were; but I do know that *mother, father, sister, teacher* were among them — words that were to make the world blossom for me, "like Aaron's rod, with flowers." It would have been difficult to find a happier child than I was as I lay in my crib at the close of that eventful day and lived over the joys it had brought me, and for the first time longed for a new day to come.

10   I recall many incidents of the summer of 1887 that followed my soul's sudden awakening. I did nothing but explore with my hands and learn the name of every object that I touched; and the more I handled things and learned their names and uses, the more joyous and confident grew my sense of kinship with the rest of the world.

11   When the time of daisies and buttercups came Miss Sullivan took me by the hand across the fields, where men were preparing the earth for the seed, to the banks of the Tennessee River, and there, sitting on the warm grass, I had my first lessons in the beneficence of nature. I learned how the sun and the rain make to grow out of the ground every tree that is pleasant to the sight and good for food, how birds build their nests and live and thrive from land to land, how the squirrel, the deer, the lion and every other creature finds food and shelter. As my knowledge of things grew I felt more and more the delight of the world I was in. Long before I learned to do a sum in arithmetic or describe the shape of the earth, Miss Sullivan had taught me to find beauty in the fragrant woods, in every blade of grass, and in the curves and dimples of my baby sister's hand. She linked my earliest thoughts with nature, and made me feel that "birds and flowers and I were happy peers."

12   But about this time I had an experience which taught me that nature is not always kind. One day my teacher and I were returning from a long ramble. The morning had been fine, but it was growing warm and sultry when at last we turned our faces homeward. Two or three times we stopped to rest under a tree by the wayside. Our last halt was under a wild cherry tree a short distance from the house. The shade was grateful, and the tree was so easy to climb that with my teacher's assistance I was able to scramble to a seat in the branches. It was so cool up in the tree that Miss Sullivan proposed that we have our luncheon there. I promised to keep still while she went to the house to fetch it.

13   Suddenly a change passed over the tree. All the sun's warmth left the air. I
knew the sky was black, because all the heat, which meant light to me, had
died out of the atmosphere. A strange odour came up from the earth. I knew it,
it was the odour that always precedes a thunderstorm, and a nameless fear
clutched at my heart. I felt absolutely alone, cut off from my friends and the
firm earth. The immense, the unknown, enfolded me. I remained still and expectant; a chilling terror crept over me. I longed for my teacher's return; but
above all things I wanted to get down from that tree.

14   There was a moment of sinister silence, then a multitudinous stirring of
the leaves. A shiver ran through the tree, and the wind sent forth a blast that
would have knocked me off had I not clung to the branch with might and main.
The tree swayed and strained. The small twigs snapped and fell about me in
showers. A wild impulse to jump seized me, but terror held me fast. I crouched
down in the fork of the tree. The branches lashed about me. I felt the inter-
mittent jarring that came now and then, as if something heavy had fallen and
the shock had traveled up till it reached the limb I sat on. It worked my sus-
pense up to the highest point, and just as I was thinking the tree and I should
fall together, my teacher seized my hand and helped me down. I clung to her,
trembling with joy to feel the earth under my feet once more. I had learned a
new lesson—that nature "wages open war against her children, and under
softest touch hides treacherous claws."

15   After this experience it was a long time before I climbed another tree. The
mere thought filled me with terror. It was the sweet allurement of the mimosa
tree in full bloom that finally overcame my fears. One beautiful spring morning
when I was alone in the summer-house, reading, I became aware of a wonderful
subtle fragrance in the air. I started up and instinctively stretched out my
hands. It seemed as if the spirit of spring had passed through the summer-
house. "What is it?" I asked, and the next minute I recognized the odour of the
mimosa blossoms. I felt my way to the end of the garden, knowing that the
mimosa tree was near the fence, at the turn of the path. Yes, there it was, all
quivering in the warm sunshine, its blossom-laden branches almost touching
the long grass. Was there ever anything so exquisitely beautiful in the world
before! Its delicate blossoms shrank from the slightest earthly touch; it seemed
as if a tree of paradise had been transplanted to earth. I made my way through
a shower of petals to the great trunk and for one minute stood irresolute; then,
putting my foot in the broad space between the forked branches, I pulled
myself up into the tree. I had some difficulty in holding on, for the branches
were very large and the bark hurt my hands. But I had a delicious sense that I
was doing something unusual and wonderful, so I kept on climbing higher and
higher, until I reached a little seat which somebody had built there so long ago
that it had grown part of the tree itself. I sat there for a long, long time, feeling
like a fairy on a rosy cloud. After that I spent many happy hours in my tree of
paradise, thinking fair thoughts and dreaming bright dreams.

16   I had now the key to all language, and I was eager to learn to use it. Children who hear acquire language without any particular effort; the words that fall from others' lips they catch on the wing, as it were, delightedly, while the little deaf child must trap them by a slow and often painful process. But whatever the process, the result is wonderful. Gradually from naming an object we advance step by step until we have traversed the vast distance between our first stammered syllable and the sweep of thought in a line of Shakespeare.

17   At first, when my teacher told me about a new thing I asked very few questions. My ideas were vague, and my vocabulary was inadequate; but as my knowledge of things grew, and I learned more and more words, my field of inquiry broadened, and I would return again and again to the same subject, eager for further information. Sometimes a new word revived an image that some earlier experience had engraved on my brain.

18   I remember the morning that I first asked the meaning of the word "love." This was before I knew many words. I had found a few early violets in the garden and brought them to my teacher. She tried to kiss me: but at that time I did not like to have any one kiss me except my mother. Miss Sullivan put her arm gently round me and spelled into my hand, "I love Helen."

19   "What is love?" I asked.

20   She drew me closer to her and said, "It is here," pointing to my heart, whose beats I was conscious of for the first time. Her words puzzled me very much because I did not then understand anything unless I touched it.

21   I smelt the violets in her hand and asked, half in words, half in signs, a question which meant, "Is love the sweetness of flowers?"

22   "No," said my teacher.

23   Again I thought. The warm sun was shining on us.

24   "Is this not love?" I asked, pointing in the direction from which the heat came. "Is this not love?"

25   It seemed to me that there could be nothing more beautiful than the sun, whose warmth makes all things grow. But Miss Sullivan shook her head, and I was greatly puzzled and disappointed. I thought it strange that my teacher could not show me love.

26   A day or two afterward I was stringing beads of different sizes in symmetrical groups—two large beads, three small ones, and so on. I had made many mistakes, and Miss Sullivan had pointed them out again and again with gentle patience. Finally I noticed a very obvious error in the sequence and for an instant I concentrated my attention on the lesson and tried to think how I should have arranged the beads. Miss Sullivan touched my forehead and spelled with decided emphasis, "Think."

27   In a flash I knew that the word was the name of the process that was going on in my head. This was my first conscious perception of an abstract idea.

28   For a long time I was still—I was not thinking of the beads in my lap, but trying to find a meaning for "love" in the light of this new idea. The sun had

been under a cloud all day, and there had been brief showers; but suddenly the sun broke forth in all its southern splendour.

29   Again I asked my teacher, "Is this not love?"

30   "Love is something like the clouds that were in the sky before the sun came out," she replied. Then in simpler words than these, which at that time I could not have understood, she explained: "You cannot touch the clouds, you know; but you feel the rain and know how glad the flowers and the thirsty earth are to have it after a hot day. You cannot touch love either; but you feel the sweetness that it pours into everything. Without love you would not be happy or want to play."

31   The beautiful truth burst upon my mind—I felt that there were invisible lines stretched between my spirit and the spirits of others.

32   From the beginning of my education Miss Sullivan made it a practice to speak to me as she would speak to any hearing child; the only difference was that she spelled the sentences into my hand instead of speaking them. If I did not know the words and idioms necessary to express my thoughts she supplied them, even suggesting conversation when I was unable to keep up my end of the dialogue.

33   This process was continued for several years; for the deaf child does not learn in a month, or even in two or three years, the numberless idioms and expressions used in the simplest daily intercourse. The little hearing child learns these from constant repetition and imitation. The conversation he hears in his home stimulates his mind and suggests topics and calls forth the spontaneous expression of his own thoughts. This natural exchange of ideas is denied to the deaf child. My teacher, realizing this, determined to supply the kinds of stimulus I lacked. This she did by repeating to me as far as possible, verbatim, what she heard, and by showing me how I could take part in the conversation. But it was a long time before I ventured to take the initiative, and still longer before I could find something appropriate to say at the right time.

34   The deaf and the blind find it very difficult to acquire the amenities of conversation. How much more this difficulty must be augmented in the case of those who are both deaf and blind! They cannot distinguish the tone of the voice or, without assistance, go up and down the gamut of tones that give significance to words; nor can they watch the expression of the speaker's face, and a look is often the very soul of what one says.

35   The next important step in my education was learning to read.

36   As soon as I could spell a few words my teacher gave me slips of cardboard on which were printed words in raised letters. I quickly learned that each printed word stood for an object, an act, or a quality. I had a frame in which I could arrange the words in little sentences; but before I ever put sentences in the frame I used to make them in objects. I found the slips of paper which represented, for example, "doll," "is," "on," "bed" and placed each name on its

object; then I put my doll on the bed with the words *is, on, bed* arranged beside the doll, thus making a sentence of the words, and at the same time carrying out the idea of the sentence with the things themselves.

37   One day, Miss Sullivan tells me, I pinned the word *girl* on my pinafore and stood in the wardrobe. On the shelf I arranged the words, *is, in, wardrobe*. Nothing delighted me so much as this game. My teacher and I played it for hours at a time. Often everything in the room was arranged in object sentences.

38   From the printed slip it was but a step to the printed book. I took my "Reader for Beginners" and hunted for the words I knew; when I found them my joy was like that of a game of hide-and-seek. Thus I began to read. Of the time when I began to read connected stories I shall speak later.

39   For a long time I had no regular lessons. Even when I studied most earnestly it seemed more like play than work. Everything Miss Sullivan taught me she illustrated by a beautiful story or a poem. Whenever anything delighted or interested me she talked it over with me just as if she were a little girl herself. What many children think of with dread, as a painful plodding through grammar, hard sums and harder definitions, is to-day one of my most precious memories.

40   I cannot explain the peculiar sympathy Miss Sullivan had with my pleasures and desires. Perhaps it was the result of long association with the blind. Added to this she had a wonderful faculty for description. She went quickly over uninteresting details, and never nagged me with questions to see if I remembered the day-before-yesterday's lesson. She introduced dry technicalities of science little by little, making every subject so real that I could not help remembering what she taught.

41   We read and studied out of doors, preferring the sunlit woods to the house. All my early lessons have in them the breath of the woods—the fine, resinous odour of pine needles, blended with the perfume of wild grapes. Seated in the gracious shade of a wild tulip tree, I learned to think that everything has a lesson and a suggestion. "The loveliness of things taught me all their use." Indeed, everything that could hum, or buzz, or sing, or bloom, had a part in my education—noisy-throated frogs, katydids and crickets held in my hand until, forgetting their embarrassment, they trilled their reedy note, little downy chickens and wildflowers, the dogwood blossoms, meadow-violets and budding fruit trees. I felt the bursting cotton-bolls and fingered their soft fiber and fuzzy seeds; I felt the low soughing of the wind through the cornstalks, the silky rustling of the long leaves, and the indignant snort of my pony, as we caught him in the pasture and put the bit in his mouth—ah me! how well I remember the spicy, clovery smell of his breath!

42   Sometimes I rose at dawn and stole into the garden while the heavy dew lay on the grass and flowers. Few know what joy it is to feel the roses pressing softly into the hand, or the beautiful motion of the lilies as they sway in the morning breeze. Sometimes I caught an insect in the flower I was plucking, and I felt the faint noise of a pair of wings rubbed together in a sudden terror, as the little creature became aware of a pressure from without.

43   Another favourite haunt of mine was the orchard, where the fruit ripened early in July. The large, downy peaches would reach themselves into my hand, and as the joyous breezes flew about the trees the apples tumbled at my feet. Oh, the delight with which I gathered up the fruit in my pinafore, pressed my face against the smooth cheeks of the apples, still warm from the sun, and skipped back to the house!

44   Our favourite walk was to Keller's Landing, an old tumble-down lumber-wharf on the Tennessee River, used during the Civil War to land soldiers. There we spent many happy hours and played at learning geography. I built dams of pebbles, made islands and lakes, and dug river-beds, all for fun, and never dreamed that I was learning a lesson. I listened with increasing wonder to Miss Sullivan's descriptions of the great round world with its burning mountains, buried cities, moving rivers of ice, and many other things as strange. She made raised maps in clay, so that I could feel the mountain ridges and valleys, and follow with my fingers the devious course of rivers. I liked this, too; but the division of the earth into zones and poles confused and teased my mind. The illustrative strings and the orange stick representing the poles seemed so real that even to this day the mere mention of temperate zone suggests a series of twine circles; and I believe that if any one should set about it he could convince me that white bears actually climb the North Pole.

45   Arithmetic seems to have been the only study I did not like. From the first I was not interested in the science of numbers. Miss Sullivan tried to teach me to count by stringing beads in groups, and by arranging kindergarten straws I learned to add and subtract. I never had patience to arrange more than five or six groups at a time. When I had accomplished this my conscience was at rest for the day, and I went out quickly to find my playmates.

46   In this same leisurely manner I studied zoölogy and botany.

47   Once a gentleman, whose name I have forgotten, sent me a collection of fossils—tiny mollusk shells beautifully marked, and bits of sandstone with the print of birds' claws, and a lovely fern in bas-relief. These were the keys which unlocked the treasures of the antediluvian world for me. With trembling fingers I listened to Miss Sullivan's descriptions of the terrible beasts, with uncouth, unpronounceable names, which once went tramping through the primeval forests, tearing down the branches of gigantic trees for food, and died in the dismal swamps of an unknown age. For a long time these strange creatures haunted my dreams, and this gloomy period formed a somber background to the joyous Now, filled with sunshine and roses and echoing with the gentle beat of my pony's hoof.

48   Another time a beautiful shell was given me, and with a child's surprise and delight I learned how a tiny mollusk had built the lustrous coil for his dwelling place, and how on still nights, when there is no breeze stirring the waves, the Nautilus sails on the blue waters of the Indian Ocean in his "ship of pearl." After I had learned a great many interesting things about the life and

habits of the children of the sea—how in the midst of dashing waves the little polyps build the beautiful coral isles of the Pacific, and the foraminifera have made the chalk-hills of many a land—my teacher read me "The Chambered Nautilus," and showed me that the shell-building process of the mollusks is symbolical of the development of the mind. Just as the wonder-working mantle of the Nautilus changes the material it absorbs from the water and makes it a part of itself, so the bits of knowledge one gathers undergo a similar change and become pearls of thought.

49   Again, it was the growth of a plant that furnished the text for a lesson. We bought a lily and set it in a sunny window. Very soon the green, pointed buds showed signs of opening. The slender, fingerlike leaves on the outside opened slowly, reluctant, I thought, to reveal the loveliness they hid; once having made a start, however, the opening process went on rapidly, but in order and systematically. There was always one bud larger and more beautiful than the rest, which pushed her outer covering back with more pomp, as if the beauty in soft, silky robes knew that she was the lily-queen by right divine, while her more timid sisters doffed their green hoods shyly, until the whole plant was one nodding bough of loveliness and fragrance.

50   Once there were eleven tadpoles in a glass globe set in a window full of plants. I remember the eagerness with which I made discoveries about them. It was great fun to plunge my hand into the bowl and feel the tadpoles frisk about, and to let them slip and slide between my fingers. One day a more ambitious fellow leaped beyond the edge of the bowl and fell on the floor, where I found him to all appearance more dead than alive. The only sign of life was a slight wriggling of his tail. But no sooner had he returned to his element than he darted to the bottom, swimming round and round in joyous activity. He had made his leap, he had seen the great world, and was content to stay in his pretty glass house under the big fuchsia tree until he attained the dignity of froghood. Then he went to live in the leafy pool at the end of the garden, where he made the summer nights musical with his quaint love-song.

51   Thus I learned from life itself. At the beginning I was only a little mass of possibilities. It was my teacher who unfolded and developed them. When she came, everything about me breathed of love and joy and was full of meaning. She has never since let pass an opportunity to point out the beauty that is in everything, nor has she ceased trying in thought and action and example to make my life sweet and useful.

52   It was my teacher's genius, her quick sympathy, her loving tact which made the first years of my education so beautiful. It was because she seized the right moment to impart knowledge that made it so pleasant and acceptable to me. She realized that a child's mind is like a shallow brook which ripples and dances merrily over the stony course of its education and reflects here a flower, there a bush, yonder a fleecy cloud; and she attempted to guide my mind on its way, knowing that like a brook it should be fed by mountain streams and

hidden springs, until it broadened out into a deep river, capable of reflecting in its placid surface, billowy hills, the luminous shadows of trees and the blue heavens, as well as the sweet face of a little flower.

53   Any teacher can take a child to the classroom, but not every teacher can make him learn. He will not work joyously unless he feels that liberty is his, whether he is busy or at rest; he must feel the flush of victory and the heart-sinking of disappointment before he takes with a will the tasks distasteful to him and resolves to dance his way bravely through a dull routine of textbooks.

54   My teacher is so near to me that I scarcely think of myself apart from her. How much of my delight in all beautiful things is innate, and how much is due to her influence, I can never tell. I feel that her being is inseparable from my own, and that the footsteps of my life are in hers. All the best of me belongs to her—there is not a talent, or an aspiration or a joy in me that has not been awakened by her loving touch.

                                                    ð

Discussion Questions

1.   Cite indications that Keller, prior to her learning language, was a sensitive and intelligent child.
2.   Describe the methods that Anne Mansfield Sullivan used to teach Keller the meaning of words. How did Keller initially respond to these efforts? At what point did the young girl first associate word with object?
3.   Summarize Keller's feelings and behavior immediately after and in the months following her having made the association between words and things.
4.   Why did Keller have difficulty learning abstract ideas? Describe the process by which she came to understand the meanings of *thought* and *love*.
5.   According to Keller, why do those who are both deaf and blind have great difficulty acquiring "the amenities of conversation" (paragraph 34)?
6.   In paragraph 52, Keller refers to her "teacher's genius." Do you think the word *genius* is appropriate to describe Anne Mansfield Sullivan? Why or why not?
*7.   By paragraph number, cite passages revealing Keller's deep appreciation of nature. Since Keller could neither see nor hear, do you find these passages unusual? Explain.
*8.   On a scale of 1 to 10, with 1 being most specific and concrete and 10 being most general and abstract, how would you rate Keller's style of writing? Explain your reasoning for your score with references to the selection.

Writing Topics

1. Keller once wrote a remarkable essay, "Three Days to See," in which she described in detail how she would spend her time if she were given the sense of sight for seventy-two hours. Assume that, beginning now, you had only three days in which to use your eyes or your ears, after which you would be permanently blind or deaf. Select one of the two senses, and in an essay describe what you would most like to see or to hear in the time allotted you. Give reasons for your choices.

2. If you share Keller's appreciation of the natural world, describe in a brief essay an outdoor locale that has special meaning for you. It might be a local, state, or national park; a favorite picnic grounds; a backyard garden; a seaside resort; or some other place. Try to make your writing so specific that your reader can visualize this place and will want to visit it.

"She was . . . that rarest of unicorns — a magical teacher, the kind who works an inexplicable and unrepeatable voodoo."

PHYLLIS PEACOCK: UNREMITTING FORCE

Reynolds Price

Widely acclaimed novelist, short-story writer, poet, play-wright, and autobiographer, [Edward] Reynolds Price (b. 1933) roots his work in the traditions and landscape of the cotton country of North Carolina, where he has lived for many years and where he is a professor of English at Duke University. He has authored more than a score of novels, among them A *Long and Happy Life* (1962), A *Generous Man* (1966), *Early Dark* (1971), *Vital Provisions* (1982), *Kate Vaiden* (1986), *The Tongues of Angels* (1990), and *Full Moon* (1993). In recent years, Price has become almost totally incapacitated by spinal cancer, an experience about which he has written in A *Whole New Life* (1994) but one that has not stopped his productivity. In 1995, with the publication of *The Promise of Rest*, Reynolds completed an ambitious trilogy begun in 1975 with *The Surface of Earth* and continued in 1981 with *The Source of Light*. In 1996 appeared *Three Gospels*, Price's translations of the gospels of Mark and John. "Phyllis Peacock: Unremitting Force" is taken from Price's memoir *Clear Pictures: First Loves, First Guides* (1989).

1   With her college-professor husband and young daughter, [Phyllis Peacock] moved to Raleigh in 1948 and began teaching junior English at Needham Broughton High School. I had a sophomore biology class in a room in which she taught the previous period; and we were always amused and a little spooked to see the crowded blackboards of grammar exercises, diagrammed sentences and barbed epigrams that the new teacher left in her wake, all in mysteriously coded colors of chalk. In her first month she put not only her own students on notice but the next generation as well; we were helplessly bound toward her.

2   And just as I'd come to the sad conclusion that my painting and film-making skills were thin and doomed, I landed in Phyllis Peacock's junior English class. At close view that first week of September 1949, I could see at

once that she was not only a formidable guardian at the gates of good old censorious, rule-ridden clear English. She was also that rarest of unicorns—a magical teacher, the kind who works an inexplicable and unrepeatable voodoo. The magic proceeds from a combination of effortless command of the subject, the discipline of a field marshal, the theatrical skills of classroom mastery and, most crucial, a fervent belief in the life-or-death importance of her subject.

3   Phyllis had them all in spades, especially the fervor. Class after class, she flung herself on the day's point—uses of the semicolon, a sonnet of Longfellow's, a story of Jack London's or the absolute demand for courteous behavior, in the classroom as in life. She was an unblinking reader of faces; so she must have known that we found her heat more than a little comic, till it turned on us. I've said that I had fine luck in teachers right along, but Phyllis was in a new league of exotic excitement. This woman plainly knew that poetry mattered like blood or money. I didn't know I'd been waiting to hear that. It turned out I had, though like my classmates I laughed awhile longer.

4   Since each year of my life had brought me fresh reasons for feeling out-landish, I began to warm to her sooner than most, though I continued perfecting my imitations of her manner—the instant smile that collapsed into the direst of frowns, the frail voice of pathos that descended and swelled to an iron contralto of scorn. By then I and my classmates were sixteen or seventeen. We were physically adult, however infantile in behavior; but we'd yet to encounter a teacher who expected us to *be* adult—to be impeccably punctual, reliant, no eyesore to look at, prepared and courteous. When we failed we were informed in terms that would have been equally appropriate at the burnt-out end of a marriage or a failed disarmament conference.

5   Life mattered, the smallest act was an important component of life, *get serious!* Strange to say, we did—with almost no exceptions. Then she said some-thing even harder to believe—we were men and women, not boys and girls. Expect no allowance for tender years. Yet with all her rigor, she laughed at herself when we least expected and could exercise mercy appropriately. Phyllis Peacock was the only teacher I've known who simply refused to let a sheep wander. He might not make an A, but he'd damned well better earn a B-minus or demonstrate some dreadful handicap. (The *damned* is mine. She'd have scorned my resort to the shorthand of mild profanity to express a meaning for which I should have worked to find a decent but forceful equivalent. Luckily for her, she retired before children began to use, every sentence, the oldest obscenities and blasphemies till now they have a language incapable of verbal outrage when needed.)

6   Eleventh-grade English concentrated on American literature, and Phyllis began to reach me powerfully when we moved into the reading of Emily Dickinson. Though the complete poems were still unavailable in a trustworthy edition, I'd for some time owned a Modern Library selection with Conrad Aiken's useful preface. Like all Dickinson's readers, I was partly seduced by the

legend of her chosen cloistered life—a choice I suspected was possible for me—but I'd also read all the poems in the volume. And in them, for the first time yet, I discovered an angle of sight and a voice that chimed uncannily with my own (later in the year I discovered the next blood-brother, Ernest Hemingway; and Phyllis proved her mettle by meeting his harsher texture with never a flinch).

7   She'd stand before us in a normal-size classroom, this small narrow-hipped woman as bare of fat as a steel bar and as coolly wild as Emily Dickinson, and read out

> *This is my letter to the world*
> *That never wrote to me. . . .*

In the act of reading alone, with no explanation, she'd make us see that it was not merely metrical language or a pathetic admission from one more dry spinster (of the sort most of us had several of in our huge families) but a not-quite-infinite shaft opening onto the adult world of knowledge and power, a glimpse of brands of feeling even more intense than our own and far more potent in the world than our pubescent howls. That first year with Phyllis Peacock taught me what I still believe—that Auden was badly wrong in his claim that "poetry makes nothing happen." Nonsense, poems change whole lives—mine for one, as the poetry of Hardy and Yeats changed the young Auden's.

8   That brief lyric of Dickinson's, and hundreds of others like it in her work and the vaster world of all poetry, was a true copy of a brave life's understanding. It could serve more purposes than a fifty-dollar Boy Scout knife—as shield, sky-scope, ice-axe, lantern, entertainment event and, maybe above all, as a hook for love. Phyllis convinced me that enduring literature was made by individual men and women much like us and that, for their pains, those heroes were due our endless praise and love. She was that romantic, that right.

9   I showed her some of my drawings, which she liked too much; and she soon asked if my vocation wasn't for the ministry rather than the desk. But by Christmas vacation of that first year, silently and in no one moment, I'd signed on in earnest for the life I thought lay behind the poems she read and we studied. I've said that, for my first prose theme in her class, I wrote a half-page sketch of Marian Anderson's recent recital downtown. And a few days later I wrote a short reaction to Olivier's film *Hamlet*. Phyllis responded with praise but she also let me know that the pieces might have been more fully imagined, more strongly braced with visual detail and less outright statement of the unproved truth I propounded so quickly.

10   Without quoting Conrad's famous claim that the prose writer can do nothing but make you *see* ("That—and no more, and it is everything"), she helped me begin to teach myself that no narrative can hope to succeed unless it takes invisible pains to make its story as visible to the audience as a good *clear* movie.

Her insistence on clear communication also began my eventual discovery of the next basic principle of narration—you can't tell your audience a story that (A) it either doesn't already know or (B) it doesn't want to hear. And each of those implies that your story had better be a good and familiar *copy*. You can tell no unprecedented stories about incomprehensible, emotionless life forms from Pluto or about Earthlings too revolting or boring to meet or watch through a two-way mirror.

11 And at a time when the more obscure works of Joyce, Eliot and Pound were fanning a high roar of narcissistic obscurity in so much American writing, Phyllis taught us otherwise. Now and then in a poem, she'd allow a little mist. But in narrative or critical prose, her own taste brought me to see how a writer must assume that his reader is a literate human being of good will and a reasonable degree of patience but of no special training or automatic allegiance to the writer. In short, she expected straightforward American English, stripped of shorthand, jargon and code and as lucid and entertaining as the complexity of the subject allowed.

12 In later years when I've sometimes known that my prose was clouding or clotting, I've pictured the frown on Phyllis's brow. And while I've occasionally slogged ahead, convincing myself that murk was implicit in my theme, I've never doubted the rightness of her principles and never regretted for an instant the fact I found in her as hardnosed an early reader as any suspendered city-editor from the grand dead days of American papers. (To be accurate and just, I'll add that Phyllis was preceded in my schooling by at least eight other English teachers, all women and five of them never-married, who inculcated principles that had been in force since the time of Samuel Johnson and are serviceable now. In thirty years of college teaching, I've met no more than a half-dozen students who've worked with teachers as firmly grounded.)

13 After that Rubicon experience in my junior year, I joined Phyllis's brand-new creative-writing class in the twelfth grade. By then she'd long since noticed my direction and urged me onward with poetry. Under her bright eye then, for another year I poured out verse. The metaphor is accurate, *poured*. However young and derivative, the lines that survive came down the fingers of my right hand with little more effort than it took to walk to the desk and hoist a pen.

14 That's not to deny that I often spent hours discarding worn thoughts or obscure language—Phyllis was one of the rare teacher-readers who could courteously say that she was confounded or bored (if more writing teachers could admit the frequency of their *boredom* with student work, what better books we'd have). But partly because of the groundwork of structure and logic built under me by Phyllis, her predecessors and a few who came later, the initial act of producing my work is mostly an occasion for excited ease, then relief and thanks. Only later, and colder, do the principles come back as battering rams to try if the thing can be breached.

15   She did me many more useful turns. In secret she sent my portrait of Olivier's Hamlet to the man himself; and back it came with a quote from the play and his signature. She and her buoyant husband Lee, who taught American literature at Meredith College, took me to New York for my first visit at age seventeen (New York then was a long way off). That was when we saw Ethel Waters and Julie Harris in *The Member of the Wedding*. In the same long Thanksgiving weekend, we also saw John Gielgud and Richard Burton in *The Lady's Not for Burning, Don Carlo* and *Manon Lescaut* at the Met. And I was addicted for thirty-four years.

16   None of her gifts lasted longer though than her endorsement of my sense, growing from the age of six, that all work which we agree to call beautiful rises from our early dealings with the unseen world of power, as the Mississippi rises in Lake Itasca. She let me know how she shared my belief that serious work — poems, mitered joints, sung songs, good bread — flows in a circle, whose final closure we cannot see, back to its source in an endless hoop. And in that closure all visible works will ultimately vanish.

17   Because of Phyllis's unremitting force . . . by the time I left her classroom in June 1951, I'd begun to suspect that every art I courted from stick-figure elephants to sonnets and stories was a facet, however fractured and cloudy, of a mirror aimed from various angles at the all-but-blinding face of a light that willed my reflected fragments into being, as it willed all else: me and the world I was helpless not to copy from here to the end, if it plans an end.

ਦੇ

Discussion Questions

*1.   Cite by paragraph number indications or evidence that as a teacher Peacock was each of the following: knowledgeable; energetic; demanding; caring; and honest.

2.   Relate why the poetry of Emily Dickinson made such a strong impression on the young Price.

*3.   Can you explain each of the uses to which, according to Price, a short lyric poem by Dickinson can be put (paragraph 8)? Is Price's claim valid or invalid?

4.   Recount what Price seems to be saying in paragraphs 16 and 17 about all "serious work." What do these paragraphs reveal about Price?

5.   What are the principles of writing that Price says he learned from Peacock (paragraphs 10 and 11)? Does Price's prose in this selection seem to adhere to Peacock's expectations as enumerated in paragraph 11? Explain.

*6. Cite by paragraph number and line examples of the following figures of speech that Price employs for stylistic purposes: *hyperbole*, a use of exaggeration for effect; *simile*, an expressed comparison between two unlike things, usually linked by *as* or *like*; *metaphor*, an implied comparison between two unlike things. For each example, try to substitute language that is equally effective.

Writing Topics

1. In paragraph 7, Price says that "poems change whole lives," including his own. If you have ever been changed by a particular poem, relate the experience in a short essay. What was the poem? What was it about? Under what circumstances did you first read it or hear it? Why did it appeal to you? What lasting effect has it had on you?

2. In paragraph 4, Price observes about his classmates and himself, "We were physically adult, however infantile in behavior. . . ." Recall your own behavior at age sixteen or seventeen, and, in an essay, relate either of the following: immature acts that you engaged in then that you would not consider repeating today, or, conversely, some things that you now do that you would have scoffed at doing as a junior in high school.

"That which to him was great evil,
to be carefully shunned, was to me a great good,
to be diligently sought . . ."

ORIGINS AND EARLY MEMORIES

Frederick Douglass

Frederick Douglass (1817?–1895) was born into slavery in Maryland, the son of a slave mother and a white father. He escaped to Massachusetts in 1838, where he was employed as a lecturer by antislavery societies. After publishing in 1845 a *Narrative of the Life of Frederick Douglass, An American Slave*, in which "Origins and Early Memories" appears, Douglass, fearing capture as a fugitive slave, fled to England and Ireland. Following a two-year stay, during which he earned enough money to buy his freedom, he returned to found the antislavery newspaper *The North Star*, which he edited for seventeen years. Douglass held a number of public offices after the Civil War and, in 1891, published the *Life and Times of Frederick Douglass*.

1   I was born in Tuckahow, near Hillsborough, and about twelve miles from Easton, in Talbot county, Maryland. I have no accurate knowledge of my age, never having seen any authentic record containing it. By far the larger part of the slaves know as little of their ages as horses know of theirs, and it is the wish of most masters within my knowledge to keep their slaves thus ignorant. I do not remember to have ever met a slave who tells of his birthday. They seldom come nearer to it than planting-time. A want of information concerning my own was a source of unhappiness to me even during childhood. The white children could tell their ages. I could not tell why I ought to be deprived of the same privilege. I was not allowed to make any inquiries of my master concerning it. He deemed all such inquiries on the part of a slave improper and impertinent, and evidence of a restless spirit. The nearest estimate I can give makes me now between twenty-seven and twenty-eight years of age. I come to this, from hearing my master say, some time during 1835, I was about seventeen years old.

2   My mother was named Harriet Bailey. She was the daughter of Isaac and Betsey Bailey, both colored, and quite dark. My mother was of a darker complexion than either my grandmother or grandfather.

3   My father was a white man. He was admitted to be such by all I ever heard speak of my parentage. The opinion was also whispered that my master was my father; but of the correctness of this opinion, I know nothing; the means of knowing was withheld from me. My mother and I were separated when I was but an infant—before I knew her as my mother. It is a common custom, in the part of Maryland from which I ran away, to part children from their mothers at a very early age. Frequently, before the child has reached its twelfth month, its mother is taken from it, and hired on some farm a considerable distance off, and the child is placed under the care of an old woman, too old for field labor. For what this separation is done, I do not know, unless it be to hinder the development of the child's affection toward its mother, and to blunt and destroy the natural affection of the mother for the child. This is the inevitable result.

4   I never saw my mother, to know her as such, more than four or five times in my life; and each of these times was very short in duration, and at night. She was hired by Mr. Stewart, who lived about twelve miles from my home. She made her journeys to see me in the night, travelling the whole distance on foot, after the performance of her day's work. She was a field hand, and a whipping is the penalty of not being in the field at sunrise, unless a slave has special permission from his or her master to the contrary—a permission which they seldom get, and one that gives to him that gives it the proud name of being a kind master. I do not recollect of ever seeing my mother by the light of day. She was with me in the night. She would lie down with me, and get me to sleep, but long before I waked she was gone. Very little communication ever took place between us. Death soon ended what little we could have while she lived, and with it her hardships and suffering. She died when I was about seven years old, on one of my master's farms, near Lee's Mill. I was not allowed to be present during her illness, at her death, or burial. She was gone long before I knew anything about it. Never having enjoyed, to any considerable extent, her soothing presence, her tender and watchful care, I received the tidings of her death with much the same emotions I should have probably felt at the death of a stranger.

5   Called thus suddenly away, she left me without the slightest intimation of who my father was. The whisper that my master was my father, may or may not be true; and, true or false, it is of but little consequence to my purpose whilst the fact remains, in all its glaring odiousness, that slaveholders have ordained, and by law established, that the children of slave women shall in all cases follow the condition of their mothers; and this is done too obviously to administer to their own lusts, and make a gratification of their wicked desires profitable as well as pleasurable, for by this cunning arrangement, the slaveholder, in cases not a few, sustains to his slaves the double relation of master and father.

6   I know of such cases; and it is worthy of remark that such slaves invariably suffer greater hardships, and have more to contend with, than others. They are, in the first place, a constant offense to their mistress. She is ever disposed to find fault with them; they can seldom do any thing to please her; she is never

better pleased than when she sees them under the lash, especially when she suspects her husband of showing to his mulatto children favors which he withholds from his black slaves. The master is frequently compelled to sell this class of his slaves, out of deference to the feelings of his white wife; and cruel as the deed may strike any one to be, for a man to sell his own children to human flesh-mongers, it is often the dictate of humanity for him to do so; for, unless he does this, he must not only whip them himself, but must stand by and see one white son tie up his brother, of but few shades darker complexion than himself, and ply the gory lash to his naked back; and if he lisp one word of disapproval, it is set down to his parental partiality, and only makes a bad matter worse, both for himself and the slave whom he would protect and defend.

7   Every year brings with it multitudes of this class of slaves. It was doubtless in consequence of a knowledge of this fact, that one great statesman of the south predicted the downfall of slavery by the inevitable laws of population. Whether this prophecy is ever fulfilled or not, it is nevertheless plain that a very different-looking class of people are springing up at the south, and are now held in slavery, from those originally brought to this country from Africa; and if their increase will do no other good, it will do away the force of the argument, that God cursed Ham, and therefore American slavery is right. If the lineal descendants of Ham are alone to be scripturally enslaved, it is certain that slavery at the south must soon become unscriptural; for thousands are ushered into the world, annually, who, like myself, owe their existence to white fathers, and those fathers most frequently their own masters.

8   I have had two masters. My first master's name was Anthony. I do not remember his first name. He was generally called Captain Anthony—a title which, I presume, he acquired by sailing a craft on the Chesapeake Bay. He was not considered a rich slaveholder. He owned two or three farms, and about thirty slaves. His farms and slaves were under the care of an overseer. The overseer's name was Plummer. Mr. Plummer was a miserable drunkard, a profane swearer, and a savage monster. He always went armed with a cowskin and a heavy cudgel. I have known him to cut and slash the women's heads so horribly, that even master would be enraged at his cruelty, and would threaten to whip him if he did not mind himself. Master, however, was not a humane slaveholder. It required extraordinary barbarity on the part of an overseer to affect him. He was a cruel man, hardened by a long life of slaveholding. He would at times seem to take great pleasure in whipping a slave. I have often been awakened at the dawn of day by the most heart-rending shrieks of an own aunt of mine, whom he used to tie up to a joist, and whip upon her naked back til she was literally covered with blood. No words, no tears, no prayers, from his gory victim, seemed to move his iron heart from its bloody purpose. The louder she screamed, the harder he whipped; and where the blood ran fastest, there he whipped longest. He would whip her to make her scream, and whip her to make her hush; and not until overcome by fatigue, would he cease to

swing the blood-clotted cowskin. I remember the first time I ever witnessed this horrible exhibition. I was quite a child, but I will remember it. I never shall forget it whilst I remember anything. It was the first of a long series of such outrages, of which I was doomed to be a witness and a participant. It struck me with awful force. It was the blood-stained gate, the entrance to the hell of slavery, through which I was about to pass. It was a most terrible spectacle. I wish I could commit to paper the feelings with which I beheld it.

9   This occurrence took place very soon after I went to live with my old master, and under the following circumstances. Aunt Hester went out one night—where or for what I do not know,—and happened to be absent when my master desired her presence. He had ordered her not to go out evenings, and warned her that she must never let him catch her in company with a young man, who was paying attention to her belonging to Colonel Lloyd. The young man's name was Ned Roberts, generally called Lloyd's Ned. Why master was so careful of her, may be safely left to conjecture. She was a woman of noble form, and of graceful proportions, having very few equals, and fewer superiors, in personal appearance, among the colored or white women of our neighborhood.

10   Aunt Hester had not only disobeyed his orders in going out, but had been found in company with Lloyd's Ned; which circumstance, I found, from what he said while whipping her, was the chief offence. Had he been a man of pure morals himself, he might have been thought interested in protecting the innocence of my aunt; but those who knew him will not suspect him of any such virtue. Before he commenced whipping Aunt Hester, he took her into the kitchen, and stripped her from neck to waist, leaving her neck, shoulders, and back entirely naked. He then told her to cross her hands, calling her at the same time a d —— d b —— h. After crossing her hands, he tied them with a strong rope, and led her to a stool under a large hook in the joist, put in for the purpose. He made her get upon the stool, and tied her hands to the hook. She now stood fair for his infernal purpose. Her arms were stretched up at their full length, so that she stood upon the ends of her toes. He then said to her, "Now you d —— d b —— h, I'll learn you how to disobey my orders!" and after rolling up his sleeves, he commenced to lay on the heavy cowskin, and soon the warm, red blood (amid heart-rending shrieks from her, and horrid oaths from him) came dripping to the floor. I was so terrified and horror stricken at the sight, that I hid myself in a closet, and dared not venture out till long after the bloody transaction was over. I expected it would be my turn next. It was all new to me. I had never seen anything like it before. I had always lived with my grandmother on the outskirts of the plantation, where she was put to raise the children of the younger women. I had therefore been, until now, out of the way of the bloody scenes that often occurred on the plantation.

11   As to my own treatment while I lived on Colonel Lloyd's plantation, it was very similar to that of the other slave children. I was not old enough to work in

the field, and there being little else than field work to do, I had a great deal of leisure time. The most I had to do was to drive up the cows at evening, keep the fowls out of the garden, keep the front yard clean, and run errands for my old master's daughter, Mrs. Lucretia Auld. The most of my leisure time I spent in helping Master Daniel Lloyd in finding his birds, after he had shot them. My connection with Master Daniel was of some advantage to me. He became quite attached to me, and was sort of a protector of me. He would not allow the older boys to impose upon me, and would divide his cakes with me.

12   I was seldom whipped by my old master, and suffered little from any thing else than hunger and cold. I suffered much from hunger, but much more from cold. In hottest summer and coldest winter, I was kept almost naked—no shoes, no stockings, no jacket, no trousers, nothing on but a coarse tow linen shirt, reaching only to my knees. I had no bed. I must have perished with cold, but that, the coldest nights, I used to steal a bag which was used for carrying corn to the mill. I would crawl into this bag, and there sleep on the cold, damp, clay floor, with my head in and feet out. My feet have been so cracked with the frost, that the pen with which I am writing might be laid in the gashes.

13   We were not regularly allowanced. Our food was coarse corn meal boiled. This was called *mush*. It was put into a large wooden tray or trough, and set down upon the ground. The children were then called, like so many pigs, and like so many pigs they would come and devour the mush; some with oyster-shells, others with pieces of shingle, some with naked hands, and none with spoons. He that ate fastest got most; he that was strongest secured the best place; and few left the trough satisfied.

14   I was probably between seven and eight years old when I left Colonel Lloyd's plantation. I left it with joy. I shall never forget the ecstasy with which I received the intelligence that my old master (Anthony) had determined to let me go to Baltimore, to live with Mr. Hugh Auld, brother to my old master's son-in-law, Captain Thomas Auld. I received this information about three days before my departure. They were three of the happiest days I ever enjoyed. I spent the most part of all these three days in the creek, washing off the planta-tion scurf, and preparing myself for my departure.

15   The pride of appearance which this would indicate was not my own. I spent the time in washing, not so much because I wished to, but because Mrs. Lucretia had told me I must get all the dead skin off my feet and knees before I could go to Baltimore; for the people in Baltimore were very cleanly, and would laugh at me if I looked dirty. Besides, she was going to give me a pair of trousers, which I should not put on unless I got all the dirt off me. The thought of owning a pair of trousers was great indeed! It was almost a sufficient motive, not only to make me take off what would be called by pigdrovers the mange, but the skin itself. I went at it in good earnest, working for the first time with the hope of reward.

16   The ties that ordinarily bind children to their homes were all suspended in my case. I found no severe trial in my departure. My home was charmless; it was not home to me; on parting from it, I could not feel that I was leaving any thing which I could have enjoyed by staying. My mother was dead, my grandmother lived far off, so that I seldom saw her. I had two sisters and one brother, that lived in the same house with me; but the early separation of us from our mother had well nigh blotted the fact of our relationship from our memories. I looked for home elsewhere, and was confident of finding none which I should relish less than the one which I was leaving. If, however, I found in my new home hardship, hunger, whipping, and nakedness, I had the consolation that I should not have escaped any one of them by staying. Having already had more than a taste of them in the house of my old master, and having endured them there, I very naturally inferred my ability to endure them elsewhere, and especially in Baltimore; for I had something of the feeling about Baltimore, that is expressed in the proverb, that "being hanged in England is preferable to dying a natural death in Ireland." I had the strongest desire to see Baltimore. Cousin Tom, though not fluent in speech, had inspired me with that desire by his eloquent description of the place. I could never point out any thing at the Great House, no matter how beautiful or powerful, but that he had seen something at Baltimore far exceeding both in beauty and strength, the object which I pointed out to him. Even the Great House itself, with all its pictures, was far inferior to many buildings in Baltimore. So strong was my desire, that I thought a gratification of it would fully compensate for whatever loss of comforts I should sustain by the exchange. I left without regret, and with the highest hopes of future happiness.

17   We sailed out of Miles River for Baltimore on a Saturday morning. I remember only the day of the week, for at that time I had no knowledge of the days of the month, nor the months of the year. On setting sail, I walked aft, and gave to Colonel Lloyd's plantation what I hoped would be the last look. I then placed myself in the bows of the sloop, and there spent the remainder of the day in looking ahead, interesting myself in what was in the distance rather than in things near by or behind.

18   In the afternoon of that day, we reached Annapolis, the capital of the State. We stopped but a few moments, so that I had no time to go on shore. It was the first large town that I had ever seen, and though it would look small compared with some of our New England factory villages, I thought it a wonderful place for its size—more imposing even than the Great House Farm!

19   We arrived at Baltimore early on Sunday morning, landing at Smith's Wharf, not far from Bowley's Wharf. We had on board the sloop a large flock of sheep; and after aiding in driving them to the slaughterhouse of Mr. Curtis on Loudon Slater's Hill, I was conducted by Rich, one of the hands belonging on board of the sloop, to my new home in Alliciana Street, near Mr. Gardner's ship-yard, on Fells Point.

20   Mr. and Mrs. Auld were both at home, and met me at the door with their little son Thomas, to take care of whom I had been given. And here I saw what I had never seen before; it was a white face beaming with the most kindly emotions; it was the face of my new mistress, Sophia Auld. I wish I could describe the rapture that flashed through my soul as I beheld it. It was a new and strange sight to me, brightening up my pathway with the light of happiness. Little Thomas was told, there was his Freddy—and I was told to take care of little Thomas; and thus I entered upon the duties of my new home with the most cheering prospect ahead.

21   I look upon my departure from Colonel Lloyd's plantation as one of the most interesting events of my life. It is possible, and even quite probably, that but for the mere circumstance of being removed from that plantation to Baltimore, I should have to-day, instead of being here seated by my own table, in the enjoyment of freedom and the happiness of home, writing this Narrative, been confined in the galling chains of slavery. Going to live at Baltimore laid the foundation, and opened the gateway, to all my subsequent prosperity. I have ever regarded it as the first plain manifestation of that kind providence which has ever since attended me, and marked my life with so many favors. I regarded the selection of myself as being somewhat remarkable. There were a number of slave children that might have been sent from the plantation to Baltimore. There were those younger, those older, and those of the same age. I was chosen from among them all, and was the first, last, and only choice.

22   I may be deemed superstitious, and even egotistical, in regarding this event as a special interposition of divine Providence in my favor. But I should be false to the earliest sentiments of my soul, if I suppressed the opinion. I prefer to be true to myself, even at the hazard of incurring the ridicule of others, rather than to be false, and incur my own abhorrence. From my earliest recollection, I date the entertainment of a deep conviction that slavery would not always be able to hold me within its foul embrace; and in the darkest hours of my career in slavery, this living word of faith and spirit of hope departed not from me, but remained like ministering angels to cheer me through the gloom. This good spirit was from God, and to him I offer thanksgiving and praise.

23   My new mistress proved to be all she appeared when I first met her at the door—a woman of the kindest heart and finest feelings. She had never had a slave under her control previously to myself, and prior to her marriage she had been dependent upon her own industry to get a living. She was by trade a weaver; and by constant application to her business, she had been in a good degree preserved from the blighting and dehumanizing effects of slavery. I was utterly astonished at her goodness. I scarcely knew how to behave towards her. She was entirely unlike any other white woman I had ever seen. I could not approach her as I was accustomed to approach other white ladies. My early instruction was all out of place. The crouching servility, usually so acceptable a

quality in a slave, did not answer when manifested toward her. Her favor was not gained by it; she seemed to be disturbed by it. She did not deem it impudent or unmannerly for a slave to look her in the face. The meanest slave was put fully at ease in her presence, and none left without feeling better for having seen her. Her face was made of heavenly smiles, and her voice of tranquil music.

24 But, alas! this kind heart had but a short time to remain such. The fatal poison of irresponsible power was already in her hands, and soon commenced its infernal work. That cheerful eye, under the influence of slavery, soon became red with rage; that voice, made all of sweet accord, changed to one of harsh and horrid discord; and that angelic face gave place to that of a demon.

25 Very soon after I went to live with Mr. and Mrs. Auld, she very kindly commenced to teach me the A, B, C. After I had learned this, she assisted me in learning to spell words of three or four letters. Just at this point of my progress, Mr. Auld found out what was going on, and at once forbade Mrs. Auld to instruct me further, telling her, among other things, that it was unlawful, as well as unsafe, to teach a slave to read. To use his own words, further, he said, "If you give a nigger an inch, he will take an ell. A nigger should know nothing but to obey his master—to do as he is told to do. Learning would *spoil* the best nigger in the world. Now," he said, "if you teach that nigger (speaking of myself) how to read, there would be no keeping him. It would be forever unfit for him to be a slave. He would at once become unmanageable, and of no value to his master. As to himself, it could do him no good, but a great deal of harm. It would make him discontented and unhappy." These words sank deep into my heart, stirring up sentiments within that lay slumbering, and called into existence an entirely new train of thought. It was a new and special revelation explaining dark and mysterious things, with which my youthful understanding had struggled, but struggled in vain. I now understood what had been to me a most perplexing difficulty—to wit, the white man's power to enslave the black man. It was a grand achievement, and I prized it highly. From that moment, I understood the pathway from slavery to freedom. It was just what I wanted, and I got it at a time when I the least expected it. Whilst I was saddened by the thought of losing the aid of my kind mistress, I was gladdened by the invaluable instruction which, by the merest accident, I had gained from my master. Though conscious of the difficulty of learning without a teacher, I set out with high hope, and a fixed purpose, at whatever cost of trouble, to learn how to read. The very decided manner with which he spoke, and strove to impress his wife with the evil consequences of giving me instruction, served to convince me that he was deeply sensible of the truths he was uttering. It gave me the best assurance that I might rely with the utmost confidence on the results which, he said, would flow from teaching me to read. What he most dreaded, that I most desired. What he most loved, that I most hated. That which to him was a great evil, to be carefully shunned, was to me a great good, to be diligently sought; and the argument which he so warmly urged, against my learning to read, only served

to inspire me with a desire and determination to learn. In learning to read, I owe almost as much to the bitter opposition of my master as to the kindly aid of my mistress. I acknowledge the benefit of both.

26   I had resided but a short time in Baltimore before I observed a marked difference, in the treatment of slaves, from that which I had witnessed in the country. A city slave is almost a freeman, compared with a slave on the plantation. He is much better fed and clothed, and enjoys privileges altogether unknown to the slave on the plantation. There is a vestige of decency, a sense of shame, that does much to curb and check those outbreaks of atrocious cruelty so commonly enacted upon the plantation. He is a desperate slaveholder, who will shock the humanity of his non-slaveholding neighbors with the cries of his lacerated slave. Few are willing to incur the odium attaching to the reputation of being a cruel master, and above all things, they would not be known as not giving a slave enough to eat. Every city slaveholder is anxious to have it known of him, that he feeds his slaves well; and it is due to them to say, that most of them do give their slaves enough to eat. There are, however, some painful exceptions to this rule. Directly opposite to us, on Philpot Street, lived Mr. Thomas Hamilton. He owned two slaves. Their names were Henrietta and Mary. Henrietta was about twenty-two years of age, Mary was about fourteen; and of all the mangled and emaciated creatures I ever looked upon, these two were the most so. His heart must be harder than stone, that could look upon these unmoved. The head, neck, and shoulders of Mary were literally cut to pieces. I have frequently felt her head, and found it nearly covered with festering sores, caused by the lash of her cruel mistress. I do not know that her master ever whipped her, but I have been an eye-witness to the cruelty of Mrs. Hamilton. I used to be in Mr. Hamilton's house nearly every day. Mrs. Hamilton used to sit in a large chair in the middle of the room, with a heavy cowskin always by her side, and scarce an hour passed during the day but was marked by the blood of one of these slaves. The girls seldom passed her without her saying, "Move faster, you *black gip!*"—continuing, "If you don't move faster, I'll move you!" Added to the cruel lashings to which these slaves were subjected, they were kept nearly half starved. They seldom knew what it was to eat a full meal. I have seen Mary contending with the pigs for the offal thrown into the street. So much was Mary kicked and cut to pieces, that she was oftener called "*pecked*" than by her name.

27   I lived in Master Hugh's family about seven years. During this time, I succeeded in learning to read and write. In accomplishing this, I was compelled to resort to various stratagems. I had no regular teacher. My mistress, who had kindly commenced to instruct me, had, in compliance with the advice and direction of her husband, not only ceased to instruct, but had set her face against my being instructed by any one else. It is due, however, to my mistress to say of her, that she did not adopt this course of treatment immediately. She at first

lacked the depravity indispensable to shutting me up in mental darkness. It was at least necessary for her to have some training in the exercise of irresponsible power, to make her equal to the task of treating me as though I were a brute.

28   My mistress was, as I have said, a kind and tenderhearted woman; and in the simplicity of her soul she commenced, when I first went to live with her, to treat me as she supposed one human being ought to treat another. In entering upon the duties of a slaveholder, she did not seem to perceive that I sustained to her the relation of a mere chattel, and that for her to treat me as a human being was not only wrong, but dangerously so. Slavery proved as injurious to her as it did to me. When I went there, she was a pious, warm, and tender-hearted woman. There was no sorrow or suffering for which she had not a tear. She had bread for the hungry, clothes for the naked, and comfort for every mourner that came within her reach. Slavery soon proved its ability to divest her of these heavenly qualities. Under its influence, the tender heart became stone, and the lamblike disposition gave way to one of tiger-like fierceness. The first step in her downward course, was in her ceasing to instruct me. She now commenced to practice her husband's precepts. She finally became even more violent in her opposition than her husband himself. She was not satisfied with simply doing as well as he had commanded; she seemed anxious to do better. Nothing seemed to make her more angry than to see me with a newspaper. She seemed to think that here lay the danger. I have had her rush at me with a face made all up of fury, and snatch from me a newspaper, in a manner that fully revealed her apprehension. She was an apt woman; and a little experience soon demonstrated, to her satisfaction, that education and slavery were incompatible with each other.

29   From this time I was most narrowly watched. If I was in a separate room any considerable length of time, I was sure to be suspected of having a book, and was at once called to give an account of myself. All this, however, was too late. The first step had been taken. Mistress, in teaching me the alphabet, had given me the *inch*, and no precaution could prevent me from taking the *ell*.

30   The plan which I adopted, and the one by which I was most successful, was that of making friends of all the little white boys whom I met in the street. As many of these as I could, I converted into teachers. With their kindly aid, obtained at different times and in different places, I finally succeeded in learning to read. When I was sent off on errands, I always took my book with me, and by going one part of my errand quickly, I found time to get a lesson before my return. I used also to carry bread with me, enough of which was always in the house, and to which I was always welcome; for I was much better off in this regard than many of the poor white children in our neighborhood. This bread I used to bestow upon the hungry little urchins, who, in return, would give me that more valuable bread of knowledge. I am strongly tempted to give the names of two or three of those little boys, as a testimonial of the gratitude and affection I bear them; but prudence forbids—not that it would injure me, but it

might embarrass them; for it is almost an unpardonable offense to teach slaves to read in this Christian country. It is enough to say of the dear little fellows, that they lived on Philpot Street, very near Durgin and Bailey's ship-yard. I used to talk this matter of slavery over with them. I would sometimes say to them, I wished I could be as free as they would be when they got to be men. "You will be free as soon as you are twenty-one, *but I am a slave for life!* Have not I as good a right to be free as you have?" These words used to trouble them; they would express for me the liveliest sympathy, and console me with the hope that something would occur by which I might be free.

✌

Discussion Questions

1. Summarize what Douglass says about his date of birth and his parentage. Why is he vague about details?

2. How often and under what conditions did Douglass's mother visit him? Why was the relationship between the two not a sustained one?

3. According to Douglass, what made the relationship between white slave owners and their mulatto children particularly complex, and what were the usual consequences for the mulatto offspring? In the author's estimation, what long-range implications for slavery did the growing number of mulatto children have?

*4. Sketch the personalities of each of the following and relate the role each played in Douglass's early life: Captain Anthony, Mr. Plummer, Aunt Hester, Colonel Lloyd, and Hugh Auld.

5. How, in general, according to Douglass, did the treatment of a slave on a plantation differ from the treatment of a slave in the city? How does Douglass account for this difference in treatment?

6. Summarize Mrs. Auld's changes in behavior toward Douglass during his seven-year stay with the Auld family. Why might slavery, as Douglass suggests, inevitably have had a corrupting effect on otherwise decent people?

7. Interpret in paragraph 25 what Douglass means by claiming now to understand "the white man's power to enslave the black man." What subsequent steps did Douglass proceed to take along "the pathway from slavery to freedom"?

*8. Whose writing style is closest to Douglass's in "Origins and Early Memories": Tarbell's, Keller's, Capote's, or Price's? In making comparisons, consider such matters as diction, sentence and paragraph length and rhythm, uses of figurative language, presence of dialogue, and tone.

Writing Topics

1. In paragraphs 21 and 22, Douglass expresses his belief that, in being chosen to move to Baltimore, divine Providence had interposed on his behalf. If you have ever had an experience about which you sensed the intervention of Providence, write about it in an essay. Relate what the situation was, who was involved, what happened, and what led you to believe that Providence played a part.

2. Douglass's learning to read was spurred on by the opposition of Hugh Auld. Recount in a short essay a time when you fulfilled a desire or reached a personal goal despite, or perhaps in part because of, the opposition of others. The desire or goal might have been that of owning a car, dating a certain person, participating in a given sport, holding a particular job, or traveling to a specific destination despite protests from parents, guardians, or friends. Whatever the desire or goal, provide sufficient details so that the reader will appreciate your determination and delight in your success.

Summary Writing Topics

*1. Dorothy West's mother apparently stayed home to raise her children. Assume that you are a parent concerned about whether children are socially or intellectually deprived by having both parents work outside the home. After examining evidence on this issue, write a report to share with other parents.

2. A friend of yours does not understand what Jay McInerney meant when he wrote, "Carver's language was unmistakably like Hemingway's—the simplicity and clarity, the repetitions, the nearly conversational rhythms, the precision of physical description." After reading at least four short stories by each author, write an essay for your friend in which you illustrate what McInerney meant.

3. Film director Robert Altman based his film *Short Cuts* on nine short stories and one poem by Raymond Carver. In a critique intended for a college magazine, compare Carver's story "A Small, Good Thing" to the sequence in the film adapted from the story. What changes from the original did Altman make? For what apparent purposes? With what effect? Which did you prefer—the original story or the film adaptation? Why?

4. Assume that you are asked on an employment form to describe the people who have had the most influence on your life. Write a response in which you pay homage to at least two individuals who you believe have been major helpers and shapers in determining who you are as a person. Provide specific examples or illustrations of ways in which each individual has influenced your development.

*5. As Indicated by Ida Tarbell, Allegheny College was once an all-male institution. Assume that you attend a single-sex college that is considering becoming coeducational. You have been asked by the board of trustees to investigate the pros and cons of your college's remaining a single-sex institution. Upon finishing your investigation, you are to write a well-supported recommendation on the kind of admissions policy your college should follow.

*6. Assume that relatives of yours have a daughter who is deaf but can see. They are unsure as to how to have their child educated—whether the girl should learn to read lips, to vocalize, to use American sign language exclusively, or something altogether different. They have asked you to look into the strengths and drawbacks of each method and to write them your recommendations, providing reasons for each.

*7. As Frederick Douglass relates, most African Americans were once deprived knowledge of how to read. They were also deprived the right to vote. Write a report for a school magazine on the historical struggle of African Americans to become enfranchised and on how their right to vote has affected politics in the United States.

*8. Like African Americans, women in the United States were unable to vote for many years. Assume that you have been asked by the local League of Women Voters to write a historical report on the women's suffrage movement, which culminated in 1920 with passage of the 19th Amendment to the Constitution, allowing women to vote. Conclude your report with suggestions on how women today might use their voting privilege to heighten their political influence.

*9. Ida Tarbell was a relative rarity for her time—a female scientist. Assume that the counselors at your college ask you to write a report titled "Women's Opportunities in Science Today." In your report, indicate women's opportunities in various branches of science, including opportunities in industry as well as in academia. Conclude your report with recommendations on how to increase women's involvement in scientific careers.

Cluster 6

Being and Becoming

Most of our days are spent routinely. We fill them by eating, sleeping, working, reading, talking, visiting, driving, viewing. We take showers, wash dishes, leaf through newspapers, empty wastebaskets, shop for groceries, call repair people, make appointments, go for interviews. We drop notes to friends, fill out questionnaires and tax forms, answer wrong numbers, write checks, toss away junk mail, balance bank accounts, fret about the weather, and speculate about what we'll have for dinner.

Though seemingly humdrum in content and monotonous in pace, such days are cumulatively important. During them, we continue to exist and to grow, to be and to become. Moreover, if we probe them carefully, turning them this way and that, we discover that no two days, no two events, are truly identical; that some hours and some moments cling to memory as being more significant than others; that despite whatever sense of ennui may occasionally threaten to swamp us, we are constantly learning new things, storing up additional information, honing our intuitions, making more refined inferences, and deepening the well of our feelings.

To test these notions, all we need to do is keep a diary for a year during which we scrupulously record the eventful happenings of each day. At year's end, we should be pleasantly surprised, if not a bit stunned, at how varied and plentiful have been both our experiences and our emotional responses to them. If we decide against keeping a diary, we should at the least take inventory at the end of each year, making note of happenings of the past twelve months that differed appreciably from those of the year preceding. Again, the variety recorded should undermine our assumptions about the depths of our ruts.

If there are telling moments in the least of our days, imagine how strikingly more meaningful to our lives are those occasions when our routines are disrupted, when inner or outer forces disturb our usual sense of equilibrium. Such occasions may result from psychological or physiological

changes occurring from within—a sudden intuition or an enlightening spiritual insight, the onset of puberty or of menopause, pregnancy, a debilitating
illness, or old age. Or the occasions may result from changes, unanticipated
or anticipated, occurring from without—marriage, divorce, parenthood, a
shift of job or location, the lingering sickness or death of a loved one, a natural calamity such as a flood or an earthquake. Whatever their origins, such
occasions disrupt the flow of our days, forcing us to reassess and reorganize
our lives and to modify our sense of being and, with it, the **I** that symbolically
bears the totality of our experiences.

In the selections that follow, you will encounter both minor ripples and
deep whirlpools in the currents of writers' lives. Through her diary, you will
share a year in the life of a precocious fourteen-year-old girl; through her brief
essay, you will share the emotionally turbulent sixteenth year of an author
recollecting her youth. You will participate in the intuitive perception of one
scientist and the puzzling but profound mystical experience of another. You
will witness the differing painful responses of two writers to their mothers'
emotional illness, and you will analyze one writer's argument against assigning chores to children. Whatever their specific content, all of the selections
should enhance your understanding and appreciation of human diversity,
of the simple and complex ways by which each of us, responding to the
demands of our environment, engages in being and becoming.

"After enough time had passed to show that the Lord had kept His side of the covenant, it fell to me to fulfill mine."

CHANGE OF LIFE

Henry Louis Gates, Jr.

Henry Louis Gates, Jr. (b. 1950) is a native of Keyser, West Virginia. After completing an undergraduate degree at Yale University and graduate degrees at Cambridge University, he taught at Yale, Cornell, and Duke Universities before becoming professor of humanities and chair of the Department of Afro-American Studies at Harvard University in 1991. Among Gates's many books are *Figures in Black* (1987), *Signifying Monkey* (1988), *The Souls of Black Folk* (1989), *Bearing Witness* (1991), *Loose Canons* (1992), and *Colored People: A Memoir* (1994), in which "Change of Life" appears.

1   Though I didn't realize it at the time, probably the biggest reason I joined the church was Mama. Mama, who knew so well how life could kill the thing that made you laugh, who remembered at every funeral what a person had hoped to be, not what he had become, seemed to be dying herself, before my eyes.

2   It came with menopause, and that's how we talked about it. Because we never had the vocabulary to talk about what it turned out to be, a depressive disorder that never quite left her. In fact, she was never the same again, but of course permanence is something you recognize afterward. I can say that a veil passed over her life, dimming her radiance, and then never quite lifted away.

3   I was twelve and she was forty-six when it started, and it was beyond my comprehension. I only knew that something had eclipsed the woman who gave birth to me and raised me, and that nothing I could do seemed to restore things. I was powerless, and so was she. Mama's "change" was the great crisis in my life, the crossroads of my childhood. I was devastated.

4   It was when Mama got sick that I began to withdraw from other kids. She'd talk about dying for hours. She told me to prepare for her death. She'd tell me she was in a lot of pain. And then she would cry. No amount of love could help. I'm very sick, she would say, and I believe I'm going to die. You'll

live with your father, and things will be OK. But it is important that you prepare yourself, she repeated.

5   I noticed smaller changes. Mama, the fearless one, suddenly became afraid of dogs. She started to alter physically, as well. Mama used to do exercises devoutly and weighed a trim ninety-eight pounds. At about this time, though, she gained fifty or sixty pounds. Then the clutter in our home started, because she would buy canned goods obsessively, as if to stock a bomb shelter we didn't have. She began to buy cloth too, bolts of material for some future occasion. Before long, there were galvanized garbage cans filled with bolts of cloth. A sense of need, born of a childhood of scarcity, now came upon her, spurring a pack rat's notion of providence—a contained panic about running short. Running out. Going without. Needing and not having. Even as the house became cluttered with her acquisitions, she became obsessed with cleanliness, spending a good part of each day vacuuming. Vacuuming and dusting. I liked trying to help her, and would cook, and clean, and even iron sometimes. I would read the pamphlets that started appearing all over our house, with titles such as "The Phases of Eve" and "The Change of Life," so that I might get a handle on this crazy, evil thing that had entered our lives.

6   I could not break the spell, no matter how ardently I labored. The depression only deepened that year, and I watched her grow sadder every day.

7   The night they took her away to the hospital, she hugged me as if that was the end. I cried until I fell asleep, afraid that she would die, afraid that I was responsible. And if I was, as I suspected, responsible, I had a good idea how.

8   You see, I had developed all sorts of rituals. I would, for instance, always walk around the kitchen table only from right to left, never the other way around. I would approach a chair from its left side, not the right. Mama had hung a beautiful oak crucifix in the hall that connected our bedrooms and the toilet, and I would nod my head as I passed it, just as I had seen my father do at the Episcopal funeral of his father. I got into and out of the same side of bed, slept on the same side, and I held the telephone with the same hand to the same ear. But most of all, as if my life depended on it, I crossed my legs right calf over left, and never, ever, the other way around.

9   Until one Sunday. For a reason that seemed compelling at the time, probably out of anger or spite, I decided that day to cross my legs in reverse. It was a dare, an act of defiance, a deliberate tempting of fate. And it took place just after Sunday supper, at about 1:00 p.m. Mama had not felt like getting dressed that day. She was having "hot flashes," as she'd started to call them, and felt "disconnected," disembodied from herself. She was going to die, she said to me, over and over and over that day. She'd had one "spell" in the middle of a funeral, just a couple of Sundays before. I wasn't there, but I heard that my aunts Helen and Hazel had taken her out of the church to Hazel's house, where the post-funeral meal was being served. Talking crazy talk, was the way Daddy still describes it. Out of her head.

10   And on this afternoon, the sense of illness lay so heavy you could have gathered it in your hands like snow and rounded it into balls to throw. We all waited for something terrible to happen. And then it was Mama who told me, through her tears, that she had to go to the hospital, that she didn't know when she would be coming back, and that if she shouldn't come back, I must never forget that she loved me.

11   She didn't die. After her hospitalization of four or five days she started taking a lot of pills prescribed by the doctors, which accumulated like everything else. She had weathered acute depression, but despite real improvement, she did not emerge healthy and whole, as I had dared to hope. Her phobias would evolve in unpredictable ways. In later years, she developed a fear that objects resting on a table or a countertop would fall off the edge. She would go around the house pushing objects farther back from perilous edges. It puzzled and vexed me: I'd point out, in a reasoning tone, that it would take an earthquake to produce the results she feared. But Mama felt her life had been shaken by just such an earthquake; she knew how easy it was to fall off the edge.

12   As did I in my own way. My metaphor was an untethered craft, battered by frigid waters, too far out for me to bring back to shore.

13   But Mama wasn't the only one to change. I could never shake the idea that if only I hadn't dared fate to punish me, by crossing my legs the wrong way around, Mama wouldn't have become sick and gone to the hospital. It was a sense of guilt so enormous that I couldn't talk about it. Except to Jesus. That Sunday when Mama went away, I started to atone. I prayed all day, all evening, and the next day: if God would just let Mama not die, as she was convinced she was going to do, I would give my life to Christ and join the church.

14   After enough time had passed to show that the Lord had kept His side of the covenant, it fell to me to fulfill mine. When I announced my intention to join the church, Daddy thought I'd taken leave of my senses. Mama, quietly wrestling with her own devils, was more tolerant, of course, but even I saw that she hoped I would outgrow it. If you go into this thing, Daddy said quietly, scarcely able to believe his ears, don't do it halfway. And don't be a quitter. Nobody likes a quitter.

15   Nobody my age had joined the church in years, at least not the Methodist church. I had been thinking about doing it for several months, since I had turned twelve. It was 1962. Each time in the service when Reverend Mon-roe would invite all who wished to make Jesus their personal Savior to come forward and enter the circle, I had been tempted to go. But I waited until a Sunday afternoon service in Keyser. Reverend Mon-roe had two churches, you see; he preached at Walden in Piedmont, but his primary pulpit was in Keyser, and he'd shuttle from one to the other, preaching in one and then the other, each Sunday.

16   I sat there throughout the service, nervous and tense. My stomach was doing flip-flops. I thought he'd never read the invitation; I thought he'd never stop that boring sermon.

17   When finally he did, I found myself rising mechanically, stumbling out of the pew, wandering to the front of the church, standing right in front of Ralph Edell Mon-roe, and wondering what would happen next. Nobody quite knew what to do. It had been so long since anyone joined the church that no one could remember what came next. Mon-roe stumbled through the book of rites until he found the right page, and then he asked me the prescribed questions.

> Do you here, in the presence of God and of this congregation, renew the solemn promise contained in the Baptismal Covenant, ratifying and confirming the same, and acknowledging yourselves bound faithfully to observe and keep the covenant, and all things contained therein?

> Have you saving faith in the Lord Jesus Christ?

> Do you entertain friendly feelings towards all the members of the Church?

> Do you believe in the doctrines of the Holy Scriptures as set forth in the articles of religion of the Methodist Church?

> Will you cheerfully be governed by the Discipline of the Methodist Church, hold sacred the ordinances of God, and endeavor, as much as in you lies, to promote the welfare of your brethren, and the advancement of the Redeemer's kingdom?

> Will you contribute of your earthly substance according to your ability, to the support of the Gospel, Church, and poor, and the various benevolent enterprises of the Church?

18   Yes, yes, and yes! I answered as forcefully as I could, and the reverend proclaimed the reception address:

> We welcome you to the communion of the Church of God; and in testimony of your Christian affection and the cordiality with which we receive you, I hereby extend to you the right hand of our fellowship; and may God grant that you may be a faithful and useful member of the Church militant till you are called to the fellowship of the Church triumphant, which is without fault before the presence of God.

19   Then, departing from the text, he invited everyone in the church—all of them older women—to march single file to the front and welcome me into the fold. God bless you, Skippy, each one said, shaking my hand warmly, or hugging me, or running her hand over my forehead or across my head. That part was so beautiful that I couldn't help but cry. I stood there crying and shaking hands, until everyone had passed by. Then I sat down again.

20 The first thing I did after joining the church was to go down to the Five and Ten Cent Store, to the school-supply section, where they stocked the boxes of twelve, twenty-four, and sixty-four Crayola crayons. There I discreetly placed $1.18, in change, down between the neatly stacked cartons. I had stolen a box of crayons when I was six, and wanted to atone for my sin by repaying the store, with interest, for my crime.

21 I began to cook most of the evening meals for the family. When Mama felt like doing the cooking, I would bake: cakes and corn pudding. I still remember the two Betty Crocker cookbooks she had. They were the same shade of green as the *Webster's Dictionary* that Daddy used for doing the crossword puzzles every day. I loved to cook *with* Mama, just to be near her, to be talking with her. But I was constantly frustrated that we never had all the ingredients a recipe would call for, so I couldn't ever get it exactly right. What is oregano? I'd ask my mother, unsure how to pronounce it. And what in the world was cumin? I'd spend hours searching for a recipe that called only for ingredients that Mama stocked. They were few and far between. Furthermore, Betty didn't season with bacon drippings or ham hocks, and she didn't cook the vegetables long enough to suit us.

22 For the next two years, I didn't play cards, I didn't go to dances, I didn't listen to rock and roll; I didn't gamble or swear, as my classmates did. I didn't even lust in my heart—except once or twice for Brenda. I went to church, and read the Bible, and spent a lot of time thinking about questions that it turned out Miss Sarah and even Reverend Mon-roe weren't prepared to answer for me.

23 I enjoyed my time alone: I had to, since I hardly went anywhere during these two years, except for school and church. It gave me distance from Daddy and Rocky, neither of whom seemed to be crazy about the person I was becoming. It gave me space to think about Mama's change and a way to use my prayers to help her. It gave me a way to stop thinking so much about nuclear war. For the world now seemed a dangerous place, and the Cuban missile crisis of 1962 provided bleak confirmation. We all went to bed one night thinking that we were going to die in some terrible, horrible, nasty way. I prayed and prayed until I fell asleep. Ain't no use worrying about bomb shelters, Daddy had said. It won't help much. I just wanted to be at home when it happened, with Mama and Daddy and Rocky. I was worried that Daddy might not get to Heaven, as much as he cussed and played cards. The church would help with my worries about Vietnam, where my cousin Jay had been sent. His mother, Aunt Marguerite, was so upset she stopped reading the papers.

24 Larger things began to worry me, now. After I became a Christian and was saved, I was terrified that an angel would show up in my room, bearing some ominous message from God, or that such a message would appear in the form of Writing on the Wall. Miss Sarah would talk of that all the time. I agonized

constantly that a bad-news message from God would delineate my role in life, my obligations to God and to our people. That was one of the reasons I was afraid of the dark. I was terrified of the Visitation that would make me an agent of salvation. More concretely, I feared that one day I'd open my mouth and somebody else's voice would come out, as the Spirit possessed me to do its bidding.

25   I didn't want it to be like that. I didn't want to be an automaton controlled by heavenly remote. What I did feel was that God spoke His will to my heart if I asked what I should do in a given situation. I still ask, and, generally, I still hear. Sooner or later.

26   In those days, I spent long hours wondering about, and worrying about, God, Jesus, being born again, eternal life, Hell, the Devil, why bad things happen to good people, why good things happen to bad people, and what is right and what wrong.

27   In the end, as I say, joining the church gave me a space of my own, and I found solace in that solitude, long after I realized that the time had come to part ways with our small white wooden church.

❧

Discussion Questions

*1.   Relate the various ways in which Mrs. Gates's "change of life" affected both her and her twelve-year-old son.

2.   Why did Gates fear that he was responsible for his mother's possible death? Under the circumstances, did his ritualistic behavior strike you as being abnormal? Explain.

3.   Recount the bargain that Gates strikes with God in hope of preserving his mother's life. How did his father and mother respond to his announced intention?

4.   Describe the changes in Gates's outward behavior that followed his becoming a member of the Methodist congregation. What personal benefits resulted from his having made these changes?

5.   Relate the inner fears that Gates experienced after he had joined the church. Did these fears seem to outweigh for Gates the value of his church membership? Explain.

*6.   From what Gates says of himself in paragraph 22, would you consider him to be each or any of the following: a religious person, a devout person, or a typical adolescent? Why or why not?

7.   In your opinion, what stylistic effects does Gates produce by mixing fragmentary sentences with complete sentences in paragraph 5?

*8.   Interpret the metaphor in paragraph 12. Rewrite the paragraph, using a different metaphor to try to express essentially the same meaning.

Writing Topics

1. Gates lists in paragraph 26 a number of matters about which he wondered and worried. If you have ever had a similar concern, relate in an essay what it was; why it troubled you; what thoughts you had about it; the sources, if any, that helped you clarify your thinking; and any conclusions to which you came.

2. Like twelve-year-old Gates, many people have superstitions and engage in ritualistic behavior to ward off bad luck or evil. If you perform any rituals to avoid ill-fortune, relate them in an essay. Tell what they are, how you acquired them, how long you have been doing them, what you fear may result if you stop performing them, how you feel on those occasions when you are unable to do them, and for what reasons you would or would not recommend them to friends.

"Oh, it is horrible to grow up!
I would suffer in hell throughout eternity if
I could only be Peter Pan in this life!!!"

DIARY OF YVONNE BLUE: 1926

Yvonne Blue

Yvonne Blue was born in Chicago, Illinois, in 1911, the daughter of an ophthalmologist who was a Methodist and an atheist mother. When Yvonne was in high school, the family, including her two younger sisters, Boo and Tickey, moved to Flossmoor, a Chicago suburb. Yvonne continued attending University High School in the city. Awkward and shy, she was two years younger than her classmates (she had learned to read at age four), and, aside from having two close friends, Bobbie and Ginny, she felt lonely and mis‑understood. Yvonne started keeping a diary at age twelve; the portion that follows was written when she was fourteen. After high school, Yvonne went on to graduate from the University of Chicago and in 1936 married B. F. Skinner, who became a noted Harvard psychologist. For many years following her marriage, Yvonne Blue Skinner taught at Boston's Museum of Fine Arts and wrote both fiction and essays on art.

1   *JANUARY 1.* For days I have pondered upon a fitting beginning for this glorious diary. If I intended this for publication, I should begin something like this:

2   "I, Yvonne Blue, being in the fourteenth year of my life, and feeling that I am old enough to convey my impressions on paper, am going to write faithfully herein, and make this book a lasting memorial of me, for those who live after I die.

3   I have been thinking seriously today about my past life, and it is but right that I record my youthful recollections. Foremost in my mind is. . . . etc. etc. etc."

4   But I most emphatically do *not* intend this for publication, so I shall begin merely by recording the events of the past hours instead of the past years.

5   At about three o'clock today, Grandpa, Grandma, Aunt Elaine, Uncle George, Bonnie, and Bobbie, arrived (note—If I intended this for publication I should tell who Bonnie and Bobbie are, but as I don't, that is unneccessary).[1] [After dinner] Bobbie and I went up to my room. We put my big Buddha stand and Buddha on the floor with an Indian candle on each side and the small Buddha incense burner before it. And we locked the door and turned out the main light and turned on the lamp and burned incense and read about the Taj Mahal from my India book.

6   *JANUARY 13.* Some people try to write differently, but there isn't any *very* different type: of course there is backhand, and beautiful writing like Grandma's, and queer writing like Grandpa's but—oh everything is like that. Everybody has to come under something classified before Cleopatra reigned. It's not fair to the present age. There aren't any *terribly* different people.

7   Whenever anyone *does* try to be different, he is ousted—kicked out. There is no room for originality in anything. Once in a while someone writes something rather different, and then he is critisized. And I critisize too. But they are different in a weird, terrible way, not in a beautiful one. They think that the more disgusting and wicked things they write, the more different they are. I don't see why we can't imagine what life on other planets is like. I suppose its just because we can't imagine anything *different*. They say that the moderns are different—bosh—they are not more modern than Cleopatra,—she would have smoked if tobacco had been discovered, and she did everything else that they do, and more too. Nothing is *different*. Of course there are all the inventions, that make our life different now. But Cleopatra was just as well off.—I can't imagine a different person—a *tremendously* different person,—and neither can anyone else, for no characters in books are very different. That word is tired, it has been worked long enough—I wish there was a different word. There it goes again.

8   And I don't know what I've been trying to say. . . . I had intended to say a little about the different sorts of handwriting,—and Something just turned it all about, and made me write a lot of nonsense that I don't understand. A whole page of it! Why—it—almost frightens me. . . .

9   *JANUARY 16.* I read in study the other day, a few entries from two diaries of very different types,—Samuel Pepys' Diary,—and *A Diary from Dixie*,—the diary of Mrs. John Rutledge. And mine is a third "type"—if it can be called such. Samuel Pepys' diary, deals with political matters, mostly, but there are things recorded there that he wouldn't want his wife to see. That is why he wrote it in code. And he didn't want it to be published, but they utterly, disregarded his wishes, and revised it and published it in book form with sundry

---

[1] Bonnie was her cousin, daughter of Aunt Elaine and Uncle George. Bobbie (Valerie) was Yvonne's closest friend.

notes and prefaces and introductions and stories of the author. And people have it in beautiful editions in their homes, and they show it to other people and exclaim "so interesting! I think it is lovely to have in a library, and so nice to have a book not meant for publication! I feel so thrilled when I read all his secrets and think how surprised he would be if he knew it."

10 A *Diary from Dixie* is rather uninteresting because it was the intention on the part of the author to have it published after her death. And it also has prefaces and pictures and facsimiles of pages in the original. And in a note in front it says, "Some few entries have been omitted because they were personal, and of local rather than general interest."

11 Just the nicest parts of course. And they leave in the political parts. (It was written during the Civil War.)

12 My diary is not in the slightest degree, of political interest. Perhaps if I had been fourteen years old during the World's War, and had lived in Belgium or France, it *might* have been. But I'm not much on politics. My diary is of interest only to myself. But possibly in years to come they might publish it, and people would say of it the same as they say of Samuel Pepys now. It makes my blood boil. It would have, of course, facsimilies of pages, illustrations, prefaces, introductions, explanations, notes and all the rest. But the worst thing is the way they correct ungramatical phrases, and put down what they *think* you meant, and switch sentences around, and leave out the most interesting parts. When *I* read a diary I want to know just the errors the author made, and the personal parts and so forth. It's not fair. They would leave out my pet parts and write a lot of junk in the front about me, and make me seem silly and sentimental and senseless. I don't want *anyone* to have fun out of what I sweated for, after I am dust and ashes. I don't *want* them to say, "What a curious person! This book is a treasure, as a relic. But I can't imagine anyone writing as much, can you?" I don't even want my decendents to have it in the original. *I don't want them to! Horrid Horrid Horrid* people! I know they will say such things because that is what I should say if I were in their place. I'm not writing all this for them to read, and get pleasure from in after years. I'm writing it for *myself*, and for no one else. They have no business to correct mistakes. When one writes stories he scratches out and scratches out and copies over and over again, or else thinks out every sentence ahead of time. But in a diary, one doesn't stop for that. It is spontaneous. (at least mine is). If I rewrote passages, I naturally would perfect them. But *they* don't understand.

13 I know what I'll do! When I'm on my death bed I'll throw *all* my diaries in the fire!

14 *FEBRUARY 8.* I told Bobbie of my determination to burn my diaries, and she said not to because she thinks it best to have something left of us, when we die. There are arguments for both sides, — I will think it over. Bobbie wants her diary published, but I don't.

15   *FEBRUARY 15*. I like things that I don't exactly understand. I like to listen to the beauty of the words and phrases, as I like to listen to harmonious music. And not to understand a thing completely, elevates it, — makes it more lofty.

16   *FEBRUARY 18*. This year, for the first time in the history of the University High School, each teacher wrote a paragraph on the work of each pupil he taught. These reports were all sent home to the parents. There is no use in trying to hide the fact that I am not a marvellous person at school. So in case I should ever get "cocky" and say to children, — my neices and nephews, for I am never going to marry, — "Now when I was a girl I *always* had my lessons well. I can never remember a time when I wasn't the star of the class etc. etc. etc." — in case I should say that, I shall copy the report down word for word, — "without softening one defect", as Jane Eyre tells herself, when she draws her picture and Blanche Ingram's.

17   *FEBRUARY 28*. Yesterday I drove to Chicago Heights with Daddy, and when we were half way there, Daddy stopped the car, and showed me how to work it in first and neutral, and then he let me drive! He is going to teach me how to drive, and when I am 16 I can take it out alone. Someday I can have it for my own. I adore to drive.

18   *MARCH 3*. I have had two queer feelings within the last week. One was on a Sunday. There is a large expanse of land behind us, and there was a patch of ice there Sunday, so I took my sisters, and went skateing on the tiny smooth patch at the end of the larger place. We had taken the waste-basket to empty in our back yard, and had carried it to the ice. I sat on the overturned waste-basket, with my head on my arms which rested on my knees, and thought that how little I dreamed when I was in my old home, that some bright sunshiny winter day, I would sit alone in the center of a great waste of rough ice, on an overturned waste-basket with my head in my lap. It was such a queer detached feeling — like I was inside my own mind, — or outside, looking down at myself.

19   The other time was tonight at nine o'clock, after Mother and I had finished the dishes. I was terrifically hot, and it was so cool and clear outdoors that I thought I would run outside a minute. I sat on the back doorstep, looking at the myriads of stars. Then I ran around in front. It was darker there and so beautiful and fresh, — like a wet white rose, at night. Then I ran out to the road, — a long way from the house. I went to the very middle of the road, where there was a little depression or hollow in the gravel, — and there I sat, gazing at the stars overhead, and the grayish blackness of the fields before me, and the lights of the houses behind me. . . . I felt again, then, that queer detached feeling, just like I had before.

20   *MARCH 5*. This afternoon I went to the dentists to have my teeth filled. I took gas. It was so queer! I was scared to death, when he stuck a big thing over my nose, and told me to breathe deeply. It had a queer dark red-brown smell too. At first I didn't feel anything, and then all of a sudden I felt all tingly, — like my foot had gone to sleep, only all over. I seemed to be sinking down and at

each breath I sank down deeper. I lost consciousness then. I didn't feel like a person at all. I seemed to see, or be, I don't know which, a funny light irregular shaped thing against a patch of darkness. It jumped up and down too like the reflection of the sun, thrown on the wall by a mirror. I heard a noise too, one short noise, and two long. . . . Even the drill went like that. Then finally, Dr. Maginnis took it off, and filled the teeth. I am to go again every Monday until all my teeth are filled. I am going to take gas too. I rather like it. I imagine it is a little like opium. I read Sax Rohmer's book called *Dope;* it is trashy, I suppose, but oh, so interesting! It describes every step of taking *chandu* which is an oriental name for opium which is smoked.

21   I would like to take opium once, if I were sure I could stop at once. Everyone thinks he has the will-power, — very often he hasn't.

22   *APRIL 3.* We had supper at the Tower Building, Mother, Daddy, and I, and then we went to the theater. I love the city at night! I love to walk along the lighted streets and watch the people pass, or stand in the doorways of sea food places, sunk below the level of the pavements, billiard rooms, and theater lobbies. I love to look up at the colossal buildings with their occasional yellow squares of light. I love to feel that I am part of the pulsing city night-life, and among the poor, walking the streets, aimlessly, and the rich driving grandly up to the lobbies of the opera-houses. I like the queer people who pass — perhaps murderers, theives, Bohemians, artists, poets, novelists, pleasure seekers, job hunters, college youths, loafers.

23   *APRIL 4.* Bobbie and I are planning to be *wonderful!* — to improve ourselves. We want to be very thin and silent, but to say unusual things when we speak, and have people hang on our words. We will wear our hair straight. We want very pale faces, and red lips, and we will dress nicely. We shall be aloof, — above the common mass, and cynical, sarcastic, sardonic, satirical, ironic. Delicious words! I would love to have a skin like Lord Byron's — with a pallor like moonlight — the genius shining thru. *He* fasted. We want to read illuminating books — like Oscar Wilde.

24   But oh! how we want to be wonderful — and thin. When it gets warmer, I shall go on a four day fast. Not a bite for four days, and see if it does any good. We want to be deep too, and perhaps, a trifle obscure.

25   We will go queer places, and do queer things. We are going to be newspaper reporters together, come what may. Maybe they will send us to Europe and we will go around there, and live in Bohemia in London, like in Arthur Ransome's book of that name. If we can do all that, we shall have achieved our heart's desire.

26   *APRIL 10.* When we die, Bobbie and I would like to be burned and have the ashes put in little jars, and each jar put in the heart of an apple tree. On the cover of my jar, I would like to have written:

"Here she lies where she longed to be,
Home is the sailor, home from the sea,
And the hunter home from the hill."

[*Robert Louis Stevenson*]

27   It was Bobbie's idea of having the ash-jar put in the heart of an a apple tree, — but I like it, so I'm copying it. If she doesn't want me too, I want them scattered on the wind, part on land and part on sea. But I like the apple tree better. I would feel horribly with part of me one place and part another. Why how could I ever get up when (?) blows the horn? It's a good thing I don't believe in the Bible.

28   *APRIL 18.* Monday Bobbie asked me to spend the night at her house. I was sure Mother wouldn't let me, but she said that I could! Bob had our night all planned out. We each got into our pajamas at about 9 o'clock, and crawled into her big double bed, after saying our prayers. We wanted to awake at 12:00 at night, but we had a hard time getting to sleep and it was 1:10 when we woke up. *Then* comes the nicest part of all. We crept downstairs in the kitchen, and Bobbie put slices of cheeze between bread, and fried them in butter — Cheeze Dreams — or — Dream Sandwitches. Then we took them, with some animal crackers and peanuts upstairs. We sat cross-legged on the bed, lit the lamp, and ate the lovely soggy, melt-in-your-mouthy-buttery sandwiches, and the rest, and read Oscar Wilde. . . .

29   *JUNE 1.* I'm way behind in all my school work. But somehow I don't care if I flunk everything. What's school? Everyone that's good in school isn't good in his chosen work, and everyone that is poor in school isn't poor outside of it.

30   *JUNE 16.* School is over — and I have an Incomplete in French, — an incomplete that I will be two months in working off next year. But, hell's bells! (a pet expression of Bobbie's and mine just now) I don't care! School is over!

31   But I am rather sorry too. Bobbie and I have been thinking over the nice things about school — things that we will miss. There will be no more Golden Moments! We have had just three of them — moments when we both had work at home, but when leaving was painful — like tearing ribs from our bodies. Lingering, delicious *Golden* Moments — like amber colored wine that goes to the head, and makes one feel estatically uplifted with the Beauty of Youth and the Thrill of Life.

32   When we came back after our Freshman year the Pirate Passion had burned dim — when we came back after our Sophmore year the India Passion was flickering low, and I suppose that when we came back after our Junior year, the Oscar Wilde Passion (though I can't conceive of such a thing now) will have almost died out. And I don't want it to! But Bobbie and I always had something — some interest — and I suppose that next year a fourth interest — the oldest of all will replace the interests of this year.

33   Oh, it is horrible to grow up! I would suffer in hell throughout eternity if I could only be Peter Pan in this life!!!

34   *JUNE 23.* Ginny [a close friend] is leaving Chicago July 1st. She sails for Europe and Asia the 3rd. I'll never get to Europe. Nice things always happen to other people — I get all the horrid ones. That is more truth than poetry — I mean it terribly. I get Flossmoor flunks in French — no vacation — maybe California — I haven't been really happy since last summer before I went to camp.

35   *JUNE 25.* Today I went to the Jackson Park [Theatre] and saw Adolph Menjou in "The Social Celebrity." It was a good picture, but I'm not going to that theatre alone, again. I sat in a row all by myself, when the play began, but after a time I became aware of a young man sitting beside me. I thought it rather odd, because if I wanted to sit in a row with only one person in it, I would sit at least a seat away. But I didn't like to move, so I just sat still. Finally I stole a look at him. He was a nice looking blond with tortose shell glasses. He said to me, "I have never seen this girl on the screen before. What is her name?" I replied as shortly as possible, "I don't know." "The man is Adolph Menjou, isn't he?" he asked. (as if Adolph Menjou isn't one of the best known and most easily recognized actors on the screen!) "Yes", I replied, determined to say no more than was necessary. He didn't say anything else, but I caught him looking at me, every time I looked away from the screen. Then I became interested in the picture, and forgot all about him until he began crowding over in his seat. I looked down at my lap. His arm was hanging over the seat-arm, and his hand was almost touching mine. I moved as far away as I could, but finally his hand did touch mine. I, of course moved mine. I thought it was an accident and I didn't like to change my seat. But it wasn't an accident. Every time I looked down and moved my hand he would take his away, and then he would put it back again, but not noticeably. First he would put it on his chair arm. And then he would slowly move it over. I still thought it was an accident, and once I waited for him to move his first. But he didn't! — at least not in the right way. Finally it dawned on me, that he intended to take my hand. I was a fool. I didn't know what to do, and I determined that he shouldn't drive me from my seat. I was there first! But as soon as it was over I got up. I saw him waiting in the lobby and I didn't want to pass him. I thought that there was another exit, but there wasn't so I finally left quickly and ran to a waiting street car.

36   *JULY 3.* I have just finished reading this diary. A more tedious, uninteresting, sentimental, forced, slushy book, it has never been my ill-fortune to read. But still, I think I have improved since I spouted this choice bit, in all seriousness, a little more than a year ago: — (speaking of my cuckoo clock) — ". . . . . If you open the little door at the top the cuckoo peeps out, and if you touch his head he will bow, flap his wings and open his beak, but alas, time has silenced his bell-like voice, and not a sound issues forth from those opened lips."

37   Still, the part about the Golden Minutes sounds suspiciously like it. From now on, I'm going to be less sentimental, and more interesting.

38   I'm so tired of being fat! I'm going back to school weighing 119 pounds — I swear it. Three months in which to lose thirty pounds — but I'll do it — or die in the attempt. There its said — whenever I weaken I'll look at this, and then I'll *have* to keep on starving. Tomorrow we have a picnic in honor of the fourth — but just the same I'm not going to eat a single bite all day. I wish there was a pair of scales in Flossmoor.

39   *JULY 9.* But of course the next morning I took a chunk of bread and ate it before I thought of my resolution. And that day I *ate*, and *ate*. But today I am keeping it. It is now a quarter to four, and so far not a crumb of food has passed my lips — not even tooth paste — or water. But I'm not at all thirsty. I've the queerest feeling though — emptiness and rather like my stomach is contracting, and I want food terribly. Some delicious cookies came just now — all my favorite kinds. I put eight away — four lucious marshmallow cocoanut covered ones and four smaller ones also of marshmallow and mounted on vanilla wafers, but covered with malted milk chocolates. I smelled them, but somehow it didn't help so awfully much.

40   Of course I know I can't get thin in a single day — but I can start to.

41   It is now just seven. I am starving. I keep close watch on the clock, I can tell you — the days don't pass any too quickly for me. And I haven't weighed myself. But tomorrow we go out for dinner. While the family goes in, I'll sit in the car and read a movie magazine. When I go in to buy it, I'll weigh myself.

42   I feel queer all over and oh! so hungry. And yet I can smell the food cooking down stairs and not snatch at it furiously the way heroes in novels who haven't eaten for two days always do. I imagine myself eating hot crusty sugary cinnamon rolls or the cookies and two bars of candy that mother bought me, which are in my bottom drawer, and I *want* them. But I'm not mad with hunger. I sent for Antionette Donnelly's book telling just how many calories each food has. "If you are trying to reduce", she says, "you would better keep your food consumption for the day down to at least 1,500 — 1,200, if possible."

43   So (after the four days) — I am going to keep them down to about 50 per day.

44   And thats absolutely *all*, at least till I lose noticeably. No cake or pie or ice-cream or cookies or candy or nuts or fruits or bread or potatoes or meat or anything. If I could *only* drink tea without cream or sugar. It has *no* calories.

45   I have been exercising very little. 100 jumps with a jump-rope a day, is all, and I'm scarcely strong enough for that.

46   *JULY 11.* I ruined the good work today. I was so weak I could hardly pull myself out of bed. My hands shook terribly and I grew hot and cold by turns. I managed to dress, but when I went downstairs Mother said I looked so shaky and pale and sick that she *made* me eat. And to tell the truth I wasn't sorry, I had gone 60 hours without food. I ate an immense breakfast — two large peaches, a cup of cocoa with three marshmallows and two pieces of toast. I don't know what to do. I weighed myself yesterday and I've lost 5 pounds — I weigh 144. But I'll get thin yet!

47 *JULY 27.* Mothcr and Daddy make me so mad! They *make* me eat. Last week I had an average of less that 140 calories a day and I lost 7 pounds. And now they won't let me diet. Last night I dropped most of the meat in my lap, rolled it in my napkin and fed it to Tar Baby [cat] and at breakfast I put half my orange and bread in my napkin and throw it away later. I hate to do it, but what am I to do. I *won't* eat it.

48 If "The Good Fäery" on my desk should take it into her pretty head to grant me three wishes I should need no time in which to make my decision. I would say:

> *Eternal Youth*
> *Genius, and*
> *to be a boy.*

49 I read an article by Fans Messan, a French sculptor who won recognition by dressing as a boy. Oh how I would love it if Bobbie and I could dress like boys, steal rides on freight trains to New York, go as stowaways to the Latin Quarter of Paris, or the Bohemian Quarter of London, rent a studio as boys, visit the queer restaurants, and write and become famous like Chatterton and Villon and all the rest of the vagabond poets.

50 I'd like sometime to write a book and call it, "The Thrill of Life." The book would be the story of my life as I would like to have it.

51 *AUGUST 1.* Today ends the second week of dieting. I haven't counted my calories this week, but I've eaten as little as Daddy let me—and not a sweet thing for two weeks! At the races they had my favorite candy—and tonight at the Sing which is to be held here, they'll have lemonade, cookies, cake and candy. But I have a will! Thats what I say when I am tempted (and I have been often!)—and I also say—"I'll be glad tomorrow that I held back"— and "Get thin first—eat afterwards." I wonder if I'll *ever* weigh 119! . . .

52 *AUGUST 16.* [At a restaurant] I ordered French Pastry. Aunt Elaine didn't want all her ice-cream, so she put a third of it on my cake. And I afterwards ate —4 pieces of candy, 5 marshmallows, 15 cookies, 1 plum, 1 banana, 1 bunch of grapes, 3 peanuts, and a half a pretzel. I knew I'd gain, so the next day, I didn't eat a thing.

53 *AUGUST 20.* I've gained two pounds! But I'll lose them. I'm not eating today. When we had supper at the Hitchcocks, I ate like a hog. I keep saying to myself "Eat, drink, and be merry, for tomorrow we die-t." But "O that this too, too solid flesh would melt!"

54 *AUGUST 23.* I have only seven pounds to go, *if* I don't gain. I've lost over 20 pounds. Aunt E. and I went to the dime museum but there were just men there. There were pistols and rifles hanging all around, and a great many slot machines where by inserting a penny, nickel or dime, motion pictures could be seen of girls not especially characterized by superfluous clothes. So we didn't stay. I

would have liked to look in one of the slot-machines, but I didn't dare with all the men around.

55   *OCTOBER 3.* [*Chicago*] School! I *hate* it. It is a seething redhot hell where tortured souls are crushed beneath despicable work. Underneath the lively chatter, underneath the hundreds of spectacled senior boys and round-eyed bewildered freshmen and laughing slim "popular" girls, underneath the apparently pleasant surface there is an iron hand that bends the students ruthlessly and molds them in a common pattern.

56   I *hate* to go back. I know what I am getting into. I see the winter ahead of me—long hours after school in the depressing— deadly study-hall, grinding over French verbs in the cheerless November afternoons—waiting frozen-footed on the cold, windy train platforms—reading in dull history books about battles I don't understand—cramming for tests—trying to memorize page after page of scientific fact. Summer is gone! blue skied—green-lawned, wild, free summer. And tomorrow—school.

57   *OCTOBER 11.* Ginny, Bobbie and I told each other, (not without much persuasion, promises not to get mad, etc) our faults, and oh horrors!—I have learned that I am obstinate, crude, loquacious, that I walk like a gorilla, and act too terribly natural. On the other hand I am self-possessed. (I'm not really. Whenever we have floor-talks I clench my fist and murmer —"Be self-possessed. That's the whole art of living", but much good it does me!) fearless, "beauty-having" and have the makings of personality. (Their words) So tomorrow I revolutionize my character. I shall walk as if I owned the world—talk slightly condesendingly, be extremely self-possessed, spout scintillating sophistication (assumed) and develop subtility. In short, I shall be supermagnaglorious personified. . . .

58   *NOVEMBER 4.* I wonder if anyone in the world has ever hated himself as I hate myself. It is just recently that I have. Formerly I thought more of myself. I thought I could write, and now that illusion too has been shattered. No one has said anything, butI have tried to write recently, and I can't—I can't. I never could. It was just illusion. Yet, tho I can form sentences better than some of those at school, they don't worry or care. And I do. I want to be able to write more than I want anything else in the world. I am not modest. I haven't an inferiority complex. I am just seeing things right for the first time, and trying to view myself detachedly, cooly, impersonally. It's not pleasant—this shattering of illusions. This last week or so I've been horribly depressed. For all my life has been bound up with illusions, and now that they have vanished I see life as it really is. It is hell. Even my own life is horrible. I hate myself. I really do. But oh why are my emotions theatrical! *This* seems theatrical—but it is one of the sincerest things I've ever written. I have a disagreeable personality, yet no one hates me as I hate myself. This fall when I came back to school I was different. It wasn't just thinness. Ginny said I was a little like Peter Pan. I was. But now I am a fat, crude, uncouth, misunderstood beast. The prospect of thinness was

not the only reason for my fasting this summer. I wanted to come nearer to the Ancient Greek ideal (only I didn't know it was Greek then)—to regard eating as an unavoidable evil—to use food only as a means of sustaining life that I might attain to higher things. I wanted to be spiritual—to cast off the bonds of material things. In part I succeeded. But now!—now I drown myself,—I flounder in a sea of meat and drink. I am obscene, earthly. I am a gibbering, blundering stupid creature. That is what my teachers and everyone at school thinks of me. I am poor in my studies. But if I fail to graduate this year I will run away, dress like a boy, vagabond to the four corners of the earth. I will get thin and be a Peter Pan, a Donatello, and forget my shattered illusions. Life is sordid, hard, cruel, here. But in sunny Italie, in Classic Hellas, life should be ideal, beautiful. I used to crave knowledge, but now I care little for education. The more intelligent people are, the more miserable they are. I shall be ignorant—and happy.

59   *NOVEMBER 7.* Chicago! There could never be another city like it. It is the modern Bagdad, the Arabian Night City where anything can happen. The slender black buildings lit by occasional yellow squares, the flashing sign-lights which seem to play hide and seek with one another, the brilliant theater lobbies, the Bohemian restaurants, the motley crowds all reek of adventure. It is like an oriental prince arrayed in sparkling, barbaric jewels. It has something that no other city however large or risqué could ever have—something symbolized by the old Field Museum. I love Chicago! I love it! I love it because it is a city of illusion, because it is beautiful and thrilling, because it is a city that like a golden tawny tiger can bare cruel fangs. But most of all I love it because it is life—and adventure! I could never be happy away from Chicago—it is in my blood, and if I tried for a thousand years, I could never express half that it means to me. . . .

60   *DECEMBER 5.* All the adolescents that have even a suggestion of writing ability came to school yesterday to take poetry tests for a young woman who looks like she writes free verse poems in the manner of Amy Lowell, and who is interested in phsycology. I am afraid that if ever I had a poetic reputation, it is sunken in the quicksand of oblivion. First we were given a list of words and we had to find as many rhymes as possible in a minute. . . . She gave us words like "butterfly" and we had to write down as many adjectives for it as we could, in a given time. Then she gave us words like "the sea" and we had to put down things it did, like—"shifts restlessly", or "dashes against rocks". Then she gave us words like "life" and we had to put down symbols, like "a grab bag". But *then* all I could think of was "hell", so I wrote it. It *is* hell when one has one's poetic ability tested by assinine tests given by modern imbeciles, with literary aspirations. Then there were couplets of poetry with words left out, and we had to fill them in ourselves. I filled in the silliest things! I think we stayed *hours*. She dropped a bomb shell when she left us—that some time next week, every person that took the test has to spend an hour with her alone. I shall collapse if she asks for my latest effort, for Ginny and I have been trying to write sentimental stuff lately.

61   Anyway I don't care if I *did* flunk the test—I don't think that there is any way a person's poetic ability can be tested except by the poems he writes! . . .

62   *DECEMBER 22.* I wonder if a person could develop an entirely new style if he tried very hard. There is really no use in my keeping a diary if I can't improve at all. I have just finished skimming over my last diaries, (*reading* them would have been too, too, great a strain) and I find that they are all written in the very same supersalious manner, except that the farther back you go, the more glaring faults you find.

63   *DECEMBER 31.* Its the last day of the old year. 1926. For exactly a year I've written here at frequent intervals. I wonder why? For the pleasure it will give me in old age? No, because I know that it will trouble me then with vain longings for youth and health. For future publication? No—that will scarcely do. A published diary is uninteresting at best when genuine, and they are written differently. Because I *must* find some outlet for the genius that is in me? Well, hardly. Because it gives me pleasure? Perhaps. It has been said that a girl's day is never complete until she has told someone about it. It may be that being possessed of an interest in writing I choose this way of telling about my more or less interesting experiences. But I think that the real reason that I keep a diary (disgusting word) is so that non omnis moriar [I shall not completely die]. . . . It is futile of course—everything I do is that—life itself is that—but it is the ultimate ideal. . . .

❧

Discussion Questions

*1.   If you had access only to paragraph 5 of Blue's diary, what might you infer about her from its content? In light of subsequent entries, would you consider your inferences to be accurate? Explain.

*2.   Relate the activities that Blue seemed to enjoy. What people— related or unrelated, dead or alive, fictional or real—did she like?

*3.   From what you learn about her through her writing, did Blue seem suited for the journalistic career she envisioned for herself in paragraph 25? Why or why not? Can you suggest other careers for which she might have had appropriate aptitudes?

4.   Recount Blue's efforts at dieting. Assuming that you were one of Blue's parents, tell why you would have either encouraged or discouraged your daughter's attempts to lose weight.

5.   In her last entry for 1926, what reasons did Blue reject for her keeping a diary? What did she claim *did* motivate her to keep a diary? Does the fact that you have been reading Blue's entries undermine or support this reason? Explain.

*6.   Cite by paragraph numbers implications or evidence that Blue was each of the following: well-read; opinionated; vain; curious; honest;

emotionally immature; imaginative; sensible; and from an affluent background.

*7. Is Blue a person you would have liked to have known when you were her age? Why or why not?

Writing Topics

1. In paragraph 59, Blue uses vivid language, including metaphors and similes, to describe the qualities about Chicago she finds most appealing. Assume that your local Chamber of Commerce is offering a trophy to the person who, in a single paragraph, can best capture the points of interest of your community. Compose your prize-winning entry.

2. Blue comments in paragraph 33, "Oh, it is horrible to grow up!" Write a short letter to Blue in which you either support or refute her assertion, offering compelling reasons for your belief that growing older is either a curse or a blessing.

❧*"Never again should I feel that I ought to believe,*
that older people were wiser and better than I was."

EARLY SORROW

Ellen Glasgow

The eighth of ten children of a kindly Episcopal mother and
a stern Presbyterian Calvinist father, Ellen Glasgow (1873–
1945) grew up in Richmond, Virginia, where her father was
director of the Tredegar Iron Works. After publishing her first
novel, *The Descendant*, in 1897, Glasgow wrote in a letter to
her publisher, "I will become a great novelist or none at all."
In general, her novels depict the effects of the new industrial
revolution upon the genteel code of the Old South and the
victimization of Southern women by a dying code of chivalry. Among them are *The Battle-Ground* (1902), *The Deliverance*
(1904), *The Romance of a Plain Man* (1909), *In Virginia* (1913),
The Builders (1919), *The Sheltered Life* (1932), and *In This Our Life*
(1941, recipient of the Pulitzer Prize). Glasgow's autobiography, *The Woman Within*, in which "Early Sorrow" appears,
was published posthumously in 1954.

1   I could not have been more than ten years old when I was overtaken by a
tragic occurrence which plunged my childhood into grief and anxiety, and
profoundly affected, not only my mind and character, but my whole future life.
In a single night, or so it seemed to us, my mother was changed from a source
of radiant happiness into a chronic invalid, whose nervous equilibrium was
permanently damaged. A severe shock, in a critical period, altered her so completely that I should scarcely have known her if I had come upon her after a
brief absence. She, who had been a fountain of joy, became an increasing
anxiety, a perpetual ache in the heart. Although she recovered her health, in a
measure, her buoyant emotion toward life was utterly lost. Even now, when
she has been dead so long, I cannot write of these things without a stab of that
old inarticulate agony. . . .

2   From the mist and sunshine of those years a few stark shapes emerge. We
had moved, now, into the big gray house on the corner of Main Street, and after

my mother's nervous breakdown, we left Jerdone Castle[1] forever. Mother had conceived a horror of the place I loved, and she could not stay on there without greater anguish of mind.

3   For Rebe,[2] and for me, leaving the farm was like tearing up the very roots of our nature. This was the only place where I found health, where I had known a simple and natural life. It was the place where I had begun to write, and had discovered an object, if not a meaning, in the complicated pattern of my inner world. It was the place, too, where I had felt hours and even days of pure happiness, where I had rushed down the road to meet the advancing storm, while I felt in my heart the fine, pointed flame that is ecstasy.

4   All this was distressing, but far worse even than this was the enforced desertion of Pat, my beautiful pointer. For years, the memory of Pat, left with an overseer who might not be kind to him, would thrust up, like a dagger, into my dreams. What would they do with Pat when they moved? What would happen to him when he grew old? Why was it people made you do things that would break your heart always? Even now, I sometimes awake with a regret, that is half for Pat himself, and half a burning remorse for some act I have committed but cannot remember.

5   Only a delicate child, rendered morbid by circumstances, could have suffered as I suffered from that change to the city in summer. Though I went to school for a few months each year, until my health grew frail again and my nervous headaches returned, I would wonder all the way home whether I should find my mother cheerful or sad. Usually, she sent us off brightly; but the brightness would fade as soon as we turned the corner, and the deep despondency would creep over her. Once in those years she went away on her only visit to her brother, whom she had adored since she was a baby. He lived in Holly Springs, Mississippi, and the doctors advised the long trip as a diversion. Rebe went with her, and they were away several months. It was my first long separation from them, and I missed them both with an ache that was like physical pain. Most of my time was spent alone, for in our large family the three elder sisters lived in a different, and a larger, world, where they had their own interests and their own pleasures. No doubt they had their own troubles also, but they seemed, to us, creatures of a more fortunate sphere.

6   I still had little Toy, but, in Mother's absence, he was set apart, though I did not suspect this, as another victim. One afternoon, I could not find him when I was urged by my father to go to walk with Lizzie Patterson,[3] and that night, after I had looked for him in vain, one of the servants told me that Father had had him put into a bag, and had given him to two men who worked at the

---

[1] **Jerdone Castle:** A farm purchased by Glasgow's father when the author was quite young. She had delighted in the freedom it provided.

[2] **Rebe:** Glasgow's younger sister, the last of Mrs. Glasgow's ten children.

[3] **Lizzie Patterson:** One of Glasgow's closest girlhood friends.

Tredegar. They told me fearfully, wondering what "Miss Annie" (my mother) "would say when she came back"; but, without a word, I turned away and went straight to Father.

7   Rage convulsed me, the red rage that must have swept up from the jungles and the untamed mind of primitive man. And this rage — I have not ever forgotten it — contained every anger, every revolt I had ever felt in my life — the way I felt when I saw the black dog hunted, the way I felt when I watched old Uncle Henry[4] taken away to the almshouse, the way I felt whenever I had seen people or animals hurt for the pleasure or profit of others. All these different rages were here; all had dissolved and intermingled with the fury of youth that is helpless. If I spoke words, I cannot recall them. I remember only that I picked up a fragile china vase on the mantelpiece and hurled it across the room. It shattered against the wall, and I can still hear the crash it made as it fell into fragments. Then I rushed into my room, and locked the door on my frightened sisters and the more frightened servants. I should never see Toy again, I knew. I had never seen Pat again. My father would not change his mind. Not once in my knowledge of him had he ever changed his mind or admitted that he was wrong — or even mistaken.

8   I poured out my heart in a letter to Mother. And she did not reply. Day after day, week after week, I waited, but when her letters came, they made no mention of her affection for my dog, or of the injustice from which I suffered so desperately. Not until long afterwards, when Mother was at home and ill again, did I discover the reason for her apparent neglect. Then, one afternoon, while I was studying my lessons in a corner of the library, I overheard my sister Emily, the eldest of the family, relate an amusing version of Toy's betrayal. It was a good opportunity to get rid of him, she explained, while Mother was away. He was sick and old and troublesome, and none of them liked him but Mother and Rebe and me. So they had meant to keep it a secret from Mother, and when they found that I had written, Emily had gone to the postmaster and asked him to return a letter which would give Mother a shock if she received it. And the postmaster had obligingly returned the letter from the post. An incredible incident to anyone who has not lived in a small Southern community.

9   The remembrance of children is a long remembrance, and the incidents often make milestones in a personal history. In those months of Mother's absence, I know that I broke forever with my childhood. For the first time I was standing alone, without the shelter and the comfort of her love and her sympathy. Her silence, inexplicable and utterly unlike her, seemed to thrust me still farther and farther into loneliness, until at last — for months may have the significance of

---

[4] **Uncle Henry:** An old, penniless, and mentally retarded African American man who was removed from his cellar and, despite his protests, forcibly taken to the poorhouse. As Glasgow indicates, she witnessed the event.

years when one is very young—I began to love, not to fear, loneliness. During this time, and indeed through all my future life, I shrank from my father's presence; and only one of my elder sisters ever won my reluctant confidence. At the time, angry, defiant, utterly unsubdued by pleadings and rebukes, I told myself, obstinately, that if they cared nothing for my feelings, I would care nothing for theirs. For weeks I hated them all. I hated the things they believed in, the things they so innocently and charmingly pretended. I hated the sanctimonious piety that let people hurt helpless creatures. I hated the prayers and the hymns, and the red images that colored their drab music, the fountains filled with blood, the sacrifice of the lamb.

10   And, then, much to Father's distress, and to my sisters' consternation, I refused to attend divine service—and there was nothing left that they could do about it. My will, which was as strong as Father's, plunged its claws into the earth. Nothing, not lectures, not deprivations, not all the pressure they could bring, could ever make me again go with them to church.

11   If I had won nothing else, I had won liberty. Never again should I feel that I ought to believe, that older people were wiser and better than I was. Never again should I feel that I ought to pretend things were different. Dumbly, obstinately, I would stare back at them when they talked to me. I could not answer them. I could not refute my father when he opened the Bible, and read aloud, in his impressive voice, the sternest psalms in the Old Testament. All I could do was to shake my ignorant head, and reply that, even if all that was true, it made no difference to me. I was finished with that way of life before I had begun it.

12   And, then, in the midst of it all, while my mother was still away, I was seized, I was overwhelmed by a consuming desire to find out things for myself, to know the true from the false, the real from the make-believe. The longing was so intense that I flung myself on knowledge as a thirsty man might fling himself into a desert spring. I read everything in our library. History, poetry, fiction, archaic or merely picturesque, works on science, and even *The Westminister Confession of Faith*. Lizzie Patterson and Carrie Coleman came frequently in the afternoon; but even with them, my two closest friends, I felt that I had changed beyond understanding and recognition. They lived happy lives on the outside of things, accepting what they were taught, while I was devoured by this hunger to know, to discover some meaning, some underlying reason for the mystery and the pain of the world.

13   For I had ceased to be a child. My mind and the very pit of my stomach felt empty. I needed the kind of reality that was solid and hard and would stay by one.

14   When, at last, Mother and Rebe returned, I felt shy with them and váguely uncomfortable. It seemed to me, for the first few days at least, that they had changed, that they had seen things I had not seen, that they treasured recollections I could not share. Or perhaps I was the one who had changed. Something

had gone out of me for good, and, in exchange, I had found something that, to me, was more precious. I had found the greatest consolation of my life; but I had found also an unconquerable loneliness. I had entered the long solitude that stretches on beyond the vanishing-point in the distance. . . .

❧

Discussion Questions

1. How did Glasgow's mother's nervous breakdown permanently affect her physically and emotionally? What immediate changes did it bring to Glasgow's life?

*2. Relate the role that each of the following people, animals, or places played in Glasgow's life: Uncle Henry; Lizzie Patterson; Pat; Holly Springs; Toy; Emily; Jerdone Castle; Father.

*3. Cite by appropriate paragraph number evidence or indications that Glasgow as a child was each of the following: intellectually precocious; unhealthy; creative; sensitive and caring; passionate; obstinate; lonely; and irreligious.

*4. Explain what you think Glasgow meant by each of the following comments: "In those months of Mother's absence, I know that I broke forever with my childhood" (paragraph 9); "If I had won nothing else, I had won liberty" (paragraph 11); "Something had gone out of me for good, and, in exchange, I had found something that, to me, was more precious" (paragraph 14).

Writing Topics

1. Glasgow refers to Pat and Toy, pets to which she had been attached. If you have ever had a pet, describe in a short essay the role it played in your life. What kind of pet was it? What were its habits? How long did you have it? What were your feelings toward it? What long range effects, if any, has it had upon you?

2. Glasgow obviously felt betrayed by the actions of her father and her sister Emily. If you have ever harbored a similar feeling because of the actions of a person or people close to you, write an essay about the experience. What incident precipitated your feeling of betrayal? Who and what were involved? How did you respond immediately? What have been the long-term consequences of the incident?

&a . . . there must often be an additional,
intuitive factor in doing first-rate scientific work."

SCIENCE ON THE RIGHT SIDE
OF THE BRAIN

Alan P. Lightman

A native of Memphis, Tennessee, Alan P. Lightman (b. 1948) did his undergraduate work at Princeton University and his doctoral studies in physics at the California Institute of Technology. After having been a professor at Harvard University and a staff scientist for the Smithsonian Astrophysical Observatory, Lightman assumed the joint position of professor of science and of writing at the Massachusetts Institute of Technology in 1988. Among his numerous books are *Time Travel and Papa Joe's Pipe* (1984), which contains "Science on the Right Side of the Brain," *A Modern Day Yankee in Connecticut Court* (1986), *Origins: The Lives and Worlds of Modern Cosmologists* (1990), *Ancient Light* (1992), and *Time for the Stars* (1992).

1   How we think is not something we often think about. Even serious mental tasks don't require much understanding of the machinery perched up there. When we do think about the mind, it seems different from our other parts, a disembodied vessel out of which thoughts flutter. And the proposition of mind studying itself flounders in a certain catch-22 absurdity. It seems almost impossible that such an entity could exist as physical matter inside our heads, but that's exactly the point of view taken, with great success, in modern brain research. In fact, a revolution in neuroscience and its applications is now underway, taking place quietly beside all the commotion in computer technology and molecular biology.

2   A major development in neuroscience has been the gradual understanding of the different functions of the right and left halves, or hemispheres, of the brain. To the untrained eye the two halves may appear identical, but it is now believed that the left hemisphere is primarily responsible for logical, linear kinds of thought processes, including language and mathematical skills, while the right is responsible for spatial relationships and holistic processes, including artistic skills. Although the two sides cooperate in normal individuals, the

degree of activity in each hemisphere varies from person to person and also from culture to culture.

3   These findings first began emerging in 1861, when Pierre Paul Broca[1] localized the center of articulate speech in the left frontal cortex. Beginning in 1953, the subject advanced dramatically with the split-brain experiments of Roger Sperry[2] and collaborators. Sperry worked with epileptic patients whose corpus callosum, the bundle of nerves connecting and allowing communication between the two hemispheres, had been surgically severed to reduce the intensity of seizures. Since each hemisphere controls and receives stimuli from only one side of the body, it then became possible to explore separately the two sides of the brain. In 1981 Sperry was awarded the Nobel Prize for his work.

4   It's always seemed obvious, without being clear in detail, that there are two different ways of approaching problems — the intuitive and the analytic. At different times one or the other approach works better, and most of us operate more comfortably in one mode or the other. Sitting at the extremes, at least in stereotype, are artists on the right and scientists on the left, both groups viewing the world at an angle. About 55 years ago Rudyard Kipling wrote the eerie poem "The Two-Sided Man," which begins, "Much I owe to the lands that grew/More to the Lives that fed/But most to the Allah Who/Gave me two separate sides to my head."

5   Having acknowledged the debts to Allah and to Sperry, how can we use all this to our advantage? An inspiring practical attempt is the recent book *Drawing on the Right Side of the Brain* by Betty Edwards. Edwards teaches art, and her thesis is that we can all learn to draw better by consciously holding at bay our left hemisphere with its preconceptions about what things *should* look like. The book gives many exercises aimed at distinguishing the handiwork of the separate hemispheres and at learning how to quiet down the interference from the left side so the right side can come out and play. My favorite exercise is one where you take a Picasso line drawing of a man sitting in a chair, turn it upside down, and copy what you see. It's crucial that you not turn the Picasso right side up during the exercise, the whole point being you're not supposed to recognize arms and chair legs and such things. Once a familiar object is identified you're in deep trouble, because the left side will take control and draw it the way you've always seen it before. I'm no artist, but after a tedious half hour, upon turning my strange jumble of lines right side up, I was astonished to see a rather nice and unstiff drawing of a man sitting in a chair.

6   Clearly, Edwards's book and its underlying ideas have meaning for any creative enterprise. I suspect that most scientists might profit by trying some of

---

[1] **Pierre Paul Broca:** A French surgeon (1824–1880).
[2] **Roger Sperry:** American neurobiologist (b. 1913) and professor emeritus of the California Institute of Technology.

these exercises, perhaps in a different version. Traditional scientific training focuses almost entirely on mastering the established body of knowledge, getting an appreciation for the scientific method of critical evaluation and learning the necessary experimental and mathematical techniques. This is almost pure left-hemisphere stuff. However, there must often be an additional, intuitive factor in doing first-rate scientific work. Mendeleyev's periodic table of the chemical elements, pointing out the similarity of every eighth element in a sequence arranged according to increasing atomic weight, resulted from years of his own meticulous accumulation of data. However, he may have been influenced by John Alexander Newlands's Law of Octaves reported several years earlier. Newlands had somehow noticed the same chemical relationships with much less data.

7   My own christening with doing science on the right side of the brain occurred a decade ago. I was a graduate student in physics at Caltech and, after waffling around with course work for well over a year, had finally settled into some genuine research. My first couple of research projects were brief and tidy. Then I fastened onto a more open-ended investigation that, in its loftiness, held the disturbing possibility of leading me off into the trees. As it was a theoretical project, all my work took place within a tiny office, equipped only with a desk, books, pencils, and paper. There were no windows. It was another world in that office. Day after day, while Kissinger[3] was announcing and unannouncing that "Peace is at hand" and Howard Hughes[4] was hiding out on the nineteenth and twentieth floors of a Vancouver hotel, I sat quietly with my equations. Getting nowhere.

8   My project concerned the implications of the well-documented fact that, neglecting air resistance, all objects fall with exactly the same acceleration under the influence of gravity. A physicist at Stanford had conjectured that this experimental result required a very special mathematical description of gravity, and I was trying to prove or disprove his conjecture. Going over and over pages of calculations, checking and rechecking each day, I knew something was amiss. An expected answer at the halfway point was not coming out right. Occasionally I ventured from my office for an outside diagnosis, but I soon realized gloomily that my colleagues couldn't help me. I was alone with the problem.

9   This went on for a couple of months. Then one day I found my mistake. And I knew immediately that the rest of the project would go without a hitch, yielding a yes to the conjecture. I don't know how I did it, but it wasn't by going from one equation to the next. Despite all attempts, I've never been able to

---

[3] **Kissinger:** Henry A. Kissinger (b. 1923), U.S. secretary of state whose term of service (1973–1977) included the closing period of the Vietnam War.

[4] **Howard Hughes:** An eccentric American multimillionaire (1905–1976), who secluded himself in hotel rooms toward the end of his life.

retrace my steps on that day. My right hemisphere, I believe, had somehow got into the act, taking off into unknown territory. Other people have tried to describe that lifting feeling when everything suddenly falls into place. For me, the best analogy is what sometimes happens when you're sailing a round-bottomed boat in strong wind. Normally, the hull stays down in the water, with the frictional drag greatly limiting the speed of the boat. But in high wind, every once in a while the hull lifts out of the water, and the drag goes instantly near zero. It feels like a great hand has suddenly grabbed hold and flung you across the surface like a skimming stone. It's called planing.

10   I've planed in my scientific career only on a few occasions and then only for seconds. Einstein and Darwin probably planed for minutes at a time. The years of details at my desk have been bearable because of those moments. I could use a lot more of them. Perhaps, at just the right time, you have to glance at the equations upside down.

❧

Discussion Questions

1.   According to Lightman, how do neuroscientists believe the two hemispheres of the brain differ in function? What scientific evidence has led to these beliefs?

2.   Describe the difference between an analytic and an intuitive approach to a problem. With which hemisphere of the brain would the analytic approach be associated? The intuitive?

3.   Which approach to a problem—analytic or intuitive—do scientists usually use? Which approach do artists normally employ? Why would the problem-solving approach of each differ?

4.   Recount Lightman's "christening with doing science on the right side of the brain"(paragraph 7): Where was he? What were his physical surroundings? What was he trying to prove? How long did he work on the problem? To what does he attribute his success in finding a solution?

*5.   Explain what you think Lightman means by each of the following statements: "It seems almost impossible that such an entity [the mind] could exist as physical matter inside our heads. . . . (paragraph 1); " I suspect that most scientists might profit by trying some of these exercises, perhaps in a different version" (paragraph 6); "Einstein and Darwin probably planed for minutes at a time" (paragraph 10).

*6.   In paragraph 9, Lightman presents an extended analogy to describe his feeling upon receiving an intuitive insight into how to solve his scientific problem. To describe that same feeling, compose another extended analogy similar to the one Lightman offered.

Writing Topics

1. Many people engage in physical activity so as to feel a wholeness between their bodies and their minds. If you exercise regularly, describe the activity in a short essay. What is it? How and why did you become interested in it? How often do you do it? Where? With whom? How do you feel during exercise and immediately afterward? How has this activity affected your life?

2. In paragraph 9, Lightman describes what some creative people have called "the 'aha!' feeling," a sudden intuitive insight into how to resolve what has been a perplexing problem. If you have ever experienced such an unanticipated insight into a problem you had been trying to solve, describe the experience in a brief essay, recounting the nature of the problem, how long you had grappled with it, and the intuitive insight that provided a solution.

"I was what they called a live wire. I was shooting out sparks that were digging a pit around me, and I was sinking into that pit."

SO THIS WAS ADOLESCENCE

Annie Dillard

Born in Pittsburg, Pennsylvania, in 1945, Annie Dillard is the versatile author of numerous books, including *Pilgrim at Tinker Creek*, awarded a Pulitzer Prize in 1975 for nonfiction; *An American Childhood* (1987), a memoir in which appears "So This Was Adolescence"; *The Writing Life* (1989), an account; *Holy the Firm* (1978), a nonfiction narrative; *Teaching a Stone to Talk* (1982), a collection of narrative essays; and *Mornings Like This* (1995), a book of poetry. Her writing has appeared in *The Atlantic Monthly, Harper's Magazine, The New York Times Magazine, Yale Review, Antaeus, American Heritage*, and in many anthologies. After living in Virginia, where she attended Hollins College, and in the Pacific Northwest, Dillard now makes her home in Connecticut with her husband, biographer Robert Richardson, Jr., and her daughter, Rosy.

1   When I was fifteen, I felt it coming; now I was sixteen, and it hit.

2   My feet had imperceptibly been set on a new path, a fast path into a long tunnel like those many turnpike tunnels near Pittsburgh, turnpike tunnels whose entrances bear on brass plaques a roll call of those men who died blasting them. I wandered witlessly forward and found myself going down, and saw the light dimming; I adjusted to the slant and dimness, traveled further down, adjusted to greater dimness, and so on. There wasn't a whole lot I could do about it, or about anything. I was going to hell on a handcart, that was all, and I knew it and everyone around me knew it, and there it was.

3   I was growing and thinning, as if pulled. I was getting angry, as if pushed. I morally disapproved most things in North America, and blamed my innocent parents for them. My feelings deepened and lingered. The swift moods of early childhood — each formed by and suited to its occasion — vanished. Now feelings lasted so long they left stains. They arose from nowhere, like winds or waves, and battered at me or engulfed me.

4   When I was angry, I felt myself coiled and longing to kill someone or bomb something big. Trying to appease myself, during one winter I whipped my bed every afternoon with my uniform belt. I despised the spectacle I made in my own eyes—whipping the bed with a belt, like a creature demented!—and I often began halfheartedly, but I did it daily after school as a desperate discipline, trying to rid myself and the innocent world of my wildness. It was like trying to beat back the ocean.

5   Sometimes in class I couldn't stop laughing; things were too funny to be borne. It began then, my surprise that no one else saw what was so funny.

6   I read some few books with such reverence I didn't close them at the finish, but only moved the pile of pages back to the start, without breathing, and began again. I read one such book, an enormous novel, six times that way—losing the binding between sessions, but not between readings.

7   On the piano in the basement I played the maniacal "Poet and Peasant Overture" so loudly, for so many hours, night after night, I damaged the piano's keys and strings. When I wasn't playing this crashing overture, I played boogie-woogie, or something else, anything else, in octaves—otherwise, it wasn't loud enough. My fingers were so strong I could do push-ups with them. I played one piece with my fists. I banged on a steel-stringed guitar till I bled, and once on a particularly piercing rock-and-roll downbeat I broke straight through one of Father's snare drums.

8   I loved my boyfriend so tenderly, I thought I must transmogrify into vapor. It would take spectroscopic analysis to locate my molecules in thin air. No possible way of holding him was close enough. Nothing could cure this bad case of gentleness except, perhaps, violence: maybe if he swung me by the legs and split my skull on a tree? Would that ease this insane wish to kiss too much his eyelids' outer corners and his temples, as if I could love up his brain?

9   I envied people in books who swooned. For two years I felt myself continuously swooning and continuously unable to swoon; the blood drained from my face and eyes and flooded my heart; my hands emptied, my knees unstrung, I bit at the air for something worth breathing—but I failed to fall, and I couldn't find the way to black out. I had to live on the lip of a waterfall, exhausted.

10   When I was bored I was first hungry, then nauseated, then furious and weak. "Calm yourself," people had been saying to me all my life. Since early childhood I had tried one thing and then another to calm myself, on those few occasions when I truly wanted to. Eating helped; singing helped. Now sometimes I truly wanted to calm myself. I couldn't lower my shoulders; they seemed to wrap around my ears. I couldn't lower my voice although I could see the people around me flinch. I waved my arm in class till the very teachers wanted to kill me.

11   I was what they called a live wire. I was shooting out sparks that were digging a pit around me, and I was sinking into that pit. Laughing with Ellin at school recess, or driving around after school with Judy in her jeep, exultant, or

dancing with my boyfriend to Louis Armstrong across a polished dining-room floor, I got so excited I looked around wildly for aid; I didn't know where I should go or what I should do with myself. People in books split wood.

12　　When rage or boredom reappeared, each seemed never to have left. Each so filled me with so many years' intolerable accumulation it jammed the space behind my eyes, so I couldn't see. There was no room left even on my surface to live. My rib cage was so taut I couldn't breathe. Every cubic centimeter of atmosphere above my shoulders and head was heaped with last straws. Black hatred clogged my very blood. I couldn't peep, I couldn't wiggle or blink; my blood was too mad to flow.

13　　For as long as I could remember, I had been transparent to myself, un-selfconscious, learning, doing, most of every day. Now I was in my own way; I myself was a dark object I could not ignore. I couldn't remember how to forget myself. I didn't want to think about myself, to reckon myself in, to deal with myself every livelong minute on top of everything else—but swerve as I might, I couldn't avoid it. I was a boulder blocking my own path. I was a dog barking between my own ears, a barking dog who wouldn't hush.

14　　So this was adolescence. Is this how the people around me had died on their feet—inevitably, helplessly? Perhaps their own selves eclipsed the sun for so many years the world shriveled around them, and when at last their inescapable orbits had passed through these dark egoistic years it was too late, they had adjusted.

15　　Must I then lose the world forever, that I had so loved? Was it all, the whole bright and various planet, where I had been so ardent about finding myself alive, only a passion peculiar to children, that I would outgrow even against my will?

16　　I quit the church. I wrote the minister a fierce letter. The assistant minister, kindly Dr. James H. Blackwood, called me for an appointment. My mother happened to take the call.

17　　"Why," she asked, "would he be calling you?" I was in the kitchen after school. Mother was leaning against the pantry door, drying a crystal bowl.

18　　"What, Mama? Oh. Probably," I said, "because I wrote him a letter and quit the church."

19　　"You—what?" She began to slither down the doorway, weak-kneed, like Lucille Ball. I believe her whole life passed before her eyes.

20　　As I climbed the stairs after dinner I heard her moan to Father, "She wrote the minister a letter and quit the church."

21　　"She—what?"

22　　Father knocked on the door of my room. I was the only person in the house with her own room. Father ducked under the doorway, entered, and put his hands in his khakis' pockets. "Hi, Daddy." Actually, it drove me nuts when people came in my room. Mother had come in just last week. My room was getting to be quite the public arena. Pretty soon they'd put it on the streetcar routes. Why not hold the U.S. Open here? I was on the bed, in uniform, trying to read a book. I sat up and folded my hands in my lap.

23   I knew that Mother had made him come—"She listens to you." He had undoubtedly been trying to read a book, too.

24   Father looked around, but there wasn't much to see. My rock collection was no longer in evidence. A framed tiger swallowtail, spread and only slightly askew on white cotton, hung on a yellowish wall. On the mirror I'd taped a pencil portrait of Rupert Brooke; he was looking off softly. Balanced on top of the mirror were some yellow-and-black FALLOUT SHELTER signs, big aluminum ones, which Judy had collected as part of her antiwar effort. On the pale maple desk there were, among other books and papers, an orange thesaurus, a blue three-ring binder with a boy's name written all over it in every typeface, a green assignment notebook, and Emerson's *Essays*.

25   Father began, with some vigor: "What was it you said in this brilliant letter?" He went on: But didn't I see? That people did these things—quietly? Just—quietly? No fuss? No flamboyant gestures. No uncalled-for letters. He was forced to conclude that I was deliberately setting out to humiliate Mother and him.

26   "And your poor sisters, too!" Mother added feelingly from the hall outside my closed door. She must have been passing at that very moment. Then, immediately, we all heard a hideous shriek ending in a wail; it came from my sisters' bathroom. Had Molly cut off her head? It set us all back a moment—me on the bed, Father standing by my desk, Mother outside the closed door—until we all realized it was Amy, mad at her hair. Like me, she was undergoing a trying period, years long; she, on her part, was mad at her hair. She screeched at it in the mirror; the sound carried all over the house, kitchen, attic, basement, everywhere, and terrified all the rest of us, every time.

27   The assistant minister of the Shadyside Presbyterian Church, Dr. Blackwood, and I had a cordial meeting in his office. He was an experienced, calm man in a three-piece suit; he had a mustache and wore glasses. After he asked me why I had quit the church, he loaned me four volumes of C. S. Lewis's broadcast talks, for a paper I was writing. Among the volumes proved to be *The Problem of Pain*, which I would find fascinating, not quite serious enough, and too short. I had already written a paper on the Book of Job. The subject scarcely seemed to be closed. If the all-powerful creator directs the world, then why all this suffering? Why did the innocents die in the camps, and why do they starve in the cities and farms? Addressing this question, I found thirty pages written thousands of years ago, and forty pages written in 1955. They offered a choice of fancy language saying, "Forget it," or serenely worded,

logical-sounding answers that so strained credibility (pain is God's megaphone) that "Forget it" seemed in comparison a fine answer. I liked, however, C. S. Lewis's effort to defuse the question. The sum of human suffering we needn't worry about: There is plenty of suffering, but no one ever suffers the sum of it.

28   Dr. Blackwood and I shook hands as I left his office with his books.

29   "This is rather early of you, to be quitting the church," he said as if to himself, looking off, and went on mildly, almost inaudibly, "I suppose you'll be back soon."

30   Humph, I thought. Pshaw.

❧

Discussion Questions

*1.   Recount some of Dillard's behaviors that reveal the emotional storminess of her sixteenth year. Do you consider her moods and actions to have been normal for a girl her age? Explain.

2.   By paragraph number, cite passages that show Dillard to have been interested in each of the following: food; boys; music; birds; books.

3.   Why do you think Dillard decided to quit the Shadyside Presbyterian Church? Relate how her father responded to her action of sending the minister a letter informing him of her decision.

4.   What can you infer from paragraph 30 about Dillard's future relationship to the church? What leads you to make this inference?

*5.   Dillard makes heavy use of simile, metaphor, and hyperbole to suggest her various states of feeling at age sixteen. Cite by paragraph number several of these figures of speech that you find particularly apt and explain why you find them so.

*6.   Does the analogy that Dillard develops in paragraph 2 effectively communicate reveal how she felt at sixteen? Why or why not? Can you propose another analogy that would be equally appropriate?

*7.   What similarities in writing style do you find in the opening sentences of paragraphs 9, 14, and 16? In the selection, what purposes do such sentences serve? Cite at least three other paragraphs with opening sentences that you find interesting or arresting and explain why you find them so.

Writing Topics

1.   Dillard likens herself at age sixteen to putty or taffy, a coiled snake, a lunatic, a live wire, and a dark object that couldn't be ignored. Recall yourself at age sixteen. Then in an essay, support with anecdotes and illustrations two or three metaphors that capture much of your nature at that age.

2. In paragraph 27, Dillard reveals that, as an adolescent, she felt deep concern about the existence of human suffering. In an essay, explore your thoughts on this subject. As a prelude to writing, consider such matters as the meaning of suffering, what constitutes needless suffering, what both the beneficial and detrimental effects of suffering may be, and whether one can reconcile the existence of human suffering with belief in a benevolent God.

And then this strange thing happened,
which I do not mean physically and cannot explain.
The man entered me."

ONE NIGHT'S DYING

Loren Eiseley

Loren Eiseley (1907–1977) was a scientist who wrote with the sensitivity and grace of a poet. Born in Lincoln, Nebraska, Eiseley did his doctoral work in anthropology at the University of Pennsylvania, where, after holding teaching positions elsewhere, he joined the faculty in 1947. At the time of his death, he was the holder of thirty-six honorary degrees and was the Benjamin Franklin and University Professor of Anthropology and History of Science. His many books, noted for the vast sweep of their subject matter and the reflective, elegaic tone of their writing, include *The Immense Journey* (1957), *Darwin's Century* (1958), *The Firmament of Time* (1960), *The Unexpected Universe* (1969), *The Invisible Pyramid* (1970), *The Night Country* (1971), source of "One Night's Dying," *Notes of an Alchemist* (1972), *The Man Who Saw through Time* (1973), *The Innocent Assassins* (1973), and *All the Strange Hours* (1975).

1   There is always a soft radiance beyond the bedroom door from a night-light behind my chair. I have lived this way for many years now. I sleep or I do not sleep, and the light makes no difference except if I wake. Then, as I awaken, the dim forms of objects sustain my grip on reality. The familiar chair, the walls of the book-lined study reassert my own existence.

2   I do not lie and toss with doubt any longer, as I did in earlier years. I get up and write, as I am writing now, or I read in the old chair that is as worn as I am. I read philosophy, metaphysics, difficult works th : sometime, soon or late, draw a veil over my eyes so that I drowse in my chair.

3   It is not that I fail to learn from these midnight examinations of the world. It is merely that I choose that examination to remain as remote and abstruse as possible. Even so, I cannot always prophesy the result. An obscure line may whirl me into a wide-awake, ferocious concentration in which ideas like animals leap at me out of the dark, in which sudden odd trains of thought drive me

inexorably to my desk and paper. I am, in short, a victim of insomnia — sporadic, wearing, violent, and melancholic. In the words of Shakespeare, for me the world "does murder sleep." It has been so since my twentieth year.

4   In that year my father died — a man well loved, the mainstay of our small afflicted family. He died slowly in severe bodily torture. My mother was stone-deaf. I, his son, saw and heard him die. We lived in a place and time not free with the pain-alleviating drugs of later decades. When the episode of many weeks' duration was over, a curious thing happened: I could no longer bear the ticking of the alarm clock in my own bedroom.

5   At first I smothered it with an extra blanket in a box beside my cot, but the ticking persisted as though it came from my own head. I used to lie for hours staring into the dark of the sleeping house, feeling the loneliness that only the sleepless know when the queer feeling comes that it is the sleeping who are alive and those awake are disembodied ghosts. Finally, in desperation, I gave up the attempt to sleep and turned to reading, though it was difficult to concentrate.

6   It was then that human help appeared. My grandmother saw the light burning through the curtains of my door and came to sit with me. A few years later, when I touched her hair in farewell at the beginning of a journey from which I would not return to see her alive, I knew she had saved my sanity. Into that lonely room at midnight she had come, abandoning her own sleep, in order to sit with one in trouble. We had not talked much, but we had sat together by the lamp, reasserting our common humanity before the great empty dark that is the universe.

7   Grandmother knew nothing of psychiatry. She had not reestablished my sleep patterns, but she had done something more important. She had brought me out of a dark room and retied my thread of life to the living world. Henceforward, by night or day, though I have been subject to the moods of depression or gaiety which are a part of the lives of all of us, I have been able not merely to endure but to make the best of what many regard as an unbearable affliction.

8   It is true that as an educational administrator I can occasionally be caught nodding in lengthy committee meetings, but so, I have observed, can men who come from sound nights on their pillows. Strangely, I, who frequently grow round-eyed and alert as an owl at the stroke of midnight, find it pleasant to nap in daylight among friends. I can roll up on a couch and sleep peacefully while my wife and chatting friends who know my peculiarities keep the daytime universe safely under control. Or so it seems. For, deep-seated in my subconscious, is perhaps the idea that the black bedroom door is the gateway to the tomb.

9   I try in that bedroom to sleep high on two pillows, to have ears and eyes alert. Something shadowy has to be held in place and controlled. At night one has to sustain reality without help. One has to hear lest hearing be lost, see lest sight not return to follow moonbeams across the floor, touch lest the sense of objects vanish. Oh, sleeping, soundlessly sleeping ones, do you ever think who knits your universe together safely from one day's memory to the next? It is the insomniac, not the night policeman on his beat.

10   Many will challenge this point of view. They will say that electric power does the trick, that many a roisterer stumbles down the long street at dawn, after having served his purpose of holding the links of the mad world together. There are parts of the nighttime world, men say to me, that it is just as well I do not know. Go home and sleep, man. Others will keep your giddy world together. Let the thief pass quickly in the shadow, he is awake. Let the juvenile gangs which sidle like bands of evil crabs up from the dark waters of poverty into prosperous streets pass without finding you at midnight.

11   The advice is good, but in the city or the country small things important to our lives have no reporter except as he who does not sleep may observe them. And that man must be disencumbered of reality. He must have no commitments to the dark, as do the murderer and thief. Only he must see, though what he sees may come from the night side of the planet that no man knows well. For even in the early dawn, while men lie unstirring in their sleep or stumble sleepy-eyed to work, some single episode may turn the whole world for a moment into the place of marvel that it is, but that we grow too day-worn to accept.

12   For example, I call the place where I am writing now the bay of broken things. In the February storms, spume wraiths climb the hundred-foot cliff to fight and fall like bitter rain in the moonlight upon the cabin roof. The earth shakes from the drum roll of the surf. I lie awake and watch through the window beyond my bed. This is no ticking in my brain; this is the elemental night of chaos. This is the sea chewing its million-year way into the heart of the continent.

13   The caves beneath the cliff resound with thunder. Again those warring wraiths shoot high over the house. Impelled as though I were a part of all those leaping ghosts, I dress in the dark and come forth. With my back against the door, like an ancient necromancer, I hurl my mind into the white spray and try to summon back, among those leaping forms, the faces and features of the dead I know. The shapes rise endlessly, but they pass inland before the wind, indifferent to my mortal voice.

14   I walk a half mile to a pathway that descends upon a little beach. Below me is a stretch of white sand. No shell is ever found unbroken, even on quiet days, upon that shore. Everything comes over the rocks to seaward. Wood is riven into splinters; the bones of seamen and of sea lions are pounded equally into white and shining sand. Throughout the night the long black rollers, like lines of frothing cavalry, form ranks, drum towering forward, and fall, fall till the mind is dizzy with the spume that fills it. I wait in the shelter of a rock for daybreak. At last the sea eases a trifle. The tide is going out.

15   I stroll shivering along the shore, and there, exposed in inescapable nakedness, I see the elemental cruelty of the natural world. A broken-winged gull, hurled by the wind against the cliff, runs before me wearily along the beach. It will starve or, mercifully, the dogs will find it. I try not to hurry it, and walk on. A little later in a quieter bend of the shore, I see ahead of me a bleeding, bedraggled blot on the edge of the white surf. As I approach, it starts warily to its

feet. We look at each other. It is a wild duck, also with a shattered wing. It does not run ahead of me like the longer-limbed gull. Before I can cut off its retreat it waddles painfully from its brief refuge into the water.

16   The sea continues to fall heavily. The duck dives awkwardly, but with long knowledge and instinctive skill, under the fall of the first two inshore waves. I see its head working seaward. A long green roller, far taller than my head, rises and crashes forward. The black head of the waterlogged duck disappears. This is the way wild things die, without question, without knowledge of mercy in the universe, knowing only themselves and their own pathway to the end. I wonder, walking farther up the beach, if the man who shot that bird will die as well.

17   This is the chaos before man came, before sages imbued with pity walked the earth. Indeed it is true, and in my faraway study my hands have often touched with affection the backs of the volumes which line my shelves. Nevertheless, I have endured the nights and mornings of the city. I have seen old homeless men who have slept for hours sitting upright on ledges along the outer hallway of one of the great Eastern stations straighten stiffly in the dawn and limp away with feigned businesslike aloofness before the approach of the policeman on his rounds. I know that on these cold winter mornings sometimes a man, like the pigeons I have seen roosting as closely as possible over warm hotel air vents, will fall stiffly and not awaken. It is true that there are shelters for the homeless, but some men, like their ice-age forebears, prefer their independence to the end.

18   The loneliness of the city was brought home to me one early sleepless morning, not by men like me tossing in lonely rooms, not by poverty and degradation, not by old men trying with desperate futility to be out among others in the great roaring hive, but by a single one of those same pigeons which I had seen from my hotel window, looking down at midnight upon the smoking air vents and chimneys.

19   The pigeon, *Columba livia*, is the city bird *par excellence*. He is a descendant of the rock pigeon that in the Old World lived among the cliffs and crevices above the caves that early man inhabited. He has been with us since our beginning and has adapted as readily as ourselves to the artificial cliffs of man's first cities. He has known the Roman palaces and the cities of Byzantium. His little flat feet, suited to high and precarious walking, have sauntered in the temples of vanished gods as readily as in New York's old Pennsylvania Station. In my dim morning strolls, waiting for the restaurants to open, I have seen him march quickly into the back end of a delivery truck while the driver was inside a store engaged in his orders with the proprietor. Yet for all its apparent tolerance of these highly adapted and often comic birds, New York also has a beach of broken things more merciless than the reefs and rollers of the ocean shore.

20   One morning, strolling sleepless as usual toward early breakfast time in Manhattan, I saw a sick pigeon huddled at an uncomfortable slant against a building wall on a street corner. I felt sorry for the bird, but I had no box, no

instrument of help, and had learned long ago that pursuing wounded birds on city streets is a hopeless, dangerous activity. Pigeons, like men, die in scores every day in New York. As I hesitantly walked on, however, I wondered why the doomed bird was assuming such a desperately contorted position under the cornice that projected slightly over it.

21   At this moment I grew aware of something I had heard more loudly in European streets as the factory whistles blew, but never in such intensity as here, even though American shoes are built of softer materials. All around me the march of people was intensifying. It was New York on the way to work. Space was shrinking before my eyes. The tread of innumerable feet passed from an echo to the steady murmuring of a stream, then to a drumming. A dreadful robot rhythm began to rack my head, a sound like the boots of Nazis in their heyday of power. I was carried along in an irresistible surge of bodies.

22   A block away, jamming myself between a waste-disposal basket and a light-post, I managed to look back. No one hesitated at that corner. The human tide pressed on, jostling and pushing. My bird had vanished under that crunching, multi-footed current as remorselessly as the wounded duck under the in-different combers of the sea. I watched this human ocean, of which I was an unwilling droplet, rolling past, its individual faces like whitecaps passing on a night of storm, fixed, merciless, indifferent; man in the mass marching like the machinery of which he is already a replaceable part, toward desks, computers, missiles, and machines, marching like the waves toward his own death with a conscious ruthlessness no watery shore could ever duplicate. I have never returned to search in that particular street for the face of humanity. I prefer the endlessly rolling pebbles of the tide, the moonstones polished by the pull-ing moon.

23   And yet, plunged as I am in dire memories and midnight reading, I have said that it is the sufferer from insomnia who knits the torn edges of men's dreams together in the hour before dawn. It is he who from his hidden, winter vantage point sees the desperate high-hearted bird fly through the doorway of the grand hotel while the sleepy doorman nods, a deed equivalent in human terms to that of some starving wretch evading Peter at heaven's gate, and an act, I think, very likely to be forgiven.

24   It is a night more mystical, however, that haunts my memory. Around me I see again the parchment of old books and remember how, on one rare evening, I sat in the shadows while a firefly flew from volume to volume lighting its small flame, as if in literate curiosity. Choosing the last title it had illuminated, I came immediately upon these words from St. Paul: "Beareth all things, believeth all things, hopeth all things, endureth all things." In this final episode I shall ask you to bear with me and also to believe.

25   I sat, once more in the late hours of darkness, in the airport of a foreign city. I was tired as only both the sufferer from insomnia and the traveler can be tired. I had missed a plane and had almost a whole night's wait before me. I could not sleep. The long corridor was deserted. Even the cleaning women had passed by.

26   In that white efficient glare I grew ever more depressed and weary. I was tired of the endless comings and goings of my profession; I was tired of customs officers and police. I was lonely for home. My eyes hurt. I was, unconsciously perhaps, looking for that warm stone, that hawthorn leaf, where, in the words of the poet, man trades in at last his wife and friend. I had an ocean to cross; the effort seemed unbearable. I rested my aching head upon my hand.

27   Later, beginning at the far end of that desolate corridor, I saw a man moving slowly toward me. In a small corner of my eye I merely noted him. He limped, painfully and grotesquely, upon a heavy cane. He was far away, and it was no matter to me. I shifted the unpleasant mote out of my eye.

28   But, after a time, I could still feel him approaching, and in one of those white moments of penetration which are so dreadful, my eyes were drawn back to him as he came on. With an anatomist's eye I saw this amazing conglomeration of sticks and broken, misshapen pulleys which make up the body of man. Here was an apt subject, and I flew to a raging mental dissection. How could anyone, I contended, trapped in this mechanical thing of joints and sliding wires expect the acts it performed to go other than awry?

29   The man limped on, relentlessly.

30   How, oh God, I entreated, did we become trapped within this substance out of which we stare so hopelessly upon our own eventual dissolution? How for a single minute could we dream or imagine that thought would save us, children deliver us, from the body of this death? Not in time, my mind rang with my despair; not in mortal time, not in this place, not anywhere in the world would blood be staunched, or the dark wrong be forever righted, or the parted be rejoined. Not in this time, not mortal time. The substance was too gross, our utopias bought with too much pain.

31   The man was almost upon me, breathing heavily, lunging and shuffling upon his cane. Though an odor emanated from him, I did not draw back. I had lived with death too many years. And then this strange thing happened, which I do not mean physically and cannot explain. The man entered me. From that moment I saw him no more. For a moment I was contorted within his shape, and then out of his body—our bodies, rather—there arose some inexplicable sweetness of union, some understanding between spirit and body which I had never before experienced. Was it I, the joints and pulleys only, who desired this peace so much?

32   I limped with growing age as I gathered up my luggage. Something of that terrible passer lingered in my bones, yet I was released, the very room had dilated. As I went toward my plane the words the firefly had found for me came automatically to my lips. "Beareth all things," believe, believe. It is thus that one day and the next are welded together, that one night's dying becomes tomorrow's birth. I, who do not sleep, can tell you this.

                           ❧

Discussion Questions

1. To what event earlier in his life did Eiseley attribute his insomnia? Following that event, how did his grandmother preserve his sanity?
2. Recount the ways in which Eiseley usually spent his time when he had insomnia. Did he always find it difficult to sleep? Explain.
*3. Relate the support that Eiseley provided for each of his following statements:". . . do you ever think who knits your universe together safely from one day's memory to the next? It is the insomniac. . . ." (paragraph 9); "This is the way wild things die, without question, without knowledge of mercy in the universe, knowing only themselves and their own pathway to the end" (paragraph 16); ". . . New York also has a beach of broken things more merciless than the reefs and rollers of the ocean shore" (paragraph 19).
*4. Interpret the extended metaphor that Eiseley developed in paragraph 22. What do you infer was Eiseley's purpose in composing the metaphor? Do you consider the implied comparison he makes to be fitting? Why or why not?
*5. Relate the closing anecdote Eiseley used to illustrate the words from St. Paul: "Beareth all things, believeth all things, hopeth all things, endureth all things." Do you find the experience Eiseley recounts to be credible or too mystical to believe? Explain.
*6. Tell why you consider the closing anecdote to be either harmonious with, or extraneous to, the content that preceded it in the selection.
*7. Which words would you choose to describe the tone—the author's implied attitude toward subject and audience—of "One Night's Dying": *formal, informal, intimate, somber, melancholy, playful, serious, resigned, clinical, ironic, meditative, condescending,* or any other possible attitudes? Justify your choices by reference to the selection.

Writing Topics

1. By the time they have reached adulthood, most people have endured in their lives many struggles of varying degrees of pain. Think of something you have had to bear—a personal illness, a family tragedy, a painful relationship, an unsatisfying job, whatever—and describe it in a short essay. Relate what it was you had to endure, under what conditions and for how long you had to endure it, and what you did to cope with the situation.
2. In his essay, Eiseley reveals that he found life on both the seashore and in New York City to be impersonal and merciless at times. Given an option between life in a large city and life in a small coastal town, which would you prefer? Consider what each site might offer that the other might not, as well as the drawbacks to either option. Then in a brief essay, reveal your choice and your reasons for it.

"Good work is not the work we assign children but the work they want to do. . . ."

THE CASE AGAINST CHORES

Jane Smiley

Jane Smiley (b. 1949) received her undergraduate degree from Vassar College and her doctorate from the University of Iowa. A professor of English at Iowa State University and a prolific writer, Smiley has authored *Barn Blind* (1980), *At Paradise Gate* (1981), *Duplicate Keys* (1984), *The Age of Grief* (1987), *The Greenlanders* (1988), *Ordinary Love and Goodwill* (1990), *A Thousand Acres* (1991), winner of the Pulitzer Prize for fiction, and *Moo* (1995). Smiley reports that she enjoys cooking, swimming, playing piano, and quilting. The June 1995 issue of *Harper's Magazine* contained "The Case against Chores," an excerpt from "Idle Hands," which appeared in the Spring 1995 issue of *Hungry Mind Review*.

1   I've lived in the upper Midwest for twenty-one years now, and I'm here to tell you that the pressure to put your children to work is unrelenting. So far I've squirmed out from under it, and my daughters have led a life of almost tropical idleness, much to their benefit. My son, however, may not be so lucky. His father was himself raised in Iowa and put to work at an early age, and you never know when, in spite of all my husband's best intentions, that early training might kick in.

2   Although "chores" are so sacred in my neck of the woods that almost no one ever discusses their purpose, I have over the years gleaned some of the reasons parents give for assigning them. I'm not impressed. Mostly the reasons have to do with developing good work habits or, in the absence of good work habits, at least habits of working. No such thing as a free lunch, any job worth doing is worth doing right, work before play, all of that. According to this reasoning, the world is full of jobs that no one wants to do. If we divide them up and get them over with, then we can go on to pastimes we like. If we do them "right," then we won't have to do them again. Lots of times, though, in a family, that *we* doesn't operate. The operative word is *you*. The practical result of almost every child-labor scheme that I've witnessed is the child doing the dirty work and the parent getting the fun: Mom cooks and Sis does the dishes; the parents plan and plant the garden, the kids weed it. To me, what this teaches the child

is the lesson of alienated labor: not to love the work but to get it over with; not to feel pride in one's contribution but to feel resentment at the waste of one's time.

3   Another goal of chores: the child contributes to the work of maintaining the family. According to this rationale, the child comes to understand what it takes to have a family, and to feel that he or she is an important, even indispensable member of it. But come on. Would you really want to feel loved primarily because you're the one who gets the floors mopped? Wouldn't you rather feel that your family's love simply exists all around you, no matter what your contribution? And don't the parents love their children anyway, whether the children vacuum or not? Why lie about it just to get the housework done? Let's be frank about the other half of the equation too. In this day and age, it doesn't take much work at all to manage a household, at least in the middle class — maybe four hours a week to clean the house and another four to throw the laundry into the washing machine, move it to the dryer, and fold it. Is it really a good idea to set the sort of example my former neighbors used to set, of mopping the floor every two days, cleaning the toilets every week, vacuuming every day, dusting, dusting, dusting? Didn't they have anything better to do than serve their house?

4   Let me confess that I wasn't expected to lift a finger when I was growing up. Even when my mother had a full-time job, she cleaned up after me, as did my grandmother. Later there was a housekeeper. I would leave my room in a mess when I headed off for school and find it miraculously neat when I returned. Once in a while I vacuumed, just because I liked the pattern the Hoover made on the carpet. I did learn to run water in my cereal bowl before setting it in the sink.

5   Where I discovered work was at the stable, and, in fact, there is no housework like horsework. You've got to clean the horses' stalls, feed them, groom them, tack them up, wrap their legs, exercise them, turn them out, and catch them. You've got to clip them and shave them. You have to sweep the aisle, clean your tack and your boots, carry bales of hay and buckets of water. Minimal horsekeeping, rising just to the level of humaneness, requires many more hours than making a few beds, and horsework turned out to be a good preparation for the real work of adulthood, which is rearing children. It was a good preparation not only because it was similar in many ways but also because my desire to do it, and to do a good job of it, grew out of my love of and interest in my horse. I can't say that cleaning out her bucket when she manured in it was an actual joy, but I knew she wasn't going to do it herself. I saw the purpose of my labor, and I wasn't alienated from it.

6   Probably to the surprise of some of those who knew me as a child, I have turned out to be gainfully employed. I remember when I was in seventh grade, one of my teachers said to me, strongly disapproving, "The trouble with you is

you only do what you want to do!" That continues to be the trouble with me, except that over the years I have wanted to do more and more.

7   My husband worked hard as a child, out-Iowa-ing the Iowans, if such a thing is possible. His dad had him mixing cement with a stick when he was five, pushing wheelbarrows not long after. It's a long sad tale on the order of two miles to school and both ways uphill. The result is, he's a great worker, much better than I am, but all the while he's doing it he wishes he weren't. He thinks of it as work; he's torn between doing a good job and longing not to be doing it at all. Later, when he's out on the golf course, where he really wants to be, he feels a little guilty, knowing there's work that should have been done before he gave in and took advantage of the beautiful day.

8   Good work is not the work we assign children but the work they want to do, whether it's reading in bed (where would I be today if my parents had rousted me out and put me to scrubbing floors?) or cleaning their rooms or practicing the flute or making roasted potatoes with rosemary and Parmesan for the family dinner. It's good for a teenager to suddenly decide that the bathtub is so disgusting she'd better clean it herself. I admit that for the parent, this can involve years of waiting. But if she doesn't want to wait, she can always spend her time dusting.

ʔ&

Discussion Questions

1. According to Smiley in paragraphs 2 and 3, what reasons do parents in the Midwest give for assigning chores to their children?

2. Relate what Smiley assumes often to be parents' real reason for giving their children work to do. Do you consider her assumption to be correct? Why or why not?

3. In paragraph 2, Smiley presents what she thinks is the lesson that assigning chores to children frequently teaches them. What is this lesson? Do you agree with Smiley? Explain.

4. Recount the differences between Smiley's upbringing and that of her husband. How have these differences apparently affected each of their lives as adults?

5. Does the fact that Smiley appears to have come from a privileged background undermine the strength of her case against chores? Explain.

6. Would you make any amendments to Smiley's assessment of the amount of time it takes to manage a middle-class household (paragraph 3)? If so, what would they be?

7. Do you sense an inconsistency between what Smiley says in paragraph 8 about what's good for teenagers and what she says in paragraph 4 about her own childhood? Explain.

8. In paragraph 2, Smiley uses a number of qualifying words or phrases—"almost no one," "mostly," "lots of times," and "almost." Clarify the purpose that these qualifiers serve in her argument.

Writing Topics

1. Smiley asserts in paragraph 8, "Good work is not the work we assign children but the work they want to do. . . . Assume that during your childhood you could have done only the work you wanted to do. In a short essay, describe what that work would have been, why you would have chosen it, what it would have involved, and how the choice to do only the work you wanted might have changed you from the person you are today.

2. Assume that the editor of *Harper's Magazine*, in which "The Case against Chores" appeared, is sponsoring a letter-writing contest on "The Case for Chores." Enter the contest, using personal experience and clear reasoning to refute Smiley's arguments.

Summary Writing Topics

*1. At the end of her entry for November 4 (paragraph 58), Yvonne Blue writes, "The more intelligent people are, the more miserable they are." Assume that the parents of a highly intelligent six-year-old girl write to you and ask whether their daughter is destined to be unhappy because of her intelligence. After reading some studies on the relationship between intelligence and happiness in life, respond to the couple in a letter, sharing your predictions about their daughter's future.

*2. The mothers of Gloria Steinem ("Ruth's Song"), Henry Louis Gates, Jr. ("Change of Life"), and Ellen Glasgow ("Early Sorrow") all suffered severe depression. In a written report to your classmates, deal with the following questions: What percentage of Americans, men and women, suffer from clinical depression at some time during their lives? What are the causes of the illness? What are its symptoms? How was it treated in the past? How is it being treated today?

3. Assume that a college magazine intends to run a series of articles under the title "Telling Moments and Times in the Lives of College Students." Think of your own "being and becoming," and in an article for the journal recount at least two events in your life that you believe have strongly influenced your present sense of self. The events to be related might be associated with childhood, school, employment, marriage, parenthood, military service, illness, death, divorce, travel, friendship, whatever. Relate each event, when it happened, the people involved, and its immediate and long-range effects upon your life.

*4. In "Science on the Right Side of the Brain," Alan P. Lightman writes in paragraph 2, "A major development in neuroscience has been the gradual understanding of the different functions of the right and left halves, or hemispheres, of the brain." Assume that members of the local Rotary Club have invited you to deliver a twenty-minute luncheon talk on current scientific understanding of the different functions of the brain's hemispheres. After investigating the topic, write the speech you intend to deliver.

5. For an essay titled "Scientists Do Not All Write Alike," intended to be published in a college literary magazine, contrast the style of Alan P. Lightman in "Science on the Right Side of the Brain" to that of Loren Eiseley in "One Night's Dying." Consider such matters as differences in the authors' subjects, diction, uses of figurative language, sentence variety and rhythm, sentence and paragraph length, and tone.

*6. As a youth, Yvonne Blue tried, apparently unsuccessfully, to diet. Millions of Americans make similar efforts each year. For a college newspaper, write an investigative report on citizens' attempts to shed weight. Who diets? Why? What companies or agencies seem to be profiting from Americans' concern about their weight? Are any popular diet programs successful? What recommendations would you make to someone who wants to lose weight?

7. In "The Case against Chores," Jane Smiley suggests that good work is that which one wants to do, not that which is assigned. Write a biographical sketch of your own work experiences. Include in it any chores you were assigned at home, jobs you held as a youth, work you are engaged in at present, and work you hope to do in the future. Relate what your compensation has been, both in money and personal satisfaction, from your various means of employment and which jobs, if any, have met Smiley's definition of good work.

*8. Assume that a pen pal from another country has read "Change of Life" by Henry Louis Gates, Jr., and is curious about religion in America. After researching the topic, write your friend a letter in which you report on such matters as Americans' religious affiliations and attendance at places of worship, the variety of religions in the nation, and the percentage of citizens who claim belief in a higher being and life after death. State your own opinion about the depth with which Americans practice their various religious beliefs.

*9. Assume that you have read little by Loren Eiseley, so you are not sure whether "One Night's Dying" is representative of Eiseley's writing style. Read at least five other essays by Eiseley, then write an essay in which you develop with supporting evidence either of the following theses:

    a. In style and content, "One Night's Dying" is typical of Eiseley's essays.

    b. In style and content, "One Night's Dying" is atypical of Eiseley's essays.

Cluster 7

NEW BEGINNINGS AND ADJUSTMENTS

For most of us, life is a never-ending series of beginnings and adjustments. We are born and immediately have to adapt to a strange new environment. We start elementary school as beginners, forced to cope with the alien new world of schooling, and eventually work our way up to the highest grade level, only to become beginners again in middle or junior high school and then once again in high school. In time, we graduate from high school and on the first day of college find ourselves novices yet again. We eventually finish college only to begin our careers as new persons on the job. Many of us become newlyweds, homeowners, and parents. Unfortunately some of us also join the ranks of the newly divorced. After working for years, most of us will retire and thus be forced once again to assimilate an entirely new way of living.

One could make the argument that no hour, no day, no year is the same as another, that each represents a new beginning, accompanied by a new set of requirements and demands, exacting from each of us the ability to make adjustments peculiar to that particular moment. This argument, though logical, treads in shallow waters: it fails to discriminate, to acknowledge that some beginnings are far more difficult to undertake than others, that some adjustments are more psychologically wrenching than others. Most of us can recall watershed events in our lives, whether they be the first day of kindergarten, the first day of life in a new neighborhood, the first day of military service, or the first day of parenthood—times imprinted indelibly in memory because of the strangeness of our situation or surroundings and because of the requirements placed upon us to accommodate that strangeness.

In the selections that follow, you are going to encounter writers who have elected or been compelled by circumstances to undertake new beginnings, ones that required major adjustments from the lives these individuals had previously lived. Some of the writers are immigrants with stories to tell about their adaptation to the United States—a Cambodian woman who discovers how to become a financial success; a blind Indian boy who learns to find his way among the sighted; a woman from Russia who challenges current notions about feminism in her adopted country; a man from Mexico who becomes an educational leader. A couple of writers are native citizens whose lives are altered by uncontrollable circumstances—a young girl who is obliged by a heretofore largely absent father to readjust the tempo of her days; a young boy who is forced by a family move to assume new responsibilities and to attend an unfamiliar school. Each of the writers we meet should remind us of the challenges, the frustrations, and often the rewards that accompany significant new beginnings.

❧ *"One of the first things you learn in America is that you need money. You can't be without money."*

THE DONUT QUEEN

Sirathra Som (as told to John Tenhula)

In his oral history *Voices from Southeast Asia* (1991), John Tenhula writes of his interview with Sirathra Som, "We meet at one of her donut shops. She is wearing a very stylish black jumpsuit, her hair pulled back tight, gold accessories, and very large sunglasses. Her new black BMW car is parked outside the window. She exudes an air of confidence and has a series of amusing anecdotes concerning cross-cultural experiences." Tenhula (b.1951) was program officer for the National Council of Churches (1977–80) and an employee of the United Nations (1980–86), during part of which time he served as legal officer for the office of United Nations High Commissioner for Refugees. A holder of two doctoral degrees—Ph.D. (Columbia University, 1972) and J.D. (University of the District of Columbia, 1984), Tenhula is an adjunct professor at Columbia University.

1   I was born in the capital, Phnom Penh, and led a very comfortable life. I can still see the school I went to as a child. I see the trees on the street and I think of the familiar things that made my life happy. I grew up a happy child with friends and school to keep me busy. My parents were educated but we were not what you would call rich. We never talked about money. Things just happened with my life, that's how I describe it—things just happened. That was the way with the war and leaving, it just happened.

What is the role of women in Cambodia?

2   The role of women in Cambodia is very defined. A woman is supposed to act in a certain way. Women are wives and mothers—those are the roles. We never questioned any of it. Not me, not my mother—we accepted it. If you grew up if a society where the rules are established and the community obeys them, then you just go along with it. You ask no questions—just go with it. I suppose it was expected. I would go to university and get an education, but more

important, I would get married and have children. Those were my duties. I gave up university when I married. My marriage, of course, was arranged. I was young, and before we left the country I had two babies. I fit the traditional role of a good wife and mother and listener.

3   No one can forget the final days in Cambodia. It was only yesterday in my mind. Cambodia fell before Vietnam, and by early April we had to leave. My husband worked for the U.S. Agency for International Development, so we would be in a dangerous position if we stayed. No question about it, we would have been killed. I was twenty-two then. We left on April 7, 1975, and went to Camp Pendleton and were released to a sponsor in Texas three weeks later.

4   All of my family and my husband's family were killed, all of my friends. No one was left. It was like a plague of death and everyone is gone. The Khmer Rouge[1] killed everyone. All of my family were educated people—those were the ones that Pol Pot[2] wanted most to destroy.

5   We arrived in California with nothing, nothing. Only the clothes we were wearing. I could not speak English and everybody looked threatening to me. Simple things seemed complicated. Colors were different, sounds were different. Each day was filled with more questions than answers.

Tell me about your first job.

6   My first job was at the Sheraton Hotel in San Francisco as a domestic, and I earned $2.50 an hour. I was lucky to get the job—there were a lot of people who wanted it. We lived in Oakland and the job was in San Francisco. To be without a car in California is like being a bird without wings. You can live but then you can't really live. So I commuted by bus with several transfers. I remember the first day when I had to transfer from the first bus to the second one and I got lost. I panicked. I could not speak and I used hand signals. A nice man took my hand and took me to the bus. He had a wonderful smile and it was that smile I will never forget.

7   I learned English but not in a classroom. That's too much wasted time, it's too tiring. If you want to learn, you listen to people on the street, listen to the radio and TV, but also you force yourself to speak. After I learned what I thought was English, although it wasn't so good, I registered for sixteen units of accounting at night school; but I had no time—work and family forced me to quit.

8   For me there was no question of whether I should work or stay at home. One of the first things you learn in America is that you need money. You can't

---

[1] **Khmer Rouge:** Native Cambodian Communists, whose soldiers gained control of more than two-thirds of the total land area of the nation in the 1970s.

[2] **Pol Pot:** Leader of the Khmer Rouge forces, who from 1975 to 1979 led a rule of terror in Cambodia.

be without money. There is no one then to help you. So we needed two incomes and I went to work. I know my husband did not like it, but it could not be helped. The journey here created problems for us and this work situation was one of them. I could work easier than he could and I began to do well and I supported the family. I became the breadwinner.

9   He had bad feelings about this, I understood this, but the feelings got worse. It's hard for me to talk about it. I understood his pain but there was nothing I could do about it to help him. Eventually, we were divorced. Divorced! This would be unheard-of in Cambodia where you are married once and that is it for life. But he could not make the changes here. The money was always a problem. Now he has a master's degree and works as a counselor in San Francisco. That part of my life is completed.

What do you think of American women?

10   I find that American women think too much about things which complicate their lives, and it seems strange to me. I suppose all women have been raised to follow, but you must take the chances while they are there. Too many American women also lack patience. They want everything so quickly and they want the impossible. No patience. Life is not that way, and it only leads to unhappiness. Our Buddhist tradition teaches us patience. Maybe it cannot be learned. When I got divorced, I felt sick; I lost twenty pounds. Silly? Well, I had three children to care for and I could not have the luxury of worrying and wasting time. So I accepted my situation and made peace.

Tell me how you started here in business.

11   Before the U.S., I had never worked. In 1976, I persuaded Winchell's Donuts to give me a manager franchise and to work off the $5,000 fee. Then I started a small Winchell's shop in Berkeley and was able to pay off the franchise fee in four months. I built up one business and sold it in five months. I doubled the money I had paid for it. In 1982, when I was visiting some friends in Stockton, I noticed a run-down Oriental food store being mismanaged, and the owners were glad to sell it. The Asia food store is doing very well today. The store is ideally located in a busy shopping center within a few blocks of a new housing subdivision full of Asian refugee farm workers.

12   I began with nothing and now I have something. For me, that's what is great about America. I know the Cambodian men say I am tough — so what? By American standards you need to be good at business to survive. So maybe I am tough. But it is very hard work. I am working every morning at four-thirty in one of my six donut stores. I want to buy that McDonald's hamburger store next door, that is my next investment.

Have you experienced discrimination in the United States?

13   I know about discrimination against Cambodians. It was not so long ago that hate groups wanted to burn down the section of Stockton where the Cambodians lived. The KKK was here, you know. I suppose we remind people of the war. But then, too, we get discrimination among our own refugee groups. Most people think we are Vietnamese, they only talk about Vietnamese refugees. Well, we are different. The Vietnamese get better training programs and other services. They are more forceful than Cambodians, but that is part of our history.

14   I have no problems as a working mother. I am remarried now. My three children are happy, and I spend time with them every day. I am at a point that if I want to take a few days off or take a vacation with them, I can do it. Just knowing you can do that is a good feeling. My kids are doing very well in school. They get rewards. For every A on the report card they get ten dollars. Anything less than an A, then they must do housework for me. It is my incentive system.

15   I care deeply about my fellow Cambodians here. I know their lives are miserable and painful. I have helped thirteen families start their own businesses around here. I share my experiences and the lessons I have learned. I get upset with refugees who live too long on welfare if they are able to work. I get upset with the welfare caseworkers, too, who encourage a lot of people to take cash assistance and to stay on welfare. They need their clients. I feel that anyone can achieve success here if they are smart and willing to work hard. I encourage people to start a business.

16   I have no regrets; how could I? I want to get my M.B.A. and I worry about the first time my twelve-year-old daughter brings home her first boyfriend. No, I have not seen *The Killing Fields* movie about Cambodia. I am not ready for that.

❧

Discussion Questions

1.   Recount Som's family background and upbringing in Cambodia. In what ways did Som fulfill the roles expected of a woman in Cambodian society?

2.   Relate the conditions that prompted Som and her husband to flee Cambodia. What difficulties did she and her spouse have in adjusting to life in the United States?

3.   In paragraph 12, Som asserts, "I began with nothing and now I have something." Describe Som's acquisitions and what she did to attain them.

*4.   In paragraph 10, Som opines that American women fail to take chances and that they lack patience. Do you agree with her assessment? Explain.

*5. Do you consider Som's own financial success to be a consequence of hard work, luck, or a combination of the two? Explain. Would you support Som's belief that "... anyone can achieve success here if they are smart and willing to work hard"? Why or why not?

*6. If you had the opportunity, what additional questions would you ask Som? Why?

Writing Topics

1. Som has apparently become a financial success. In an essay, define what you would consider to be "financial success" for yourself, relate what considerations went into your definition, and describe the steps you think necessary to take in order to achieve your goal.

2. Assume that you are one of Som's children. Think carefully of the various implications of your mother's system of reward or punishment for grades in school. Then write her a letter in which you provide her with sound reasons for either continuing or discontinuing her present practice.

"Sometime try to find a door in the dark,
and believe me, ma'am,
you'll find even you have some facial vision."

A DONKEY IN A WORLD OF HORSES
Ved Mehta

Blind since he was three, Ved Mehta (b. 1934) was one of seven children of a medical administrator in the Indian government. Wishing a better education than he could find in his native country, he came to the United States in 1949 to attend the Arkansas School for the Blind, the setting of "A Donkey in a World of Horses." Mehta, who went on to obtain an undergraduate degree from Pomona College and graduate degrees from Harvard and Oxford universities, has been a staff writer for *The New Yorker* since 1961. Appointed a distinguished professor at Vassar College in 1994, he is the author of numerous books, among them *Face to Face* (1958), *Walking the Indian Streets* (1960), *Fly and the Fly-Bottle* (1963), *Portrait of India* (1970), *John Is Easy to Please* (1971), *The New India* (1978), *Daddyjii* (1972), *Mamajii* (1979), *Vedi* (1982), *The Stolen Light* (1989), and *Up at Oxford* (1993).

1   After the initial few weeks of school, when everything seemed gloomy and I still brooded a great deal about having left home, things started to get easier. I stopped going to the elementary-grade arithmetic class, and with a little coaching from our high school math teacher now and then, I could keep up with my own class quite handsomely. I sometimes even got better marks than Ray[1] in English and civics. Whereas before I had spent hours on homework, I could now finish it all in thirty or forty minutes. Often, however, I felt discouraged that the classes were not hard enough, that most of the time in the classrooms was spent just talking rather than learning.

2   Big Jim once remarked, "What good does it do us to keep on learning about adjustment, when we are with blind people in school all the time and might even end up working in workshops for the blind, where no one could tell

---

[1] **Ray:** A half-sighted, sixteen-year-old fellow student.

whether you ate with hands or silverware, wiped your mouth with a shirt sleeve or a napkin, or wore a navy-blue shirt with brown pants." Indeed, the programme for "social adjustment"got more attention than our academic education. We met in classes, sometimes twice, sometimes four times a week, to learn about social graces and adjustments to a sighted society, which, at least at our school for the blind, would not have been represented at all, were it not for some of our seeing teachers.

3   Mr Chiles, almost totally blind himself, introducing one of the social-adjustment classes, had remarked, "To be blind is an up-hill struggle. You've got to sell yourself to every seeing man. You've got to show him that you can do things that he thinks you can't possibly do."

4   It was true enough—if you were a donkey in a world of horses, you had to justify your worth and existence to the horses. You had, somehow, to prove to them that you could carry as much weight as they could, and if you couldn't move as fast, you at least were willing to work harder and put in longer hours.

5   "Anything you do wrong in the world of the seeing," Mr Chiles had said, "like dressing untidily or putting your elbows on the table while eating, even if half the sighted world themselves commit these sins, people around you will chalk it up to your blindness. They'll call you poor wretches, feel sorry for you, and they will commit the worst sin of all by excusing it because you're blind."

6   So we were marshalled in groups and marched into classes where we were given good common-sense lessons—that you had to introduce young to old, rather than vice versa, that it was good to avoid wearing brown and blue together, even if you did not know what brown or blue signified, and that if you could not eat an orange half with a spoon, it was better not to eat oranges at all. At the same time, we were told that, no matter how independent blind people became, they must always accept help from the sighted graciously, recognizing that the feeling for helping the blind was the result of a generous impulse.

7   When Ernest asked, "If you went to a restaurant and they served you oranges in halves and you couldn't eat them and the waitress offered to feed you, should you accept the help?" he was abruptly told not to make light of serious matters.

8   As part of the social adjustment programme, we also had personal, private conferences with the faculty, who pointed to individual defects which they did not care to criticize in public. Ernest told us that his adviser suggested that he wash his feet more often. Joe reported that he was to start using a deodorant. Kenneth said he got a lecture to keep his mouth closed at least some of the time.

9   No blind person should be caught dead petting in public, and one teacher went so far as to say that it might be better to avoid kissing your wife or husband in public, just in case there might be a misunderstanding. We were carefully examined on this material in written tests, and it was a tribute to the teachers that no one failed.

10   The more serious side of the social-adjustment programme was concerned
with facial vision and the teaching of "mobility." One day early in spring, all
the totally blind students were herded into the gymnasium and asked to run
through an obstacle course. Plastic and wooden slabs of all sizes and weights
were suspended from the ceiling around the gymnasium. Some of them hung
as low as the waist; others barely came down to the forehead. These slabs were
rotated at varying speeds, and the blind were asked to walk through the labyrinth at as great a speed as possible without bumping into the obstacles. The
purpose of keeping the slabs moving was to prevent the students from getting
accustomed to their position and to force them to strain every perceptory ability
to sense the presence of the obstacles. The thinner the slab and the higher its
position, the harder it was to feel or hear it—that is to say, to sense the pressure
of the object against the skin—a pressure felt by the myriad of pores above,
below and next to our ears. Some of the slabs were of an even fainter mass than
the slimmest solitary lamp-post on a street corner. This obstacle course helped
gauge how well an individual could distinguish one shadow-mass from another
and, having located the one closest to him, circumvent it without running into
yet another. Here was where the wheat was separated from the chaff.

11   A person who has knocked about fearlessly—and it is a help if he was
blinded in his childhood—will do much better in this test of facial vision than
an individual who either lost his sight late in life, or has been restrained from
developing the full range of his co-ordinated senses. Having, of course, during
my childhood jumped from banister to banister, from roof to roof, and ridden
my bicycle through unfamiliar places crowded with unlocated objects—and
that, too, at a much faster rate of speed—for me, going through this obstacle
course was child's play. The gymnasium was kept quiet so that the blind people
could hear the obstacles, although I could not help feeling that I could have run
through the labyrinth with a jet buzzing overhead. When someone cracked his
head against one of the slabs, and the others discovered who had done it, they
would laugh mercilessly, until, of course, they themselves ran smack into one.

12   After we had spent three or four class sessions running through this obstacle course, we were given a theoretical briefing on the importance of facial
vision—that the blind ought to put the same emphasis on it as sighted do on
seeing, and that the way to develop it was through abandonment of fear and
through complete relaxation. We were also briefed on a few stock secrets of
the trade, such as that the head should always be held high in order to more
easily walk a straight line, that some found that a hardly perceptible arching of
the back helped to minimize any injuries frontally received, and that compass
directions—determined sometimes by the sun against the cheek—were better
than remembering lefts and rights. In time, we would get the knack of such
things as going into unfamiliar stores and finding the right counter or finding
an elevator in a strange building.

13   We were also advised that in crossing streets it was safer to walk with the traffic rather than to follow pedestrians, as they might be crossing against the light. In crossing streets without lights, safety depended entirely upon the ingenuity of the blind individual in gauging the distance of the cars correctly, although it was helpful in crossing wider streets to take them in parts or in halves. Above all, one must never get panicky and run across a street.

14   Each instructor then was assigned two or three students, and with cane in hand, bus token in pocket, we separated for downtown. My instructor gave me a list of trifling, if not embarrassing, things to purchase from scattered counters in a Rexall drug store, and then asked me to meet him at the coffee shop of a departmental store for a milk shake, the treat being dependent upon my success in making the purchases. I was specifically told not to ask for help, and even if it were voluntarily offered, I should try to decline, provided I could do so gracefully. I did not know whether the instructor would keep his watchful eye on me, but whether he did or not, it was important to me that I should do well on this first day of independence.

15   I started out by tapping the cane in front of each foot before taking a step, as I had been taught. This was supposed to ward off tripping over a kerb, dropping into a manhole or meeting some other such obstacle, inclining or declining. I found that the noise of the cane made me very self-conscious and was quite distracting, so I flung it into the gutter at the end of the driveway in front of the school, and having made a mental note of the spot so that I might pick up the cane on my return, I started walking rapidly towards the bus stop, with my hands thrust into my pockets. Rather than wait at the nearest bus stop, I decided I would walk three or four blocks to the next one. Just to test my facial vision, I counted the lamp-posts and tried to guess the distance from which I first perceived them.

16   The sun was out in its full noon glory, although there was just the right proportion of breeze, making the heat not severe, but pleasant. In fact, the breeze was so gentle that it disturbed my facial vision not at all, and I could even perceive the curves and slight upgrades on the street, though that street was totally unfamiliar to me. However, when I unexpectedly stepped off a kerb, that fraction of a second between the kerb and the street was so frightening I almost wished I had my cane back—that cane which my instructor called the third leg of a blind man, although Big Jim had remarked that it was more like a displaced tail. I found, though, that soon my foot started registering a slight indentation before the end of the sidewalk, and that was clue enough. To my left, on the street, there was a steady stream of cars going both ways, at, I guessed, about forty miles an hour. There were sounds of Ford motors, Chevrolets, and I even remember hearing a few Buick engines. Walking on that street, I felt as confident and happy as I imagined a driver would feel with a ton of machine at the command of his feet. Then I heard the clanging vibration of the electric wire just above the traffic. My instructor had told me to listen for it

as a sign of the approaching trackless trolley. Then, almost a block behind me, I distinguished the sound of the trolley motor from the rest of the traffic. The bus stop was still a block and a half ahead of me and I knew I had to catch that trolley, because it would be twenty minutes before the next one. With the ever-increasing sound of the trolley motor in my ears, I started running as fast as I could to the bus stop. I wished there were the shadow of a wall or a fence, to my right, to run by. As it was, there was empty space to my right and the hindering noise of the traffic to my left, a narrow sidewalk with a string of lamp-posts, and heaven knew what other hazards. I skirted one lamp-post by a hair's breadth, and another actually caught my shoulder, but not my head.

17   When I got to the next intersection, the trolley was almost abreast. If I waited to listen for the sound of the traffic, I could not possibly make it, so I dashed across the street, thinking of what I had repeated to my mother a long time ago.

18   "Death comes only once," I had said.

19   "But," she had said, "what if you lose a leg?"

20   That had been frightening, all right.

21   "After that I wouldn't want to live. I don't mind being blind, but a wheel chair . . ."

22   Maybe if I had a white cane in my hand, I wouldn't have to worry as much about the traffic, and the bus driver would know I was blind and would wait for me. But it is better this way, I thought.

23   Just when I perceived the looming shadow of the bench at the bus stop, about ten or fifteen feet away from me, the trolley passed me. If only someone would be waiting there, I wished, so that the trolley will at least stop. But no one was, and I missed the trolley.

24   With a discouraged heart I slowly walked up to the bench, out of breath, and sat down. It would be twenty minutes more, twenty whole long minutes, and maybe I wouldn't get my milk shake after all. I took out my Braille watch and kept my fingers fixed on the hands, and I heard car after car pass by. I felt as envious of the drivers inside as a man standing in a rainstorm trying to thumb a ride, although I myself had no intention of flagging down a car.

25   At last there was another trolley. I heard its door open a few feet ahead of me. Walking parallel to the shadow of the trolley, I felt the gap of the door and climbed the three steps, slightly nervous, wondering if I could drop my coins in the box without having to be shown. I found the box, and the driver must have thought I could see a little, because he did not say anything about a vacant seat. The trolley was moving already. I walked down the aisle, feeling the vague shadows of the people, hearing the crackling sounds of packages or newspapers, until I felt the shadow of an empty seat and sat down. All of a sudden I was trembling all over. Arlie had been right when he said, "I don't give a damn about being blind, but I do give a damn about being blind in a world where people have eyes." I was glad I did not have a cane, because this way probably no one

was watching me. No, I assured myself, I would rather be blind than deaf, any day. I was surer about it that time than ever before.

26   I did not pay any attention to the half-bends of the trolley. My instructor had told me, "Just wait for the second right-angle turn, where the trolley goes from Markham to Main Street." It was such an obvious turn that I could not miss it. We were going south now (I always oriented myself with the direction of one street), and the Rexall drug store was on Fifth Street. My instructor had said, "Don't bank on the bus halting at every bus or light stop. Try to get used to the distance of a block, and that way you can't go wrong."

27   I got off on Fifth all right, and crossing Main, I went into the Rexall drug store. Since it was my first time, I asked the man in the front where I could pick up some shoelaces.

28   "Straight to the back," he said, "and the second counter to the right."

29   After five minutes I had bought all that my instructor had asked for, and I started walking rapidly a block up to the department store, dodging the window shoppers by using facial vision to keep a proper distance between the windows and myself, and the luncheon crowd by a watchful ear. By counting the gaps in the sustained shadow of the windows, I knew how many stores there were on that block. Next time I came to town, I would get the various stores located by keeping track of how many doors up they were from the street corner. It was as simple as that.

30   My instructor had said that there were a number of ways of telling when you got to the street corner. It could be done by the noise of the traffic, the draft of air, or the receding shadow of the windows. At last I was at the double doors of the department store. I went in and started walking back towards the elevator, listening for the sound of its door. Inside the elevator, I found my instructor.

31   As soon as we sat down in the restaurant, he said laughingly, "You shouldn't have asked that man for the shoelace counter."

32   "And how was I to know where to find it?" I retorted. "By the smell of it?"

33   "You gave me the slip," he said, "that is, until I saw you running, from inside the trolley that you missed. But I picked you up again at the drug store." So he had watched me!

34   "The first thing," he was saying admonishingly, "is that you've got to admit to yourself that you are blind and that there are certain things you just can't do, like throwing away your cane and crossing streets without listening for traffic."

35   He was right, of course. I wouldn't make a habit of crossing streets that way, but the cane—that was another matter. I had never hooked a cane in front of my bicycle when I rode it, so I did not see why I had to carry one when walking, if I did not mind taking the chance of falling into a manhole. As for letting drivers know I was blind, I felt safer relying on myself than on their judgement. Maybe it was all rationalization, like that of Benjamin Franklin when he stopped being a vegetarian because he saw a little fish in the open stomach of a big fish about to be cooked.

36   "You'll carry that cane," my instructor said threateningly. "If not, you won't be allowed to leave campus."

37   "Yes, sir," I replied.

38   The milk shake was there now, and putting the straw between my teeth, I let it drain down my throat. It was cool and delicious, and I forgot about the cane. All of a sudden I felt weak and empty. "It must have been tougher than I admitted," I said.

39   "It always is the first day you are on the road by yourself," the instructor agreed. After we had finished the milk shakes, he asked, "Can you find your way home? I have some other business in town."

40   "Yes," I said.

41   We walked out of the department store together, and then separated. I could have caught the bus on that corner, but I decided I would walk all the way down to Markham (or First) Street. I must have passed a nut shop on the way, because there was the smell of roasting peanuts. And from the next open door, a fresh smell of leather. Must be a shoe store, I thought, or maybe a luggage shop. Then there was a swinging door which creaked as it was opened and closed, letting out a burst of air which breathed of dime store. At Markham Street there were three or four buses standing. I knew which was a trolley because of the motor. A number of people were getting on it, and I got in line. I felt in my pocket and there were two bus tokens. I had been given one extra for the trip, just in case I lost one or took the wrong bus. They would be good for another trip downtown, I thought, that is, if I did not use one now. So I left the line, crossed Main Street, and started walking west on Markham. I could not think of walking home, because the distance was at least a couple of miles. Besides, I did not know the way.

42   Half-way down the block, I stepped off the kerb and, standing about a foot away from it, tried to thumb a ride. The trolley whizzed past in front of me. Cars kept on passing me until finally a woman stopped.

43   "Are you going towards Stiff Station?" I asked.

44   "Going right there," she said.

45   I climbed in.

46   "I bet you go to the school for the blind," she said. Why did my eyes always give me away? I thought. Maybe if I had glass eyes and kept my eyes open all the time, no one would ever know. But that was useless. My mother wouldn't think of it, and from my left eye everyone would always know that I was blind.

47   "How much can you see?" she asked.

48   "Just enough to get around," I replied. That way, I thought, there would be no fuss about her taking me right to the door of the school and helping me in.

49   "You know," she said—we had just overtaken the trolley—"you half-sighted people are the link between the world of the blind and the world of the seeing."

50   "Yes, ma'am," I said. That was the first time the words "half-sighted" had ever sounded good to me.

51   "The blind must have a world all their own, don't you think?" she asked.

52   "It's just a world minus eyes," I said. "It's what one might call a world of four senses, instead of five."

53   "But you have developed your senses so much more acutely, and to see a blind person get around is so amazing to me, until, of course, I remind myself that they have extra senses."

54   "They don't have any extra senses, ma'am," I said, "unless you call facial vision that. Sometime try to find a door in the dark, and believe me, ma'am, you'll find even you have some facial vision."

55   "They must have extra senses," she said emphatically. She probably had not even listened to what I had said. "If you were totally blind you would know what I am talking about."

56   I was too tired to argue, and, leaning back against the seat, I relaxed while she lectured me about the extra senses of the blind, the car all the time moving swiftly through traffic.

57   Bringing the car to a stop, she said, "Here we are." I thanked her and got out of the car right in front of the long driveway leading to the school. She drove away. I found my cane where I had left it. It had a spring at the tip so that when you tapped it the cane would automatically spring up. I stood there, just springing the cane up and down, listening to the tapping sound. The more I tapped, the less I liked it. I knew I couldn't get used to it even if I wanted to. The spring made it worse rather than better.

58   I heard then, above the roar of the traffic, a clattering noise beginning a block away. Clack, clack, clack, and I could almost forecast the next one. Some blind man was walking on the sidewalk, finding his way with the help of a cane. He must have very bad facial vision, I thought, to have to locate every wretched lamp-post with a cane. Clack, clack, clack. I stood there, running my hand up and down my new long, thin cane, with a fancy strap instead of a handle at the top. I took the two ends of the cane in my hands, and putting my foot at the centre, pulled hard and broke it in two. And flinging it back into the gutter, I walked rapidly towards the school building. I reached the building almost running, with "clack, clack, clack," still ringing in my ears.

59   I took the steps in front of the building two at a time and reached the lounge out of breath. As always, there was Joe humming a tune.

60   "Who's there?" he asked.

61   "It's me," I said. "You ought to be able to recognize my steps by now."

62   "I guess so," he said languidly, and went back to humming his tune.

⟡

Discussion Questions

1. What are the indications that Mehta adjusted rather quickly to his new school?

*2. Tell how the title "A Donkey in a World of Horses" relates to the social-adjustment classes required of Mehta. Do you consider the social graces taught in these classes to be important to blind people? To sighted people? Explain.

3. Relate the purpose of having blind students try to run through an obstacle course, one consisting of suspended rotating plastic and wooden slabs of different heights, weights, and speeds. Why did Mehta consider the course to be "child's play"?

4. Describe the test of Mehta's ability to find his way downtown and around the stores. What risks did he take, and what errors did he make in completing the assignment?

5. Cite evidence of Mehta's sensory acuity during his trip to and from town. What made his hitchhiked ride home ironically amusing?

*6. Explain the symbolic importance in paragraph 57 of Mehta's breaking his cane in two. What traits of Mehta's character did the act reveal?

*7. On a scale of 1 to 10, with 1 being simple and lucid and 10 being complex and opaque, how would you rate Mehta's writing style? Defend your rating with evidence from the selection.

Writing Topics

1. In paragraphs 19–21, Mehta indicates he would rather be dead than be blind and confined to a wheelchair. Assume that Mehta had unfortunately lost a leg in trying to board the trolley car. Write him a letter disagreeing with his position and explaining why you believe he should elect to continue living.

2. Mehta disregards the advice of others and fortunately suffers no dire consequences. Think of advice you have been given in the past, such as, "Obey traffic laws," "Don't smoke," "Stay close to home," "Get your homework in on time." Then, in an essay, recount a time when your disregard of a piece of advice resulted in unfortunate consequences. Include details about the circumstances involved, the advice given, the behavior you displayed, and the results it brought, as well as the lesson learned, if any, from the experience.

❧ *"We did not know how to welcome a strange*
man . . . into the life we had created for ourselves;
what's more, we didn't want to."

MY FATHER THE STRANGER

Virginia Bell Dabney

In 1917, Virginia Dabney's mother, Alice, moved to a farm
in Virginia, taking her two daughters with her and leaving
behind her husband, fifteen years her elder, to continue his
work as an insurance actuary in Chicago. From that time
until his retirement some seventeen years later, Dabney's
father, Hugh, saw his family only during two-week summer
vacations and over Christmases, an arrangement both
parents seemed to find "perfectly acceptable," according
to Dabney, who was born in 1919. "My Father the Stranger "
appears in Dabney's memoir, *Once There Was a Farm*: A
Country Childhood Remembered (1990). For further information
about the author, see the biographical sketch on page 126.

1   My father and I really became acquainted for the first time in 1934, when
I was fifteen and he sixty-five; he retired then from the insurance company he
had been a part of for over thirty years and came home to stay. Our relationship
during his vacation visits over the years had been formal and polite. He brought
presents on those visits and I thanked him; then I was expected to take them
somewhere else to play.

2   As I grew older and closer to his age at that time, I tried to understand him
as I could not then. Now I believe that he came with an idealized picture in his
mind of long days of reading and walking around the farm, with perhaps some
cozy, friendly exchanges with my mother and possibly with me, though I do not
think he thought much about me at all.

3   Mother did not prepare herself adequately for my father's retirement,
though I am sure she must have had misgivings about it that she did not tell me.
She didn't prepare me for it either; perhaps there was no way she could have.
I had my own idealized scenario of at last getting to know my father in the way
I thought other girls knew theirs. At first I thought that he and I might now
become good friends, that he would like the way I was growing up, that there

were many things he could tell me about subways, museums and stage plays—
the exciting life of the city I wondered about.

4 　　That he loved all of us I was sure. I remembered all the barrels and boxes he
had sent us in the early twenties. Tins of Chinese delicacies that my mother liked
to have on hand—preserved ginger, tinned crisp noodles, dried mushrooms,
canned water chestnuts. Food we could not buy in local stores: maple sugar,
canned and candied pineapple, canned apricots, as exotic to us then as litchi
nuts would be now. There were sweets we never saw in stores in our small
towns: Scotch shortbread, chocolate butter creams, butterscotch patties and
ribbon candies. Toys shining and smelling of new lacquer, emerging magically
from the excelsior they were packed in. We derived a quiet pleasure from the
care he showed in making these choices for us.

5 　　But the truth dawned on my mother and me after my father had been with
us for a few months: We did not know how to welcome a strange man—or
perhaps any man—into the life we had created for ourselves; what's more, we
didn't want to. In small carpings we revealed to each other that he was an
intruder, complicating our satisfactory existence. Of course Mother was aware
that we owed much of that existence to his regular checks sent over the years,
and she may have hoped that he would be mellowed with age now, glad to be
home at last, content to let life go on as it had before he came.

6 　　My father did not bring with him much in the way of personal effects: suits
and a heavy overcoat, a bookcase, books on psychic research, atheism and
religious cults, and two large file cabinets of clippings. But his clothes shoved
my mother's over in the closet, and soon hers smelled of his, a curious blend of
coal smoke, Chiclets and apartment-house mixed cuisine. He occupied the
her twin bed in her bedroom, and he dropped his pocket watch, comb and
br sh, nail clip and desk calendar on her dresser among her pretty jars and
pow er box. The combination washroom and linen closet that she had furnished with basin and pitcher, towel rack and chamber pot (we still had no
electric or plumbing) became a place whose primitive facilities he swore at
every mc ing. His filing cabinets and bookcase took up most of one wall in
the small r m that Mother used for sewing.

7 　　The roc g chair in the living room became my father's favorite and he
rocked and read there for hours at a time. The only desk was a sturdy mahogany drop leaf that was full of my mother's canceled checks, letters, receipts,
account books and, tucked into a pigeonhole, the bit of embroidery she worked
on when she found time, so when he wrote anything, he did it on his knees. I
don't know if he cared where he wrote, but in our house everyone had had a
desk except my father. I don't wish to imply that he was not permitted or encouraged to have one; probably it didn't matter to him.

8 　　I found that if I was in the living room when my father was there and made
a rustle looking through records I would like to play, or said something to my
mother while she worked in the kitchen, I would find his eyes fixing me with a

chilly stare over his half glasses. Naturally I left, unable to ignore what I read as hostility and probably was. I usually went up to my room and stayed there until he climbed the stairs at bedtime; then I could go down and play a few records, trying to keep the volume low. That was hard to do with hand-cranked phonographs; the only way to play records softly was to use fiber instead of steel needles and they gave a slightly muted sound to those old 78's. I always closed the doors, but Liszt must have hummed through the double floors anyway.

9   Sometimes my father was the one to sigh, pick up his book and go upstairs so he wouldn't have to listen to my mother and me talking about dress patterns, what went on at school or her work. She had by then been employed as executive secretary of the Lewis County Farm Loan Association for nearly two years. She enjoyed discussing what she was doing in those years, the people she met and the farms she visited as part of her job, but my father could bear only so much of this before he would say, "Do I know these people? No. Do I want to know these people? No. So let me read and you talk about your job with Mary Marshall[1] or Vallie.[2]"

10   I rarely said anything to my father except when I had to. I tried to at first, but even if I spoke to him directly there would be a pause before he focused his blue eyes on me and said, "Were you speaking to me?" I would clear my throat and repeat the question, and he would shake his head, say, "I don't know what you're talking about," and return without another word to his plate or his book. Anything more I thought to say was swallowed forthwith. After this happened several times, I stopped trying. I think now that if I had been less timid and had insisted on his attention, I might have broken through that barrier. I wonder if it was his slight deafness that kept him from hearing my wispy voice. But of course he wasn't trying either, and felt no impulse to exchange ideas with me.

11   He had been a solitary man in the city, and he spoke of only one man, dead by then for twenty years, as a friend, apparently the only one he ever had. It was solely letters that had kept him in touch with his children after my mother moved to Virginia, and he barely knew me at all. By adolescence I was as much a stranger in the house he shared with his wife as he was to me in the house I shared with my mother. I could not know that his profound aloneness was what had molded him into the old man he was by then. And I could not recognize that his translation from bustling city to unhurried country must have been unsettling.

12   My mother was unable to help me appreciate my father's dislocation; though understanding in many ways, she was prevented from seeing it by old antagonisms between them. She felt it was *her* life that was being disrupted and

---

[1] **Mary Marshall:** A neighbor who does housework for Mrs. Bell and is her confidante.
[2] **Vallie:** A family name for the author.

moved from its center. When the two of them had separated and she removed to Virginia—partly because, she said, she could not bring up the children to be targets of his sarcasm—she may have thought he would not live to retire to the farm. He was much older than she, and in those years fewer men lived to be sixty-five. Now that he was home, in seeming good health, she did not know what to do with him. For a while she left him to his reading and went on with her work. It was when he decided he should take part in the running of the farm that matters became uncomfortable. To do anything out of doors he had to communicate with Solomon, and this was difficult for him because he could not get the hang of southern black speech.

13 "Why can't he talk like other people?" he would say to me testily after I had translated for him, and Solomon was out of earshot.

14 "He does," I said. "He talks like Susan and other colored people."

15 From the time that my father started showing interest in the farm, Solomon found himself caught in the middle. He would begin a job, perhaps making a new pigpen, and my father would stand there and watch, wearing one of his old office shirts and worn gray business pants.

16 "Why are you doing it that way?" he would ask.

17 "This what Mrs. Bell tole me to do," Solomon would say.

18 "She *told* you to do it this way?" Incredulously.

19 "Yes sir. They's a hole s'posed to be here for to pour slops through."

20 "Pour *what* through?"

21 "Slops. What we feeds to pigs."

22 "Slops," my father would repeat a little nastily. "Now that's a nice word." To which, of course, Solomon could give no answer, and he would try to go on with his work of setting a trough in the hole. In a few minutes my father would say, "Don't you ever measure anything before you saw?" or "I knew you weren't making that board the right length," until Solomon was so discomfited that he would suddenly discover it was time to milk the cows.

23 Later my father would report to my mother about Solomon's sloppy carpentry. "Do you think the pig will mind?" Mother asked more tartly than my father was prepared to appreciate.

24 "Then you don't care if our money goes for shoddy work?" my father asked severely.

25 My mother's chin went into the air and her voice became a little harsh. "You know very well we don't pay Solomon much, and we don't need expert builders for a pigpen. I hope you are not telling Solomon how to do things when you don't know what you're talking about."

26 There were more words between them, impolite words, even ugly words, since my father did not take kindly to being told he was ignorant and my mother was indignant that her judgment was questioned.

27 Unfortunately, it was not just the pigpen. When my father had read for several hours he grew restless and walked out to check on what Solomon was

doing. He hovered around as Solomon fixed a fence, cleaned eggs or washed his hands in preparation for milking. Realizing that Solomon might summarily quit, Mother tried to avert disaster. She started taking my father to Richmond whenever she could—he did not drive—so that he could have lunch in a restaurant, go to the movies and have a beer afterward. But that worked for only two days. She tried a gentle-voiced diplomacy: "You know, hon, we won't be able to find anyone else as capable as Solomon. If you keep standing over him I'm afraid we'll lose him."

28   My father said, "Himpf" through his nose. Then, "He doesn't even know how to wash his hands. He needs to scrub—*scrub*—before he handles milk equipment."

29   Mother kept her voice calm. "He's been doing the milking for ten years now and we've never had a problem."

30   "You don't know; you can't see germs."

31   "I know we haven't been sick." Then she turned to coaxing. "Maybe while he is doing what he has to outside you could be putting up shelves in the pantry. We really need those."

32   The pantry had never been finished; it was only a junk room with a window. My father agreed to work on it. He gathered nails, a saw, hammer and boards, laid them all out neatly, put on old clothes and brought a level. After he had put up wooden braces he cut the first shelf. It was a quarter inch too short. My father swore mildly and tensely cut another. This time it was not short enough and he had to trim it. It was the nailing that undid him; he could not drive the nails he chose to use straight down. They curled without going through the boards. He tried four times to pound them in, each time with the same results.

33   We—or at least I, who was in the dining room—heard the crash of his hammer as my father flung it against a wall, and a string of swear words that I did not know were in the language. He told my mother later, "That lumber is no good. I can't drive a nail through any of those boards." He put up one precarious shelf and quit. This did not deter him from overseeing how other work was done, however, and my mother worried.

34   "If only your father could meet someone he could talk to," she said to me several times.

35   "How about Mr. Ford?" I said. Mr. Ford was a local minister who did not press his religious views when he called.

36   "Oh dear, no." She was emphatic. "He would crucify Mr. Ford. Your father would be sarcastic about his church and beliefs, and I can't have him doing that."

37   We really couldn't think of anybody. All my father wanted to talk about was his dislike of churches, his scorn of organized religion and how stupid people were to believe there was a God and a heaven and hell. He liked to tell visitors in solemn tones: "When the fire burned our old house all my books

burned except my books on religion." When the visitor made sounds of amaze-
ment, he would say smugly, "All my religious books were in Chicago," and enjoy
our guest's weak smile.

38   Finally, in the days and months after Solomon had resigned (for the reasons my mother feared) and gone to work for a neighbor who was delighted to
hire him, my father, who now cleaned the eggs brought in by a hired man who
came for two hours a day, found a friend—an improbable friend whom we
expected would be chewed up and spat out after half an hour in our house.

39   He came to our front door with a Bible under his arm, and I looked at him
in surprised recognition. He was Robert Dunlap, a farm boy who had been two
classes ahead of me in school.

40   "Hello, Vallie," he said when I opened the door. "Your father home? I'd like
to talk to him if he has time."

41   "Certainly," I said. "Come in, won't you?" I was mimicking my mother,
and wished I could tell him to hide the Bible. I walked ahead of him to the
living room, said, "Father?" and waited for him to turn his head. "This is
Robert Dunlap. He lives on a farm near here and he wants to talk to you."

42   Robert put out a hand and gave my father a warm, firm shake. "Do you
have a little time for me, sir?"

43   "Time is what I have the most of," my father said, noting the Bible and
getting a gleam in his eye. "Sit down, sit down. Not many people want to see
me. Most of them want to see my wife."

44   That was when I left; I decided to go out and take a long walk down the
pasture that now had lush green grass where once there had been ashes. I went
across the creek into the woods, which were gradually sending up bushes from
the burned stumps, to a place I liked to sit when I wanted to be really alone. I
stayed there a long time and hoped my father would not gloat later over his
attack on Robert's beliefs, which I presumed were strictly Southern Baptist.

45   But when I came into the kitchen, Mother, starting on supper preparation,
put her finger to her lips, and I could hear Robert's eager voice, and my father's
equally eager one answering him. They were talking, not arguing, and my father
was listening politely. When Robert said well, he had to go home and help with
the milking, my father went with him to the door and said, "Young man, I have
enjoyed your visit very much."

46   "I'd like to come again next week, sir, if that would be all right."

47   "You come whenever you like." My father actually sounded pleased. "This
is the first intelligent conversation I've had since I came to Virginia."

48   Mother and I stared at each other in disbelief. My father came out to the
kitchen and poured himself a glass of wine, obviously in good humor. "Now
there is a fine young man," he said. "I brought out some of my clippings on
biblical history and he wanted to hear what I thought about all of it. We didn't

agree on all points, but he read the Bible versions of the same history and we compared them. He's coming back next week."

49   Robert was back as he had said he would be, polite and smiling as before, and for months thereafter. He and my father sometimes strolled outside on pleasant days, Robert with his Bible, my father with copies of *Truthseeker*, a publication for atheists. They were often still deep in talk when I came home from school. Most of the conversation seemed to be about what was in the Bible, but frequently I heard my father talking about the city he had lived in for so long, telling Robert all the details I used to wish he would tell me.

50   I know now that it was Robert's gentle persistence and innate dignity, impervious to ridicule, that could bypass my father's outer defenses to touch his terrible need for a friend. Robert was still coming to visit when I went away to college, and continued to do so until he volunteered for the army in 1940. My mother said that my father was as desolate as if he had lost a son. Until Robert was killed in the Pacific, they exchanged letters, and Mother made cookies that my father could send him. When Robert's family came to tell my father of his death, they came in a body: his one brother who farmed and his three sisters, who had never married and stayed on the farm. My father subsequently made a rare gesture—he visited Robert's family as they awaited the return of their brother's body. Mother said later that it was the only time she had known my father to reach outside of himself to others in pain.

❧

Discussion Questions

1.   What does Dabney now believe her father had looked forward to in his retirement? What were her own expectations about his homecoming?

2.   Relate how Mrs. Bell responded to her husband's permanent presence in her house. What details about him seemed to annoy her in particular?

3.   Why did the relationship between Dabney's father and Robert Dunlap surprise Dabney and her mother? What unanticipated traits about Mr. Bell were revealed by his association with Dunlap?

*4.   By paragraph number, cite evidence indicating that Mr. Bell was on occasion each of the following: considerate; nonmaterialistic; proud; lonely; meddling; unsociable; and congenial.

*5.   Recount what the selection reveals about Dabney's own interests when she was fifteen years old. Do her tastes seem unusual for someone her age? Explain.

Writing Topics

1. Like many people, if not most, Mr. Bell seems to display a number of contradictory personality traits. Think about your own character: Are you sociable and generous at times, unfriendly and stingy toward others? Are you perhaps vain in one situation and humble in another? In an essay, illustrate through anecdotes at least two sets of conflicting characteristics about your personality.

2. Assume that you are Robert Dunlap and that you keep a diary. You have just returned home after your first encounter with Mr. Bell. Write an entry in which you give your impressions of the man, suggest how your discussion with him went, and tell what you look forward to in your relationship with him.

❧ *"What happens is you become binational and bicultural. You're comfortable in both countries but never fully integrated in either."*

BETWEEN TWO CULTURES

Celestino Fernández (as told to Marilyn P. Davis)

For many years, anthropologist Marilyn P. Davis has divided her time between California and a pueblo in western Mexico, where she taught elementary school and became godmother to twenty-five children. To them she dedicated her oral history *Mexican Voices/American Dreams* (1990), in which Celestino Fernández tells of his life between two cultures. Born in Santa Ines, Michoacan, Mexico, in 1949, Fernández moved to California when he was eight. He is a graduate of Sonoma State University (B.A., 1973) and Stanford University (M.A., 1974; Ph.D., 1976). By accepting an appointment as Associate Vice President at the University of Arizona when he was thirty-three, Fernández became one of the youngest college administrators in the United States. In 1995, when he was in his early forties, he was promoted to Executive Vice- President and Provost of the University's new campus in Pima County. His publications include *Resistance to Naturalization among Mexican Immigrants* (1988), *Mexican Horse Races and Cultural Values* (1988), *The Lighter Side of Immigration* (1989), and *Knowing No Boundaries* (1992).

1   The change was so dramatic. It was complete culture shock. We went from a small town in Mexico with a population of about 700 to a community of about 48,000 in California. The traffic seemed like it never stopped in Santa Rosa, whereas in Santa Inez we'd see a bus or a truck go by only once in a while. There we had the cobblestone streets, here it was all pavement. Santa Rosa is almost rural, but coming from a community of 700 people, it looked like a megalopolis. I was eight and a half.

2   Yes, the size was different, but there was much more than that. Everything and anything, all the way from hot running water to electricity, at any time of the day. In Mexico we had electricity maybe a couple of hours a day, but we didn't know when, so one never depended on it. No refrigerators, no stoves, no

washing machines, and we moved into a home with all those things. Beyond that, it was very enclosed. There were a lot of windows, but it was enclosed. In Mexico our bedrooms were enclosed, the kitchen was enclosed, but that was it. The rest of the time we were, in a sense, living outdoors.

3   The food of course was radically different. My mother continued to cook the same, but it tasted different because she cooked over a gas stove as opposed to an open fire. She still made her own tortillas, but they didn't taste the same either. There we used lard for cooking and here it was mostly oil. Nothing tasted the same.

4   The milk! Coming across the border here in Nogales between Arizona and Sonora took a long time, with all the shots and questions. Finally we came through customs. So my dad was going to treat us to a special lunch. He knew what American kids liked, so we went to an A&W Root Beer and he ordered hamburgers, fries, and milk. Now a hamburger, we'd never seen anything like that, and we weren't about to touch it. My sister and I were not about to eat it. Even my mother was very apprehensive. Then he explained to us that the French fries were potatoes. We knew what potatoes were, but we had never had them cooked that way, so we kind of nibbled on those. But the worst thing of all was the milk. It came in this mug that had been in the freezer, so it was cold—ice-cold milk. I was used to getting up in the morning, taking my glass to my grandfather, who would fill it directly from the cow. Of course milk from the cow has steam coming off it because it's so warm. Then during the day we would drink it as it sat on the counter, room temperature, but it was never refrigerator cold. It was never processed. Here milk is very thin, it doesn't have any taste. There, depending on the time of year and the type of grass the cows were eating, you could taste the difference. That was a big shock for me because I liked the cattle. I hung around with my grandfather and helped him milk the cows. It took me years to get adjusted to the milk here.

5   Today I drink milk here, it's fine. But my grandfather is still alive, he's ninety-two. When I go back, we go out in the morning and fill the glass; I drink a couple of glasses of that milk. I like it.

6   We knew everybody in Santa Inez and everybody knew us, not only in that little town, but in all the towns and ranches around. Everybody was family in that respect. In the evening we would go to my grandmother's and sit around the fire and chat. Even when I visit now, that's what we do; we sit around the kitchen and talk. We moved from that to Santa Rosa, California, where we didn't know anyone.

7   My dad knew his boss before our coming. He had worked several seasons with this particular gentleman and his family. He helped us obtain our documents when we all came up in 1957. My sister and I didn't know anyone, and we couldn't communicate. That fall my sister entered the fourth grade and I entered second. I mean we just sat there. There was no one else in the school who spoke Spanish. There was one black family and one American Indian

family, and we were the foreigners. It was a lot of emotional stress. I remember telling my parents to send me back, that I would go back and live with my grandparents. I didn't want to live here. I didn't know what any of the kids were saying. They'd come around at recess and try to talk to me, and they were laughing and stuff. They weren't necessarily laughing at me, but I didn't know what they were saying, and I couldn't say anything to them at all.

8   School was different from in Mexico. There I had gone to kindergarten and Catholic school with the nuns, and I was one of their favorites. The teachers were friends of my family, it was all family. Here, I had a very nice second grade teacher, Mrs. Albright. She was very warm. We still communicate. We were close but it was very different. She made sure that I was taken care of. We would walk together and she would hold my hand. It was real important because I was scared.

9   There are good memories too. The principal would come around, take me out of class, and we'd walk around the schoolyard. He'd try to teach me English. Now I know that's what he was trying to do because I only learned one word and that was *coat*. I had this huge coat that had been given to me. My parents' boss had five boys, so they gave me a lot of clothes. There I was in this coat that was too big for me; the sleeves hung down below my hands, way down. He would tug on this and say, "Coat, coat, coat."

10   During that first year I never said a word. The teacher wouldn't have known if I was mute or not. I never said a word. It was after that summer, coming back, that I remember speaking. I could do mathematics. That was it. I was very well mannered, not one of the assertive middle-class kids of the United States, not at all.

11   I still remember all these people who were good to me, attempted to teach me to speak without an accent. In fifth grade, Mrs. Neff would have me take *WH* words like *when*, *where*, and *why* and have me hold my hand about six inches from my mouth and overcompensate for the *WH* sound 'til I could feel the breath on my hand. I would practice twenty minutes at a time almost every day — *wh–a–ere, wh–a–en, wh–a–y*. I can still feel that air on my palm.

12   Kindergarten in Mexico is almost like second grade here, particularly with the nuns. There was no nonsense, no playtime, you don't take your little mat and have naps or cookies and milk. We had to learn how to read and write and mathematics and so on. So that gave me a good start.

13   That first year I was actually a couple of years ahead of the kids here in mathematics. The teachers saw that. They knew that I wasn't a dumb kid — I just couldn't speak. So I think they gave me a good deal of attention. I also believe that being a foreigner in this country is different than being a minority student. We were clearly foreigners. We were like a novelty. Everybody was interested in us in the school. They had never had any other foreigners there. We were the center.

14   My parents always stressed the importance of education, but they themselves never really had that much opportunity. My dad had a sixth grade education and my mom a third grade education in the Catholic school in Santa Inez.

15   From elementary school on I worked after school and weekends. In the winter, picking up brush in the apple orchard after they prune, and in the summer picking apples off the ground, then later in the packing house. In high school I worked at a golf course and in a bakery. I always had a job, so I never had the opportunity for sports or anything like that. I'd just rush off from school to work.

16   So, it wasn't easy. My dad owed a good deal of money in simply bringing us here. He used to work in the apple orchards, but in the winter it rained and there was no work. So he would save up in the summers and we'd use it up in the winter, and it went around like that. But we all worked to help.

17   High school was tracked. There was remedial, intermediate, and advanced; advanced was college-bound. Well I was in the advanced in everything except somehow, for my junior year, I was assigned to Mr. Hanson. He taught remedial English. It was hard to get out of there, and it became easier to stay rather than hassle. All I got in there were Cs. An Anglo friend of mine in there got nothing but As. He and I were real close, so toward the end of the academic year I said, "You know, all you ever get are As and all I ever get are Cs. Next time we get an assignment, you do yours and I'll do mine and then we'll exchange. Then you copy mine in your own writing and I'll copy yours in my handwriting. So I'll have my name on yours." I kept telling myself Mr. Hanson doesn't care what I do. He really doesn't read what I do, he just gives me a C no matter what. Well, it turned out I was right. He got an A on my paper and I got a C on his. I said, "Well, tough."

18   I applied to several universities and colleges and was accepted at almost all of them, but my parents couldn't afford it. I was offered a scholarship at Santa Rosa Junior College, so I took that. I was still in community college when I married. My wife really put me through college. By the time I got to Stanford I had a number of fellowships and scholarships, but she always worked and maintained the household.

19   At Stanford I worked on a research project with five other graduate students and a faculty member who had received a very large grant. We worked on this project all the way from developing a survey instrument to collecting the data and analyzing it. About five dissertations and a book came out of that, a big, big project. In our first publication together the professor had assigned different chapters to each of us. We prepared them, and then another student and I wrote the introduction and conclusion. Finally we sent it out to preview readers before submitting it for publication. Well, it came back. They didn't know me, we didn't have names on the chapters, but mine was judged the best, the most clearly written. There were three different readers and they all had the same comments. Then I knew that Mr. Hanson was wrong.

20   I feel Mexican and I behave American. Inside, my feelings, my values, my attitudes, my beliefs are based in Mexican culture, but my behavior is very American. I feel very comfortable here. I understand the system and I can work it. My wife says when I'm in Mexico I'm Mexican. I know that system as well and can fit in and behave Mexican. I'm the only one in my family who is a naturalized American citizen.

21   I haven't left Mexico behind. I always carry a letter in my briefcase from my grandmother, written four years ago when I was promoted to Associate Vice President for Academic Affairs. She knows that I work at a university. She doesn't know exactly what I do, but she knows that I have an important position. She wrote me a letter of congratulations. She says, "We know that you've done a lot in terms of education and your career, but you never make us feel uncomfortable. When you come here you're Tino. You treat us as if we were equals." I know exactly what she was talking about because I have cousins who, after being in the United States for five or ten years, will go back to Santa Inez and dress in a tie and a suit—in this little town. It makes no sense whatsoever, right? It's presumptuous, it's irritating to people, and rightly so. When I go there I help milk the cows because I enjoy it. I enjoy riding horses in the country. There are different chances, different opportunities.

22   Mexican culture has a certain wisdom I appreciate. My grandfather is *Don* Chema. You don't just call yourself by the title of *Don*. I can't be *Don*; I'm not old enough, I'm not wise enough. Unlike American culture, Mexicans value age. There is respect for someone for simply being older. They don't feel bad if they are ninety, because they are still respected. Here, people are channeled out of the job market when they're too old and sent off to retirement communities. It's a different orientation. When they're old here, they want to be young instead.

23   In a faceless kind of society there are people who are bigots. My wife has experienced it in some strange kinds of ways. She's blond, blue-eyed, but people have said to her, "Oh, you don't look like a Fernández." People have a mind-set as to what they expect a Fernández to look like. There are other things, people asking if our kids are Mexican or half Mexican. Parents tell their kids stories about Mexicans that come back to our kids. For my wife it's real upsetting. We experience it all the time, even in an educational environment. There are people here in our lovely university who still have certain images about Mexicans, about Mexican-Americans, about non-Anglo-Saxons. You affect the people you can, you try to change them, and the rest, that's their problem. It really comes back to what my dad used to say to us, "*Así son los americanos.*" We would come home from school and complain about something and he'd say, "That's the way they are." It's like, we're okay but that's just the way they are. Don't worry about it; you have to figure out how to work with them. We were *mexicano*, we were proud of that. We had an identity. We were just living in the United States and working here.

24   We came up here with almost the same idea all Mexicans come up with. We'd work for a couple of years and then go back and do something down there. That something changed over the years. At one time it was putting up *a granja*, a chicken farm, another time it was pigs, the next time a little store. It changed but we never really lost that emotion of going back.

25   One time we went back for about six months because my parents thought they were going to make it. Later we went back for another four months and tried again. It never worked out. Then one thing happened and another and years passed and my parents said, "Let's wait till the kids are out of school." Of course we're not all the same age, so we were never all out of school. My dad just retired last year and they still maintain a home in Santa Inez. They've been fixing it up over the years. They were saying they're going to go back and retire there. I think they'll go back for some months there and some months here, but they'll never go back to live there. What happens is you become binational and bicultural. You're comfortable in both countries but never fully integrated in either. You don't want to be, because you know the best world is in the margins, in between, where you can choose and take what is best from each culture.

ʒ●

Discussion Questions

1.   Describe how the environment that Fernández left in Mexico compared to that he encountered in the United States. What adjustment in his diet seemed particularly difficult for Fernández to make as a young boy? Why?

2.   Relate how Fernández's schooling in Mexico differed from that in the United States. To what and to whom does Fernández attribute his eventual elementary-school success in this country?

*3.   In paragraph 13, Fernández expresses his belief that foreign students in the United States are treated differently than minority students. Tell why you think he is either correct or mistaken in his belief.

*4.   Provide evidence from the selection that could support Fernández's assertion, "I feel Mexican and I behave American."

*5.   Explain why you would either agree or disagree with Fernández's conclusion that being binational and bicultural, without being fully integrated into either country, is preferable to being integrated into a single nation.

*6.   Relate the significance to Fernández of each of the following people, places, activities, or phrases: *Así son los americanos*; Stanford; *Don Chema*; Mrs. Neff; picking apples; Santa Rosa Junior College; Mr. Hanson; Santa Inez; his wife; and Tino.

Writing Topics

1. Assume that the mayor of your community has asked you to submit a report suggesting ways in which elderly citizens might make valuable contributions to the community. Give reasons for your suggestions.

2. Almost every nationality, ethnic group, religious denomination, occupation, and stage of life has been stereotyped in one way or another. In an essay, describe the stereotypes of at least two groups into which you could be classified and the ways in which the stereotypes do and do not seem applicable to you.

❧"Like all would-be revolutionaries,
the radical feminists seek to subordinate private life to
ideology—an endeavor that I find . . . frightening."

KEEPING WOMEN WEAK

Cathy Young

Born in Moscow, Russia, in 1963, Cathy Young came to the United States with her family in 1980 and was educated at Syracuse University. She is the author of *Growing Up in Moscow* (1989) and a contributor to the *Washington Post*, *The New York Times*, *Newsday*, the *Philadelphia Inquirer*, *The New Republic*, and other publications. Since 1987, Young has been a translator in New York City for the Center for Democracy in the U.S.S.R. She makes her home in Neptune, New Jersey.

1   Not long ago, I attended a conference on women's research and activism in the nineties, attended by dozens of feminist academics, writers, and public figures. At the wrap-up session, a middle-aged history professor from the Midwest introduced a discordant note into the spirit of celebration. "The fact," she said, "is that young women just aren't interested in feminism or feminist ideas, even though they are leading feminist lives—planning to become lawyers, doctors, professionals. What is it about feminism, and about our approach, that puts young women off?"

2   In response, some blamed "the backlash," others "homophobia." One woman protested that there *were* young feminists out there, citing sexual harassment lawsuits filed by high-school girls—apparently a greater accomplishment than merely preparing for a career. Another declared that what feminist educators needed to give their students was "an understanding of the power dynamic," not "quote-unquote objectivity." (Could it be something about comments like these that turns female students off?) Missing from this picture was any serious discussion of what modern feminism has to offer modern young women.

3   Feminism meant a great deal to me when I came to the United States thirteen years ago, after a childhood spent in the Soviet Union. Indeed, one of the things that elated me the most about America was women's liberation.

4   The society in which I had grown up was one that officially proclaimed sexual equality and made it a point of great pride yet stereotyped men and

women in ways reminiscent of the American fifties. At school, we had mandatory home economics for girls and shop for boys, a practice no one thought of challenging. At the music school for the gifted where my mother taught piano, to say that someone played "like a girl"—pleasantly, neatly, and without substance—was a commonly used putdown; in literary reviews, the highest compliment to be paid a woman writer or poet was that she wrote like a man.

5   As I approached college age, I learned that there was tacit but widely known discrimination against women in the college-entrance exams, on the assumption that a less-capable male would in the end be a more valuable asset than a bright female, who would have boys and makeup and marriage on her mind. And all too many smart, ambitious girls seemed to accept this injustice as inevitable, assuming simply that they had to be twice as good as the boys to prove themselves.

6   It was just as unquestioningly accepted that housework, including the arduous task of Soviet shopping, was women's work; when the problem of women's excessive double burden at home and on the job was mentioned at all, the proposed solution was always for men to be paid more and for women to spend more time at home, not for men to pitch in with domestic chores. And although my parents' relationship was an uncommonly equal one, my father still quoted to me the dictum (coming from Karl Marx, a thinker he generally did not regard as much of an authority) that "woman's greatest strength is her weakness."

7   My discovery of America was also a discovery of feminism—not only *Ms.* magazine and *The Feminine Mystique*[1] but also the open and straightforward manner of young American women I met. This was in stark contrast to the style that so many Russian women reverently equated with "femininity"—a more-or-less affected air of capriciousness and frailty, a flirtatious deference to men. I admired the easy camaraderie between boys and girls on American college campuses, the independence and self-confidence of young women who invited guys on dates and picked up the tab, drove when they were out with male companions, and wouldn't let anyone treat them like frail, helpless little things.

8   Those early impressions may have been too optimistic, perhaps somewhat superficial, perhaps incomplete. But I don't think they were wrong.

9   Becoming an American as a teenager in 1980, I joined the first generation of American women who had grown up assuming not only that they would work most of their lives but also that they were the equals of men and that they could be anything they wanted to be (except maybe a full-time homemaker). This was also the first generation, really, to have grown up after the sexual revolution—at a time when, at least among the educated, the nice-girls-don't

---

[1] *The Feminine Mystique:* A popular book by Betty Friedan, first published in 1963.

sexual standard vanished almost completely. In a somewhat dizzying reversal of traditional norms, many girls felt embarrassed telling their first lovers that they were virgins (at least that's how I felt).

10   Of course new choices meant new pressures. I never thought a world of sexual equality would be a utopia of peace and harmony. I did believe that our generation of women, and men, was on its way to achieving a world in which people were judged as individuals and not on the basis of their gender; a world in which men and women worked and loved in equal partnership—even if, inevitably, they continued every so often to make each other miserable and furious.

11   And then something funny happened on the way to that feminist future. We were told that we were victims, with little control over our lives and our choices; we were told that we needed to be protected.

12   When the right said that women were victimized by career opportunities and sexual freedom, it didn't matter much—at least to the middle-class, college-educated women who were the main beneficiaries of these new opportunities. Who, in those social circles, was going to listen to people who said that wives should obey their husbands and stick to the kitchen and nursery—to Phyllis Schlafly[2] or Jerry Falwell,[3] notorious reactionaries with little impact on mass culture?

13   But the message of victimhood also came from the feminist left. Everywhere around us, we were told, was a backlash seeking to snatch from us the freedoms we had gained. We were told that we were the targets of a hidden war and had better start acting like ones, searching for subtle signs of enemy forays everywhere. If we believed that we had never experienced gender-based injustice and had never felt particularly restricted by our gender, we were not just naive but dangerous: we were turning our backs on feminism and fostering the myth that its major battles had been won.

14   Whenever a campus study has shown that young people of both sexes increasingly share the same values and aspirations and that most college women are quite confident of their ability to succeed in the workplace and to combine family and career, older feminists seem far from pleased. Their warnings—oh, just wait until these young women get a taste of the real world and find that they still face prejudice and discrimination—can sound almost gleeful.

15   Older feminists talk a good line about empowering young women and letting them speak in their own voices; but that goes only as long as these voices say all the approved things. At a university workshop on peer sexual harassment in schools I attended in the spring of 1993, some of the panelists

---

[2] **Phyllis Schlafly:** Spokesperson for The Eagle Forum, an organization that promotes conservative values.

[3] **Jerry Falwell:** Baptist clergyman, founder in 1979 of Moral Majority, Inc.

complained that many girls didn't seem to understand what sexual harassment was; when boys made passes or teased them sexually they just shrugged it off, or they thought it was funny and actually liked it. "They need to be educated," one speaker said earnestly, "that the boys aren't just joking around with you, that it's harassment."

16   Ignored in all this discussion was intriguing evidence of the assertive, even aggressive sexuality of many of today's teenage girls, who apparently do a bit of harassing of their own. If girls seemed to revel in sexual attention, that could only be a sign of "low self-esteem" or inability to say no.

17   Judging by all those complaints about the unraised consciousness of the young, the preoccupation with the sexual and other victimization of high-school and college females is not coming, by and large, from young women themselves. Most of them, I believe, tend to regard all the extreme rhetoric as a sort of background noise; if they think about feminism at all, they often decide that they want no part of it — even if they're all for equal rights. The kind of feminists they usually see in their midst may further contribute to this alienation.

18   When I was still in college, I began to notice, alongside the spirited, independent, ambitious young women I admired, a different product of the feminist age: the ever-vigilant watchdog on the alert for signs of sexism. Occasionally, she made a good point; when our environmental science professor blamed overpopulation in part on Third World women "choosing" to have lots of babies, a student spoke up to note that for most Third World women, childbearing was hardly a matter of choice.

19   More typical, alas, was the young woman in my human sexuality class who was constantly pouncing on the professor for saying something like "People who suffer from premature ejaculation . . ." ("Are you implying that only men are people?"). When he had the audacity to cite data indicating that some rapists were motivated primarily by hatred of women and the desire to dominate them but others were driven primarily by sexual impulses, she went ballistic: "The ONLY thing that causes rape is men wanting to control and terrorize women, and you're trying to make it SEXY!" Later, this person bragged about having caused the poor prof "a lot of trouble" by filing a complaint with the dean.

20   *Paranoid* is a red-flag word to many feminists — understandably so, since it has been used all too often to dismiss women's rightful concerns about sexism. But what other word can come to mind when a woman claims that her writing instructor's selection of a sample of bad writing — a conservative Christian screed linking pornography and communism — was a personal insult directed at her, since she had sometimes worn a Women Against Pornography button in school?

21   And what can one expect when Naomi Wolf,[4] a writer hailed as a trailblazer of a new "Third Wave" of feminism for the younger generation, urges

---

[4] **Naomi Wolf:** Author of *The Beauty Myth* (1991) and *Fire with Fire* (1993).

women to undertake—and men, to gracefully (and gratefully) second—"the arduous, often boring, nonnegotiable *daily chore of calling attention to sexism*" (emphasis mine)? In the essay "Radical Heterosexuality, or, How to Love a Man and Save Your Feminist Soul" (published in the twentieth-anniversary issue of *Ms.*), Wolf describes how even well-intentioned men tend to be blind to the horrific things women have to put up with:

> *Recently, I walked down a New York City avenue with a woman friend, X, and a man friend, Y. I pointed out to Y the leers, hisses, and invitations to sit on faces. Each woman saw clearly what the other woman saw, but Y was baffled. . . . A passerby makes kissy-noises with his tongue while Y is scrutinizing the menu of the nearest bistro. "There, there! Look! Listen!" we cried. "What? Where? Who?" wailed poor Y, valiantly, uselessly spinning.*

22   Like poor Y, I am baffled. God knows, I've been taking walks in Manhattan at least once or twice a week for nearly thirteen years now, and not a single invitation to sit on a face, not even a single hiss as far as I recall—nothing more dramatic than the occasional "You look gorgeous today" or "That's a pretty outfit," and certainly nothing like the constant barrage Wolf describes. Even the time I wore a new dress that exposed much more cleavage than I realized, all it cost me was one fairly tame remark (as I was stepping into a subway car, a man who was stepping off stared at my bosom and muttered, "Very nice"). Applied to everyday life and interpersonal relations, "eternal vigilance is the price of liberty" strikes me as a rather disastrous motto to adopt.

23   Like all would-be revolutionaries, the radical feminists seek to subordinate private life to ideology—an endeavor that I find, quite simply, frightening. You don't have to spend part of your life under a totalitarian system (though maybe it helps) to realize that social and political movements that subordinate life to ideology have a nasty way of turning coercive, whether it's the mass violence of communism or the neo-Puritan controls of "P.C."[5]

24   This is not to say that there is no room for rethinking traditional attitudes, on things ranging from who picks up the check in the restaurant to who takes care of the baby. Millions of women and men are grappling with these issues at home and in the workplace, some more successfully than others. But that doesn't mean they have to walk around with their eyes glued to a microscope.

25   Eternal vigilance is a tempting trap for post-baby-boomer feminists. It has been often remarked that women of earlier generations had to struggle against visible and overt barriers, such as being denied admission to law school, or told

---

[5] **P.C.:** Abbreviation for *political correctness.* Either the initials or the term is used to stigmatize behavior or language ostensibly used to avoid offending any group.

that only men need apply for certain jobs or that married women shouldn't work. It seemed that once such barriers dropped, equality would come quickly. It didn't quite turn out that way; there were other, more insidious roadblocks, from a working mother's guilt over taking a business trip to a professor's unconscious tendency to call on the boys in the class. The problem, however, is that subtle sexism is an elusive target, with plenty of room for error and misinterpretation. If you complain to your professor that you find the course work too difficult and he says, "Well, I've always thought girls didn't belong in this class anyway," there's not a shadow of a doubt that he's a sexist pig. But suppose he says, "Hey, start working harder or drop the class, but don't come whining to me." Is he being insensitive to you as a woman? (An incident of this sort figured in a recent sex-discrimination suit at the University of Minnesota.) Or is he simply a blunt fellow who believes people should stand on their own two feet and who would have treated a male student exactly the same? And if he had been tough on a man but sensitive and solicitous toward a woman student, wouldn't that have been exactly the kind of paternalism feminists used to oppose?

26   But then, certain aspects of cutting-edge feminism do smack of a very old-fashioned paternalism, a sort of chivalry without the charm. At some campus meetings, it is considered P.C. for men who are first in line for the microphone to cede their place to a woman in order to ensure that female speakers — apparently too timid to just get up and get in line — get a proper hearing. Ladies first?

27   Definitions of "hostile environment" sexual harassment often seem like a throwback to prefeminist, if not positively Victorian, standards of how to treat a lady: no off-color jokes, no sexual remarks, no swearing and, God forbid, no improper advances. Surveys purporting to gauge the prevalence of harassment lump together sexual blackmail — demands for sex as a condition of promotion, good grades, or other rewards — with noncoercive advances from coworkers or fellow students, with sexual jokes or innuendo, "improper staring" or "winking."

28   Well, guess what: women too make off-color jokes and risqué comments, and even sexual advances. Sure, many women at one time or another also have to deal with obnoxious, lecherous, and/or sexist jerks. But in most cases, especially if the man is not a superior, they're perfectly capable of putting a jerk back in his place. Of course, radical feminists such as Catharine MacKinnon[6] tell us that there is *always* an imbalance of power between a man and a woman: even if you're studying for an MBA and have a prestigious job lined up, you're still powerless. Now there's a message guaranteed to build up self-confidence and self-esteem.

---

[6] **Catharine MacKinnon:** University of Michigan law professor noted for her strong opposition to pornography.

29   A video on sexual harassment, broadcast on public television twice in January 1993 and available free through an 800 number, includes a segment on a university experiment in which unwitting male students are assigned to supervise the computer work of an attractive girl. Before leaving them alone, the male research assistant pretends to take small liberties with the young woman (putting a hand on her shoulder, bending closely over her) while explaining the work process, and in most cases the male student proceeds to imitate this behavior or even push it a little further.

30   Then, the young woman—who, of course, has known what's been going on the whole time—talks on camera about how the experience has helped her understand what it's like to feel powerless. But doesn't this powerlessness have at least something to do with the fact that she was undoubtedly instructed not to show displeasure? Is it such a good idea to teach young women that, short of legal intervention, they have no way of dealing with such annoyances?

31   I don't believe that our views or our allegiances are determined solely or primarily by age. Still, one might have expected our generation to articulate a feminism rooted in the experience of women who have never felt subordinated to men, have never felt that their options were limited by gender in any significant way or that being treated as sexual beings diminished their personhood. This is not, of course, the experience of all young women; but it is the experience of many, and an experience that should be taken as a model. Perhaps those of us who have this positive view of our lives and our relationships with men have not lived up to our responsibility to translate that view into a new feminist vision.

32   In an *Esquire* article about sexual politics and romantic love on campus in the nineties, Janet Viggiani, then-assistant dean for coeducation at Harvard, was quoted as saying, "I think young women now are very confused. . . . They don't have many models for how to be strong females and feminine. Many of their models are victim models—passive, weak, endangered." In recent years, feminist activism has focused almost entirely on negatives, from eating disorders to sexual violence and abuse. Sadly, these problems are all too real, and they certainly should be confronted; what they should not be is the central metaphor for the female condition or for relations between women and men, or for feminism. What does it mean when the only time young women and girls think of feminism is not when they think of achievement but when they think of victimization?

33   The emphasis on victimhood has had an especially dramatic effect on attitudes toward sexuality. We didn't revel in our sexual freedom for too long; as if the shadow of AIDS weren't bad enough, sex was suddenly fraught with danger and violence as much as possibilities of pleasure, or even more so. A cartoon in the *Nation* shows a girl grooming herself before a mirror, with the caption, "Preparing for a date"—and in the next frame, a boy doing the same, with the caption, "Preparing for a date rape." Pamphlets on sexual assault warn that one out of every five dates ends in a rape, and that up to 25 percent of college

women become victims: "Since you can't tell who has the potential for rape by simply looking, be on your guard with every man."

34   If these numbers are true, women would be well advised either to forswear dating altogether or to carry a can of Mace on every date. But what about these numbers? When one looks at how they are obtained, and how rape is defined, it becomes clear that the acquaintance-rape hysteria not only gives young women an exaggerated picture of the dangers they face in the company of men but essentially demeans women, absolving or stripping them of all responsibility for their behavior.

35   The question is not whether a woman's provocative dress, flirtatious behavior, or drinking justifies sexual assault; that attitude is now on the wane, for which the women's movement certainly deserves credit. It's not even a question of whether a woman should have to fight back and risk injury to prove that she did not consent to sex. The latest crusade makes a woman a victim of rape if she did not rebuff a man's sexual advances because she was too shy or didn't want to hurt his feelings, or if she had sex while drunk (not passed out, just sufficiently intoxicated so that her inhibitions were loosened) and felt bad about it afterwards. In a typical scenario, a couple is making out and then the woman pulls back and says, "I really think we shouldn't," and the man draws her back toward him, *nonforcibly*, and continues to fondle her, or says, "Oh come on, you know you want it," and eventually they end up having sex. If the woman feels that the intercourse was "unwanted," she can — according to the anti-date-rape activists — claim to be a victim, no different from the woman who's attacked at knifepoint in a dark, empty parking lot.

36   A few years ago, I was at the apartment of an ex-boyfriend with whom I was still on friendly terms; after a couple of beers, we started kissing. When his hand crept under my skirt, I suddenly sobered up and thought of several good reasons why I should not go to bed with the guy. I wriggled out of his arms, got up, and said, "That's enough." Undaunted, he came up from behind and squeezed my breasts. I rammed my elbow into his chest, forcefully enough to make the point, and snapped, "Didn't you hear me? I said, enough."

37   Some people might say that I overreacted (my ex-boyfriend felt that way), but the logic of modern-day radical feminists suggests the opposite: that I displayed a heroism that cannot be required of any woman in a situation like that because she could expect the guy to beat her up, to maim her, even if he hadn't made any threats or shown any violent tendencies. A "reasonable" woman would have passively submitted and then cried rape.

38   Even "no means no" is no longer enough; some activists want to say that yes means no, or at least the absence of an explicit yes means no. Feminist legal theorist MacKinnon suggests that much of what our society regards as consensual sex hardly differs from rape and that, given women's oppression, it is doubtful "whether consent is a meaningful concept" at all. Which is to say that, like underage children and the mentally retarded, women are to be presumed

incapable of valid consent. MacKinnon's frequent ally, polemicist Andrea Dworkin, states bluntly that all intercourse is rape.

39   This reasoning is still very far from mainstream acceptance. Even MacKinnon only expresses such views when addressing fairly narrow and converted audiences, not when she's interviewed on TV. Yet a 1992 report by the Harvard Date Rape Task Force recommended that university guidelines define rape as "any act of sexual intercourse that occurs without the expressed consent of the person." What does this mean—that a consent form must be signed before a date? Or that, as a couple moves toward the bed after passionate and mutual heavy petting, the man should ask the woman if she's quite sure she wants to? (A friend who just graduated from college tells me that some men are actually beginning to act that way.) And perhaps he has to keep asking every time: the couple's prior sexual relationship, the advocates say, makes no difference whatsoever.

40   Clearly, this vision leaves no room for spontaneity, for ambiguity, for passionate, wordless, animal sex. What's more, it is, in the end, deeply belittling to women, who apparently cannot be expected to convey their wishes clearly or to show a minimum of assertiveness. It also perpetuates a view of woman as the passive and reticent partner who may or may not want sex and man as the pursuer who is naturally presumed to want it: *she* is not required to ask for *his* consent (even though, given some current definitions, plenty of women must have committed rape at least a few times in their lives; I'm sure I have). Sex is something men impose on women. We're back full circle to fragile, chaste, nineteenth-century womanhood.

41   And some people think that's good. Recently, I got into a discussion with a conservative Catholic male who vehemently argued that the campaign against date rape was nothing more than a distorted expression of women's legitimate rejection of sexual freedom, a thing so contrary to their chaste natures. Casual sex, he said, makes women (but not men) feel cheap and used, and what they're doing now is using the extreme language of rape to describe this exploitation; things were really better under the much-maligned double standard, when women were expected to say no to sex, and thus accorded more protection from male lust. To some conservatives, the outcry about sexual harassment confirms what conservatives have known all along: women want to be put on a pedestal and treated like ladies; they find sexual advances insulting because they are chaster than men.

42   I don't think that's true. Most young women have no wish to return to the days when they were branded as sluts if they said yes. It may be, however, that this generation's confusion over sexual boundaries has to do with the pains of transition from one set of morals to another, of contradictory cultural messages: the traditional ones of chastity as the basis of female self-respect and reputation and the new ones of sexual liberation and female desire. Sometimes, we may not think we're "cheap" if we go to bed with a man we just met—at least, we're

no worse than the guy is for going to bed with a woman he just met—yet when we wake up the next morning we may find that *he* thinks less of us but not of himself. And we may find, to our chagrin, that feminine coyness is not quite as extinct as we might like to think. The other day, a very liberated fortysomething friend of mine breezily said, "Oh, of course no modern woman says no when she means yes." Alas, recent studies (done by feminist researchers) show that *by their own admission*, about half of college women sometimes do.

43   But there may be another reason, too, for this generation's susceptibility to the victim mentality: overconfidence in the perfectibility of life. The sexual-liberation rhetoric itself overlooked the complexity of human emotions and fostered the belief that sexual relationships could be free of all manipulation or unfair pressure. More generally, there is the idealistic arrogance of middle-class boys and girls who have grown up in a sheltered, affluent environment, accustomed to the notion that getting one's way is a basic right. The old cliché "Life isn't fair" is not only unpopular nowadays but profoundly suspect, seen as a smokescreen designed by the oppressors to keep the oppressed—women and minorities, in particular—in their place. Yes, it has been used for such purposes often enough. But often it happens to be true, and to disregard that is to invite disastrous consequences—like the belief that anyone, male or female, is entitled to an annoyance-free life.

44   The danger in the new radical feminism is not only that it legitimizes what is, deep down, an extremely retrograde view of women; it also seeks to regulate personal relationships to a degree unprecedented since the Puritans roamed the earth. If you feel that a man has enticed or pressured you into having unwanted sex, you don't confront him and call him a manipulative creep; you run to a campus grievance committee and demand redress. If you don't like the way a coworker has been putting his hand on your shoulder, you don't have to tell him to stop it—you can go and file a lawsuit instead. Courts and law-enforcement authorities are being asked to step into situations where, short of installing hidden cameras in every bedroom and every office hallway, they have no way of finding out on whose side the truth is. Of course, many millions of women and men remain relatively unaffected by this relentless politicization of the personal. Still, the damage is being done.

45   Again, it may be my Soviet background that makes me especially sensitive to the perils of this aggressive, paternalistic interventionism. In the Soviet *ancien régime*, it was not uncommon to report one's unfaithful spouse to the Communist party bureau at his (or, less commonly, her) workplace, and conflicts between husband and wife—particularly if both were party members—were often settled at public meetings that satisfied both the voyeuristic and the viciously moralistic impulses of the other comrades.

46   What are we going to be, then? Assertive, strong women (and sometimes, surely, also needy and vulnerable, because we *are* human), seeing ourselves as no better or worse than men; aware of but not obsessed with sexism; interested

in loving and equal relationships but with enough confidence in ourselves, and enough understanding of human foibles, to know better than to scrutinize every move we or our partners make for political incorrectness? Or full-time agents of the gender-crimes police?

47   Women's liberation is not yet a completed task. Sexism still lingers and injustice toward women still exists, particularly in the distribution of domestic tasks. We are still working on new standards and values to guide a new, equal relationship between men and women. But "Third Wave" feminism, which tries to fight gender bias by defining people almost entirely in terms of gender, is not the way to go.

48   We need a "Third Way" feminism that rejects the excesses of the gender fanatics *and* the sentimental traditionalism of the Phyllis Schlaflys; one that does not seek special protections for women and does not view us as too socially disadvantaged to take care of ourselves. Because on the path that feminism has taken in the past few years, we are allowing ourselves to be treated as frail, helpless little things — by our would-be liberators.

ક

Discussion Questions

1. Recount Young's experiences with sexual stereotyping and gender discrimination in the Soviet Union. What were her initial impressions of feminism when she first arrived in the United States?

2. How, according to Young, did the assumption of her generation of teenage women differ from the assumptions held by prior generations of women?

*3. Identify the people and ideas that Young holds responsible for undermining the assumptions of her generation of women. Does her criticism seem valid to you? Why or why not?

*4. Is Young's argument against presenting women as victims weakened in the least by her failure to present in paragraph 16 any of the "intriguing evidence of the assertive, even aggressive sexuality of today's teenage girls"? Do her later comments in paragraphs 28 and 40 offer the evidence lacking from paragraph 16? Explain.

5. Tell why you agree or disagree that, by and large, young women do not seem preoccupied "with the sexual and other victimization of high-school and college females" (paragraph 17). Are there other matters with which they are equally or more concerned? If so, what are they?

6. Young seems to dismiss as frivolous some claims by women of sexual harassment. What, if anything, do you think she would consider to be reasonable grounds for a woman's decision to file a case of sexual harassment against a professor or an employer?

*7. Does the feminism that one might have expected Young's generation to articulate seem to offer a sound and adequate model for
feminists today (paragraph 31)? Why or why not? What attitudinal
and societal changes would be necessary for such a model to
flourish?

*8. What do you infer to be the primary intent of Young's essay—to
report, to entertain, to persuade, or to obtain some other objective?
Do you believe that Young successfully achieves her intent? Why or
why not?

Writing Topics

1. Assume that "Keeping Women Weak" has appeared in a magazine
you regularly read. Write a letter to the editor, no more than five
hundred words, expressing your reasons for agreeing or disagreeing with Young's point of view.

2. In paragraph 43, Young observes that the cliché "Life isn't fair" is
often true. Think of times in your past when life seemed unfair, and,
in an essay, describe at least one such occasion. Be sure to include
enough details to convince your reader that life did indeed treat
you unjustly or inequitably.

*"I cannot recover much of that first winter of school.
It was not an experience to remember for its charm."*

OUR FIRST WINTER ON THE PRAIRIE

Hamlin Garland

Short-story writer, novelist, and autobiographer, Hamlin
Garland (1860–1940) is known for his realistic depiction of
the frustrations of farm life in his native Midwest. After
experiencing the harsh labor of farm life in Wisconsin, his
birth state, and in Iowa and South Dakota, Garland moved
to Boston in his early twenties. There he began to write the
stories and sketches published in *Main-Traveled Roads* (1891).
Numerous stories and novels followed, many of them dealing with the realities of prairie life or promoting populist
ideology. However, Garland is best known today for two of
his eight autobiographical narratives, *A Son of the Middle
Border* (1917), in which appears "Our First Winter on the
Prairie," and *A Daughter of the Middle Border* (1921), recipient
of a Pulitzer Prize for autobiography.

1   For a few days my brother and I had little to do other than to keep the cattle
from straying, and we used our leisure in becoming acquainted with the region
round about.

2   It burned deep into our memories, this wide, sunny, windy country. The
sky so big, and the horizon line so low and so far away, made this new world of
the plain more majestic than the world of the Coulee. — The grasses and many
of the flowers were also new to us. On the uplands the herbage was short and
dry and the plants stiff and woody, but in the swales the wild oat shook its
quivers of barbed and twisted arrows, and the crow's foot, tall and sere, bowed
softly under the feet of the wind, while everywhere, in the lowlands as well as
on the ridges, the bleaching white antlers of by-gone herbivora lay scattered,
testifying to "the herds of deer and buffalo" which once fed there. We were just
a few years too late to see them.

3   To the south the sections were nearly all settled upon, for in that direction
lay the county town, but to the north and on into Minnesota rolled the un-
plowed sod, the feeding ground of the cattle, the home of foxes and wolves, and
to the west, just beyond the highest ridges, we loved to think the bison might
still be seen.

4   The cabin on this rented farm was a mere shanty, a shell of pine boards, which needed re-enforcing to make it habitable and one day my father said, "Well, Hamlin, I guess you'll have to run the plow-team this fall. I must help neighbor Button wall up the house and I can't afford to hire another man."

5   This seemed a fine commission for a lad of ten, and I drove my horses into the field that first morning with a manly pride which added an inch to my stature. I took my initial "round" at a "land" which stretched from one side of the quarter section to the other, in confident mood. I was grown up!

6   But alas! my sense of elation did not last long. To guide a team for a few minutes as an experiment was one thing — to plow all day like a hired hand was another. It was not a chore, it was a job. It meant moving to and fro hour after hour, day after day, with no one to talk to but the horses. It meant trudging eight or nine miles in the forenoon and as many more in the afternoon, with less than an hour off at noon. It meant dragging the heavy implement around the corners, and it meant also many ship-wrecks, for the thick, wet stubble matted with wild buckwheat often rolled up between the coulter and the standard and threw the share completely out of the ground, making it necessary for me to halt the team and jerk the heavy plow backward for a new start.

7   Although strong and active I was rather short, even for a ten-year-old, and to reach the plow handles I was obliged to lift my hands above my shoulders; and so with the guiding lines crossed over my back and my worn straw hat bobbing just above the cross-brace I must have made a comical figure. At any rate nothing like it had been seen in the neighborhood and the people on the road to town looking across the field, laughed and called to me, and neighbor Button said to my father in my hearing, "That chap's too young to run a plow," a judgment which pleased and flattered me greatly.

8   Harriet cheered me by running out occasionally to meet me as I turned the nearest corner, and sometimes Frank consented to go all the way around, chatting breathlessly as he trotted along behind. At other times he was prevailed upon to bring to me a cookie and a glass of milk, a deed which helped to shorten the forenoon. And yet, notwithstanding all these ameliorations, plowing became tedious.

9   The flies were savage, especially in the middle of the day, and the horses, tortured by their lances, drove badly, twisting and turning in their despairing rage. Their tails were continually getting over the lines, and in stopping to kick their tormentors from their bellies they often got astride the traces, and in other ways made trouble for me. Only in the early morning or when the sun sank low at night were they able to move quietly along their ways.

10   The soil was the kind my father had been seeking, a smooth dark sandy loam, which made it possible for a lad to do the work of a man. Often the share would go the entire "round" without striking a root or a pebble as big as a walnut, the steel running steadily with a crisp craunching ripping sound which I rather liked to hear. In truth work would have been quite tolerable had it not

been so long drawn out. Ten hours of it even on a fine day made about twice too many for a boy.

11   Meanwhile I cheered myself in every imaginable way. I whistled. I sang. I studied the clouds. I gnawed the beautiful red skin from the seed vessels which hung upon the wild rose bushes, and I counted the prairie chickens as they began to come together in winter flocks running through the stubble in search of food. I stopped now and again to examine the lizards unhoused by the share, tormenting them to make them sweat their milky drops (they were curiously repulsive to me), and I measured the little granaries of wheat which the mice and gophers had deposited deep under the ground, storehouses which the plow had violated. My eyes dwelt enviously upon the sailing hawk, and on the passing of ducks. The occasional shadowy figure of a prairie wolf made me wish for Uncle David and his rifle.

12   On certain days nothing could cheer me. When the bitter wind blew from the north, and the sky was filled with wild geese racing southward, with swiftly-hurrying clouds, winter seemed about to spring upon me. The horses' tails streamed in the wind. Flurries of snow covered me with clinging flakes, and the mud "gummed" my boots and trouser legs, clogging my steps. At such times I suffered from cold and loneliness — all sense of being a man evaporated. I was just a little boy, longing for the leisure of boyhood.

13   Day after day, through the month of October and deep into November, I followed that team, turning over two acres of stubble each day. I would not believe this without proof, but it is true! At last it grew so cold that in the early morning everything was white with frost and I was obliged to put one hand in my pocket to keep it warm, while holding the plow with the other, but I didn't mind this so much, for it hinted at the close of autumn. I've no doubt facing the wind in this way was excellent discipline, but I didn't think it necessary then and my heart was sometimes bitter and rebellious.

14   The soldier did not intend to be severe. As he had always been an early riser and a busy toiler it seemed perfectly natural and good discipline, that his sons should also plow and husk corn at ten years of age. He often told of beginning life as a "bound boy" at nine, and these stories helped me to perform my own tasks without whining. I feared to voice my weakness.

15   At last there came a morning when by striking my heel upon the ground I convinced my boss that the soil was frozen too deep for the mold-board to break. "All right," he said, "you may lay off this forenoon."

16   Oh, those beautiful hours of respite! With time to play or read I usually read, devouring anything I could lay my hands upon. Newspapers, whether old or new, or pasted on the wall or piled up in the attic, — anything in print was wonderful to me. One enthralling book, borrowed from Neighbor Button, was *The Female Spy*, a Tale of the Rebellion. Another treasure was a story called *Cast Ashore*, but this volume unfortunately was badly torn and fifty pages were missing so that I never knew, and do not know to this day, how those indomitable

shipwrecked seamen reached their English homes. I dimly recall that one man carried a pet monkey on his back and that they all lived on "Bustards.[1]"

17   Finally the day came when the ground rang like iron under the feet of the horses, and a bitter wind, raw and gusty, swept out of the northwest, bearing gray veils of sleet. Winter had come! Work in the furrow had ended. The plow was brought in, cleaned and greased to prevent its rusting, and while the horses munched their hay in well-earned holiday, father and I helped farmer Button husk the last of his corn.

18   Osman Button, a quaint and interesting man of middle age, was a native of York State and retained many of the traditions of his old home strangely blent with a store of vivid memories of Colorado, Utah and California, for he had been one of the gold-seekers of the early fifties. He loved to spin yarns of "When I was in gold camps," and he spun them well. He was short and bent and spoke in a low voice with a curious nervous sniff, but his diction was notably precise and clear. He was a man of judgment, and a citizen of weight and influence. From O. Button I got my first definite notion of Bret Harte's[2] country, and of the long journey which they of the ox team had made in search of Eldorado.

19   His family "mostly boys and girls" was large, yet they all lived in a low limestone house which he had built (he said) to serve as a granary till he should find time to erect a suitable dwelling. In order to make the point dramatic, I will say that he was still living in the "granary" when last I called on him thirty years later!

20   A warm friendship sprang up between him and my father, and he was often at our house but his gaunt and silent wife seldom accompanied him. She was kindly and hospitable, but a great sufferer. She never laughed, and seldom smiled, and so remains a pathetic figure in all my memories of the household.

21   The younger Button children, Eva and Cyrus, became our companions in certain of our activities, but as they were both very sedate and slow of motion, they seldom joined us in our livelier sports. They were both much older than their years. Cyrus at this time was almost as venerable as his father, although his years were, I suppose, about seventeen. Albert and Lavinia, we heard, were much given to dancing and parties.

22   One night as we were all seated around the kerosene lamp my father said, "Well, Belle, I suppose we'll have to take these young ones down to town and fit 'em out for school." These words so calmly uttered filled our minds with visions of new boots, new caps and new books, and though we went obediently to bed we hardly slept, so excited were we, and at breakfast next morning not

---

[1] **bustards:** Large European and Australian birds, chiefly terrestrial, related to cranes.
[2] **Bret Harte:** American author (1839–1902) of popular stories of gold-rush days in California.

one of us could think of food. All our desires converged upon the wondrous expedition—our first visit to town.

23   Our only carriage was still the lumber wagon but it had now two spring seats, one for father, mother and Jessie, and one for Harriet, Frank and myself. No one else had anything better, hence we had no sense of being poorly outfitted. We drove away across the frosty prairie toward Osage[3]—moderately comfortable and perfectly happy.

24   Osage was only a little town, a village of perhaps twelve hundred inhabitants, but to me as we drove down its Main Street, it was almost as impressive as LaCrosse[4] had been. Frank clung close to father, and mother led Jessie, leaving Harriet and me to stumble over nail-kegs and dodge whiffle trees what time our eyes absorbed jars of pink and white candy, and sought out boots and buckskin mittens. Whenever Harriet spoke she whispered, and we pointed at each shining object with cautious care.—Oh! the marvellous exotic smells! Odors of salt codfish and spices, calico and kerosene, apples and ginger-snaps mingle in my mind as I write.

25   Each of us soon carried a candy marble in his or her cheek (as a chipmunk carries a nut) and Frank and I stood like sturdy hitching posts whilst the storekeeper with heavy hands screwed cotton-plush caps upon our heads,—but the most exciting moment, the crowning joy of the day, came with the buying of our new boots.—If only father had not insisted on our taking those which were a size too large for us!

26   They were real boots. No one but a Congressman wore "gaiters" in those days. War fashions still dominated the shoe-shops, and high-topped cavalry boots were all but universal. They were kept in boxes under the counter or ranged in rows on a shelf and were of all weights and degrees of fineness. The ones I selected had red tops with a golden moon in the center but my brother's taste ran to blue tops decorated with a golden flag. Oh! that deliciously oily *new* smell! My heart glowed every time I looked at mine. I was especially pleased because they did *not* have copper toes. Copper toes belonged to little boys. A youth who had plowed seventy acres of land could not reasonably be expected to dress like a child.—How smooth and delightfully stiff they felt on my feet.

27   Then came our new books, a McGuffey reader, a Mitchell geography, a Ray's arithmetic, and a slate. The books had a delightful new smell also, and there was singular charm in the smooth surface of the unmarked slates. I was eager to carve my name in the frame. At last with our treasures under the seat (so near that we could feel them), with our slates and books in our laps we jolted home, dreaming of school and snow. To wade in the drifts with our fine high-topped boots was now our desire.

---

[3] **Osage:** Now a town of approximately four thousand, near Mason City, Iowa, and close to the Minnesota border.
[4] **La Crosse:** A city in Wisconsin with a current population of over ninety thousand.

28   It is strange but I cannot recall how my mother looked on this trip. Even my father's image is faint and vague (I remember only his keen eagle-gray terrifying eyes), but I can see every acre of that rented farm. I can tell you exactly how the house looked. It was an unpainted square cottage and stood bare on the sod at the edge of Dry Run ravine. It had a small lean-to on the eastern side and a sitting room and bedroom below. Overhead was a low unplastered chamber in which we children slept. As it grew too cold to use the summer kitchen we cooked, ate and lived in the square room which occupied the entire front of the two story upright, and which was, I suppose, sixteen feet square. As our attic was warmed only by the stove-pipe, we older children of a frosty morning made extremely simple and hurried toilets. On very cold days we hurried down stairs to dress beside the kitchen fire.

29   Our furniture was of the rudest sort. I cannot recall a single piece in our house or in our neighbors' houses that had either beauty or distinction. It was all cheap and worn, for this was the middle border, and nearly all our neighbors had moved as we had done in covered wagons. Farms were new, houses were mere shanties, and money was scarce. "War times" and "war prices" were only just beginning to change. Our clothing was all cheap and ill fitting. The women and children wore home-made "cotton flannel" underclothing for the most part, and the men wore rough, ready-made suits over which they drew brown denim blouses or overalls to keep them clean.

30   Father owned a fine buffalo overcoat (so much of his song's promise was redeemed) and we possessed two buffalo robes for use in our winter sleigh, but mother had only a sad coat and a woolen shawl. How she kept warm I cannot now understand—I think she stayed at home on cold days.

31   All of the boys wore long trousers, and even my eight year old brother looked like a miniature man with his full-length overalls, high-topped boots and real suspenders. As for me I carried a bandanna in my hip pocket and walked with determined masculine stride.

32   My mother, like all her brothers and sisters, was musical and played the violin—or fiddle, as we called it,—and I have many dear remembrances of her playing. *Napoleon's March, Money Musk, The Devil's Dream* and half-a-dozen other simple tunes made up her repertoire. It was very crude music of course but it added to the love and admiration in which her children always held her. Also in some way we had fallen heir to a Prince melodeon—one that had belonged to the McClintocks, but only my sister played on that.

33   Once at a dance in neighbor Button's house, mother took the "dare" of the fiddler and with shy smile played *The Fisher's Hornpipe* or some other simple melody and was mightily cheered at the close of it, a brief performance which she refused to repeat. Afterward she and my father danced and this seemed a very wonderful performance, for to us they were "old"—far past such frolicking, although he was but forty and she thirty-one!

34   At this dance I heard, for the first time, the local professional fiddler, old Daddy Fairbanks, as quaint a character as ever entered fiction, for he was not

only butcher and horse doctor but a renowned musician as well. Tall, gaunt and sandy, with enormous nose and sparse projecting teeth, he was to me the most enthralling figure at this dance and his queer "Calls" and his "York State" accent filled us all with delight. "*Ally* man left," "Chassay *by* your pardners," "Dozy-*do*" were some of the phrases he used as he played *Honest John* and *Haste to the Wedding*. At times he sang his calls in high nasal chant, "*First* lady lead to the *right*, deedle, deedle dum-dum —*gent* foller after — dally-deedle-do-do — *three* hands round"—and everybody laughed with frank enjoyment of his words and action.

35   It was a joy to watch him "start the set." With fiddle under his chin he took his seat in a big chair on the kitchen table in order to command the floor. "Farm on, farm on!" he called disgustedly. "Lively now!" and then, when all the couples were in position, with one mighty No.14 boot uplifted, with bow laid to strings he snarled, "Already — GELANG!" and with a thundering crash his foot came down, "Honors TEW your pardners — right and left FOUR!" And the dance was on!

36   I suspect his fiddlin' was not even "middlin'," but he beat time fairly well and kept the dancers somewhere near to rhythm, and so when his ragged old cap went round he often got a handful of quarters for his toil. He always ate two suppers, one at the beginning of the party and another at the end. He had a high respect for the skill of my Uncle David and was grateful to him and other better musicians for their noninterference with his professional engagements.

37   The school-house which was to be the center of our social life stood on the bare prairie about a mile to the southwest and like thousands of other similar buildings in the west, had not a leaf to shade it in summer nor a branch to break the winds of savage winter. "There's been a good deal of talk about setting out a wind-break," neighbor Button explained to us, "but nothing has as yet been done." It was merely a square pine box painted a glaring white on the outside and a desolate drab within; at least drab was the original color, but the benches were mainly so greasy and hacked that original intentions were obscured. It had two doors on the eastern end and three windows on each side.

38   A long square stove (standing on slender legs in a puddle of bricks), a wooden chair, and a rude table in one corner, for the use of the teacher, completed the movable furniture. The walls were roughly plastered and the windows had no curtains.

39   It was a barren temple of the arts even to the residents of Dry Run, and Harriet and I, stealing across the prairie one Sunday morning to look in, came away vaguely depressed. We were fond of school and never missed a day if we could help it, but this neighborhood center seemed small and bleak and poor.

40   With what fear, what excitement we approached the door on that first day, I can only faintly indicate. All the scholars were strange to me except Albert and Cyrus Button, and I was prepared for rough treatment. However, the experience was not so harsh as I had feared. True, Rangely Field did throw me

down and wash my face in snow, and Jack Sweet tripped me up once or twice, but I bore these indignities with such grace as I could command, and soon made a place for myself among the boys.

41   Burton Babcock was my seat-mate, and at once became my chum. You will hear much of him in this chronicle. He was two years older than I and though pale and slim was unusually swift and strong for his age. He was a silent lad, curiously timid in his classes and not at ease with his teachers.

42   I cannot recover much of that first winter of school. It was not an experience to remember for its charm. Not one line of grace, not one touch of color relieved the room's bare walls or softened its harsh windows. Perhaps this very barrenness gave to the poetry in our readers an appeal that seems magical, certainly it threw over the faces of Frances Babcock and Mary Abbie Gammons a lovelier halo. — They were "the big girls" of the school, that is to say, they were seventeen or eighteen years old, — and Frances was the special terror of the teacher, a pale and studious pigeon-toed young man who was preparing for college.

43   In spite of the cold, the boys played open air games all winter. "Dog and Deer," "Dare Gool" and "Fox and Geese" were our favorite diversions, and the wonder is that we did not all die of pneumonia, for we battled so furiously during each recess that we often came in wet with perspiration and coughing so hard that for several minutes recitations were quite impossible. — But we were a hardy lot and none of us seemed the worse for our colds.

44   There was not much chivalry in the school — quite the contrary, for it was dominated by two or three big rough boys and the rest of us took our tone from them. To protect a girl, to shield her from remark or indignity required a good deal of bravery and few of us were strong enough to do it. Girls were foolish, ridiculous creatures, set apart to be laughed at or preyed upon at will. To shame them was a great joke. — How far I shared in these barbarities I cannot say but that I did share in them I know, for I had very little to do with my sister Harriet after crossing the school-house yard. She kept to her tribe as I to mine.

45   This winter was made memorable also by a "revival" which came over the district with sudden fury. It began late in the winter — fortunately, for it ended all dancing and merry-making for the time. It silenced Daddy Fairbanks' fiddle and subdued my mother's glorious voice to a wail. A cloud of puritanical gloom settled upon almost every household. Youth and love became furtive and hypocritic.

46   The evangelist, one of the old-fashioned shouting, hysterical, ungrammatical, gasping sort, took charge of the services, and in his exhortations phrases descriptive of lakes of burning brimstone and ages of endless torment abounded. Some of the figures of speech and violent gestures of the man still linger in my mind, but I will not set them down on paper. They are too dreadful to perpetuate. At times he roared with such power that he could have been heard for half a mile.

47   And yet we went, night by night, mother, father, Jessie, all of us. It was our theater. Some of the roughest characters in the neighborhood rose and professed repentance, for a season, even old Barton, the profanest man in the township, experienced a "change of heart."

48   We all enjoyed the singing, and joined most lustily in the tunes. Even little Jessie learned to sing *Heavenly Wings, There is a Fountain filled with Blood,* and *Old Hundred.*

49   As I peer back into that crowded little school-room, smothering hot and reeking with lamp smoke, and recall the half-lit, familiar faces of the congregation, it all has the quality of a vision, something experienced in another world. The preacher, leaping, sweating, roaring till the windows rattle, the mothers with sleeping babes in their arms, the sweet, strained faces of the girls, the immobile wondering men, are spectral shadows, figures encountered in the phantasmagoria of disordered sleep.

❧

Discussion Questions

1. Relate the various reasons that plowing was more like a demanding job than a chore for Garland.

2. Why did Garland fear complaining to his father about the arduous work he had been assigned? What finally put an end to his plowing?

3. Describe the physical layout of the school Garland attended and the relationship there between the boys and girls. What do you think accounted for the "barbarities" Garland mentions in paragraph 44? Does such behavior continue in schools today?

4. Recount Garland's remembrances of his father, his mother, and his siblings. Would you consider his family to have been a close-knit one? Explain.

5. What do you think Garland meant by referring to the evangelical services as "our theater" (paragraph 47)? Do you consider his remark to be sacrilegious? Why or why not?

*6. By paragraph number, cite evidence that Garland as a ten-year-old was sociable; proud; keenly observant of his surroundings; poor; studious; and timorous.

Writing Topics

1. Garland recalls the excitement of the shopping trip he and his family took to Osage. Recall a shopping trip that excited you, and describe it in an essay. Before writing, consider these questions: How old were you? Where did you go? Who went with you? What did you see that you wanted, and what did you buy, if anything? What feelings did you experience? Would you consider the trip to have been a success or a failure?

2. Garland found plowing to have been a tedious, demanding job. Consider chores that you have done and jobs that you have held. In a brief essay, describe what you consider to be the worst work you have ever been given to do. What was it? Who or what led you to do it? What made it so difficult or distasteful? What, if anything, did you learn from having done it?

Summary Writing Topics

*1. You wonder whether Sirathra Som is correct about how best to learn English. Investigate the issue by speaking to teachers of English as a second language, by interviewing immigrants who have learned English, and by reading relevant materials. Afterwards, write your recommendations, providing evidence and reasons, on how nonnative speakers can best learn English after their arrival in the United States.

2. Assume that you have a five-year-old child who is blind. You are concerned with your child's future education. Would you send your child to a school for the blind similar to the one Ved Mehta attended, to a private school, or to a public school? If either of the latter, would you want your child "mainstreamed" into classes with sighted students? After carefully investigating the options, write your child a letter to be read twenty years from now on why you chose for him or her the educational environment that you did.

3. When Ved Mehta thumbs a ride back to school from a woman driver, he allows—even encourages—her to believe he is half-sighted. In an essay, describe a time when you pretended to have done something that you hadn't done or to have been someone or something that you weren't. Include details about both the circumstances that led to your deception and the consequences of your behavior.

4. If you have ever experienced new beginnings and adjustments as the consequence of a move from one environment to another, relate the experience in an essay. Include detailed information about what necessitated your move, how your new environment differed from the old one (neighborhood, schools, population, weather, friends, and so on), and what adjustments you had to make.

5. If you have spent at least six months in a country other than the United States or emigrated to this country from another, relate in an essay the difficulties you encountered in your new environment, the adjustments you had to make, and the advice you would give to those who might follow in your footsteps.

*6. Celestino Fernández was once a good student and is now a successful educator. But a high percentage of Mexican-American students leave school before completing the twelfth grade. As a member of a school board concerned with this problem, you have been asked to investigate how high the national dropout rate is for Mexican-American students, both males and females, and what the causes for that rate might be. Following your investigation, you are to write a report revealing your findings to the board as well as your recommendations on what the district might do to retain more of its Mexican-American students in its schools.

*7. Celestino Fernández describes how, as a high-school student, he was "tracked" into academic courses, a practice that some charge is elitist and undemocratic and one that others maintain is fairest for all students, gifted, average, or slow. As the principal of a new high school, you have decided to investigate the controversy over tracking and then to write to your faculty a report of your findings, followed by your recommendations with regard to the practice.

8. Assume that a friend is confused by what "equality between the sexes" really means. Respond in a letter in which you enumerate, with reasons and illustrative examples, the conditions that you believe would allow for a meaningful equality between the sexes to exist.

*9. "You've come a long way, baby" has been used as a rallying cry to convince women that they are playing increasingly major roles in society. In an essay to be shared with classmates, assess how far you believe women have come socially, politically, and economically since 1920, the year in which women were granted the right to vote. Indicate whether or not you believe women have attained by now the same rights as men.

*10. The kind of one-room schoolhouse that Hamlin Garland attended was once commonplace. Write an article for an educational journal on the history of such schools—on their locations, their organization, their curricula, their students, and their teachers.

*11. Hamlin Garland mentions a number of games he and his classmates played at the school they attended. For a magazine intended for grammar-school students, write an article describing games that were once very popular but are almost unheard of today. Indicate why some games lost their popularity and whether you believe some ought to be revived.

Cluster

8

Walls and Barriers

The primary founding document of the United States—the Declaration of Independence—reads in part: "We hold these truths to be self-evident, that all men are created equal, that they are endowed by their Creator with certain unalienable Rights, that among these are Life, Liberty, and the pursuit of Happiness." In spite of the noble principles proclaimed on July 4, 1776, the institution of slavery was not abolished until after the bloody struggle of the Civil War (1861–1865), and women were not granted the right to vote until the adoption of the nineteenth amendment to the Constitution in 1920.

Prejudice is a universal human feeling often inspired by an irrational fear of the Different, the Other, the Divergent. That fear can often turn into dislike and even hatred, resulting in the building of walls and barriers to keep the Other away, separate, on the outside. The most powerful of these walls and barriers are invisible, imposed by law or custom. Probably no human being has ever lived who has not felt prejudice aganist the Other, and who has not been in some way the victim of prejudice. These feelings in their rawest manifestations often explode to the surface on the playgrounds of our elementary schools, when one group of children gangs up on a classmate who does not conform in appearance, dress, speech, color—the ugly, the fat, the beanpole, the egghead, the crippled, the stutterer, the dwarf, the misshapen, the sissy, the teacher's pet, the mama's boy, and so on.

In the essays that follow, victims of prejudice vividly describe how it feels to find their lives circumscribed by walls walling them out, their possibilities diminished by barricades blocking their paths. In reading these essays, keep in mind your own past group associations. Did you ever join a group ganging up on a loner? Were you ever the target of such behavior by others?

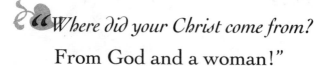

"Where did your Christ come from? From God and a woman!"

AREN'T I A WOMAN?

Sojourner Truth

Sojourner Truth (1797–1883) delivered the following speech in 1851 at the Ohio Women's Rights Convention in Akron, Ohio. Her spontaneous words were taken down by the organizer of the conference and later appeared in the 1878 edition of *Narrative of Sojourner Truth*, an autobiography dictated to Olive Gilbert and first published in 1850. Truth was born into slavery in Ulster County, New York, and was given the name Isabella Baumfree by her master. After New York abolished slavery in 1828, she changed her last name to that of an employer who befriended her (Van Wagener). In the early 1840s, she committed herself fully to evangelical Christianity, hearing voices and having visions. She then adopted what she believed to be the God-given name that reflected her life in the service of all humankind—Sojourner Truth.

1   Well, children, where there is so much racket there must be something out of kilter. I think that, twixt the Negroes of the South and the women at the North, all talking about rights, the white men will be in a fix pretty soon.

2   But what's all this here talking about? That man over there says that women need to be helped into carriages, and lifted over ditches, and to have the best place everywhere. Nobody ever helps me into carriages, or over mud-puddles, or gives my any best place. And aren't I a woman? Look at me! Look at my arm. I have plowed and planted and gathered into barns, and no man could head me. And aren't I a woman? I could work as much and eat as much as a man—when I could get it—and bear the lash as well. And aren't I a woman? I have borne thirteen children, and seen them most all sold off into slavery, and when I cried out with a mother's grief, none but Jesus heard me! And aren't I a woman?

3   Then they talk about this thing in the head; what's this they call it? ["Intellect," whispered someone near.] That's it, honey. What's that got to do with women's rights or Negroes' rights? If my cup won't hold but a pint and

yours holds a quart, wouldn't you be mean not to let me have my little half-measure full?

4   Then that little man in black there, he says women can't have as much rights as men, 'cause Christ wasn't a woman. Where did your Christ come from? Where did your Christ come from? *Where did your Christ come from?* From God and a woman! Man had nothing to do with Him.

5   If the first woman God ever made was strong enough to turn the world upside down all alone, these together ought to be able to turn it back and get it right side up again. And now they is asking to do it, the men better let them.

6   Obliged to you for hearing on me, and now old Sojourner hasn't got nothing more to say.

🖎

Discussion Questions

  1.   Sojourner Truth's speech appears to be devoted to answering three basic objections made by men at the convention against women's rights—that women need to be helped, that women's intellects are not comparable to the intellects of men, and that Christ was a man, not a woman. How does Truth answer these arguments?

 *2.   In answering the argument about male and female intellect introduced in paragraph 3, Truth uses a metaphor: "If my cup won't hold but a pint and yours holds a quart, wouldn't you be mean not to let me have my little half-measure full?" Explain the use of the metaphor and discuss the effectiveness of Truth's reply to the argument about intellects of the two genders.

Writing Topics

  1.   Judging from this speech alone, does Truth appear to be an effective or ineffective speaker in arguing for women's rights? Note the way she opens and closes her brief speech as well as the way she handles her points of rebuttal. Also assess the personal impression she must have made on her listeners given the way she spoke and her method of argument. Write a brief essay stating your opinion about Truth's effectiveness and defend the points you make by referring to passages in the text.

  2.   Write a brief speech you would give today at a women's rights conference on hearing the same objections to such rights that Truth heard in 1851 but using different points of rebuttal.

❧"The present condition of woman causes a horrible perversion of the marriage relation."

A DISAPPOINTED WOMAN

Lucy Stone

Lucy Stone (1818–1893) is considered a pioneer leader in the movements for the abolition of slavery and the establishment of women's rights. Her first male opponent was her father, who refused to subsidize her education. She was able, however, after several years of teaching, to finance her attendance at Oberlin College in Ohio, from which she graduated in 1854. "A Disappointed Woman" is the speech she delivered at the National Woman's Rights Convention in Cincinnati, Ohio, in 1855. She married Henry Blackwell that same year, but she kept her maiden name. Together they edited the *Woman's Journal*, sponsored by the American Woman Suffrage Association.

1   The last speaker alluded to this movement as being that of a few disappointed women. From the first years to which my memory stretches, I have been a disappointed woman. When, with my brothers, I reached forth after the sources of knowledge, I was reproved with "It isn't fit for you; it doesn't belong to women." Then there was but one college in the world where women were admitted, and that was in Brazil. I would have found my way there, but by the time I was prepared to go, one was opened in the young state of Ohio—the first in the United States where women and Negroes could enjoy opportunities with white men. I was disappointed when I came to seek a profession worthy an immortal being—every employment was closed to me, except those of the teacher, the seamstress, and the housekeeper. In education, in marriage, in religion, in everything, disappointment is the lot of woman. It shall be the business of my life to deepen this disappointment in every woman's heart until she bows down to it no longer. I wish that women, instead of being walking showcases, instead of begging of their fathers and brothers the latest and gayest new bonnet, would ask of them their rights.

2   The question of woman's rights is a practical one. The notion has prevailed that it was only an ephemeral idea, that it was but women claiming the right to smoke cigars in the streets and to frequent barrooms. Others have supposed it

a question of comparative intellect; others still, of sphere. Too much has already been said and written about woman's sphere. Trace all the doctrines to their source and they will be found to have no basis except in the usages and prejudices of the age. This is seen in the fact that what is tolerated in woman in one country is not tolerated in another. In this country women may hold prayer meetings, etcetera, but in Mohammedan countries it is written upon their mosques, "Women and dogs, and other impure animals, are not permitted to enter." Wendell Phillips says, "The best and greatest thing one is capable of doing, that is his sphere."

3   I have confidence in the Father to believe that when He gives us the capacity to do anything He does not make a blunder. Leave women, then, to find their sphere. And do not tell us before we are born even, that our province is to cook dinners, darn stockings, and sew on buttons. We are told woman has all the rights she wants; and even women, I am ashamed to say, tell us so. They mistake the politeness of men for rights—seats while men stand in this hall tonight, and their adulations; but these are mere courtesies. We want rights. The flour merchant, the house builder, and the postman charge us no less on account of our sex; but when we endeavor to earn money to pay all these, then, indeed, we find the difference. . . . Women working in tailor shops are paid one-third as much as men. Someone in Philadelphia has stated that women make fine shirts for twelve and a half cents apiece; that no woman can make more than nine a week, and the sum thus earned, after deducting rent, fuel, etcetera, leaves her just three and a half cents a day for bread. Is it a wonder that women are driven to prostitution? Female teachers in New York are paid fifty dollars a year, and for every such situation there are five hundred applicants. I know not what you believe of God, but I believe He gave yearnings and longings to be filled, and that He did not mean all our time should be devoted to feeding and clothing the body.

4   The present condition of woman causes a horrible perversion of the marriage relation. It is asked of a lady, "Has she married well?" "Oh, yes, her husband is rich." Woman must marry for a home, and you men are the sufferers by this; for a woman who loathes you may marry you because you have the means to get money which she cannot have. But when woman can enter the lists with you and make money for herself, she will marry you only for deep and earnest affection.

5   A woman undertook in Lowell to sell shoes to ladies. Men laughed at her, but in six years she has run them all out and has a monopoly of the trade. Sarah Tyndale, whose husband was an importer of china and died bankrupt, continued his business, paid off his debts, and has made a fortune and built the largest china warehouse in the world. Mrs. Tyndale, herself, drew the plan of her warehouse, and it is the best plan ever drawn. A laborer to whom the architect showed it, said: "Don't she know e'en as much as some men?" I have seen a woman at manual labor turning out chair legs in a cabinet shop, with a

dress short enough not to drag in the shavings. I wish other women would imitate her in this. . . . The widening of woman's sphere is to improve her lot. Let us do it, and if the world scoff, let it scoff—if it sneer, let it sneer—but we will go on emulating the example of the sisters Grimké and Abby Kelley. When they first lectured against slavery they were not listened to as respectfully as you listen to us. So the first female physician meets many difficulties, but to the next the path will be made easy.

❧

Discussion Questions

1. In the first paragraph, Stone says, "In education, in marriage, in religion, in everything, disappointment is the lot of woman." Explain her meaning of *disappointment* in religion and/or in marriage. Does the author literally mean disappointment "in everything"?
*2. What does the author mean when she begins paragraph two, "The question of woman's rights is a practical one"? How does the statement relate particularly to the focus on money in the latter part of her speech?

Writing Topics

1. Write a letter to Stone explaining how her list of disappointments as a woman, made in the middle of the nineteenth century, needs to be modified or changed now, some one hundred fifty years later?
2. Record an interview with an older woman in your family or community, covering such subjects as her attitude toward the women's rights movement and encouraging her to focus on her own personal experience in growing up female. Devise questions about her experience in education, in the world of work, in marriage (or remaining single), in raising children (or remaining childless). To what extent did gender play a role in determining what she did or became?

"Here's my list of dirty chores:
buying groceries, carting them home and
putting them away;
cooking meals and washing dishes and pots;
doing the laundry;
digging out the place when things get out of control;
washing floors."

THE POLITICS OF HOUSEWORK

Pat Mainardi

Pat Mainardi, born in Paterson, New Jersey, in 1942, earned a B.A. at Vassar in 1963 and then studied at Columbia University from 1963 to 1965 and at New York Studio School from 1965 to 1966. She was awarded an M.F.A. at the City University of New York in 1976, an M.A. at Hunter College in 1980, an M.Phil. at the City University of New York in 1981, followed by a Ph.D. in 1984. She served as founding editor of *Women and Art* (1971–1972) and *Feminist Art Journal* (1973–1974). After teaching visual arts at a number of institutions, she assumed her position as a professor at Brooklyn College and the Graduate School, City University of New York, in 1985. In *Sisterhood Is Powerful* (1970), source of "The Politics of Housework," the editor, Robin Morgan, wrote of the author of this essay: "Pat Mainardi is a member of Redstockings [of the Women's Liberation Movement] and a painter. She attributes her insights into male culture to her mother, her grandmother, and her mother's four sisters. The seven women have collectively put in over two hundred years of housework and all that feeling, speaking, and sharing pain has resulted in 'The Politics of Housework.' May our daughters be spared."

> *Though women do not complain of the power of husbands, each*
> *complains of her own husband, or of the husbands of her friends. It*
> *is the same in all other cases of servitude; at least in the*
> *commencement of the emancipatory movement. The serfs did not at*
> *first complain of the power of the lords, but only of their tyranny.*
> —*John Stuart-Mill,* On the Subjection of Women

1   Liberated women—very different from women's liberation! The first signals all kinds of goodies, to warm the hearts (not to mention other parts) of the most radical men. The other signals—*housework*. The first brings sex without marriage, sex before marriage, cozy housekeeping arrangements ("You see, I'm living with this chick") and the self-content of knowing that you're not the kind of man who wants a doormat instead of a woman. That will come later. After all, who wants that old commodity anymore, the Standard American Housewife, all husband, home and kids. The New Commodity, the Liberated Woman, has sex a lot and has a Career, preferably something that can be fitted in with the household chores—like dancing, pottery, or painting.

2   On the other hand is women's liberation—and housework. What? You say this is all trivial? Wonderful! That's what I thought. It seemed perfectly reasonable. We both had careers, both had to work a couple of days a week to earn enough to live on, so why shouldn't we share the housework? So I suggested it to my mate and he agreed—most men are too hip to turn you down flat. "You're right," he said, "It's only fair."

3   Then an interesting thing happened. I can only explain it by stating that we women have been brainwashed more than even we can imagine. Probably too many years of seeing television women in ecstasy over their shiny waxed floors or breaking down over their dirty shirt collars. Men have no such conditioning. They recognize the essential fact of housework right from the very beginning. Which is that it stinks. Here's my list of dirty chores: buying groceries, carting them home and putting them away; cooking meals and washing dishes and pots; doing the laundry, digging out the place when things get out of control; washing floors. The list could go on but the sheer necessities are bad enough. All of us have to do these things, or get some one else to do them for us. The longer my husband contemplated these chores, the more repulsed he became, and so proceeded the change from the normally sweet considerate Dr. Jekyll into the crafty Mr. Hyde who would stop at nothing to avoid the horrors of—*housework*. As he felt himself backed into a corner laden with dirty dishes, brooms, mops, and reeking garbage, his front teeth grew longer and pointier, his fingernails haggled and his eyes grew wild. Housework trivial? Not on your life! Just try to share the burden.

4   So ensued a dialogue that's been going on for several years. Here are some of the high points:

5   "I don't mind sharing the housework, but I don't do it very well. We should each do the things we're best at."

Meaning: Unfortunately I'm no good at things like washing dishes or cooking. What I do best is a little light carpentry, changing light bulbs, moving furniture (*how often do you move furniture?*).

Also Meaning: Historically the lower classes (black men and us) have had hundreds of years experience doing menial jobs. It would be a waste of manpower to train someone else to do them now.

Also Meaning: I don't like the dull stupid boring jobs, so you should do them.

6   "I don't mind sharing the work, but you'll have to show me how to do it."

Meaning: I ask a lot of questions and you'll have to show me everything everytime I do it because I don't remember so good. Also don't try to sit down and read while I'm doing my jobs because I'm going to annoy hell out of you until it's easier to do them yourself.

7   "We used to be so happy!" (Said whenever it was his turn to do something.)

Meaning: I used to be so happy.

Meaning: Life without housework is bliss. (*No quarrel here. Perfect agreement.*)

8   "We have different standards, and why should I have to work to your standards. That's unfair."

Meaning: If I begin to get bugged by the dirt and crap I will say "This place sure is a sty" or "How can anyone live like this?" and wait for your reaction. I know that all women have a sore called "Guilt over a messy house" or "Household work is ultimately my responsibility." I know that men have caused that sore — if anyone visits and the place *is* a sty, they're not going to leave and say, "He sure is a lousy housekeeper." You'll take the rap in any case. I can outwait you.

Also Meaning: I can provoke innumerable scenes over the housework issue. Eventually doing all the housework yourself will be less painful to you than trying to get me to do half. Or I'll suggest we get a maid. She will do my share of the work. You will do yours. It's women's work.

9   "I've got nothing against sharing the housework, but you can't make me do it on your schedule."

Meaning: Passive resistance. I'll do it when I damned well please, if at all. If my job is doing dishes, it's easier to do them once a week. If taking out laundry, once a month. If washing the floors, once a year. If you don't like it, do it yourself oftener, and then I won't do it at all.

10   "I *hate* it more than you. You don't mind it so much."

Meaning: Housework is garbage work. It's the worst crap I've ever done. It's degrading and humiliating for someone of *my* intelligence to do it. But for someone of *your* intelligence . . .

11 "Housework is too trivial to even talk about."
Meaning: It's even more trivial to do. Housework is beneath my status. My purpose in life is to deal with matters of significance. Yours is to deal with matters of insignificance. You should do the housework.

12 "This problem of housework is not a man-woman problem! In any relationship between two people one is going to have a stronger personality and dominate."
Meaning: That stronger personality had better be *me*.

13 "In animal societies, wolves, for example, the top animal is usually a male even where he is not chosen for brute strength but on the basis of cunning and intelligence. Isn't that interesting?"
Meaning: I have historical, psychological, anthropological, and biological justification for keeping you down. How can you ask the top wolf to be equal?

14 "Women's liberation isn't really a political movement."
Meaning: The Revolution is coming too close to home.
Also Meaning: I am only interested in how *I* am oppressed, not how I oppress others. Therefore the war, the draft, and the university are political. Women's liberation is not.

15 "Man's accomplishments have always depended on getting help from other people, mostly women. What great man would have accomplished what he did if he had to do his own housework?"
Meaning: Oppression is built into the System and I, as the white American male receive the benefits of this System. I don't want to give them up.

Postscript

16 Participatory democracy begins at home. If you are planning to implement your politics, there are certain things to remember.

1. He *is* feeling it more than you. He's losing some leisure and you're gaining it. The measure of your oppression is his resistance.

2. A great many American men are not accustomed to doing monotonous repetitive work which never ushers in any lasting let alone important achievement. This is why they would rather repair a cabinet than wash dishes. If human endeavors are like a pyramid with man's highest achievements at the top, then keeping oneself alive is at the bottom. Men have always had servants (us) to take care of this bottom strata of life while they have confined their efforts to the rarefied upper regions. It is thus ironic when they ask of women—where are your great painters, statesmen, etc? Mme.

Matisse ran a millinery shop so he could paint. Mrs. Martin Luther King kept his house and raised his babies.

3. It is a traumatizing experience for someone who has always thought of himself as being against any oppression or exploitation of one human being by another to realize that in his daily life he has been accepting and implementing (and benefiting from) this exploitation; that his rationalization is little different from that of the racist who says "Black people don't feel pain" (women don't mind doing the shitwork); and that the oldest form of oppression in history has been the oppression of 50 percent of the population by the other 50 percent.

4. Arm yourself with some knowledge of the psychology of oppressed peoples everywhere, and a few facts about the animal kingdom. I admit playing top wolf or who runs the gorillas is silly but as a last resort men bring it up all the time. Talk about bees. If you feel really hostile bring up the sex life of spiders. They have sex. She bites off his head.

    The psychology of oppressed people is not silly. Jews, immigrants, black men, and all women have employed the same psychological mechanisms to survive: admiring the oppressor, glorifying the oppressor, wanting to be like the oppressor, wanting the oppressor to like them, mostly because the oppressor held all the power.

5. In a sense, all men everywhere are slightly schizoid—divorced from the reality of maintaining life. This makes it easier for them to play games with it. It is almost a cliché that women feel greater grief at sending a son off to war or losing him to that war because they bore him, suckled him, and raised him. The men who foment those wars did none of those things and have a more superficial estimate of the worth of human life. One hour a day is a low estimate of the amount of time one has to spend "keeping" oneself. By foisting this off on others, man gains seven hours a week—one working day more to play with his mind and not his human needs. Over the course of generations it is easy to see whence evolved the horrifying abstractions of modern life.

6. With the death of each form of oppression, life changes and new forms evolve. English aristocrats at the turn of the century were horrified at the idea of enfranchising working men—were sure that it signaled the death of civilization and a return to barbarism. Some working men were even deceived by this line. Similarly with the minimum wage, abolition of slavery, and female suffrage. Life changes but it goes on. Don't fall for any line about the death of

everything if men take a turn at the dishes. They will imply that you are holding back the Revolution (their Revolution). But you are advancing it (your Revolution).

7. Keep checking up. Periodically consider who's actually *doing* the jobs. These things have a way of backsliding so that a year later once again the woman is doing everything. After a year make a list of jobs the man has rarely if ever done. You will find cleaning pots, toilets, refrigerators and ovens high on the list. Use time sheets if necessary. He will accuse you of being petty. He is above that sort of thing—(housework). Bear in mind what the worst jobs are, namely the ones that have to be done every day or several times a day. Also the ones that are dirty—it's more pleasant to pick up books, newspapers etc. than to wash dishes. Alternate the bad jobs. It's the daily grind that gets you down. Also make sure that you don't have the responsibility for the housework with occasional help from him. "I'll cook dinner for you tonight" implies it's really your job and isn't he a nice guy to do some of it for you.

8. Most men had a rich and rewarding bachelor life during which they did not starve or become encrusted with crud or buried under the litter. There is a taboo that says that women mustn't strain themselves in the presence of men: we haul around 50 pounds of groceries if we have to but aren't allowed to open a jar if there is someone around to do it for us. The reverse side of the coin is that men aren't supposed to be able to take care of themselves without a woman. Both are excuses for making women do the housework.

9. Beware of the double whammy. He won't do the little things he always did because you're now a "Liberated Woman," right? Of course he won't do anything else either . . .

17   I was just finishing this when my husband came in and asked what I was doing. Writing a paper on housework. Housework? he said, *Housework?* Oh my god how trivial can you get. A paper on housework.

❧

Discussion Questions

1. According to Mainardi, what is the difference between the terms *liberated women* and *women's liberation?* Which does she favor? Why? What seems to be her attitude toward the other?

*2. Beginning with paragraph 5, the author presents several paragraphs in which there is a quotation followed by what are apparently translations of the quoted comment. Who is being quoted? Who is providing the real or hidden meaning? Discuss the effect of Mainardi's technique in these paragraphs.

3. In the Postscript, item 4, the author writes, "Talk about bees. If you feel really hostile bring up the sex life of spiders. They have sex. She bites off his head." Explain the significance of these references to bees and spiders.

*4. In the last paragraph, Mainardi writes that her husband came in just as she was finishing her essay and asked what she was doing. When she tells him, what does he answer? What is the effect of letting her husband have the last word (or words) in her essay?

Writing Topics

1. In the Postscript, item 5, Mainardi writes, "It is almost a cliché that women feel greater grief at sending a son off to war or losing him to that war because they bore him, suckled him, and raised him. The men who foment those wars did none of those things and have a more superficial estimate of the worth of human life." Is this a profound or superficial observation? Write an essay in which you analyze and characterize Mainardi's observation and marshal arguments of your own to support your position.

2. Mainardi's essay is full of sweeping statements or strong opinions. Find a statement that you want to support or refute and, in an essay, enumerate your own arguments for or against it. One example opens item 6 in the Postscript: "With the death of each form of oppression, life changes and new forms evolve." Another example is found in item 8 of the Postscript: "Most men had a rich and rewarding bachelor life during which they did not starve or become encrusted with crud or buried under the litter."

*❧❧Before the sit-in, I had always hated
the whites in Mississippi.
Now I knew it was impossible for me to hate sickness.
The whites had a disease,
an incurable disease in its final stage.
What were our chances against such a disease?"*

THE MOVEMENT

Anne Moody

Anne Moody was born in 1940 in Centreville, Mississippi. She was a star pupil in high school and attended both Natchez Junior College and Tougaloo College in Tougaloo, Mississippi, receiving a B.S. in 1963. At college, she became involved in the Civil Rights movement and participated in a sit-in organized by the NAACP at a Woolworth lunch counter in Jackson, Mississippi, described in "The Movement." After graduation, Moody became active in the Council on Racial Equality (CORE) and other movements, working for a time in 1967 in New York City's antipoverty program. There she discovered that the problems plaguing the poor were as intractable as those plaguing the blacks and other racial minorities. In 1968, she published *Coming of Age in Mississippi*, source of "The Movement." The book won the "Best Book of the Year Award" from the American Library Association and the "Gold Medal Award" from the National Council of Catholics and Jews. It has been translated into seven languages. During the 1970s, Moody went to Europe to devote herself to studying and writing, and her work *Mr. Death: Four Stories* appeared in 1975. She now lives in New York City, teaching, lecturing, and writing.

1   During my senior year at Tougaloo, my family hadn't sent me one penny. I had only the small amount of money I had earned at Maple Hill. I couldn't afford to eat at school or live in the dorms, so I had gotten permission to move

off campus. I had to prove that I could finish school, even if I had to go hungry every day. I knew Raymond and Miss Pearl were just waiting to see me drop out. But something happened to me as I got more and more involved in the Movement. It no longer seemed important to prove anything. I had found something outside myself that gave meaning to my life.

2   I had become very friendly with my social science professor, John Salter, who was in charge of NAACP activities on campus. All during the year, while the NAACP conducted a boycott of the downtown stores in Jackson, I had been one of Salter's most faithful canvassers and church speakers. During the last week of school, he told me that sit-in demonstrations were about to start in Jackson and that he wanted me to be the spokesman for a team that would sit-in at Woolworth's lunch counter. The two other demonstrators would be classmates of mine, Memphis and Pearlena. Pearlena was a dedicated NAACP worker, but Memphis had not been very involved in the Movement on campus. It seemed that the organization had had a rough time finding students who were in a position to go to jail. I had nothing to lose one way or the other. Around ten o'clock the morning of the demonstrations, NAACP headquarters alerted the news services. As a result, the police department was also informed, but neither the policemen nor the newsmen knew exactly where or when the demonstrations would start. They stationed themselves along Capitol Street and waited.

3   To divert attention from the sit-in at Woolworth's, the picketing started at J. C. Penney's a good fifteen minutes before. The pickets were allowed to walk up and down in front of the store three or four times before they were arrested. At exactly 11 A.M., Pearlena, Memphis, and I entered Woolworth's from the rear entrance. We separated as soon as we stepped into the store, and made small purchases from various counters. Pearlena had given Memphis her watch. He was to let us know when it was 11:14. At 11:14 we were to join him near the lunch counter and at exactly 11:15 we were to take seats at it.

4   Seconds before 11:15 we were occupying three seats at the previously segregated Woolworth's lunch counter. In the beginning the waitresses seemed to ignore us, as if they really didn't know what was going on. Our waitress walked past us a couple of times before she noticed we had started to write our own orders down and realized we wanted service. She asked us what we wanted. We began to read to her from our order slips. She told us that we would be served at the back counter, which was for Negroes.

5   "We would like to be served here," I said.

6   The waitress started to repeat what she had said, then stopped in the middle of the sentence. She turned the lights out behind the counter, and she and the other waitresses almost ran to the back of the store, deserting all their white customers. I guess they thought that violence would start immediately after the whites at the counter realized what was going on. There were five or six other people at the counter. A couple of them just got up and walked away.

A girl sitting next to me finished her banana split before leaving. A middle-aged white woman who had not yet been served rose from her seat and came over to us. "I'd like to stay here with you," she said, "but my husband is waiting."

7   The newsmen came in just as she was leaving. They must have discovered what was going on shortly after some of the people began to leave the store. One of the newsmen ran behind the woman who spoke to us and asked her to identify herself. She refused to give her name, but said she was a native of Vicksburg and a former resident of California. When asked why she had said what she had said to us, she replied, "I am in sympathy with the Negro movement." By this time a crowd of cameramen and reporters had gathered around us taking pictures and asking questions, such as Where were we from? Why did we sit-in? What organization sponsored it? Were we students? From what school? How were we classified?

8   I told them that we were all students at Tougaloo College, that we were represented by no particular organization, and that we planned to stay there even after the store closed. "All we want is service," was my reply to one of them. After they had finished probing for about twenty minutes, they were almost ready to leave.

9   At noon, students from a nearby white high school started pouring in to Woolworth's. When they first saw us they were sort of surprised. They didn't know how to react. A few started to heckle and the newsmen became interested again. Then the white students started chanting all kinds of anti-Negro slogans. We were called a little bit of everything. The rest of the seats except the three we were occupying had been roped off to prevent others from sitting down. A couple of the boys took one end of the rope and made it into a hangman's noose. Several attempts were made to put it around our necks. The crowds grew as more students and adults came in for lunch.

10   We kept our eyes straight forward and did not look at the crowd except for occasional glances to see what was going on. All of a sudden I saw a face I remembered—the drunkard from the bus station sit-in. My eyes lingered on him just long enough for us to recognize each other. Today he was drunk too, so I don't think he remembered where he had seen me before. He took out a knife, opened it, put it in his pocket, and then began to pace the floor. At this point, I told Memphis and Pearlena what was going on. Memphis suggested that we pray. We bowed our heads, and all hell broke loose. A man rushed forward, threw Memphis from his seat, and slapped my face. Then another man who worked in the store threw me against an adjoining counter.

11   Down on my knees on the floor, I saw Memphis lying near the lunch counter with blood running out of the corners of his mouth. As he tried to protect his face, the man who'd thrown him down kept kicking him against the head. If he had worn hard-soled shoes instead of sneakers, the first kick probably would have killed Memphis. Finally a man dressed in plain clothes identified himself as a police officer and arrested Memphis and his attacker.

12   Pearlena had been thrown to the floor. She and I got back on our stools after Memphis was arrested. There were some white Tougaloo teachers in the crowd. They asked Pearlena and me if we wanted to leave. They said that things were getting too rough. We didn't know what to do. While we were trying to make up our minds, we were joined by Joan Trumpauer. Now there were three of us and we were integrated. The crowd began to chant, "Communists, Communists, Communists." Some old man in the crowd ordered the students to take us off the stools.

13   "Which one should I get first?" a big husky boy said.

14   "That white nigger," the one man said.

15   The boy lifted Joan from the counter by her waist and carried her out of the store. Simultaneously, I was snatched from my stool by two high school students. I was dragged about thirty feet toward the door by my hair when someone made them turn me loose. As I was getting up off the floor, I saw Joan coming back inside. We started back to the center of the counter to join Pearlena. Lois Chaffee, a white Tougaloo faculty member, was now sitting next to her. So Joan and I just climbed across the rope at the front end of the counter and sat down. There were now four of us, two whites and two Negroes, all women. The mob started smearing us with ketchup, mustard, sugar, pies, and everything on the counter. Soon Joan and I were joined by John Salter, but the moment he sat down he was hit on the jaw with what appeared to be brass knuckles. Blood gushed from his face and someone threw salt into the open wound. Ed King, Tougaloo's chaplain, rushed to him.

16   At the other end of the counter, Lois and Pearlena were joined by George Raymond, a CORE field worker and a student from Jackson State College. Then a Negro high school boy sat down next to me. The mob took spray paint from the counter and sprayed it on the new demonstrators. The high school student had on a white shirt; the word "nigger" was written on his back with red spray paint.

17   We sat there for three hours taking a beating when the manager decided to close the store because the mob had begun to go wild with stuff from the other counters. He begged and begged everyone to leave. But even after fifteen minutes of begging, no one budged. They would not leave until we did. Then Dr. Beittel, the president of Tougaloo College, came running in. He said he had just heard what was happening.

18   About ninety policemen were standing outside the store; they had been watching the whole thing through the windows, but had not come in to stop the mob or do anything. President Beittel went outside and asked Captain Ray to come and escort us out. The captain refused, stating the manager had to invite him in before he could enter the premises, so Dr. Beittel himself brought us out. He had told the police that they had better protect us after we were outside the store. When we got outside, the policemen formed a single line that blocked the mob from us. However, they were allowed to throw at us everything

they had collected. Within ten minutes, we were picked up by Reverend King in his station wagon and taken to the NAACP headquarters on Lynch Street.

19   After the sit-in, all I could think of was how sick Mississippi whites were. They believed so much in the segregated Southern way of life, they would kill to preserve it. I sat there in the NAACP office and thought of how many times they had killed when this way of life was threatened. I knew that the killing had just begun. "Many more will die before it is over with," I thought. Before the sit-in, I had always hated the whites in Mississippi. Now I knew it was impossible for me to hate sickness. The whites had a disease, an incurable disease in its final stage. What were our chances against such a disease? I thought of the students, the young Negroes who had just begun to protest, as young interns. When these young interns got older, I thought, they would be the best doctors in the world for social problems.

           ❧

Discussion Questions

1. How did Moody become involved in the sit-in to begin with?
2. What was the purpose of the picketing at J. C. Penney's (referred to in the opening of paragraph 3)?
3. What happened to the other customers when the sit-in began at the lunch counter?
4. Compare and contrast the conduct of the students who did the sitting in and the others who gathered around.
5. What role did the news reporters play? The police? Dr. Beittel, president of Tougaloo College?
*6. What change in attitude did the experience bring about in Moody?

Writing Topics

1. Many moral questions are raised by the behavior of the individuals and groups described in "The Movement." Reread the work with care, making a moral assessment of such behavior in accord with your own moral antennae, and then write an essay defending your judgment as to the blameworthy and the blameless. You might want to concentrate on one segment—those sitting in, the individual bystanders, or the figures of authority (the NAACP members, the store officials, the police, Dr. Beittel.)
2. The world has changed considerably since the Tougaloo sit-in. Using the community in which you have lived, and your knowledge of race relations in it, write a letter to Moody assuring her that things have changed for the better—or worse—in the United States.

"Schoolwork, my two Black Power chanting elementary-school classmates and I decided, was for white people."

THE BLACK ACADEMIC ENVIRONNMENT

Hugh Pearson

Hugh Pearson was born in 1957 in Fort Wayne, Indiana. After graduation from Brown University in 1979, he did graduate work in urban planning at the New School for Social Research from 1983 to 1984 and worked briefly as a project manager for the Harlem Urban Development Corporation. "I decided," he has explained, "to return to writing, in which I had made my mark as a high school and college student." He is the author of *The Shadow of the Panther: Huey Newton and the Price of Black Power in America*, published in 1994. The *New Yorker* reviewer wrote of the work: "This book will awaken profound misgivings—about gun-barrel rhetoric, about armed rebellion, about the ambiguities of justice." "The Black Academic Environment," which describes the influence of the Black Power movement on the author as a boy, was published in *The Wall Street Journal* on November 23, 1994. Pearson served as associate editor for the Pacific News Service from 1990 to 1994 and is currently on the editorial staff of *The Wall Street Journal*. His work has appeared in many publications, including *The New York Times*, the *Los Angeles Times*, and *The New Republic*. Asked to comment on "learning to write," Pearson said, "My favorite writing instructor was my eleventh grade teacher in Fort Wayne who taught me to always get to the point as soon as possible in my writing, and always write in a clear prose style. Ever since then I've done my best to follow those instructions. In 1974 they led to my being the sole high school student in a metropolitan area of 350,000 residents to receive the National Council of Teachers of English Achievement Award in Writing."

When I was in the third grade an idea caught on among two of my fellow African-American classmates and me as we walked back and forth from our predominantly white elementary school adjacent to the small black middle-class enclave in which we lived in Fort Wayne, Ind. The year was 1966, and it was characterized by news accounts of a dynamic 25-year-old named Stokely Carmichael, a leader of the Student Nonviolent Coordinating Committee (SNCC), who was popularizing something called Black Power.

If you believed in Black Power and you were a male, you stopped cutting your hair close to the scalp. You started wearing sunglasses, even in the dark. You took a liking to black leather jackets and black turtleneck sweaters. And, most important, you put on a black leather glove and began balling your hand into a fist, then raising your fist above your head in a salute as you repeated the mantra, "Black Power!" After the youthful activists in SNCC erroneously concluded that as a result of their failure to gain power in Mississippi and Alabama the electoral avenues to power were closed off to blacks, something first uttered by the recently assassinated Malcolm X was added to the slogan: "By Any Means Necessary!"

Youthful Romanticism

That addendum ushered in a youthful romanticism with guns, and large-scale black support for the 1967 riots in Newark and Detroit. Other SNCC leaders such as H. Rap Brown fanned the flames, encouraging violence in places like Cambridge, Maryland. Simultaneously Huey Newton's Black Panthers dazzled us with their rifles, berets, leather-jacketed military formations, and impressive drills. And hundreds of thousands of black youths became convinced that the society we were to enter as adults held no future for us.

Schoolwork, my two Black Power chanting elementary-school classmates and I decided, was for white people. Our take on Black Power meant not only that we were supposed to stop excelling in "the white man's school," but that we were to glorify one segment of the black community. The Black Panthers called them the lumpen proletariat.

They said that the lumpen proletariat, who constituted the poorest and least-skilled blacks, were the noblest of us all. So my two classmates and I reasoned that our middle-class families—particularly ones like mine in which my father was a physician—weren't truly black. How could my father be? Every time I used the English language improperly, he corrected me. The lumpen proletariat had their own speech patterns. Every time he took me to the barbershop and I attempted to let my hair stay put, he insisted that it be cut short. To my young mind he wasn't "acting black."

It wasn't long before, due to the D's and occasional F's on my report cards, my third-grade teacher began calling home insisting that I be held back from promotion to the fourth grade.

7   Black Power sloganeering be damned, thought my father. The idea that a violent American revolution could be pulled off by blacks was foolish. The notion that excelling in school meant "acting white" was beyond silly. To my father, the naive youthful behavior encouraged by the Black Power movement could only popularize once again the racist belief the civil rights movement originally set out to destroy: that blacks were a different species of human from whites.

8   And now the threat that that belief will become popular is presented once again. Only this time it comes from a new book written by a pair of white researchers. *The Bell Curve* by Charles Murray and Richard Herrnstein argues that, on average, black IQs are naturally lower than white IQs, raising the possibility that the nation will witness something that has never happened before. Black and white weariness due to the issue of race could combine with conclusions drawn from the book by certain decision-makers to induce a national retreat from commitment to equal opportunity.

9   However, if read closely enough with a clear eye for reality, "The Bell Curve" could contain the ingredients for a different response. The authors discuss something called the Flynn Effect, in which over time IQ scores tend to drift upward among groups of people, a phenomenon that could only be due to improvements in the environment overriding any possible genetic basis for IQ performance. According to the Flynn Effect, over time the average IQ scores among a nation's population have been shown to increase by as much as one point per year, posting gains comparable to the 15 points separating black and white IQ averages today. The only catch is that the authors argue it's doubtful the 15-point gap in average IQ scores between blacks and whites will be closed, since the Flynn Effect will happen equally among blacks and whites.

10   Apparently the authors didn't observe the educational environment among large numbers of black youths closely enough. Even today numerous black students tell of being made to feel uncomfortable if they apply themselves and get good grades. Such a tactic is the legacy of the type of behavior I experienced in the sixth grade.

11   My father ignored my third-grade teacher's advice, and I was not held back from promotion to the fourth grade. Neither was I held back from promotion to the fifth or sixth grades, despite my poor report cards. By the time I reached the sixth grade I was determined to enter junior high school at the highest level of the tracking system. So I applied myself in class and registered the greatest improvement in test scores of any student in my predominantly white school, only to hear a black classmate say, "I guess you think you're like the white students now."

12   That a black child would think that way about excelling academically underscores the indelible damage done to my classmates by the Black Power movement, though the movement also left many of us with a lasting racial pride. However, in the long run, the damage may have outweighed that benefit. Plenty

of rap music performers have picked up where the Black Power movement left off, as they promote the notion among black youths that there is a unique black language and way of seeing the world that need only be defended to outsiders with the simple phrase: "It's a black thing. You wouldn't understand." So instead of applying themselves in English and math, thousands of black youths dedicate their energy to scratching records, mixing samples of music, and using their voices to create staccato rhymes.

13 Energy and industriousness that create an entire new window of economic opportunity should, on the one hand, be admired. Yet on the other hand, like black accomplishment in professional basketball, rap delivers the skewed message to black youths that their hopes and dreams need only be applied in a few limited directions. It signals that diversity of ambition and industry is "a white thing that blacks wouldn't understand."

14 The magnitude of the problem suggests that turning such attitudes around could more than make up for any natural environmental improvement that will occur among other youths through the Flynn Effect. A concerted effort to do so could mean that within 15 years the 15-point gap in black and white IQ averages would be closed.

Too Balkanized

15 The question is whether our society will commit to such a turnaround. At the moment that doesn't appear likely. We're too balkanized, too determined to read what we wish to read into research findings, a tendency that is seen in the authors of *The Bell Curve*. Because our Constitution is dedicated to providing equal opportunity rather than a road map to the creation of a caste society, turning this situation around is the first step needed if we are to glean anything useful from a book like *The Bell Curve*.

❧

Discussion Questions

1. In Pearson's description of the Black Power movement's effect on him and his schoolmates, what part did personal appearance and dress play? What kind of "statement" does such dress and behavior appear to make?

2. According to Pearson, what benefit, if any, did the Black Power movement have?

3. What is Pearson's attitude toward rap music? Explain.

*4. Why does Pearson introduce and discuss *The Bell Curve*, by Charles Murray and Richard Herrnstein? According to *The Bell Curve*, what is the "Flynn Effect," and why does Pearson focus on it?

Writing Topics

1. Write a short essay first explaining Pearson's meaning in one of the following statements and then agreeing or disagreeing with him:
    a. ". . . like black accomplishment in professional basketball, rap delivers the skewed message to black youths that their hopes and dreams need only be applied in a few limited directions" (paragraph 13).
    b. "Because our Constitution is dedicated to providing equal opportunity rather than a road map to the creation of a caste society, turning this situation [balkanization] around is the first step needed if we are to glean anything useful from a book like *The Bell Curve*" (paragraph 15).
2. Obviously, the influence the Black Power movement had on Pearson's attitude toward education when he was a boy was a negative one. Reflect on any past affiliations you may have had to various groups, such as a sports team, a religious group, a theater group, and so forth. Did this group's particular ideology have any effect, positive or negative, on your own values? If so, write about the experience, describing the circumstances involved and the lessons learned.

"It was what I was looking for,
something to guide myself by, a way of life,
a compendium of the wise, the true and the beautiful."

KIPLING AND I

Jesús Colón

Born in Puerto Rico, Jesús Colón (1901–1974) stowed away on a ship bound for New York at the age of seventeen. He wrote for the communist newspaper, the *Daily Worker*, and was later called to testify before the House Committee on Un-American Activities in its infamous search for left-leaning "pinkoes" who were "un-American." Although he ran for public office in New York (U.S. Senate, Comptroller of the City of New York), he never won an election. When Colón died in 1974, he requested that his ashes be sprinkled over his native Puerto Rico. In 1961, he published *A Puerto Rican in New York and Other Sketches*, which has become recognized as a key early work in Hispanic-American literature. It was reprinted in 1982. "Kipling and I" is an excerpt from this work.

1   Sometimes I pass Debevoise Place at the corner of Willoughby Street . . . I look at the old wooden house, gray and ancient, the house where I used to live some forty years ago . . .

2   My room was on the second floor at the corner. On hot summer nights I would sit at the window reading by the electric light from the street lamp which was almost at a level with the windowsill.

3   It was nice to come home late during the winter, look for some scrap of old newspaper, some bits of wood and a few chunks of coal, and start a sparkling fire in the chunky fourlegged coal stove. I would be rewarded with an intimate warmth as little by little the pigmy stove became alive puffing out its sides, hot and red, like the crimson cheeks of a Santa Claus.

4   My few books were in a soap box nailed to the wall. But my most prized possession in those days was a poem I had bought in a five-and-ten-cent store on Fulton Street. (I wonder what has become of these poems, maxims and sayings of wise men that they used to sell at the five-and-ten-cent stores?) The

poem was printed on gold paper and mounted in a gilded frame ready to be hung in a conspicuous place in the house. I bought one of those fancy silken picture cords finishing in a rosette to match the color of the frame.

5   I was seventeen. This poem to me then seemed to summarize, in one poetical nutshell, the wisdom of all the sages that ever lived. It was what I was looking for, something to guide myself by, a way of life, a compendium of the wise, the true and the beautiful. All I had to do was to live according to the counsel of the poem and follow its instructions and I would be a perfect man — the useful, the good, the true human being. I was very happy that day, forty years ago.

6   The poem had to have the most prominent place in the room. Where could I hang it? I decided that the best place for the poem was on the wall right by the entrance to the room. No one coming in and out would miss it. Perhaps someone would be interested enough to read it and drink the profound waters of its message . . .

7   Every morning as I prepared to leave, I stood in front of the poem and read it over and over again, sometimes half a dozen times. I let the sonorous music of the verse carry me away. I brought with me a handwritten copy as I stepped out every morning looking for work, repeating verses and stanzas from memory until the whole poem came to be part of me. Other days my lips kept repeating a single verse of the poem at intervals throughout the day.

8   In the subways I loved to compete with the shrill noises of the many wheels below by chanting the lines of the poem. People stared at me moving my lips as though I were in a trance. I looked back with pity. They were not so fortunate as I who had as a guide to direct my life a great poem to make me wise, useful and happy.

9   And I chanted:

> *If you can keep your head when all about you*
> *Are losing theirs and blaming it on you . . .*
>
> *If you can wait and not be tired by waiting,*
>   *Or being lied about, don't deal in lies,*
> *Or being hated don't give way to hating . . .*
>
> *If you can make one heap of all your winnings;*
>   *And risk it on one turn of pitch-and-toss,*
> *And lose, and start again at your beginnings . . .*

10   "If—," by Kipling, was the poem. At seventeen, my evening prayer and my first morning thought. I repeated it every day with the resolution to live up to the very last line of that poem.

11   I would visit the government employment office on Jay Street. The conversations among the Puerto Ricans on the large wooden benches in the employment office were always on the same subject. How to find a decent place to live. How they would not rent to Negroes or Puerto Ricans. How Negroes and Puerto Ricans were given the pink slips first at work.

12   From the employment office I would call door to door at the piers, factories and storage houses in the streets under the Brooklyn and Manhattan bridges. "Sorry, nothing today." It seemed to me that that "today" was a continuation and combination of all the yesterdays, todays and tomorrows.

13   From the factories I would go to the restaurants, looking for a job as a porter or dishwasher. At least I would eat and be warm in a kitchen.

14   "Sorry" . . . "Sorry" . . .

15   Sometimes I was hired at ten dollars a week, ten hours a day including Sundays and holidays. One day off during the week. My work was that of three men: dishwasher, porter, busboy. And to clear the sidewalk of snow and slush "when you have nothing else to do." I was to be appropriately humble and grateful not only to the owner but to everybody else in the place.

16   If I rebelled at insults or at a pointed innuendo or just the inhuman amount of work, I was unceremoniously thrown out and told to come "next week for your pay." "Next week" meant weeks of calling for the paltry dollars owed me. The owners relished this "next week."

17   I clung to my poem as to a faith. Like a potent amulet, my precious poem was clenched in the fist of my right hand inside my secondhand overcoat. Again and again I declaimed aloud a few precious lines when discouragement and disillusionment threatened to overwhelm me.

If you can force your heart and nerve and sinew
To serve your turn long after they are gone . . .

18   The weeks of unemployment and hard knocks turned into months. I continued to find two or three days of work here and there. And I continued to be thrown out when I rebelled at the ill treatment, overwork and insults. I kept pounding the streets looking for a place where they would treat me half decently, where my devotion to work and faith in Kipling's poem would be appreciated. I remember the worn-out shoes I bought in a secondhand store on Myrtle Avenue at the corner of Adams Street. The round holes in the soles that I tried to cover with pieces of carton were no match for the frigid knives of the unrelenting snow.

19   One night I returned late after a long day of looking for work. I was hungry. My room was dark and cold. I wanted to warm my numb body. I lit a match and began looking for some scraps of wood and a piece of paper to start a fire. I searched all over the floor. No wood, no paper. As I stood up, the glimmering flicker of the dying match was reflected in the glass surface of the framed poem.

If you can talk with crowds and keep your virtue,
  Or walk with Kings—nor lose the common touch,
If neither foes nor loving friends can hurt you,
  If all men count with you, but none too much;
If you can fill the unforgiving minute
  With sixty seconds' worth of distance run,
Yours is the Earth and everything that's in it,
  And—which is more—you'll be a Man, my son!

1. Read the poem aloud with vigor and listen for the tone that captured the imagination of the destitute seventeen-year-old Colón. How does the virtuous advice of the four-stanza poem relate specifically to the experiences Colón had in looking for a job in New York?

2. How does the narrator Colón differ from the Colón described in the essay?

3. How does the stove, introduced in paragraph 3, figure later in the essay?

*4. Characterize the attitude and behavior of all those Colón encountered in his search for employment in New York.

5. What case might be made that Colón, in the end, was following the advice of the poem, especially as expressed in the last lines of the third stanza?

*6. In what ways might the "goals" of a life's endeavor, as expressed in the last two lines of the poem, be considered worthy or unworthy? Discuss.

Writing Topics

1. "I clung to my poem as to a faith. Like a potent amulet, my precious poem was clenched in the fist of my right hand inside my second-hand overcoat." Is it possible that Colón depended too much on the poem? In a brief essay, set forth your answer to this question.

2. At the end of the essay, Colón describes how he burned his "precious" poem in order "to warm [his] numb body." Is it possible that Colón destroyed the thing he held dearest for reasons beyond simply trying to keep warm? In an essay, explore the possible symbolism in this act.

I unhooked the poem from the wall. I reflected for a minute, a minute tl
like an eternity. I took the frame apart, placing the square glass upon th‹
table. I tore the gold paper on which the poem was printed, threw its
inside the stove and, placing the small bits of wood from the frame on top
paper, I lit it, adding soft and hard coal as the fire began to gain strengt
brightness.

20   I watched how the lines of the poem withered into ashes inside the :
stove.

❧

Discussion Questions

"If—," by the British poet Rudyard Kipling (1865–1936), was once so popu
that in 1961 Colón could write his essay confident that his readers wou
know the poem. Here is the entire poem:

> If you can keep your head when all about you
>   Are losing theirs and blaming it on you,
> If you can trust yourself when all men doubt you,
>   But make allowance for their doubting too;
> If you can wait and not be tired by waiting,
>   Or being lied about, don't deal in lies,
> Or being hated don't give way to hating,
>   And yet don't look too good, not talk too wise:
>
> If you can dream—and not make dreams your master;
>   If you can think—and not make thoughts your aim,
> If you can meet with Triumph and Disaster
>   And treat those two impostors just the same;
> If you can bear to hear the truth you've spoken
>   Twisted by knaves to make a trap for fools,
> Or watch the things you gave your life to, broken,
>   And stoop and build 'em up with worn-out tools:
>
> If you can make one heap of all your winnings;
>   And risk it on one turn of pitch-and-toss,
> And lose, and start again at your beginnings
>   And never breathe a word about your loss;
> If you can force your heart and nerve and sinew
>   To serve your turn long after they are gone
> And so hold on when there is nothing in you
>   Except the Will which says to them: "Hold on!"

❧"Our country was built on, and remains glued by, the idea that everybody deserves a fair shot and that we must work together to guarantee that opportunity — the original American Dream."

A CHINAMAN'S CHANCE:
REFLECTIONS ON THE AMERICAN DREAM

Eric Liu

Eric Liu's "A Chinaman's Chance" is taken from *Next: Young American Writers on the New Generation* (1994), a volume he edited. Included in the volume is a brief biographical sketch that, as editor, he probably wrote: "Eric Liu, twenty-five, is the founder and editor of *The Next Progressive*, a journal of opinion produced by writers in their twenties. He has served as a legislative aide to U.S. Senator David Boren and as a speechwriter for Secretary of State Warren Christopher and for President Clinton." Liu, the son of Chinese immigrant parents, was born in 1968, in Poughkeepsie, New York. He tells of his father "painting the yellow line down a South Dakota interstate" and of his mother "filing pay stubs for a New York restaurant." By seizing every opportunity, he relates, his parents were able to provide him a "breadth of resources"—"arts, travel, and an Ivy League education." Liu went to Yale University (graduating in 1990), and, during the summers, he enrolled in the Marine Corps Officer Candidates' School at Quantico, Virginia. Although he finished the course successfully, he turned down the commission offered him because it would have required four years of active duty. He instead wanted to spend those four years moving ahead with his busy life, not the least part of which was the creating and editing of *The Next Progressive*. He is enrolled now in the Harvard Law School, class of 1998, and is working on a new book "on Asian Americans and the Politics of Race."

1   A lot of people my age seem to think that the American Dream is dead. I think they're dead wrong.

2   Or at least only partly right. It is true that for those of us in our twenties and early thirties, job opportunities are scarce. There looms a real threat that we will be the first American generation to have a lower standard of living than our parents.

3   But what is it that we mean when we invoke the American Dream?

4   In the past, the American Dream was something that held people of all races, religions, and identities together. As James Comer has written, it represented a shared aspiration among all Americans—black, white, or any other color—"to provide well for themselves and their families as valued members of a democratic society." Now, all too often, it seems the American Dream means merely some guarantee of affluence, a birthright of wealth.

5   At a basic level, of course, the American Dream is about prosperity and the pursuit of material happiness. But to me, its meaning extends beyond such concerns. To me, the dream is not just about buying a bigger house than the one I grew up in or having shinier stuff now than I had as a kid. It also represents a sense of opportunity that binds generations together in commitment, so that the young inherit not only property but also perseverance, not only money but also a mission to make good on the strivings of their parents and grandparents.

6   The poet Robert Browning once wrote that "a man's reach must exceed his grasp—else what's a heaven for?" So it is in America. Every generation will strive, and often fail. Every generation will reach for success, and often miss the mark. But Americans rely as much on the next generation as on the next life to prove that such struggles and frustrations are not in vain. There may be temporary setbacks, cutbacks, recessions, depressions. But this is a nation of second chances. So long as there are young Americans who do not take what they have—or what they can do—for granted, progress is always possible.

7   My conception of the American Dream does not take progress for granted. But it does demand the *opportunity* to achieve progress—and values the opportunity as much as the achievement. I come at this question as the son of immigrants. I see just as clearly as anyone else the cracks in the idealist vision of fulfillment for all. But because my parents came here with virtually nothing, because they did build something, I see the enormous potential inherent in the ideal.

8   I happen still to believe in our national creed: freedom and opportunity, and our common responsibility to uphold them. This creed is what makes America unique. More than any demographic statistic or economic indicator, it animates the American Dream. It infuses our mundane struggles—to plan a career, do good work, get ahead—with purpose and possibility. It makes America the only country that could produce heroes like Colin Powell—heroes who rise from nothing, who overcome the odds.

9   I think of the sacrifices made by my own parents. I appreciate the hardship of the long road traveled by my father—one of whose first jobs in America was painting the yellow line down a South Dakota interstate—and by my mother— whose first job here was filing pay stubs for a New York restaurant. From such beginnings, they were able to build a comfortable life and provide me with a breadth of resources—through arts, travel, and an Ivy League education. It was an unspoken obligation for them to do so.

10   I think of my boss in my first job after college, on Capitol Hill. George is a smart, feisty, cigar-chomping, take-no-shit Greek-American. He is about fifteen years older than I, has different interests, a very different personality. But like me, he is the son of immigrants, and he would joke with me that the Greek-Chinese mafia was going to take over one day. He was only half joking. We'd worked harder, our parents doubly harder, than almost anyone else we knew. To people like George, talk of the withering of the American Dream seems foreign.

11   It's undeniable that principles like freedom and opportunity, no matter how dearly held, are not enough. They can inspire a multiracial March on Washington, but they can not bring black salaries in alignment with white salaries. They can draw wave after wave of immigrants here, but they can not provide them the means to get out of our ghettos and barrios and Chinatowns. They are not sufficient for fulfillment of the American Dream.

12   But they are necessary. They are vital. And not just to the children of immigrants. These ideals form the durable thread that weaves us all in union. Put another way, they are one of the few things that keep America from disintegrating into a loose confederation of zip codes and walled-in communities.

13   What alarms me is how many people my age look at our nation's ideals with a rising sense of irony. What good is such a creed if you are working for hourly wages in a dead-end job? What value do such platitudes have if you live in an urban war zone? When the only apparent link between homeboys and housepainters and bike messengers and investment bankers is pop culture— MTV, the NBA, movies, dance music—then the social fabric is flimsy indeed.

14   My generation has come of age at a time when the country is fighting off bouts of defeatism and self-doubt, at a time when racism and social inequities seem not only persistent but intractable. At a time like this, the retreat to one's own kind is seen by more and more of my peers as an advance. And that retreat has given rise again to the notion that there are essential and irreconcilable differences among the races—a notion that was supposed to have disappeared from American discourse by the time my peers and I were born in the sixties.

15   Not long ago, for instance, my sister called me a "banana."

16   I was needling her about her passion for rap and hip-hop music. Every time I saw her, it seemed, she was jumping and twisting to Arrested Development or Chubb Rock or some other funky group. She joked that despite being the daughter of Chinese immigrants, she was indeed "black at heart." And then

she added, lightheartedly, "You, on the other hand—well, you're basically a banana." Yellow on the outside, but white inside.

17   I protested, denied her charge vehemently. But it was too late. She was back to dancing. And I stood accused.

18   Ever since then, I have wondered what it means to be black, or white, or Asian "at heart"—particularly for my generation. Growing up, when other kids would ask whether I was Chinese or Korean or Japanese, I would reply, a little petulantly, "American." Assimilation can still be a sensitive subject. I recall reading about a Korean-born Congressman who had gone out of his way to say that Asian-Americans should expect nothing special from him. He added that he was taking speech lessons "to get rid of this accent." I winced at his palpable self-hate. But then it hit me: Is this how my sister sees me?

19   There is no doubt that minorities like me can draw strength from our communities. But in today's environment, anything other than ostentatious tribal fealty is taken in some communities as a sign of moral weakness, a disappointing dilution of character. In times that demand ever-clearer thinking, it has become too easy for people to shut off their brains: "It's a black/Asian/Latino/ white thing," says the variable T-shirt. "You wouldn't understand." Increasingly, we don't.

20   The civil-rights triumphs of the sixties and the cultural revolutions that followed made it possible for minorities to celebrate our diverse heritages. I can appreciate that. But I know, too, that the sixties—or at least, my generation's grainy, hazy vision of the decade—also bequeathed to young Americans a legacy of near-pathological race consciousness.

21   Today's culture of entitlement—and of race entitlement in particular—tells us plenty about what we get if we are black or white or female or male or old or young.

22   It is silent, though, on some other important issues. For instance: What do we "get" for being American? And just as importantly, What do we owe? These are questions around which young people like myself must tread carefully, since talk of common interests, civic culture, responsibility, and integration sounds a little too "white" for some people. To the new segregationists, the "American Dream" is like the old myth of the "Melting Pot": an oppressive fiction, an opiate for the unhappy colored masses.

23   How have we allowed our thinking about race to become so twisted? The formal obstacles and the hateful opposition to civil rights have long faded into memory. By most external measures, life for minorities is better than it was a quarter century ago. It would seem that the opportunities for tolerance and cooperation are commonplace. Why, then, are so many of my peers so cynical about our ability to get along with one another?

24   The reasons are frustratingly ambiguous. I got a glimpse of this when I was in college. It was late in my junior year, and as the editor of a campus magazine, I was sitting on a panel to discuss "The White Press at Yale: What Is to Be

Done?" The assembly hall was packed, a diverse and noisy crowd. The air was heavy, nervously electric.

25   Why weren't there more stories about "minority issues" in the Yale *Daily News?* Why weren't there more stories on Africa in my magazine, the foreign affairs journal? How many "editors of color" served on the boards of each of the major publications? The questions were volleyed like artillery, one round after another, punctuated only by the applause of an audience spoiling for a fight. The questions were not at all unfair. But it seemed that no one—not even those of us on the panel who *were* people of color—could provide, in this context, satisfactory answers.

26   Toward the end of the discussion, I made a brief appeal for reason and moderation. And afterward, as students milled around restlessly, I was attacked: for my narrow-mindedness—How dare you suggest that Yale is not a fundamentally prejudiced place!—for my simplemindedness—Have you, too, been co-opted?

27   And for my betrayal—Are you just white inside?

28   My eyes were opened that uncomfortably warm early summer evening. Not only to the cynical posturing and the combustible opportunism of campus racial politics. But more importantly, to the larger question of identity—my identity—in America. Never mind that the aim of many of the loudest critics was to generate headlines in the very publications they denounced. In spite of themselves—against, it would seem, their true intentions—they got me to think about who I am.

29   In our society today, and especially among people of my generation, we are congealing into clots of narrow commonality. We stick with racial and religious comrades. This tribal consciousness-raising can be empowering for some. But while America was conceived in liberty—the liberty, for instance, to associate with whomever we like—it was never designed to be a mere collection of subcultures. We forget that there is in fact such a thing as a unique American identity that transcends our sundry tribes, sets, gangs, and cliques.

30   I have grappled, wittingly or not, with these questions of identity and allegiance all my life. When I was in my early teens, I would invite my buddies overnight to watch movies, play video games, and beat one another up. Before too long, my dad would come downstairs and start hamming it up—telling stories, asking gently nosy questions, making corny jokes, all with his distinct Chinese accent. I would stand back, quietly gauging everyone's reaction. Of course, the guys loved it. But I would feel uneasy.

31   What was then cause for discomfort is now a source of strength. Looking back on such episodes, I take pride in my father's accented English; I feel awe at his courage to laugh loudly in a language not really his own.

32   It was around the same time that I decided that continued attendance at the community Chinese school on Sundays was uncool. There was no fanfare; I simply stopped going. As a child, I'd been too blissfully unaware to think of

Chinese school as anything more than a weekly chore, with an annual festival (dumplings and spring rolls, games and prizes). But by the time I was a peer-pressured adolescent, Chinese school seemed like a badge of the woefully un-assimilated. I turned my back on it.

33   Even as I write these words now, it feels as though I am revealing a long-held secret. I am proud that my ancestors—scholars, soldiers, farmers—came from one of the world's great civilizations. I am proud that my grandfather served in the Chinese Air Force. I am proud to speak even my clumsy brand of Mandarin, and I feel blessed to be able to think idiomatically in Chinese, a language so much richer in nuance and subtle poetry than English.

34   Belatedly, I appreciate the good fortune I've had to be the son of immigrants. As a kid, I could play Thomas Jefferson in the bicentennial school play one week and the next week play the poet Li Bai at the Chinese school festival. I could come home from an afternoon of teen slang at the mall and sit down to dinner for a rollicking conversation in our family's hybrid of Chinese and English. I understood, when I went over to visit friends, that my life was different. At the time, I just never fully appreciated how rich it was.

35   Yet I know that this pride in my heritage does not cross into prejudice against others. What it reflects is pride in what my country represents. That became clear to me when I went through Marine Corps Officer Candidates' School. During the summers after my sophomore and junior years of college, I volunteered for OCS, a grueling boot camp for potential officers in the swamps and foothills of Quantico, Virginia.

36   And once I arrived—standing 5'4", 135 pounds, bespectacled, a Chinese Ivy League Democrat—I was a target straight out of central casting. The wiry, raspy-voiced drill sergeant, though he was perhaps only an inch or two taller than I, called me "Little One" with as much venom as can be squeezed into such a moniker. He heaped verbal abuse on me, he laughed when I stumbled, he screamed when I hesitated. But he also never failed to remind me that just because I was a little shit didn't mean I shouldn't run farther, climb higher, think faster, hit harder than anyone else.

37   That was the funny thing about the Marine Corps. It is, ostensibly, one of the most conservative institutions in the United States. And yet, for those twelve weeks, it represented the kind of color-blind equality of opportunity that the rest of society struggles to match. I did not feel uncomfortable at OCS to be of Chinese descent. Indeed, I drew strength from it. My platoon was a veritable cross section of America: forty young men of all backgrounds, all regions, all races, all levels of intelligence and ability, displaced from our lives (if only for a few weeks) with nowhere else to go.

38   Going down the list of names—Courtemanche, Dougherty, Grella, Hunt, Liu, Reeves, Schwarzman, and so on—brought to mind a line from a World War II documentary I once saw, which went something like this: The reason why it seemed during the war that America was as good as the rest of the world put together was that America *was* the rest of the world put together.

39   Ultimately, I decided that the Marines was not what I wanted to do for four years and I did not accept the second lieutenant's commission. But I will never forget the day of the graduation parade: bright sunshine, brisk winds, the band playing Sousa as my company passed in review. As my mom and dad watched and photographed the parade from the rafters, I thought to myself: this is the American Dream in all its cheesy earnestness. I felt the thrill of truly being part of something larger and greater than myself.

40   I do know that American life is not all Sousa marches and flag-waving. I know that those with reactionary agendas often find it convenient to cloak their motives in the language of Americanism. The "American Party" was the name of a major nativist organization in the nineteenth century. "America First" is the siren song of the isolationists who would withdraw this country from the world and expel the world from this country. I know that our national immigration laws were once designed explicitly to cut off the influx from Asia.

41   I also know that discrimination is real. I am reminded of a gentle old man who, after Pearl Harbor, was stripped of his possessions without warning, taken from his home, and thrown into a Japanese internment camp. He survived, and by many measures has thrived, serving as a community leader and political activist. But I am reluctant to share with him my wide-eyed patriotism.

42   I know the bittersweet irony that my own father — a strong and optimistic man — would sometimes feel when he was alive. When he came across a comically lost cause — if the Yankees were behind 14-0 in the ninth, or if Dukakis was down ten points in the polls with a week left — he would often joke that the doomed party had "a Chinaman's chance" of success. It was one of those insensitive idioms of a generation ago, and it must have lodged in his impressionable young mind when he first came to America. It spoke of a perceived stacked deck.

43   I know, too, that for many other immigrants, the dream simply does not work out. Fae Myenne Ng, the author of *Bone*, writes about how her father ventured here from China under a false identity and arrived at Angel Island, the detention center outside the "Gold Mountain" of San Francisco. He got out, he labored, he struggled, and he suffered "a bitter no-luck life" in America. There was no glory. For him, Ng suggests, the journey was not worth it.

44   But it is precisely because I know these things that I want to prove that in the long run, over generations and across ethnicities, it *is* worth it. For the second-generation American, opportunity is obligation. I have seen and faced racism. I understand the dull pain of dreams deferred or unmet. But I believe still that there is so little stopping me from building the life that I want. I was given, through my parents' labors, the chance to bridge that gap between ideals and reality. Who am I to throw away that chance?

45   Plainly, I am subject to the criticism that I speak too much from my own experience. Not everyone can relate to the second-generation American story. When I have spoken like this with some friends, the issue has been my perspective. *What you say is fine for you. But unless you grew up where I did, unless you've had people avoid you because of the color of your skin, don't talk to me about common dreams.*

46 But are we then to be paralyzed? Is respect for different experiences supposed to obviate the possibility of shared aspirations? Does the diversity of life in America doom us to a fractured understanding of one another? The question is basic: Should the failure of this nation thus far to fulfill its stated ideals incapacitate its young people, or motivate us?

47 Our country was built on, and remains glued by, the idea that everybody deserves a fair shot and that we must work together to guarantee that opportunity—the original American Dream. It was this idea, in some inchoate form, that drew every immigrant here. It was this idea, however sullied by slavery and racism, that motivated the civil-rights movement. To write this idea off—even when its execution is spotty—to let American life descend into squabbles among separatist tribes would not just be sad. It would be a total mishandling of a legacy, the squandering of a great historical inheritance.

48 Mine must not be the first generation of Americans to lose America. Just as so many of our parents journeyed here to find their version of the American Dream, so must young Americans today journey across boundaries of race and class to rediscover one another. We are the first American generation to be born into an integrated society, and we are accustomed to more race mixing than any generation before us. We started open-minded, and it's not too late for us to stay that way.

49 Time is of the essence. For in our national political culture today, the watchwords seem to be *decline* and *end*. Apocalyptic visions and dark millennial predictions abound. The end of history. The end of progress. The end of equality. Even something as ostensibly positive as the end of the Cold War has a bittersweet tinge, because for the life of us, no one in America can get a handle on the big question, "What Next?"

50 For my generation, this fixation on endings is particularly enervating. One's twenties are supposed to be a time of widening horizons, of bright possibilities. Instead, America seems to have entered an era of limits. Whether it is the difficulty of finding jobs from some place other than a temp agency, or the mountains of debt that darken our future, the message to my peers is often that this nation's time has come and gone; let's bow out with grace and dignity.

51 A friend once observed that while the Chinese seek to adapt to nature and yield to circumstance, Americans seek to conquer both. She meant that as a criticism of America. But I interpreted her remark differently. I *do* believe that America is exceptional. And I believe it is up to my generation to revive that spirit, that sense that we do in fact have control over our own destiny—as individuals and as a nation.

52 If we are to reclaim a common destiny, we must also reach out to other generations for help. It was Franklin Roosevelt who said that while America can't always build the future for its youth, it can—and must—build its youth for the future. That commitment across generations is as central to the American

Dream as any I have enunciated. We are linked, black and white, old and young, one and inseparable.

53   I know how my words sound. I am old enough to perceive my own naïveté but young enough still to cherish it. I realize that I am coming of age just as the American Dream is showing its age. Yet I still have faith in this country's unique destiny—to create generation after generation of hyphenates like me, to channel this new blood, this resilience and energy into an ever more vibrant future for *all* Americans.

54   And I want to prove—for my sake, for my father's sake, and for my country's sake—that a Chinaman's chance is as good as anyone else's.

❧

Discussion Questions

  1. What is "a Chinaman's chance"? In what way did Liu's father use the term, and to what effect does Liu introduce the term in the title and text of his essay?

*2. In the opening paragraphs, but especially in paragraphs 5–8, Liu explores various views of the American Dream in order to highlight, by contrast, his view of the American Dream. Analyze the opening of the essay, and particularly these paragraphs, pointing out his view of the American Dream as compared with other views introduced directly or implicitly.

  3. In paragraph 11, Liu writes, "It's undeniable that principles like freedom and opportunity, no matter how dearly held, are not enough." Why, according to Liu, are they not enough? What part do they play, then, in the American Dream?

  4. Liu's sister claims to be "black at heart" and calls him a "banana"—"yellow on the outside, but white inside." How does Liu use this incident for his own purposes in refining his definition of the American Dream?

*5. In paragraph 30, Liu describes his father's presence when he had his "buddies overnight to watch movies." Explain his comment in paragraph 31, "I take pride in my father's accented English."

*6. Liu begins the account (paragraphs 35–39) of his experience at the Marine boot camp for potential officers by describing the drill sergeant's calling him the "Little One" and heaping "as much venom" on him as could "be squeezed into such a moniker." Yet, he concludes of this experience, "those twelve weeks . . . represented the kind of color-blind equality of opportunity that the rest of society struggles to match." Explain.

Writing Topics

1. In paragraph 29, Liu writes, "We forget that there is in fact such a thing as a unique American identity that transcends our sundry tribes, sets, gangs, and cliques." In an essay, analyze the comment in context to get at its full meaning, and then show why you agree or disagree with the statement.
2. Write an essay in which you agree or disagree with Liu's belief in the American Dream, drawing on your own experience throughout your life and the experiences of your parents and/or grandparents.

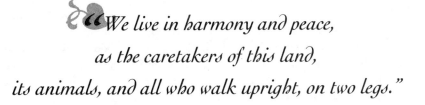

We live in harmony and peace,
as the caretakers of this land,
its animals, and all who walk upright, on two legs."

PAUM-MAN-AKE

Elaine Johnson

Elaine Johnson was born in 1930 in Brooklyn, New York. Her mother was a descendant of the Shinnecock tribe, whose ancestors were settled on Paumanok (Paum-man-ake), or Long Island, at the time of the arrival there in 1609 of the English led by Henry Hudson. She identifies as African her "other ancestor" (evidently through her mother) who had long ago intermarried with the Indians. There is no mention in her account of growing up of the presence of a father. In her early education, her classmates made her the butt of racist jokes, sometimes accompanied by violence. Johnson was devastated by their hostility. After the early death of her husband, Johnson was offered the opportunity to go to college on a fellowship when she was in her fifties. She decided to accept the offer, primarily because it presented an opportunity to "research and validate [her] ancestry." The result is contained in "Paum-man-ake," reprinted from *Legacies: Stories of Courage, Humor and Resilience, of Love, Loss, and Life-Changing Encounters,* by *New Writers Sixty and Older* (1993), edited by Maury Leibovitz and Linda Solomon. Johnson, having established close ties with her ancestral relatives, continues to live in Brooklyn.

1   In the year of the great snow, around 1609, Henry Hudson, an Englishman, dropped anchor off the shores of Paum-man-ake. That is the Delaware Indian name for "land that is long"; we know it today as Long Island. Along these eastern shores the Algonquian language was spoken, as far north as the cold land of the Onondaga, the Mohawk, and the Seneca. I know, for we greet each other as cousins. The crew of the ship, *Half Moon,* was met by either the Rockaway or Canarsie Indians, in canoes called mushee. The Indians were friendly, staring in awe at the sight of men with blue eyes (like a clear summer day), blond hair (with the sun caught in it), and white skin. You see, in their custom of painting

themselves for war, white meant peace, so they did not fear these strange-looking men. The whites landed at a place known today as Coney Island, in the village of Broken Land, now called Brooklyn, my birthplace.

2   I was a shy, lonely, only child who loved to read books. The stories my mother told me became a reality as I grew older, but the kids at school made fun of me whenever I repeated the Indian myths, legends, and ghost stories. They called me "Shittycock" instead of Shinnecock; they said, "Gee, you don't look like Tonto," or "Hey, Elaine, where are your feathers and your bow and arrows?" I was the butt of so many jokes, tricks, and nasty remarks that I shut up and stayed to myself. But one nut kept it up. He had a good time putting my braids in the inkwell, or throwing my dress up over my head, or stealing my pennies.

3   As a child I couldn't understand why I got beat up at school and beat up again when I got home. One time I ran away, but when it got dark I had cried myself out, and I was hungry and cold. I went home, and to my surprise I was greeted with open arms. "Oh, baby, Lainee-bunch, where were you?" I thought all kinds of things. We both cried, but we talked to each other, and thus began my first fighting lesson. "I'm going to teach you to hit first and ask questions later," my mother said. "I'm not going to be with you always, and you have no sisters or brothers."

4   The next day I waited for the nut to swagger into the classroom and hit him with all my might. His big mouth was swollen, his lips and eyes were black-and-blue. I jumped on his back and was pounding his head on the floor when the teachers finally got me off him. He went home crying, with a sore head along with his bruises. What could the principal do? They all knew how he had been tormenting me. I know one thing: after that he walked around me, no more did he call me names.

5   As time went on, I kept wondering about the truth of the oral history repeated to me by my mother. My husband died young, and in my fifties I was granted a scholarship to college. I was scared about going to school with kids young enough to be my grandchildren, but something said, "Go ahead and try it. You can always back out if it gets too hard." A whole new world opened up to me, and I was able to research and validate my ancestry.

6   I know there were thirteen tribes on Long Island. The Shinnecock descendants still live there, along the shores of Peconic and Shinnecock bays, and in the hills that still bear their name. The great chief Nowendonah took his braves to help the Americans transport a ship from one shore to another, since the British were coming. They carried the ship on their strong shoulders and backs, as was their custom, walking and swimming the bright waters. All were lost, leaving a village full of grieving women. When winter came the other tribes stole the fat, plump squaws to their lodges, as their bodies produced heat and shelter from the bitter-cold nights, but in the summer months they enticed the maidens away from their mothers. At the Battle of Long Island, on August 27,

1776, the warriors served as scouts and guides under the American general George Washington, marching to the northern parts of the state, using old Indian trails as shortcuts. Again the women were left alone, so they worked on the farms of the wannux (white men) and taught their children. The last known full-breed on record was Rebecca Kellis, "Aunt Becky," who lived and taught on the reservation for a hundred years. If you've seen the motion picture *The Amityville Horror*, it's the Shinnecocks who haunt that house; there are forgotten graves all over these sacred lands.

7   On dark nights, before the campfires, many ghost stories, deeds of bravery, and legends are told by the senior citizens. At their center traditional beadwork, needlepoint, sewing, music, and the ancient dances are performed. At sixty-three I join them to reminisce over tales told over and over again, then add my own to theirs. The English did not visit our village until 1640. We went to their churches, and until this day they come to our annual powwow, where we give thanks to God for a good harvest. We are the largest remaining confederacy of Long Island. We live in harmony and peace, as the caretakers of this land, its animals, and all who walk upright, on two legs. Wanitonka, the creator, planned it so. I am now a weena (old lady) and I grow tired, but I must repeat these words spoken by the ancestors and the great war chiefs Wyandanch, Poggattecut, Culluloo, Telewana, and Occom:

> *For as long as the grass grows green*
> *and the rivers flow.*
> *This the land of the indian!*
> *Forever this will be so.*

8   I know nothing of my other ancestor, the African. I'm just glad he found the Indians in the woods of Paum-man-ake and that those caretakers fed him, clothed him, and taught him the Indian way of surviving in this sometimes harsh land. They intermarried and stayed with the tribe, and became peaceful warriors and chiefs.

❧

Discussion Questions

1.   What are the rhetorical advantages or disadvantages of Johnson's beginning her essay with a paragraph-long historical sketch?

2.   What purpose is served by Johnson's describing some vividly re-membered episodes from her childhood? In your experience, is the behavior of Johnson's classmates normal or unusual? Explain.

3.   What is the meaning of the words inherited by the author from the great war chiefs: "For as long as the grass grows green / and the rivers flow. / This the land of the indian! / Forever this will be so"?

*4. What in the end do we find out about the author's "other ancestor"? What is the effect of the conclusion?

Writing Topics

1. Conduct interviews with your parents, grandparents, or other relatives to find out as much as you can about your origins, especially about how you have come to be an American. Write an account of your "ancestral line," including whatever varieties you find in race, ethnicity, wealth or poverty, fame or notoriety.

2. Consider whether Johnson, in searching out and identifying so closely with her ethnic group, lived up to or violated the principle set forth by Liu in "A Chinaman's Chance": ". . . there is in fact such a thing as a unique American identity that transcends sundry tribes, sets, gangs, and cliques" (paragraph 29). Write an essay stating and defending your view.

*For better or worse,
America is going to look more and
more like me in the next century — that is to say,
individuals are going to be walking embodiments
of the melting pot."*

MIXED LIKE ME

David Bernstein

David Bernstein was born in Washington, D.C., in 1967, to a black mother and a Jewish father. In 1970, his father, who operated a furniture-rental store, was transferred to the "redneck mill town" of Reading, Pennsylvania. In the period during which the family lived there (1970–1977), Bernstein was enrolled in private schools and attended Hebrew school in the afternoons. Upon the family's return to Washington, Bernstein again attended a private school in Georgetown. His first year of college he attended Allegheny College in Meadville, Pennsylvania, which he disliked intensely, transferring after his freshman year to the University of Maryland, which was more to his liking and nearer to his home. He was elected president of the campus College Republicans. After graduation, his interest in racial politics led to his founding and editing a magazine that "looks at race relations in America from the perspective of young people." His biographical note in *Next* reads: "David Bernstein, twenty-six, is the founding editor of *Diversity & Division* magazine. He lives in Washington, D.C."

1 I am a twenty-six-year-old man, half black and half Jewish, who founded and edits a conservative magazine that deals with race relations and culture. Such a statement would have been extraordinary thirty years ago; today we treat it with mild interest and move along. No one would argue that my life has been typical—typical of the "black experience," of the "Jewish experience," or of any other dubious paradigm associated with a particular race or ethnicity. I have not overcome racism or poverty, and people become visibly disappointed

when I tell them that my mixed background has not been a cause of distress, or any other difficulty for that matter.

2 However, my story may be of some interest. For better or worse, America is going to look more and more like me in the next century—that is to say, individuals are going to be walking embodiments of the melting pot. The argument over whether America is more like cheese dip or the multiculturalist "tossed salad" (Are you getting hungry yet?) will be made moot by the increasing incidence of mixed marriage and of the growing class of mutts like me who have more ethnicities than the former Yugoslavia.

3 My parents married in 1965, in Washington, D.C. If they had lived then in the comfortable suburb where they now reside, they would have been breaking the law—miscegenation, as marriage between blacks and whites was known in those days, was still illegal in Maryland. My mother was a native Washingtonian who, until her teen years, felt sorry for the few white people who lived near her, her mother, and two siblings; she thought they were albinos. Her parents—both of whom had moved from the country to Washington when they were teenagers—were separated when my mother was just a toddler. She was raised, along with an older sister and brother, in a small brownstone apartment in downtown D.C. Her brother, the oldest child, went off to fight in the Korean War, one of the first black airmen to participate in the integrated armed forces. While in Korea, he fell in love with and married a Korean girl. Meanwhile, my mother attended segregated public schools until senior high school, when she was in the first class that integrated Eastern Senior High School in the wake of the Supreme Court's *Brown* decision. After graduation, she opted not to attend college, because she didn't know what she wanted to do—and "didn't want to waste" my grandmother's money.

4 My father grew up in North Philadelphia, one of those old working-class neighborhoods where there were Jewish blocks, Italian blocks, Irish blocks, and so on. His parents were second-generation Americans: Grandpa Bernstein's family was from Poland; my grandmother's family from Leeds, England. (I understand the Blasky family still lives there, apparently running a successful wallpaper-hanging business.) My grandfather and my father's two brothers fought in World War II; my father, who was too young to go, became a paratrooper soon after the war ended. After leaving the Army in the early 1950s, he moved to Washington, where he and my mother eventually ended up working at the same furniture-rental place.

5 Despite the rich possibilities for mischief making presented by their union, my parents did not marry to make a political statement. While their contemporaries marched for civil rights and held sit-ins, they hung out with a mixed-race group of cool cats at various jazz nightclubs in downtown D.C. Most of these establishments were burned to the ground after Martin Luther King's assassination in 1968, bringing to an end that unique era of naive integration. Since those riots, race relations in this country have been tinged with guilt, fear, and lies.

6   In 1970, my father's company transferred him to the redneck mill town of Reading, Pennsylvania. My mother hated it; my father tolerated it; and I went about the business of growing up. I went to a mostly white private school and Monday afternoons attended Hebrew school with the children of Reading's prosperous and assimilated Jewish community. My Cub Scout group and summer camp were at the local Jewish community center, which had been bombed recently by Reading's prominent community of neo-Nazis.

7   It was also at the center that I was first called a "nigger." My mother had been preparing me my entire life for that to happen, but when it did, I was hardly bothered at all. I actually felt sorry for the kid who shouted it at me during a softball game; he genuinely felt bad afterward and apologized about six times. (Even though it's out of sequence in our little narrative, I should recount the only other time I have been called a "nigger." A couple of years ago, I was riding on D.C.'s Metro with two white liberal friends when a white homeless person approached me and stated, "You niggers get all the jobs." My friends were horrified and silent. I laughed and told the bum that he was right; that was how it should be.)

8   We moved back to Washington in 1977. Again, I attended private school, this time at Georgetown Day School, a place founded in the 1940s as Washington's first integrated school. Despite the forty-year tradition, there were still not many blacks at GDS. The students were largely from well-to-do, secular Jewish families with traditions of liberal political activism. My family, though secular, was not well-to-do or politically active. My parents were somewhat liberal, but it was a liberalism of function rather than form; in other words, they might be considered budding neoconservatives. I inherited from my parents a healthy suspicion of conventional wisdom—which, in the case of my teachers and peers, was overwhelmingly on the left. By 1980, I was one of six kids in my junior-high class to vote for Ronald Reagan in our mock election.

9   My "political awakening" was just beginning. In high school I cowrote a piece in the school newspaper on what it meant to be conservative, an awfully crafted piece of literature that nearly caused a riot, despite its (by my standards today) extremely mushy conservatism. I started to realize that you could make liberals mad just by saying the "c" word. On election day 1984, I wore a jacket and tie to school to celebrate President Reagan's impending victory. One friend didn't talk to me for a week.

10   It never dawned on me that, as a "person of color," I ought to be "mortally" opposed to this Reagan guy. All I ever heard come out of his mouth just sounded like good sense to me. I heard over and over again on TV that the man was a racist and that he was bad for black people. But what stuck with me from all this was that the people who repeated this charge were buffoons. Early on, the idea of race was not central to my view of politics. This would change rather sharply later on.

11   My freshman year in college was spent at Allegheny College in lovely Meadville, Pennsylvania. Within weeks, it was apparent to me and several of my friends there that the school was lousy. A group of us dedicated our lives to the idea of transferring out of that freezing mud hole of a campus. In one of our brainstorming sessions on how to make our transfer applications look beefier, we locked onto the idea of starting a "Conservative Club," which would be a forum for discussing ideas on the right. It sounded like fun, and more importantly, we would all be made vice presidents of the club, an ideal way to bolster our extracurricular résumés.

12   Once again, just using the word *conservative* nearly brought the campus down around our ears. Two of the conspirators in our résumé-building scheme went before the student government in order to get the necessary recognition, supposedly just a formality. Forty-five minutes later, after shrieks of outrage from the so-called student leaders of this $13,000-a-year institution of higher learning, we were told that the student government was afraid to get involved in "neo-Nazi" groups and that we should come back in a month with a detailed statement of just what we stood for. Only one member of the SG stood up for us—a young woman who pointed out that on a campus with absolutely no political activity, people who showed some initiative to do something, anything, ought to be encouraged.

13   But this was a college where political discourse was typified by this statement from the school's chaplain: "We should divest from South Africa. Harvard and Princeton already have, and if we want to be as good as them, we must do so as well." In this kind of environment, which is now typical at liberal-arts colleges around the country, it should have come as no surprise that conservatism was associated with evil. It wasn't the last time that the supposed characteristics of conservatives like me—that we were narrow-minded, ignorant, and shrill— were to be embodied better by our critics.

14   I did finally escape from Allegheny College, going back home to the University of Maryland. At UM, I decided to make politics a full-time vocation. I worked in Washington afternoons and evenings at various political jobs, first at the Republican National Committee and later at a small, conservative non-profit foundation. In between, I took a semester off to work for Senator Bob Dole's ill-fated presidential campaign. Returning to Maryland, I was soon elected president of the campus College Republicans, a position that occasionally put me at the center of campus political attention.

15   This was not because I was a vocal, articulate (some would say loud-mouthed) conservative but because I was a *black* conservative. Conservatives are a dime a dozen, smart ones are common, but a black one? "Nelly, wake the kids! They have to *see* this!"

16   Other conservatives loved having me around. After all, most of them were presumed to be Nazis from the get-go by the ultrasensitive P.C. crowd; having a black person say you're okay was temporary protection from the scholastic

inquisition. Further, as a black conservative, I was thought to have special insight into why more blacks didn't identify with the Republican party. Again and again, I was asked how conservatives could find more blacks (or African-Americans, if the petitioner wanted to be sensitive). After a while, I think I actually began to believe that, somehow, I had special understanding of the souls of black folk, and with increasing confidence I would sound off about the political and social proclivities of African-Americans.

17   In a perverted way, liberals and left-radicals liked having me around as well—because I helped justify their paranoia. I was living proof that imperialist, racist forces were at work, dividing black people and turning us against one another. How else, they theorized, could a black person so obviously sell out both his race and the "progressive" whites who were the only thing standing between him and a right-wing lynch mob? The ardor (and obvious pleasure) with which they alternatively ignored and condemned me demonstrated their belief that I was more than just the opposition: I was a traitor, a collaborator in my own oppression. Finally, one particularly vitriolic black militant suggested in the school newspaper that black conservatives ought to be "neutralized." I took it personally.

18   And I got fired up. There comes a time in every conservative activist's life when he gets the heady rush of realization at how much fun (and how easy) it is to annoy liberals. Indeed, it was something I had been doing for years. People on the left, with their self-righteousness, humorless orthodoxies, and ultra-sensitivity to their own and everyone else's "oppression" are only fun at parties if you get them pissed off. Naturally, then, it is something that conservatives spend a lot of time doing.

19   Rush Limbaugh, R. Emmett Tyrell, P. J. O'Rourke, hundreds of editors of conservative college newspapers like the *Dartmouth Review*, and thousands of College Republican activists turned the 1980s into one long laugh for conservatives at the expense of the P. C. crowd. The staleness of liberal beliefs, the inability of the campus activists to move beyond sloganeering to real thought, and the creation of a regime on campus by college professors and administrators that treats open discussion as anathema offered fertile ground for conservative humorists.

20   But it also allowed many conservatives to dismiss leftism as a political force, and they were unprepared when it was resurrected as such in the person of Bill Clinton—thus in 1992, it was the right that too often degenerated into empty sloganeering. The intellectual stagnation of liberalism contributed to the intellectual sloth of too many conservatives, concerned more with one-liners than actually formulating policy.

21   I was no exception. I slipped easily into the world of leftist haranguing. I was always good for a sound bite in the school newspaper, and as a unique case—a black Jewish conservative—I had opportunities to comment with some built-in authority on a range of issues. Controversy with the Black Student

Union? I would have a comment. Someone wants the university to divest from South Africa? I would be there with other conservatives holding a press conference presenting the other side. Controversy between Arab students and Jewish students? The College Republicans would uphold the Reagan tradition of unswerving support for Israel as long as I was in charge. Tensions rising between black and Jewish students? I was there to denounce genuine bigots brought to campus in the name of "black awareness" and "free speech" like Louis Farrakhan and Stokely Carmichael (this, of course, did not further endear me to the radical black students).

22   I tried not to lose sight of why I was doing this; that annoying liberals was just a means, not an end. But like every young right-winger, I'm sure that more than once I've annoyed just for annoyance's sake. There are worse sins, but this is the only one I'll admit to in print.

23   Since those heady college days, I have become a magazine editor. *Diversity & Division* looks at race relations in America from the perspective of young people, particularly of its black Jewish editor and white male managing editor. Do I still go after liberals? Yeah, sure. But the issues we talk about—those bearing on the future on how we are all going to get along—are not very funny. And the things that leftists advocate on these issues, from radical multiculturalism to quotas, promise to make it next to impossible for us to survive as a multicultural society.

24   There are two lessons, I think, that my little autobiography teaches. First is my comfort in moving between worlds of different cultures and colors. The conventional wisdom about us mixed-race types, that we are alienated, never feeling comfortable in either culture, is baloney. I am black. I am Jewish. I am equally comfortable with people who identify themselves as either one, or neither one. Why? Because to me the most defining characteristic of who I am is not my race, ethnicity, religious beliefs, political party, or Tupperware club membership. Rather, I see myself as an individual first, part of the larger "human family" with all the suballegiances reduced to ancillary concerns.

25   This is obviously a very romantic and idealistic notion. It is also, equally as obviously, the only ideology that will allow us to overcome prejudice and bigotry and enable everyone to get along. In me, the melting pot the idea has become the melting pot the reality, with (I must immodestly say) reasonably positive results. My commonality with other people is not in superficial appeals to ethnic solidarity—it is far more fundamental.

26   That is why I am sickened by people who continue to insist that we must all cling to our ancestors' "cultures" (however arbitrarily defined at that moment) in order to have self-awareness and self-esteem. The notion of "self" should not be wrapped up in externalities like "culture" or "race"—unless you want to recreate the United States as Yugoslavia, Somalia, or any other such place where people's tribal identities make up their whole selves. Indeed, true self-awareness stands opposed to grouping human beings along arbitrary lines like race,

gender, religion, weight, or preferred manner of reaching orgasm. Groupthink is primitive. It is not self-awareness; rather it is a refuge for those afraid of differences.

27   At the contemporary university, students are exhorted to "celebrate diversity" by people who practice just the opposite. There is nothing "diverse" about having racially segregated housing (black students at many colleges have their own dorms), tribalized curricula (Black Studies, Women's Studies, Gay Studies, etc.), or any of the numerous other pathological policies that enlightened administrators foist off on students in the name of tolerance.

28   What we ought to teach kids to celebrate is their individuality and their accomplishments, not to take phony pride in what their ancestors did. So what if a black man invented the traffic light? Do I really shine in his reflected glory? If so, then I really do have a self-esteem problem.

29   Those who preach about diversity believe that tolerance means not exulting one class of human being over another, by recognizing that every race and culture has made a contribution to modern civilization: a worthy goal, especially if this were true. But this way of thinking ignores a powerful truth, an obvious solution to the bigotry and suspicion that these sensitivity warriors say they are out to eliminate. The reality is that groups aren't equal; individuals are. If it is "self-evident that all men are created equal" isn't it even more self-evident that blacks and whites, men and women, Christians and Jews are created equal?

30   Granted, we haven't lived up to this absolute ideal. But we are beginning to see the implications of setting our aspirations below what we know to be the best. Here's the second lesson I think my story tells.

31   Despite my obvious distaste for the entire notion of group politics, I have become wrapped up in it. By editing a magazine that deals primarily with racial issues, I am not doing what I would most like to be doing. But I am doing what is expected. Under our phony system of racial harmony, college-educated blacks are expected to do something that is, well, black. Black academics are concentrated in Afro-American studies, sociology, and other "soft" fields where they can expound at length about the plight of the American Negro. Everyone, it seems, needs an expert on what it means to be black. Corporations need human-relations specialists to tell them about the "special needs" of black employees. Newspapers need "urban beat" reporters. Foundations, political parties, unions, and any other organizations you can name all need black liaisons to put them "in touch with the community." And, of course, conservatives need a magazine that reassures them that many of the ideas that they have about race relations are not evil and fascistic. These jobs are generally, somewhat lucrative, fairly easy to do, and carry just one job requirement—you have to be black.

32   No one is forced to follow this course; there should be no whining about that. But in life, as in physics, currents flow along the path of least resistance. As long as it is easy to make a living as a professional race man, the best and

brightest blacks will be siphoned off into this least-productive field in our service economy. The same is true, of course, of Hispanics, Asians, or whatever minority group is in vogue in a specific region or profession. Our educational system, our country's entire way of thinking about race, is creating a class of professionals whose entire raison d'être is to explore and explain—and thus perpetuate—the current regime. All the preaching of sensitivity, all the Afrocentric education, all the racial and ethnic solidarity in the world will not markedly improve race relations in America. Indeed, the smart money says that this obsession with our differences, however well-meaning, will make things much, much worse.

33   But this is a point that, blessedly, may well be rendered moot for the next generation. Intermarriage is the great equalizer; it brings people of different races together in a way that forced busing, sensitivity training, and affirmative action could never hope to—as individuals, on equal footing, united by common bonds of humanity. Four hundred years ago Shakespeare wrote of intermarriage:

> *Take her, fair son, and from her blood raise up*
> *Issue to me; that the contending kingdoms . . .*
> *May cease their hatred; and this dear conjunction*
> *Plant neighbourhood and Christian-like accord*
> *In their sweet bosoms . . .*

34   Eventually, if all goes well, America's melting pot will be a physical reality, bringing with it the kind of healing Shakespeare had in mind. Let's just hope we don't file for an ethnic divorce before then.

❧

Discussion Questions

1.   In paragraph 2, Bernstein writes, "The argument over whether America is more like cheese dip or the multiculturalist 'tossed salad' (are you getting hungry yet?) will be made moot by the increasing incidence of mixed marriage and of the growing class of mutts like me who have more ethnicities than the former Yugoslavia." Explore the meaning and the effect of this sentence, characterizing its style (witty or sober; light or heavy-handed). Find other sentences that would buttress your view of the essay's style.

*2.   What was the event that, according to Bernstein, brought about a distinct change in race relations in America, tingeing them with "guilt, fear, and lies"? Explain Bernstein's attitude, and why you agree or disagree with it.

3. Recount the two times the author was called "nigger" and characterize—or analyze—his responses.

4. What does Bernstein mean when he writes in paragraph 8, "My parents were somewhat liberal, but it was a liberalism of function rather than form; in other words, they might be considered budding neoconservatives"?

*5. In the last few pages of the essay (beginning with paragraph 24), Bernstein says that his "little autobiography" teaches two lessons. What is the first lesson, and what is your reaction to it?

6. The second lesson taught by Bernstein is summed up metaphorically in this sentence, "But in life, as in physics, currents flow along the path of least resistance." Apply the terms of this metaphor to the author's "second lesson."

Writing Topics

1. Bernstein writes in his last paragraph, "Eventually, if all goes well, America's melting pot will be a physical reality." Why does Bernstein continue to use a term—melting pot—that has been attacked as misleading by some, especially liberals? Write an essay arguing for or against Bernstein's use of this term and his view that "intermarriage," the "great equalizer," will bring about racial peace in the next generation or so.

2. In paragraph 24, Bernstein asserts that the most defining characteristic of who he is is not in his "race, ethnicity, religious beliefs, political party, or Tupperware club membership," but rather in himself as an individual—"part of the larger 'human family' with all the suballegiances reduced to ancillary concerns." Write an essay in which you agree or disagree with Bernstein's position, setting forth your own basic beliefs.

Summary Writing Topics

1. In the era of women's liberation, some people have called into question the courtesies men have been supposed traditionally to extend to women—opening doors for them, letting them enter or exit first, walking on the street-side of a sidewalk, rising when they enter a room, and so on. These and other courtesies are found in the slogan presumably followed on sinking ships: "Women and Children First." Write an essay describing your view on this subject: that such courtesies were never practiced except hypocritically; that they were followed but have become irrelevant in an age of women's liberation; that they are in fact compatible with women's liberation; that they are relevant because women's liberation itself is irrelevant.

2. Seek out two older women with children for an interview—one who has chosen to fill the role of mother and housekeeper, and one who has entered the workforce. Solicit their views as to the role they have chosen and the role they have rejected. Write an essay describing the interviews and comparing/contrasting the views expressed by the two women. Conclude with a summary of what you have learned by this experience and what you have concluded about the views of the two interviewees.

3. In the Introduction to Cluster 8, we present a list of individuals who are often the victims of ridicule by the "crowd": the ugly, the fat, the beanpole, the egghead, the crippled, the stutterer, the dwarf, the misshapen, and so on. You can probably remember a time in your life when you became the victim. Write a narrative in which you describe as vividly as you can your experience as a victim of prejudice.

4. At some point in your life, you might have joined a gang or crowd in teasing, ridiculing, or mistreating some individual who did not fully conform to the norm. Write a narrative describing the behavior of the members of the crowd and the reaction of the victim.

5. Convert the final episode in Pat Mainardi's "The Politics of Housework" into the beginning of a one-act play, with the husband coming home to find his wife at her desk and asking her what she is doing. Her reply is, "Writing a paper on housework." He answers: "Housework? Housework? Oh my god how trivial can you get. A paper on housework." Call your play, perhaps, "A Trivial Supper," and imagine shortly after coming home he yells from the shower: "What's for supper?" What is her reply—and what is the conversation over trivial food trivially prepared that she serves him in a lively scene?

6. Anne Moody concludes "The Movement": "Now I knew it was impossible for me to hate sickness. The whites had a disease, an incurable disease in its final stage. What were the chances against such a disease?" Do you agree or disagree that racism is an "incurable

disease"? Have you eliminated racial feeling that you have experienced? Have you ever known people who changed their racist views? Write an essay in which you explain and defend your position.

7. A key sentence in Hugh Pearson's "The Black Academic Environment" says, "Schoolwork, my two Black Power chanting elementary-school classmates and I decided, was for white people." When Pearson later changed his mind and became an achiever in school, he was ridiculed by his classmates. A slight change of the sentence may get at another kind of prejudice: "Schoolwork, my jeering classmates chanted, was for sissies and teacher's pets." Do you know someone who was so singled out for ridicule? Have you ever been the target of such ridicule? Write a narrative in which you describe the experience (your own or one you observed) and explore the anti-intellectual implications of such an episode.

8. Compare and contrast the nature of the racism described in Anne Moody's "The Movement" and Jesús Colón's "Kipling and I," with particular focus on its ferocity and on the seemingly bleak endings of the two essays.

9. Although both Eric Liu ("A Chinaman's Chance") and David Bernstein ("Mixed Like Me") have been victims of racism in America, they are poles apart on the political spectrum, with Liu on the left and Bernstein on the right. In a careful reconsideration of their essays, speculate as to why Liu has ended up a liberal and Bernstein has ended up a conservative. Write an analysis as to why, in your view, they have become what they have become, and then indicate which conclusions about America's future, Liu's or Bernstein's, seem more persuasive to you and why.

10. One of Eric Liu's prime beliefs in "A Chinaman's Chance" is contained in the sentence, "We forget that there is in fact such a thing as a unique American identity that transcends our sundry tribes, sets, gangs, and cliques." In an analytical essay, show how Liu reached this conclusion and then select two other writers from this cluster, each representing presumably a tribe, set, gang, or clique, and show how their positions in their essays are compatible or incompatible with Liu's statement. Use your best judgment in assessing the statements you encounter in all the essays you analyze.

Cluster

9

Roads Taken and Not Taken

We seem in life to be confronted at every turn with choices requiring us to make decisions. Who hasn't stopped to wonder now and again whether a past decision was the right one, whether the road taken is really leading to the destination desired. Robert Frost captures something of this dilemma in his 1915 poem, "The Road Not Taken":

> Two roads diverged in a yellow wood,
> And sorry I could not travel both
> And be one traveler, long I stood
> And looked down one as far as I could
> To where it bent in the undergrowth;
>
> Then took the other, as just as fair,
> And having perhaps the better claim,
> Because it was grassy and wanted wear;
> Though as for that the passing there
> Had worn them really about the same,
>
> And both that morning equally lay
> In leaves no step had trodden black.
> Oh, I kept the first for another day!
> Yet knowing how way leads on to way,
> I doubted if I should ever come back.
>
> I shall be telling this with a sigh
> Somewhere ages and ages hence:
> Two roads diverged in a wood, and I—
> I took the one less traveled by,
> And that has made all the difference.

Just what that difference was Frost leaves us to guess. The little word *all* tells us how big the long-ago decision loomed in his memory. Frost's poem, recalling a crucial decision in his past, portrays a universal experience. In this cluster of essays, the writers describe such critical moments in their past, revealing not only the nature of the roads taken but often also the experiences that shaped their choices. Sometimes they realize they should have chosen a "road not taken."

> *"Leaving the Rubicon incident away back where it belongs, I can say with truth that the reason I am in the literary profession is because I had the measles when I was twelve years old."*

"THE TURNING POINT OF MY LIFE"
Mark Twain

Mark Twain (1835–1910) is a pseudonym for Samuel L. Clemens, who grew up in Hannibal, Missouri, and became a printer-journalist-writer-humorist, gaining his first recognition from stories he heard and retold in publications out west when it was still frontier country. He is credited with establishing a distinctively American literary style in such books as *Tom Sawyer* (1876), *Life on the Mississippi* (1883), and *Adventures of Huckleberry Finn* (1884). "The Turning Point of My Life" is taken from *What Is Man?* first published in 1917. For more biographical information, see the headnote on page 96.

I

1 If I understand the idea, the *Bazar* invites several of us to write upon the above text [the title]. It means the change in my life's course which introduced what must be regarded by me as the most *important* condition of my career. But it also implies—without intention, perhaps—that that turning point was *itself*, individually, the creator of the new condition. This gives it too much distinction, too much prominence, too much credit. It is only the *last* link in a very long chain of turning points commissioned to produce the weighty result; it is not any more important than the humblest of its ten thousand predecessors. Each of the ten thousand did its appointed share, on its appointed date, in forwarding the scheme, and they were all necessary; to have left out any one of them would have defeated the scheme and brought about *some other* result. I know we have a fashion of saying "such and such an event was *the* turning point in my life," but we shouldn't say it. We should merely grant that its place as *last* link in the chain makes it the most *conspicuous* link; in real importance it has no advantage over any one of its predecessors.

2   Perhaps the most celebrated turning point recorded in history was the crossing of the Rubicon. Suetonius says:

> *Coming up with his troops on the banks of the Rubicon, he halted for a while, and, revolving in his mind the importance of the step he was on the point of taking, he turned to those about him and said, "We may still retreat; but if we pass this little bridge, nothing is left for us but to fight it out in arms."*

3   This was a stupendously important moment. And all the incidents, big and little, of Caesar's previous life had been leading up to it, stage by stage, link by link. This was the *last* link — merely the last one, and no bigger than the others; but as we gaze back at it through the inflating mists of our imagination, it looks as big as the orbit of Neptune.

4   You, the reader, have a *personal* interest in that link, and so have I; so has the rest of the human race. It was one of the links in your life-chain, and it was one of the links in mine. We may wait, now, with bated breath, while Caesar reflects. Your fate and mine are involved in his decision.

> *While he was thus hesitating, the following incident occurred. A person remarkable for his noble mien and graceful aspect, appeared close at hand, sitting and playing upon a pipe. When not only the shepherds, but a number of soldiers also, flocked to listen to him, and some trumpeters among them, he snatched a trumpet from one of them, ran to the river with it, and sounding the advance with a piercing blast, crossed to the other side. Upon this, Caesar exclaimed, "Let us go whither the omens of the gods and the iniquity of our enemies call us. The die is cast."*

5   So he crossed — and changed the future of the whole human race, for all time. But that stranger was a link in Caesar's life-chain, too; and a necessary one. We don't know his name, we never hear of him again, he was very casual, he acts like an accident; but he was no accident, he was there by compulsion of *his* life-chain, to blow the electrifying blast that was to make up Caesar's mind for him, and thence go piping down the aisles of history forever.

6   If the stranger hadn't been there! But he *was*. And Caesar crossed. With such results! Such vast events — each a link in the *human race's* life-chain; each event producing the next one, and that one the next one, and so on: the destruction of the republic; the founding of the empire; the breaking up of the empire; the rise of Christianity upon its ruins; the spread of the religion to other lands — and so on: link by link took its appointed place at its appointed time, the discovery of America being one of them; our Revolution another; the inflow of English and other immigrants another; their drift westward (my ancestors

among them) another; the settlement of certain of them in Missouri—which resulted in *me*. For I was one of the unavoidable results of the crossing of the Rubicon. If the stranger, with his trumpet blast, had stayed away (which he *couldn't*, for he was an appointed link), Caesar would not have crossed. What would have happened, in that case, we can never guess. We only know that the things that did happen would not have happened. They might have been replaced by equally prodigious things, of course, but their nature and results are beyond our guessing. But the matter that interests me personally is, that I would not be *here*, now, but somewhere else; and probably black—there is no telling. Very well, I am glad he crossed. And very really and thankfully glad, too, though I never cared anything about it before.

II

7   To me, the most important feature of my life is its literary feature. I have been professionally literary something more than forty years. There have been many turning points in my life, but the one that was the last link in the chain appointed to conduct me to the literary guild is the most *conspicuous* link in that chain. *Because* it was the last one. It was not any more important than its predecessors. All the other links have an inconspicuous look, except the crossing of the Rubicon; but as factors in making me literary they are all of the one size, the crossing of the Rubicon included.

8   I know how I came to be literary, and I will tell the steps that led up to it and brought it about.

9   The crossing of the Rubicon was not the first one, it was hardly even a recent one; I should have to go back ages before Caesar's day to find the first one. To save space I will go back only a couple of generations, and start with an incident of my boyhood. When I was twelve and a half years old, my father died. It was in the spring. The summer came, and brought with it an epidemic of measles. For a time, a child died almost every day. The village was paralyzed with fright, distress, despair. Children that were not smitten with the disease were imprisoned in their homes to save them from the infection. In the homes there were no cheerful faces, there was no music, there was no singing but of solemn hymns, no voice but of prayer, no romping was allowed, no noise, no laughter, the family moved spectrally about on tiptoe, in a ghostly hush. I was a prisoner. My soul was steeped in this awful dreariness—and in fear. At some time or other every day and every night a sudden shiver shook me to the marrow, and I said to myself, "There, I've got it! and I shall die." Life on these miserable terms was not worth living, and at last I made up my mind to get the disease and have it over, one way or the other. I escaped from the house and went to the house of a neighbor where a playmate of mine was very ill with the malady. When the chance offered I crept into his room and got into bed with him. I was discovered by his mother and sent back into captivity. But I had the disease;

they could not take that from me. I came near to dying. The whole village was interested, and anxious, and sent for news of me every day; and not only once a day, but several times. Everybody believed I would die; but on the fourteenth day a change came for the worse and they were disappointed.

10   This was a turning point of my life. (Link number one.) For when I got well my mother closed my school career and apprenticed me to a printer. She was tired of trying to keep me out of mischief, and the adventure of the measles decided her to put me into more masterful hands than hers.

11   I became a printer, and began to add one link after another to the chain which was to lead me into the literary profession. A long road, but I could not know that; and as I did not know what its goal was, or even that it had one, I was indifferent. Also contented.

12   A young printer wanders around a good deal, seeking and finding work; and seeking again, when necessity commands. N. B. Necessity is a *Circumstance*; Circumstance is man's master—and when Circumstance commands, he must obey; he may argue the matter—that is his privilege, just as it is the honorable privilege of a falling body to argue with the attraction of gravitation—but it won't do any good, he must *obey*. I wandered for ten years, under the guidance and dictatorship of Circumstance, and finally arrived in a city of Iowa, where I worked several months. Among the books that interested me in those days was one about the Amazon. The traveler told an alluring tale of his long voyage up the great river from Para to the sources of the Madeira, through the heart of an enchanted land, a land wastefully rich in tropical wonders, a romantic land where all the birds and flowers and animals were of the museum varieties, and where the alligator and the crocodile and the monkey seemed as much at home as if they were in the Zoo. Also, he told an astonishing tale about *coca*, a vegetable product of miraculous powers; asserting that it was so nourishing and so strength-giving that the native of the mountains of the Madeira region would tramp up-hill and down all day on a pinch of powdered coca and require no other sustenance.

13   I was fired with a longing to ascend the Amazon. Also with a longing to open up a trade in coca with all the world. During months I dreamed that dream, and tried to contrive ways to get to Para and spring that splendid enterprise upon an unsuspecting planet. But all in vain. A person may *plan* as much as he wants to, but nothing of consequence is likely to come of it until the magician *Circumstance* steps in and takes the matter off his hands. At last Circumstance came to my help. It was in this way. Circumstance, to help or hurt another man, made him lose a fifty-dollar bill in the street; and to help or hurt me, made me find it. I advertised the find, and left for the Amazon the same day. This was another turning point, another link.

14   Could Circumstance have ordered another dweller in that town to go to the Amazon and open up a world-trade in coca on a fifty-dollar basis and been obeyed? No, I was the only one. There were other fools there—shoals and shoals of them—but they were not of my kind. I was the only one of my kind.

15   Circumstance is powerful, but it cannot work alone, it has to have a partner. Its partner is man's *temperament*—his natural disposition. His temperament is not his invention, it is *born* in him, and he has no authority over it, neither is he responsible for its acts. He cannot change it, nothing can change it, nothing can modify it,—except temporarily. But it won't stay modified. It is permanent; like the color of the man's eyes and the shape of his ears. Blue eyes are gray, in certain unusual lights; but they resume their natural color when that stress is removed.

16   A Circumstance that will coerce one man, will have no effect upon a man of a different temperament. If Circumstance had thrown the bank note in Caesar's way, his temperament would not have made him start for the Amazon. His temperament would have compelled him to do something with the money, but not that. It might have made him advertise the note—and *wait*. We can't tell. Also, it might have made him go to New York and buy into the government; with results that would leave Tweed nothing to learn when it came his turn.

17   Very well, Circumstance furnished the capital, and my temperament told me what to do with it. Sometimes a temperament is an ass. When that is the case the owner of it is an ass, too, and is going to remain one. Training, experience, association, can temporarily so elevate him that people will think he is a mule, but they will be mistaken. Artificially he *is* a mule, for the time being, but at bottom he is an ass yet, and will remain one.

18   By temperament I was the kind of person that *does* things. Does them, and reflects afterwards. So I started for the Amazon, without reflecting, and without asking any questions. That was more than fifty years ago. In all that time my temperament has not changed, by even a shade. I have been punished many and many a time, and bitterly, for doing things first and reflecting afterward, but these tortures have been of no value to me; I still do the thing commanded by Circumstance and Temperament, and reflect afterward. Always violently. When I am reflecting, on those occasions, even deaf persons can hear me think.

19   I went by the way of Cincinnati, and down the Ohio and Mississippi. My idea was to take ship, at New Orleans, for Para. In New Orleans I inquired, and found there was no ship leaving for Para. Also, that there never had *been* one leaving for Para. I reflected. A policeman came and asked me what I was doing, and I told him. He made me move on; and said if he caught me reflecting in the public street again he would run me in.

20   After few days I was out of money. Then Circumstance arrived, with another turning point of my life—a new link. On my way down, I had made the acquaintance of a pilot; I begged him to teach me the river, and he consented. I became a pilot.

21   By and by Circumstance came again—introducing the Civil War, this time, in order to push me ahead a stage or two toward the literary profession. The boats stopped running, my livelihood was gone.

22   Circumstance came to the rescue with a new turning point and a fresh link. My brother was appointed secretary to the new Territory of Nevada, and he invited me to go with him and help him in his office. I accepted.

23   In Nevada, Circumstance furnished me the silver fever and I went into the mines to make a fortune and enter the ministry. As I supposed; but that was not the idea. The idea was, to move me another step toward literature. For amusement I scribbled things for the Virginia City *Enterprise*. One isn't a printer ten years without setting up acres of good and bad literature, and learning—unconsciously at first, consciously later—to discriminate between the two, within his mental limitations; and meantime he is unconsciously acquiring what is called a "style." One of my efforts attracted attention, and the *Enterprise* sent for me, and put me on its staff.

24   And so I became a journalist—another link. By and by Circumstance and the Sacramento *Union* sent me to the Sandwich Islands for five or six months, to write up sugar. I did it; and threw in a good deal of extraneous matter that hadn't anything to do with sugar. But it was this extraneous matter that helped me to another link.

25   It made me notorious, and San Francisco invited me to lecture. Which I did. And profitably. I had long had a desire to travel and see the world, and now the platform had furnished me the means. So I joined the "Quaker City Excursion."

26   When I returned to America, Circumstance was waiting on the pier—with the *last* link: I was asked to *write a book*, and I did it, and called it *The Innocents Abroad*. Thus at last I became a member of the literary guild. That was forty-two years ago, and I have been a member ever since. Leaving the Rubicon incident away back where it belongs, I can say with truth that the reason I am in the literary profession is because I had the measles when I was twelve years old.

III

27   Now what interests me, as regards these details, is not the details themselves, but the fact that none of them was foreseen by me, none of them was planned by me, I was the author of none of them. Circumstance, working in harness with my temperament, created them all and compelled them all. I often offered help, and with the best intentions, but it was rejected: as a rule, uncourteously. I could never plan a thing and get it to come out the way I planned it. It came out some other way—some way I had not counted upon.

28   And so I do not admire the human being—as an intellectual marvel—as much as I did when I was young, and got him out of books, and did not know him personally. When I used to read that such and such a general did a certain brilliant thing, I believed it. Whereas it was not so. Circumstance did it, by help of his temperament. The circumstances would have failed of effect with a general of another temperament: he might see the chance, but lose the advantage

by being by nature too slow or too quick or too doubtful. Once General Grant was asked a question about a matter which had been much debated by the public and the newspapers; he answered the question without any hesitancy: "General, who planned the march through Georgia?" "The enemy!" He added that the enemy usually makes your plans for you. He meant that the enemy, by neglect or through force of circumstances, leaves an opening for you, and you see your chance and take advantage of it.

29   Circumstances do the planning for us all, no doubt, by help of our temperaments. I see no great difference between a man and a watch, except that the man is conscious and the watch isn't, and the man *tries* to plan things and the watch doesn't. The watch doesn't wind itself, and doesn't regulate itself—these things are done exteriorly. Outside influences, outside circumstances, wind the *man* and regulate him. Left to himself he wouldn't get regulated at all, and the sort of time he would keep would not be valuable. Some rare men are wonderful watches, with gold case, compensation balance, and all those things, and some men are only simple and sweet and humble Waterburys. I am a Waterbury. A Waterbury of that kind, some say.

30   A nation is only an individual, multiplied. It makes plans, and Circumstance comes and upsets them—or enlarges them. A gang of patriots throws the tea overboard; it destroys a Bastile. The plans stop there; then Circumstance comes in, quite unexpectedly, and turns these modest riots into a revolution.

31   And there was poor Columbus. He elaborated a deep plan to find a new route to an old country. Circumstance revised his plan for him, and he found a new *world*. And *he* gets the credit of it, to this day. He hadn't anything to do with it.

32   Necessarily the scene of the real turning point of my life (and of yours) was the Garden of Eden. It was there that the first link was forged of the chain that was ultimately to lead to the emptying of me into the literary guild. Adam's *temperament* was the first command the Deity ever issued to a human being on this planet. And it was the only command Adam would *never* be able to disobey. It said, "Be weak, be water, be characterless, be cheaply persuadable." The later command, to let the fruit alone, was certain to be disobeyed. Not by Adam himself, but by his *temperament*—which he did not create and had no authority over. For the *temperament* is the man; the thing tricked out with clothes and named Man, is merely its Shadow, nothing more. The law of the tiger's temperament is, Thou shalt kill; the law of the sheep's temperament is, Thou shalt not kill. To issue later commands requiring the tiger to let the fat stranger alone, and requiring the sheep to imbue its hands in the blood of the lion is not worth while, for those commands *can't* be obeyed. They would invite to violations of the law of *temperament*, which is supreme, and takes precedence of all other authorities. I cannot help feeling disappointed in Adam and Eve. That is, in their temperaments. Not in *them*, poor helpless young creatures—afflicted with temperaments made out of butter; which butter was commanded to get

into contact with fire and *be melted*. What I cannot help wishing is, that Adam and Eve had been postponed, and Martin Luther and Joan of Arc put in their place — that splendid pair equipped with temperaments not made of butter, but of asbestos. By neither sugary persuasions nor by hellfire could Satan have beguiled *them* to eat the apple.

33   There would have been results! Indeed yes. The apple would be intact to-day: there would be no human race; there would be no *you*; there would be no *me*. And the old, old creation-dawn scheme of ultimately launching me into the literary guild would have been defeated.

⮳

Discussion Questions

   1.   According to Twain, how did the "die" get "cast" in Caesar's crossing of the Rubicon? Explain the reasoning that leads Twain to say, ". . . I was one of the unavoidable results of the crossing of the Rubicon."

   2.   How is it that Twain can conclude Part II of his essay: ". . . I can say with truth that the reason I am in the literary profession is because I had the measles when I was twelve years old"?

   3.   How does Twain refine the definitions of *circumstance* and *temperament* to suit his ends in "The Turning Point of My Life"?

   *4.   Explain Twain's comment in Part III of his essay, "Some rare men are wonderful watches, with gold case, compensation balance, and all those things, and some men are only simple and sweet and humble Waterburys."

   *5.   In Part III, Twain gives several examples of the plans carefully laid by nations or men being upset completely by "Circumstance": "A gang of patriots throws the tea overboard"; "it destroys a Bastille"; it "re-vised [Columbus's] plan for him, and he found a new *world*." Explain Twain's meaning in each of the examples he cites.

   6.   Explain Twain's comment near the end of his essay, "What I can-not help wishing is that Adam and Eve had been postponed, and Martin Luther and Joan of Arc put in their place—that splendid pair equipped with temperaments not made of butter, but of asbestos."

Writing Topics

   1.   Twain is known as a great comic writer, and it is axiomatic that hu-mor can alter or undermine literal meaning in a work of literature. Write an analytical essay in which you focus on examples of wit or humor in Twain's essay that might affect meaning in some way. Con-clude with an estimate of how much the comic dimension should or should not shape our reading of "The Turning Point of My Life."

2. Compare and contrast the attitude toward "turning points" in Frost's "The Road Not Taken" and in Twain's "The Turning Point of My Life." In your conclusion, explain why you think one or the other is closer to the "truth"—or how you believe that both have some measure of validity.

"Writers did not have to ring doorbells.
So far as I could make out,
what writers did couldn't even be classified as work."

TOP-DRAWER SEVENTH GRADE PROSE

Russell Baker

Russell Baker was born in Virginia in 1925 and earned a B.A. at Johns Hopkins University in 1947. After graduation he launched his journalistic career at The Baltimore Sun before moving to The New York Times in 1954. In 1962, he began writing a personal column, "Observer," for the Times. Many of his books contain collections of his newspaper writings, including Baker's Dozen (1964), All Things Considered (1965), Poor Russell's Almanac (1972), and So This Is Depravity? (1980). He is also the author of a book for children, The Upside Down Man (1977), and a musical play, Home Again (1979). He won his first Pulitzer Prize for his newspaper columns published in 1979. And he won his second for Growing Up, a series of autobiographical sketches published in 1983. Growing Up is the source for "Top-Drawer Seventh Grade Prose." His columns continue to appear in The New York Times.

1   I began working in journalism when I was eight years old. It was my mother's idea. She wanted me to "make something" of myself and, after a level-headed appraisal of my strengths, decided I had better start young if I was to have any chance of keeping up with the competition.

2   The flaw in my character which she had already spotted was lack of "gumption." My idea of a perfect afternoon was lying in front of the radio rereading my favorite Big Little Book, *Dick Tracy Meets Stooge Viller*. My mother despised inactivity. Seeing me having a good time in repose, she was powerless to hide her disgust. "You've got no more gumption than a bump on a log," she said. "Get out in the kitchen and help Doris do those dirty dishes."

3   My sister Doris, though two years younger than I, had enough gumption for a dozen people. She positively enjoyed washing dishes, making beds, and cleaning the house. When she was only seven she could carry a piece of short-weighted cheese back to the A&P, threaten the manager with legal action, and

come back triumphantly with the full quarter-pound we'd paid for and a few ounces extra thrown in for forgiveness. Doris could have made something of herself if she hadn't been a girl. Because of this defect, however, the best she could hope for was a career as a nurse or schoolteacher, the only work that capable females were considered up to in those days.

4   This must have saddened my mother, this twist of fate that had allocated all the gumption to the daughter and left her with a son who was content with Dick Tracy and Stooge Viller. If disappointed, though, she wasted no energy on self-pity. She would make me make something of myself whether I wanted to or not. "The Lord helps those who help themselves," she said. That was the way her mind worked.

5   She was realistic about the difficulty. Having sized up the material the Lord had given her to mold, she didn't overestimate what she could do with it. She didn't insist that I grow up to be President of the United States.

6   Fifty years ago parents still asked boys if they wanted to grow up to be President, and asked it not jokingly but seriously. Many parents who were hardly more than paupers still believed their sons could do it. Abraham Lincoln had done it. We were only sixty-five years from Lincoln. Many a grandfather who walked among us could remember Lincoln's time. Men of grandfatherly age were the worst for asking if you wanted to grow up to be President. A surprising number of little boys said yes and meant it.

7   I was asked many times myself. No, I would say, I didn't want to grow up to be President. My mother was present during one of these interrogations. An elderly uncle, having posed the usual question and exposed my lack of interest in the Presidency, asked, "Well, what *do* you want to be when you grow up?"

8   I loved to pick through trash piles and collect empty bottles, tin cans with pretty labels, and discarded magazines. The most desirable job on earth sprang instantly to mind. "I want to be a garbage man," I said.

9   My uncle smiled, but my mother had seen the first distressing evidence of a bump budding on a log. "Have a little gumption, Russell," she said. Her calling me Russell was a signal of unhappiness. When she approved of me I was always "Buddy."

10   When I turned eight years old she decided that the job of starting me on the road toward making something of myself could no longer be safely delayed. "Buddy," she said one day, "I want you to come home right after school this afternoon. Somebody's coming and I want you to meet him."

11   When I burst in that afternoon she was in conference in the parlor with an executive of the Curtis Publishing Company. She introduced me. He bent low from the waist and shook my hand. Was it true as my mother had told him, he asked, that I longed for the opportunity to conquer the world of business?

12   My mother replied that I was blessed with a rare determination to make something of myself.

13   "That's right," I whispered.

14   "But have you got the grit, the character, the never-say-quit spirit it takes to succeed in business?"

15   My mother said I certainly did.

16   "That's right," I said.

17   He eyed me silently for a long pause, as though weighing whether I could be trusted to keep his confidence, then spoke man-to-man. Before taking a crucial step, he said, he wanted to advise me that working for the Curtis Publishing Company placed enormous responsibility on a young man. It was one of the great companies of America. Perhaps the greatest publishing house in the world. I had heard, no doubt, of the *Saturday Evening Post?*

18   Heard of it? My mother said that everyone in our house had heard of the *Saturday Post* and that I, in fact, read it with religious devotion.

19   Then doubtless, he said, we were also familiar with those two monthly pillars of the magazine world, the *Ladies Home Journal* and the *Country Gentleman.*

20   Indeed we were familiar with them, said my mother.

21   Representing the *Saturday Evening Post* was one of the weightiest honors that could be bestowed in the world of business, he said. He was personally proud of being a part of that great corporation.

22   My mother said he had every right to be.

23   Again he studied me as though debating whether I was worthy of a knighthood. Finally: "Are you trustworthy?"

24   My mother said I was the soul of honesty.

25   "That's right," I said.

26   The caller smiled for the first time. He told me I was a lucky young man. He admired my spunk. Too many young men thought life was all play. Those young men would not go far in this world. Only a young man willing to work and save and keep his face washed and his hair neatly combed could hope to come out on top in a world such as ours. Did I truly and sincerely believe that I was such a young man?

27   "He certainly does," said my mother.

28   "That's right," I said.

29   He said he had been so impressed by what he had seen of me that he was going to make me a representative of the Curtis Publishing Company. On the following Tuesday, he said, thirty freshly printed copies of the *Saturday Evening Post* would be delivered at our door. I would place these magazines, still damp with the ink of the presses, in a handsome canvas bag, sling it over my shoulder, and set forth through the streets to bring the best in journalism, fiction, and cartoons to the American public.

30   He had brought the canvas bag with him. He presented it with reverence fit for a chasuble. He showed me how to drape the sling over my left shoulder and across the chest so that the pouch lay easily accessible to my right hand, allowing the best in journalism, fiction, and cartoons to be swiftly extracted and sold to a citizenry whose happiness and security depended upon us soldiers of the free press.

31   The following Tuesday I raced home from school, put the canvas bag over my shoulder, dumped the magazines in, and, tilting to the left to balance their weight on my right hip, embarked on the highway of journalism.

32   We lived in Belleville, New Jersey, a commuter town at the northern fringe of Newark. It was 1932, the bleakest year of the Depression. My father had died two years before, leaving us with a few pieces of Sears, Roebuck furniture and not much else, and my mother had taken Doris and me to live with one of her younger brothers. This was my Uncle Allen. Uncle Allen had made something of himself by 1932. As salesman for a soft-drink bottler in Newark, he had an income of $30 a week; wore pearl-gray spats, detachable collars, and a three-piece suit; was happily married; and took in threadbare relatives.

33   With my load of magazines I headed toward Belleville Avenue. That's where the people were. There were two filling stations at the intersection with Union Avenue, as well as an A&P, a fruit stand, a bakery, a barber shop, Zuccarelli's drugstore, and a diner shaped like a railroad car. For several hours I made myself highly visible, shifting position now and then from corner to corner, from shop window to shop window, to make sure everyone could see the heavy black lettering on the canvas bag that said THE SATURDAY EVENING POST. When the angle of the light indicated it was supper-time, I walked back to the house.

34   "How many did you sell, Buddy?" my mother asked.

35   "None."

36   "Where did you go?"

37   "The corner of Belleville and Union Avenues."

38   "What did you do?"

39   "Stood on the corner waiting for somebody to buy a *Saturday Evening Post*."

40   "You just stood there?"

41   "Didn't sell a single one."

42   "For God's sake, Russell!"

43   Uncle Allen intervened. "I've been thinking about it for some time," he said, "and I've about decided to take the *Post* regularly. Put me down as a regular customer." I handed him a magazine and he paid me a nickel. It was the first nickel I earned.

44   Afterwards my mother instructed me in salesmanship. I would have to ring doorbells, address adults with charming self-confidence, and break down resistance with a sales talk pointing out that no one, no matter how poor, could afford to be without the *Saturday Evening Post* in the home.

45   I told my mother I'd changed my mind about wanting to succeed in the magazine business.

46   "If you think I'm going to raise a good-for-nothing," she replied, "you've got another think coming." She told me to hit the streets with the canvas bag and start ringing doorbells the instant school was out next day. When I objected that I didn't feel any aptitude for salesmanship, she asked how I'd like to lend her my leather belt so she could whack some sense into me. I bowed to superior will and entered journalism with a heavy heart.

47   My mother and I had fought this battle almost as long as I could remember. It probably started even before memory began, when I was a country child in northern Virginia and my mother, dissatisfied with my father's plain workman's life, determined that I would not grow up like him and his people, with calluses on their hands, overalls on their backs, and fourth-grade educations in their heads. She had fancier ideas of life's possibilities. Introducing me to the *Saturday Evening Post*, she was trying to wean me as early as possible from my father's world where men left with their lunch pails at sunup, worked with their hands until the grime ate into the pores, and died with a few sticks of mail-order furniture as their legacy. In my mother's vision of the better life there were desks and white collars, well-pressed suits, evenings of reading and lively talk, and perhaps—if a man were very, very lucky and hit the jackpot, really made something important of himself—perhaps there might be a fantastic salary of $5,000 a year to support a big house and a Buick with a rumble seat and a vacation in Atlantic City.

48   And so I set forth with my sack of magazines. I was afraid of the dogs that snarled behind the doors of potential buyers. I was timid about ringing the doorbells of strangers, relieved when no one came to the door, and scared when someone did. Despite my mother's instructions, I could not deliver an engaging sales pitch. When a door opened I simply asked, "Want to buy a *Saturday Evening Post*?" In Belleville few persons did. It was a town of 30,000 people, and most weeks I rang a fair majority of its doorbells. But I rarely sold my thirty copies. Some weeks I canvassed the entire town for six days and still had four or five unsold magazines on Monday evening; then I dreaded the coming of Tuesday morning, when a batch of thirty fresh *Saturday Evening Post*s was due at the front door.

49   "Better get out there and sell the rest of those magazines tonight," my mother would say.

50   I usually posted myself then at a busy intersection where a traffic light controlled commuter flow from Newark. When the light turned red I stood on the curb and shouted my sales pitch at the motorists.

51   "Want to buy a *Saturday Evening Post*?"

52   One rainy night when car windows were sealed against me I came back soaked and with not a single sale to report. My mother beckoned to Doris.

53   "Go back down there with Buddy and show him how to sell these magazines," she said.

54   Brimming with zest, Doris, who was then seven years old, returned with me to the corner. She took a magazine from the bag, and when the light turned red she strode to the nearest car and banged her small fist against the closed window. The driver, probably startled at what he took to be a midget assaulting his car, lowered the window to stare, and Doris thrust a *Saturday Evening Post* at him.

55   "You need this magazine," she piped, "and it only costs a nickel."

56   Her salesmanship was irresistible. Before the light changed half a dozen times she disposed of the entire batch. I didn't feel humiliated. To the contrary. I was so happy I decided to give her a treat. Leading her to the vegetable store on Belleville Avenue, I bought three apples, which cost a nickel, and gave her one.

57   "You shouldn't waste money," she said.

58   "Eat your apple." I bit into mine.

59   "You shouldn't eat before supper," she said. "It'll spoil your appetite."

60   Back at the house that evening, she dutifully reported me for wasting a nickel. Instead of a scolding, I was rewarded with a pat on the back for having the good sense to buy fruit instead of candy. My mother reached into her bottomless supply of maxims and told Doris, "An apple a day keeps the doctor away."

61   By the time I was ten I had learned all my mother's maxims by heart. Asking to stay up past normal bedtime, I knew that a refusal would be explained with, "Early to bed and early to rise, makes a man healthy, wealthy, and wise." If I whimpered about having to get up early in the morning, I could depend on her to say, "The early bird gets the worm."

62   The one I most despised was, "If at first you don't succeed, try, try again." This was the battle cry with which she constantly sent me back into the hopeless struggle whenever I moaned that I had rung every doorbell in town and knew there wasn't a single potential buyer left in Belleville that week. After listening to my explanation, she handed me the canvas bag and said, "If at first you don't succeed . . ."

63   Three years in that job, which I would gladly have quit after the first day except for her insistence, produced at least one valuable result. My mother finally concluded that I would never make something of myself by pursuing a life in business and started considering careers that demanded less competitive zeal.

64   One evening when I was eleven I brought home a short "composition" on my summer vacation which the teacher had graded with an A. Reading it with her own schoolteacher's eye, my mother agreed that it was top-drawer seventh grade prose and complimented me. Nothing more was said about it immediately, but a new idea had taken life in her mind. Halfway through supper she suddenly interrupted the conversation.

65   "Buddy," she said, "maybe you could be a writer."

66   I clasped the idea to my heart. I had never met a writer, had shown no previous urge to write, and hadn't a notion how to become a writer, but I loved stories and thought that making up stories must surely be almost as much fun as reading them. Best of all, though, and what really gladdened my heart, was the ease of the writer's life. Writers did not have to trudge through the town peddling from canvas bags, defending themselves against angry dogs, being rejected by surly strangers. Writers did not have to ring doorbells. So far as I could make out, what writers did couldn't even be classified as work.

67 I was enchanted. Writers didn't have to have any gumption at all. I did not dare tell anybody for fear of being laughed at in the schoolyard, but secretly I decided that what I'd like to be when I grew up was a writer.

❧

Discussion Questions

1. Does Baker seem to be striving for tragedy, pathos, or comedy in his characterization of his relationship with his mother and his sister, Doris? Support your answer by citing specific passages in the text.
2. When asked by his uncle what he wanted to be when he grew up, what led Baker to answer the way he did?
3. What role did Baker's mother play in his interview with the executive of the Curtis Publishing Company?
4. Describe the part his mother's maxims played in Baker's career selling magazines.
*5. Baker reveals that his mother, as long as he could remember, was determined to see that he would not grow up to live the kind of life his dead father had lived. Explain.
*6. What finally led to Baker's decision to become a writer?

Writing Topics

1. Write a comparison/contrast essay showing how Russell and his sister, Doris, are alike and how different, taking into account their mother's role in shaping them both.
2. Baker's mother appears in his recollection the way he, *as a boy*, saw her and felt about her. Write a description and assessment of the mother's role in his life as you can see her through your own eyes.

In the days of my adventure,
Vermont had no law restricting the age or youth
of a teacher, but shortly after my experience,
and possibly consequent thereto,
the state passed a law making sixteen the earliest age
at which one might begin. . . ."

TEACHING IN THE LITTLE RED SCHOOLHOUSE

Lucia B. Downing

Lucia B. Downing (1868–1945) began teaching at the age of fourteen in 1882 in a farm village in Vermont. She had to decide what to teach and figure out how to obtain texts; on her own, she had to devise methods of classroom discipline. She taught several years and obtained a degree from the University of Vermont in 1889. The following account of her first year of teaching comes from her essay "Teaching in the Keeler 'Deestrict' School," from *Vermont Quarterly: A Magazine of History*, October 1951.

> *Still sits the schoolhouse by the road,*
> *A ragged beggar sunning;*
> *Around it still the sumacs grow,*
> *And blackberry vines are running.*

1   It is still standing—the little red schoolhouse where I, a little girl barely four-teen, began my career as a teacher; still standing, though with sunken roof and broken windows, a solitary reminder of the days of long ago. No longer does its door's worn sill resound to the clatter of copper-toed boots; no longer does its smoking box-stove drive pupils and teacher out into the frosty air; never again on a summer's day will the passer-by hear the droning sound of the ab-abs, or the singsong recital of the multiplication table. The children, if there are any now in the old "Keeler Deestrict," clamber into a bus and ride merrily away to a central seat of learning five miles distant. "Time rolls his ceaseless course!"

2   In the days of my adventure, Vermont had no law restricting the age or youth of a teacher, but shortly after my experience, and possibly consequent thereto, the state passed a law making sixteen the earliest age at which one might begin what Thompson, who probably never taught a day in his life, calls

> *Delightful task! to rear the tender thought,*
> *To teach the young idea how to shoot.*

3   In our little town, the duties of a school superintendent were not burdensome, nor the position lucrative, and for many years our superintendent was the village doctor (Dr. L.C. Butler), who was probably the best-educated man in town, not even excepting the minister! The doctor could easily combine the two occupations—I had almost said "kill two birds with one stone!" For instance, he could visit the school on Brigham Hill when he had a patient up there, and save a trip up a steep hill with narrow, rocky road, which even to a Ford presents difficulties to this day. The doctor lived about two miles out of the village (Page's Corners) in a lovely old colonial house, once used as an inn and a popular Mecca for horseback parties in the good old days. There was a schoolhouse— red, of course—just across the road, and the doctor could drop in there any time. But to the teachers in outlying districts it was a decided advantage to have a doctor for supervisor. The teacher always knew if any one in the neighborhood was sick, and she could keep watch of the road. When old white Dolly, drawing the easy low phaeton, hove in sight, there was time to furbish up a little, and call out a class of the brightest pupils!

4   The doctor had vaccinated me when a little girl came from Canada with symptoms of that dreaded disease, small pox, and all the parents were calling him in. And he had brought me through measles and chicken pox, and his wife was my Sunday School teacher, and I was not a bit afraid of him. So when my sister, already a teacher, went to take another examination, the spring I was thirteen, I went along too, and said to the doctor, who was only a superintendent that day, that, if he had enough papers, I should like to see how many questions I could answer. The doctor smiled at me, and gave me an arithmetic paper for a starter. It proved to be easy, for it brought in some favorite problems in percentage, which would be an advantage to a merchant, as they showed how to mark goods in such a way that one could sell below the marked price, and still make a profit. I guess all merchants must have studied Greenleaf's *Arithmetic!* There was either a problem under the old Vermont Annual Interest Rule, or we were asked to write the rule. As it covered a half page in the book, writing it out involved some labor. I felt quite well pleased with my paper, and then proudly started on Grammar. I knew I could do something with that, for I loved to parse and analyze and "diagram," according to Reed and Kellogg. In fact, my first knowledge, and for many years my only knowledge, of "Paradise Lost" was gleaned from a little blue parsing book, and I have always been puzzled to know whether "barbaric" modifies "kings" or "pearl and gold":

High on a throne of royal state, which far
Outshone the wealth of Ormus and of Ind,
Or where the gorgeous East with richest hand
Showers on her kings barbaric pearl and gold,
Satan exalted sat.

Next came Geography. Though I had never traveled farther than Burlington, I knew, thanks to Mr. Guyot and his green geography, that Senegambia was "rich in gold, iron ore and gum-producing trees." (I always supposed it was "spruce gum," so popular before gutta-percha and licorices were combined and put up in slabs.) History and Civil Government were pretty hard for me, but next came Physiology, and I made the most of my bones and circulatory system, hoping to impress the physician. But it was in Theory and School Management that I did myself proud. I discoursed at length on ventilation and temperature, and, knowing that "good government" is a most desirable and necessary qualification for a teacher, I advocated a firm, but kind and gentle method, with dignity of bearing. In giving my views of corporal punishment, I related a story I had read of the Yankee teacher who was asked his views on the subject. He said, "Wal, moral suasion's my theory, but lickin's my practice!" When I reported at home that I had told that story, my Father laughed, but Mother expressed deep disgust.

5   When I compared notes with my sister, in regard to my answers, I began to feel that I did not know as much as I thought I did! An anxious week followed, and I haunted the post office. Finally, one morning, there was an envelope addressed in Dr. Butler's scholarly hand, but it bore my sister's name, and there was none for me. I was heartbroken—evidently my record was so poor that he was not going to tell me how I stood. But, as my sister opened her envelope, out fluttered two yellow slips—two certificates, entitling the recipients to teach in Vermont for one year. And one was in my name! I cannot recall any subsequent joy equal to what I felt at that moment—even a college diploma and a Phi Beta Kappa key, in later years, brought less of a thrill.

6   Of course, the eight or ten districts in town were already supplied with teachers, and no doubt that was why I was given a certificate, instead of a mere statement of standing. But one day my chum (Lena Brown) told me that in her Grandfather Keeler's district they planned to open up the old schoolhouse, unused for years because there were no children. Now there were at least four, of school age, and a school was demanded. She said the committeeman was Mr. Nichols (Charles Nichols), a friend of my father, and I insisted that he be interviewed. Thinking it was the "big girl" Father was talking about, Mr. Nichols talked very encouragingly, but when he found it was I who thus aspired, he laughed scornfully. Although Father told him I had a certificate, and was really bigger than the "big" one, the case looked hopeless. Sometime later he came to the house, and I happened to be the only member of the family at

home. After various circumlocutions he told me that I might try it. He said they could not pay much, as there probably would be only four scholars, and said he would let me know when school would open and where I should board — "boarding-around" was gone by at that time. I was the happiest person in town that night, but later I heard he had said to others that, with so few scholars, it didn't matter much anyway — and I made up my mind to do or die.

7 Before the term opened I had a birthday and attained the mature age of fourteen, but, in spite of unusual height for my years, I really did not look very old, and my chief anxiety was to acquire the appearance that for many years now I have made every effort to avoid! My skirts were fearfully short, and though Mother let out the last tuck and hem, they only reached to the tops of my buttoned boots, and, unless I was careful in seating myself, there was a glimpse of my stockings that no modest young woman, especially a teacher, should permit! However, Mother sewed a watch-pocket in my little dresses, and gave me her watch, a lovely little Swiss, with wide-open face, and there was a gorgeous long chain. You can't think how much dignity was added thereby! The next difficulty was my hair, heavy and long, and the only way I could fix it was to make a long, thick, childish braid. But, after many experiments, I achieved a way of folding it up, under and under, tying it close to my head, and I thought it resembled a real pug.

8 It was to be a fall term, and it probably opened late in August. The morning dawned when I was to begin "the glorious adventure." Father harnessed old Diamond — he was just my age, but what is old age for a horse is youth to a human being — and I came out with a little black bag, borrowed from Mother, and wearing my blue gingham dress. I had insisted on wearing that one, because it was a half-inch longer than any other. I can visualize it now — rather tight at the waist, fortunately for the watch-pocket, with ruffles at the bottom.

9 I was supposed to board in the family of a Mr. Vespasian Leach, a former merchant, who, like many such, had retired to a farm. As we jogged along, we met Mr. Leach taking his milk to the cheese factory, and he told us that, owing to sickness, they could not take a boarder. My father expressed his regret, and, with fine old-fashioned courtesy, said he had counted on my being looked after by these old friends. Presently we met Mr. Nichols, and he said that I was to board in *his* family. Father said he was delighted to know that, and he would not worry about me at all. After we passed along I said, "Why, Father, you told Mr. Leach how sorry you are, and now you tell Mr. Nichols how glad you are." I do not recall his explanation, except that it sounded very reasonable, and that was my first lesson in diplomacy. I see now that there was no dishonesty in my father's mind or language.

10 Well, we journeyed on, passing the schoolhouse on the way to the Nichols farm. I don't know how I felt — that is one of the things I can't remember! I was to go home week-ends, though of course we called it "over Sunday," and it looked to me like a long, long week. Mr. Nichols was a wealthy farmer, with a

grown-up family; and one son, with his wife and two babies (only one baby the first week), lived at home. There were menservants and maidservants galore, and we all sat down to most marvelous meals at a long table in a big dining-room. And what wonderful food! Picture it, even if you have not had the experience, and have not the imagination, of an Ichabod Crane! We did not have exactly the things to eat that made the pedagogue's mouth water in anticipation, but in retrospection it seems that nothing could be so good again as what was daily set before us. We did not have a young roast pig, but we had delicious home-smoked ham and tender roasts, and milk-fed chickens and honey with biscuits rich with cream, and then all the fruits and vegetables that early fall makes possible on a rich "interval" farm, besides plenty of eggs and cream and butter.

11   Then, too, I was treated like an honored guest, and given the "spare room" with blue walls and curtains, and was always addressed as "Teacher"—much to my satisfaction. I had really worried over that matter, for to call me Miss B. was absurd, and I feared I might be addressed by a familiar nickname, or pet name, which was most undignified. But, with the new title, my self-respect increased amazingly, and also my *conceit*. After four o'clock I was free from school duties, and I enjoyed the family life, playing with the two babies, or listening to the little parlor organ, played by some member of the family, and often there was a song by the son. I remember how he sang "Finnegan's Wake," and the song about the man from India, who ate ice cream and could never get warm again.

12   From nine to twelve and from one to four I was supposed to spend in the schoolhouse, and I can't see how I ever managed to put in the time—six long hours every day—with four pupils! Most of the time there were only four (four—all named Leach—two families), but one morning the number was increased. I was startled to see a young lady in trailing gown (how I envied her) approach and ask if she might come to school, adding that she loved me, just seeing me go by the house! She brought with her a little purple primer, with such lucid and inspiring sentences as, "Lo, I go! See me go up." She had learned to read out of that antiquated book before I was born, but in the intervening years reading had become a lost art, and she was ready to begin all over. It was a wonderful help to me in killing time, for each day we could go over and over the same thing, never too often to please her, as she stood by me and picked out the sentences, letter by letter.

13   But I still wonder how I put in the time. I did not knit or crochet, for I had heard of teachers who had made trouble for themselves by so doing. I was not skilful at drawing, and I couldn't sing much, being like the old woman who knew just two tunes—"Old Hundred" and "Doxology"! and when each pupil had read and ciphered and spelled and passed the water and recessed and recessed and passed the water and spelled and had a lesson in geography and read and spelled, there was usually an hour before I dared dismiss them. I sometimes carried my watch key to school and turned the hands ahead, but

that took me home to the committee-man's too early. Parents, what few there were, I suppose were glad to be relieved of the care of their offspring, and no one ever suggested a shortening of the hours. I had to earn my salary! We had few books, and my principal memorizing had been confined to the Westminster Catechism with its one hundred and seven long answers, but I knew a few poems, and I taught the children all I knew. I devised what I thought was a wonderful set of "Instructive Questions and Answers," suggested by a *New England Primer* that had come down in our family, but I did not limit the field of instuction to matters Biblical, attempting rather to cover the entire realm of knowledge in art, science, history, literature what you will.

14   My pride suffered several falls. I did not have very good discipline, for one thing. Then, when I was proud of my success in teaching a boy to read by the word method, just coming into use, I ventured to suggest that words were made up of letters, and began to point them out. He said, "Yes, I knew my letters last year, and that's why I know how to read." Then there was one *big* boy who was *peeved* because I would not allow him the same privilege as the little ones who always wanted to kiss "Teacher" good night. And my oldest pupil took a dislike to her teacher, as sudden and as inexplicable as her erstwhile fondness.

15   The glorious autumn days flew by, and the ten weeks' term was drawing to a close. One of the most arduous tasks was "keeping the register," and the consequent figuring up of averages at the end of the term. There was the total number of days' attendance by all pupils; the average attendance per day, which would have been a fine record, except for the defection of the oldest pupil, and the number of days' attendance per pupil. My sister showed me how to do all those things, but there was a vital question that I was obliged to leave until the last moment, namely, the amount of salary received. Except that it would be a small salary, the subject had never been mentioned. I was worried; just suppose I did not get enough to pay my board! I really had eaten a great deal, and I knew Father would not want to pay my board, even if he had the money. Waiting until the last possible moment to finish my register, I approached Mr. Nichols after one of the fine dinners we always had. When I spoke of my difficulty in completing the register, he looked worried—maybe he had heard of those averages! But, as I told him my *real* difficulty, he looked relieved, and smiled, as he said, in his delightful, cultured Yankee drawl, that the *district calculated* they could afford to pay three dollars and a half a week, to cover salary and board, the proportion to be determined by the committeeman, and he had decided to give me two dollars a week for my work, and take only a dollar and a half for board, which, I may say, was a most generous arrangement, in view of everything!

16   But the last days of school were busy ones. I drilled the scholars on the pieces they were to speak—I can remember one of them now, "Little Dan"—and I told the children how important it was that they should behave well the last day, if never before or later. And school ended in a blaze of glory, a vast and

terrifying audience having assembled—entirely out of proportion to the number of pupils. There were fond parents, and grandparents, and aunts and uncles and cousins thrice removed. I think there were twenty-five visitors and only four scholars, but the children did very well. They went through some specially prepared lessons in the various subjects they had been studying; they spoke their pieces without prompting, and they went glibly through the "Instructive Questions and Answers," though if I had made a slip and asked the questions out of order, the results might have been disastrous. They might have said that Vermont is the largest state in the Union, or that George Washington had sailed the ocean blue in 1492, or that Rome was built by Julius Caesar, but I do not recall that any such contretemps occurred. I do fear, however, that "Teacher," herself, was at that time a bit uncertain as to whether the *I. Watts* who wrote hymns was the *I. Watt* whose mother had a teakettle. Everything went off well, and I presented the children with cards, for which I had borrowed the money from my sister, and my pupils and their friends said goodbye, and I went proudly home with twenty dollars, the remuneration for ten weeks of toil. But never before or since has that sum of money gone so far. I went to Burlington the next week, and I bought blue flannel for a dress, a photograph album, a cage for my canary, a beaver hat, and numerous small things, besides paying up for my cards.

17   I went back to school, picking up my work at the Academy, and I felt rather superior to my classmates. When spring came, I was flattered to be asked to go back and teach another term. I was told that children had moved into the neighborhood, some had become of school age, and some had even been born, in the hope of going to school to me! I went back, and completed my second term as a teacher while I was fourteen. I had fifteen scholars, and probably more salary, though I do not remember. As a matter of fact, I do not recall much about that second term and the other terms I taught there and elsewhere during my school and college course. But the incidents of that first term are still vivid in my mind after nearly half a century. It was an unusual experience, and the events of each week were told over at home, and repeated to any one who would listen, as I did a "round, unvarnished tale deliver." In the telling I have not exaggerated or drawn upon my imagination, but as I call the old time back, memories rush upon me, and I can visualize the scene, and it is all as fresh as if it had happened yesterday.

❧

Discussion Questions

1.   As explained by Downing, why was the village doctor also appointed the school superintendent? How did the teacher help him in his role as doctor?

*2. Under what circumstances did the thirteen-year-old Downing take the examination for certification? How did she find out about her certification, and what was her reaction?

3. What concern did Downing have about her physical appearance as she was about to launch her teaching career? What did she do about it?

4. Describe the system of "boarding" the teacher in Downing's day and community, along with her experience in boarding for her first job. What is the "lesson in diplomacy" she learns from her father when he takes her to her boarding family?

5. What were the school hours and how did Downing feel about filling these hours for her four pupils?

*6. What is revealed about Downing's teaching methods when she writes of the last day, when parents and other relatives assembled to hear the pupils exhibit their learning (penultimate paragraph), "[The students] went through some specially prepared lessons in the various subjects they had been studying; they spoke their pieces without prompting, and they went glibly through the 'Instructive Questions and Answers,' though if I had made a slip and asked the questions out of order, the results might have been disastrous"?

Writing Topics

1. When asked in her "examination" for certification by the superintendent about "corporal punishment," the young Downing says she related a story of the Yankee teacher who was asked to give "his views on the subject." He answered: "Wal, moral suasion's my theory, but lickin's my practice." In a brief essay, explain the meaning of this answer and the differing reactions of Downing's mother and father when she related the story to them. Explain why you agree with the mother or father, or with neither.

2. Downing seemed to have relied mainly on memorization of material, or "rote" learning, in her teaching. Given her circumstances, she may have taught this way out of necessity. Write an essay in which you explore her reasons for using this method of teaching and give your own assessment of the virtue or shortcomings of such a method.

"In an era when men of his class wore dark suits and white shirts and monochromatic neckties, Father appeared to have outfitted himself at the Salvation Army."

IT WAS ENOUGH TO HAVE BEEN A UNICORN

Kurt Vonnegut

Kurt Vonnegut was born in Indianapolis, Indiana, in 1922 and, after high school, began studying biochemistry at Cornell University in Ithaca, New York. But he was drafted as a G.I. (Government Issue) in the U.S. Army to fight in World War II. Captured by the Germans, he ended up imprisoned in an underground slaughterhouse in Dresden, Germany, and he was there when Dresden was firebombed by Allied planes flying from England. He emerged to find the city transformed into a moonscape. On his discharge from the Army after the war, he enrolled at the University of Chicago to earn an M.A. in anthropology, but his completed M.A. thesis was rejected and he withdrew. (Later, after he achieved fame as a novelist, the University of Chicago reversed its decision and awarded him the degree.) Although Vonnegut worked for a time for General Electric, he turned more and more to the writing of fiction, publishing *Player Piano* in 1952 and *Sirens of Titan* in 1959. He early established himself as something of a cult novelist read and recommended by the young. His melding of science fiction style and plots with real-world events and places seemed to capture the essence of the postwar nightmare world of the atomic age, particularly in such widely read novels as *Mother Night* (1961), *Cat's Cradle* (1963), and *God Bless You, Mr. Rosewater* (1965). It was, however, his experience as a prisoner of war in Dresden and the firebombing of the city—and him—by his own forces that shaped his ironic vision of the world. It appears that he could not trust himself to recreate this traumatic experience in fiction until his sixth book, a quite moving, semiautobiographical novel, *Slaugh-terhouse Five: or The Children's Crusade* (1969). Although he has continued to write—*Jailbird* (1979) and *Deadeye Dick* (1982) among others—no other of his books has achieved the power of *Slaughterhouse Five*. The following essay comes from *Fates Worse Than Death: An Autobiographical Collage of the* 1980s (1991).

1   When my father was sixty-five and I was twenty-seven, I said to him, thinking him a very old man, that it must have been fun for him to be an architect. He replied unexpectedly that it had been no fun at all, since architecture had everything to do with accounting and nothing to do with art. I felt that he had mousetrapped me, since he had encouraged me up until that moment to believe that architecture for him had indeed been a lark.

2   I now perceive his deception, so suddenly discontinued, as having been a high order of gallantry. While my two siblings and I were growing up, he gave us the illusion that our father was jauntily content with his professional past and excited about all the tough but amusing challenges still to come. The truth was that the Great Depression and then World War II, during which almost all building stopped, came close to gutting him as an architect. From the time he was forty-five until he was sixty-one he had almost no work. In prosperous times those would have been his best years, when his evident gifts, reputation, and maturity might have caused some imaginative client to feel that Father was entitled to reach, even in Indianapolis, for greatness or, if you will, for soul-deep fun.

3   I am not about to speak of soup kitchens, much in the news again of late. We never missed a meal during the Great Depression. But Father had to close down his office, started up by *his* father, the first licensed architect in Indiana, and let his six employees go. Small jobs still came his way now and then, jobs so uninteresting, I now understand, that they would have been soporific to a high school drafting class. If we hadn't needed the money, Father might have said what I heard him say to a would-be client after World War II, when prosperity had returned to the land: "Why don't you get some pencils and squared paper, and see what you and your wife can do?" He said this pleasantly. He was trying to be helpful.

4   During the war he stopped being an architect entirely, and went to work in inventory control at the Atkins Saw Company, which was making weapons of some sort, maybe bayonets. It was then that his wife died. It became clear to him, too, that none of his three children would live in Indianapolis when the war was over. We would be following careers which would require us to live far away. So he was all but gutted yet again.

5   When prosperity, but not his children, returned to Indianapolis, Father became a partner of much younger men in a new architectural firm. His reputation was still excellent, and he was one of the most universally loved men in town, a founder, by the way, of the city's now world-famous Children's Museum. He was especially admired for his design of the Bell Telephone headquarters on North Meridian Street, a project conceived before the stock market crash.

6   After the war, Bell Telephone resolved to add more floors to the building, their exteriors to be identical with those of the eight below. They hired another architect, although Father was not senile or alcoholic or in any other way impaired. To Bell Telephone, an architect was an architect. Bell got the job done and it looked OK. So much for the romance of architecture.

7   Father retired alone to Brown County, Indiana, soon after that, to spend the rest of his life as a potter. He built his own potter's wheel. He died down there in the hills in 1957, at the age of seventy-two.

8   When I try to remember now what he was like when I was growing up and he had so little satisfying work to do, I see him as Sleeping Beauty, dormant in a brier patch, waiting for a prince. And it is easy to jump from that thought to this one: All architects I have known, in good times or bad, have seemed to be waiting forever for a generous, loving client who will let them become the elated artists they were born to be.

9   So my father's life might be seen as a particularly lugubrious fairy tale. He was Sleeping Beauty, and in 1929 not one but several princes, including Bell Telephone, had begun to hack through the briers to wake him up. But then they all got sick for sixteen years. And while they were in the hospital a wicked witch turned Sleeping Beauty into Rip Van Winkle instead.

10   When the Depression hit I was taken out of private school and put into public school. So I had a new set of friends to bring home to have a look at whatever my father was. These were the ten-year-old children of the yeomanry of Hoosierdom, and it was they who first told me that my father was as exotic as a unicorn.

11   In an era when men of his class wore dark suits and white shirts and monochromatic neckties, Father appeared to have outfitted himself at the Salvation Army. Nothing matched. I understand now, of course, that he had selected the elements of his costume with care, that the colors and textures were juxtaposed so as to be interesting and, finally, beautiful.

12   While other fathers were speaking gloomily of coal and iron and grain and lumber and cement and so on, and yes, of Hitler and Mussolini, too, my father was urging friends and startled strangers alike to pay attention to some object close at hand, whether natural or manmade, and to celebrate it as a masterpiece. When I took up the clarinet, he declared the instrument, black studded with silver, to be a masterpiece. Never mind whether it could make music or not. He

adored chess sets, although he could not play that game worth a nickel. My new friends and I brought him a moth one time, wanting to know what sort of moth it was. He said that he did not know its name, but that we could all agree wholeheartedly on this much: that it was a masterpiece.

13 And he was the first planetary citizen my new friends had ever seen, and possibly the last one, too. He was no more a respecter of politics and national boundaries than (that image again) a unicorn. Beauty could be found or created anywhere on this planet, and that was that.

14 AT&T has completed yet another building, this one on the island of Manhattan, near where I live. The telephone company has again done without the services of my father, who could not now be awakened in any case. AT&T hired Philip Johnson instead, a Sleeping Beauty who throughout his adult life has been tickled awake by ardent princes.

15 Should I now rage at Fate for not having enabled my father to have as much fun as Mr. Johnson?

16 I try to imagine my father speaking to me across the abyss between the dead and the living, and I hear him saying this: "Do not pity me because I in my prime awaited romantic challenges which never came. If you wish to carve an epitaph on my modest headstone in Crown Hill Cemetery at this late date, then let it be this: IT WAS ENOUGH TO HAVE BEEN A UNICORN."

❧

Discussion Questions

1. What did Vonnegut, age twenty-seven, find out about his father, age sixty-five, that he had not known before? Why does Vonnegut feel that his father had "mousetrapped" him?

2. What brought about the turning point in the senior Vonnegut's career as an architect?

3. Describe the older Vonnegut's career beginning in 1929 until his death in 1957.

*4. In paragraph 9, Vonnegut uses fictional characters (Sleeping Beauty, Rip Van Winkle) to describe the course of the career of his father. Explain.

5. How did Vonnegut learn that his father was "exotic as a unicorn"? Explain the description.

*6. How was Vonnegut's father different from other fathers? How do his traits of character, described in paragraphs 11–13, seem to be pluses or minuses?

Writing Topics

1. Overwhelming national or world events, such as the Great Depression, World War II, the Korean War, or the Vietnam War, have intervened in—and altered—the lives of all involved. Conduct an interview with a relative or older friend who was caught up in such an event and ask how the event changed his or her life. Write an account of your interview, beginning with an identification and description of the individual you have interviewed.

2. Often small or seemingly trivial events (for example, an illness, disappearance, tardiness, or misunderstanding) change a person's life. Think over your own life and consider the choices you have made or been denied because of matters (happenings, episodes) beyond your control. Write an account of this time of your life, considering what might have been different had there not been the "intervention." (Are you in the class in which this book is a text, for example, because of your own detailed planning or have other factors brought you to the chair you occupy?)

*"I suppose I am talking about just that:
the ambiguity of belonging to a
generation distrustful of political highs,
the historical irrelevancy of growing up convinced that
the heart of darkness lay not in some error of
social organization but in man's own blood."*

ON THE MORNING AFTER THE SIXTIES

Joan Didion

Born in 1934 in Sacramento, California, Joan Didion identifies not with the sixties but with the fifties generation. She
attended the University of California at Berkeley, graduating
in the mid-1950s, that decade of the "quiet" (or conformist)
generation, sharply different from the activist (or rebellious)
generation that came along the following decade (the
"notorious" 1960s). As a college senior, she won a literary
prize from *Vogue* magazine and immediately embarked on a
writing career. She was written a number of novels, including *River Run* (1963), *Play It as It Lays* (1970), and *Run River*
(1994). She is, however, more widely known for her essays
and journalistic reports, the first of which, *Slouching toward
Bethlehem* (1968), attracted wide attention with its penetrating cultural criticism. Other similar collections include *The
White Album* (1979), from which the essay below is taken,
and *Sentimental Journeys* (1993). In such books as *Salvador*
(1983), *Miami* (1987), and *After Henry* (1992), she assumes
the role of a journalist—but one with a keenly perceptive
and critical eye.

1   I am talking here about being a child of my time. When I think about the
Sixties now I think about an afternoon not of the Sixties at all, an afternoon
early in my sophomore year at Berkeley, a bright autumn Saturday in 1953. I
was lying on a leather couch in a fraternity house (there had been a lunch for
the alumni, my date had gone on to the game, I do not now recall why I had

stayed behind), lying there alone reading a book by Lionel Trilling and listening to a middle-aged man pick out on a piano in need of tuning the melodic line to "Blue Room." All that afternoon he sat at the piano and all that afternoon he played "Blue Room" and he never got it right. I can hear and see it still, the wrong note in "We will thrive on / Keep alive on," the sunlight falling through the big windows, the man picking up his drink and beginning again and telling me, without ever saying a word, something I had not known before about bad marriages and wasted time and looking backward. That such an afternoon would now seem implausible in every detail—the idea of having had a "date" for a football lunch now seems to me so exotic as to be almost czarist—suggests the extent to which the narrative on which many of us grew up no longer applies.

2   The distance we have come from the world in which I went to college was on my mind quite a bit during those seasons when not only Berkeley but dozens of other campuses were periodically shut down, incipient battlegrounds, their borders sealed. To think of Berkeley as it was in the Fifties was not to think of barricades and reconstituted classes. "Reconstitution" would have sounded to us then like Newspeak, and barricades are never personal. We were all very personal then, sometimes relentlessly so, and, at that point where we either act or do not act, most of us are still. I suppose I am talking about just that: the ambiguity of belonging to a generation distrustful of political highs, the historical irrelevancy of growing up convinced that the heart of darkness lay not in some error of social organization but in man's own blood. If man was bound to err, then any social organization was bound to be in error. It was a premise which still seems to me accurate enough, but one which robbed us early of a certain capacity for surprise.

3   At Berkeley in the Fifties no one was surprised by anything at all, a *donnée* which tended to render discourse less than spirited, and debate nonexistent. The world was by definition imperfect, and so of course was the university. There was some talk even then about IBM cards, but on balance the notion that free education for tens of thousands of people might involve automation did not seem unreasonable. We took it for granted that the Board of Regents would sometimes act wrongly. We simply avoided those students rumored to be FBI informers. We were that generation called "silent," but we were silent neither, as some thought, because we shared the period's official optimism nor, as others thought, because we feared its official repression. We were silent because the exhilaration of social action seemed to many of us just one more way of escaping the personal, of masking for a while that dread of the meaningless which was man's fate.

4   To have assumed that particular fate so early was the peculiarity of my generation. I think now that we were the last generation to identify with adults. That most of us have found adulthood just as morally ambiguous as we expected it to be falls perhaps into the category of prophecies self-fulfilled: I am simply not sure. I am telling you only how it was. The mood of Berkeley in those years

was one of mild but chronic "depression," against which I remember certain small things that seemed to me somehow explications, dazzling in their clarity, of the world I was about to enter: I remember a woman picking daffodils in the rain one day when I was walking in the hills. I remember a teacher who drank too much one night and revealed his fright and bitterness. I remember my real joy at discovering for the first time how language worked, at discovering, for example, that the central line of *Heart of Darkness* was a postscript. All such images were personal, and the personal was all that most of us expected to find. We would make a separate peace. We would do graduate work in Middle English, we would go abroad. We would make some money and live on a ranch. We would survive outside history, in a knid of *idée fixe* referred to always, during the years I spent at Berkeley, as "some little town with a decent beach."

5   As it worked out I did not find or even look for the little town with the decent beach. I sat in the large bare apartment in which I lived my junior and senior years (I had lived awhile in a sorority, the Tri Delt house, and had left it, typically, not over any "issue" but because I, the implacable "I," did not like living with sixty people) and I read Camus and Henry James and I watched a flowering plum come in and out of blossom and at night, most nights, I walked outside and looked up to where the cyclotron and the bevatron glowed on the dark hillside, unspeakable mysteries which engaged me, in the style of my time, only personally. Later I got out of Berkeley and went to New York and later I got out of New York and came to Los Angeles. What I have made for myself is personal, but is not exactly peace. Only one person I knew at Berkeley later discovered an ideology, dealt himself into history, cut himself loose from both his own dread and his own time. A few of the people I knew at Berkeley killed themselves not long after. Another attempted suicide in Mexico and then, in a recovery which seemed in many ways a more advanced derangement, came home and joined the Bank of America's three-year executive-training program. Most of us live less theatrically, but remain the survivors of a peculiar and inward time. If I could believe that going to a barricade would affect man's fate in the slightest I would go to that barricade, and quite often I wish that I could, but it would be less than honest to say that I expect to happen upon such a happy ending.

ੴ

Discussion Questions

1. Didion wrote this essay in 1970, after the sixties were over. Considering the distinctions she draws between her fifties generation and the sixties generation, what do you take to be the meaning of the title, "On the Morning after the Sixties"?

2. In the first paragraph, Didion describes an afternoon of the fifties on the campus at Berkeley. What was she doing, and why does she say "That such an afternoon would now seem implausible in every detail—the idea of having had a 'date' for a football lunch now seems to me so exotic as to be almost czarist—suggests the extent to which the narrative on which many of us grew up no longer applies"?

3. Explain Didion's comment in paragraph 3, "We were that generation called 'silent,' but . . . we were silent because the exhilaration of social action seemed to many of us just one more way of escaping the personal, of masking for a while that dread of the meaningless which was man's fate."

*4. In paragraph 4, Didion remembers "certain small things that seemed to [her] somehow explications, dazzling in their clarity, of the world [she] was about to enter." Explain how all of the examples Didion cites could appear "dazzling in their clarity."

Writing Topics

1. Read (or reread) Joseph Conrad's *Heart of Darkness* and, in an analytical essay, explore Didion's meaning when she says she discovered that the "central line" of the work "was a postscript."

2. Didion concludes her essay, "If I could believe that going to a barricade would affect man's fate in the slightest I would go to that barricade, and quite often I wish that I could, but it would be less than honest to say that I expect to happen upon such a happy ending." Write an essay in which you agree with Didion's skeptical view of activism, or in which you see her attitude as a cop-out, as self-centered, or as essentially defeatist.

"I do not think my medical education has been extraordinarily well designed, and I think that some of the most effectively conveyed lessons have been the unadvertised teachings about behavior, ethics, style, and power."

BECOMING A BABY DOCTOR

Perri Klass

Perri Klass was born in Tuna-puna, Trinidad, to an American citizen in 1958. She earned a B.A. from Harvard in 1979 and studied at the University of California from 1979 to 1981. She received her M.D. from Harvard University in 1986 and became a resident in pediatrics that same year at Boston's Children's Hospital. She began writing fiction and essays at a very early age. One of her stories was accepted by *Mademoiselle* just before she entered medical school, and she continued her writing throughout her medical training. Her works include two novels, *Recombinations* (1985) and *Other Women's Children* (1992), a book of short stories, *I Am Having an Adventure* (1986), and a professional book, *Baby Doctor* (1992). She published A *Not Entirely Benign Procedure: Four Years as a Medical Student* in 1987; portions of the "Introduction" and "Conclusion," describing the way in which she became first a medical student and then a pediatrician, are included in "Becoming a Baby Doctor."

1   I did not originally intend to go to medical school, and when I started medical school, I certainly did not intend to write about it. I had majored in biology in college, thinking at first about becoming a doctor, but moved off in the direction of biological research. I began to picture myself going into the jungle to study animals, and so I took the first step toward the jungle and went off to graduate school in zoology. The animals I chose to study were parasitic organisms, and I was interested in questions of ecology and evolution as applied

to parasites; I wondered how a life cycle could evolve that required two, or even three, different hosts, all synchronized into the development of the parasite. But hanging around parasitology you meet a lot of doctors and biomedical researchers, and after a couple of years I decided that I was interested in the human hosts as well as the parasites, so I applied to medical school. I make it all sound casual and a little lighthearted; in fact I had to put a great deal of effort into areas in which I am not talented—notably learning enough chemistry and physics to do decently on the eight-hour multiple-choice test required of all medical school applicants. I had come close to flunking these courses in college and needed to convince medical schools that I had since learned the material. I filled in applications, and when the time came I bought a suit and flew around the country for interviews. I smiled and looked enthusiastic and got asked all sorts of exciting questions, including why had I almost failed chemistry and physics in college (I rehearsed a good many answers to that one, finally went with a disarmingly sincere statement about being out of my depth back in those first years of college, and simply not knowing how to study properly—it wasn't exactly true, but it was disarmingly sincere). I toured any number of medical schools, asking the questions applicants all ask on these tours, most notably, "How many students to a cadaver?" At some schools it's four, at others it's five or six. Is this a basis on which to choose your medical school? No, but it's one of the few questions for which you can get a firm objective answer. I no longer remember which schools have how many students to a cadaver.

2   I have been writing for most of my life; I come from a family in which most people write, and publish (though no one makes a living at it), and I had been writing fiction all through high school, college, and graduate school. It never occurred to me that I wouldn't go on writing fiction in medical school, and it never occurred to me that I might start writing nonfiction. The summer before I started medical school, I achieved my first publication: a story of mine was printed in *Mademoiselle* magazine. Although I was of course pleased to get into medical school, I have to say that the acceptance from *Mademoiselle* was easily ten times as exciting. I mean, it's hard to get into medical school, but thousands of people do it every year.

3   I had gone to college at Harvard, then moved out to Berkeley for graduate school. The year I was applying to medical school, I took some time off from school of any kind and went to Italy with my friend Larry Wolff. He researched his doctoral dissertation in the Vatican archives while I worked in a lab and did some writing. In September of 1982, we moved back to Cambridge, Massachusetts, and settled in.

4   Medical school was sort of a great unknown for me. No one in my family had ever gone, and for the last few years I had been hanging out with graduate students. I didn't know what to expect, and I had only limited confidence that the process was going to be successful, that I was going to come out the other end a real doctor. Most of what I knew about medicine was what I had seen on

television; as a child, I had been a great devotee of *Marcus Welby, M.D.*, and *Medical Center*. But I started medical school without any very clear idea of what my training would be like, of what would come after medical school, of what choices I might have in front of me.

5   Toward the end of my first year of medical school, an editor at *Mademoiselle* suggested that I write an article for the magazine about being a woman in the first year of medical school. I had never written anything like this before, and I more or less blundered my way through it. The article was published, and later I was offered other opportunities to write about my training. I had entered a world which was as mysterious to most people as it had been for me, and it seemed that there were readers interested in hearing the details. I wrote a weekly column in *The New York Times* for nine weeks, then later began doing regular columns for two other magazines, *Discover*, aimed at a general readership interested in science, and *Massachusetts Medicine*, which goes to doctors and medical students. I have also done articles for a variety of other publications.

6   Meanwhile, I went through medical school. I also had a baby; I got pregnant toward the end of my first year and had the baby in the middle of the second year, and I ended up writing about that too.

7   The experience of writing about medical school while going through it has changed my medical education tremendously. I have found that in order to write about my training so that people outside the medical profession can understand what I am talking about I have had to preserve a certain level of naiveté for myself. I have to hear and see things not only as a doctor, who would take most hospital sights, most medical locutions, completely for granted, but also as a nondoctor. Instead of trying to forget, as quickly as possible, what it felt like to be in the operating room for the first time (Who are all these people? What are they doing? What are all these machines? What are those tubes for? Where am I supposed to stand? What am I supposed to do? This is completely disgusting; what if I faint?), I had to try to preserve all those disorienting sensations and impressions.

8   The general pressure in medical school is to push yourself ahead into professionalism, to start feeling at home in the hospital, in the operating room, to make medical jargon your native tongue—it's all part of becoming efficient, knowledgeable, competent. You want to leave behind that green, terrified medical student who stood awkwardly on the edge of the action, terrified of revealing limitless ignorance, terrified of killing a patient. You want to identify with the people ahead of you, the ones who know what they're doing. And instead, I have found it necessary to retain some of that greenness, so I could explain the hospital to people for whom it was not familiar turf.

9   Of course, it becomes a little artificial after a while, and there are sensations I can no longer remember. The hospital no longer feels alien or threatening to me, the medical jargon is familiar in my ears. Once you have come to understand a language, it is probably impossible to recapture exactly what it felt like to hear it as gibberish.

10 There are things I find funny which are funny only to doctors or medical students. I can laugh at a fellow student doing an imitation of an inept medical student trying and trying to draw blood from a patient; I laugh in recognition, in identification with the student, but nondoctors cringe in horror, identifying with the poor abused patient. And so I have to acknowledge that despite a very deliberate attempt to remember the perceptions of someone without medical training, I have in fact become someone with medical training, and with the attendant perceptions.

11 The essays in this book were written during the four years I spent in medical school. The essay about the first year was in fact written at the end of my first year. The essay on beginning clinical training, drawing blood from a patient for the first time, was written during my first months in the hospital. I have not altered these pieces to make them more uniform, because it seems to me that if my voice has changed through medical school, then that change should be part of the education process I have been writing about.

12 Medical school divides into two parts. For the first two years, I was mostly in the classroom, listening to lectures, carrying out various kinds of lab exercises (looking at slides under a microscope, dissecting a cadaver). Then the second two years I was "on the wards," in the hospitals. I spent a month or two in each of a number of specialties, a month in radiology, two months in surgery, a month in psychiatry, and so on. And sometime during this clinical training, I decided what branch of medicine I wanted to enter—pediatrics.

❖   ❖   ❖

13 I am going to be a pediatrician. This is a decision that I started to make even before I had done any pediatrics. During my first three months in the hospital, my general medicine clerkship, I became aware that something was wrong. I was not finding clinical medicine as interesting or as rewarding as I had hoped to. It was more interesting to take care of patients than it had been to memorize diseases for a test, but it wasn't fascinating and all-absorbing—as I had sort of hoped it would be. This, after all, was the big apple, the goal of all those courses, the hospital ward. Why wasn't I more involved, more excited about what I was doing? Some of the answer had to do with my circumstances, the particular hospital I had been assigned to, some of the people with whom I had to work closely, some of those who were supposedly teaching me. But I also began to wonder whether I might prefer working with pediatric patients.

14 And sure enough, when I got to pediatrics I loved it. I was even reasonably happy most of the time—which is not bad for someone who is in the hospital all day every day and all night every fourth night. I felt profoundly involved with my team, with my patients.

15 The kind of adult medicine I was exposed to in a famous teaching hospital does not of course represent all adult medicine. But when I did adult medicine,

we seemed to spend a great deal of our time fighting to save people who have very very limited prospects. A nursing home would send in an elderly patient who had not walked or talked in two years, who had developed a temperature. A person with a rare and fascinating case of something or other would be referred in for more tests—there would be nothing in particular we could do to help, but everyone would repeat, like a mantra, "Great teaching case." In addition, many of the patients had problems that required other kinds of interventions besides medical treatment—people with chronic lung disease who couldn't stop smoking, for example. As doctors, or medical students, we had to leave these things alone; they were outside our domain, and besides, who had time to talk about smoking or diet or exercise or stress? There are, of course, doctors who address all these subjects, but from my point of view it was just another frustration.

16 But this may all be rationalizing. It's true that in pediatrics you are almost always fighting a battle for a whole lifetime. It's true that you deal much less in what are unfairly stigmatized as "self-induced" problems—the effects of smoking, drinking. (I don't mean to belittle the suffering these substances cause, or imply that sufferers are not entitled to good medical care. I just didn't really get much satisfaction myself from dealing with these problems.) It's also true that in pediatrics you never get to ignore what we rather pompously call the psychosocial aspect of your patients; you always have to deal with the parents, who provide you with the kind of context which is often missing in adult medicine. But maybe what I really discovered about myself was that I like children, as a group, much better than I like adults. And I also tend to like pediatricians more than I like other doctors. I like them because they are not able to be stiff—the adult doctor can stride grandly into the patient's room and announce, we have decided to do this and that, and command respect from many patients. The pediatrician who says, apologetically, to a small patient that such and such a procedure is necessary and will only hurt a tiny bit, is frequently bitten or kicked.

17 Of course, since I had my own child during medical school, and he has grown to the ripe and stubborn age of two and a half while I was a student, I have had a certain amount of contact with pediatrics from the parent's side of the examining table. When I was applying for residency, I tried to pretend that having had a baby naturally gifted me with tremendous expertise, gave me an advantage over other applicants. This, naturally, was nonsense. Of course, there are a few things I know that come in useful in the hospital. I can change diapers in my sleep, for example. And I know all the developmental milestones, when a child can be expected to smile, walk, talk—except I know them only up as far as Benjamin's age. In other words, I could evaluate any child two and a half or under to see if everything was going on schedule, but I would be lost with three-year-olds (can they build tall towers with blocks? catch baseballs? operate heavy machinery? child-raising is full of surprises). By the end of

residency, a three-year process, I expect to be fully competent with any child up to five and a half.

18   No, the real advantage of having had a child is that I know a great deal more about parents than I otherwise would have. I have brought my own child to the emergency room where I will begin working in a few months, and I will not forget what it felt like to sit in the waiting room, holding a feverish and alarmingly quiet little boy on my lap, wishing that all the other patients would get out of the way so my child could be seen. I have also in my time called the pediatrician because my tiny baby had a funny-looking poop. One night a year or so ago my son had an ear infection, and his temperature went up over 104, and I began to worry that his brain was melting. Now, I happen to know for a fact that brains do not melt; I even had in my notes a lecture I had attended on the syndrome of so-called fever phobia—all the myths parents believe about the ill effects of fever, all the damage they can cause their children by overdosing them with antifever drugs. I read over those notes, then I called the pediatrician and told him that I was worried that my baby's brain might be melting. The doctor on call that night was actually someone who knew me; he had taught me during my pediatrics rotation. And he said to me, gently, come on now, Perri, is this kind of fever really unusual in severe otitis media? And of course I blubbered into the phone, don't ask me any questions, dammit, just tell me my baby is going to be okay, his brain isn't cooking. And does he need a spinal tap? Does he need to be admitted to the hospital? And all of this, I suppose, is valuable experience for a pediatrician to have had. Last summer, when I was doing my advanced pediatrics rotation, I admitted a young boy with what we were pretty sure was viral meningitis. We were putting him on antibiotics in case it was bacterial, a much more severe disease, but we weren't really worried. And after I had explained all this to his mother, she suddenly clutched my arm and began to cry. "You can tell me the truth," she sobbed. "He's going to die, he's never going to come out of the hospital alive, is he? My baby's going to die!" It was worth my remembering, right then, despite my impatience that she hadn't heard a word of my brilliant and sensitive explanation, that I am fully capable of the same kind of uncontrollable fears.

19   Like most medical students, and I suspect like many doctors, I tend to deal with my own illness by denying it. Sometimes I indulge myself, especially if I think I can claim a day off, but basically I don't go to doctors and I don't take medicines—or at least not until I absolutely have to. And as an intern, of course, you aren't allowed to be sick. But for my kid, I am a demanding, frightened, overanxious consumer of medical care. For myself, I accept the various unhealthy constraints of residency—no fresh food, no regular hours, no time for exercise, no stress reduction, no doing any of the things we tell patients to do. But for my kid, I want what everyone wants, healthy circumstances and a life tailored to his needs. So having a child has enlarged my perspective on medicine, and on my chosen branch of medicine in particular, in a number of ways.

My son has been and will, I expect, continue to be a steady reminder to me of what my patients represent. They are not their diseases, they are—well, I know what they are. I have one of my own.

20 And my own reactions to my child have been and will, I expect, continue to be reminders to me of what parents feel when their children are sick, of the hopes, expectations, and fears with which they bring a child to the doctor.

21 So I am going to be a pediatrician. Two years of preclinical courses, two years of hospital work, and now medical school is ending. I have a great many doubts about the education I have undergone, and most of those doubts are included in these various essays. I do not think my medical education has been extraordinarily well designed, and I think that some of the most effectively conveyed lessons have been the unadvertised teachings about behavior, ethics, style, and power.

22 As I wrote in the introduction, the process of writing about medical school has changed the last four years for me. I think that in many ways it has helped me through; many of the frustrations and furies of medical school have been essentially small and petty (it's amazing how petty you can be when you're really tired and you really want to go home), and trying to put my grievances in writing has sometimes helped me sort that out. In the end, I suppose I under-stand what has happened to me much better for having written about it; there are people who can keep track of themselves without writing anything down, but I am not like that.

23 I feel obliged to sum it up: am I glad I did it, would I do it again, would I do it differently? I can't answer for myself of four years ago, but I suppose I'm glad, I'd probably do it again. And of course I'd do it differently; I'd do it *right*, whatever that means. I wouldn't let myself be so intimidated, right? I'd defend my dignity, I wouldn't truckle to my superiors, right? I'd really learn everything thoroughly and properly, come out completely *prepared* for internship, right? Well, maybe not.

24 And so, what I am left with is an appreciation that the last four years have certainly accomplished something. Maybe not all they were intended to accom-plish, and maybe also some things they were not meant to do, but one way or another, they have served as an initiation. An initiation of blood (not mine) and pain (mine was the least of it), weariness and confusion, of books and cadavers, needles and plastic tubing, patients and doctors. And I, having been initiated, am left saying, well, here I am—a different person. And, as of this writing, almost but not quite a doctor.

ॐ

Discussion Questions

1. What led Klass in her thinking and experience to begin medical school? Characterize the process: was it a straight road or was it a somewhat curving or roundabout road? Explain.
2. What led Klass to write about her experience, thus combining one strong interest and talent with another?
3. How did writing about her experience in medical school affect the very experience Klass was writing about?
4. What were the primary considerations that led Klass to become a pediatrician?
5. What difference did having a baby make in her training as a pediatrician?
*6. In the end, what does Klass say about her experience of writing about medical school while enrolled in it?
*7. In her last paragraph, Klass writes, "And so, what I am left with is an appreciation that the last four years [in medical school] have certainly accomplished something." What have these years "accomplished" as compared with what they were intended to accomplish?

Writing Topics

1. Write a letter to a friend who is considering the possibility of becoming a doctor, recommending the reading of these excerpts from Klass's A Not Entirely Benign Procedure and pointing out what features in them might be useful in such consideration. (You may want to read more deeply into the book in preparation for writing.)
2. Write a letter to your parents revealing your current thinking about your own career: What do you think you would like to become? Are you torn between two or more possibilities and having difficulty making a choice? Have you changed your mind in the distant or recent past about your future? What are the various factors you feel you must take into account in your decision? To whom if anyone do you turn for advice?

"We studied the ads in the glossy magazines
and saw every movie we could,
chewing our little-girl nails and
dreaming of the day when they would be long
and scarlet and, of course, holding a cigarette."

THE GRAND DELUSION:
SMOKING WAS COOL TILL IT LEFT ME COLD

Eileen Herbert Jordan

Eileen Herbert Jordan reveals in the opening of "The Grand Delusion" that she was sixteen years old in 1942 when she was mesmerized by the scenes in the World War II movie *Casablanca*—those scenes in Rick's Café Américain that were played out in the soft fog of the smoke from innumerable cigarettes. She joined those on the screen by smoking her first cigarettes ever while sitting discreetly in the balcony watching Humphrey Bogart and Ingrid Bergman declare their doomed love—the doom intensified somehow by all that smoke! Jordan has served as a senior editor for *Good Housekeeping* and *Woman's Day* magazines and is now a free-lance writer. She has published both fiction and nonfiction in numerous publications, including *Modern Maturity*, a monthly publication of the American Association of Retired People. "The Grand Delusion" was taken from the June 1994 issue of *Modern Maturity*.

1   *I am sitting in a darkened, dank and claustrophobia-inducing basement room. The room is in a hospital, tucked away amid pipes and gauges and awesome walls of machinery. I am sitting here staring at a screen that has been unrolled before me. A woman is standing next to the screen, tapping a picture projected on it with the pointer she holds in one hand. Whatever it is, the picture is malevolently evil. Why am I here? What am I doing? This is my story.*

2   In the first 45 minutes of *Casablanca* Humphrey Bogart smoked ten cigarettes. I smoked two. It was 1942, I was 16, and so wrapped was I in the enchanted shadowy haze of Rick's Café Américain that I paid no attention—I could have smoked a pack. Everybody in *Casablanca* moved about in a wonderful soft-focus fog, the air about their heads ever cloudy. The piano, muffled in the smoke, had a special kind of intimacy that made one ache just listening to the notes. I was convinced as I watched that love, doomed or otherwise, never would flourish in any other atmosphere quite so well. I was very young and my sense of doom ran high.

3   It was the first time I smoked. The two cigarettes in question were my allotment from a pack a group of us, all underage, had purchased jointly at a local stationery store while one of our number stood guard outside, a lookout for parents and nuns. The potential horror of encountering either while in possession of something so contraband as cigarettes was also the reason we then repaired to the very back of the balcony, as far away from Humphrey Bogart and anyone else as possible.

4   In fact, our parents' objections to smoking were mild enough, possibly because a good many of them smoked themselves (and died for it, some of them). When they said anything, it was usually that old saw warning that smoking would stunt our growth. In my lifetime I have never met a single woman stopped by the stunt-the-growth theory. Personally, since I had reached five feet six inches by the time I was 13 and was sure that half the men in the world were already lost to me as a result, stunting further growth seemed a marvelous idea.

5   The nuns, however, were quite another matter. *Ladies*, they said, do not smoke. And people (presumably including men) soon shunned women who did. Their convent school curriculum included teaching us to pour tea—apparently on the theory that this would be of some use to us in the future—forbidding all cosmetics, and monitoring our legs (lest we go without stockings), our hands (to be gloved, preferably in white, almost anywhere outdoors), and our heads (to be covered with a veil or a hat in chapel). The ban on smoking capped all this. What gave that one particular clout was the threat of immediate expulsion if caught.

6   We believed the nuns. We *knew* that a lady did not smoke. Whoever said she did? Neither did a drudge in lisle stockings and a chapel veil. Smoking was something done by beautiful women in silver rooms, women who waved jeweled cigarette holders and slithered down staircases blowing rings into the air until there were halos all about their heads. As for being shunned: Those creatures practically needed sabers to fight their suitors off.

7   We studied the ads in the glossy magazines and saw every movie we could, chewing our little-girl nails and dreaming of the day when they would be long

and scarlet and, of course, holding a cigarette. Our dreams never omitted the company of men.

8   At one point we came upon Paul Henreid lighting two cigarettes, one for himself and one for Bette Davis, in *Now, Voyager*. This feat became one important criterion for a devastating date, a romantic gesture beyond all others; we could die for it.

9   *Nobody told us we actually might. Danger? Why, danger was only delicious—back then.*

10   Better even than Henreid was something we learned from one of our group who had an older, married sister: the magic of the postcoital cigarette. This was a really new thought. It was spoken of in whispers behind closed doors and with much giggling; notes concerning it were passed back and forth. Obviously it was a landmark that lay ahead for us all, and we looked forward to it with some of the anticipation we had for the act itself. Probably more. At least we knew a little bit about smoking—we had absolutely no idea what we were getting into with *coitus*.

11   In 1951, a man named Herbert Brean published a book called *How to Stop Smoking*. It is interesting today only because it sold three-quarters-of-a-million copies; its arguments were really very mild.

12   For example, Brean said that smoking wastes time. He broke this into a mathematical equation: Smoking one cigarette takes slightly longer than one minute, he said. This includes the time it takes to remove it from the pack, light it, place it in an ashtray as it burns, pick it up and lay it down again. He conceded that one can accomplish other things, perhaps even think, while doing all this; nonetheless, at the rate of 30 cigarettes a day (evidently a norm in 1951), a week of one's life is, shall we say, blown away every year in smoking.

13   No hints that down the road you might be losing years of your life. There were not even as yet any warning drums along the Mohawk. Those came later.

14   First there were superficial signs that smoking's fashionability was on the wane. Gold cigarette cases clasped with gems had not been at the top of anyone's wish list for years. Nobody gave silver table lighters as wedding presents anymore (and not because they didn't work anyway). In all the photographs of the beautiful people frequenting the beautiful places there was not a cigarette to be seen—though that was subliminal and you might not have noticed it right away.

15   Then in 1964 the Surgeon General of the United States released a report linking smoking to lung cancer and other diseases. Thereafter, a warning to that effect appeared on every pack of cigarettes. Eventually the best prospects in personal ads were looking for nonsmoking mates. The number of places where you could smoke, if you did, began to dwindle.

16   At the bay where I spent childhood summers, when it was high tide there was only one sand dune tall enough to stand on and not be underwater. That's

the way I began to feel with cigarettes in my hand in public places. Movies and railroad stations, lobbies and offices and airlines, taxis and waiting rooms, and great sweeping areas in restaurants—all gone. Something was beginning to nudge me, too; some vagrant thought I could not quite capture yet.

17   You see, when you are hooked, you are hooked. Change does not come like shortening the hem of a skirt; you spend more time kicking and screaming and denying than you spend thinking. For one thing, you have to marshal all your excuses. Here are my favorites:

18   *Smoking helps me keep my figure:* That's a big one, though to use it effectively you must have some semblance of a figure to begin with.

19   *Smoking relaxes me:* A goofing-off mechanism; impractical for full-time use.

20   *Smoking helps my concentration:* A comment beloved by sedentary workers who stay at their desks because the ashtray is there.

21   *I'm a liberated woman, free to do as I please:* This fails to take into consideration the fact that an addict is never free.

22   At length, I ran out of excuses.

23   "The patch is not guaranteed," the doctor said to me. "Nothing is. It depends on you."

24   The patches were small, made up of thin layers of plastic containing a solution of nicotine in amounts ranging from 21 milligrams down to seven milligrams. Every day I was going to paste a fresh patch on a part of my upper body (a different part each time) and it was going to dispense nicotine into my system, replacing the cigarettes that used to do the job. It was going to cure me of smoking. It was my recognition that my time had come.

25   Along with the box of patches came a serious warning: Under no circumstances, no matter what, was I to smoke a cigarette while wearing one—*that could kill me.* It might well bring on a fatal heart attack; if not, I could simply succumb to nicotine poisoning from the combination of the two.

26   I am very gung-ho about not being dead, so this got to me. The doctor said I should walk out of his office happy; I walked out petrified.

27   Along with the patch, I had a booklet of tips on how to face the future without cigarettes. I found as I settled in and tried them that they were Band-Aids, not tourniquets—I continued to bleed. Still, I had not yet reached my moment of truth and these tips were better than nothing, so I set them down here for you:

28   *Keep ice water in your refrigerator and sip it whenever you have the urge to smoke.*

29   *Buy a fake cigarette (they are made of plastic and smell of mint) and play with it.*

30   *Several times during the day open a window and breathe deeply, counting to ten with each breath.*

31   *Get a large supply of lollipops and start sucking them.*

32   *Put all the butts and ashes you can gather together in a glass jar; then position the jar conspicuously where it will look particularly revolting each time you pass it.*

33   *Take the money you save from no longer buying cigarettes, drop it in another jar, and dream of the extravagant present you will buy for yourself with it.*

34   *Use your hands: Do needlepoint, knit, tat, crochet, write letters. Do crossword puzzles, jigsaw puzzles, cook, bake, garden, paint.*

35   And accept the fact that life never stops putting roadblocks in your way. What happened to me, for example, was the weight gain. People tell you that when you stop smoking you add weight because your metabolism slows down. After a while it seemed that mine had ground to a dead stop. I blamed my new Rubenesque proportions on that, ignoring other factors. The thing is, I was so profoundly sorry for myself that only regular, protracted indulgence in the richest of chocolates could ease my pain.

36   But it was not just chocolate — it was food of every variety. I began planning my lunch while finishing breakfast, my dinner as lunch was ending. Television food commercials I had scorned in the past now drove me wild with desire; I knew all the Häagen-Dazs flavors by heart.

37   And, unwittingly, this led to my final salvation.

38   "Medically, your weight is all right," the doctor said.

39   Medical opinions about one's weight bear no relation to what one sees in a full-length mirror. I told him as much.

40   "Well, if you're unhappy," he said, "try a support group. Here. . . ." He handed me a card with the vital information. "Talk about it with them."

41   *My name is Eileen and I am a smoker.* I wrote it, along with my telephone number, on the pad passed around the long table where I sat. No last names, please. No addresses. Overhead a light was beating down, making shadows. My chair was stiff and unyielding. I was anonymous, trapped in this forbidding room, unsure how to leave. The woman standing beside the screen holding a pointer was a nurse. She was tapping a picture of a lung. It was a smoker's lung. It could have been mine.

42   *What was I doing here? What was it all about? This was not what I had in mind. Ever. All those years ago — those years when smoking had been a part of music that broke your heart, of silver staircases and savoir-faire — all gone, all gone.*

43   The night before I had watched a television movie and, from a host of suspects, had picked at once the serial killer — and I am not usually good at that. He was the one who smoked. Of course. Oh yes, the mystique was altogether gone.

44   Maybe it had only ever been the stuff of dreams. And once you lose it, you are free. I was free. There was a chill in the air in the room the way there is in basements, but it didn't matter; I didn't have to stay there anymore. I didn't need patches or jars of ashes, either. I didn't need chocolates at midnight. The money I was saving went into a ruby-red Pontiac, a car so sportive my son said it needed only fuzzy dice on its rear-view mirror — but I didn't even need that. Most of all, I didn't need a cigarette. Try it. It feels wonderful.

45   Oh, once in a while now, when smoke blows my way, I have a memory—of a certain night, a certain weekend, a certain song. I close my eyes and sniff, and then go on. In my next coming I'm going to feature fitness as my lifestyle; my body will be superb as I run and jump and jog with my beloved, instead of languishing in smoke-filled rooms. I suppose in *that* life thereafter I will shiver with nostalgia every time I catch the scent of sweat. You simply never know.

Discussion Questions

1. In what way did the movies influence the young Jordan and her friends to begin smoking?
2. What were the warnings against smoking in 1942, when Jordan and her friends began? What effect did the warnings have?
*3. According to Jordan, what differences in attitude toward smoking were brought about by the publication in 1951 of Herbert Brean's book, *How to Stop Smoking?* Explain.
4. What changes does Jordan cite as brought about by the Surgeon General's report on smoking issued in 1964?
5. Explain Jordan's meaning in paragraph 17 when she writes, "Change does not come like shortening the hem of a skirt; you spend more time kicking and screaming and denying than you spend thinking."
*6. In paragraph 37, Jordan writes, "And, unwittingly, this led to my final salvation." What does *this* refer to? What weight of meaning does *unwittingly* carry? What, exactly, was Jordan's "final salvation"?

Writing Topics

1. Beginning with paragraph 18, Jordan lists the excuses she "marshaled" for continuing to smoke. Write an essay analyzing the excuses on her list, indicating why you think they are valid or invalid. Add any other excuses you have heard or can think of and analyze them. Then give your considered opinion about beginning—or continuing—to smoke.
2. In the latter part of her essay, Jordan sets forth in detail all the ways she attempted to stop smoking, and finally, at the end, the way that led "unwittingly" to her "final salvation." Write a long letter to a friend or relative who probably wants to stop smoking, setting forth the ways you suggest that he or she try to stop. Give whatever advice you think might be effective.

Why do I tell you this little boy's story of medusas,

rays, and sea monsters,

nearly sixty years after the fact?

Because it illustrates, I think,

how a naturalist is created."

PARADISE BEACH

Edward O. Wilson

Edward O. Wilson was born in Birmingham, Alabama, in 1929. At the University of Alabama, he was awarded a B.S. degree in 1949 and an M.S. in 1950. He earned his Ph.D. in biology at Harvard in 1955. His many books,which are as accessible to the common reader as to the specialist, include *The Insect Societies* (1971), *Sociobiology: The New Synthesis* (1975), *On Human Nature* (1978), and *Success and Dominance in Ecosystems: The Case of the Social Insects* (1990). His book *The Ants* (1990), coauthored by Bert Hölldobler, was winner of the 1991 Pulitzer Prize in nonfiction prose. Wilson is Pellegrino University Professor and curator of entomology at the Museum of Comparative Zoology, Harvard University. "Paradise Beach" comes from *Naturalist*, his autobiography published in 1994.

1   What happened, what we *think* happened in distant memory, is built around a small collection of dominating images. In one of my own from the age of seven, I stand in the shallows off Paradise Beach, staring down at a huge jellyfish in water so still and clear that its every detail is revealed as though it were trapped in glass. The creature is astonishing. It existed outside my previous imagination. I study it from every angle I can manage from above the water's surface. Its opalescent pink bell is divided by thin red lines that radiate from center to circular edge. A wall of tentacles falls from the rim to surround and partially veil a feeding tube and other organs, which fold in and out like the fabric of a drawn curtain. I can see only a little way into this lower tissue mass. I want to know more but am afraid to wade in deeper and look more closely into the heart of the creature.

2   The jellyfish, I know now, was a sea nettle, formal scientific name *Chrysaora quinquecirrha*, a scyphozoan, a medusa, a member of the pelagic fauna that drifted in from the Gulf of Mexico and paused in the place I found it. I had no idea then of these names from the lexicon of zoology. The only word I had heard was *jellyfish*. But what a spectacle my animal was, and how inadequate, how demeaning, the bastard word used to label it. I should have been able to whisper its true name: *scyph-o-zo-an!* Think of it! I have found a scyphozoan. The name would have been a more fitting monument to this discovery.

3   The creature hung there motionless for hours. As evening approached and the time came for me to leave, its tangled undermass appeared to stretch deeper into the darkening water. Was this, I wondered, an animal or a collection of animals? Today I can say that it was a single animal. And that another outwardly similar animal found in the same waters, the Portuguese man-of-war, is a colony of animals so tightly joined as to form one smoothly functioning super-organism. Such are the general facts I recite easily now, but this sea nettle was special. It came into my world abruptly, from I knew not where, radiating what I cannot put into words except—*alien purpose and dark happenings in the kingdom of deep water*. The scyphozoan still embodies, when I summon its image, all the mystery and tensed malignity of the sea.

4   The next morning the sea nettle was gone. I never saw another during that summer of 1936. The place, Paradise Beach, which I have revisited in recent years, is a small settlement on the east shore of Florida's Perdido Bay, not far from Pensacola and in sight of Alabama across the water.

5   There was trouble at home in this season of fantasy. My parents were ending their marriage that year. Existence was difficult for them, but not for me, their only child, at least not yet. I had been placed in the care of a family that boarded one or two boys during the months of the summer vacation. Paradise Beach was paradise truly named for a little boy. Each morning after breakfast I left the small shorefront house to wander alone in search of treasures along the strand. I waded in and out of the dependably warm surf and scrounged for anything I could find in the drift. Sometimes I just sat on a rise to scan the open water. Back in time for lunch, out again, back for dinner, out once again, and, finally, off to bed to relive my continuing adventure briefly before falling asleep.

6   I have no remembrance of the names of the family I stayed with, what they looked like, their ages, or even how many there were. Most likely they were a married couple and, I am willing to suppose, caring and warmhearted people. They have passed out of my memory, and I have no need to learn their identity. It was the animals of that place that cast a lasting spell. I was seven years old, and every species, large and small, was a wonder to be examined, thought about, and, if possible, captured and examined again.

7   There were needlefish, foot-long green torpedoes with slender beaks, cruising the water just beneath the surface. Nervous in temperament, they kept you in sight and never let you come close enough to reach out a hand and catch them. I wondered where they went at night, but never found out. Blue crabs with skin-piercing claws scuttled close to shore at dusk. Easily caught in long-handled nets, they were boiled and cracked open and eaten straight or added to gumbo, the spicy seafood stew of the Gulf coast. Sea trout and other fish worked deeper water out to the nearby eelgrass flats and perhaps beyond; if you had a boat you could cast for them with bait and spinners. Stingrays, carrying threatening lances of bone flat along their muscular tails, buried themselves in the bottom sand of hip-deep water in the daytime and moved close to the surf as darkness fell.

8   One late afternoon a young man walked past me along the beach dangling a revolver in his hand, and I fell in behind him for a while. He said he was hunting stingrays. Many young men, my father among them, often took guns on such haphazard excursions into the countryside, mostly .22 pistols and rifles but also heavier handguns and shotguns, recreationally shooting any living thing they fancied except domestic animals and people. I thought of the sting-ray hunter as a kind of colleague as I trailed along, a fellow adventurer, and hoped he would find some exciting kind of animal I had not seen, maybe something big. When he had gone around a bend of the littoral and out of sight I heard the gun pop twice in quick succession. Could a bullet from a light handgun penetrate water deep enough to hit a stingray? I think so but never tried it. And I never saw the young marksman again to ask him.

9   How I longed to discover animals each larger than the last, until finally I caught a glimpse of some true giant! I knew there were large animals out there in deep water. Occasionally a school of bottlenose porpoises passed offshore less than a stone's throw from where I stood. In pairs, trios, and quartets they cut the surface with their backs and dorsal fins, arced down and out of sight, and broke the water again ten or twenty yards farther on. Their repetitions were so rhythmic that I could pick the spot where they would appear next. On calm days I sometimes scanned the glassy surface of Perdido Bay for hours at a time in the hope of spotting something huge and monstrous as it rose to the surface. I wanted at least to see a shark, to watch the fabled dorsal fin thrust proud out of the water, knowing it would look a lot like a porpoise at a distance but would surface and sound at irregular intervals. I also hoped for more than sharks, what exactly I could not say: something to enchant the rest of my life.

10   Almost all that came in sight were clearly porpoises, but I was not com-pletely disappointed. Before I tell you about the one exception, let me say something about the psychology of monster hunting. Giants exist as a state of the mind. They are defined not as an absolute measurement but as a propor-tionality. I estimate that when I was seven years old I saw animals at about twice the size I see them now. The bell of a sea nettle averages ten inches across, I

know that now; but the one I found seemed two feet across—a grown man's two feet. So giants can be real, even if adults don't choose to classify them as such. I was destined to meet such a creature at last. But it would not appear as a swirl on the surface of the open water.

11   It came close in at dusk, suddenly, as I sat on the dock leading away from shore to the family boathouse raised on pilings in shallow water. In the failing light I could barely see to the bottom, but I stayed perched on the dock anyway, looking for any creature large or small that might be moving. Without warning a gigantic ray, many times larger than the stingrays of common experience, glided silently out of the darkness, beneath my dangling feet, and away into the depths on the other side. It was gone in seconds, a circular shadow, seeming to blanket the whole bottom. I was thunderstruck. And immediately seized with a need to see this behemoth again, to capture it if I could, and to examine it close up. Perhaps, I thought, it lived nearby and cruised around the dock every night.

12   Late the next afternoon I anchored a line on the dock, skewered a live pinfish on the biggest hook I could find in the house, and let the bait sit in six feet of water overnight. The following morning I rushed out and pulled in the line. The bait was gone; the hook was bare. I repeated the procedure for a week without result, always losing the pinfish. I might have had better luck in snagging a ray if I had used shrimp or crab for bait, but no one gave me this beginner's advice. One morning I pulled in a Gulf toadfish, an omnivorous bottom-dweller with a huge mouth, bulging eyes, and slimy skin. Locals consider the species a trash fish and one of the ugliest of all sea creatures. I thought it was wonderful. I kept my toadfish in a bottle for a day, then let it go. After a while I stopped putting the line out for the great ray. I never again saw it pass beneath the dock.

13   Why do I tell you this little boy's story of medusas, rays, and sea monsters, nearly sixty years after the fact? Because it illustrates, I think, how a naturalist is created. A child comes to the edge of deep water with a mind prepared for wonder. He is like a primitive adult of long ago, an acquisitive early *Homo* arriving at the shore of Lake Malawi, say, or the Mozambique Channel. The experience must have been repeated countless times over thousands of generations, and it was richly rewarded. The sea, the lakes, and the broad rivers served as sources of food and barriers against enemies. No petty boundaries could split their flat expanse. They could not be burned or eroded into sterile gullies. They were impervious, it seemed, to change of any kind. The waterland was always there, timeless, invulnerable, mostly beyond reach, and inexhaustible. The child is ready to grasp this archetype, to explore and learn, but he has few words to describe his guiding emotions. Instead he is given a compelling image that will serve in later life as a talisman, transmitting a powerful energy that directs the growth of experience and knowledge. He will add complicated details and context from his culture as he grows older. But the core image stays intact. When an adult he will find it curious, if he is at all reflective, that he has the urge to travel all day to fish or to watch sunsets on the ocean horizon.

14   Hands-on experience at the critical time, not systematic knowledge, is what counts in the making of a naturalist. Better to be an untutored savage for a while, not to know the names or anatomical detail. Better to spend long stretches of time just searching and dreaming. Rachel Carson, who understood this principle well, used different words to the same effect in *The Sense of Wonder* in 1965: "If facts are the seeds that later produce knowledge and wisdom, then the emotions and the impressions of the senses are the fertile soil in which the seeds must grow. The years of childhood are the time to prepare the soil." She wisely took children to the edge of the sea.

15   The summer at Paradise Beach was for me not an educational exercise planned by adults, but an accident in a haphazard life. I was parked there in what my parents trusted would be a safe and carefree environment. During that brief time, however, a second accident occurred that determined what kind of naturalist I would eventually become. I was fishing on the dock with minnow hooks and rod, jerking pinfish out of the water as soon as they struck the bait. The species, *Lagodon rhomboides*, is small, perchlike, and voracious. It carries ten needlelike spines that stick straight up in the membrane of the dorsal fin when it is threatened. I carelessly yanked too hard when one of the fish pulled on my line. It flew out of the water and into my face. One of its spines pierced the pupil of my right eye.

16   The pain was excruciating, and I suffered for hours. But being anxious to stay outdoors, I didn't complain very much. I continued fishing. Later, the host family, if they understood the problem at all (I can't remember), did not take me in for medical treatment. The next day the pain had subsided into mild discomfort, and then it disappeared. Several months later, after I had returned home to Pensacola, the pupil of the eye began to cloud over with a traumatic cataract. As soon as my parents noticed the change, they took me to a doctor, who shortly afterward admitted me to the old Pensacola Hospital to have the lens removed. The surgery was a terrifying nineteenth-century ordeal. Someone held me down while the anesthesiologist, a woman named Pearl Murphy, placed a gauze nose cone over my nose and mouth and dripped ether into it. Her fee for this standard service, I learned many years later, was five dollars. As I lost consciousness I dreamed I was all alone in a large auditorium. I was tied to a chair, unable to move, and screaming. Possibly I was screaming in reality before I went under. In any case the experience was almost as bad as the cataract. For years afterward I became nauseous at the smell of ether. Today I suffer from just one phobia: being trapped in a closed space with my arms immobilized and my face covered with an obstruction. The aversion is not an ordinary claustrophobia. I can enter closets and elevators and crawl beneath houses and automobiles with aplomb. In my teens and twenties I explored caves and underwater recesses around wharves without fear, just so long as my arms and face were free.

17   I was left with full sight in the left eye only. Fortunately, that vision proved to be more acute at close range than average — 20/10 on the ophthalmologist's chart — and has remained so all my life. I lost stereoscopy but can make out fine print and the hairs on the bodies of small insects. In adolescence I also lost, possibly as the result of a hereditary defect, most of my hearing in the uppermost registers. Without a hearing aid, I cannot make out the calls of many bird and frog species. So when I set out later as a teenager with Roger Tory Peterson's *Field Guide to the Birds* and binoculars in hand, as all true naturalists in America must at one time or other, I proved to be a wretched birdwatcher. I couldn't hear birds; I couldn't locate them unless they obligingly fluttered past in clear view; even one bird singing in a tree close by was invisible unless someone pointed a finger straight at it. The same was true of frogs. On rainy spring nights my college companions could walk to the mating grounds of frogs guided only by the high-pitched calls of the males. I managed a few, such as the deep-voiced barking tree frog, which sounds like someone thumping a tub, and the eastern spadefoot toad, which wails like a soul on its way to perdition; but from most species all I detected was a vague buzzing in the ears.

18   In one important respect the turning wheel of my life came to a halt at this very early age. I was destined to become an entomologist, committed to minute crawling and flying insects, not by any touch of idiosyncratic genius, not by foresight, but by a fortuitous constriction of physiological ability. I had to have one kind of animal if not another, because the fire had been lit and I took what I could get. The attention of my surviving eye turned to the ground. I would thereafter celebrate the little things of the world, the animals that can be picked up between thumb and forefinger and brought close for inspection.

❧

Discussion Questions

1. Compare and contrast the impression made by the jellyfish sighted off Paradise Beach on the seven-year-old Wilson with the impression of a sea nettle summoned to mind sixty years later by the entomologist Professor Wilson.

2. Why and with whom did Wilson spend the summer of his seventh year on Paradise Beach?

3. In paragraph 7, Wilson describes how he saw needlefish, blue crabs, sea trout, and stingrays. What is it about these creatures that attracted or fixed his attention?

4. At one point in his boyhood (paragraph 8), Wilson encountered a young man walking along the beach. What was the man doing, and why did the boy see him as a "fellow adventurer"?

*5. What happened as a kind of climax to the boy's longing to see ever-larger sea creatures, to catch a "glimpse of some true giant"? In his effort to catch the gigantic creature he finally spotted, the boy put out a hook and line. What was the "catch" and what was the attitude of the boy?

*6. Near the end of the essay, Wilson says that his summer at Paradise Beach was for him "not an educational exercise planned by adults, but an accident in a haphazard life"; he then says that there was a "second accident." What was the second accident? How did the two accidents shape his choice of a profession?

Writing Topics

1. Write an analytical essay exploring the ways Wilson's narrative about his long-ago summer bears out his comment at the opening of paragraph 14, "Hands-on experience at the critical time, not systematic knowledge, is what counts in the making of a naturalist."

2. Wilson limits his statement to the "making of a naturalist." Is it possible that "hands-on experience" counts more than "systematic knowledge" in the making of a historian, a poet, a doctor, a literary critic, a farmer, a druggist, a dentist, a teacher, a secretary, a computer programmer, and so on? After interviewing a relative or friend, or reviewing your own experience, use the applicable material in an analytical essay supporting or rejecting Wilson's view as it may be universally applied.

Summary Writing Topics

1. In "The Turning Point of My Life," Mark Twain appears to be taking the side of "determinists" against supporters of "free will" in the centuries-long debate between the two. Reflect on and think deeply about a choice you believe you have made—for example, deciding to come to the college in which you find yourself—and then write an argumentative essay in which you demonstrate that you acted out of your own free will or that forces beyond your control determined your course of action.

2. Examine Kurt Vonnegut's father, as portrayed in "It Was Enough to Have Been a Unicorn," applying the terms *circumstance* and *temperament* as defined by Mark Twain in "The Turning Point of My Life." Assume the attitude of Twain and mount an argument in an essay on the senior Vonnegut, showing how his career and end were in effect determined by the circumstances in which he found himself and the temperament he inherited at birth.

3. As writers, Mark Twain and Russell Baker are known for their humor. Select a series of examples of the wit or comedy of each and analyze them in an essay, comparing and contrasting the kinds of humor each writer uses. Entertain such questions as to whether one plays with ideas or philosophical propositions more than the other or finds more comedy in domestic relationships or in behavioral ticks. Does either writer make himself the target of his wit? Consider these and any other questions that might enable you to characterize the humor of both authors.

4. We might identify Eileen Herbert Jordan ("The Grand Delusion") as a product of the forties generation and Joan Didion ("On the Morning after the Sixties") as a product of the fifties—as she herself claims. In effect, both claim in their essays to have been influenced by what might be termed the "cultural climate"—in the case of Jordan, the movies (*Casablanca*, for example); in the case of Didion, the "silence" of the "silent generation." Revisit their essays and write a comparison/contrast piece in which you explore the similarities and differences in the experiences they narrate in their essays.

5. Eric Liu writes in his preface to the book he edited, *Next: Young American Writers on the New Generation* (1994): "Over the last few years, there has been no shortage of disparaging commentary about Americans in their twenties and early thirties. Neither has there been a shortage of negative labels for us, from 'Generation X' to 'Twentynothings' to 'Lost Generation' . . . Mainstream media coverage of this age group has been a study in caricature. Are we drifters or career-obsessed young fogies? Are we spoiled whiners? Apathetic slackers?" A movie released in 1995 entitled *Kids* portrayed the

younger generation as amoral, randomly violent in behavior, and lacking all capacity for human sympathies. Take a poll of your classmates and ask them to characterize the generation to which they belong (or test the labels listed above). On the basis of the answers, write an essay presenting your findings and then give your own answer to the questions you have asked others.

6. A number of books have appeared with similar titles, *Growing Up Black*, *Growing Up Latino*, *Growing Up Native American*, *Growing Up Asian American*. Invent a title for a book for which you intend to write a brief narrative of your life: *Growing Up Nobody*, *Growing Up Poor*, *Growing Up Shy*, *Growing Up Rich*, *Growing Up Bewildered*, *Growing Up Common American*, *Growing Up without TV*, *Growing Up with TV*, *Growing Up in a Chaotic Household*, and so on. Join with a few classmates and decide together what title might be applicable to all your lives. Then, to begin, write a joint letter to a publisher (your instructor can play this role) describing the book you want to publish and explaining why you think it would be popular by including sample incidents from your lives that will be included in the narrative essays. If this publisher encourages you, write your autobiographical narratives.

7. Mark Twain (in "The Turning Point of My Life") says that he read a book about the Amazon that affected the course of his life markedly. Joan Didion (in "The Morning after the Sixties") names Conrad's *Heart of Darkness* as a book from which she learned. Eileen Herbert Jordan (in "The Grand Delusion") names movies and books that made a difference in her life. Think back on your life: what story, poem, book, play, movie, or TV production has made a difference in your life. Write a brief narrative in which you tell what led to your reading a work or watching a production that affected you profoundly and how the effect fixed itself in your imagination where it has, long after the original experience, somehow contributed to your life and its course.

8. Reexamine your past and discover any hidden "turning points" of your life that did not reveal themselves at the time they took place. Write a narrative in which you describe your behavior as you viewed it then and as you view it in hindsight. Where has the road that you took led you? Where could the other or untravelled road have possibly led you? Were you asked to join a gang and didn't (or did)? Were you offered a cigarette (or drink, or drugs, or some forbidden experience) and refused (or accepted)?

9. Interview your mother or father, an older sibling, or another relative and ask him or her to tell you about a long-past choice that he or she looks back on with satisfaction or regret. Find out as much as you can about how and why the choice was made, and then write a narrative account of the nature of the choice, the factors weighed in

making the choice, the nature of the road traveled because of the choice, and the possible destination of the road not taken. Conclude with the interviewee's present attitude toward that past choice.

10. Reread Eileen Herbert Jordan's "The Grand Delusion" and Edward O. Wilson's "Paradise Beach," focusing on the similarities in their notions about the way chance happenings or accidents affect the lives we live in fundamental ways. In an analytical essay, report your findings. In your conclusion, indicate and explain your agreement or disagreement with their notions.

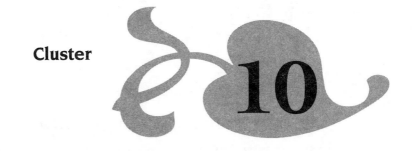

Cluster

10

Country Life, City Life: Then and Now

Assume you were asked by a foreigner, "What is the American way of life I hear so much about?" What would you answer? Much would depend, probably, on the way you grew up. If you grew up on a farm, you might praise it as an idyllic, magical place where you learned to become self-reliant or damn it as an isolated, primitive place where you learned only the lessons of poverty and loneliness. If you grew up in a city, you might describe vividly the city library, where you turned yourself into an avid reader of books, or you might describe the city streets at night, where you experienced fear for your life. And if you grew up in a small town, you might focus on the friendliness of small-town folks, or you might remember your boredom and desire to escape to big-city life.

The truth is that the American way of life has always been—and still is—quite varied. There has long been much debate about the virtues of country life versus the virtues of city life. The tendency has been to idealize the simple ways of life on the farm, ways that produce rugged individualists with great strength of character. During the twentieth century, however, the United States has witnessed a decrease in the number of farms and farmers and an explosive growth of its big and mid-size cities.

The latest movement has been to the suburbs, rows and rows of houses nestled around large cities—not really in the country, but not quite in the city either. Shopping malls have replaced main streets and have developed a social structure of their own. Some might argue that these changes have ended in creating a homogenized culture, resulting in an emphasis on conformity. Others may reply that the cities and their suburbs are fine places, offering opportunities for experiencing the best of two worlds—the exciting cultural opportunities of the city alongside the quiet retreat of a home in a neighborhood.

The essays that follow offer a variety of views of country life and city life, all shaped by the personal experiences of the writers. In spite of their differences, they all testify explicitly or implicitly to the powerful influence of place—where they grew up, where they lived—on who they are, what they have become, and how they see the world.

"My father told me:
you only need three store-bought things.
They are salt, sugar and a little kerosene."

ONE MULE AND A WALKING PLOW

Luther Haines (as told to John Baskin)

Luther Haines is one of the farmers whose oral histories are presented in *New Burlington: The Life and Death of an American Village*, written (or "recorded") by John Baskin and published in 1976. The oral histories were recorded in the mid-1970s, at which time Haines was seventy-nine years old. He was born in Ohio, near New Burlington, on land that had first been farmed by his great-great grandfather. The time of his birth would have been around 1895–1896. His primary teacher, as he indicates, was his father and his main subject, farming. In the introduction to his book, Baskin writes, "I came to New Burlington, Ohio, three years ago, by the accidents of my life. The villagers told me that before long they would be gone. The U.S. Army Corps of Engineers was building a reservoir over their village and soon children would water-ski in 175-year-old cornfields." Baskin set out to write an "obituary," which turned out to be something of a history. "I think of New Burlington," he said, "as a book of stories and voices in which the characters ponder some of their time on earth. It could be said, then, that it is no more than a book about loneliness."

My great-great grandfather Isaac Haines was the first of the Haineses here. He came out and began to clear land. Later he found it was not his and he had to move and begin again. It was quite a bit of land, too. I was raised here and my father before me and my son and his sons. I can tell you everyone who has owned this land. Except for seven years it has remained in two families for over 175 years. The land did not change. Nothing changed. My father told me: you only need three store-bought things. They are salt, sugar and a little kerosene. When company came we went to the cellar, not the grocery.

2   I began with one mule and a walking plow. He turned and went down the right row. Later on, we thought the tractor was wonderful but the horses were sacred. The teams thought for a man in the fields and he cared for them. The tractor gave us nothing. But the machinery was coming on, you know. You had to compete. My dad and I bought a Fordson in 1919 and a three bottom plow. They cost us $900. Gasoline was fifteen cents. We used the horses to save gas. We tried to keep the money at home. When we got behind, we used the tractor. But we were independent with the horse. I wonder how it would have been to have continued that way. I raised young horses. I made money on my power by that. My power cost me only my feed. It took two acres for a horse. We had eight at one time.

3   Sometimes I long for those days. We thought we worried very little. If my father got pinched he didn't go to a bank. He went to his neighbors. One looked under the carpet on the stairs and got what he wanted. It was $300.

4   The disassociation began after the First World War. The factory seemed most attractive to the young men. When I was a boy, town boys made light of us. They thought us backward. Of course they had some of the conveniences. They had water under pressure, and lights. I think perhaps now city boys would like to get back to the country but it is an alien place.

5   I have been in the large cities and I am never happy there. I cannot imagine a boy growing up in these places. What does he find? Here he is among the animals in the fields and woods and growing things. When I was young a bunch of boys hoed in the fields and sang coming home.

6   Now there is so much propaganda by the big industries. We look up to the fellow in the office. Why is that? Well, crackers are not sold in a barrel anymore and young girls know nothing of lard. I do worry about the future. I say: I am glad I lived in my own time.

ॐ

Discussion Questions

1. In paragraph 2, explain the sentence, "The teams thought for a man in the fields and he cared for them."

2. Why was there no need for banks in Haines's life?

*3. According to Haines, what advantages did city boys have over farm boys, and why didn't these advantages outweigh the farm boys' disadvantages? Explain.

*4. In the last paragraph, what does Haines mean both explicitly and implicitly by the sentence, "Well, crackers are not sold in a barrel anymore and young girls know nothing of lard"?

Writing Topics

1. Write a brief argumentative essay explaining why you agree or disagree with Haines's view of farm life versus city life.
2. Haines is remembering his life near the beginning of the twentieth century. Your experience growing up some decades later has probably been quite different. Write a brief essay comparing and contrasting your life with the farm life/city life Haines pictures.

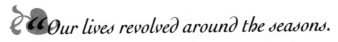

"Our lives revolved around the seasons.
Spring was each year's genesis,
the beginning of new life,
the awakening of the sleeping land."

HILLTOP WORLD

Ben Logan

Ben Logan's *The Land Remembers: The Story of a Farm and Its People* was first published in 1975 and is the source of "Hilltop World." In an "Afterword" written for its second appearance in 1985, Logan writes, "Because of all the dialogue and detail in the book, people sometimes ask me how factual it is. I tell them that it is feeling-level truth. Certainly I took small liberties in my efforts to create a world for the reader to walk into and became a participant." Logan was born in 1920 on the Wisconsin farm described in "Hilltop World." He has served as broadcast producer with Methodist Communications and as a member of the board of directors of Media Action Research Center. The note on him at the end of the 1985 printing of *The Land Remembers* reads, "Ben Logan—novelist, nonfiction writer, lecturer, producer/writer of films and television—lives in two separate worlds. While he pursues his livelihood in New York City, another part of him remains rooted in the southwestern Wisconsin hill country of his childhood. . . . [He] will soon return to his native state, to live on the home farm, the site of *The Land Remembers*." Indeed he is now living in his boyhood home in Wisconsin and has commented, "You can go home again, as long as you don't try to be who you were when you left." Logan is coauthor of *Television Awareness Training: The Viewer's Guide for Family and Community*, published in 1979.

1   There is no neat and easy way to tell the story of a farm. A farm is a process, where everything is related, everything happening at once. It is a circle of life; and there is no logical place to begin a perfect circle. This is an unsolved paradox for me. Part of the folly of our time is the idea that we can see the whole of something by looking at the pieces, one at a time.

2   Yet how else tell the story of a farm?

3   There were two hundred sixty acres of cultivated fields, woods, and pasture land sprawled out along the narrow branching ridgetop. There was the cluster of buildings, dominated by the main barn with its stanchions for dairy cows, stalls for work horses. Attached to the barn was a tall silo, which oozed the strong smell of fermented silage when it was filled and made a marvelous, echoing place to yell into when it was empty. A second barn, mostly for hay and young cattle, had a machine-shed lean-to. An eight-foot-tall wood windbreak connected the two barns. Across the barnyard, like the other side of the compound in a fort, was the great tobacco shed. It stood on poles rather than foundations and it creaked and groaned in the wind.

4   There were the bulging granary, with bins for oats; a slatted corncrib with white and yellow ears showing; a hog house with roof ventilators turning restlessly in the wind; a milkhouse next to the tall steel-towered windmill; and a woodshed with sticks of oak for the kitchen range and heating stoves.

5   There was the house. It had two wings, the walls of the old one very thick because the siding hid what it had once been—a log house. "You can say you grew up in a log cabin, even if it doesn't show," Mother used to tell us.

6   In the yard around the house were lilacs, elms, box elders, junipers, and one immense soft maple tree that looked as if it had been there forever. On the east side of the yard was the orchard with its overgrown apple, cherry, and plum trees. On the west was the rich black soil of the garden.

7   The farmstead stood on a hilltop, like a castle, like the center of the world. A dusty road went straight into the woods to the west and wound over knolls and swales to the east until it disappeared down the big hill that led to Halls Branch Valley. Look in any direction and there were other ridges, with dots of houses and barns, and the blue shadows of other ridges still beyond them, each a full world away from the next narrow ridge. Down below, in the valley, was yet another world. The valleys had different trees and animals. Even the seasons were different—watercress stayed green all winter in the valley springs.

8   Below our orchard, a ravine led down to a timbered hollow which broadened and joined the crooked valley of the Kickapoo River. That ravine and hollow brought to us the whistle of the "Stump Dodgers," the steam locomotives of the Kickapoo Railroad, so loud on foggy nights the engine seemed to be coming right through the house. That whistle was joined sometimes, when the wind was in the west and the air just right, by the sound of trains along the Mississippi, nine miles to the west.

9   The nearest neighbors were a half mile away and seemed farther because the buildings were half hidden by a hill and because each farm was its own busy place.

10   In our own hilltop world there were Father, Mother, and four boys: Laurance, the oldest; then Sam, Junior; then Lee, and me, the youngest. There were two years between each of us. We were as alike as peas in a pod, as different from one another as the four seasons.

11   There was someone else to make seven of us. Lyle Jackson came as a hired man the year I was born. He stayed on and became such a part of us that even the neighbors sometimes called him the oldest Logan boy.

12   If the farm had a name before Lyle came, it was soon lost. Lyle, who had grown up near the village of Gays Mills, was used to more people. He took one look out along that isolated ridge, shook his head, and said, "Hell and tooter. We better call it Seldom Seen."

13   From then on Seldom Seen was the only name ever used for that farm. The seven of us, and the land with all its living things, were like a hive of bees. No matter how fiercely independent any one of us might be, we were each a dependent part of the whole, and we knew that.

14   Father was the organizer of our partnership with the land. Because he had come from out beyond the hill country, I was always searching for his past, but I could not easily ask him questions, nor could he easily answer. It was as though his earlier years did not belong to us. That part of his life had happened in a foreign language and did not translate into a new place and time.

15   He came from the Old Country, as he put it. That meant southern Norway and the community of Loga, which was once a little kingdom. "You are descendants of royalty," our Uncle Lou used to tell us.

16   Born fourth of eight sons and daughters, Father was named Sigvald Hanson Loga. The year was 1880. I know his world included the rising and falling of the tides, storms along a rocky coast, midnight sun and winter snow. I know he fished in open dories, offshore and up into the canyonlike fjords. And always at Christmas there was a sheaf of grain for the birds. What kind of birds in his childhood land? What color? Which ones stayed all winter? I never knew. I didn't ask.

17   There is a picture in my mind of Father, in the incredibly long summer evenings, running along dark paths close to the cold North Sea. He ran sometimes toward an old mill to surprise whoever, or whatever, made a light shine from the window of that long-deserted place. He would get to the mill and find nothing, no light, no sound except for the rushing water that was no longer harnessed to work for man.

18   "Yet," Father would say, "my brothers watching me from home said the light never left the window."

19   "But I was there," he would tell them.

20   "So was somebody else," they would say.

21   They pursued that light summer after summer, one running, the others watching, but the end was always the same.

22   "Maybe it was the reflection of the moon or the Northern Lights," I once suggested.

23   Father nodded and smiled. "We thought of that. There was no glass in the window."

24   It was one of the few stories he told me of his boyhood. I loved the mystery of it, though another mystery was even greater — the idea that my father had once been as young as I.

25   Father ran away from home and went to sea when he was fifteen, on an old schooner sailing with timbers for the coal mines of England. "Windjammers," he called the ships, with a mixture of ridicule and pride. For three years he lived with the windjammers. Then there was a voyage when a great storm took his ship. For eleven days it was carried far out into the open Atlantic. Finally the storm ended. Half starved, the crew rerigged enough sail to get the battered schooner headed back toward Norway. Almost every crewman was from that one little community. They came home to families who thought they were dead.

26   Father was eighteen then.

27   Here glimpses of his mother appear, the grandmother I never knew, though she lived to be ninety: a stern-faced woman in a metal picture with mountains in the background, a brass candlestick, a tin box of matches, a letter in a foreign language each Christmas, and a silver spoon inscribed with the words *Sigvald, fra Mudder*.

28   She gathered her sons after that stormy voyage and told them, "I would rather never see you again than to have you lost, one by one, to the sea."

29   She brought out the box. To each son went passage money to the New World. To the village silversmith she took a pair of old candlesticks. He melted them down and made for each son a silver serving spoon.

30   Father and three brothers landed in New York in 1898. At Ellis Island an immigration official suggested they add an "n" to the name Loga to make it "more American." They didn't know if they had a choice or not, so they left Ellis Island with the name Logan.

31   Father also left that island with "not a word of English, ten dollars in my pocket, and the whole country before me." The ten dollars took him to south central Wisconsin, where his first job was grubbing stumps from newly cleared land. His pay — fifty cents a day. "Young Norwegians were cheaper than blasting powder in those days," he told us.

32   Father had worked as a hired man on many different farms. He and Lyle talked about their experiences sometimes on summer evenings under the big maple tree. It was endless, adult talk. I could run a mile into the dark woods and come back to find the talk still going on.

33   They had seen what happens on farms given mostly to tobacco, with the other fields going to ruin. They learned about different combinations of beef, dairy cattle, and hogs. They had worked for men who loved the land, treating it with respect, working with it. Other farmers seemed to hate the land, taking a living from it, giving nothing back.

34   They found people were different on ridge and valley farms. Some were happier down below where the days were shorter, the wind gentle, storms hidden by steep hillsides. Others were happier on the hilltop, where you could

prove yourself by standing against the summer storms and winter blizzards, enduring the stony fields and loneliness, with other ridges beyond yours, like great rollers on the sea.

35   When he was ready to buy land, Father chose the ridge.

36   People who came to visit us on our hilltop talked as if they were on an expedition to the end of the world. A cousin of Mother's always drove miles out of the way to avoid the steep hill coming up from Halls Branch Valley. Outsiders just weren't used to the ups and downs of south-western Wisconsin. It was a small area, missed by the glaciers that had flattened out the country all around it.

37   Lyle nodded when he first heard about the glaciers. "That figures. Even the ice had sense enough to stay out of these hills. Now wouldn't you think people would be as smart as ice?"

38   Some of our visitors were from towns. They climbed carefully out of their cars, looking down at the ground with every step, expecting a bear or timber wolf or rattlesnake to get them any minute. They recoiled from every leaf because it might be poison ivy, and they asked questions we couldn't answer. It would have meant educating them about a world they didn't even know existed.

39   One of the summer-night voices I remember is that of a bachelor neighbor who shaved once a month, whether he needed it or not. He didn't care much for town people. "I got relatives," he said, "that come when the strawberries are ripe and leave before milkingtime. I guess it must be different in town. Don't know. Never lived there. I guess in town a man can be a banker, barber, store-keeper, just be good at one job. A farm needs a man who's some kind of revolving son of a bitch. You got to help calves get born, nursemaid a dozen different crops, be your own blacksmith, cut the testicles out of male pigs, fix machinery, keep the windmill going. . . ."

40   "Of course, that's just before breakfast," Lyle interrupted with his cat-that-ate-the-canary grin.

41   The hill country was filled with voices that I remember. Some of them, the older ones mostly, were forever trying to put the past in proper order. I heard them at ice-cream socials, at school picnics, at stores in town, and under our own big maple tree.

42   "Was it eighteen ninety-five that we didn't get but fourteen inches of rain?"

43   "I thought it was twelve inches."

44   "When was it frost came in the middle of August? Never saw so much soft corn in my life."

45   A small group might come over to Father. "Say, Sam, we been talking about your farm. Wasn't it Banty McPherson who broke the first land?"

46   "That's what we been told."

47   "Well, when was that?"

48   "The deed says eighteen sixty-four."

49   "There, I told you! I said the Civil War was still going on."

50 "Well, I thought Pat Mullaney lived there then. He used to tell about Indians crossing his land just below where the buildings are now. They was carrying lead from some little mines down in Halls Branch. Carried it down to the Kickapoo and took it by canoe clean down to Illinois someplace. Was lead still that scarce after the war was over?"

51 The voices went on and on, putting events and past years together.

52 Years were hard to separate on the farm. A year is an arbitrary, calendar thing. Our lives revolved around the seasons. Spring was each year's genesis, the beginning of new life, the awakening of the sleeping land. Summer was heat, sun, harvest, and always work, with muscles aching, shirts covered with dust and sweat and the white rings of salt from earlier sweat.

53 Fall was the end of harvest, end of the growing season, a glorious burst of color and sun-warmth before killing frost turned the land gray and cold. Fall was a moody time, full of both life and death, a time when we were reminded of the power outside us, reminded that the seasons happen to us. We do not invite the change to come.

54 Winter was in-between time, the frozen land resting under blowing snow. The farm seemed to shrink in winter, with the farmstead bigger and more important. The animals were inside the barns, the fields were empty. Even the winter birds gathered near the buildings. We were in the house more, and it was a time when we reached out past the frozen fields to explore a bigger world in our books and conversation.

55 Then, magically, spring again, the rebirth of the rolling seasons, the unfailing promise of the awakening land.

ੴ

Discussion Questions

1. Logan says in paragraph 2, "Yet how else tell the story of a farm?" Explain the meaning of this statement as it relates to what is said in paragraph 1, and then as it relates to the paragraphs following it—particularly as they begin "There were . . . ," "There were . . . ," "There was . . . ."

2. Explain the title "Hilltop World" as it is revealed in the body of the essay.

3. What did the author's Norwegian grandmother do to prevent her sons from running away to sea, as the author's father once had done? What was her motive? What was her sacrifice?

4. Why did the author's father choose to buy land on the ridge rather than in the valley?

5. What was the reaction of town people when they came to visit the "hilltop world" the author describes?

*6. In paragraph 52, the author writes, "Years were hard to separate on the farm." What does he mean, and how does the statement relate to the argumentative nature of the endless conversations the author remembers overhearing?

Writing Topics

1. Write an analytical essay exploring the ways that Logan has found to overcome the difficulties he cites in his first paragraph to telling "the story of a farm." (What, for example, determines the order in which he introduces the various elements he describes?) In your conclusion, assess his success.

2. Consider beginning an essay with "There is no neat and easy way to tell the story of _____." Fill in the blank with a word of your choice and write a descriptive essay, overcoming the difficulties your sentence implies. You might, for example, write about high school, summer camp, a family trip on a holiday, or a summer job.

3. "Logan romanticizes life in his hilltop world." After careful consideration of this controversial statement, write an analytical essay setting forth the extent to which you agree or disagree, citing specific passages to support your position.

❧ "*That tiredness that feels so good to the occasional laborer and the athlete is disturbing to a man destined to it eight months of every year.*"

GETTING TIRED

Carol Bly

Born in Duluth, Minnesota, in 1930, Carol Bly earned a B.A. at Wellesley College in 1951 and did graduate work at the University of Minnesota in 1954 and 1955. She married the poet Robert Bly in 1955 and joined him in managing a little magazine he had founded named after the decade, The Fifties (later to become The Sixties and The Seventies). The marriage ended in divorce in 1979, after which she settled in Madison, Minnesota, with a population of 2,242, and began in her writing to focus on the small-town rural life of America. This interest resulted in the publication of Letters from the Country in 1981 (reissued in 1988). It is the source of "Getting Tired" reprinted here. Bly joined with two other writers to publish a volume of short stories, Backbone, in 1985. She also published two volumes of essays, Soil and Survival and Bad Government and Silly Literature in 1986. In that same year, Bly became associated with the creative writing program at the University of Minnesota.

1   The men have left a gigantic 6600 combine a few yards from our grove, at the edge of the stubble. For days it was working around the farm; we heard it on the east, later on the west, and finally we could see it grinding back and forth over the windrows on the south. But now it has been simply squatting at the field's edge, huge, tremendously still, very professional, slightly dangerous.

2   We all have the correct feelings about this new combine: this isn't the good old farming where man and soil are dusted together all day; this isn't farming a poor man can afford, either, and therefore it further threatens his hold on the American "family farm" operation. We have been sneering at this machine for days, as its transistor radio, amplified well over the engine roar, has been grinding up our silence, spreading a kind of shrill ghetto evening all over the farm.

3   But now it is parked, and after a while I walk over to it and climb up its neat little John Deere-green ladder on the left. Entering the big cab up there is

like coming up into a large ship's bridge on visitors' day—heady stuff to see the inside workings of a huge operation like the Queen Elizabeth II. On the other hand I feel left out, being only a dumbfounded passenger. The combine cab has huge windows flaring wider at the top; they lean forward over the ground, and the driver sits so high behind the glass in its rubber moldings it is like a movie-set spaceship. He has obviously come to dominate the field, whether he farms it or not.

4   The value of the 66 is that it can do anything, and to change it from a combine into a cornpicker takes one man about half an hour, whereas most machine conversions on farms take several men a half day. It frees its owner from a lot of monkeying.

5   Monkeying, in city life, is what little boys do to clocks so they never run again. In farming it has two quite different meanings. The first is small side projects. You monkey with poultry, unless you're a major egg handler. Or you monkey with ducks or geese. If you have a very small milk herd, and finally decide that prices plus state regulations don't make your few Holsteins worthwhile, you "quit monkeying with them." There is a hidden dignity in this word: it precludes mention of money. It lets the wife of a very marginal farmer have a conversation with a woman who may be helping her husband run fifteen hundred acres. "How you coming with those geese?" "Oh, we've been real disgusted. We're thinking of quitting monkeying with them." It saves her having to say, "We lost our shirts on those darn geese."

6   The other meaning of monkeying is wrestling with and maintaining machinery, such as changing heads from combining to cornpicking. Farmers who cornpick the old way, in which the corn isn't shelled automatically during picking in the field but must be elevated to the top of a pile by belt and then shelled, put up with some monkeying.

7   Still, cornpicking and plowing is a marvelous time of the year on farms; one of the best autumns I've had recently had a few days of fieldwork in it. We were outside all day, from six in the morning to eight at night—coming in only for noon dinner. We ate our lunches on a messy truck flatbed. (For city people who don't know it: *lunch* isn't a noon meal; it is what you eat out of a black lunch pail at 9 A.M. and 3 P.M. If you offer a farmer a cup of coffee at 3:30 P.M. he or she is likely to say, "No thanks, I've already had lunch.") There were four of us hired to help—a couple to plow, Celia (a skilled farmhand who worked steady for our boss), and me. Lunch was always two sandwiches of white commercial bread with luncheon meat, and one very generous piece of cake-mix cake carefully wrapped in Saran Wrap. (I never found anyone around here self-conscious about using Saran Wrap when the Dow Chemical Company was also making napalm.)

8   It was very pleasant on the flatbed, squinting out over the yellow picked cornstalks—each time we stopped for lunch, a larger part of the field had been plowed black. We fell into the easy psychic habit of farmworkers: admiration

of the boss. "Ja, I see he's buying one of those big 4010s," someone would say. We always perked up at inside information like that. Or "Ja," as the woman hired steady told us, "he's going to plow the home fields first this time, instead of the other way round." We temporary help were impressed by that, too. Then, with real flair, she brushed a crumb of luncheon meat off her jeans, the way you would make sure to flick a gnat off spotless tennis whites. It is the true feminine touch to brush a crumb off pants that are encrusted with Minnesota Profile A heavy loam, many swipes of SAE 40 oil, and grain dust.

9   All those days, we never tired of exchanging information on how *he* was making out, what *he* was buying, whom *he* was going to let drive the new tractor, and so on. There is always something to talk about with the other hands, because farming is genuinely absorbing. It has the best quality of work: nothing else seems real. And everyone doing it, even the cheapest helpers like me, can see the layout of the whole—from spring work, to cultivating, to small grain harvest, to cornpicking, to fall plowing.

10   The second day I was promoted from elevating corncobs at the corn pile to actual plowing. Hour after hour I sat up there on the old Alice, as she was called (an Allis-Chalmers WC that looked rusted from the Flood). You have to sit twisted part way around, checking that the plowshares are scouring clean, turning over and dropping the dead crop and soil, not clogging. For the first two hours I was very political. I thought about what would be good for American farming—stronger marketing organizations, or maybe a law like the Norwegian Odal law, preventing the breaking up of small farms or selling them to business interests. Then the sun got high, and each time I reached the headlands area at the field's end I dumped off something else, now my cap, next my jacket, finally my sweater.

11   Since the headlands are the last to be plowed, they serve as a field road until the very end. There are usually things parked there—a pickup or a corn trailer—and things dumped—my warmer clothing, our afternoon lunch pails, a broken furrow wheel someone picked up.

12   By noon I'd dropped all political interest, and was thinking only: how unlike this all is to Keats's picture of autumn, a "season of mists and mellow fruitfulness." This gigantic expanse of horizon, with everywhere the easy growl of tractors, was simply teeming with extrovert energy. It wouldn't calm down for another week, when whoever was lowest on the totem pole would be sent out to check a field for dropped parts or to drive away the last machines left around.

13   The worst hours for all common labor are the hours after noon dinner. Nothing is inspiring then. That is when people wonder how they ever got stuck in the line of work they've chosen for life. Or they wonder where the cool Indian smoke of secrets and messages began to vanish from their marriage. Instead of plugging along like a cheerful beast working for me, the Allis now smelled particularly gassy. To stay awake I froze my eyes onto an indented

circle in the hood around the gas cap. Someone had apparently knocked the screw cap fitting down into the hood, so there was a moat around it. In this moat some overflow gas leapt in tiny waves. Sometimes the gas cap was a castle, this was the moat; sometimes it was a nuclear-fission plant, this was the horrible hot-water waste. Sometimes it was just the gas cap on the old Alice with the spilt gas bouncing on the hot metal.

14   Row after row. I was stupefied. But then around 2:30 the shadows appeared again, and the light, which had been dazing and white, grew fragile. The whole prairie began to gather itself for the cool evening. All of a sudden it was wonderful to be plowing again, and when I came to the field end, the filthy jackets and the busted furrow wheel were just benign mistakes: that is, if it chose to, the jacket could be a church robe, and the old wheel could be something with some pride to it, like a helm. And I felt the same about myself: instead of being someone with a half interest in literature and a half interest in farming doing a half-decent job plowing, I could have been someone desperately needed in Washington or Zurich. I drank my three o'clock coffee joyously, and traded the other plowman a Super-Valu cake-mix lemon cake slice for a Holsum baloney sandwich because it had garlic in it.

15   By seven at night we had been plowing with headlights for an hour. I tried to make up games to keep going, on my second wind, on my third wind, but labor is labor after the whole day of it; the mind refuses to think of ancestors. It refuses to pretend the stalks marching up to the right wheel in the spooky light are men-at-arms, or to imagine a new generation coming along. It doesn't care. Now the Republicans could have announced a local meeting in which they would propose a new farm program whereby every farmer owning less than five hundred acres must take half price for his crop, and every farmer owning more than a thousand acres shall receive triple price for his crop, and I was so tired I wouldn't have shown up to protest.

16   A million hours later we sit around in a daze at the dining-room table, and nobody says anything. In low, courteous mutters we ask for the macaroni hot-dish down this way, please. Then we get up in ones and twos and go home. Now the farm help are all so tired we *are* a little like the various things left out on the headlands—some tools, a jacket, someone's thermos top—used up for that day. Thoughts won't even stick to us any more.

17   Such tiredness must be part of farmers' wanting huge machinery like the Deere 6600. That tiredness that feels so good to the occasional laborer and the athlete is disturbing to a man destined to it eight months of every year. But there is a more hidden psychology in the issue of enclosed combines versus open tractors. It is this: one gets too many impressions on the open tractor. A thousand impressions enter as you work up and down the rows: nature's beauty or nature's stubbornness, politics, exhaustion, but mainly the feeling that all this repetition—last year's cornpicking, this year's cornpicking, next year's cornpicking—is taking up your lifetime. The mere repetition reveals your eventual death.

18   When you sit inside a modern combine, on the other hand, you are so isolated from field, sky, all the real world, that the brain is dulled. You are not sensitized to your own mortality. You aren't sensitive to anything at all.

19   This must be a common choice of our mechanical era: to hide from life inside our machinery. If we can hide from life in there, some idiotic part of the psyche reasons, we can hide from death in there as well.

❧

Discussion Questions

1.   Explain how the following words and phrases are used in the first three paragraphs to characterize the "gigantic 6600 combine": *Squatting at the field's edge; grinding up our silence, spreading a kind of shrill ghetto evening all over the farm; the inside workings of a huge operation like the* Queen Elizabeth II; *it is like a movie-set spaceship.*

2.   How does the author define *monkeying* and *lunch* and why does she spend time providing the definitions?

3.   After the author's job is switched to "actual plowing" (paragraph 10), she describes the various emotional and physical stages she passes through during a full day lasting until "seven at night." What are her thoughts and feelings in the morning? At noon and after? At mid-afternoon? At the end of the day?

4.   What is the meaning and effect of the reference to John Keats's ode "To Autumn" in paragraph 12? The poem opens, "Season of mists and mellow fruitfulness, / Close bosom-friend of the maturing sun; / Conspiring with him how to load and bless/With fruit the vines that round the thatch-eaves run."

*5.   Paragraph 16 opens, "A million hours later we sit around in a daze at the dining-room table, and nobody says anything." What image of the "farm help" is created by this hyperbole and other figures of speech in the paragraph? Explain.

6.   What revelation does such "tiredness" felt by the farm help lead to as described by Bly in paragraph 17?

*7.   Explain why Bly returns at the end of her essay to the "gigantic 6600 combine" she had introduced at the beginning. How does her initial description relate to her conclusion?

Writing Topics

1.   Write an analytical essay exploring how Bly arrives at the statement opening the last paragraph, "This must be a common choice of our mechanical era: to hide from life inside our machinery."

2. A skeptical reader might say of Bly's conclusion, "If I have to choose between the mind-numbing work described in the day's plowing of the fields on Allis-Chalmers WC and a day's work in the comfort of the glassed-in big cab of the 6600 combine, I'll take the 6600 combine, thank you. I'll be better able in that 'comfort' to contemplate my own mortality and the linkage of life and death than I would sitting exposed and dirty on an ancient motorized tractor requiring constant attention." Write an argumentative essay in which you agree or disagree with this view.

There was still daylight, shining softly and with a tarnish, like the lining of a shell; and the carbon lamps lifted at the corners were on in the light, and the locusts were started, and the fire flies were out, and a few frogs were flopping in the dewy grass, by the time the fathers and the children came out."

KNOXVILLE: SUMMER OF 1915

James Agee

James Agee (1909–1955) was born in Knoxville, Tennessee, and earned a B.A. at Harvard in 1932. His volume of poems *Permit Me Voyage* was published in the Yale Series of Younger Poets in 1934. He worked for a time on the staffs of *Fortune* and *Time* and was assigned by *Fortune* to write a study of southern farm life, which was then (like the country at large) in the grips of the Great Depression. The work when submitted was found unsuitable for *Fortune* and was published as a book in 1941, with photographs by Walker Evans, and entitled *Let Us Now Praise Famous Men*. It is an extraordinarily vivid and moving portrayal of the marginal existence of three Alabama sharecropper families, presented largely through their own oral histories. Agee became a film critic for *Nation*, *Time*, and other journals in the latter part of his career, and he tried his hand at scriptwriting. A collection of his film criticism, *Agree on Film*, appeared in 1958, and a collection of his film scripts, *Agee on Film* II, appeared in 1960. His semiautobiographical novel *A Death in the Family* (1957) won a Pulitzer Prize, as did the popular play made from it, *All the Way Home* (1960). His letters to his old school teacher and long-time friend, written from age sixteen to his death, were published as *Letters to Father Flye* in 1962. "Knoxville: Summer of 1915," published in *Partisan Review* in 1938, is presented here in its entirety. Composer Samuel Barber and choreographer Alvin Ailey collaborated in creating a version for the stage.

1   We are talking now of summer evenings in Knoxville, Tennessee in the time that I lived there so successfully disguised to myself as a child. It was a little bit mixed sort of block, fairly solidly lower middle class, with one or two juts apiece on either side of that. The houses corresponded: middle-sized gracefully fretted wood houses built in the late nineties and early nineteen hundreds, with small front and side and more spacious back yards, and trees in the yards, and porches. These were softwooded trees, poplars, tulip trees, cottonwoods. There were fences around one or two of the houses, but mainly the yards ran into each other with only now and then a low hedge that wasn't doing very well. There were few good friends among the grown people, and they were not poor enough for the other sort of intimate acquaintance, but everyone nodded and spoke, and even might talk short times, trivially, and at the two extremes of the general or the particular, and ordinarily next door neighbors talked quite a bit when they happened to run into each other, and never paid calls. The men were mostly small businessmen, one or two very modestly executives, one or two worked with their hands, most of them clerical, and most of them between thirty and forty-five.

2   But it is of these evenings, I speak.

3   Supper was at six and was over by half past. There was still daylight, shining softly and with a tarnish, like the lining of a shell; and the carbon lamps lifted at the corners were on in the light, and the locusts were started, and the fire flies were out, and a few frogs were flopping in the dewy grass, by the time the fathers and the children came out. The children ran out first hell bent and yelling those names by which they were known; then the fathers sank out leisurely in crossed suspenders, their collars removed and their necks looking tall and shy. The mothers stayed back in the kitchen washing and drying, putting things away, recrossing their traceless footsteps like the lifetime journeys of bees, measuring out the dry cocoa for breakfast. When they came out they had taken off their aprons and their skirts were dampened and they sat in rockers on their porches quietly.

4   It is not of the games children play in the evening that I want to speak now, it is of a contemporaneous atmosphere that has little to do with them: that of the fathers of families, each in his space of lawn, his shirt fishlike pale in the unnatural light and his face nearly anonymous, hosing their lawns. The hoses were attached at spigots that stood out of the brick foundations of the houses. The nozzles were variously set but usually so there was a long sweet stream of spray, the nozzle wet in the hand, the water trickling the right forearm and the peeled-back cuff, and the water whishing out a long loose and low-curved cone, and so gentle a sound. First, an insane noise of violence in the nozzle, then the still irregular sound of adjustment, then the smoothing into steadiness and a pitch as accurately tuned to the size and style of stream as any violin. So many qualities of sound out of one hose; so many choral differences out of those several hoses that were in earshot. Out of any one hose, the almost dead silence

of the release, and the short still arch of the separate big drops, silent as a held breath, and the only noise the flattering noise on leaves and the slapped grass at the fall of each big drop. That, and the intense hiss with the intense stream; that, and that same intensity not growing less but growing more quiet and delicate with the turn of the nozzle, up to that extreme tender whisper when the water was just a wide bell of film. Chiefly, though, the hoses were set much alike, in a compromise between distance and tenderness of spray (and quite surely a sense of art behind this compromise, and a quiet, deep joy, too real to recognize itself), and the sounds therefore were pitched much alike; pointed by the snorting start of a new hose; decorated by some man playful with the nozzle; left empty, like God by the sparrow's fall, when any single one of them desists; and all, though near alike, of various pitch; and this in unison. These sweet pale streamings in the light lift out their pallors and their voices all together, mothers hushing their children, the hushing unnaturally prolonged, the men gentle and silent and each snaillike withdrawn into the quietude of what he singly is doing, the urination of huge children stood loosely military against an invisible wall, and gently happy and peaceful, tasting the mean goodness of their living like the last of their suppers in their mouths; while the locusts carry on this noise of hoses on their much higher and sharper key. The noise of the locust is dry, and it seems not to be rasped or vibrated but urged from him as if through a small orifice by a breath that can never give out. Also there is never one locust but an illusion of at least a thousand. The noise of each locust is pitched in some classic locust range out of which none of them varies more than two full tones; and yet you seem to hear each locust discrete from all the rest, and there is a long, slow, pulse in their noise, like the scarcely defined arch of a long and high set bridge. They are all around in every tree, so that the noise seems to come from nowhere and everywhere at once, from the whole shell heaven, shivering in your flesh and teasing your eardrums, the boldest of all the sounds of night. And yet it is habitual to summer nights, and is of the great order of noises, like the noises of the sea and of the blood her precocious grandchild, which you realize you are hearing only when you catch yourself listening. Meantime from low in the dark, just outside the swaying horizons of the hoses, conveying always grass in the damp of dew and its strong green-black smear of smell, the regular yet spaced noises of the crickets, each a sweet cold silver noise three-noted, like the slipping each time of three matched links of a small chain.

5   But the men by now, one by one, have silenced their hoses and drained and coiled them. Now only two, and now only one, is left, and you see only ghostlike shirt with the sleeve garters, and sober mystery of his mild face like the lifted face of large cattle enquiring of your presence in a pitch-dark pool of meadow; and now he too is gone; and it has become that time of evening when people sit on their porches, rocking gently and talking gently and watching the street and the standing up into their sphere of possession of the trees, of birds, hung

havens, hangars. People go by; things go by. A horse, drawing a buggy, break-ing his hollow iron music on the asphalt: a loud auto: a quiet auto: people in pairs, not in a hurry, scuffling, switching their weight of aestival body, talking casually, the taste hovering over them of vanilla, strawberry, pasteboard and starched milk, the image upon them of lovers and horsemen, squared with clowns in hueless amber. A street car raising its iron moan; stopping; belling and starting, stertorous; rousing and raising again its iron increasing moan and swimming its gold windows and straw seats on past and past and past, the bleak spark crackling and cursing above it like a small malignant spirit set to dog its tracks; the iron whine rises on rising speed; still risen, faints; halts; the faint stinging bell; rises again, still fainter; fainting, lifting, lifts, faints forgone: forgotten. Now is the night one blue dew.

Now is the night one blue dew, my father has drained, he has coiled the hose.
Low on the length of lawns, a frailing of fire who breathes.
Content, silver, like peeps of light, each cricket makes his comment over and over in the drowned grass.
A cold toad thumpily flounders.
Within the edges of damp shadows of side yards are hovering children nearly sick with joy of fear, who watch the unguarding of a telephone pole.
Around white carbon corner lamps bugs of all sizes are lifted elliptic, solar systems. Big hardshells bruise themselves, assailant: he is fallen on his back, legs squiggling.
Parents on porches: rock and rock. From damp strings morning glories: hang their ancient faces.
The dry and exalted noise of the locusts from all the air at once enchants my eardrums.

7   On the rough wet grass of the back yard my father and mother have spread quilts. We all lie there, my mother, my father, my uncle, my aunt, and I too am lying there. First we were sitting up, then one of us lay down, and then we all lay down, on our stomachs, or on our sides, or on our backs, and they have kept on talking. They are not talking much, and the talk is quiet, of nothing in particular, of nothing at all in particular, of nothing at all. The stars are wide and alive, they seem each like a smile of great sweetness, and they seem very near. All my people are larger bodies than mine, quiet, with voices gentle and meaningless like the voices of sleeping birds. One is an artist, he is living at home. One is a musician, she is living at home. One is my mother who is good to me. One is my father who is good to me. By some chance, here they are, all on this earth; and who shall ever tell the sorrow of being on this earth, lying, on quilts, on the grass, in a summer evening, among the sounds of the night. May God bless my people, my uncle, my aunt, my mother, my good father, oh, remember them kindly in their time of trouble; and in the hour of their taking away.

8   After a little I am taken in and put to bed. Sleep, soft smiling, draws me unto her: and those receive me, who quietly treat me, as one familiar and well-beloved in that home: but will not, oh, will not, not now, not ever; but will not ever tell me who I am.

୨෧

Discussion Questions

*1.   The opening sentence appears to signal not a beginning but a continuation: "We are talking now of summer evenings in Knoxville, Tennessee in the time that I lived there so successfully disguised to myself as a child." Explore the meaning and the effect of this opening sentence as it is illuminated by the essay as a whole.

2.   The entire second paragraph reads, "But it is of these evenings, I speak." The opening word *but* signals a shift in subject or focus. Define this shift.

*3.   Paragraph 4 opens, "It is not of the games children play in the evening that I want to speak now, it is of a contemporaneous atmosphere that has little to do with them. . . ." Analyze paragraph 4, with emphasis on identifying the various images introduced, appealing to the various senses (sight, sound, smell, touch, taste). How does this imagery evoke the "atmosphere" Agee identifies as his focus? Describe the atmosphere as evoked.

4.   Analyze paragraphs 5 and 6 with an eye to explaining why Agee shifts from what appears to be poetic prose in 5 to poetic lines in 6. How do the lines of paragraph 6 relate to the images and "atmosphere" introduced and evoked in paragraph 4?

*5.   Paragraph 7 seems to end in a kind of prayer. Explore the relationship of the paragraph's various rhetorical devices—imagery, repetition, incantatory tone—to its closing prayerlike lines.

*6.   Paragraph 8 portrays the author as a boy, being put to bed by his elders, struggling with a mystery: no one will "ever," "will not ever tell me who I am." Explore in depth the meaning of this ending. How might it relate to the author's reference to himself as "so successfully disguised to myself as a child" in the opening paragraph?

Writing Topics

1.   " 'Knoxville: Summer of 1915' is really a prose-poem, or a kind of poem in the process of becoming. Now it is neither fish nor fowl. It would have made for better reading if Agee had worked it over into a real poem!" Write an argumentative essay agreeing or disagreeing with this statement.

2. Recall a "moment" from your past that sticks in your mind because it seems the distillation of a period or place in your life, perhaps because it bestowed some insight about life or yourself that you treasured or perhaps because it withheld an insight it seemed on the verge of revealing. Write a descriptive essay of recollection of that moment, evoking whatever atmosphere seems appropriate by whatever rhetorical devices that seem to work.

"If this talk of musical discipline gives the impression that there were no forces working to nourish one who would one day blunder, after many a twist and turn, into writing, I am misleading you."

NEGRO OKLAHOMA CITY

Ralph Ellison

Ralph Ellison (1914–1994) was born in Oklahoma City. His father named him Ralph Waldo Ellison after the famous American writer Ralph Waldo Emerson, perhaps with the intention of influencing his son to become a writer. If so, his intent was admirably realized. Ellison attended Tuskegee Institute in Alabama to study music but left after his junior year. He went to New York and, after meeting novelist Richard Wright there, began to write and publish book reviews and short stories. In 1952, he published his novel, Invisible Man, which dazzled reviewers and readers; it won the National Book Award in 1955. The novel has often been called the classic novel about black experience in America. Although he worked on his second novel for the rest of his life, he never brought it to completion. But, at his death, he left a mass of manuscripts from which a posthumous novel will eventually be published. He issued two volumes of his collected essays, Shadow and Act (1964) and Going to the Territory (1986). During his career, Ellison held a number of academic posts, including the Albert Schweitzer Professor of Humanities at New York University from 1970 to 1980. "Negro Oklahoma City" comes from an autobiographical essay in Shadow and Act, "Hidden Name and Complex Fate."

1   Negro Oklahoma City was starkly lacking in writers. In fact, there was only Roscoe Dungee, the editor of the local Negro newspaper and a very fine editorialist in that valuable tradition of personal journalism which is now

rapidly disappearing; a writer who in his emphasis upon the possibilities for justice offered by the Constitution anticipated the antisegregation struggle by decades. There were also a few reporters who drifted in and out, but these were about all. On the level of *conscious* culture the Negro community was biased in the direction of music.

2   These were the middle and late twenties, remember, and the state was still a new frontier state. The capital city was one of the great centers for southwestern jazz, along with Dallas and Kansas City. Orchestras which were to become famous within a few years were constantly coming and going. As were the blues singers, Ma Rainey and Ida Cox, and the old bands like that of King Oliver. But best of all, thanks to Mrs. Zelia N. Breaux, there was an active and enthusiastic school music program through which any child who had the interest and the talent could learn to play an instrument and take part in the band, the orchestra, the brass quartet. And there was a yearly operetta and a chorus and a glee club. Harmony was taught for four years and the music appreciation program was imperative. European folk dances were taught throughout the Negro school system, and we were also taught complicated patterns of military drill.

3   I tell you this to point out that although there were no incentives to write, there was ample opportunity to receive an artistic discipline. Indeed, once one picked up an instrument it was difficult to escape. If you chafed at the many rehearsals of the school band or orchestra and were drawn to the many small jazz groups, you were likely to discover that the jazzmen were apt to rehearse far more than the school band; it was only that they seemed to enjoy themselves better and to possess a freedom of imagination which we were denied at school. And once one learned that the wild, transcendent moments which occurred at dances or "battles of music," moments in which memorable improvisations were ignited, depended upon a dedication to a discipline which was observed even when rehearsals had to take place in the crowded quarters of Halley Richardson's shoeshine parlor. It was not the place which counted, although a large hall with good acoustics was preferred, but what one did to perfect one's performance.

4   If this talk of musical discipline gives the impression that there were no forces working to nourish one who would one day blunder, after many a twist and turn, into writing, I am misleading you. And here I might give you a longish lecture on the Ironies and Uses of Segregation. When I was a small child there was no library for Negroes in our city, and not until a Negro minister invaded the main library did we get one. For it was discovered that there was no law, only custom, which held that we could not use these public facilities. The results were the quick renting of two large rooms in a Negro office building (the recent site of a pool hall), the hiring of a young Negro librarian, the installation of shelves and a hurried stocking of the walls with any and every book possible. It was, in those first days, something of a literary chaos.

5　　But how fortunate for a boy who loved to read! I started with the fairy tales and quickly went through the junior fiction; then through the Westerns and the detective novels, and very soon I was reading the classics—only I didn't know it. There were also the Haldeman Julius Blue Books, which seem to have floated on the air down from Girard, Kansas; the syndicated columns of O. O. McIntyre, and the copies of *Vanity Fair* and the *Literary Digest* which my mother brought home from work—how could I ever join uncritically in the heavy-handed attacks on the so-called Big Media which have become so common today?

6　　There were also the pulp magazines and, more important, that other library which I visited when I went to help my adopted grandfather, J. D. Randolph (my parents had been living in his big rooming house when I was born), at his work as custodian of the law library of the Oklahoma State Capitol. Mr. Randolph had been one of the first teachers in what became Oklahoma City; and he'd also been one of the leaders of a group who walked from Gallatin, Tennessee, to the Oklahoma Territory. He was a tall man, as brown as smoked leather, who looked like the Indians with whom he'd herded horses in the early days.

7　　And while his status was merely the custodian of the law library, I was to see the white legislators come down on many occasions to question him on points of law, and often I was to hear him answer without recourse to the uniform rows of books on the shelves. This was a thing to marvel at in itself, and the white lawmakers did so, but even more marvellous, ironic, intriguing, haunting—call it what you will—is the fact that the Negro who knew the answers was named after Jefferson Davis. What Tennessee lost, Oklahoma was to gain, and after gaining it (a gift of courage, intelligence, fortitude and grace), used it only in concealment and, one hopes, with embarrassment . . .

8　　In the loosely structured community of that time, knowledge, news of other ways of living, ancient wisdom, the latest literary fads, hate literature—for years I kept a card warning Negroes away from the polls, which had been dropped by the thousands from a plane which circled over the Negro community—information of all kinds, found its level, catch-as-catch can, in the minds of those who were receptive to it. Not that there was no conscious structuring—I read my first Shaw and Maupassant, my first Harvard Classics in the home of a friend whose parents were products of that stream of New England education which had been brought to Negroes by the young and enthusiastic white teachers who staffed the schools set up for the freedmen after the Civil War. These parents were both teachers and there were others like them in our town.

9　　But the places where a rich oral literature was truly functional were the churches, the schoolyards, the barbershops, the cotton-picking camps; places where folklore and gossip thrived. The drug store where I worked was such a place, where on days of bad weather the older men would sit with their pipes and tell tall tales, hunting yarns and homely versions of the classics. It was here that I heard stories of searching for buried treasure and of headless horsemen, which I was told were my own father's versions told long before. There were even recitals of popular verse, "The Shooting of Dan McGrew," and, along with these, stories of Jesse James, of Negro outlaws and black United States marshals, of slaves who became the chiefs of Indian tribes and of the exploits of Negro cowboys. There was both truth and fantasy in this, intermingled in the mysterious fashion of literature.

10   Writers, in their formative period, absorb into their consciousness much that has no special value until much later, and often much which is of no special value even then—perhaps, beyond the fact that it throbs with affect and mystery and in it "time and pain and royalty in the blood" are suspended in imagery. So, long before I thought of writing, I was claimed by weather, by speech rhythms, by Negro voices and their different idioms, by husky male voices and by the high shrill singing voices of certain Negro women, by music; by tight spaces and by wide spaces in which the eyes could wander; by death, by newly born babies, by manners of various kinds, company manners and street manners; the manners of white society and those of our own high society; and by interracial manners; by street fights, circuses and minstrel shows; by vaudeville and moving pictures, by prize fights and foot races, baseball games and football matches. By spring floods and blizzards, catalpa worms and jack rabbits; honeysuckle and snapdragons (which smelled like old cigar butts); by sunflowers and hollyhocks, raw sugar cane and baked yams; pigs' feet, chili and blue haw ice cream. By parades, public dances and jam sessions, Easter sunrise ceremonies and large funerals. By contests between fire-and-brimstone preachers and by presiding elders who got "laughing-happy" when moved by the spirit of God.

11   I was impressed by the expert players of the "dozens" and certain notorious bootleggers of corn whiskey. By jazz musicians and fortunetellers and by men who did anything well; by strange sicknesses and by interesting brick or razor scars; by expert cursing vocabularies as well as by exalted praying and terrifying shouting, and by transcendent playing or singing of the blues. I was fascinated by old ladies, those who had seen slavery and those who were defiant of white folk and black alike; by the enticing walks of prostitutes and by the limping walks affected by Negro hustlers, especially those who wore Stetson hats, expensive shoes with well-starched overalls, usually with a diamond stickpin (when not in hock) in their tieless collars as their gambling uniforms.

12   And there were the blind men who preached on corners, and the blind men who sang the blues to the accompaniment of washboard and guitar, and the white junkmen who sang mountain music and the famous hucksters of fruit and vegetables.

13   And there was the Indian-Negro confusion. There were Negroes who were part Indian and who lived on reservations, and Indians who had children who lived in towns as Negroes, and Negroes who were Indians and traveled

back and forth between the groups with no trouble. And Indians who were as wild as wild Negroes and others who were as solid and steady as bankers. There were the teachers, too, inspiring teachers and villainous teachers who chased after the girl students, and certain female teachers who one wished would chase after young male students. And a handsome old principal of military bearing who had been blemished by his classmates at West Point when they discovered on the eve of graduation that he was a Negro. There were certain Jews, Mexicans, Chinese cooks, a German orchestra conductor and an English grocer who owned a Franklin touring car. And certain Negro mechanics— "Cadillac Slim," "Sticks" Walker, Buddy Bunn and Oscar Pitman—who had so assimilated the automobile that they seemed to be behind a steering wheel even as they walked the streets or danced with girls. And there were the whites who despised us and the others who shared our hardships and our joys.

14　　There is much more, but this is sufficient to indicate some of what was present even in a segregated community to form the background of my work, my sense of life.

❧

Discussion Questions

1. According to Ellison, what opportunities for a musical education did a black student have in "Negro Oklahoma City" in the middle and late twenties? Why does he discuss these?

*2. In paragraph 3, what does Ellison mean by the phrase, "moments in which memorable improvisations were ignited"? How does the phrase relate to its context?

3. In paragraph 4, Ellison says, "And here I might give you a longish lecture on the Ironies and Uses of Segregation." What does the sentence mean and how does it apply to what he goes on to tell about use of the city library?

4. What role does J. D. Randolph, "custodian of the library of the Oklahoma State Capitol," play in his relationship with the legislators? What role does he play in Ellison's development?

*5. Explain the statement in paragraph 7, "marvellous, ironic, intriguing, haunting . . . is the fact that the Negro who knew the answers was named after Jefferson Davis."

6. What is *oral literature* (paragraph 9) and what role does it play in Ellison's literary development?

7. What purpose is served by the long lists or catalogs found in paragraphs 10–13?

Writing Topics

1. Write a brief character sketch of Ralph Ellison as revealed to you in "Negro Oklahoma City." What, for example, was his attitude toward segregation between the races at school, libraries, and other places? What is revealed by sentences like, "And there were the whites who despised us and the others who shared our hardships and our joys."

2. Write a brief descriptive/narrative essay in which you touch on the key events, situations, and aspects of your past that formed you into what you have become today. First set forth a succinct summary of what, indeed, you have become today—a prospective janitor, doctor, hamburger flipper, politician, teacher, writer, or indecisive freshman hoping to become a sophomore.

❧"A man walks his tedious miles through
the same interminable street every day,
elbowing his way through a buzzing multitude of men,
yet never seeing a familiar face,
and never seeing a strange one the second time."

NEW YORK: A SPLENDID DESERT

Mark Twain

Mark Twain (1835–1910) is considered by many to be America's greatest humorist and satirist. He is credited with inventing the American prose style in such works as The Innocents Abroad (1869), Life on the Mississippi (1883), and Adventures of Huckleberry Finn (1884). Twain grew up in Hannibal, Missouri, on the Mississippi River, and after a stint of piloting steamboats on the great river went out west to observe life in the gold-mining country of California. He reveals his distinctively western (or "frontier") perspective in the letter on New York City (below) published in a California newspaper in 1867. For more biographical information on Twain, see the headnotes on pages 96 and 457.

New York, June 5th, 1867.

Editors Alta:

1   I have at last, after several months' experience, made up my mind that it is a splendid desert—a domed and steepled solitude, where the stranger is lonely in the the midst of a million of his race. A man walks his tedious miles through the same interminable street every day, elbowing his way through a buzzing multitude of men, yet never seeing a familiar face, and never seeing a strange one the second time. He visits a friend once—it is a day's journey—and then stays away from that time forward till that friend cools to a mere acquaintance, and finally to a stranger. So there is little sociability, and, consequently, there is little cordiality. Every man seems to feel that he has got the duties of two lifetimes to accomplish in one, and so he rushes, rushes, rushes, and never has time to be companionable—never has any time at his disposal to fool away on matters which do not involve dollars and duty and business.

2   All this has a tendency to make the city-bred man impatient of interruption, suspicious of strangers, and fearful of being bored, and his business interfered with. The natural result is, that the striking want of heartiness observable here, sometimes even among old friends, degenerates into something which is hardly even chilly politeness towards strangers. A large party of Californians were discussing this matter yesterday evening, and one said he didn't believe there was any genuine fellow-feeling in the camp. Another said: "Come, now, don't judge without a full hearing—try all classes; try everybody; go to the Young Men's Christian Association." But the first speaker said: "My son, I have been to the Young Men's Christian Association, and it isn't any use; it was the same old thing—thermometer at 32°, which is the freezing notch, if I understand it. They were polite there, exasperatingly polite, just as they are outside. One of them prayed for the stranger within his gates—meaning me—but it was plain enough that he didn't mean his petition to be taken in earnest. It simply amounted to this, that he didn't know me, but would recommend me to mercy, anyhow, since it was customary, but didn't wish to be misunderstood as taking any personal interest in the matter."

3   Of course that was rather a strong exaggeration, but I thought it was a pretty fair satire upon the serene indifference of the New Yorker to everybody and everything without the pale of his private and individual circle.

4   There is something about this ceaseless buzz, and hurry, and bustle, that keeps a stranger in a state of unwholesome excitement all the time, and makes him restless and uneasy, and saps from him all capacity to enjoy anything or take a strong interest in any matter whatever—a something which impels him to try to do everything, and yet permits him to do nothing. He is a boy in a candy-shop—could choose quickly if there were but one kind of candy, but is hopelessly undetermined in the midst of a hundred kinds. A stranger feels unsatisfied, here, a good part of the time. He starts to a library; changes, and moves toward a theatre; changes again and thinks he will visit a friend; goes within a biscuit-toss of a picture-gallery, a billiard-room, a beer-cellar and a circus, in succession, and finally drifts home and to bed, without having really done anything or gone anywhere. He don't go anywhere because he can't go everywhere, I suppose. This fidgetty, feverish restlessness will drive a man crazy, after a while, or kill him. It kills a good many dozens now—by suicide. I have got to get out of it.

5   There is one thing very sure—I can't keep my temper in New York. The cars and carriages always come along and get in the way just as I want to cross a street, and if there is any thing that can make a man soar into flights of sublimity in the matter of profanity, it is that. You know that, yourself. However, I must be accurate—I must speak truth, and say there is one thing that is more annoying. That is to go down West Tenth street hunting for the Art building, No. 51. You are tired, and your feet are hot and swollen, and you wouldn't start, only you calculate that it cannot be more than two blocks away, and you

almost feel a genuine desire to go and see the picture on exhibition without once changing your mind. Very well. You come to No. 7; and directly you come to 142! You stare a minute, and then step back and start over again—but it isn't any use—when you are least expecting it, comes that unaccountable jump. You cross over, and find Nos. 18, 20, 22, and then perhaps you jump to 376! Your gall begins to rise. You go on. You get on a trail, at last, the figures leading by regular approaches up toward 51—but when you have walked four blocks they start at 49 and begin to run the other way! You are perspiring and furious by this time, but you keep desperately on, and speculate on new and complicated forms of profanity. And behold, in time the numbers become bewilderingly complicated: on one door is a 3 on a little tin scrap, on the next a 17 in gold characters a foot square, on the next a 19, a 5 and a 137, one above the other and in three different styles of figuring! You do not swear any more now, of course, because you can't find any words that are long enough or strong enough to fit the case. You feel degraded and ignominious and subjugated. And there and then you say that you will go away from New York and start over again; and that you will never come back to settle permanently till you have learned to swear with the utmost fluency in seventeen different languages. You become more tranquil, now, because you see your way clearly before you, how that, when you are properly accomplished, you can live in this great city and still be happy; you feel that in that day, when a subject shall defy English, you can try the Arabic, the Hungarian, the Japanese, the Kulu-Kaffir, and when the worst comes to the worst, you can come the Hindostanee on it and conquer. After this, you go tranquilly on for a matter of seventeen blocks and find 51 sandwiched in between Nos. 13 and 32,986. Then you wish you had never been born, to come to a strange land and suffer in this way.

6 Well, I intended, when I started out, to give my views of the pleasant side of New York, but I perceive that I have wandered into the wrong vein, and so I will stop short and give it up until I find myself in a more fortunate humor. I do not think that I could twist myself around now any easier than I could turn myself inside out.

❧

Discussion Questions

1. What, according to Twain in paragraphs 1 and 2, makes the "city-bred man" so inhospitable?
2. Explain the statement in paragraph 2 made supposedly by a fellow Californian, "My son, I have been to the Young Men's Christian Association, and it isn't any use; it was the same old thing—thermometer at 32°, which is the freezing notch, if I understand it."

3. What in paragraph 5 caused Twain to lose his temper? What solution did he work out for himself that caused him to "become more tranquil"?

*4. What was Twain's original plan in the essay, and what caused him to change the plan?

Writing Topics

1. Write an analytical essay about the humor of exaggeration in Twain's short piece. In your conclusion, indicate to the reader how and what to take seriously in Twain in spite of his humor.

2. Ever since the publication of *The Lonely Crowd* in 1950 (by David Reisman, et al.), it has become a commonplace that, in cities with immense populations, the loneliness of the individual is intensified. In a brief argumentative essay, agree or disagree with this idea, relying on your own experience of big cities or on that of someone you know.

"New York has no pity: it's every man for himself, and since you are yourself-and-a-half, you fall behind."

PREGNANT IN NEW YORK

Anna Quindlen

Anna Quindlen was born in Philadelphia, Pennsylvania, in 1952 and earned a B.A. from Barnard College in 1974. On graduation, she went to work for the *New York Post* and after three years moved to *The New York Times*, serving as a city hall reporter until 1981. From 1981 to 1983, she wrote the "About New York" column for the newspaper. After serving as deputy editor from 1983 to 1985, she began, at the invitation of the editor, a new personal column entitled "Life in the Thirties," which appeared weekly beginning in 1986. Later, beginning in 1990, she became author of the column entitled "Public and Private." In 1992, she won the Pulitzer Prize for commentary in journalism. In 1988, she published a volume of her columns entitled *Living Out Loud*, from which "Pregnant in New York" has been taken; the essay originally appeared in her column on March 27, 1986. Her other books include a best-selling novel, *Object Lessons* (1991); a children's book, *The Tree That Came to Stay* (1992); a collection of essays, *Thinking Out Loud: On the Personal, the Political, the Public and the Private* (1993); and a second novel, *One True Thing* (1994).

1   I have two enduring memories of the hours just before I gave birth to my first child. One is of finding a legal parking space on Seventy-eighth Street between Lexington and Park, which made my husband and me believe that we were going inside the hospital to have a child who would always lead a charmed life. The other is of walking down Lexington Avenue, stopping every couple of steps to find myself a visual focal point—a stop sign, a red light, a pair of $200 shoes in a store window—and doing what the Lamaze books call first-stage breathing. It was 3:00 A.M. and coming toward me through a magenta haze of what the Lamaze books call discomfort were a couple in evening clothes whose eyes were popping out of their perfect faces. "Wow," said the man when I was at least two steps past them. "She looks like she's ready to burst."

2   I love New York, but it's a tough place to be pregnant. It's a great place for half sour pickles, chopped liver, millionaires, actors, dancers, akita dogs, nice leather goods, fur coats, and baseball, but it is a difficult place to have any kind of disability and, as anyone who has filled out the forms for a maternity leave lately will tell you, pregnancy is considered a disability. There's no privacy in New York; everyone is right up against everyone else and they all feel compelled to say what they think. When you look like a hot-air balloon with insufficient ballast, that's not good.

3   New York has no pity: it's every man for himself, and since you are yourself-and-a-half, you fall behind. There's a rumor afoot that if you are pregnant you can get a seat on the A train at rush hour, but it's totally false. There are, in fact, parts of the world in which pregnancy can get you a seat on public transportation, but none of them are within the boundaries of the city—with the possible exception of some unreconstructed parts of Staten Island.

4   What you get instead are rude comments, unwarranted instrusions and deli countermen. It is a little-known fact that New York deli countermen can predict the sex of an unborn child. (This is providing that you order, of course. For a counterman to provide this service requires a minimum order of seventy-five cents.) This is how it works: You walk into a deli and say, "Large fruit salad, turkey on rye with Russian, a large Perrier and a tea with lemon." The deli counterman says, "Who you buying for, the Rangers?" and all the other deli countermen laugh.

5   This is where many pregnant women make their mistake. If it is wintertime and you are wearing a loose coat, the preferred answer to this question is, "I'm buying for all the women in my office." If it is summer and you are visibly pregnant, you are sunk. The deli counterman will lean over the counter and say, studying your contours, "It's a boy." He will then tell a tedious story about sex determination, his Aunt Olga, and a clove of garlic, while behind you people waiting on line shift and sigh and begin to make Zero Population Growth and fat people comments. (I once dealt with an East Side counterman who argued with me about the tea because he said it was bad for the baby, but he was an actor waiting for his big break, not a professional.) Deli countermen do not believe in amniocentesis. Friends who have had amniocentesis tell me that once or twice they tried to argue: "I already know it's a girl." "You are wrong." They gave up: "Don't forget the napkins."

6   There are also cabdrivers. One promptly pulled over in the middle of Central Park when I told him I had that queasy feeling. When I turned to get back into the cab, it was gone. The driver had taken the $1.80 on the meter as a loss. Luckily, I never had this problem again, because as I grew larger, nine out of ten cabdrivers refused to pick me up. They had read the tabloids. They knew about all those babies christened Checker (actually, I suppose now most of them are Plymouths) because they're born in the back seat in the Midtown Tunnel. The only way I could get a cabdriver to pick me up after the sixth

month was to hide my stomach by having a friend walk in front of me. The exception was a really tiresome young cabdriver whose wife's due date was a week after mine and who wanted to practice panting with me for that evening's childbirth class. Most of the time I wound up taking public transportation.

7   And so it came down to the subways: men looking at their feet, reading their newspapers, working hard to keep from noticing me. One day on the IRT I was sitting down—it was a spot left unoccupied because the rainwater had spilled in the window from an elevated station—when I noticed a woman standing who was or should have been on her way to the hospital.

8   "When are you due?" I asked her. "Thursday," she gasped. "I'm September," I said. "Take my seat." She slumped down and said, with feeling, "You are the first person to give me a seat on the subway since I've been pregnant." Being New Yorkers, with no sense of personal privacy, we began to exchange subway, taxi, and deli counterman stories. When a man sitting nearby got up to leave, he snarled, "You wanted women's lib, now you got it."

9   Well, I'm here to say that I did get women's lib, and it is my only fond memory of being pregnant in New York. (Actually, I did find pregnancy useful on opening day at Yankee Stadium, when great swarms of people parted at the sight of me as though I were Charlton Heston in *The Ten Commandments*. But it had a pariah quality that was not totally soothing.)

10   One evening rush hour during my eighth month I was waiting for a train at Columbus Circle. The loudspeaker was crackling unintelligibly and ominously and there were as many people on the platform as currently live in Santa Barbara, Calif. Suddenly I had the dreadful feeling that I was being surrounded. "To get mugged at a time like this," I thought ruefully. "And this being New York, they'll probably try to take the baby, too." But as I looked around I saw that the people surrounding me were four women, some armed with shoulder bags. "You need protection," one said, and being New Yorkers, they ignored the fact that they did not know one another and joined forces to form a kind of phalanx around me, not unlike those that offensive linemen build around a quarterback.

11   When the train arrived and the doors opened, they moved forward, with purpose, and I was swept inside, not the least bit bruised. "Looks like a boy," said one with a grin, and as the train began to move, we all grabbed the silver overhead handles and turned away from one another.

&a

Discussion Questions

1. What are the "two enduring memories" Quindlen describes in her first paragraph, and how did they affect her?

*2. Quindlen asserts in paragraph 2 that New York is a "tough place to be pregnant," but then adds that New York is "a great place" for—a long list of items. Analyze the items on the list and give your best rhetorical sense of why they are there.

3. Describe Quindlen's "pregnant experiences" (paragraphs 4–9) with deli countermen, with cabdrivers, on the subways, and at Yankee Stadium. What constant theme seems to run through these experiences?

4. At the end of paragraph 10, Quindlen describes her experience waiting to get on a subway. How does this experience differ from the foregoing experiences? What happened at the conclusion of the experience that indicates that Quindlen is still in the New York she has described earlier?

Writing Topics

1. Write a letter to Quindlen telling her how her experience of being pregnant in New York would be the same—or different—from her experience of being pregnant in a city or town you know.

2. Take a poll of other members of the class asking whether they would offer their seat to a pregnant woman and why or why not? To encourage responses, you might cite as an example of one attitude the departing statement of the subway rider quoted by Quindlen, "You wanted women's lib, now you got it." Write a letter to the editorial page of the local newspaper offering your findings and setting forth your own views.

*❧ "With all the problems in the world,
who cares about change for a quarter?"*

RUDE? YEAH, YOU ARE

Robert V. Levine

Robert V. Levine was born in Brooklyn, New York, in 1945 and took a B.A. at the University of California in 1967. He studied clinical psychology in the graduate program at Florida State University, earning an M.A. in 1969. He was awarded a Ph.D. at New York University in 1974, specializing in personality and social psychology. Levine is currently a professor of psychology at California State University, Fresno, where he has won several teaching awards, including Outstanding Professor of the Year in 1990. He has published extensively in his field and is completing a book on "the pace of life in different cities." His "Rude? Yeah, You Are" appeared in *The New York Times* on July 29, 1995.

1   Thomas Wolfe once wrote that city people "have no manners, no courtesy, no consideration for the rights of others and no humanity." American urbanites would deny that they see more than their share of nastiness. But when I was growing up in Brooklyn, I was taught that big cities simply have more of everything—the good and the bad.

2   Over the last several years, my students and I have conducted a series of experiments in different cities to test the likelihood that a stranger in need will be offered help.

3   In our comparisons of 36 cities of various sizes, we asked not for Schindler-like acts of heroism but for simple acts of civility: Does a man with a hurt leg receive assistance in picking up a dropped magazine? Will a blind person be helped across a busy street? Is an "unnoticed" dropped pen retrieved by a passerby? Will a stranger try to make change for a quarter? Do people take the time to mail a stamped and addressed "lost" letter?

4   True to its stereotype, New York City made a poor showing. It was 35th in the hurt leg, dropped pen and making-change experiments, 26th in returning lost letters and 16th on the helping-the-blind measure. In an overall helping index, New York finished last.

5 I catch a lot of flak for my studies. When a social scientist—from Fresno, no less—goes around rating people's home towns, it goes with the territory. But to our surprise, New Yorkers, whom you would think would be inured to charges of rudeness, have been some of the most sensitive.

6 New Yorkers told me: "It doesn't prove that people don't care." "How do you know the blind guy wanted to be helped?" "With all the problems in the world, who cares about change for a quarter?"

7 Perhaps the most frequent critique was: New Yorkers are the world's friendliest people; you just need to pierce that exterior. But experiments are not about what people are like on the inside or how they treat their loved ones or whether the ominous looking taxi driver turns out to be a great conversationalist. They compare the probabilities, under systematic conditions, that a needy stranger will receive help in different places. And New York performs dismally.

8 New Yorkers were not only least likely to help a stranger but often showed a lack of civility when they did. When an experimenter dropped a pen, for example, altruistic New Yorkers would typically call back that he had dropped his pen and then quickly move away. Compare this with those in Rochester (the most helpful city of the 36), who were more likely to pick up and return the pen, sometimes running to catch up with the experimenter.

9 Upon seeing the blind person, helpful New Yorkers would often wait until the light turned green, tersely announce that it was safe to cross and then quickly walk ahead. In Rochester, helpers were more likely to offer to walk the person across the street and sometimes even offer further aid.

10 An especially vivid and uncivil instance of help occurred in the lost letter experiment. In many cities, we received envelopes that had clearly been opened. In almost all of these cases, the finder had then resealed it or remailed it in new envelopes.

11 Only from New York did we receive an envelope that had its entire side ripped and left open. On the back of it the helper had scribbled a nasty accusation in Spanish. Below that, he (she?) added an even more straight-forward obscenity in English. I've tried to picture this angry New Yorker, perhaps cursing my irresponsibility all the way to the mailbox, somehow feeling compelled to pick up after a stranger he already hated. And this letter counted in the helping column for New York's score.

12 Paradoxically, there was less uncivil behavior from New York's nonhelpers than from those in some other low-scoring cities. One experimenter said that in Los Angeles (34th out of 36) people sometimes went out of their way to avoid helping. In New York, it seemed that they were just too busy to help. "It was like they saw me but didn't really notice—not just me, but everything else around them," he said.

13 To the stranger in need, thoughts don't count for much. When it comes to deeds, the prospects are even bleaker in New York than they are in Los Angeles.

❧

Discussion Questions

1. Explain Levine's meaning when he writes (paragraph 3), "In our comparisons of 36 cities of various sizes, we asked not for Schindler-like acts of heroism but for simple acts of civility."

*2. When told that New York finished last in an "overall helping index," some New Yorkers replied, "New Yorkers are the world's friendliest people; you just need to pierce that exterior." What did Levine think of this reply? What do you think?

*3. Levine says that New Yorkers often added insult to injury by being uncivil even when they did help. What examples does he cite? What is your reaction to them?

4. In the "lost letter" experiment, New York scored in "helping" but not in "civility." Explain.

Writing Topics

1. Write an argumentative essay as to why you think Levine's experiment is valid or not. In your conclusion, explore what purpose the experiment serves.

2. Try out some of Levine's experiments (or similar experiments of your own) on campus or in some other locations and write a descriptive account, comic or serious, about the results.

I always had great respect for whores.
The many I've known were kind and generous.
Some of them supported whole families. . . ."

THE RED-LIGHT DISTRICT
IN PHILADELPHIA

Ethel Waters

Ethel Waters (1896–1977) was born in Chester, Pennsylvania, and, after working as a maid, began a singing career in black nightclubs. She became a star with the leading role in the Broadway hit *Mamba's Daugthers* in 1939 and had important roles in such films as *Cabin in the Sky* and *Pinky*. Among the songs she made her own are "Stormy Weather" and "Am I Blue?" She is best remembered for playing the black cook in both the stage and film versions (1950 and 1952) of Carson McCullers's novel *Member of the Wedding* (1946). The selection below is taken from her autobiography, *His Eye Is on the Sparrow* (1950). The title comes from the hymn she frequently sang after joining Billy Graham's revivalist crusades in the latter part of her life.

1   I did have one childhood home for more than a few weeks. It was a three-room shanty in an alley just off Clifton Street. Prostitution was legal in Philadelphia then, and Clifton Street, located in the old Bloody Eighth Ward, lay in the heart of the red-light district.

2   There was always something interesting to watch in that lively neighborhood. Every night the whores, black and white, paraded up and down Clifton Street. They all wore the same outfit, a regular uniform consisting of a voile skirt with taffeta underneath, cork-heeled shoes, a black velvet neckband, and big whores' hoop earrings. Of course their unmistakable trade-mark was their hip-wriggling walk.

3   I was not yet six years old when we moved there and seven when we left, but I had one hell of a time for myself in that plague spot of vice and crime. I came to know well the street whores, the ladies in the sporting houses, their pimps, the pickpockets, shoplifters, and other thieves who lived all around us. I played with the thieves' children and the sporting women's trick babies. It was they who taught me how to steal.

4   Things at home didn't change much, but I remember that little alley home as the heaven on earth of my childhood. For once we were all together in a whole house—Vi, Ching, Charlie, me, Mom on her days off. And after a while Louise also came to live with us.

5   We stayed in Clifton Street for fifteen months. That was the only time I could feel that I had a family that wasn't continually disrupting and belonged in one neighborhood. My family kept on squabbling, but I lived more in the street than at home.

6   All of us dead-end kids ran errands for the whores. Some of them were good for as much as fifteen, twenty, or twenty-five cents in tips. We spent most of our earnings on candy and food. You could buy a frankfurter for three cents at a street stand, yat-gaw-mein cost a nickel in the Chinese joints, and for a dime you could get a whole plate of fish and French-fried potatoes at a food stand called See Willie's.

7   A bunch of us would often sleep all night out on the street, over the warm iron gratings of bakeries or laundries. Our families didn't care where we were, and these nesting places, when you put your coat under you, were no more uncomfortable than the broken-down beds with treacherous springs or the bedbug-infested pallets we had at home. Being so large for my age, I was accepted as an equal by older boys and girls. My biggest asset as a street child in the tenderloin was my ability to keep my mouth shut.

8   Along with a few other Clifton Street youngsters I acted as a semiofficial lookout girl for the sporting houses. Though prostitution was a legalized business, there were occasional police raids. These came when church groups bore down heavily on the authorities or after one body too many, stabbed, shot, or cut up very untidily, had been found in some dark alley.

9   Any of us slum children could smell out a cop even though he was a John, a plain-clothes man. These brilliant sleuths never suspicioned that we were tipsters for the whole whoring industry. Usually we'd be playing some singing game on the street when we spotted a cop, a game like Here Come Two Dudes A-Riding or the one that begins:

> "King William was King James's son,
> Upon his breast he wore a star,
> And that was called . . ."

10   On smelling out the common enemy, we boys and girls in the know would start to shout the songs, accenting certain phrases. If we happened to be playing a singing game we'd whistle the agreed-on tune. The other kids, even those who weren't lookouts, would innocently imitate us, and in no time at all the whole neighborhood would be alerted. The street women would disappear, the lights would go out, and the doors would be locked in the sporting houses.

11   Some of the friendlier policemen tried to be nice to us, but that got them nowhere. It was an unwritten law among us not to accept candy from cops or have anything to do with them. It was the only law that was never broken on Clifton Street.

12   The Bloody Eighth at that time was not exclusively a Negro slum. We had plenty of white neighbors, Hunkies and Jews, and some Chinese. The few respectable families, white and black, forced by circumstances to live in that slum kept to themselves as much as possible.

13   I didn't know much about color then. There was no racial prejudice at all in that big melting pot running over with vice and crime, violence, poverty, and corruption. I never was made to feel like an outcast on Clifton Street. All of us, whites, blacks, and yellows, were outcasts there together and having a fine time among ourselves.

14   Anyway, racial prejudice couldn't have existed in that neighborhood where vice was the most important business. The white and Negro street whores worked together, lived and slept together. The two men who owned and protected most of them were Lovey Joe and Rosebud, both of them Negroes. It was not considered unusual for a colored prostitute to have a trick baby white as a lily.

15   I've always had great respect for whores. The many I've known were kind and generous. Some of them supported whole families and kept at their trade for years to send their trick babies through college. I never knew a prostitute who did harm to anyone but herself. I except, of course, the whores who are real criminals and use knockout drops and bring men to their rooms to be robbed, beaten, and blackmailed.

16   No woman in my immediate family ever turned to prostitution. Neither were they saints. Sometimes they lived with men they weren't married to. This is true of my mother and my two aunts, Vi and Ching. And they never saw anything wrong in getting what presents they could from their men—shoes for themselves or for me, clothes, or money.

17   My grandmother hated the idea of my growing up in the red-light district and strongly disapproved of prostitution. But there was nothing she could do about it. The alley shanty was the best home she could find or afford.

❧

Discussion Questions

1.   What according to Waters was the "uniform" of the whores in Philadelphia's red-light district?
2.   Describe the six-year-old Waters's "street education" in Philadelphia.
*3.   How did Waters feel about her family life at home during this period? Explain.

4   Define by context (or the dictionary) the following terms used by Waters: (paragraph 6) *dead-end kids*; (paragraph 7) *nesting places*; *bedbug infested pallets*; *in the tenderloin*; (paragraph 8) *the sporting houses*.

5.   What were the duties of Waters and the other slum children who acted as "tipsters for the whole whoring industry"? Describe their techniques.

6.   In paragraph 15, Waters says that she "always had great respect for whores." Did her respect extend to all the whores? Explain.

Writing Topics

1.   In paragraph 14, Waters writes, "Racial prejudice couldn't have existed in that neighborhood where vice was the most important business." In a brief analytical essay, summarize the evidence in her account for Waters making such a statement. In your conclusion, show whether you believe that her statement has or has not been adequately supported.

2.   In the last paragraph, Waters writes, "My grandmother hated the idea of my growing up in the red-light district and strongly disapproved of prostitution." Conduct an interview with someone who holds the same opinion as the grandmother (or with yourself in which you imagine yourself as the grandmother). In an essay, present the results of the interview and then indicate your approval or disapproval of the grandmother's view.

❧Terrified as I was at this angle, which, I surmised,
must steadily increase toward ninety degrees,
I had sense enough now to realize quickly the
connection between the bridge and the boat."

HELD UP BY THE
DEARBORN STREET BRIDGE, CHICAGO

Mary Ellen Chase

Mary Ellen Chase (1887–1973) was born in Blue Hill, Maine and took a B.A. from the University of Maine in 1909. She did graduate work in English at the University of Minnesota, earning an M.A. in 1918 and a Ph.D. in 1922 and had a full career as a professor of English, spent mainly at Smith College (1926–1955). She is the author of numerous books, including novels, biographies, children's books, and books on the Bible. Her fiction ranges from *The Girl from the Big Horn Country* (1916) to *The Lovely Ambition* (1960) and her nonfiction from *The Art of Narration* (1926) to *The Story of Lighthouses* (1965). Her books on the Bible include *Life and Language of the Old Testament* (1955) and *Prophets for the Common Reader* (1963). In addition to all these books, she wrote three autobiographical works, *A Goodly Heritage* (1932), *A Goodly Fellowship* (1939), and *The White Gate* (1954). In the following essay, taken from the second of these volumes, Chase is twenty-two years old; the time is around the year 1909.

1   I was sitting up in my berth and peering from the window the next morning long before it was light enough to see. The flat expanse of country, with the harvest already cut and with corn stacked in golden huts upon the shorn ground, was as fascinating to my eyes when it had once come into vision as the tumbling Berkshire hills. It made up in newness what it lacked in beauty. I suddenly remembered how Stevenson in *Across the Plains* had named as beautiful the words *Ohio, Indiana, Illinois*. Now they seemed beautiful to me also although I had never thought of them in that way before.

2   When we at last swept through the sordid outskirts of Chicago in the early afternoon, I was well-nigh exhausted even more from excitement than from Middle Western heat. But my fervor knew no lessening, and I pinned on one of my father's large handkerchiefs in almost painful curiosity and agitation. The elderly gentleman promised by the Bible Institute was awaiting me, similarly marked. I thought even then, I remember, that I should have recognized him without his handkerchief since, among all the many persons on the platform, he alone could have emerged from a Bible Institute.

3   He conducted me with a benevolent and, I felt, faintly disapproving air to the elevated railroad, and I staggered after him bearing my suit-case, which he did not offer to carry and which I was too embarrassed to give to any importuning porter, not being sure of them and their ways. Once we had landed within the Bible Institute and I had been shown my very hot and somewhat musty room, I decided that benevolence and faint disapproval were two of the current attitudes of that institution. By the time I had eaten my supper in company with others of its inmates, I had added to these, suspicion and a very unattractive zeal.

4   My mother was quite right in assuming that I should be safe within its doors. Surely no one would enter it who was not compelled by inner or by outer force to do so! It was a place devoted to one purpose, namely the saving of souls, and even to me, whose religious background had been extremely simple, not to say fervent at times, it was the most embarrassing of hostels. All the dozen or so young women whom it housed were training to be evangelists, as I learned to my great confusion at supper when two of them asked me if I had made the great decision. Upon my vowing hastily and stoutly that I had, their suspicion of me somewhat relaxed for the moment, but their zeal was fired to anecdotal vigor by their very relief.

5   I stayed two weeks in the Bible Institute. It was the only place I have ever known which grew increasingly unpalatable from constant association. I never quite knew whether to admire or to dislike the single-minded young women, who, when they were not at prayer, at oral testimonials, or at Bible study, went about doing good; but I think my only genuine emotion toward them and their activities was an extreme sense of embarrassment. We never had quite enough to eat, I remember, although perhaps my hunger partly resulted from the uncomfortable knowledge that everyone but me was dedicated to the principle that man does not live by bread alone. Before we sat down to each scanty meal, we sang a hymn with a chorus which said,

"O to be nothing, nothing!"

Since I had come to Chicago with the express purpose of being something, I found this hymn exceedingly irritating. I think I regarded it with superstition as well, fearing that the thrice-daily repetition of its refrain might result in my becoming precisely nothing at all!

6   We had nightly prayer circles at which my presence was tacitly expected and my habitual silence the cause of renewed suspicion. This atmosphere of constant petition with which the entire establishment was redolent got somewhat on my nerves, not to say my conscience, especially since the only praying of which I was capable throughout the fortnight was of a most selfish and antisocial nature, namely that I might get a job.

7   Had I not, indeed, like St. Paul been intent only upon "this one thing," had I not been tormented by fears lest I should fail therein, I might conceivably have become interested in the Bible Institute and in the study of its strange, tenacious, fervid minds. But the more intent I became upon my own future as the jobless days went on, the more its curious existence seemed a law unto itself and quite divorced from life outside its grimy, comfortless walls. I learned, however, that it was known elsewhere. For when Mr. B. F. Clark, the manager of the teachers' agency which held my future in its hands, asked me upon the occasion of my first call upon him where I was living in Chicago, and I told him, he rose from his chair and cried, "My God!"

8   I shall always remember my first visit to Mr. Clark's office in Steinway Hall on Van Buren Street. He told me some years afterwards that he remembered it, too, in fact that it had always stood him in good stead as a source of amusement when he needed entertainment in his thoughts. I am sure that no young teacher from Maine had ever before journeyed jobless to Chicago to cast herself upon his mercy. I am sure, too, that he was quite unprepared to meet such eager ingenuousness in a young woman, even in those days when artlessness was still not uncommon among the young.

9   I went to see him the first morning after my arrival in Chicago, when I had ascertained from the most worldly of the Bible students how I should get to Van Buren Street. I went on the street-car since I did not dare essay the elevated railroad by myself, and I carried my suit-case with me. I do not know just why I thus encumbered myself. Perhaps I was still conscious of my mother's adjurations to keep my most valuable possessions with me as much as possible in such a city. But I think rather that I needed a generous receptacle for more letters of recommendation and for the themes which I had written in college and which, I thought, might give added proof to Mr. Clark that I knew something about the teaching of English.

10   When I had once reached Van Buren Street with my suit-case and had taken the elevator to the eleventh floor of Steinway Hall, I was in a frightful state of nervous excitement, which did not lessen upon my discovery that no one of a dozen young women in a dozen different offices had ever so much as heard of me. After a long wait during which the furious beating of my heart sent added blood to my already very red cheeks, I was, however, ushered, still with my suit-case, into the presence of him upon whose probably long since forgotten suggestion I had come to Chicago. Mr. Clark, seeing my suit-case, quite

naturally thought I had only just arrived; and when I explained that it contained documents which might be of interest to him, he leaned back in his chair and laughed long and loudly.

11   He was a small, round man of perhaps fifty, with intensely blue round eyes set in a very smooth, pink face. He had brushy white hair parted in the middle, and he was dressed in a light gray suit with a red tie. As I stood there much embarrassed before him, I thought of George Meredith, who had recently died and who, I had read somewhere, favored light gray suits with red ties. For a moment I thought self-consciously of impressing Mr. Clark by the comparison and then thought better of it.

12   I asked instead whether he really thought I should get a position, and I remember that he said he felt sure of it, since he could not allow some school to be deprived of me. I took this as a compliment at the moment and felt much encouraged, although later I realized that another meaning lurked within his words. My heart leaped at his next announcement.

13   "Let me see," he said. "There may be something this minute. What about Mason City, Iowa? They want a Latin teacher."

14   My heart fell as quickly as it had risen.

15   "I'm afraid Iowa is beyond the Mississippi, isn't it?" I said.

16   "Why the Mississippi?" asked Mr. Clark, fumbling among other papers on his desk. "It's a nice river. Got anything against it?"

17   "No," said I. "It's only that my mother would prefer me not to go beyond the Mississippi unless it's really necessary."

18   Mr. Clark laughed again. I could see that our interview was unusual to him in many respects. Then he told me with great encouragement that he felt reasonably sure some opening this side of the Mississippi would put in an appearance before many days had passed. I in turn assured him that with his permission I should look in at the office every morning at this hour, and he did not seem to object to my proposal.

19   The morning of my first visit to Mr. Clark is also memorable to me because of a somewhat terrifying as well as humorous accident which befell me before I was again safely within the walls of the Bible Institute. There is always, I think, an element of pathos in inexperience and the mishaps which it often calls down upon itself, humorous as such mishaps may be. Perhaps for this very reason much of the humor of today lacks a kind of mellowness since inexperience has become so relatively impossible in an age like our own.

20   I had lived all of my twenty-two years in the country and in the most countrified country at that. The college which I attended was a country college, situated in a small town, the nearest city being the inconsiderable one of Bangor. I knew nothing of great cities and their ways, and had I not been so eager to enjoy my new freedom to its limit and to learn all that I could about my new surroundings, I should have felt terrified by Chicago, its dirt, its uproar, and its frenzied rush.

21   Strange and frightening as everything seemed to me, however, I determined upon leaving Mr. Clark's office on Van Buren Street to walk to the Bible Institute. I was impelled to do so by a variety of desires: to make my next letter home as dramatic and interesting as possible; to see what Chicago was really like; to avoid another street-car since in the first I had felt extremely self-conscious and ill at ease; and above all else to postpone as long as possible my re-entry into the Bible Institute. Even with my suitcase the distance did not seem long to me when the impatient door-man at Steinway Hall had explained to me with many pointings of a scornful finger the requisite blocks west and the turn northward.

22   I reached Dearborn Street with no disaster and turned northward. The day was warm, and I took my time, seemingly the only person, I thought, on the street who was not in a hurry. There was and still is, unless I am mistaken, a bridge on Dearborn Street which crosses the Chicago River. The structure of this bridge meant nothing to me, but I lingered thereon, being fascinated by the filthy water of the river and by a peculiar craft coming upstream. This struck me, I remember, as odd since there was obviously no way by which it might proceed beyond the bridge. I walked on slowly, studying the steady progress of the boat, when I was startled by the blowing of whistles and the apparent haste of everyone but me. Whether I was hidden by the iron uprights of the bridge from the sight of the men responsible for its manipulation, I do not know; but by the time I had come to my senses and was hurrying to reach the other side, I felt to my horror the solid boards beneath my feet begin to rise in the air and to place me and my suit-case in an ever-increasing precarious position at an angle of some forty-five degrees.

23   Terrified as I was at this angle, which, I surmised, must steadily increase toward ninety degrees, I had sense enough now to realize quickly the connection between the bridge and the boat. Since the bridge had parted in its middle and was rising in the air to allow the passage of the boat, I knew that it was destined to come down again. I had not come to Chicago to meet my death, and I instantly decided upon the only way to avoid it. I wedged my suit-case between two of the iron supports which met at an angle and somehow cast myself upon it with my arms clinging to whatever there was to cling to. I would hold on, I determined, with all my strength until the bridge once again assumed its normal position, when I would extricate myself and walk off with what dignity I could muster.

24   But by the time my decisions were made and I was placed in my desperate position, the men in charge of this curious feat of engineering had spotted me. There were shouts, more blowing of whistles, the gathering of a crowd on the nearer bank of the river. The boat backed downstream; the bridge began to descend. I felt it slowly dropping backward behind me. It clanged and bumped into position; and I was lifted to my feet by two policemen who had run onto the bridge from the nearer pavement.

25   Once on the street I found myself the center of a strange assortment of men and women, many with foreign faces, who, used to such bridges as this, had been awaiting its normal behavior in order to cross the river. I instantly recognized that my courage in the face of danger meant nothing whatever to them. They thought I was either mad or senseless and were curiously waiting to discover which.

26   The bigger policeman, who had not relinquished his hold upon me, began at once to question me.

27   "Young woman," he screamed, "are you tired of life? Just what do you mean by not heeding signals?"

28   I explained as best I could, while the crowd increased and I wanted terribly to die, that I had never before seen such a bridge and that I had not understood the connection between the signals and myself.

29   "Will you kindly tell us," asked the other policeman, who still held my suit-case, looking upon it occasionally with disdain and scorn, "who you are and where on earth you hail from?"

30   I strove to hold back my nervous tears as I gave my name and the state of my kindly engendure, which at that moment I devoutly wished I had never left.

31   The crowd howled with unkind amusement and repeated the howl when, upon further harsh inquiry, I was obliged to tell where I was staying in the city; I thought for some terrible moments that I was not to be allowed to proceed on my way unattended by the law; but my obvious innocence and the sight of my tears apparently convinced the policemen that I was truthful, if a fool, and they at last let me go.

32   A kind-faced woman walked five blocks with me. She insisted upon carrying my suit-case, and, although I could not speak a word to her, I have always felt toward her a gratitude which I have felt toward few persons before or since.

33   The Bible Institute for the only time during my stay in Chicago looked good to me when I had once reached it. I hurried to my room to burst into tears of utter humiliation upon my miserable bed. For days I suffered paroxysms of dread lest my exploit appear in the papers and reach the round, blue eyes of Mr. Clark, who would then and there decide that such ignorance deserved no confidence. But apparently, I concluded, when I again felt safe, it was of importance only as a story to be told as a joke by all the strange and awful people who had witnessed it.

34   It was months before I saw that it had its humorous aspects, not, indeed, until it had been received with high amusement by friends whom I was soon to make. Most of them, I think, never really believed the story in spite of my asseverations. But it was so true in every detail that it even now reappears in certain dreams of terror. For when in the night I find myself, like De Quincey, jeered at by monsters in human form, I know that far back somewhere in my mind the Dearborn Street bridge still stands, flanked by Chinamen and negroes and two burly policemen, and that I, even in my sleep, am searching somewhere for a kind-faced woman to thank her after many years.

35   I have often since wondered exactly what I did during that fortnight in Chicago. I think it was a period not of action so much as of certain concentrated and extremely limited states of mind. I was too beset by fear and uncertainty to read much, as I should otherwise have done. My bodily frame attended prayer circles and went occasionally under the chaperonage of the elderly gentleman with the handkerchief to hysterical, revivalistic gatherings in certain undesirable portions of the city; but my mind rarely accompanied it. I am sure I walked miles on bridgeless streets and along the Lake front, hopeful at times, at others fearful. I grew thin during that fortnight, partly from scanty, ill-cooked meals, mostly from anxiety.

36   But at last on an afternoon early in September Mr. Clark summoned me to Van Buren Street, and I went in a fever of excitement. He said, while I stood opposite him trembling with hope, that a certain school in Wisconsin had been so favorably impressed by a letter concerning me that its headmistresses wished to see me. They wanted a teacher of history who would assist in English. Above everything else they wanted one who knew and liked the country. The school, Mr. Clark said, was a rather unusual boarding-school known as the Hillside Home School; and although its mistresses preferred a teacher with more experience than mine, he thought it might afford the very place for me. He said that with my approval he would inform the Lloyd-Jones sisters that I would arrive at Spring Green, Wisconsin, which was the nearest town to Hillside, on the following afternoon at six o'clock.

37   I presume I walked back to the Bible Institute on ordinary pavements, but they were to me high and wide pathways toward my future. The dirty city which had terrified and humiliated me seemed clothed in light, shining and kind. I caught myself smiling at strangers on the street who, surprised, smiled shyly back at me. I was now freed from anxiety and fear, for in my new resiliency I had not a doubt in my mind that, whoever the Lloyd-Jones sisters were, they were as eagerly awaiting me as I was awaiting them. This assurance prompted me to pack my trunk before supper so that, when I was once engaged to teach at the Hillside Home School, I might not have to return to Chicago at all. I would then, I thought, write the Bible Institute to send it after me so that I might never again have to climb its steps to peal its clanging, dissonant bell.

38   I remember that at supper that night I asked boldly for another piece of cake and a second helping of custard. The horrified silence which greeted my request was broken at last by the most serious of the would-be evangelists, who offered me her portion, which she assured me she did not want. I do not think I even demurred at accepting it or blushed at my temerity. For I was leaving this odd house where the desire of everyone was to be nothing and embarking on my way where I was to be something at last.

                                   ॐ

Discussion Questions

1. Chase reveals in paragraph 3 that she concluded soon after her arrival at the Chicago Bible Institute that those enrolled there held certain attitudes, "benevolence and faint disapproval," together with "suspicion and a very unattractive zeal." What evidence do you find in her essay to support this conclusion? Explain.

2. In paragraph 4, two of the evangelists-to-be asked Chase if she had "made the great decision." What did the question mean, and what was Chase's response?

*3. How does the chorus of a hymn sung before each meal—"O to be nothing, nothing!"—figure in Chase's attitude toward the Bible Institute, particularly at the end of the essay? Explain.

4. When Chase went to see about the teaching job promised by Mr. Clark at the teachers' agency, what was his reaction: when she told him where she was living in Chicago; when she asked about the possibility of her finding a job; when she said her mother would prefer for her not to locate beyond the Mississippi?

*5. Why did Chase end up in danger on the Dearborn Bridge? What was the attitude of the police and assembled onlookers toward her? How did she extricate herself from the scene and return to the Bible Institute? In what way did the experience have a lasting effect on Chase?

6. How did Chase's view of the world change after she learned from Mr. Clark that the Hillside Home School in Wisconsin wished to see her?

7. Describe Chase's feelings and behavior on her last night at the Bible Institute.

Writing Topics

1. On the basis of the scenes with Mr. Clark Chase presents in her essay, write a character sketch of him, stressing those attributes revealed by the scenes. In your conclusion, make an assessment of Clark's performance in his job.

2. Both Chase and the evangelists-to-be of the Bible Institute appear to be religious, but Chase's attitude toward life contrasts sharply with the evangelists' attitude. Write a brief essay setting forth the two attitudes as you are able to find them in the essay; then in a conclusion indicate which attitude you find more compatible with your own.

"There is no here, here, only there, here.
One friend lives there, another there,
and there is where you can buy the best cheesecake."

WHERE DO WE GO IN L.A.?

Liza Williams

Liza Williams was born in New York City in 1928 and attended Reed College (1948–1949) and New York University (1949–1951). She also studied briefly at La Grand Chaumier (1951–1952) and the Central School of Art in London (1952). In her introduction to *Up the City of Angels* (1971), from which the essay below comes, Williams writes, "My parents lived with me in Greenwich Village in the thirties and forties. They sent me to expensive progressive private schools where I learned to believe in justice and the divine right of individuality. It was a space age preparation for a grounded society. . . . Almost all of these columns, pieces, poems, ravings, effluvia, regurgencies, appeared in the Los Angeles *Free Press*." The title of her column in the Los Angeles *Free Press* was "Liza Williams," and it appeared from 1966 to 1972. She published *Art Deco Los Angeles* in 1978.

1   Where do we go for anywhere in this city? Where do we go for central joy, like Times Square at midnight on New Year's Eve? We go to the Thrifty Drugstore, open twenty-four hours a day, and play with the plastic bargains, or read the magazines and marvel at the perpetual Jackie on the cover, never interviewed but always top copy. Where do we go to celebrate in this blobtown, amorphous city, melted metropolis? We skit along the freeway oblivious to the containers of existence on either side, the endless Bo-peep houses in their rhythm of ugh pink and yich blue, the cement office blocks, pastrami stands, hot dog houses, we zip along the freeway to one house in particular, a friend, a party, we are vagrants in our own land with no visible means of support except the directions memorized, turn left at the 76 sign and right at the dry cleaners.

2   Bea Lillie, according to a story in the LA *Times*, asked (while on the *Queen Mary*), "When does this place get there?" We are there, though where we are is privately devised. This city is a game of stops, separated by nothingland, by stretches of streets which will never be familiar. There is no here, here, only

there, here. One friend lives there, another there, and there is where you can buy the best cheesecake. The Movie is playing there, but the Restaurant is over there, miles of city, like miles of desert, separate goals from each other.

3   Describe me this place, tell me this city, where is downtown, oh I know, and aptly named, very downtown. But downtown is not where the town is, though that's where it used to be, downtown is everywhere there is a parking lot and a laundromat/giftshop/barber/supermarket/dress store—that's where downtown is now.

4   There are areas. Beverly Hills, sprawled on gold, and Bel Air, sprawled on purer gold. There is Laurel Canyon doing its Thing in the street and behind doors, contemporary *à la* pot, and La Cienega contemporary *à la mode*, and Echo Park, *au courant à la* poverty. Everyone says Venice and there is Venice, surely Venice, decaying wooden houses and new developments and European Heartache memories by the sea. Artists, that's where the artists live, though I doubt it, being in the street with paint on your pants doesn't make art, artists live in trees everywhere like monkeys, making mockery and joy.

5   There is the Other End, which at last names the place that bumps and grinds from Vermont and Hoover and Franklin, and Sunset and Silverlake in residential spirals and has views of houses with views, and views of lakes, and garages with views and streets with curves and trees with tired branches. The Other End has a Renaissance now, boutiques and antiques and frantics and fanatics and romantics and homosexuals, who may be also any of the above. It's cheaper than Echo Park, which is cheaper than Laurel Canyon, which is cheaper than Beverly Glen Canyon, though Beverly Glen Canyon is nearer to UCLA where some things happen. Everything is cheaper than Truesdale Estates unless you're speaking of taste, in which case nothing is cheaper than Truesdale Estates.

6   Pasadena has junk shops and junk shops and junk shops. Glendale is near Pasadena and has Nazis and junk shops. Eagle Rock is near Glendale and has Nazis.

7   Griffith Park has trees and rapes, depending on who you are—if you're out for a picnic it has trees, if you're a cop it has rapes.

8   This place, or collection, or unhomogenized urban nonrenewal is what you make-take of it (as long as you have a car). It is a body with cement veins, a universe connected by cement, a sprawling, messed-up old tart with occasional decorations in unusual places. This city doesn't make you—you have to make it.

Discussion Questions

*1. In the first paragraph, Williams asks, "Where do we go to celebrate in this blobtown, amorphous city, melted metropolis?" Is something of an answer contained in the question? Explain. What is the answer according to the sentence that follows the question?

*2. The last paragraph begins, "This place, or collection, or unhomogenized urban nonrenewal is what you make-take of it (as long as you have a car)." Explain as fully as you can the explicit/implicit meanings of the sentence and assess its effectiveness as the beginning of a concluding paragraph to the essay.

Writing Topics

1. " 'Where Do We Go in L.A.?' conveys very little information about the city but evokes a good sense of what kind of city Los Angeles is." Write an analytical essay agreeing or disagreeing with this statement, citing passages from the essay to support your view. In your conclusion, assess the success of the essay in achieving what you believe to be its intended effect.

2. Williams said of the selections in *Up the City of Angels* that they were "columns, pieces, poems, ravings, effluvia, regurgencies." Write a brief descriptive essay about a subject familiar to you (perhaps your own city or town) in which you attempt to capture its essence, emphasizing an appropriate style rather than direct description in evoking the effect you want.

3. Write a letter to Williams explaining to her why, after having read "Where Do We go in L.A.?" you would or would not want to live in Los Angeles.

Summary Writing Topics

1. Luther Haines ("One Mule and a Walking Plow"), Ben Logan ("Hilltop World"), and Carol Bly ("Getting Tired") all write about life on a farm. Write a comparison/contrast essay on a topic of your choice, such as: Love of the Land; The Complications of Farming Brought about by "Improved" Farm Implements; The Isolation of Farm Life; The Virtues of Farm Life.

2. Choose one of the essays involving farm life listed above as the most impressive in conveying a sense of living and working on a farm. Write an analytical essay in which you highlight and explore those features that made it successful in achieving its effect.

3. James Agee's "Knoxville: Summer of 1915" and Liza Williams's "Where Do We Go in L.A.?" appear to share many elements of what might be called a poetic or lyric style. Write a two-part comparison/contrast essay in which you (1) explore the similarities of style and (2) focus on and consider the reasons for the differences of effect.

4. Write a brief essay on a subject of your choice in imitation of the length and poetic style of either the Agee or the Williams essay. As you decide on the subject, also consider the effect you intend— witty or sober, comic or tragic. Possible subjects include: A Disappointing Christmas; An Extraordinary Birthday Party; The Day I Discovered _____; The Night I Dreamed _____.

5. The essays by Twain ("New York: A Splendid Desert"), Quindlen ("Pregnant in New York"), and Robert V. Levine ("Rude? Yeah, You Are") all express negative attitudes toward the Big Apple. Write a comparison/contrast essay in which you examine and sort out the various attitudes expressed, showing the subtle differences—especially those underlying the apparent differences.

6. Choose one of the essays in Question 5 and set it beside the Williams essay ("Where Do We Go in L.A.?") in order to compare the two. Write an essay in which you describe your sense of the two cities, New York and Los Angeles, as shaped by the two accounts. Which leaves you with a more vivid picture of the "essence" of a city? Explore the possible reasons for this difference in effect.

7. Ralph Ellison (in "Negro Oklahoma City") and Ethel Waters (in "The Red-Light District in Philadelphia") write of periods in their past that shaped their futures. Write a comparison/contrast essay in which you explore the kinds of education in experience the two received and the ways that education made a difference in their lives. In your conclusion, consider what part racial prejudice played in their experiences.

8. Using the Ellison and Waters essays as models, write a narrative essay about some experience in your past that you now see was important to your future. Keep in mind—and explore— a possible distinction between your feelings at the time and your feelings now in recollection.

9. Chase describes, in "Held Up by the Dearborn Street Bridge, Chicago," her horror at the time she was carried into the air by the rising bridge and her mortification when the police and crowd verbally attacked her. But she also reveals that as time passed she came to see the episode's "humorous aspects." This is a not an uncommon experience. Perhaps you remember a similar incident in your past, tragic at the time but shifting gradually to the comic as time passed. Write a narrative essay recounting this experience, using the Chase essay as a model.

10. In this cluster of essays, there are descriptions of country life and city or town life but no account of life in the suburbs. If you have experienced life in the suburbs, write an account of a part or piece of your experience that you believe catches its essence, and then send it to the editors of this book, pointing out in a letter why it should be included in the anthology. Possible subjects include: The Importance of Lawns in Suburbia; The Quarrels over Property Lines in Suburbia; The Unneighborliness of Neighborhoods in Suburbia.

11. Humor has been defined as the "juxtaposition of the ludicrously incongruous." Put in simple language, this definition might be translated as "the bringing together of things that become funny side-by-side." Often one of the elements is present only by implication, as in hyperbole or exaggeration. Tentatively accepting this definition, find an essay in this or any other cluster that you find humorous and analyze the humor in it in light of this definition. The Twain, Quindlen, and Williams essays in this cluster might be candidates.

12. Choose the essay that has most impressed you in this cluster and write a letter to the author in which you point out why the author has persuaded you to find, one day in the future, the kind of place he or she has described. You might want to turn this assignment upside down: Choose the essay that definitively turned you off in its description of a place and write the author explaining how the essay convinced you to stay away.

Cluster

Everyday Realities

"The trouble with life is that it's so damned daily!" No doubt you have either heard or said this—or at least know what it means. At some moments in our lives, we come to realize that "this" is "it." Hopes or ambitions of the past have receded into fantasy, and we find ourselves "trapped" in the drudgery of daily living. Perhaps we are "trapped" in unemployment without the skills to get a job and without the possibility of getting those skills. Perhaps we are "trapped" in an eight-hour-a-day job requiring repetitive actions that are inherently uninteresting, sometimes even tedious. Or we may have sought and found a rewarding job free of such routine but have gradually come to feel that "something is missing."

It is an "everyday reality" that much of life is beyond our personal control, with chance itself often playing a major role. Whereas we might want to march through life briskly to the lively sound of a military band, we may well find ourselves instead slogging up a rugged road, requiring stamina and ingenuity to endure.

The truth is that there are "everyday realities" waiting even for those who appear to have cleared the initial hurdles and seem to be on their chosen road. It is more likely than not that they will run into stretches of uncertainty and even slick patches of intense frustration. And if they make it through these obstructions without detouring, they may arrive at their destination only to find themselves asking, "Is this *it?*" Indeed, they may conclude that the journey itself was more exhilarating than the arrival.

There is, apparently, no way to plan our lives so as to avoid being ambushed at unexpected intersections by these "everyday realities." They may tie us up in knots of frustration or even plunge us for a time into pits of gloom. Some say, "That's life," and shrug. Others say, "Life is basically unfair," and go on. During the Great Depression, people tried to lift their spirits by singing "Life is just a bowl of cherries," while everywhere they looked, they knew it was not.

"I live from the refuse of others. I am a scavenger. I think it a sound and honorable niche, although if I could I would naturally prefer to live the comfortable consumer life. . . ."

ON DUMPSTER DIVING

Lars Eighner

Lars Eighner was born in Texas in 1948 and attended the University of Texas from 1955 to 1969 but did not take a degree. His publications have included contributions to *Bayou Boy and Other Stories*, published in 1985 and reprinted in 1993, *Lavender Blue* (1988), and BMOC (1993). It was not until the publication in 1993 of *Travels with Lizbeth* (from which "On Dumpster Diving" is taken) that Eighner gained wide attention. His account of wandering homeless and hungry from Texas to California in prosperous America captured the imaginations of readers and inspired comparisons with such works as George Orwell's *Down and Out in Paris and London* (1933) and William Least Heat Moon's *Blue Highways* (1982). As Eighner reports in *Travels with Lizbeth*, he quit a job (just before getting fired) at a "lunatic asylum" in Austin, Texas, and set out for California to get a job with one of the gay magazines that had published his fiction. He and his dog, Lizbeth, became homeless vagabonds and both became adept at "dumpster diving" in order to survive.

1   Long before I began Dumpster diving I was impressed with Dumpsters, enough so that I wrote the Merriam-Webster research service to discover what I could about the word *Dumpster*. I learned from them that it is a proprietary word belonging to the Dempster Dumpster company. Since then I have dutifully capitalized the word, although it was lowercased in almost all the citations Merriam-Webster photocopied for me. Dempster's word is too apt. I have never heard these things called anything but Dumpsters. I do not know anyone who knows the generic name for these objects. From time to time I have heard a wino or hobo give some corrupted credit to the original and call them Dipsy Dumpsters.

2   I began Dumpster diving about a year before I became homeless.

3   I prefer the word *scavenging* and use the word *scrounging* when I mean to be obscure. I have heard people, evidently meaning to be polite, use the word *foraging*, but I prefer to reserve that word for gathering nuts and berries and such, which I do also according to the season and the opportunity. *Dumpster diving* seems to me to be a little too cute and, in my case, inaccurate because I lack the athletic ability to lower myself into the Dumpsters as the true divers do, much to their increased profit.

4   I like the frankness of the word *scavenging*, which I can hardly think of without picturing a big black snail on an aquarium wall. I live from the refuse of others. I am a scavenger. I think it a sound and honorable niche, athough if I could I would naturally prefer to live the comfortable consumer life, perhaps — and only perhaps — as a slightly less wasteful consumer, owing to what I have learned as a scavenger.

5   While Lizbeth and I were still living in the shack on Avenue B as my savings ran out, I put almost all my sporadic income into rent. The necessities of daily life I began to extract from Dumpsters. Yes, we ate from them. Except for jeans, all my clothes came from Dumpsters. Boom boxes, candles, bedding, toilet paper, a virgin male love doll, medicine, books, a typewriter, dishes, furnishings, and change, sometimes amounting to many dollars — I acquired many things from the Dumpsters.

6   I have learned much as a scavenger. I mean to put some of what I have learned down here, beginning with the practical art of Dumpster diving and proceeding to the abstract.

7   What is safe to eat?

8   After all, the finding of objects is becoming something of an urban art. Even respectable employed people will sometimes find something tempting sticking out of a Dumpster or standing beside one. Quite a number of people, not all of them of the bohemian type, are willing to brag that they found this or that piece in the trash. But eating from Dumpsters is what separates the dilettanti from the professionals. Eating safely from the Dumpsters involves three principles: using the senses and common sense to evaluate the condition of the found materials, knowing the Dumpsters of a given area and checking them regularly, and seeking always to answer the question "Why was this discarded?"

9   Perhaps everyone who has a kitchen and a regular supply of groceries has, at one time or another, made a sandwich and eaten half of it before discovering mold on the bread or got a mouthful of milk before realizing the milk had turned. Nothing of the sort is likely to happen to a Dumpster diver because he is constantly reminded that most food is discarded for a reason. Yet a lot of perfectly good food can be found in Dumpsters.

10   Canned goods, for example, turn up fairly often in the Dumpsters I frequent. All except the most phobic people would be willing to eat from a can, even if it came from a Dumpster. Canned goods are among the safest of foods to be found in Dumpsters but are not utterly foolproof.

11   Although very rare with modern canning methods, botulism is a possibility. Most other forms of food poisoning seldom do lasting harm to a healthy person, but botulism is almost certainly fatal and often the first symptom is death. Except for carbonated beverages, all canned goods should contain a slight vacuum and suck air when first punctured. Bulging, rusty, and dented cans and cans that spew when punctured should be avoided, especially when the contents are not very acidic or syrupy.

12   Heat can break down the botulin, but this requires much more cooking than most people do to canned goods. To the extent that botulism occurs at all, of course, it can occur in cans on pantry shelves as well as in cans from Dumpsters. Need I say that home-canned goods are simply too risky to be recommended.

13   From time to time one of my companions, aware of the source of my provisions, will ask, "Do you think these crackers are really safe to eat?" For some reason it is most often the crackers they ask about.

14   This question has always made me angry. Of course I would not offer my companion anything I had doubts about. But more than that, I wonder why he cannot evaluate the condition of the crackers for himself. I have no special knowledge and I have been wrong before. Since he knows where the food comes from, it seems to me he ought to assume some of the responsibility for deciding what he will put in his mouth. For myself I have few qualms about dry foods such as crackers, cookies, cereal, chips, and pasta if they are free of visible contaminates and still dry and crisp. Most often such things are found in the original packaging, which is not so much a positive sign as it is the absence of a negative one.

15   Raw fruits and vegetables with intact skins seem perfectly safe to me, excluding of course the obviously rotten. Many are discarded for minor imperfections that can be pared away. Leafy vegetables, grapes, cauliflower, broccoli, and similar things may be contaminated by liquids and may be impractical to wash.

16   Candy, especially hard candy, is usually safe if it has not drawn ants. Chocolate is often discarded only because it has become discolored as the cocoa butter de-emulsified. Candying, after all, is one method of food preservation because pathogens do not like very sugary substances.

17   All of these foods might be found in any Dumpster and can be evaluated with some confidence largely on the basis of appearance. Beyond these are foods that cannot be correctly evaluated without additional information.

18   I began scavenging by pulling pizzas out of the Dumpster behind a pizza delivery shop. In general, prepared food requires caution, but in this case I knew when the shop closed and went to the Dumpster as soon as the last of the help left.

19   Such shops often get prank orders; both the orders and the products made to fill them are called *bogus*. Because help seldom stays long at these places, pizzas are often made with the wrong topping, refused on delivery for being cold, or baked incorrectly. The products to be discarded are boxed up because inventory is kept by counting boxes: A boxed pizza can be written off; an unboxed pizza does not exist.

20   I never placed a bogus order to increase the supply of pizzas and I believe no one else was scavenging in this Dumpster. But the people in the shop became suspicious and began to retain their garbage in the shop overnight. While it lasted I had a steady supply of fresh, sometimes warm pizza. Because I knew the Dumpster I knew the source of the pizza, and because I visited the Dumpster regularly I knew what was fresh and what was yesterday's.

21   The area I frequent is inhabited by many affluent college students. I am not here by chance; the Dumpsters in this area are very rich. Students throw out many good things, including food. In particular they tend to throw everything out when they move at the end of a semester, before and after breaks, and around midterm, when many of them despair of college. So I find it advantageous to keep an eye on the academic calendar.

22   Students throw food away around breaks because they do not know whether it has spoiled or will spoil before they return. A typical discard is a half jar of peanut butter. In fact, nonorganic peanut butter does not require refrigeration and is unlikely to spoil in any reasonable time. The student does not know that, and since it is Daddy's money, the student decides not to take a chance. Opened containers require caution and some attention to the question, "Why was this discarded?" But in the case of discards from student apartments, the answer may be that the item was thrown out through carelessness, ignorance, or wastefulness. This can sometimes be deduced when the item is found with many others, including some that are obviously perfectly good.

23   Some students, and others, approach defrosting a freezer by chucking out the whole lot. Not only do the circumstances of such a find tell the story, but also the mass of frozen goods stays cold for a long time and items may be found still frozen or freshly thawed.

24   Yogurt, cheese, and sour cream are items that are often thrown out while they are still good. Occasionally I find a cheese with a spot of mold, which of course I just pare off, and because it is obvious why such a cheese was discarded, I treat it with less suspicion than an apparently perfect cheese found in similar circumstances. Yogurt is often discarded, still sealed, only because the expiration date on the carton had passed. This is one of my favorite finds because yogurt will keep for several days, even in warm weather.

25   Students throw out canned goods and staples at the end of semesters and when they give up college at midterm. Drugs, pornography, spirits, and the like are often discarded when parents are expected—Dad's Day, for example. And spirits also turn up after big party weekends, presumably discarded by

the newly reformed. Wine and spirits, of course, keep perfectly well even once opened, but the same cannot be said of beer.

26   My test for carbonated soft drinks is whether they still fizz vigorously. Many juices or other beverages are too acidic or too syrupy to cause much concern, provided they are not visibly contaminated. I have discovered nasty molds in vegetable juices, even when the product was found under its original seal; I recommend that such products be decanted slowly into a clear glass. Liquids always require some care. One hot day I found a large jug of Pat O'Brien's Hurricane mix. The jug had been opened but was still ice cold. I drank three large glasses before it became apparent to me that someone had added the rum to the mix, and not a little rum. I never tasted the rum, and by the time I began to feel the effects I had already ingested a very large quantity of the beverage. Some divers would have considered this a boon, but being suddenly intoxicated in a public place in the early afternoon is not my idea of a good time.

27   I have heard of people maliciously contaminating discarded food and even handouts, but mostly I have heard of this from people with vivid imaginations who have had no experience with the Dumpsters themselves. Just before the pizza shop stopped discarding its garbage at night, jalapeños began showing up on most of the thrown-out pizzas. If indeed this was meant to discourage me, it was a wasted effort because I am a native Texan.

28   For myself, I avoid game, poultry, pork, and egg-based foods, whether I find them raw or cooked. I seldom have the means to cook what I find, but when I do I avail myself of plentiful supplies of beef, which is often in very good condition. I suppose fish becomes disagreeable before it becomes dangerous. Lizbeth is happy to have any such thing that is past its prime and, in fact, does not recognize fish as food until it is quite strong.

29   Home leftovers, as opposed to surpluses from restaurants, are very often bad. Evidently, especially among students, there is a common type of personality that carefully wraps up even the smallest leftover and shoves it into the back of the refrigerator for six months or so before discarding it. Characteristic of this type are the reused jars and margarine tubs to which the remains are committed. I avoid ethnic foods I am unfamiliar with. If I do not know what it is supposed to look like when it is good, I cannot be certain I will be able to tell if it is bad.

30   No matter how careful I am I still get dysentery at least once a month, oftener in warm weather. I do not want to paint too romantic a picture. Dumpster diving has serious drawbacks as a way of life.

31   I learned to scavenge gradually, on my own. Since then I have initiated several companions into the trade. I have learned that there is a predictable series of stages a person goes through in learning to scavenge.

32   At first the new scavenger is filled with disgust and self-loathing. He is ashamed of being seen and may lurk around, trying to duck behind things, or

he may try to dive at night. (In fact, most people instinctively look away from a scavenger. By skulking around, the novice calls attention to himself and arouses suspicion. Diving at night is ineffective and needlessly messy.)

33   Every grain of rice seems to be a maggot. Everything seems to stink. He can wipe the egg yolk off the found can, but he cannot erase from his mind the stigma of eating garbage.

34   That stage passes with experience. The scavenger finds a pair of running shoes that fit and look and smell brand-new. He finds a pocket calculator in perfect working order. He finds pristine ice cream, still frozen, more than he can eat or keep. He begins to understand: People throw away perfectly good stuff, a lot of perfectly good stuff.

35   At this stage, Dumpster shyness begins to dissipate. The diver, after all, has the last laugh. He is finding all manner of good things that are his for the taking. Those who disparage his profession are the fools, not he.

36   He may begin to hang on to some perfectly good things for which he has neither a use nor a market. Then he begins to take note of the things that are not perfectly good but are nearly so. He mates a Walkman with broken earphones and one that is missing a battery cover. He picks up things that he can repair.

37   At this stage he may become lost and never recover. Dumpsters are full of things of some potential value to someone and also of things that never have much intrinsic value but are interesting. All the Dumpster divers I have known come to the point of trying to acquire everything they touch. Why not take it, they reason, since it is all free? This is, of course, hopeless. Most divers come to realize that they must restrict themselves to items of relatively immediate utility. But in some cases the diver simply cannot control himself. I have met several of these pack-rat types. Their ideas of the values of various pieces of junk verge on the psychotic. Every bit of glass may be a diamond, they think, and all that glisters, gold.

38   I tend to gain weight when I am scavenging. Partly this is because I always find far more pizza and doughnuts than water-packed tuna, nonfat yogurt, and fresh vegetables. Also I have not developed much faith in the reliability of Dumpsters as a food source, although it has been proven to me many times. I tend to eat as if I have no idea where my next meal is coming from. But mostly I just hate to see food go to waste and so I eat much more than I should. Something like this drives the obsession to collect junk.

39   As for collecting objects, I usually restrict myself to collecting one kind of small object at a time, such as pocket calculators, sunglasses, or campaign buttons. To live on the street I must anticipate my needs to a certain extent: I must pick up and save warm bedding I find in August because it will not be found in Dumpsters in November. As I have no access to health care, I often hoard essential drugs, such as antibiotics and antihistamines. (This course can be recommended only to those with some grounding in pharmacology. Antibiotics, for example, even when indicated are worse than useless if taken in

insufficient amounts.) But even if I had a home with extensive storage space, I could not save everything that might be valuable in some contingency.

40   I have proprietary feelings about my Dumpsters. As I have mentioned, it is no accident that I scavenge from ones where good finds are common. But my limited experience with Dumpsters in other areas suggests to me that even in poorer areas, Dumpsters, if attended with sufficient diligence, can be made to yield a livelihood. The rich students discard perfectly good kiwifruit; poorer people discard perfectly good apples. Slacks and Polo shirts are found in the one place; jeans and T-shirts in the other. The population of competitors rather than the affluence of the dumpers most affects the feasibility of survival by scavenging. The large number of competitors is what puts me off the idea of trying to scavenge in places like Los Angeles.

41   Curiously, I do not mind my direct competition, other scavengers, so much as I hate the can scroungers.

42   People scrounge cans because they have to have a little cash. I have tried scrounging cans with an able-bodied companion. Afoot a can scrounger simply cannot make more than a few dollars a day. One can extract the necessities of life from the Dumpsters directly with far less effort than would be required to accumulate the equivalent value in cans. (These observations may not hold in places with container redemption laws.)

43   Can scroungers, then, are people who must have small amounts of cash. These are drug addicts and winos, mostly the latter because the amounts of cash are so small. Spirits and drugs do, like all other commodities, turn up in Dumpsters and the scavenger will from time to time have a half bottle of a rather good wine with his dinner. But the wino cannot survive on these occasional finds; he must have his daily dose to stave off the DTs. All the cans he can carry will buy about three bottles of Wild Irish Rose.

44   I do not begrudge them the cans, but can scroungers tend to tear up the Dumpsters, mixing the contents and littering the area. They become so specialized that they can see only cans. They earn my contempt by passing up change, canned goods, and readily hockable items.

45   There are precious few courtesies among scavengers. But it is common practice to set aside surplus items: pairs of shoes, clothing, canned goods, and such. A true scavenger hates to see good stuff go to waste, and what he cannot use he leaves in good condition in plain sight.

46   Can scroungers lay waste to everything in their path and will stir one of a pair of good shoes to the bottom of a Dumpster, to be lost or ruined in the muck. Can scroungers will even go through individual garbage cans, something I have never seen a scavenger do.

47   Individual garbage cans are set out on the public easement only on garbage days. On other days going through them requires trespassing close to a dwelling. Going through individual garbage cans without scattering litter is almost

impossible. Litter is likely to reduce the public's tolerance of scavenging. Individual cans are simply not as productive as Dumpsters; people in houses and duplexes do not move so often and for some reason do not tend to discard as much useful material. Moreover, the time required to go through one garbage can that serves one household is not much less than the time required to go through a Dumpster that contains the refuse of twenty apartments.

48   But my strongest reservation about going through individual garbage cans is that this seems to me a very personal kind of invasion to which I would object if I were a householder. Although many things in Dumpsters are obviously meant never to come to light, a Dumpster is somehow less personal.

49   I avoid trying to draw conclusions about the people who dump in the Dumpsters I frequent. I think it would be unethical to do so, although I know many people will find the idea of scavenger ethics too funny for words.

50   Dumpsters contain bank statements, correspondence, and other documents, just as anyone might expect. But there are also less obvious sources of information. Pill bottles, for example. The labels bear the name of the patient, the name of the doctor, and the name of the drug. AIDS drugs and antipsychotic medicines, to name but two groups, are specific and are seldom prescribed for any other disorders. The plastic compacts for birth-control pills usually have complete label information.

51   Despite all of this sensitive information, I have had only one apartment resident object to my going through the Dumpster. In that case it turned out the resident was a university athlete who was taking bets and who was afraid I would turn up his wager slips.

52   Occasionally a find tells a story. I once found a small paper bag containing some unused condoms, several partial tubes of flavored sexual lubricants, a partially used compact of birth-control pills, and the torn pieces of a picture of a young man. Clearly she was through with him and planning to give up sex altogether.

53   Dumpster things are often sad—abandoned teddy bears, shredded wedding books, despaired-of sales kits. I find many pets lying in state in Dumpsters. Although I hope to get off the streets so that Lizbeth can have a long and comfortable old age, I know this hope is not very realistic. So I suppose when her time comes she too will go into a Dumpster. I will have no better place for her. And after all, it is fitting, since for most of her life her livelihood has come from the Dumpster. When she finds something I think is safe that has been spilled from a Dumpster, I let her have it. She already knows the route around the best ones. I like to think that if she survives me she will have a chance of evading the dog catcher and of finding her sustenance on the route.

54   Silly vanities also come to rest in the Dumpsters. I am a rather accomplished needleworker. I get a lot of material from the Dumpsters. Evidently sorority girls, hoping to impress someone, perhaps themselves, with their

mastery of a womanly art, buy a lot of embroider-by-number kits, work a few stitches horribly, and eventually discard the whole mess. I pull out their stitches, turn the canvas over, and work an original design. Do not think I refrain from chuckling as I make gifts from these kits.

55   I find diaries and journals. I have often thought of compiling a book of literary found objects. And perhaps I will one day. But what I find is hopelessly commonplace and bad without being, even unconsciously, camp. College students also discard their papers. I am horrified to discover the kind of paper that now merits an A in an undergraduate course. I am grateful, however, for the number of good books and magazines the students throw out.

56   In the area I know best I have never discovered vermin in the Dumpsters, but there are two kinds of kitty surprise. One is alley cats whom I meet as they leap, claws first, out of Dumpsters. This is especially thrilling when I have Lizbeth in tow. The other kind of kitty surprise is a plastic garbage bag filled with some ponderous, amorphous mass. This always proves to be used cat litter.

57   City bees harvest doughnut glaze and this makes the Dumpster at the doughnut shop more interesting. My faith in the instinctive wisdom of animals is always shaken whenever I see Lizbeth attempt to catch a bee in her mouth, which she does whenever bees are present. Evidently some birds find Dumpsters profitable, for birdie surprise is almost as common as kitty surprise of the first kind. In hunting season all kinds of small game turn up in Dumpsters, some of it, sadly, not entirely dead. Curiously, summer and winter, maggots are uncommon.

58   The worse of the living and near-living hazards of the Dumpsters are the fire ants. The food they claim is not much of a loss, but they are vicious and aggressive. It is very easy to brush against some surface of the Dumpster and pick up half a dozen or more fire ants, usually in some sensitive area such as the underarm. One advantage of bringing Lizbeth along as I make Dumpster rounds is that, for obvious reasons, she is very alert to ground-based fire ants. When Lizbeth recognizes a fire-ant infestation around our feet, she does the Dance of the Zillion Fire Ants. I have learned not to ignore this warning from Lizbeth, whether I perceive the tiny ants or not, but to remove ourselves at Lizbeth's first pas de bourée. All the more so because the ants are the worst in the summer months when I wear flip-flops if I have them. (Perhaps someone will misunderstand this. Lizbeth does the Dance of the Zillion Fire Ants when she recognizes more fire ants than she cares to eat, not when she is being bitten. Since I have learned to react promptly, she does not get bitten at all. It is the isolated patrol of fire ants that falls in Lizbeth's range that deserves pity. She finds them quite tasty.)

59   By far the best way to go through a Dumpster is to lower yourself into it. Most of the good stuff tends to settle at the bottom because it is usually weightier than the rubbish. My more athletic companions have often demonstrated to me that they can extract much good material from a Dumpster I have already been over.

60 To those psychologically or physically unprepared to enter a Dumpster, I recommend a stout stick, preferably with some barb or hook at one end. The hook can be used to grab plastic garbage bags. When I find canned goods or other objects loose at the bottom of a Dumpster, I lower a bag into it, roll the desired object into the bag, and then hoist the bag out—a procedure more easily described than executed. Much Dumpster diving is a matter of experience for which nothing will do except practice.

61 Dumpster diving is outdoor work, often surprisingly pleasant. It is not entirely predictable; things of interest turn up every day and some days there are finds of great value. I am always very pleased when I can turn up exactly the thing I most wanted to find. Yet in spite of the element of chance, scavenging more than most other pursuits tends to yield returns in some proportion to the effort and intelligence brought to bear. It is very sweet to turn up a few dollars in change from a Dumpster that has just been gone over by a wino.

62 The land is now covered with cities. The cities are full of Dumpsters. If a member of the canine race is ever able to know what it is doing, then Lizbeth knows that when we go around to the Dumpsters, we are hunting. I think of scavenging as a modern form of self-reliance. In any event, after having survived nearly ten years of government service, where everything is geared to the lowest common denominator, I find it refreshing to have work that rewards initiative and effort. Certainly I would be happy to have a sinecure again, but I am no longer heartbroken that I left one.

63 I find from the experience of scavenging two rather deep lessons. The first is to take what you can use and let the rest go by. I have come to think that there is no value in the abstract. A thing I cannot use or make useful, perhaps by trading, has no value however rare or fine it may be. I mean useful in a broad sense—some art I would find useful and some otherwise.

64 I was shocked to realize that some things are not worth acquiring, but now I think it is so. Some material things are white elephants that eat up the possessor's substance. The second lesson is the transience of material being. This has not quite converted me to a dualist, but it has made some headway in that direction. I do not suppose that ideas are immortal, but certainly mental things are longer lived than other material things.

65 Once I was the sort of person who invests objects with sentimental value. Now I no longer have those objects, but I have the sentiments yet.

66 Many times in our travels I have lost everything but the clothes I was wearing and Lizbeth. The things I find in Dumpsters, the love letters and rag dolls of so many lives, remind me of this lesson. Now I hardly pick up a thing without envisioning the time I will cast it aside. This I think is a healthy state of mind. Almost everything I have now has already been cast out at least once, proving that what I own is valueless to someone.

67 Anyway, I find my desire to grab for the gaudy bauble has been largely sated. I think this is an attitude I share with the very wealthy—we both know

there is plenty more where what we have came from. Between us are the rat-race millions who nightly scavenge the cable channels looking for they know not what.

68   I am sorry for them.

❮❯

Discussion Questions

1. What distinctions does Eighner draw among the words *scavenging*, *scrounging*, *foraging*, and *dumpster diving*? Why does he think *scavenging* suits his purposes better than the others?

2. In paragraph 6, Eighner says that he will relate what he has learned as a scavenger, "beginning with the practical art of Dumpster diving and proceeding to the abstract." What does he mean by the distinction he draws? Explain by citing examples.

3. When considering taking any item from a dumpster, Eighner emphasizes, it is important to ask, "Why was this discarded?" How does the answer to the question help? Explain.

4. What areas did Eighner find the best to settle in for dumpster diving? What times, in accord with a schedule in these areas, were more productive than others for the scavenger?

5. Did Eighner ever become ill from his scavenging? Explain.

*6. According to Eighner in paragraphs 31–37, what stages does the beginning scavenger pass through before becoming a skilled scavenger?

7. What does Eighner advise concerning the temptation for scavengers to begin and maintain collections? Explain.

8. According to Eighner in paragraphs 41–46, who were the "can scroungers" and what problems did they present for the regular scavengers?

*9. Why did Eighner (paragraphs 47–48) prefer to stick to dumpsters rather than also scavenging "individual garbage cans"?

10. What according to Eighner (paragraph 49) were "scavenger ethics"?

11. In paragraph 52, Eighner relates a "story" scavenged from a dumpster. How did he extract a tale from the varied items he has found?

12. What at the end are the "two rather deep lessons" Eighner has learned from the experience of scavenging? Why "deep"?

Writing Topics

1. There are many references by Eighner to his companion Lizbeth throughout "On Dumpster Diving." Write a brief character sketch of the two in which you draw on the essay to explore the bond between them. Be sure to include Lizbeth's role doing the "Dance of the Zillion Fire Ants."

2. In paragraph 67, Eighner says, "Between us [Eighner and the very wealthy] are the rat-race millions who nightly scavenge the cable channels looking for they know not what." Write an analytical/ argumentative essay in which you explain fully what Eighner seems to mean and then why you agree or disagree with the distinctions and the characterizations he draws. Feel free to cite any personal experience you have that seems relevant.

*"In the city of New York last year, firemen responded
to 72,060 false alarms — an average of 197 daily.
Yet, the courts and the Police Department do not look
on the pulling of a false alarm as a serious offense."*

REPORT FROM ENGINE CO. 82

Dennis Smith

Dennis Smith was born in New York City in 1940 and took a B.A. at New York University in 1970 and an M.A. in 1972. He served in the U.S. Air Force from 1957 to 1960 and as a firefighter in the New York Fire Department from 1963 to 1981. He founded *Firehouse Magazine* in 1975 and served in various positions on the popular magazine until 1990, when it was sold. From 1988 to 1990, he acted as chairman of the board and founding trustee of the New York Fire Museum, housing a collection of documents, materials, and equipment related to the fighting of fires. Throughout his career, Smith has been a prolific writer of both fiction and nonfiction works. His novels include *The Final Fire* (1975), *Glitter and Ash* (1980), and a work for children, *The Little Fire Engine that Saved the City* (1990). His nonfiction works include *Dennis Smith's History of Firefighting in America: 300 Years of Courage* (1978), *The Aran Islands: A Personal Journey* (1980), and *Firefighters: Their Lives in Their Own Words* (1980). In 1972, he published a personal account of his life as a firefighter entitled *Report from Engine Co. 82*, the second chapter of which appears below. The volume won the Christopher Book Award in 1973.

1   My name is Dennis Smith, and I'm a New York City fireman—one of New York's bravest. "New York's bravest," that's what the writers of newspaper editorials call us. There are almost eight million people in this city, and twelve thousand of us are firemen. We are different from the rest of the people who work in this town: bankers, ad-men, truck drivers, secretaries, sellers and buyers, all have a high degree of assurance that they will return home from work in the evening the same way they left in the morning—on their feet. A little tired perhaps, but on their feet. Firemen are never sure. When a fireman's

wife kisses him as he leaves for work, she makes a conscious wish that he will return to her. She hopes that she will not have to make those fast, desperate arrangements for a baby-sitter so that she can visit him in the hospital, and each time the doorbell rings she hopes that there will not be a chief, a chaplain, and a union official there, all coming to say kind things about her husband, how good he was, how dedicated, how brave.

2   I'm part of Engine Company 82. The firehouse I work out of is on Intervale Avenue and 169th Street in a ghetto called the South Bronx. Of the three biggest ghettos in New York City, the South Bronx is the least talked about. You've heard of Harlem, Adam Clayton Powell came from Harlem; and you may have heard of Bedford-Stuyvesant, Shirley Chisholm comes from Bedford-Stuyvesant. Nobody you've ever heard of comes from the South Bronx.

3   Around the corner from the firehouse is the Forty-first Precinct House. It is the busiest police station in the city. There are more homicides per square mile in this precinct than anywhere in the United States, more drug traffic, more prostitution.

4   There are four companies working out of the firehouse on Intervale Avenue. Engine 82 and Engine 85 do the hose work in the district. Ladder Company 31 and Tactical Control Unit 712 do the rescue work, the ladder work, and the ax work.

5   Until recently my company and Engine 85 responded to many of the same alarms. Then, two years ago, we responded a record number of times. Engine 85 went out 8,386 times in a twelve month period. Ladder Company 31 went to 8,597 alarms, and my company, Engine 82, went to 9,111. The Fire Department saw that a change was needed, and arranged that engines 82 and 85 would not respond to the same alarms. The plan worked. Last year my company's responses dropped to 6,377, and Engine 85's to 5,012. But the plan worked only for the engine companies; Ladder Company 31's responses increased to 8,774. Another plan was then devised, and Tactical Control Unit 712 was created to respond only within the high incidence hours between three in the afternoon and one in the morning. The four companies on Intervale Avenue are now each averaging 700 runs a month. It is safe to say that ours is the busiest firehouse in the city—and probably the world.

6   An average of eight firemen die each year while doing their duty in New York City. Only six died last year, and I don't want to think about how many will die this year, or next. Almost five thousand firemen were injured in the line of duty last year. The injuries cost the city 65,000 days in medical leaves.

7   There is a sign in the kitchen of my firehouse. It is inconspicuously hung, and it reads with a proper amount of ambiguity: THIS COULD BE THE NIGHT! We don't talk about the hazards of the trade in the firehouse. There is no sense in talking about what we hope never becomes a reality for us, and for our families. It's all part of the job, and like committed Calvinists we accept what's written in the cards for us.

8   Just yesterday a man was killed. He was assigned to Rescue Company 1, and he was working on the roof of a burning warehouse. The roof had been weakened by the fire, and it gave in. The man fell through the roof and into an air shaft. He passed eight floors before he hit the bottom.

9   I was sitting in the kitchen of the firehouse when the bells came in. First five short rings, a pause, five more, a pause, another five, another pause, and the final five. Signal 5-5-5-5 has a special meaning to us. Put the flag at half mast, and listen to the department radio for the message.

10   There is a five-by-five cubicle at the front of the firehouse. Inside the small partition there is a man writing the signal in the department company journal. He turns the volume of the department radio up as we gather around it. This is the man assigned housewatch duty, and he knows what he has to do. After recording the signal, he moves to the outside of the firehouse and brings the colors to half-mast. He returns to the watch-desk and prepares to write the message in the company journal. His face is pensive, and he is asking himself the same question we all ask ourselves: I wonder if I know the guy?

11   The radio begins to squawk the message, and the housewatchman begins to write. "*The signal 5-5-5-5 has been transmitted, and the message is as follows: It is with deep regret that the department announces the death of Fireman 1st Grade Edward Tuite which occurred while operating at Box 583, at 1125 hours this date.*"

12   None of us there knew the man personally, but we all felt the loss. We went about our work for the rest of the day without talking about it.

13   I had a friend we don't talk about either. His name was Mike Carr, and he was an upstanding kind of a guy. He was the union delegate of Engine 85. Only a few days before his death I had mentioned to him that we should clean out an old locker and use it for our union business. It was a shabby old locker, but it could be used to store medical forms, work contracts, information bulletins, and other union material. Mike thought it was a good idea, and within the hour he had the locker cleared and had begun painting it. Anything that had the smallest benefit for firemen would interest Mike, and he worked untiringly for the men in the firehouse.

14   Then a nine-year-old boy reached up and pulled the alarm-box handle. Kids do this a lot in the South Bronx. His friends giggled, and they all ran up the street to watch the fire engines come. The box came in on the bells—2787—Southern Boulevard and 172nd Street. Mike pulled himself up on the side step of the apparatus. The heavy wheels turned up Intervale Avenue, the officer's foot pressing hard on the siren. At Freeman Street the apparatus turned right, and Mike lost his grip. He spun from the side step like a top. Marty Hannon and Juan Moran jumped off the apparatus even before it came to a screeching stop. There was blood all over. They could see that Mike had stopped breathing. Marty cleared some of the blood away with a handkerchief, and began mouth-to-mouth resuscitation. He told me all he remembers of those agonizing minutes was the Battalion Chief's voice blaring over the Department radio: "*Transmit signal ten ninety-two for Box 2787. Malicious false alarm.*"

15   The following day the city's newspapers ran the story stating that the Uniformed Firefighters Association was offering a thousand dollars reward for information leading to the arrest of the person who pulled the box. That afternoon a nine-year-old boy was led through the heavy iron doors of the Forty-first Precinct House. News spreads quickly in the South Bronx, and the boy's friends told their parents, who called the cops.

16   While the boy was being questioned at the police station, people from the Hoe Avenue Association, a neighborhood action group, painted alarm box number 2787 black, and hung a sign around it. The sign was in two parts, the top half in Spanish, and the bottom in English. It read: A FIREMAN WAS KILLED WHILE COMING HERE TO A FALSE ALARM. Before the paint was dry another false alarm was pulled at the same box, and the men of Engine 85 took the sign down.

17   Mike had two sons, one seven, the other nine—two brave and frightened boys now walking on either side of their mother, walking slowly behind a shining red fire engine that moves between endless rows of their school chums, and hundreds of firemen. They look up at the flag-draped casket on top of the fire engine and feel proud that their daddy is the cause of all this ceremony, but they are also frightened because they are old enough to realize that there is a tomorrow, and it is going to be different without him.

18   The young boy in the police station is frightened too, but in a different way. He is confused, and wonders why everyone is so upset. All the kids pull false alarms. At least the kids he pals around with do. He came to this country from Puerto Rico five years ago, and the kids on the block taught him that you have to make your own fun in the South Bronx. You can play in the abandoned buildings, they told him, or on the towering trash heaps in the backyards, or in musty, rat-infested cellars. There used to be a boys' club in the neighborhood, but it burned down and never reopened. He learned, too, that pulling the handle of a fire-alarm box causes excitement, and a certain pleasure that comes with being responsible for all the noise, the sirens, the air horns. Why is everyone so upset?

19   I know why I am upset. My company alone, Engine 82, responded to over two thousand false alarms last year. Many of them were caused by kids like this. Kids with no place to go, nothing to do. Kids whose parents never talk to them, never have a surprise gift for them, or a warm squeeze. Kids whose real meaning in the family is that they symbolize a few extra dollars in the welfare check each month. Kids whose parents did not know anything about contraception to begin with, and never learned to love what they did not ask for. Kids born of poverty and ignorance into a system of deprivation.

20   What do you do with a nine-year-old boy who has pulled a false alarm that has resulted in a death? It is easy to say that the death was unfortunate, but peripheral to the crime of pulling a false alarm. It is even easier to say that the perpetrator is only nine years old, and so should be made aware of the severity of his actions merely by being given over to the social services for guidance care. This, in fact, is what happened to the child.

21   I do not advocate cutting off the child's hand, but I do think he should have been institutionalized for a year. I understand the sad social conditions in which this child has been forced to live, but I have lost sympathy for the cry that poverty founded the crime, not the boy. Anyone found guilty of pulling a malicious false alarm should be sent to jail for a year, or, if under sixteen, to a reform school. But, in the eight years I have been a fireman, I have seen only one man jailed, and I have responded to thousands of alarms that proved to be maliciously false.

22   In the city of New York last year, firemen responded to 72,060 false alarms — an average of 197 daily. Yet, the courts and the Police Department do not look on the pulling of a false alarm as a serious offense. Few are arrested, fewer are found guilty, and fewer still are punished.

23   Besides Mike Carr, I know of two other firemen who were killed en route to false alarms in New York City in the past eight years. But, it is not just firemen who are victimized by false alarms. Often while firemen are answering a false alarm at one end of their district, a serious fire breaks out at the other end. Time is the most important factor in fighting fires. I can remember many fires where, had we been there a minute or two sooner, we probably would have saved someone's life. Three hundred and seven people died in New York City fires last year. Statistics are not available, but you can be sure that some of those deaths could have been avoided if firemen had not been answering a false alarm minutes before.

24   Mike Carr is dead, and his widow will have to make it on just half the salary she was used to. It's strange, but had Mike come through the accident with a disabling injury, he would have been pensioned off with three-fourths of his salary. His wife would have been happy to have him alive. But he died, and she gets half his salary to support his family. The same will go to the widow of the man who fell through the roof yesterday.

25   We don't talk about Mike Carr in the firehouse. We think about him often, but we don't talk about him. Words of sentiment and emotion do not come easily.

26   The day following Mike's death the firehouse was busy with journalists and television news camera crews. Marty Hannon and Juan Moran were not working, and the television people decided to film an interview with Charlie McCartty, who is the biggest man in Ladder 31. And he is as tough a fireman as he is big. He is respected around the firehouse, not only because of his size and his ability as a fireman, but also because he is known to do the right thing — always. Never pretentious, McCartty is willing to stand up for anything or anyone when he thinks the cause is right.

27   Charlie applied the mechanical resuscitator to Mike Carr as the ambulance careened its way to the hospital. He stayed with Mike the whole time the doctors worked on him. He tried to make small talk with the members of Engine 85 at the hospital, to take their minds off Mike. He tried to console Nick Riso, who was punishing himself because he was driving the apparatus from which Mike

fell. He said, "God Almighty, Nick, how many times did you turn that corner before when nothing ever happened? The Big Guy upstairs called the shots, that's all. You gotta look at it that way." But Nick just sobbed, with his face in his hands.

28   Charlie understood what was happening, and he had full control over his own feelings. Now, though, the television people wanted to film him, and I could see his lips moving in that uncontrollable way a person's lips do when he is nervous.

29   "You knew Mike Carr?" The television commentator pushed the microphone to Charlie's twitching lips.

30   "Yes, I knew him. I worked with him here for the past three years," Charlie said, looking directly at the ground.

31   "What did you think of him, and what do you think of what's happened?"

32   "He was a great guy," Charlie answered, still looking at the ground. "It's a shame this had to happen, and, and . . ." Charlie turned away, his shoulders shaking. He turned back, tears were running from his eyes, and said, "I'm sorry—I just can't do this," and the toughest guy in the firehouse walked away.

33   I am sitting now, along with eight other men, in the kitchen of the firehouse. It is a long, narrow room at the rear of the apparatus floor. The walls are tiled brown, and there are four tables set against the side wall, with room enough to seat twenty-eight men. A soda machine and a refrigerator are set against the opposite wall. A sink, a stove, and another refrigerator are at the front of the room, at the entrance.

34   Billy O'Mann is at the stove preparing the night's meal—tenderloin, boiled potatoes, and cabbage. A couple of men are playing cards, a few read magazines, and the rest are watching the television, which is sitting on a shelf in the corner.

35   Charlie McCartty has forgotten about the accident, the funeral, the news telecaster. It is almost time to eat, and he is yelling over the sound of the T.V.

36   "Yessir, men, Mrs. O'Mann is cooking Irish footballs tonight, and she requests that you clean off the tables."

37   Billy-o hears the remark, and approaches waving a long-pronged fork in his hand. "Listen, Charlie," he says, "I don't mind you calling me Mrs. O'Mann, just as long as you don't try to touch my body."

38   "He doesn't need you Billy-o," Jerry Herbert says, "because he can get his own Mrs. McCartty for a deuce anytime he wants."

39   Everyone laughs. Charlie makes a motion as if he was pulling a spear from his chest. "Got me," he says. "But, a deuce is a lot of money. It doesn't cost that much, does it?"

40   "Well, it depends on whether you want coupons or not," Billy-o says.

41   "Ahh, got me again."

42   Charlie, Billy-o, and Jerry have worked together for the past seven years—in fires and above fires, where it is roughest. Each has saved the other's life at

one time or another, and they can say anything about each other, or each other's family, with impunity.

43 The laughing over, the men in the kitchen begin to gather empty coffee cups and soda cans from the tables. One man goes to the sink to wash the cups and the pots Billy-o has finished with. Another sweeps the floor. It is ten minutes after nine, and we'll eat early.

44 There is a list of men on the kitchen blackboard. Twenty-four men are eating tonight, and the price of the meal is seventy-five cents. I go to the cabinet and count twenty-four plates.

45 As I arrange the plates on the table I think of how slow it has been since I began duty at six o'clock. We answered three alarms—a false alarm and two garbage fires burning in corner trash cans. The plates arranged, I go to count the silverware. I count off twenty-four forks, and begin counting knives when the bells start ringing. I count each gong: two—five—nine—six. Box 2596.

46 "That's right up the block," Jerry says. "Home and Simpson."

47 The housewatchman begins yelling, "Eighty-two and seven twelve, get out. Chief goes too." Men scramble out of the kitchen and run to the apparatus, passing others who are sliding down the brass poles. The Battalion Chief, who has an office on the top floor of the firehouse, watches as 712's truck and 82's pumper leave the house. He will respond behind us.

48 As we leave the firehouse we can see a large crowd of people standing in the middle of Home Street. We pass the intersection of Simpson Street, but that is as far as we are going to get. The sirens are screaming, but the crowd won't move. We get off the rigs and push our way through.

49 The attraction is a ten-year-old boy lying on the street. He is in great pain, but he is not crying. A handsome boy, with long, wavy, black hair. His face is tense, and he is biting his teeth together with all his energy. The cause of his pain is his leg, which is broken and lying under him like a contortionist's trick. He has been hit by a car.

50 The Chief sees what the conditions are, and uses his walkie-talkie to tell his aide to call for an ambulance and for the cops to control the crowd. Chief Niebrock has been around for a long time, almost thirty years, and nothing shakes him. He spent all his time as a fireman in Harlem, and as a fire officer in the South Bronx. He has seen it all, and if the whole block were burning he would act as he acts now—with cool and confidence. "Make the kid comfortable," he says, "but don't move him. And try to move this crowd back a bit." He is not talking to anyone in particular, but we all move to do as he says.

51 I take off my rubber coat, fold it, and place it under the boy's head. John Nixon, of Ladder 712, is feeling around his body for other injuries. The boy is really in pain, and I feel sorry for him, but I can't help thinking how lucky the boy is that he seems to have only a broken leg.

52 There is a lot of hysterical screaming and yelling. A woman is trying to get close to the boy, but she is being restrained by three men. She is a heavy woman,

and the men are finding it difficult to hold her. They are screaming at her in Spanish. It is the boy's mother, and she wants to pick her son up. Luckily, the men understand that the boy should not be moved, and they carry her away.

53   Soon Spanish passion infects two other women who evidently know the boy, and they, too, are carried from the street by their neighbors. There are about three hundred people gathered now in the middle of Home Street. The boy seems confused by the crowd and the noise, but he still doesn't cry. I lean down close to him, and ask, "Does it hurt anywhere else?"

54   "No, just my leg," he replies in a mild Spanish accent.

55   "Just hold on, son. The ambulance will be here soon."

56   John Nixon covers him with a blanket, and starts to say those reassuring words kids need to hear. There is nothing to do now but wait for the ambulance, so I push my way through to the rim of the crowd.

57   I put a cigarette between my lips, and I'm about to ask Bill Valenzio, the chauffeur of our pumper, for a light when I hear an urgent cry: "Hey Dennis. Bill. Here, quick!"

58   It is our captain, Al Albergray, and he has his arm around a bleeding man. It is the driver of the car that hit the boy. His eye is closed, and blood drips from his lip. Captain Albergray has managed to get him away from a group of eight men who have beaten him. The leader of the group reminds me of a Hollywood stereotype of the Mexican bandito. His eyes are close together, and one is slightly turned. He has a wide, thick mustache on his dark face, and he wears a bandanna around his forehead. He stands squarely in front of the others, in a flowered wool jacket, yelling "Peeg, peeg," but I'm not sure at whom.

59   "These guys are looking to kill this man," Captain Albergray says. "Put him in the cab of the pumper, and sit in there with him. And call for police assistance." As Bill and I hustle the man into the pumper, I can see Captain Albergray trying to talk to the group of men, but they want nothing to do with him and walk away.

60   A police car arrives. Bill and I take the man from the pumper and put him in the back seat of the squad car. Captain Albergray tells the cops what has happened. The eight men have now been joined by others, and there is a crowd of hostile people surrounding the car. The cops put in a call for additional assistance.

61   The early winter cold is penetrating my sweatshirt, and I silently wish that the ambulance would get there so I could get my coat back. Many of the men around the car have cans of beer in their hands, and they are screaming for the man sitting in the back seat. Their words fly into the night in English and Spanish. I can understand only the English. "Give 'im to us, man, he needs a lesson, give 'im to us," they are saying.

62   Suddenly, the man in the flowered wool jacket jerks open the rear door and begins to swing wildly at the man in the back seat. The two cops struggle with him, and the crowd surges toward the car on all sides. Captain Albergray

and I are pressed against the rear door on the other side of the car, and people are trying to push us away so they can get at him. But we stand firm. As long as the punches don't fly at us, it is a little like playing tug of war.

63 The man in the back seat is crying, but his tears come more from fear than pain. Just a few minutes before he was speeding happily through the streets of the South Bronx in a souped-up Chevy sedan, and now he sits in the back of a police car, looking out at a panorama of hating eyes. He came close to killing a boy who doesn't cry, and now he sobs because he is not sure if a few cops and firemen can hold off the crowd that wants to kill him.

64 It is not very long before two more squad cars arrive at the scene. The noise of their screaming sirens alarms the crowd, and they back off. The newly arrived cops clear a path between the people, and the beleaguered squad car backs out of the street carrying the sobbing driver to safety. The disappointed crowd returns to mill around the boy.

65 The ambulance finally appears. It has been thirty minutes since the Chief's aide called for it. The attendant pulls out a stretcher and hands it to Benny Carroll, one of the men in my company. John Nixon, two other firemen, and I carefully lift the boy as Benny shoves the stretcher beneath him. The boy cries out in agony as he feels his leg being moved. "It's all right, Joseph," John says. "In a little while it will be all over, and all the kids on the block will want to sign their names on the big white cast the doctor will fix you up with." The boy feels reassured, and he holds John's hand as we lift him into the ambulance.

66 Our job is done as we watch the ambulance carry little Joseph Mendez away. Captain Albergray will make an entry in the company journal: "*Assisted injured civilian, rendered first aid, 35 minutes.*"

67 Most of the people have re-entered the buildings now, and the street is near normal as we drive up toward Southern Boulevard. On the way back to the firehouse, Benny Carroll says to me, "A lady back there told me why they were trying to do that guy in. It seems that he's the neighborhood hot-rodder. Drives up and down the street like a maniac. They warned him a couple of times that they were going to break his ass if he didn't slow down, and tonight was his night."

68 "You can't blame them, I guess," I say.

69 "Hell no," Benny replies. "If that was my kid I'd make sure I had a piece of him, especially after he was warned and everything."

70 We have backed into the firehouse, and are taking off our rubber gear at the rear of the apparatus floor when the bells start. Box 2596, again, Home and Simpson streets. In ten seconds we are out the door.

71 I had forgotten about the souped-up Chevy, but I can see it now completely engulfed in flames. In his haste to leave the scene, the driver forgot about it, and the police who are now questioning him evidently figured it would be safe double-parked on Home Street.

72   There is no crowd now in the middle of the street, except for a small group involved in a crap game at the corner. The car burns, and few watch as we pull the hose off and extinguish the fire. All the windows are broken, and all the tires are flat.

73   It was a good-looking car, deep violet, and well cared for. All the chrome was removed, in hot-rod fashion, and the rear end set lower than the front. It was probably the most valuable thing the driver ever owned, and now it is destroyed. As we roll up the hose, I think about how much longer this will hurt him than the beating he took tonight.

74   As we turn the corner at Simpson Street, the men playing dice stop to watch us pass. The man with the close eyes and the flowered wool jacket is there, and he waves to us, and smiles, in that ironic way that means he knows more than we do.

75   It is now after 10:00 P.M. as we back again into the firehouse. The men of Engine 85 and Ladder 31 have already eaten the Irish footballs, and are now washing their dishes and cleaning up. Billy-o sees us coming and begins to cut the meat for us. McCartty already has a big pot on the table, and he is forking cabbage quarters onto each plate.

76   I have taken only one bite of tenderloin when the bells come in again: two—seven—three—seven. That's a lucky break for us. The housewatchman yells, "Get out, Engine 85 and Ladder 712. Chief goes too. Vyse Avenue and 172nd Street."

77   The Chief was sitting behind me, and he walks past with a paper napkin to his lips, saying, "It never fails, never fails." I once kept a running account of how many meals I could eat in the firehouse without interruption. It went for three and a half months, and in that time I never ate one uninterrupted meal.

78   I am eating now as fast as I can, but the bells come in. At least I have finished half—enough to satisfy me anyway. The housewatchman yells, "Two, Seven, Nine, Three, Boston and 169. Get out 82 and 31." Forty seconds later we are racing up 169th Street, past Stebbins Avenue, past Prospect Avenue, past Union Avenue. Benny Carroll leans to the side of the apparatus and looks up the street. He looks at us now—me and the other men working tonight: Vinny Royce, Ed Montaign, and Carmine Belli. We are huddled on the back step of the fire engine, gripping the crossbar. He says, "Looks like this is our night for accidents. There's a guy up there just knocked down the traffic signal."

79   The pumper stops in the middle of Boston Road, a broad, main thoroughfare in the Bronx. There was once a traffic stanchion standing in the middle of the road. It is now laying flat on the ground, partly covered by a new Continental. The car evidently climbed five feet up the pole before the pole came crashing down.

80   There are six people in the car. Four are unconscious, and one, a woman, is dazed, and muttering incoherently. The driver has the steering post through his chest and looks dead.

81   Herbert and McCartty come with Ladder 31's first-aid box. They begin unraveling bandages and applying them to head wounds. The two other women begin to come to, and one starts screaming, "Rufus, Rufus, Rufus." She is hysterical, and Herbert and O'Mann lift her out of the car and lay her on the ground. The conscious woman gets out of the car and sits down next to her. The third woman is moaning, and bleeding badly from the mouth. All her front teeth have been knocked out. I climb into the back seat and sit next to her. I put my arm around her, and her head falls onto my shoulder. I begin to clean her with a gauze sponge.

82   A lanky youth, about nineteen or twenty, leans in the car, with his hands on the floor. "What do you want?" I ask.

83   "It's okay," he replies. "I'm the man, man."

84   "Well you go be the man somewhere else," I tell him.

85   There is a crowd around the car, and people keep poking their heads in the rear. I keep telling them to keep back, until Carmine comes over and stands guard by the door.

86   Chief Niebrock responds from the other alarm—it was an MFA (malicious false alarm). He holds his portable lamp close to the driver. "Better take him out," he says to Ken Lierly, Ladder 31's lieutenant.

87   The man is obviously the worst off of the six, and the only way to give first aid is to remove him from the car. He is a heavy man, and it takes four firemen to lift him. He may be dead, but only a doctor can say that for sure, so Bill Finch, the Chief's aide, applies the resuscitator to him. The other two men in the front seat have hit the windshield, and their foreheads are wide open. McCartty and Herbert have more room to work on them now.

88   Two police cars are at the scene, one from the Forty-first Precinct, and the other from the Forty-eighth. The boundary between the two precincts is Boston Road, and the car has crashed dead in the middle of it. There is some disagreement as to which car will take the accident. All those forms and reports that have to be filled out means one of the cars will be a loser, and the other a winner. They finally decide. The two men in the car from the Forty-first will take it, and the other car drives off.

89   After twenty-five minutes or so, two ambulances arrive. The men are quickly stretchered and driven away. The two seriously hurt women are put in the other ambulance. The third woman is walking around the car crying, "Has anybody seen my pocketbook? Please give it back. You can have the money. I need my keys and my cards. Please, oh God, please, PLEASE give me back my pocketbook!"

90   The crowd looks wonderingly at her, and the cops and the firemen search in, under, and around the car. A cop goes back to the ambulance, and returns saying that the other two women don't have their pocketbooks either. The crying woman falls to the ground amid broken glass and drying blood. "I am not leaving until I have my pocketbook!" she screams. Herbert and I gently lift her

to her feet, and she becomes passive. We lead her to the ambulance, and sit her in the corner seat. The yearning cries, "Rufus, Rufus!" will occupy her mind until they reach the hospital.

91   We are about to return to the firehouse, but I ask Bill to drive past the squad car, where the two cops are recording the information in their logbooks. "Hey, Officer," I yell. "Which one was Rufus?"

92   "The driver," he replied.

93   Bill directs the pumper toward the firehouse, stopping for the red lights along the way. We are about to turn onto Intervale Avenue when the apparatus begins to go faster, and the siren begins to penetrate the air. The Captain has received an alarm over the department radio.

94   We turn down Hoe Avenue. There is a small crowd of about thirty people waving to us. Bill stops the pumper next to the crowd, and as we push through them Benny Carroll says, to no one in particular, "Looks like an O.D."

95   There is a boy, about fifteen years old, lying on the hood of a car. His eyes are closed and his arms spread out, like he was crucified on the '69 Oldsmobile. The car is white, and the boy's black face seems darker against the solid white background.

96   I get to him first, and as I check his arms, I can hear Captain Albergray asking "Does anybody know him?" There is no reply from the crowd. The boy's friends are probably there, but if they are, they are high, and know they can't get involved.

97   The boy's wrists and forearms are covered with holes, and round, purple scars. I raise his eyelids and see that his eyes haven't rolled back yet. They stare straight out as if belonging to a catatonic.

98   "Someone go get some ice for us!" Benny yells to the crowd. A man turns to a woman, talks to her in Spanish, and she runs into one of the tenements.

99   The boy is breathing, but his breath is dangerously slow. An overdose of heroin slows up the system until everything stops completely. We lift the boy up and begin to slap his face and shake him. He isn't conscious enough to walk around. If this boy lives it will be because his blood begins to circulate normally again.

100   The woman returns from her apartment with a small pot filled with ice. Benny takes it and thanks her. He puts a half dozen cubes into his handkerchief, and knots the top. "Pull his drawers down, Dennis," he says to me.

101   Ladder 31 and the Chief have pulled into the block now. Billy-o comes over with a blanket, and he and Vinny Royce lift the boy up as I pull his dungarees and shorts to his knees. Carmine Belli has the blanket, and shoves it under him. Benny takes the ice pack and places it under the scrotum. He covers his arm and the boy's legs with the blanket ends.

102   The crowd looks on with interest. There is no yelling or pushing, only the fast syllables of conversational Spanish. A man once told me that he was told by an immigration officer in Puerto Rico to call the Fire Department if he ever

needed emergency help in New York City. The people in the South Bronx know that when the corner alarm box is pulled the firemen always come. If you pick up a telephone receiver in this town you may, or may not, get a dial tone. If you get on a subway you may, or may not, get stuck in a tunnel for an hour. The wall socket in your apartment may, or may not, contain electricity. The city's air may, or may not, be killing you. The only real sure thing in this town is that the firemen come when you pull the handle on that red box.

103 Billy-o is rapidly squeezing the boy's cheeks. Bill Finch has the resuscitator turned to the inhalator position, and puts the face piece an inch from the boy's mouth. The boy finally begins to moan and move slightly. The crisis is over for him, at least until the next time he squats in a vacant building, wraps a belt around his arm, and puts a match under a bottle cap filled with white powder.

104 "Put in another call for an ambulance" Chief Niebrock says to Captain Albergray. It is now near 11:30 P.M., and I make a mental note to pick up a container of milk and a piece of cake on the way back to the firehouse. I have lost any hope of being satisfied with dried-out Irish football.

105 We have been here a half hour when the ambulance arrives. We are able now to walk the boy to the ambulance, although he still cannot support his own weight. The nurse in the ambulance looks at me and says, "What a night!" I know what she means.

106 Some nights our job has little to do with fire. Since the O.D. case on Hoe Avenue, we have responded to eleven alarms. One was a water leak — a guy's bathtub overflowed at four in the morning. Another was a fallen street wire, which required the emergency crew of Con Edison. And the other nine were false alarms — one each hour from midnight to eight.

107 It is a little after 8:00 A.M. now, and I am sitting in the kitchen having coffee and a roll. The men working the day tour begin to arrive, but I'm too tired to say much more than "Good morning." Instead of driving the sixty miles to where I live, I think that I'll take the subway to my mother's apartment in Manhattan. At least there I'll be able to get six solid hours of sleep in. I'll have to get up at four, because I'm due in again tonight at six.

Discussion Questions

1. What is the difference, according to Smith, between firefighters and the other people who work in New York—"the bankers, ad-men, truck drivers, secretaries, sellers and buyers"?

2. How is the South Bronx, where Engine 82 is located, different from the two other poorest neighborhoods in New York? Why is this important to the story Smith is preparing to tell?

3. In paragraphs 8–12, Smith describes the death the day before of a firefighter from Rescue Company 1. How did the firefighters at Smith's firehouse learn about this death, and what was their reaction to this news?

4. What do we learn about Mike Carr, Smith's friend who was killed in the response of Engine Company 85 to a false alarm? What was the immediate cause of Carr's death? How will his family fare in the future?

5. Describe the result of the Hoe Avenue Association's attempt to prevent more false alarms from alarm box number 2787, at which the boy pulled the alarm handle that led to Carr's death.

6. What happened to the nine-year-old boy who pulled the false alarm, and what was Smith's reaction to the court's decision?

7. Describe Charlie McCartty, his actions after the Carr accident, and his response when the television people began to film him.

*8. Smith says (paragraph 42) of Charlie, Billy-o, and Jerry that "they can say anything about each other, or each other's family, with impunity." What had they been saying—and in what tone? Explain.

Writing Topics

1. In paragraphs 18–22, Smith discusses the background of the boy who pulled the false alarm, describes the boy's light punishment, and states his own view that the boy should have "been institutionalized for a year." In a brief essay, agree or disagree with Smith's opinion.

2. Investigate the fire alarm apparatus in your hometown and interview the firefighters at one of the firehouses to find out how the alarm system has been working. Write a letter to the editorial page of your local newspaper indicating either that the city can be reassured about the fire department and its alarm system or should worry that what happened in New York could happen at home.

"We are a deaf family; we are different but we are not crazy freaks and we mean no one any harm. We are silent when we speak, but noisy when we call to one another."

STOP YOUR INFERNAL NOISE

Ruth Sidransky

Ruth Sidransky was born in New York City in 1929 and graduated from Hunter College with a B.A. in 1950 and an M.A. in 1953. In 1990, she published *In Silence: Growing Up Hearing in a Deaf World*, from which "Stop Your Infernal Noise" was taken. Her story of society's careless treatment of her deaf parents is an eloquent account of the double pain handicapped people often suffer—first from their handicap but more brutally perhaps from thoughtless and irrational responses to them from irritated, nonhandicapped people. Sidransky has contributed widely to periodicals, including *Reader's Digest*.

1   We had new neighbors. They moved in one day when I was at school. My mother greeted me with the news as soon as I entered the apartment. "New people downstairs, they have a daughter your age. You will have a new friend."

2   Ina Levy was a homely teenager, bent with a gentle dowager's hump, a sweet smile of loneliness on her face. She was an only child and her parents were old. It was a family aged by Mr. Levy's premature illness. His thick white hair framed his thin crushed face. He stooped when he walked and complained little. Mrs. Levy, in matriarchal splendor, wrapped her graying black hair into a tight knot on the back of her head. Although she carefully pushed two locks of hair into soft waves on her forehead, her face remained pinched and ugly. She wore expensive clothes that were easily ten years old.

3   Their apartment was crowded with furniture that had graced a large house. The furniture was heavy, dark, and spoke of the family's economic collapse. There was no walking space and no light. I felt as though I were in a crammed furniture store. The curtains were always drawn, hiding the massive mahogany pieces from the sun. I did like their rugs. They were soft under my feet. They were the first people I ever knew who had a rug in their apartment.

4   Ina and I began our relationship shyly. Before our friendship had a chance to mature, it ended in bitter anger.

5   The quarrel began soon after their arrival. One early evening as we sat eating our quiet supper in the kitchen there was a loud thumping noise under our feet. My father jumped up from his chair and signed rapidly, "What's that?"

6   The thumping continued. I knew instantly what it was. Someone in Mrs. Levy's apartment was banging a broom against the ceiling. I explained what it was. My mother's hands were quick. "Ruth, go downstairs. Maybe something is wrong. You go help."

7   I walked down one flight of stairs and rang Mrs. Levy's doorbell.

8   She opened the door and when she saw me she raged at me. "How dare you make so much noise! My husband is a sick man. Stop your infernal noise!"

9   I looked at her dumbfounded. "We were not making any noise. We were eating our dinner."

10   She ranted, "You people are always banging on the floor. Are you roller skating up there?"

11   "No," I answered in a still voice, hiding my fright at her rampage.

12   She didn't stop. "You people are impossible. Stop making a racket. The next time I hear a noise I shall call the police."

13   She kept shrieking at me as I climbed the stairs back to our apartment.

14   "Well," my father asked, "what's wrong?"

15   I didn't have the heart to tell him. I lifted my eyes to his and kept my hands at my sides. My mother touched my shoulder and turned my face to hers. With her mouth she formed the words, "Ruth, tell me what is the matter."

16   "Mrs. Levy," I signed, "says we make too much noise." My signs were tight to my chest.

17   "Oh," my mother breathed.

18   Her face slackened. It was a look I knew well.

19   "It is because we are deaf," she signed sadly.

20   Our voices didn't and couldn't call to each other. Automatically we stomped one foot on the floor, vibrating our message foot to foot. As soon as the vibration was transmitted, my mother or my father turned to the caller. It is a common method of communication among the deaf. We did it without thinking. Foot stomping eliminated the need to get up and call someone to conversation. It was natural to us and we had never considered the shock to the neighbors who lived beneath our uncarpeted floors.

21   We looked at each other, my brother, my father, my mother and I.

22   "What shall we do?" my mother asked.

23   I shrugged and said nothing. My brother was silent.

24   "We are helpless. The hearing people do not understand that we are deaf." My mother's signs were firm. Her hands flew and she raged at the injustice of her deafness.

25   How would we call to one another? How could someone stop us from talking in our own home? We used our bodies, hands and feet, mouth and eyes to talk. Would we have to cut down on our already diminished speech? A rock settled in my heart. My chest tightened as my mother spent her fury. Our dinner was left unfinished. Cold spaghetti snaked over our chipped unmatched china.

26   My mother cried and put her head down on the kitchen table. I put my arms around her and said, "Don't worry Momma, we will tap, tap our shoulders to call each other. Let us try."

27   My father, who had remained impassive, flared his nostrils and hands and said directly to my mother, "To hell with them. This is our home. We finish to eat our good supper now!"

28   In the days that followed, I listened to the opening and closing of apartment doors until I could identify the Levys' door. I learned their schedule and avoided them. At home we made the colossal effort of curtailing our natural speaking rhythms. As the weeks passed the broom thumping stopped and we comfortably reverted to calling each other by foot.

29   Mrs. Levy began her broom banging again. Each time we ignored her and lived as we always did. When we passed in the hallway, she glared at me and I sneered at her. My legs were fast, and I raced past her whenever I could, avoiding her gray eyes. She snarled words at me. I ran into our apartment, closed the door behind me, and held my breath until her scathing words left my mind.

30   One afternoon, without a thought of Mrs. Levy in my head, I dashed up the stairs and heard horrible screams. I knew they were my mother's screams. At the third-floor landing, against a window guarded by two iron bars, my mother had her hands around Mrs. Levy's throat, screeching in a deaf soprano voice, "You son-of-a-bitch woman, son-of-bitch, go to hell!" No one would have understood her, but I did. Her beautiful face was contorted and blotched with red anger.

31   I moved swiftly and separated my mother from her prey. I had never seen her use physical force. She never, ever raised a hand to me or my brother. Loose from my mother's powerful hands, Mrs. Levy shouted, "You freaks, you are all freaks. You are not fit to live with normal people. You belong in an institution for crazy freaks!" She raved on.

32   I shuddered. I took my mother by the arm as Mrs. Levy fled into her apartment and bolted the door.

33   My mother, still furious, would have none of me. Her anger was cresting. "Wait," she punctured the air with her hands, "I am not ready."

34   I waited for her to regain her composure. I hadn't noticed the pillowcase filled with wet wash laundry. She bent down and hoisted the heavy load of wash onto her left shoulder. She washed clothes in the basement washing machine every Thursday.

35   She spoke the words, "Come, we go up now. I feel better."

36   She moved swiftly up the stairs energized by her outburst. She plunged the key into the lock and opened the door. Together we removed the shirts and underwear, socks and blouses from the pillowcase and strung them out in the small bathroom to dry.

37   My mother said, "I make tea and we have cookies. Go to kitchen."

38   I sat at our gray wooden table watching her prepare tea. We had tea in the afternoons to celebrate the day's end. She filled the dented tea kettle with water, lit the gas stove and settled the pot on the flame. She slid the unopened box of cookies on the table.

39   "You open!" she commanded.

40   I wanted to tell her that she had forgotten to turn off the tap, that water was streaming into the sink. She often left the tap running, not hearing the water. When her back was turned to the sink, she didn't know whether the water gushed or dripped from the faucet. I didn't tell her this time. Let it run, I thought. This was not the time to call attention to her deafness. Instead, I tore the cellophane wrapping from the box of sweet shortbread cookies and heard the crackle of the cellophane crescendo into the room. And I thought, she cannot hear that either. I liked the sound of the paper in my fingers, glad that I was not deaf.

41   After her first sip of lemon-laced tea she said to me, "You know that Mrs. Levy is crazy woman. She screamed her face at me, moving her mouth up and down, she pushed her fingers on my chest. She made the sign for *crazy* and pointed to me. She hurt me. I am not crazy. I am sensitive woman. I try to pass her on the stairs. She stayed to my body. I could not pass her. I cannot speak. I grab her. I so very angry. I choke this woman to make her stop insulting me."

42   "It is all right, Momma. I understand."

43   "It is hard to be deaf in hearing world."

44   "I know," I answered, calming my own anger. I kept my anger hidden from her and from me. It was too dangerous to be angry; I had to remain her link to the uncomprehending, unfeeling world that eyed her with revulsion. I was her bridge to normalcy.

45   When we finished I went to the sink and shut the tap, stopping the flow of water.

46   "Why did you not tell me that water was still running?"

47   "It made a nice sound Momma."

48   "Tell me," she asked with childlike curiosity, "what is sound of water?"

49   "It sounds like it feels on your hands, soft and clean. It washes the dirt away. It washes Mrs. Levy away."

50   She liked that, and laughed. We grinned and hugged each other. She was feeling better.

51   Two days later, at four in the afternoon, the doorbell rang. I went to the door and shouted, "Who is it?"

52   "Is this the Sidransky residence?"

53   "Who is it?" I queried again.

54   "I have a court summons for Mrs. Sidransky."

55   I opened the door as far as the chain latch would permit. A strange man stood there.

56   "What do you want?"

57   "Who are you?" he asked cordially.

58   "I am Mrs. Sidransky's daughter."

59   He thrust an enevlope into my hand and said, "Give this to your mother. She has to appear in court in two weeks. It's all explained in the papers." He turned and left.

60   Stunned, I held the document in my hands until my mother came to the door and asked, "What is the matter with you?"

61   We went into the living room, sat on the deep rose sofa and opened the envelope. It was a summons. Mrs. Levy was the plaintiff and my mother the defendant. I wasn't clear about judicial procedure. My knowledge of the law consisted of movie courtroom scenes.

62   My mother was agitated. As the family caretaker I assured her that I would handle the entire matter. I was cast into the role of omnipotence once more; the sense of power was overwhelming. I did not recognize that this power was an abuse of my childhood. No one was to blame for this abuse. It was simply so.

63   It continued to be so as my mother pleaded, "Who will help us?"

64   "I will do it," I said.

65   I read the summons carefully, absorbing each word. I was fifteen and in my second year of high school. I had to concentrate to get through the incomprehensible legal jargon.

66   "Will I go to jail?" my mother asked with fear in her fingers.

67   "Of course not, no one is going to jail!"

68   My father's only concern when he arrived home was the cost of a lawyer to defend my mother against the charges of assault and disturbing the peace.

69   "We have no money. We cannot pay a lawyer. We do not know a lawyer."

70   "I will be the lawyer," I told my father.

71   "You can be lawyer in two weeks?" He laughed at me.

72   "I will be absent from school and I will go to the library and learn to be a lawyer." My signs were courtly.

73   I had no doubts about my capacity to learn anything and to learn it quickly. My father caught my spirit and was about to relent, when he shook his head at the enormity of my task. I didn't allow him to soften. I demanded, "Trust me! Don't I always help you and Momma? I can do it again."

74   He took my hands in his heavy square hands, kissed me on the forehead and said with his voice, "Good girl baby Ruth."

75   That was settled.

76   I went to my beloved library in search of a two-week law degree. The library had no law books, just books about law. I rushed through book after book, scanning chapter headings, looking for answers to my legal dilemma. I

found none. I searched my memory for the cinematic courtroom scenes I remembered and decided that if I could not learn to be a lawyer, I could learn to act like one.

77   The day arrived and we walked up the impressive stone steps to the Bronx County Courthouse. My father, my mother, and I were together. My father had taken the day off from work to be with us; it meant the loss of a day's pay. We were immaculately dressed. I had selected my clothes the night before with great care, choosing a black and white checked woolen skirt and a starched white cotton blouse.

78   When I looked in the mirror in the morning I decided that I looked too old. I wanted the judge to pity me, to pity all of us. I hated the pity I had seen in the faces of so many, but this time I would use it to my advantage. I braided my long dark hair into two thick braids and wrapped the ends with two white silky ribbons. I was ready to take on the Bronx judicial system.

79   We found our assigned courtroom and pushed the swinging doors into the large room. It looked like all the courtrooms I had seen in the movies. The judge sat at his bench and the court stenographer sat beneath him. The American flag and the New York State flag were in plain view. There were two long tables, one for each of the lawyers. I sighed with relief. The courtroom was familiar.

80   I showed the summons to the guard and he ushered us to the first row of the long brown wooden benches. Mrs. Levy and her husband arrived moments after we did, accompanied by their lawyer, and sat down behind us. We waited for over an hour until we were called to the bench.

81   I explained for my parents the petty cases that were heard before ours, with my hands hidden in my lap. Then I heard the names Sidransky and Levy. Mrs. Levy's lawyer rose from his seat and walked forward. I followed him.

82   The judge was a kindly looking man. His bifocals sat at the tip of his nose and his fat face had deep laugh lines. I liked him. His voice was firm, his manner fair. I was not afraid of him.

83   Mrs. Levy's lawyer presented himself. The judge peered down at me and asked, "And who are you?"

84   "I am Ruth Sidransky and I am here to represent my parents."

85   "Where is your lawyer?"

86   "We do not have a lawyer. We cannot afford one. I shall act both as lawyer and interpreter."

87   He treated me seriously. "Where are your parents?"

88   "They are over there." I turned and pointed to them.

89   "Tell them to come forward and speak for themselves."

90   "They can come forward, Your Honor, but they cannot speak for themselves. They are deaf."

91   "Deaf and dumb?"

92   "No," I answered, suppressing my anger at his question, "they are deaf, *not* dumb."

93   I beckoned to my parents to approach and they came forward. Mr. and Mrs. Levy followed behind them. We were all standing in position, my parents behind me and the Levys behind their lawyer. The lawyer presented his case, citing our continual floor thumpings and bangings. Mrs. Levy interrupted her lawyer and in a loud whisper complained that since the summons had been issued, the noise was worse.

94   I said nothing, but each night when my parents were asleep, Freddie and I, behind our closed bedroom door, had taken one heavy shoe and dropped it mightily on the floor. We never dropped the other.

95   I remained silent during the proceedings until Mrs. Levy shouted, "She's a slut, look at her, pretending to be so innocent. There are boys in and out of their apartment all the time. Damned prostitute!"

96   I felt myself redden at her outrageous mouthings and said nothing.

97   The judge said calmly, "You are out of order, Mrs. Levy. She is not charged; her mother is."

98   My mother looked at me, pleading with her eyes for me to interpret the words that were said. I did not lift my hands to language.

99   Mrs. Levy's lawyer began again, this time describing my mother's attempt to choke her to death.

100   I interrupted. "Your Honor, may I speak?"

101   "Yes, you may speak."

102   In a loud clear voice I recounted the story of my mother's attack on Mrs. Levy. As I spoke my hands signed the words at the same time. This was difficult to do, for the words of my mouth had to match the words of my hands. I was slow and deliberate, explaining how Mrs. Levy had goaded my mother, how she had insulted her and how my mother, in her own fright and rage, had attempted to silence Mrs. Levy's incomprehensible rantings. I paused and looked at my mother and father nodding their approval at my words.

103   I then put down my hands and spoke with my mouth only, and repeated Mrs. Levy's charge that we were freaks and should be made to move away from normal people. My voice dropped to a lower pitch so that the judge leaned forward in order to hear me. I continued, "We are a deaf family; we are different but we are not crazy freaks and we mean no one any harm. We are silent when we speak, but noisy when we call to one another."

104   The judge peered at me in sympathy.

105   I stopped speaking. The judge sat upright on his bench and turned his attention to Mrs. Levy's lawyer, who softened his voice and demanded that we be ordered by the court to buy carpets for our entire apartment to diminish the noise level. I turned to my parents as I signed the lawyer's words. My father looked horrified; this was something he could not afford to do.

106   I said to the judge, "We are poor people. If we couldn't afford a lawyer we can certainly not afford to buy rugs."

107   The judge ignored my remarks and asked me directly, "How did you learn sign language?"

108   "I learned sign language as a baby, long before I could speak orally. I learned to speak as you do when I went to school."

109   He motioned to Mrs. Levy's lawyer and to me to come close to him. When we were close enough that no one else could hear, he said, "This is an unusual case and has no place in the courtroom. I shall dismiss this case and refer the Sidransky family to a social worker."

110   He banged his gavel and declared, "Case dismissed."

111   I smiled deeply and said, "Thank you, Your Honor."

112   "Miss Sidransky, you are a remarkable girl." I had heard those words before and hated them, but this time I gloated.

113   My mother asked me as I turned from the bench, "What does it mean?"

114   I signed in small letters with my left hand at my side, "We won, say nothing, I will tell you outside."

115   We walked out the swinging doors together. Mrs. Levy and my mother brushed shoulders but made no attempt to communicate. I said, "Mrs. Levy, we will try to be quiet if you will try to be patient with us," magnanimous before her courtroom loss.

116   In the wide hallway, I explained what had happened to my parents. My father soared with delight. "So," he signed, "you are lady lawyer now."

117   "No," I answered, "I am your daughter Ruth."

118   I thought of Sammy and I wanted to share my victory with him. It was Tuesday and I had to wait until Friday to see him. Friday came and the night air was filled with the hint of springtime. The stripped trees quivered with barely discernible buds in Crotona Park's cool soft wind.

119   "I have something to tell you, Sammy," I said as we sat down on our park bench.

120   "Well, tell me. I'm waiting."

121   Slowly, I told him my Mrs. Levy tale. He did not interrupt me.

122   His face was pensive; he looked sad.

123   "Sammy, what's wrong? Aren't you happy for me?"

124   He swallowed his breath and in even tones said, "I have something to tell you."

125   I waited for him to continue.

126   "I don't know how to say this."

127   I waited.

128   "Ruthie, my Star Eyes, I cannot marry you. I do not want to have deaf children."

129   I sat still, wordless.

❧

Discussion Questions

1. In the opening paragraphs of "Stop Your Infernal Noise," we learn that Sidransky has an eye for detail as she describes the new occupants in the apartment below. What do we find out about the Levys from her observations?

2. After the first loud thumping from below, Sidransky went down to "help." How was she treated by Mrs. Levy?

3. What motivated Sidransky's mother to choke Mrs. Levy in the stairwell?

4. What sources did Sidransky have at her disposal to learn how to be a lawyer for her mother when she obeyed the summons and appeared in court? Which source proved to be the most useful?

*5. At the appearance in court, Mrs. Levy told her lawyer in a loud whisper that the noise from the Sidransky apartment had increased, not decreased, after the fight in the stairwell. What did Sidransky reveal to the reader as the cause of this noise? Explain.

6. What was the judge's decision in the case?

*7. In the concluding scene, what did Sammy tell Sidransky that left her "wordless"? Explain.

Writing Topics

1. Write a letter to Mrs. Levy, pointing out how she might have handled the situation differently and brought about a peaceful resolution of the conflict with the Sidranskys through compromise.

2. Write a character sketch of Sidransky based on what is revealed about her in her narrative. Set forth her most important traits, both strong and weak, and support your points by citing passages in the text. Conclude with an overall assessment of her as an individual.

❧"Our third move (in the ninth year of my overschlepped Sealy) kicked the mattress situation into crisis mode; the queen-size box spring couldn't make it up the stairs."

GOING TO THE MATTRESSES

Sarah Mahoney

Sarah Mahoney was a senior editor for *Smart Money: The Wall Street Journal's Magazine of Personal Business* and contributed to the "Expert Shopper" column, in which "Going to the Mattresses" appeared in the September 1994 issue. Born in 1960, Mahoney grew up in Amityville, a suburb on the north shore of Long Island. She graduated from the University of Michigan in 1982 with a major in English. She has worked for many publications, including *Advertising Age*, *Adweek*, *Success*, *Savvy*, and *Smart Money*. She has also contributed to a variety of magazines, including *Glamour*, *Working Woman*, and *Redbook*. Although Mahoney is executive editor of *Parents Magazine* and the mother of two small children, she remains an avid reader. She writes, "I read as much as I can get my hands on, but try especially hard to keep up with books from writers I'm crazy about: Anna Quindlen, Mary Kay Blakely, Ellen Goodman, Molly Ivins, Anne LaMott, etc . . . [Personal essays] are the most fun [to write]—when I'm working on a story where I can get immersed in the reporting and still get to talk about me, I find the piece just writes itself. In fact, that's why my current job (as executive editor of *Parents*, I assign and edit many essays and first-person pieces) is easily the most fun I've ever had. People are passionately interested in their kids, and everything about their kids—and it usually shows in the quality of the work. Even writers who aren't all that talented can turn out beautiful essays about the things that matter most to them— passion, focus, and honest reflection go a long, long way."

1 I can't say for certain when the bounce went out of our bed, or when the mattress started to resemble a relief map of Death Valley. But either Jack and I were aging at four times the normal rate, or our lumpy love nest was responsible for our chronic backaches. Another couple would have replaced it immediately, but thanks to the recent trauma of a shared couch-buying experience, we feared hurrying into another major conjugal furniture purchase.

2 Besides, I wasn't quite ready to let go of the old bed. It was mine, initially, and I have fond memories of acquiring it back in simpler days with one of my first paychecks and a tall boyfriend in tow. After several years, it followed me into marriage to a shorter man, but one who tossed and turned a lot more. "We'll use my mattress," I insisted. "It's newer."

3 When morning backaches began dogging us both, we blamed our discomfort on other things. After all, we had two babies, and who could tell where baby-bouncing backaches left off and worn-out-mattress backaches began? Plus, we could always name five ways to spend money that seemed more pressing or more fun.

4 Our third move (in the ninth year of my overschlepped Sealy) kicked the mattress situation into crisis mode; the queen-size box spring couldn't make it up the stairs. I conjured up Cardinal Richelieu, who so loathed waking up that he had his servants tote him around in bed. If his hosts' door frames couldn't accommodate the royal four-poster, his staff simply tore down the walls.

5 Of course, Richelieu didn't have to worry about his damage deposit. We did, and after much pushing, pulling, ceiling-scraping and swearing in the movers' mother tongue, we agreed to throw the damn thing out.

6 The following week we whisk down to the local Stern's department store, convinced we'll find a bed within an hour. After all, it took us that long to buy a car. But there's a reason most couples hang on to their beds for around 20 years, according to the Better Sleep Council, when they're usually good for only eight to 10 years: Two bounces exposed marital strife as stark as the battle over blankets on a chilly night. Jack's idea of heaven is a mattress made of stone; I prefer something softer.

7 Thus begins our bedding education. Through examining a few hideous cross-sections, we learn that most modern mattresses start with a system of springs, or wire coils. There can be as few as 250 coils, or as many as 1,000; top-of-the-line full-size mattresses usually have at least 300. Next, the springs are wrapped in a coarse padding, like burlap or coconut fiber. Then more padding is added—as few as two layers or as many as eight. Most padding is synthetic foam; more expensive mattresses rely on natural fibers—cotton, silk, even animal hair. The mattress is covered in fabric ticking, which may be quilted to add softness. And some mattresses are finished off with a pillow top, a thick quilt stitched onto both sides.

8 After trying every mattress at Stern's we settle upon a queen-size Sealy Esquire Posturepedic. A salesperson says it would cost $894 during a sale

scheduled to start the following Thursday. That includes a split box spring that would fit up our narrow stairs, a feature that can add $100 or so to the cost.

9 Jack reaches for his wallet, but I decide, at the very least, to get a competitive bid from Macy's—which doesn't carry the Esquire, but rather a similar Sealy model dubbed the Madiera. Thus I learn that brand-name mattresses are marketed under different monikers.

10 "Something might be called the Declaration at Macy's and the Eton at Bloomingdale's, so you can't price-compare," explains Nanette, a bedding specialist at Dial-A-Mattress. Simply by dialing 1-800-MATTRES ("Leave off the last S for savings"), you can find out the alias of any bed you like, and get a price. The Esquire that I like, a.k.a. the Trilogy, would cost $849 through Dial-A-Mattress, plus $29 for delivery. In other words, I'd save $16 over Stern's sale price. If I don't love it, Nanette assures me, the delivery guys will take it back. "We have it in stock," she says alluringly. "We can have it to you today." (It's 1:00 p.m.)

11 That night, we have another lights-off conference. "I wish," Jack says, "that there was some way we could find a bed that was soft on your side and harder on mine."

12 "I'll look into it," I say. I see one advertised—the Select Comfort air bed—and send away for the video. The bed comes with two hand-held controls that allow each person to pump up one side, like a high-tech basketball shoe. Through the miracle of Velcro, you can assemble it yourself; queens run about $770.

13 Somehow, though, I think mattresses should be simple. And besides, there's no independent evidence that a bed filled with air (or water, for that matter) is better for you. In fact, when I contact one of the experts cited in Select Comfort's sales brochures—Jim Jones, an engineering-resource manager at the Hillenbrand Biomedical Engineering Center of Purdue University—he says that there's no scientific proof that air is inherently more comfortable. Jones himself sleeps on "an old junker from Sears—it's been shot for a while." His dream bed? A mattress made of tiny, fluidized silicone beads, currently available only for burn patients.

14 We dismiss space-age beds, and I coax Jack to Manhattan's ABC Carpets & Home in New York. Here we try the $3,000 Dux bed imported from Sweden. "Let me warn you," Norris, our salesman, says. "The spring system is very sensitive. If your husband tosses and turns, you won't like it. It jiggles too much." Dux beds are based on the premise that softer, not firmer, is better for your back. Jack hates it.

15 For fun, I ask if we can test-drive ABC's most expensive bed, and Jack and I flop our weary bones on an $8,000 Heal's of London model. Big mistake. We both feel we've gone straight to heaven, and Norris leaves us there for a full five minutes before talking.

16   Waving to a mattress cross-section stuffed with curly tendrils of what looks like nose hair, Norris explains that Heal's uses only natural materials, such as lamb's wool and cattle- and horsehair. The horsehair, he tells us, used to come from an Argentinian who would clip his horses' manes, then weave the hair into a mat that wrapped around the springs. Since the Argentinian went out of business, Heal's craftsmen have had to wrestle wads of hair around the springs by hand.

17   According to Norris, John Wayne had a Heal's mattress custom-made while filming in London, and Buckingham Palace asked Heal's to whip up a special bed for a state visit from Charles "Too Tall" de Gaulle. (The Queen herself may sleep on a Heal's mattress, but the aide answering the press phone the day I call the palace snaps, "We'd never release that information.") Heal's beds are also popular with the owners of antique bedsteads, which often require oddly sized mattresses.

18   But what makes this bed so special isn't the mattress. In fact, bucking today's trend toward pillow tops and thicker mattresses, the Heal's mattress is surprisingly thin. The bed's comfort comes from the hand-tied box springs, with each spring connected to eight others, distributing weight evenly over the bed. (Most box springs are machine-tied; one spring connects to just four others.) For a couple of widely disparate weights, Norris swears, it makes a tremendous difference.

19   He then directs us to the ABC custom-made "natural" bed. Like Heal's, it gets its softness from all-natural padding—cotton batting, cushy lamb's wool. Even with a split queen box, we can have the whole thing for less than $1,000. The best part, Norris explains, is that natural fibers are far more durable than the synthetics. The "natural" bed should go more than a dozen years without sagging, compared with synthetic mattresses, which he says will last half that time.

20   I tell Jack to put his Visa card away; this natural-fibers claim sounds fishy to me. I track down a fibers genius, one Owen H. Sercus, professor of textile development and marketing at New York's Fashion Institute of Technology, and run the ABC theory by him. "Man-made fibers can be made to do whatever you want them to do. I'm not throwing rocks at the naturalists, but I think they're taking advantage of consumer vulnerability."

21   Disillusioned, we head home to New Jersey and stroll through Stern's one more time. We lie down on all the beds, returning over and over to the Sealy Posturepedic Esquire Firm Plus—exceedingly firm, but with a luscious pillow top. I roll on my side, digging in with my decidedly unbony hip. Jack assumes his usual position, on his back, spreadeagled. I throw an arm across the line into his territory, he crosses his legs into mine.

22   "This is it. This is the bed," he says. "Let's get the king size."

23   "No," I say. "The bedroom's too small. There'd be nothing in the room but bed."

24   "Okay," he sighs.

25   A saleswoman says the list price is $2,000, including box springs with a tension cross bar for improved weight distribution. A sale just ended, she says, "but if you order the bed today, I can sneak it in at $968, including the split queen." Delivery will take about a week; Stern's will throw in a free clock-radio.

26   We tell her we'll think it over and race home to call Dial-A-Mattress. This time, my operator is Anthony. His price: $1,057, including the delivery charge; it's about $90 more than Stern's. "We'll take away your old mattress for free," he says. I am silent. "We have it in stock," he says, lowering his voice an octave. "We can have it for you tonight."

27   The temptation is too great. I rationalize that $90 is a small price to pay for six nights of quality sleep. But I'm too zonked to face immediate delivery. "How about first thing in the morning?"

28   "We'll be there between 8 and 11," he says cheerfully.

29   Immediately, the phone rings: It's Dr. Neil Kavey. While assuring me that there is no medical proof that any type of mattress promotes better sleep than another, he's convinced that a mattress that supports each part of your back makes a critical difference. (He should know: As director of the Sleep Disorders Center at New York's Columbia-Presbyterian Medical Center, he helps over 700 new patients a year get a better night's rest.) "The sleep environment is very important, especially as we get older," says Kavey. "Every year, sleep tends to lighten. We become more sensitive to things that can disturb sleep, like a poor-quality mattress," he says. Size is an important factor: "As a couple gets older, maybe they should get something a little bigger."

30   Kavey might not have hard evidence on this, but Simmons claims to: In 1957, Zalmon Simmons, the company's founder, discovered that the average adult moves between 20 and 45 times per night, which allows each muscle to rest and relax. With couples, there's a phenomenon known as "link movement," familiar to anyone who's ever dodged an elbow jab: One person's moves generally cause the other to readjust, too. Moving a couple to a larger bed reduces their movements by 50 percent and, theoretically, improves their sleep.

31   The Dial-A-Mattress team arrives a few minutes before 8 a.m. the next morning. Within 10 minutes, the new bed is assembled. The old mattress is whisked away.

32   The movers wait for me to test the bed, standing by. I try to ignore them, and lie down to commune with it. I smile blissfully. I roll over, and over again, but I run out of room when I try to roll a third time. I realize my husband and Kavey are right.

33   "Take it back," I say sadly. "I'm sorry, but we should have gotten the king."

34   The two mattress men are stunned—clearly, few people take Dial-A-Mattress at its word. "She wants us to take it back," they keep muttering to one another. Finally, one asks to use the phone. "She wants to talk to you," he says, thrusting the receiver at me.

35 "Hi, this is Donna in customer service," a perky voice says. "What's the problem?"

36 I explain that I should have ordered the bigger bed. "No problem," she says cheerfully. "We'll send you the king."

37 Now I backpedal furiously. While Stern's was about $90 cheaper on the queen, the sale price on the king was more like $200 cheaper. "Well," I say, "It's not just the size that was wrong. It was too . . . high," I add lamely. "I didn't realize how tall the pillow top and frame would make it."

38 "No problem," she says, still cheerful. "The pillow top will settle about an inch, and we can send a low-boy frame—it's four and a half inches instead of seven."

39 I dodge desperately. "Sorry," I say. "I need to ask my husband first."

40 I return to Stern's, order the bed, and resign myself to waiting a week for the bed and the free clock-radio. (We've had to tune ours with a pencil for years.) At last, the day dawns, and with it, a sharp reminder that there's a reason specialty retailers like Dial-A-Mattress flourish while department stores like Stern's are facing hard times: One tiny screw is missing from the frame, and I'm left with an unassembled bed tipped on its end, and our old mattress leaning against the dresser. I call the customer-service department, where I'm promptly told that the only solution is to send me a new frame, which should take about a week.

41 "A week?" I wail. "How are we going to live in a bedroom overflowing with a split-box-spring set, a king-size mattress and the old queen for a week?" The woman answering my call tries four times—unsuccessfully—to transfer me to her supervisor. I wait a half hour, then call again; this operator manages to transfer me to her supervisor after three tries. "Look," I say. "If you can't get this bed assembled, I want it out of here now—I'll just get my bed somewhere else." She says nothing. "I'll call Dial-A-Mattress. *They* know how to deliver beds," I say vindictively. "Fine," she says coolly, "we'll send a truck to take it away this afternoon."

42 Moments later, a man calls from Stern's warehouse. I explain the problem again. "Okay," he says. "I got a couple of guys here—someone will be over to fix it this afternoon. We don't want no animosity." I go out for a quick errand, and when I return, the bed, miraculously, is fully assembled. That night, we fall into bed, and find the comfort disorienting.

43 The next morning, I wake up rested, feeling as if I've been on a long vacation. Our new clock-radio has somehow been tuned to the easy-listening station I hate, but when you feel this good, "Indiana Wants Me" doesn't sound half bad.

❧

Discussion Questions

1. What "kicked the mattress situation into crisis mode" in the Mahoney household?
2. At the outset, what difficulty did the Mahoneys face in coming to a decision on which mattress to buy?
3. What did Mahoney find out about the practice of mattress manufacturers when she tried to compare prices at two stores on the same Sealy mattress?
4. Why did Mahoney change her mind about the bed delivered and installed by Dial-A-Mattress?
*5. When Stern's department store finally delivered a bed, what caused Mahoney to realize that "there's a reason specialty retailers like Dial-A-Mattress flourish while department stores like Stern's are facing hard times"?

Writing Topics

1. Mahoney's prose flashes with a considerable amount of wit. Write a brief analytical essay in which you present and examine a number of the witty passages and venture some generalizations on the nature of her humor. Example (paragraph 1): "I can't say for certain when the bounce went out of our bed, or when the mattress started to resemble a relief map of Death Valley."
2. You have no doubt had at some point in your life an adventure shopping or renting a room or apartment. Write a brief narrative of the problems encountered, the frustrations suffered, and the final outcome. You might also add the lessons learned—if any.

❧"For boredom speaks the language of time,
and it teaches you the most valuable lesson of your life:
the lesson of your utter insignificance."

LISTENING TO BOREDOM

Joseph Brodsky

Joseph Brodsky (1940–1996) was born in Leningrad (now again Saint Petersburg), Russia, and attended schools there until 1956. He began writing poems in 1958 while he worked at various jobs—sailor, photographer, coroner's assistant. Charged with being a "social parasite" in 1964, he was exiled to Siberia for five years of hard labor and was released after some twenty months. In 1972, after being exiled by the Soviet government, he emigrated to the United States and became poet-in-residence at the University of Michigan. He became an American citizen in 1977. His first book of poems was published in the United States in 1965, while he was still in Siberia. His *Selected Poems* appeared in 1973 and *A Part of Speech* in 1979. A volume of his essays, *Less Than One*, appeared in 1986 and received the National Book Award. In 1987, Brodsky was awarded the Nobel Prize for literature. In 1991, he served as Poet Laureate of the United States. "Listening to Boredom" was originally delivered as a commencement address at Dartmouth College and is taken from the March 1995 issue of *Harper's Magazine*.

1   A substantial part of what lies ahead of you is going to be claimed by boredom. The reason I'd like to talk to you about it today, on this lofty occasion, is that I believe no liberal arts college prepares you for that eventuality. Neither the humanities nor science offers courses in boredom. At best, they may acquaint you with the sensation by incurring it. But what is a casual contact to an incurable malaise? The worst monotonous drone coming from a lectern or the most eye-splitting textbook written in turgid English is nothing in comparison to the psychological Sahara that starts right in your bedroom and spurns the horizon.

2   Known under several aliases—anguish, ennui, tedium, the doldrums, humdrum, the blahs, apathy, listlessness, stolidity, lethargy, languor, etc.—boredom

is a complex phenomenon and by and large a product of repetition. It would seem, then, that the best remedy against it would be constant inventiveness and originality. That is what you, young and newfangled, would hope for. Alas, life won't supply you with that option, for life's main medium is precisely repetition.

3   One may argue, of course, that repeated attempts at originality and inventiveness are the vehicle of progress and, in the same breath, civilization. As benefits of hindsight go, however, this one is not the most valuable. For if we divide the history of our species by scientific discoveries, not to mention new ethical concepts, the result will not be very impressive. We'll get, technically speaking, centuries of boredom. The very notion of originality or innovation spells out the monotony of standard reality, of life.

4   The other trouble with originality and inventiveness is that they literally pay off. Provided that you are capable of either, you will become well-off rather fast. Desirable as that may be, most of you know firsthand that nobody is as bored as the rich, for money buys time, and time is repetitive. Assuming that you are not heading for poverty, one can expect your being hit by boredom as soon as the first tools of self-gratification become available to you. Thanks to modern technology, those tools are as numerous as boredom's symptoms. In light of their function — to render you oblivious to the redundancy of time — their abundance is revealing.

5   As for poverty, boredom is the most brutal part of its misery, and escape from it takes more radical forms: violent rebellion or drug addiction. Both are temporary, for the misery of poverty is infinite; both, because of that infinity, are costly. In general, a man shooting heroin into his vein does so largely for the same reason you rent a video: to dodge the redundancy of time. The difference, though, is that he spends more than he's got, and that his means of escaping become as redundant as what he is escaping from faster than yours. On the whole, the difference in tactility between a syringe's needle and a stereo's push button roughly corresponds to the difference between the acuteness of time's impact upon the have-nots and the dullness of its impact on the haves. But, whether rich or poor, you will inevitably be afflicted by monotony. Potential haves, you'll be bored with your work, your friends, your spouses, your lovers, the view from your window, the furniture or wallpaper in your room, your thoughts, yourselves. Accordingly, you'll try to devise ways of escape. Apart from the self-gratifying gadgets I mentioned before, you may take up changing your job, residence, company, country, climate; you may take up promiscuity, alcohol, travel, cooking lessons, drugs, psychoanalysis.

6   In fact, you may lump all these together, and for a while that may work. Until the day, of course, when you wake up in your bedroom amidst a new family and a different wallpaper, in a different state and climate, with a heap of bills from your travel agent and your shrink, yet with the same stale feeling toward the light of day pouring through your window. You'll put on your loafers only to discover that they're lacking bootstraps by which to lift yourself

up from what you recognize. Depending on your temperament and your age, you will either panic or resign yourself to the familiarity of the sensation, or else you'll go through the rigmarole of change once more. Neurosis and depression will enter your lexicon; pills, your medicine cabinet.

7　　Basically, there is nothing wrong with turning life into the constant quest for alternatives, into leapfrogging jobs, spouses, and surroundings, provided that you can afford the alimony and jumbled memories. This predicament, after all, has been sufficiently glamorized onscreen and in Romantic poetry. The rub, however, is that before long this quest turns into a full-time occupation, with your need for an alternative coming to match a drug addict's daily fix.

8　　There is yet another way out of boredom, however. Not a better one, perhaps, from your point of view, and not necessarily secure, but straight and inexpensive. When hit by boredom, let yourself be crushed by it: submerge, hit bottom. In general, with things unpleasant, the rule is: The sooner you hit bottom, the faster you surface. The idea here is to exact a full look at the worst. The reason boredom deserves such scrutiny is that it represents pure, undiluted time in all its repetitive, redundant, monotonous splendor.

9　　Boredom is your window on the properties of time that one tends to ignore to the likely peril of one's mental equilibrium. It is your window on time's infinity. Once this window opens, don't try to shut it; on the contrary, throw it wide open. For boredom speaks the language of time, and it teaches you the most valuable lesson of your life: the lesson of your utter insignificance. It is valuable to you, as well as to those you are to rub shoulders with. "You are finite," time tells you in the voice of boredom, "and whatever you do is, from my point of view, futile." As music to your ears, this, of course, may not count; yet the sense of futility, of the limited significance of even your best, most ardent actions, is better than the illusion of their consequences and the attendant self-aggrandizement.

10　　For boredom is an invasion of time into your set of values. It puts your existence into its proper perspective, the net result of which is precision and humility. The former, it must be noted, breeds the latter. The more you learn about your own size, the more humble and the more compassionate you become to your likes, to the dust aswirl in a sunbeam or already immobile atop your table.

11　　If it takes will-paralyzing boredom to bring your insignificance home, then hail the boredom. You are insignificant because you are finite. Yet infinity is not terribly lively, not terribly emotional. Your boredom, at least, tells you that much. And the more finite a thing is, the more it is charged with life, emotions, joy, fears, compassion.

12　　What's good about boredom, about anguish and the sense of meaninglessness of your own, of everything else's existence, is that it is not a deception. Try to embrace, or let yourself be embraced by, boredom and anguish, which are larger than you anyhow. No doubt you'll find that bosom smothering, yet try to endure it as long as you can, and then some more. About all, don't think you've goofed somewhere along the line, don't try to retrace your steps to correct the error. No, as W. H. Auden said, "Believe your pain." This awful bear hug is no mistake. Nothing that disturbs you ever is.

ह

Discussion Questions

1. Brodsky lists "several aliases" for boredom in paragraph 2, "anguish, ennui, tedium, the doldrums, humdrum, the blahs, apathy, listlessness, stolidity, lethargy, languor, etc." Why does Brodsky use the term *aliases* rather than *synonyms*?

2. What does Brodsky mean in paragraph 3 when he writes, "For if we divide the history of our species by scientific discoveries, not to mention new ethical concepts, the result will not be very impressive"?

*3. Brodsky opens paragraph 4, "The other trouble with originality and inventiveness is that they literally pay off." What is the *first* trouble Brodsky assumes you know, and why does Brodsky consider it another "trouble" that "originality and inventiveness . . . literally pay off"?

4. In paragraph 5, what does Brodsky mean when he writes, "In general, a man shooting heroin into his vein does so largely for the same reason you rent a video: to dodge the redundancy of time"?

*5. In paragraphs 4–7, Brodsky discusses the responses to boredom by the "haves" and the "have-nots." How are their responses different and how are they alike?

*6. Brodsky refers to "another way out of boredom" in paragraph 8. What is it? Explain.

*7. Explain Brodsky's meaning in paragraph 10 when he writes, "The more you learn about your own size, the more humble and the more compassionate you become to your likes, to the dust aswirl in a sunbeam or already immobile atop your table."

Writing Topics

1. In paragraph 11, Brodsky says that boredom brings home to us our insignificance, our finiteness, "And the more finite a thing is, the more it is charged with life, emotions, joy, fears, compassion." In a brief philosophical/argumentative essay, show why you agree or disagree with his idea of "boredom" and the good it does by teaching us our own insignificance.

2. In "A Psalm of Life," Henry Wadsworth Longfellow writes, "Life is real! Life is earnest! / And the grave is not its goal; / Dust thou art, to dust returnest, / Was not spoken of the soul." Write an essay in which you consider Longfellow's view in light of Brodsky's essay. (You might want to look up the whole of the Longfellow poem.) In your conclusion, set forth your own views on the questions raised.

"I think slavery was a mighty bad thing,
though it's been no bed of roses since,
but then no one could whip me no more."

SLAVERY WAS A MIGHTY BAD THING

Jacob Manson (as edited by Belinda Hurmence)

Jacob Manson's "Slavery Was a Mighty Bad Thing" is reprinted from *My Folks Don't Want Me to Talk about Slavery: Twenty-One Oral Histories of Former North Carolina Slaves*, edited by Belinda Hurmence and published in 1984. It was named the Best Adult Book for Young Adult Readers in 1990. Jacob Manson was eighty-six years old when he was interviewed in Raleigh, North Carolina, by T. Pat Matthews in the late 1930s (probably 1937). Slavery was abolished at the end of the Civil War (1861–1865). Thus, the period Manson is recalling lies some sixty-five years or so in his past, when he was between ten and fifteen years old. As he indicates, he "belonged to" a plantation owner in Warren County, North Carolina. He married around 1881, some twenty-five years after he had been freed, and had six sons and three daughters. At the time he was interviewed, his wife, one son, and two daughters were still alive.

Editor Belinda Hurmence, as a biographical note says, "was born in Oklahoma, raised in Texas, and educated at the University of Texas [graduated 1942] and Columbia University [studies in creative writing, 1946–1948]." She has served in editorial positions on *Mademoiselle* and *Flair* and has held appointments teaching creative writing at a number of institutions. She has written novels for young people, one of which, *A Girl Called Boy*, won the Parents' Choice Award as well as the NCTE Teachers' Choice Award. Her editions of other oral histories of slaves include *Before Freedom: When I Can Just Remember* (1988) and *We Lived in the Little Cabin in the Yard* (1988). A primary source for her work has been the recorded interviews with former slaves conducted under the auspices of the Federal Writers' Project, a New Deal program implemented by President Roosevelt during the

Great Depression to give jobs to unemployed writers. Over two thousand oral histories of former slaves were recorded from 1936 to 1938 and deposited in the Library of Congress. Facsimile copies were published in 1941 (reprinted in 1972) in nineteen volumes under the title *The American Slave: A Composite Biography*. In her editing, Hurmence omitted material that appeared repetitive or hearsay and corrected dialect spelling to enhance readability.

1   I belonged to Colonel Bun Eden. His plantation was in Warren County, and he owned about fifty slaves or more. There was so many of them there he did not know all his own slaves.

2   Our cabins was built of poles and had stick-and-dirt chimneys, one door, and one little window at the back end of the cabin. Some of the houses had dirt floors. Our clothing was poor and homemade.

3   Many of the slaves went bareheaded and barefooted. Some wore rags around their heads, and some wore bonnets. We had poor food, and the young slaves was fed out of troughs. The food was put in a trough, and the little niggers gathered around and et. The chillun was looked after by the old slave women who were unable to work in the fields, while the mothers of the babies worked. The women plowed and done other work as the men did. No books or learning of any kind was allowed. No prayer meetings was allowed, but we sometimes went to the white folks' church. They told us to obey our marsters and be obedient at all times.

4   When bad storms come, they let us rest, but they kept us in the fields so long sometimes that the storm caught us before we could get to the cabins. Niggers watched the weather in slavery time, and the old ones was good at prophesying the weather.

5   Marster lived in the great house. He did not do any work but drank a lot of whiskey, went dressed up all the time, and had niggers to wash his feet and comb his hair. He made me scratch his head when he lay down, so he could go to sleep. When he got to sleep, I would slip out. If he waked up when I started to leave, I would have to go back and scratch his head till he went to sleep again. Sometimes I had to fan the flies away from him while he slept.

6   Marster would not have any white overseers. He had nigger foremen. Ha! Ha! He liked some of the nigger womens too good to have any other white man playing around them. He had his sweethearts among his slave women. I ain't no man for telling false stories. I tells the truth, and that is the truth. At that time, it was a hard job to find a marster that didn't have women among his slaves. That was a general thing among the slave owners. One of the slave girls on a plantation near us went to her missus and told her about her marster forcing her to let him have something to do with her, and her missus told her, "Well, go on, you belong to him."

7   A lot of the slave owners had certain strong, healthy slave men to serve the slave women. Generally they give one man four women, and that man better not have nothing to do with the other women, and the women better not have nothing to do with other men.

8   We worked all day and some of the night, and a slave who made a week, even after doing that, was lucky if he got off without getting a beating. We got mighty bad treatment, and I just want to tell you, a nigger didn't stand as much show there as a dog did. They whipped for most any little trifle. They whipped me, so they said, just to help me get a quicker gait.

9   The pattyrollers come sneaking around often and whipped niggers on Marster's place. They nearly killed my uncle. They broke his collarbone when they was beating him, and Marster made them pay for it 'cause Uncle never did get over it.

10   One morning the dogs begun to bark, and in a few minutes the plantation was covered with Yankees. They told us we was free. They asked me where Marster's things was hid. I told them I could not give up Marster's things. They told me I had no marster, that they had fighted four years to free us and that Marster would not whip me no more. Marster sent to the fields and had all the slaves to come home. He told me to tell them not to run but to fly to the house at once. All plowhands and women come running home. The Yankees told all of them they was free.

11   Marster offered some of the Yankees something to eat in his house, but they would not eat cooked food, they said they wanted to cook their own food.

12   After the war, I farmed around, one plantation to another. I have never owned a home of my own. When I got too old to work, I come and lived with my married daughter in Raleigh. I been here four years.

13   I think slavery was a mighty bad thing, though it's been no bed of roses since, but then no one could whip me no more.

🐚

Discussion Questions

1. In accord with Manson, describe the cabins the slaves lived in, the clothes they wore, the food they ate, the books and papers they were given to read, and the churches they attended.

2. Why did Manson's "Marster" use black overseers rather than white? Describe his relationship with his female slaves.

3. Describe the system of punishment for the slaves.

4. How did Manson and his master react when the Yankees arrived to free the slaves?

*5. How did Manson fare after he was freed?

Writing Topics

1. Write a brief character sketch of Manson from what you can glean of his character, his wit, his wisdom, his interests, and his philosophy of life from his oral history.
2. Many abolitionists believed that slavery was not only immoral and unjust, but that it also degraded the slave owners, the institution of slavery holding them and their slaves in a kind of mutual bondage. One poet, James Jeffrey Roche, wrote, "The blow that liberates the slave / But sets the master free." Assuming that Manson's description of the slaves' and master's lives and behavior is generally valid, write an essay agreeing or disagreeing with the abolitionist view as expressed in the Roche lines.

❧"Yeah, the years don' stop now, they roll around.
Sure do. One year roll round,
an here come another one agin!"

I DONE WORKED!

Lottie Jackson (as told to Sherry Thomas)

The source for "I Done Worked!" is We Didn't Have Much, But We Sure Had Plenty: Stories of Rural Women by Sherry Thomas, which was published in 1981. As we learn from her oral history, Lottie Jackson believes herself to be well along in her seventies. She never attended school but worked as a field hand virtually her entire life, from the time she was raised by her aunt until she was on her own, during her marriage to Richard Jackson and throughout his bout with cancer, and after his death. At the time she was interviewed, the farm where she had worked for many years had been sold, and she found herself worrying about where she was going to live.

Oral historian/editor Sherry Thomas was born in Georgia in 1948 and attended Brown University (1966–1969). She became a contributor to feminist publications and, with Jeanne Tetrault, founded the magazine Country Women. Together they published Country Women: Handbook for the New Farmer (1976). She set out from her sheep farm in California in 1978 to explore "the state of farms and farming, of communities and families, of traditional women's lives," gathering the oral histories and photographs she published in We Didn't Have Much, But We Sure Had Plenty.

1   I been out all day planting watermelon vines. Lord, if I didn' work I couldn't make it. No, if I didn' work, I'd jus die! I been workin ever day, *ever* day, in those big fields by myself. I *like* to work. I jus *want* to work, cause that keep me goin. I be jus settin round, I get so *stiff*, you know. I walked through the fields, worked out there every day, workin for Mr. John, you know. Yes suh, I been here ever since forty, right here on this place. Been here ever since forty! Been a *long* time. Came here young and done got old.

2   An I tole Mr. John, he better *not* throw me away! I done *raised* his chillun that's got grown and gone away. I said, "Now you better see bout me!"

3   An he say, "Lottie, I'm gonna see bout ya."

4   I said, "I knowed it cause if you don', I'm a-comin to your house! You ain't gettin rid of Lottie!"

5   An he jus laughed. "Lottie, we ain't gonna throw you away."

6   "You better not, cause I'm almos one of the family, I'm one *in* the family!" That what I tell him.

7   I hate movin so *bad!* But he say, "Lottie, I cain't help it, I had to do it."

8   It got confused in the famly some way. I tole him he ought've looked out for us, though, he ought've leaved a space for us. I ain't goin to no town, not Dawson an not Americus, neither! An I cain't find me no house, cause they ain't no houses, ain't no house cause people is tearin 'em down soon's as people move out. I got to try to get me a trailer house or somethin. Somethin to live in. There ain't no houses.

9   Lord, I don' like no town, for sure I don'! I like to stay out where I can get *somptin* fer nothin! I kin go to somebody's house they give me some greens, peas, anything. If I go to town, I got to go to the market. Town ain't no place to live!

10   I fish a lot, I sure do. How come I goin to miss this place, we got a lot of fishin on this place. An I hate to leave here, on account of that fishin. I like to fish! There's a heap of dams down there where the beavers done dammed and jus left a little stream, made ponds out of it. I go from one pond to another, I catch 'em, I sure do! Trout, bass, catfish, all kinds!

11   Oooh, I had one of the purrtiest gardens. But I don' have one now. See, I didn' know where I was gonna be. See, I'd've had this place cleaned up all the way around, but I let it growed up cause I didn' know *where* I was gonna be. My garden, I jus let it growed up. I grow beans, greens, peas, everthing like that. Oh, I have plenty of flowers in my yard, all kind of flowers in my yard.

12   Irene older than I am, I know that. I was born in Calhoun County but I don't know when I was born. Don't even know my mama because she died in chil'bed. Didn't never even see my mama. I had one brother, he die when I be a little thing like that; an one sister, she died year before last. Ain't nobody left but me. My aunt, one of my aunts, raised me. Didn't know my dad till I was bout grown! Sure didn't. Sure *didn't!*

13   Our aunt raised us. Not my brother, he died when us wasn't but little things. He was older than us. He had a *heap* of sense, you know. An he went over to fix the cane mill, they had a cane mill what had stopped, you know; and it caught him and it broke his neck.

14   My aunt had some more chilrun, you know, what their parents had died and she was raisin them with us. She didn't have none of her own. She had a husband that died; she were a widda. Her good. She was *good* to us. She was on her own place, she had hands workin for her, an a big old stove. She took care of us good. Dad, he'd come for us, but she'd tell us that wadn't our daddy, you know. Us'd run from him, us'd *run* from him! She did that to keep our daddy from gittin us, you know, and us didn' know no better, us'd jus *run* from him.

15   When I were at my aunt's, I jes worked in the field. Worked in the fields! Didn't get time to go to school fer in the fields! Yeah'm that what I did, work in the fields or in da house. Weren't nothin to do in the fields, then I were in the house. You go on in there, an they put you to work. I growed up workin, growed *up* workin! Sure did.

16   No'm they never tell me how old I was. Wouldn't tell you cause they think that make you grown! No, they sure wouldn't. Didn't do nothin but work ye, sure would work ye now. I'm *glad* they did it. I'm glad of it. Sure 'nough. Made me willin to do it right on.

17   Now my sista, she wasn't much of a worker, an I'd work hard, you know. I work hard enough fer her, where her wouldn't get a whuppin! She was older than I was, an I'd work *hard*. I'd show up right smart, you know, to keep her from a-whuppin us. My sista cared that they whup her, but she jest a slow worker, couldn't work much. She scared of a whupping but she couldn't make work. I'd ruther be like I am.

18   Irene sure had a hard life. I didn't have it hard like she did. I have worked *hard*, but she have done some things *I* didn' do.

19   When I were a little girl, I were choppin cotton, pickin cotton, all of that. Tha's right. First of the year, start plowin, pickin them old stalks, pilin them up. You didn' have no time for sittin around! Sure didn'. Ooooh girl, you better get up afore the sun rise, better get on out there afore the sun be up, or she be there with a strap. Yes ma'am! You better get up. Yes ma'am, you *better* get out of that bed! I'd wake up and wake the others up. She'd fix a breakfast for us, and she'd have that breakfast ready where we could hit the field. Soon's we was done, we had to git on. Sure did! They jes tell me what they want done. I never was hard to learn nothin. They tell me or show me *one* time, that be it, I'd do it.

20   We didn' have no birthdays, none of that, just "Go to the field!" No, we didn' know nothin bout birthdays! Christmas they bring us a little Santa Claus at night, give you an apple or orange, little candy, somptin like that. Bake a little cake, or somptin. Chillun gettin so much now, they don' want *this* an they don' want *that*, they kin get anything they want! Us was glad to git a biscuit on Sunday mornin!

21   An I done some of everthing in the field that could be done. I done plowed. Me an my huband, we worked that farm up there, just me an him. An I worked! I'd help him plow an he'd help me hoe. And come time together, we'd get our supper ourself. An then get out and help the other. Plowin with mules. We were sharecroppin. That where my huband died, up there. I think my huband died in . . . fifty-two . . . fifty-three! That right, he died in fifty-three. An I didn' have not nair a chile, not nair a one. Sure didn't.

22   I left my aunt's house after I married. I don' know how old I was. Round fifteen, sixteen year old, I think. I think I were that old cause they wouldn't let you marry along then fore you got old enough, you know. Chillun nowadays, they don' marry, they jus shack up together, they don' marry no more! Now an then, you find one that will marry, but mos they jest git together an say, "That

my huband, that my wife." But you had to *marry* along in then. I think it better to get married.

23   You ask what'd I *do* when I got married!? Worked a farm! I moved to a place, jes me and my huband. An Lord, I jes work, work, work, work. I work harder here though, than I did then. I done some WORK on this place. An I wud be doin it now, if Mr. John be farmin it still! I'd be in the fields right now, sure I would. All over this place, I worked jus by myself. Nobody wif me. He'd come back and forth, see if nothin got at me. I'd be workin way out back and he'd come ever night an see if anything got me! He'd tell me what to do, but a heap a time, I'd tell him. "This place need to be worked, Mr. John."

24   "Well, Lottie, go ahead and do it," he'd say.

25   I never drove no tractor, I wished I'd've but if I did, I wudn't know how to turn it around! I tole him, "Mr. John, jus learn me how to turn it around, I'll drive it!" But he never did learn me. I hated fer the mules to go. I hated that. I like mules. I wanted to go *fast*. I wanted a fast mule, I didn't want no mule draggin. I wanted one gotta *go* when I went.

26   An I liked to shake peanuts an pick cotton. I liked-ed that. I put peanuts up, fast as my huband could plow them up. He'd get mad an take out the mule an go to the house! He wanted me to be slow where he could help shake some. He mad, he *mad*! Sure was!

27   I love to cook. I likes to cook, if I gots somethin to cook, I likes to do it. My huband cooked when I be workin sometimes. When we got through with our farmin, he wouldn't want me to go out nowhere an work. But I'd go out anyhow, an he'd stay home, look out for the cows and cook! I'd work and he'd fuss . . . you know, I'd work my farm, then I'd go out an work, but he'd stay home and cook. He'd say when I done did my work, I ought to stay home an rest. But I'd go work an help other folks. Sometime he'd go, an most time he wudn't.

28   I worked, you *know* I worked. I'd plow an I'd plant. Get done plantin, it be hoein time. Yes sir, I done some work. And I still would be, followin them tractors, handin seed, *everthing*.

29   Them tractors put a lot of folks out of work. It were a bad time. Don't know what gonna happen to us now either, I jus don' know! Lately now, I been figurin maybe they fixin to put us in *slavery times* agin!

30   You cain't get this an you cain't get that. No work, an no houses, no gas, *nothin*. Food up yonder so high you cain't buy it. I jus don' know what gonna happen. Ever year but this, I growed my food, but this year everthing done turned around. I don' have a garden cause I didn' know where I was gonna be. I jus don' know what we goin to do! I ain't hear none of 'em talk bout slavery times lately, but I think on it.

31   It sure was worser in slavery times! In my times, we wudn't make much, but we'd get some, sure would! Maybe two hundred dollars fer the whole year. But fer us, that'd be—you know, when I first came here on this place, they weren't givin but fifty cent a day. An my huband were gittin sixty cent. He got

sixty cause he was a man, I reckon, and I were a lady. An I worked harder than him, cause he couldn't work like me. That right! Sure did seem wrong to me, but I jus couldn't do no better. I hear some of 'em say they work for a quarter a day. I ain't never worked for no twenty-five cent a day, but I hear some of these folk round here say they *have* worked for twenty-five cents a day!

32 An I'm talkin bout you had to go to the field before sunup an work till the *bell* rang, an go back at one o'clock an work till *dark*. That right! For that money! Fifty cent! An come back an wash, an cook, an all that in the dark.

33 One time, my huband an me, we was with some white people wouldn't give us nothin. Was *worthless* folk, an wouldn't give us nothin. We couldn't hardly git somptin to eat. So we moved over here. We stayed at that other place two years. Sure did. Cause we couldn't git nothin, we moved over here. I had knowed bout this place fore we came here. When we was down at them white folks, we'd visit some people, that stayed over here. So that how we knowed bout this place an we moved on over here. Been here ever since. I stayed here till my huband died, and I'm *still* here. Done pretty good on this place.

34 My huband had cancer. He was sick about two year. Sure was. Ooooh Lord, like to have bout worked me to *death!* I had to see bout him, an work that crop, an I had two mules, and four or five head of cows to see bout. You know, people'd come over there an help me wid him; Irene an them, they help me wid him. I had to keep a fire goin, you know, all day long, an I jus bout cleaned up them woods up there cuttin wood! To keep him warm. When some of them be there wif him, I'd go cut wood.

35 An he'd tell me, "Honey, I ain't gonna hurt right now, you kin go ahead an do what you gotta do. I ain't gonna hurt right now."

36 So, I'd get out an go do, an run back. I'd work out in the field an jus run back see bout him, sure would! When he went down, I worked, sure 'nough, cause I had *all* it to do! The cows an the mules, an seein bout him. His name Richard Jackson, but everbody called him Shorty. He bout a high as Irene. But he weren't little, he were stout!

37 My life didn' change much after he were gone. I got on just bout as good as when he was livin.

38 I couldn't do without my huband, you know, cause he was *good* to me. But I wouldn't have nair an un now! Uh uh, I'm doin *too* good!

39 You know, the Lord is removing the men, cause they ain't no good. More men die than the women, cause they ain't no good! Sure does! Why I coulda married the next week after my huband had died. The next *week*, they talkin bout marryin me! They knowed I was a hard worker an they thought I might take care of 'em! But I didn't want none of 'em! NOOOOOO! My huband been gone all that long, an I ain't married yet. An I'm doin all right. But my huband was good to me, sure was.

40 I never liked frolickin like Irene did. No, I *never* liked that. I always been *old*, all of my days! Yeah, my sista was fast, like Rene. She'd get mad, you know, if I wudn't go out with her.

41   She'd tell me, "You'm too *slow!*"

42   "Yeah, I aim to be here a *long* time slow!"

43   I took care of myself, sure did. After my huband died, my sista and her fella'd come here trying to take me out. But I wudn't come out the door. I wudn't run my life out, uh uh! Got to take *care* of myself! I ain't missed a thing, not nothin. My sista's dead and *gone* now an I'm still right here.

44   Irene, she still here, but she ain't no *good* fer anything. She *here* all right. She can do her work round the house an everthing, she might could do a little work in the field maybe, but it wouldn't be much. Rene want to do, and she sure got the will. She sure do got the *will*. She ain't lazed up a bit. But sometime she cain't, cause she be hurtin. I know she older than I am. An I is old, I'm pushin well on over seventy. I is *old*.

45   I seen some young people look older than I do! Young folk! Look older than I do! This day, OLD women look better than the chillun. Some of these old folk that got grown chillun look better than the chillun, that right! You know, I be *thankful* that I'm old an can be doin anything that I've been doin. I'm thankful! I do the *same* work I ever done. I thank the Lord for bein old an doin what I want to do!

46   Plenty old ones and plenty young ones cain't do nothin. Everthing I ever done, I still do now: cut wood, tote wood, work in the field, tote them big buckets ever day, time I put the buckets down, I got to hoe, hoe this big place, just me, that's right, fillin up them big tractors with peanuts an gettin them things. Big five-gallon buckets full of peanuts, one in each hand, and all them boys be turnin them big tractors, "All right, come on!" An I got to be right there with 'em.

47   I work ever day *now*. I work wif a man that go round an hire hands, you know. He hires hands an tell you what place to work. The man pay us eighteen dollar a day. Some works by the hour, different places, but he just pay so much a day. We go to the field at eight ever day and work till eleven, an then we go back at one-thirty an work till six after noon. Not bad pay, when I have worked for fifty cent a day!

48   But I cain't work much an get my Social Security. They don' like you to be workin. I kin make more money workin than I kin on Social Security. Sure! See, if I were on Social Security they don' pay but once a month an I can get money ever day workin!

49   Yeah, that Mr. John, he a good one. He look out for me. I said to his boy, I said to Mr. Dave, "If I get where I cain't do nothin, you better see bout me! I done set up wif you all day an all night when you was a little bitty thing, couldn't do nothin. An you better see bout me now!"

50   I bathed them chillun, bathed 'em an put 'em to bed! I set up there with 'em all night. Mr. John and them be gone, an I set up there *all* night till he come back, till *day* the next morning. An them chillun are bout grown now.

51   Yeah, the years don' stop now, they roll around. Sure do. One year roll round, an here come another one agin! An still here, thank the Lord! Yes sir, I been here with these people a *long* time!

❧

Discussion Questions

1. In the opening of the essay, Jackson expresses her attitude toward work. What is it? Does it change in the course of the interview or remain the same? Explain.
2. How does Jackson view her relationship with Mr. John and his son Mr. Dave?
3. Does Jackson prefer to live in the country or in town? What does she cite as the advantages of her choice?
*4. In paragraphs 12–20, Jackson recalls growing up. What kind of family life did she have, and what does she remember of her close relatives?
5. When Jackson married, what kind of arrangement did she and her husband make about household chores and working? Explain.
6. What reasons does Jackson give for not remarrying?
*7. In paragraph 48, Jackson says, "But I cain't work much an get my Social Security. They don' like you to be workin. I kin make more money workin than I kin on Social Security. Sure! See, if I were on Social Security they don' pay but once a month an I can get money ever day workin!" Explain Jackson's meaning. What does her statement reveal about her?

Writing Topics

1. Jackson says in the final paragraph, "Yeah, the years don' stop now, they roll around. Sure do. One year roll round, an here come another one agin! An still here, thank the Lord! Yes sir, I been here with these people a *long* time!" Find other poetic passages in the essay that have similar effect and write an analytical essay exploring the sources of the effect of her poetic style of speech.
2. Jackson observes in paragraph 29, "Them tractors put a lot of folks out of work. It were a bad time. Don't know what gonna happen to us now either, I jus don' know! Lately now, I been figurin maybe they fixin to put us in *slavery times* again!" Although Jackson never went to school, she is clearly a perceptive observer, and her essay is filled with an authentic folk wisdom, as in the example quoted. Find other such examples and write an essay setting forth Jackson's view of the world, human behavior, male-female relationships , male-female differences, human destiny—and anything else you find significant.

"Whenever I was a boy growing up
I wanted to go in the mines more than anything.
That's all I lived for;
that's all a person could [live for] back then."

COAL DUST IN YOUR BLOOD

Milburn Jackson (as told to Laurel Shackelford and Bill Weinberg)

Our Appalachia: An Oral History, edited by Laurel Shackelford and Bill Weinberg and published in 1977, is the source for "Coal Dust in Your Blood." Appalachia is a region covered by the Appalachian Mountains running through several eastern states of the United States—the whole of West Virginia and portions of New York, Pennsylvania, Ohio, Maryland, Kentucky, Virginia, Tennessee, North Carolina, South Carolina, Alabama, and Georgia. The coal fields of the region flourished during World War II, but employment declined drastically during the 1950s with the introduction of the "continuous miner," or mechanized mining, enabling companies to produce more coal more efficiently with far fewer workers. Milburn Jackson, from a coal-mining family, worked in the mines throughout the period of radical change. He describes the problems of miners adjusting to working "as the machine tells you." He was living in Cranes Nest, Virginia, when his oral history was recorded.

The editors of Our Appalachia say in their introduction, "The impetus of this book grew out of the need for a social history of Central Appalachia. It has provided the opportunity to let residents of the region tell their own story—an opportunity they have seldom had. It presents the struggles and the joys, the high points and the low, the strengths and the weaknesses of being part of America's largest geographically contiguous subculture." The interviews for the oral histories were collected over a period of five years, beginning in 1971, by students of four schools (public and private) located in Appalachia and participating in the Appalachian Oral History Project. In 1973, the editors of Our Appalachia began sifting through the thousands of oral histories collected for those to be published in their book.

1   I don't believe that a person who works in the coal mines is any more endangered than my wife sitting there on the porch. The whole house could fall in on her. I would say that a person is about as safe in a coal mine as [he is working] in a garage checking automobiles because there is a lot more men working in the coal mines than there would be in any garage. There are a lot of people who get killed in garages and there are a lot of people who get killed in the mines.

2   I never worry about slate falls, which happen every day, but one thing that I would be worried about is insufficient air. I know what smothering [is like], buddy, for I've had asthma ever since I was about four years old. I believe I would rather a rock mash me up and kill me instantly than to cut air off of me and make me smother. I would wake up a lot of times in the morning fighting and slinging my arms because I'm smothering. A person that has never smothered don't know what a feeling that is. There is a health hazard in the coal mines: you ain't got sufficient air and that causes lung trouble, you get rock dust. That's why I hope and pray nary one of my kids will go into the mines [but] they probably will.

3   In certain ways I think [the new machinery] is a great improvement; on the other hand, it has cut a lot of poor laboring men out of work. In the [mechanized] mines you have to work as the machine tells you. Every day that you go in there, you're in danger, you have got to stay one step ahead of [the machine]. In West Virginia forty or fifty people were killed. Some people say, "It will never happen to us over here." It could happen here just as it could happen in West Virginia. If that rock has a certain time to fall, it's got no special person. I don't believe that a person has got a time to be called. I do believe if you'll take safety precautions and watch yourself you can prevent that. A lot of people say you can't keep death from slipping up on you, but you *can* shorten your days. If a person will watch hisself and see that he is safe he will never die in the coal mines. You've got to respect [the mine] and not be afraid of it. Fear in a coal mine is one of the biggest dangers. If you get scared in a coal mine [while] driving cars and look up, you'll kill yourself or kill somebody else.

4   I've always wanted to work in the mines and I'll be in the mines for the rest of my life. Whenever I was a boy growing up I wanted to go in the mines more than anything. That's all I lived for; that's all a person could [live for] back then.

5   *In other words, once coal dust gets in your blood you can't get it out?*

6   That's right. I believe that with all my heart. I can't stand that hot sun. When I come in from work I don't set foot in the garden until that sun has gone down on the other side of the mountain. It burns me up. I sweat in the house. If you change jobs you'll sweat. If I change from one side of the machine to the other, I'll sweat and burn up. If I get back on that other side of the machine, I don't sweat.

7   One time I was working in the mines and a [boss] hired a colored person to work with me and I had knowed the colored boy all of my life. It wasn't long after that until I got me a different job with more money. [In] about three or four weeks [the boss] come back up and said, "Jackson, if you will come back to work for me I'll fire every damn Nigger on the job."

8   He thought I quit because he had hired that colored feller, but I would just as soon work with a colored feller as anybody. I said, "Lordy have mercy, that's the furthest thing from my mind. I would just as soon work with him as with my twin brother as far as that's concerned," which I would because I was in there to make a living, not to take partiality on no man. I said, "I ain't coming back because I am working for more money." If a colored person is a friend to you, he's a friend to you. Our neighbors right around us here is a lot worse than a colored person as far as the friendly part. There's some of them that won't even speak to you. If you speak to them, they'll drop their damn lip down to their ankles and walk off.

9   I've had some dreams, some awful dreams, about coal mines and I've told my wife that I would give anything not to go to work. I've dreamed that nothing would happen to me, but I would be digging my buddies out from under a rock fall. You talk about something that would really hurt, that would.

10   *Do you ever stay home from work after a dream like that?*

11   No, I never have; I'll tell you the reason why. If I was there maybe I could help him if it did happen. When I got that finger cut off that about drove me crazy. That's the worse I was ever hurt in the coal mines. I got that finger cut off the twenty-sixth day of January [1963]. The third day of February those guys got killed [in the mine where I was working] and I was off with my finger. I went to the doctor that day and here come Jimmy, my brother, and told me about the fall. I didn't know whether [Little] Bud was killed or not. He's my twin brother. I couldn't get no information nowhere. I was walking the floors. I took off and went to the mines. I don't guess there was a prouder person ever walked up in front of a mines [than I was] when I saw Bud standing there. I would have give a hundred dollars to have been in there when it happened to find out what was going on. I couldn't have stopped it but I would have knowed what was happening.

ʖᵁ

Discussion Questions

1. In the opening paragraph, Jackson seems to deny that the mines were very dangerous, "I don't believe that a person who works in the coal mines is any more endangered than my wife sitting there on the porch." What do we discover later that seems to suggest a different attitude?

*2. In paragraph 2, Jackson reveals his primary fear about working in the mines. What was this fear, and why did he have it?

3. Has mechanization made the mines safer? Explain.

4. What does the incident described in paragraphs 7–8, involving Jackson's working with an African American, show about Jackson's racial feelings and his humanity?

5. What was Jackson's recurring dream and how did it affect him?

*6. When Jackson was forced to take hospital leave from his work, what happened in the mines? What do we learn about Jackson by his behavior in this episode?

Writing Topics

1. Write a brief character sketch of Jackson as you have come to know him from his oral history, supporting your points by reference to the text. What are his main traits of character, and how would you summarize him as a family man as well as a man of the community?

2. Jackson describes two recurring dreams (or nightmares) that he has, one that he is smothering, the other that he is digging in the mines for his buddies. Both have some clear relationship to his working life. Reflect on your own dreams, especially any nightmares that frighten you. Write an essay in which you explore your own dream psyche, describing as vividly as you can your recurring dreams and what you make of them as related to your waking world.

Summary Writing Topics

1. Write an essay in which you compare and contrast the human values found in Lars Eighner's "On Dumpster Diving" (as reflected in his concept, paragraph 67, of "the rat-race millions who nightly scavenge the cable channels looking for they know not what") and Joseph Brodsky's "Listening to Boredom" (as suggested by his paragraph 11, "And the more finite a thing is, the more it is charged with life, emotions, joy, fears, compassion").

2. Lars Eighner's essay presents a rather comprehensive picture of the life of college students. Describe the college life he depicts and, according to your college experience, indicate where you believe him to be wrong and where right. In your conclusion, assess the validity of the picture he draws of college life.

3. Joseph Brodsky, in paragraph 5 of "Listening to Boredom," says "whether rich or poor, you will inevitably be afflicted by monotony." The poor he sees turning to violence and drugs, the rich to devising "ways of escape" through change. Adopt the point of view of Sarah Mahoney in "Going to the Mattresses," Lottie Jackson in "I Done Worked!" or Dennis Smith in "Report from Engine Co. 82" and write an essay showing how Brodsky is wrong, that one can be absorbed in ordinary life or work and be relieved of boredom.

4. In an argumentative essay, indicate whether you agree or disagree with Joseph Brodsky's views on boredom and support your position by reference to your own experience.

5. Jacob Manson ("Slavery Was a Mighty Bad Thing") and Lottie Jackson ("I Done Worked!") represent two accounts of black experience during two very different periods of U.S. history. Write an essay comparing and contrasting the two essays, showing how there are both differences and similarities in the experiences related. In your conclusion, you might want to make some comparisons of their accounts with the kinds of experiences African Americans have today.

6. Assume that you have applied for a job and have been asked to write a letter describing what kind of activity during a full day of work you would find both challenging and absorbing. Consider whether you would like to sit at a desk most of the day, involved with the keeping of records of some kind; or to move about, encountering others related to your enterprise; or to go on frequent business trips; or to go from house to house talking with potential customers; or to sit in meetings and make reports; and so on. In short, describe your ideal workday.

7. You have probably had enough experience doing chores and odd jobs, working for short periods during summer or at part-time jobs during school. Write an essay presenting an account of your work

experience, both "amateur" and professional, indicating how you made a difference or a contribution through your work and how the experience in turn helped to shape you. For example, did you learn any skills you did not know you had? Did you discover that some skills do not interest you at all?

8. Assume that you learn of a family having difficulties with neighbors over noise like Ruth Sidransky's in "Stop Your Infernal Noise". You want to give the family the Sidransky piece. Write a letter to accompany the essay, pointing out how you think the family might find it useful or even valuable.

9. Find an older relative or neighbor who has been a "manual laborer"—that is, made his or her living by working with his or her hands in the coal mines, in the oil fields, in a moving and hauling business, or in any job that required a lot of muscle and sweat. Using the essays by Milburn Jackson ("Coal Dust in Your Blood") and Lottie Jackson ("I Done Worked!") as models, take down an oral history, asking questions you prepared in advance. Introduce your oral history with a description of your "author" and a brief account of who he or she is and your experience in obtaining the oral history from him or her.

10. Both the Lottie Jackson and the Milburn Jackson essays touch on the effect of mechanization displacing workers from their jobs. There is similar concern today about advances in technology, especially in computerization, downsizing the workforces of large companies. After some library research, write an essay bringing the point of view of the two Jacksons up-to-date: What is happening? What concern, especially political, is expressed about it? What, if any, are the proposed solutions? What is your assessment of such possible solutions?

Cluster 12

Disruptions and Disasters

Whereas "everyday realities" are monotonously familiar to us all, "disruptions and disasters" are those sporadic *unrealities* that take as their victims "inferior" beings and "hated" enemies. We set aside here "natural" catastrophes—floods, earthquakes, hurricanes—and limit ourselves to the "human" kind: the twentieth century has been replete with mass destructions and mass extinctions—enough to engage the whole of our collective imagination. Many of us who have not been the victims have been complicit in our silent assent to acts we find repugnant. It is probably not that humankind has become more evil or degenerate, but that technology has in this century provided the means to destroy the whole of the human race and render the planet itself uninhabitable.

We do not need to be historians to be aware of the critical turning-points of this century—the Holocaust in Germany, which saw the extinction of nearly ten million Jews, Gypsies, homosexuals, and other "undesirables"; the dropping of the atomic bomb on Hiroshima and Nagasaki, wiping out two cities and killing over a hundred thousand people in a flash; the fighting of the inexplicable Vietnam War, lasting over ten years and resulting in several hundred thousand Vietnamese and American casualties. These are only the major markers of recent history that have made us—not just Americans but the whole world—rethink what history is and how it might now *literally* end.

In fact, we Americans have rethought our own history, perhaps because we were so repulsed by what was found when the death camps in Germany were liberated at the end of World War II. What about our treatment of the Native Americans in the nineteenth century? And what about our internment of Japanese Americans in detention camps during World War II? Just as prejudice is universal, the fear, hatred, and greed that lie behind these appalling events are also universal human traits, not confined to any one group, country, or race. Our real enemy lurks within ourselves—all of us who belong to the *human* race.

Most of the voices heard in this cluster are the voices of victims; they are the lucky survivors who can speak most eloquently of what happened to them. Among the exceptions is an American pilot who flew both missions that dropped atomic bombs on Hiroshima and Nagasaki; included here is his account published for the first time fifty years after the event that changed all our lives.

"And then I heard that we would all go into the Soldiers' Town when the grass should appear, and that Crazy Horse had untied his pony's tail and would not fight again."

WALKING THE BLACK ROAD AND THE KILLING OF CRAZY HORSE

Black Elk (as told through John G. Neihardt)

Black Elk (1863–1950) was an Ogalala holy man of the Lakota-Sioux Indians, the son of a Black Elk who was a medicine man. A peace treaty signed by Ogalala Chief Red Cloud, allowing the Indians to keep their lands in Dakota's Black Hills, was being violated by the U.S. government, which was permitting settlers to move into the area and eventually selling the land to the Wasichus (the whites). In 1875, the Indians, near starvation because of a harsh winter, began to leave their reservations and renew their buffalo hunts. General Custer was sent out with troops to force the Indians back to their reservations, resulting in the battle of the Little Bighorn in 1876, at which Custer and many of his men were killed by Indians led by Chiefs Sitting Bull and Crazy Horse. Black Elk, only in his early teens at the time, has related these events as well as those that followed in his oral autobiography recorded by the Nebraska poet John G. Neihardt in *Black Elk Speaks* (1932). In the excerpt below, Black Elk relates the events after Little Bighorn, in which government troops pursued and fought the Indians, persuading some to give up the fight and finally forcing the remainder to return into "the Soldiers' Town" (Fort Robinson) under the surveillance of the troops. These events culminated in 1877 when Crazy Horse tried to escape but was caught and, as he resisted being imprisoned, killed. Black Elk died in 1950. John G. Neihardt (1881–1973) was born near Sharpsburg, Illinois, but migrated with his family to the Great Plains area, settling finally in the frontier town of Wayne, Nebraska. His passionate interest in the stories, legends, and lives of the Plains Indians developed into a life-long involvement with them and became a source of material for his many volumes of poetry, fiction, and essays. Neihardt was named poet laureate of Nebraska by the state legislature in 1921.

1   Wherever we went, the soldiers came to kill us, and it was all our own country. It was ours already when the Wasichus made the treaty with Red Cloud, that said it would be ours as long as grass should grow and water flow. That was only eight winters before, and they were chasing us now because we remembered and they forgot.

2   After that we started west again, and we were not happy anymore, because so many of our people had untied their horses' tails[1] and gone over to the Wasichus. We went back deep into our country, and most of the land was black from the fire, and the bison had gone away. We camped on the Tongue River where there was some cottonwood for the ponies; and a hard winter came on early. It snowed much; game was hard to find, and it was a hungry time for us. Ponies died, and we ate them. They died because the snow froze hard and they could not find the grass that was left in the valleys and there was not enough cottonwood to feed them all. There had been thousands of us together that summer, but there were not two thousand now.

3   News came to us there in the Moon of the Falling Leaves (November) that the Black Hills had been sold to the Wasichus and also all the country west of the Hills—the country we were in then.[2] I learned when I was older that our people did not want to do this. The Wasichus went to some of the chiefs alone and got them to put their marks on the treaty. Maybe some of them did this when they were crazy from drinking the minne wakan (holy water, whiskey) the Wasichus gave them. I have heard this; I do not know. But only crazy or very foolish men would sell their Mother Earth. Sometimes I think it might have been better if we had stayed together and made them kill us all.

4   Dull Knife was camping with his band of Shyelas on Willow Creek in the edge of the Big Horn Mountains, and one morning very early near the end of the Moon of Falling Leaves the soldiers came there to kill them.[3] The people were all sleeping. The snow was deep and it was very cold. When the soldiers began shooting into the tepees, the people ran out into the snow, and most of them were naked from their sleeping robes. Men fought in the snow and cold with nothing on them but their cartridge belts, and it was a hard fight, because

---

[1] Left the war-path. (J. Neihardt)
[2] The treaty was signed in October, 1876. (J. Neihardt)
[3] Colonel Mackenzie attacked the Cheyenne village as stated on November 26, 1876. (J. Neihardt)

the warriors thought of the women and children freezing. They could not whip the soldiers, but those who were not killed and did not die from the cold, got away and came to our camp on the Tongue.

5   I can remember when Dull Knife came with what was left of his starving and freezing people. They had almost nothing, and some of them had died on the way. Many little babies died. We could give them clothing, but of food we could not give them much, for we were eating ponies when they died. And afterwhile they left us and started for the Soldiers' Town on White River to surrender to the Wasichus; and so we were all alone there in that country that was ours and had been stolen from us.

6   After that the people noticed that Crazy Horse was queerer than ever. He hardly ever stayed in the camp. People would find him out alone in the cold, and they would ask him to come home with them. He would not come, but sometimes he would tell the people what to do. People wondered if he ate anything at all. Once my father found him out alone like that, and he said to my father: "Uncle, you have noticed me the way I act. But do not worry; there are caves and holes for me to live in, and out here the spirits may help me. I am making plans for the good of my people."

7   He was always a queer man, but that winter he was queerer than ever. Maybe he had seen that he would soon be dead and was thinking how to help us when he would not be with us any more.

8   It was a very bad winter for us and we were all sad. Then another trouble came. We had sent out scouts to learn where the soldiers were, and they were camping at the mouth of the Tongue. Early in the Moon of Frost in the Tepee (January), some of our scouts came in and said that the soldiers were coming up the Tongue to fight us, and that they had two wagon guns (cannon) with them.

9   There was no better place to go, so we got ready to fight them; and I was afraid, because my father told me we had not much ammunition left. We moved the village a little way off up stream, and our warriors were ready on a high bluff when the walking soldiers and their wagons came in the morning.[4] The soldiers built fires and ate their breakfast there in the valley while our people watched them and were hungry. Then they began shooting with the wagon guns that shot twice, because the iron balls went off after they fell. Some of them did not go off, and we boys ran after one of these and got it.

10   Then the walking soldiers started up the bluff, and it began to snow hard and they fought in the blizzard. We could not stop the soldiers coming up, because we had not much ammunition. The soldiers had everything. But our men used spears and guns for clubs when the soldiers got there, and they fought hand to hand awhile, holding the soldiers back until the women could

---

[4] General Miles attacked the village of Crazy Horse on the Tongue River, January 8, 1876. (J. Neihardt)

break camp and get away with the children and ponies. We fled in the blizzard southward up the Tongue and over to the Little Powder River. The soldiers followed us awhile, and there was fighting in our rear. We got away, but we lost many things we needed, and when we camped on the Little Powder, we were almost as poor as Dull Knife's people were the day they came to us. It was so cold that the sun made himself fires, and we were eating our starving ponies.

11   Late in the Moon of the Dark Red Calf (February) or early in the Moon of the Snowblind (March), Spotted Tail, the Brule, with some others, came to us. His sister was Crazy Horse's mother. He was a great chief and a great warrior before he went over to the Wasichus. I saw him and I did not like him. He was fat with Wasichu food and we were lean with famine. My father told me that he came to make his nephew surrender to the soldiers, because our own people had turned against us, and in the spring when the grass was high enough for the horses, many soldiers would come and fight us, and many Shoshones and Crows and even Lakotas and our old friends, the Shyelas, would come against us with the Wasichus. I could not understand this, and I thought much about it. How could men get fat by being bad, and starve by being good? I thought and thought about my vision, and it made me very sad; for I wondered if maybe it was only a queer dream after all.

12   And then I heard that we would all go into the Soldiers' Town when the grass should appear, and that Crazy Horse had untied his pony's tail and would not fight again.

13   In the Moon of the Grass Appearing (April) our little band started for the Soldiers' Town ahead of the others, and it was early in the Moon When the Ponies Shed (May) that Crazy Horse came in with the rest of our people and the ponies that were only skin and bones. There were soldiers and Lakota policemen in lines all around him when he surrendered there at the Soldiers' Town. I saw him take off his war bonnet. I was not near enough to hear what he said. He did not talk loud and he said only a few words, and then he sat down.

14   I was fourteen years old. We had enough to eat now and we boys could play without being afraid of anything. Soldiers watched us, and sometimes my father and mother talked about our people who had gone to Grandmother's Land with Sitting Bull and Gall, and they wanted to be there. We were camped near Red Cloud's Agency, which was close to the Soldiers' Town. What happened that summer is not a story.

✿   ✿   ✿

15   One night early in the Moon When the Calf Grows Hair (September) we broke camp there at Red Cloud Agency without making any noise, and started. My father told me we were going to Spotted Tail's camp, but he did not tell me why until later. We traveled most of the night and then we camped.

16   But when we were moving again next day, a band of Red Cloud's people overtook us and said there would be bad trouble if we did not come back right away. Some of us turned around then and went back, and soldiers sent the others back a little later; but Crazy Horse went on to his uncle's camp.

17   After what happened my father told me why Crazy Horse had done this. He was afraid somebody might start trouble down there where all the soldiers were, and the Wasichus had taken our guns away from us, so that we could do nothing if there was bad trouble. The Wasichus had made Spotted Tail head chief of all the Lakotas because he would do what they wanted, and Crazy Horse thought we might be safer there with his uncle. Afterwards, the Hang-Around-the-Fort people said that he was getting ready to tie up his horse's tail again and make war on the Wasichus. How could he do that when we had no guns and could not get any? It was a story the Wasichus told, and their tongues were forked when they told it. Our people believe they did what they did because he was a great man and they could not kill him in battle and he would not make himself over into a Wasichu, as Spotted Tail and the others did. That summer, my father told me, the Wasichus wanted him to go to Washington with Red Cloud and Spotted Tail and others to see the Great Father there; but he would not go. He told them that he did not need to go looking for his Great Father. He said: "My Father is with me, and there is no Great Father between me and the Great Spirit."

18   In the evening of the next day after we got back to Red Cloud's Agency, some soldiers came there bringing Crazy Horse with them. He was riding his horse alone a little way ahead. They did not stay there long, but rode on over to the Soldiers' Town, and my father and I went along with many others to see what they were going to do.

19   When we got over there we could not see Crazy Horse, because there were soldiers and Lakota policemen all around where he was and people crowding outside.

20   In just a little while I could feel that something very bad was happening in there, and everybody was excited all at once, and you could hear voices buzzing all around. Then I heard a loud cry in our own language, and it said: "Don't touch me! I am Crazy Horse!" And suddenly something went through all the people there like a big wind that strikes many trees all at once. Somebody in there yelled something else, but everybody around me was asking or telling everybody what had happened, and I heard that Crazy Horse was killed, that he was sick, that he was hurt; and I was frightened, because everything felt the way it did that day when we were going up to kill on the Greasy Grass, and it seemed we might all begin fighting right away.

21   Then everything got quiet, and everybody seemed to be waiting for something. Then the people began to break up and move around, and I heard that Crazy Horse had just taken sick and maybe he would be all right soon.

22   But it was not long until we all knew what had happened in there, because some of the people saw it happen, and I will tell you how it was.

23   They told Crazy Horse they would not harm him if he would go to the Soldiers' Town and have a talk with the Wasichu chief there. But they lied. They did not take him to the chief for a talk. They took him to the little prison

with iron bars on the windows, for they had planned to get rid of him. And when he saw what they were doing, he turned around and took a knife out of his robe and started out against all those soldiers. Then Little Big Man, who had been his friend and was the one who told us boys that we were brave before my first fight when we attacked the wagons on War Bonnet Creek, took hold of Crazy Horse from behind and tried to get the knife away. And while they were struggling, a soldier ran a bayonet into Crazy Horse from one side at the back and he fell down and began to die. Then they picked him up and carried him into the soldier chief's office. The soldiers stood all around there and would not let anybody in and made the people go away. My father and I went back to our camp at Red Cloud Agency.

24   That night I heard mourning somewhere, and then there was more and more mourning, until it was all over the camp.

25   Crazy Horse was dead. He was brave and good and wise. He never wanted anything but to save his people, and he fought the Wasichus only when they came to kill us in our own country. He was only thirty years old. They could not kill him in battle. They had to lie to him and kill him that way.

26   I cried all night, and so did my father.

🐚

Discussion Questions

1. Explain what Black Elk means in paragraph 3, "But only crazy or very foolish men would sell their Mother Earth."
2. Black Elk observes at the beginning of paragraph 6, "After that the people noticed that Crazy Horse was queerer than ever." What do the words "after that" refer to that might explain Crazy Horse's behavior?
3. In paragraph 11, what do we learn about Spotted Tail's relation to Crazy Horse, and why did he go to see him? Explain Black Elk's observation, "How could men get fat by being bad, and starve by being good?"
4. What did Crazy Horse and his followers attempt to do in paragraphs 15–16, and what was the result?
*5. Explain Black Elk's comment in paragraph 20, "And suddenly something went through all the people there like a big wind that strikes many trees all at once."
6. Describe Crazy Horse's death in accord with Black Elk's description in paragraph 23.
*7. Paragraph 25 has something of the effect of a eulogy for the dead at a funeral. How does it achieve this effect?

Writing Topics

1. In paragraph 1, Black Elk says, "It [the land] was ours already when the Wasichus [white people] made the treaty with Red Cloud, that said it would be ours as long as grass should grow and water flow." The sentence clearly reflects a lyrical or poetic element in Black Elk's speech. Find other such passages and write an analytical essay on the style of the piece, exploring the rhetorical devices that result in the poetic effect.

2. From listening to Black Elk's voice and taking the measure of his language, what kind of individual do you take him to have been? Write a brief character sketch in which you explore three or four of his leading traits, supporting your views with references to the text. Close with an overall assessment of the man.

"As we opened the door, the SS was there.
They pushed us aside and came into the house.
"Guten Morgen," *they said,* "Guten Morgen,"
I remember. They were very polite and then
they went about this utter destruction with axes."

THEN CAME THE FAMOUS
KRISTALLNACHT

Elise Radell (as told to Joan Morrison and Charlotte Fox Zabusky)

Elise Radell's "Then Came the Famous *Kristallnacht*" appeared in *American Mosaic: The Immigrant Experience in the Words
of Those Who Lived It* (1980) by Joan Morrison and Charlotte
Fox Zabusky. A headnote to Radell's oral history tells us:
"She has fresh coloring, crisp graying hair, and a casual,
matter-of-fact manner—no accent at all. After working as a
dietitian for several years, she now teaches consumer economics at a community college. She and her husband, a
highly successful real-estate man, live with their two sons
in a spacious house on a hill, overlooking two ponds and a
golf course." We learn from the oral history itself that she
was born in Ludwigshafen, Germany, in 1931, and was provided a private tutor after she was forced as a Jew to leave
the public schools. In 1938, after the "famous *Kristallnacht*"
(crystal night, when anti-Jewish forces destroyed Jewish
possessions and imprisoned Jewish men), Radell and her
family began to search for a way to escape, finally obtaining
visas for the United States in 1939. The family settled in New
Jersey with relatives. After going through American public
schools, Radell attended Pratt Institute in Brooklyn, New
York, graduating with honors.

Joan Morrison, one of the editors of *American Mosaic*, was
born in 1922 and took a B.A. at the University of Chicago in
1944. She has contributed frequently to such publications
as *The New York Times and Mademoiselle*. She and her collaborator, Charlotte Fox Zabusky, spent four years collecting the

oral histories of *American Mosaic.* Morrison has also published, with Robert K. Morrison, *From Camelot to Kent State: The Sixties Experience in the Words of Those Who Lived It* (1984).

1   I was born in 1931 and Hitler came to power in 1933. As a little girl I never noticed anything. We were much integrated into the society. We had friends that were Jewish, that were non-Jewish. There never seemed to be any difference. But by 1937 or 1938, the Brown Shirts came along. All of a sudden, we became very much aware that we were Jews. We didn't know quite what to do with it. I remember going to school one day and somebody said to me, "You're Jewish," and threw a rock at me. I came home and I said to my mom and dad, "What is this being Jewish? Other people are Catholic. There are a lot of Lutherans and there are all kinds of churches, and why are they throwing stones at me?" And my parents said, "Well, that's the way it is." And then they took me out of regular public school and they took a private tutor for me—a young man who used to come to our house every day. I remember sitting in the dining room with him and we studied. I didn't study very well because I liked him more as a friend than as a teacher. I was about seven or eight then.

2   My grandfather owned a very large apartment house, where we lived. In fact, it was the first apartment house in Ludwigshafen, where I was born, that had glass doors that opened and an elevator. It was on the main street, and I remember the Nazis, on the days when there were parades for the Nazis, coming onto our dining room balcony; because our dining room balcony faced the main street in Ludwigshafen and it had to have a flagpole holder. And they came in every time there was a parade and put up the swastika flag. I didn't like that. I didn't like them and I didn't like that.

3   Then came the famous *Kristallnacht.* I don't remember the exact date. That morning, Mina, the maid, and I were going to get milk from the milk store. As we opened the door, the SS was there. They pushed us aside and came into the house. "*Guten Morgen,*" they said, "*Guten Morgen,*" I remember. They were very polite and then they went about this utter destruction with axes. They knew exactly how to do it. We had a breakfront in the dining room and it was one piece of teakwood, maybe seven feet long, and they knew just how to wreck it with one ax. Zzaszhh! Just ruined the whole thing. And the china closet was knocked all over and the pictures on the wall, with just one rip in each, and the furniture all just went. They were scientific about it. They had been told exactly how to go about it with the least amount of work. The pillows were ripped and the feathers—at that time there were feathers, you know—they just flew all over the house, and it was total destruction. Just ruined everything. My grandmother locked herself in the bathroom. The rest of us just stood and watched

this destruction. Everyone was in shock. There was no fighting back. We were just stunned. Afterward, they took all the Jewish men, put them in jail, and then transported them to Dachau.

4　　My father had been out of town on business and didn't come home until the next day. And then, out of some strange, unbelievable loyalty or honor or whatever the Germans were brought up to believe, when he came home and saw that all the Jewish men were gone, he went to the police station and gave himself up.

5　　Now, I, as a Jew, can't quite understand how the German Jews did this; how my father could come back and turn himself in. But, being raised his whole life as an honorable citizen, to him this was the height of being honorable. And it's very hard for me to accept. I can understand intellectually; I don't understand it emotionally. . . .

6　　After this, all the German Jewish women and children began to live together. I remember a cousin, a neighbor, another neighbor; we all lived in our apartment. We had the largest apartment. The train from Dachau to Ludwigshafen came at 2:10 every morning, and everybody woke up at 2:10 A.M. because you never knew who would come home. We had a distant aunt and her daughter living with us, and one night her husband came home and it was my Uncle Julius. I loved him dearly before that. And he walked into our house and I wouldn't look at him and I said, "How come you didn't bring my daddy?" I just couldn't understand how he came home without my daddy.

7　　Later, much later, eventually my daddy came home. My father was six-foot-one then, and tall and handsome, as a daughter sees her daddy—an eight-year-old daughter. And he had all his hair shaved off and he was down to ninety pounds. He came home and he never spoke about it again. Never mentioned it. It must have been so unbelievably terrible. But he came home. All I remember is his shaven head and that he was very skinny. But he hugged me and he kissed me and he said hello. "*Guten Tag*, Lisel. Everything's all right."

8　　Those who could got boat tickets then to America, to Shanghai, wherever they could go. You couldn't get a visa to America unless you had relatives there. I think Roosevelt could have tried to open the quota a little bit. Maybe he did try; I don't know. But we had an aunt who had come to the U.S. in 1936, and she did everything she could for us. We had to go to Stuttgart, which was the center where all the visas and passports were given. My mother always took me along because I didn't look Jewish. I had blue eyes and blond hair at the time. We had to go by train, I remember. We finally managed to get the visas and everything, and we got on a boat and landed here in August 1939. The last trip over.

9　　We begged my grandparents to come with us, but my grandfather was a great German nationalist. Not a religious man. He just didn't believe in God, and, therefore, what sense did temple make or religion make? He was an atheist. He was a German. And he said, "No. Nothing will happen to me." He wouldn't go. But now I think back—I have a feeling my grandfather knew my grandmother wouldn't make it through the physical. She was a very sick woman then. So he stayed with her. First they were deported to France, and then they were on one of those trains. The last we ever heard. In fact, we have a picture of them going on one of those trains—stepping up to the car that was going to go to Poland or wherever they went to be gassed. A friend of a friend saw them and took a picture. I have the picture now. I never look at it. . . . Right to the bitter end they were properly dressed. My grandfather had on a tie and a white shirt, and my grandmother had a dress on and a brooch and whatever shoes she had. And they got into that train! That's what I say about the German Jews. Down to the bitter end they had a false dignity. That's what they knew and that's what they were told to do, and they did it in the most elegant and dignified way they knew how. Right down to the gas chamber. And I'm sure that they walked into that gas chamber with their heads held high and that was it. . . . [*Breaks down.*]

10   I say, "Why didn't they fight? Why didn't we all fight back?" But if you're raised in a certain milieu, you cannot change. And besides, the fight would have been hopeless. That's something we know. The Poles' fight was hopeless, too, but at least they did it. You know, I'm torn. I always knew, after I got my senses back and was settled, I said, "I never could marry a German Jew," because I don't quite believe in going into the death chamber with your head held high, without somehow, somewhere, fighting back. It might be a terrible thing for me to say. In a way, I feel like a traitor when I think that, and, in another way, I feel, "Well, I'm an individual. I'm a free soul. I can begin to believe the way I would believe—and choose what I would choose." I don't blame my parents, because there were too many who did it the same way. But I don't think I could do it. . . .

11   We landed in Hoboken. We sat on our suitcases on the docks there, waiting for my uncle and aunt to come and pick us up. And they did and they took us to Seymour Avenue in Newark. They had an apartment and we moved in with them. My aunt and my uncle and my cousin, who was three years older than I was. That night I remember waking up. I had a terrible stomachache, and my aunt and uncle had taken my mother and father out for their first American ice cream cone. There were no ice cream cones in Germany, you know. I woke up with this terrible stomachache, and my cousin came over and said, "What's the matter?" And I couldn't speak English and I said, "My stomach hurts," in German. And he said, "Wait a little bit. I'll look out the window." And he looked out the window and the ice cream parlor was just down the street and he called and they came home. And my parents came in, and my aunt and uncle too, and they saw I was really sick. The family doctor came over at two in the morning and he said, "Uh, oh, Elise has appendicitis." The very first night. I had had it on the boat, but the boat doctors kept saying, "She's seasick. Yes, she's seasick." Anyhow, I was rushed over to the hospital and they operated

on me and took out the appendix, and I had a little peritonitis afterward. It was all free of charge, because we couldn't pay.

12   In the hospital, I couldn't speak English. I didn't know anything. I couldn't even ask for a bedpan. It was dreadful. Short visiting hours; parents could only come once a day. And the girls in the room with me were Margo, Margaret, Marsha, Mildred—all the *M*'s. And I couldn't tell one from the other. It was awful. The first thing I learned in English was: "Please, may I have a bedpan?" And the second was: "What time is it, please?" so I could know when my parents could come. The other children were all American. If they spoke, I couldn't understand them. They served corn on the cob one night, and in Germany, corn on the cob only went for the pigs. Nobody ever served corn on the cob, and I didn't know what to do with it and I started to cut it with a knife and fork and they all laughed and I was mortified and humiliated. I remember it was a terrible time. But I came home finally and I was all right.

13   And then it was time to start school. I was eight and a half by then. They put me in kindergarten. I was the big girl and I couldn't understand one word and I was put in with all these little ones. I never opened my mouth. Once the teacher asked me to get something from the back of the room. She wanted the scissors and I brought the crayons, because I didn't understand. And the whole class laughed and I was mortified and I said, "I'm not going to school anymore." But I went again—September, October, November. In December I opened my mouth and I started to speak the way I do now. I never practiced. I was just determined not to have an accent, and I wasn't going to be laughed at and I wasn't going to be left out. And when I knew I could speak, I opened my mouth and spoke. Then I got moved up right away. I went to first grade. I could pass that. Arithmetic is arithmetic, you know. And then I went up to second grade and then third grade and, then, right up to fourth grade. They skipped me.

14   My father got a job in a fabric store as a stockboy. He had owned a large textile firm in Ludwigshafen. Now he earned eleven dollars a week. And my mother was working as a seamstress in a dress shop and she was earning seven dollars a week. Finally we earned enough money, and we moved out from my aunt and uncle's house and got a one-room apartment of our own, which was nicer.

15   I finished grade school and high school and then had to pick out a college that was very inexpensive and where I could live at home, because we still had no money. I really had no right to go to college, but my parents' pride was to have braces on Elise's teeth and to send her to college. So we managed. I had braces on my teeth and I commuted every day from Newark to Pratt Institute in Brooklyn. I never knew it was dreadful, because I always had companions who commuted too. We got up at six in the morning. We were there for an eight-thirty class. And I did four years at Pratt Institute and I graduated with honors. I was going to go on to graduate school, but my father got sick: ulcers. I had been accepted at NYU Graduate School, but my mother and I were standing on the sundeck at Beth Israel Hospital and my mother said, "Elise.

Poppa's sick. We got no more money. You can't go to graduate school." And I said, "Okay. You know what? I'm going to go downstairs to the dietician and I'm going to ask her if she needs a therapeutic dietician." And I was hired at once. Right there. I had my training. I was qualified. I could get to the hospital by bus. I had my degree and I went to work. And I worked until I met Ray and we got married.

16   My husband's an East European Jew. I had always said I couldn't marry a German Jew. But we're both Americans. To us, Judaism is a religion, not a patriotic thing. We're both Americans.

17   We send our children to a cultural Jewish school because we don't belong to a temple. We don't know if there is a God or not. I hate to say I'm an atheist; maybe "an agnostic" is better. I don't know. And yet, I feel the children need something, somehow, somewhere, for our Jewishness. So there is this cultural Jewish school, an offshoot of the Workmen's Circles in New York. Eastern Jews, garment workers, who were not religious, started those schools. They've been carried on and there's one here now. That's where my sons learned about the Holocaust. I've never mentioned it and my parents never mentioned it, and until a year ago, when they studied it in Sunday School, my own children didn't even know that their grandpa was in Dachau. . . .

18   Last year my husband had a heart attack. I knew what the dangers were. We decided it wasn't going to destroy our family or us. That was the time I looked back and I said, "If my parents could have gone through all the Holocaust in Europe and all that danger, I can go through this." And Ray made it, and he's well now, knock wood. . . .

19   I remember when all this first started with the Jews in Germany. There was a chance that you could send your children to England on children's transports. My mother wrote a letter to my father in Dachau in some kind of jabberwocky so that the censors would not understand. You should excuse me, the German censors are not the brightest. Anyway, she quoted from Goethe and, somehow, she coded it, asking whether she should send me with the child transport to England, where the English will take the children into their homes; not quite as their children, but as their companions, maids, helpers. And my father wrote back, again quoting from Goethe. I don't know the exact translation, but it means: "When I return I want to find you all there." And that ended it. In other words, he was saying, "Do not do that. If we're going to go under, we're going to go under all together. We're not going to do this."

20   I have my children. I have my husband. We enjoy each day whatever we do. And the children, we always take the children with us when we go. We enjoy having them. We see things that we wouldn't see without them—look up at the clouds. I don't walk around looking up at the clouds, but my children tell me to and I do. . . . I understand now why my father sent my mother that message from Dachau.

❧

Discussion Questions

1. As related in paragraph 1, how did Radell become aware of her Jewishness?
2. What was the reaction of the Radell family to the behavior of the SS men on *Kristallnacht*?
3. What happened to the men on *Kristallnacht*?
4. Since Radell's father was absent, he was not taken. What did he do when he came home? Explain.
5. What was Radell's father's physical and mental condition when he returned home after being in Dachau?
6. Why did Radell's mother take Radell along when she went to get the proper documents for travel abroad?
7. In paragraph 9, Radell tells of a picture she has of her grandparents getting on a train, probably for Poland. Explain.
*8. What brought Radell to resolve (paragraph 10), "I never could marry a German Jew"?
9. Why was Radell hospitalized shortly after her arrival in the United States? What problems did she describe having had in the hospital?

Writing Topics

1. Write a brief essay, entitled perhaps, "Succeeding in America," in which you show, in accord with what is revealed in the essay and your own knowledge of life in the United States, why Radell and her parents were able to overcome the many obstacles in their path and do as well as they did?
2. The narrative ends, "I understand now why my father sent my mother that message from Dachau." In a brief essay, explain fully the meaning of this sentence as revealed in the narrative and then explore how its sentiment reflects a particular set of values and/or an attitude toward the living of a life.

*For me at least, the near catastrophe of June 6
diminished forever the credibility of the concepts of
strategic planning and of tactical order;
it provided me instead with a sense of chaos,
random disaster, and vulnerability. "*

ON OMAHA BEACH

William Preston, Jr.

William Preston, Jr., was born in 1924 and received his Ph.D. in American history at the University of Wisconsin. He is the author of *Aliens and Dissenters: Federal Suppression of Radicals, 1903–1933* (1963, reprinted 1994) and a coauthor of *Hope and Folly: The United States and UNESCO* (1989). After teaching at Denison University in Ohio, Preston became professor of history at the John Jay College of the City University of New York. He is now retired. He served for a time as history editor of *Lies of Our Time: A Magazine to Correct the Record*. In 1944, he was a nineteen-year-old soldier in the U.S. Army when he participated in the World War II D-Day landings on the beaches of Normandy in France. His account of the experience, "On Omaha Beach," appeared in *The New York Review of Books* on July 14, 1994.

1   Fifty years ago, on D-Day, June 6, 1944, Company C of the 743rd Tank Battalion landed on Omaha Beach at H hour minus ten minutes. The invasion of Normandy was the first modern amphibious assault in which tanks went ashore first in order to provide fire power that would protect the infantry and engineers who followed. A Hungarian-born inventor living in England, Nicholas Straussler, made this extraordinary development possible, for he had found a way to float and move a 32-ton Sherman tank without reducing its armor or armaments.

2   As a nineteen-year-old gunner in Company C, I first heard we might lead the invasion in waterborne tanks in January 1944, soon after our arrival in England. The idea seemed about as plausible as going to sea in a bathtub, even apart from the fact that German forces behind the Atlantic Wall would also be

shooting at us. In the next six months of training, however, most of us became used to the idea; its logic and daring and our ignorance of military mishaps and invasion disasters sustained our optimism. To be singled out for such an apparently foolhardy attempt to gain tactical surprise probably fed our egotistical fantasies of some sort of glory, the military equivalent of fifteen minutes of fame. Besides, I'd grown up on the New England coast, so that being launched 5,000 yards off the French coast in a nine-foot-high canvas boat with a 32-ton keel and twin propellers running off the tank's moving tracks was an innovation in seamanship I could admire.

3   As we learned how to use this novel assault weapon, our confidence increased. It did float, although with only three feet of the boat above water. It was launched from a 150-foot-long landing craft (LCT) far from shore and churned forward slowly but steadily. So far as safety and surprise were concerned, it seemed better for us to approach the shore this way than to come close to it while packed into large naval ships that would be easy targets. The German defenders, spotting dozens of small craft, would, or so it was supposed, hold their fire until the little boats discharged soldiers, who would then be obliterated with machine guns and mortars. Instead, as the canvas screen support dropped down in shallow water, the enemy would suddenly discover tanks charging up the beach.

4   Yet other more ominous dangers also loomed for us. "Should your tank start to sink," we were told, "you have only twenty seconds to get out," since the 32-ton keel would quickly reach a depth at which the water pressure would make escape impossible. The training included the same practice as submarine crews go through, and we learned how to quickly put on oxygen masks and swim to the surface.

5   In a practice maneuver in the English Channel, we saw how the waves could roll over the three feet of canvas that stayed above water and swamp us, and how the channel waters in springtime could drown anyone who stayed in them too long. I suppose, however, that most of us simply believed that our strange boat-tanks would fool the enemy and get us safely ashore. We trusted the experts and their grand strategy, and had no reason to imagine that nature would take the side of the Nazis on D-Day.

6   Other preparations also encouraged us. A model of the Normandy beach and the terrain behind it familiarized us with every feature of the area's geography. We knew exactly what each part of the coast we were assigned to assault looked like. Aerial photographs of the shore revealed three rows of defenses (visible at the low tide set for the landing), but preinvasion bombing was supposed to destroy many of them. The anticipated day-by-day lines of advance also seemed to confirm our commanders' confidence that we could move quickly off the beach and into the countryside. Why, we'd be in Paris in no time.

7   As we awaited our orders to board, many of us had taken some sort of lucky token along with us. The assistant driver hung a pair of baby shoes inside our tank, while I had a letter from a favorite uncle who was serving with the US Economic Mission in London. Known for his black humor, he had ended his farewell note with the hope that we would "take the Germans the way Custer took the Indians." In a postscript, he added, "See you under a little white cross." But virtually all the combat-bound GIs I knew assumed that whatever the odds, each of us individually would be the one that survived.

8   The first hint of trouble occurred on June 4 after our convoy left Portland for the landings on June 5. We were well on our way across, steaming forward, when quite late in the day the group was ordered to return to base. A communications foul-up almost let us show up off Normandy alone when the rest of the fleet had already been notified to abort the invasion until June 6.

9   As the armada gathered the next day, its vast size seemed to promise victory, notwithstanding the channel gale and high seas. Our LCT pitched ominously while waiting for a signal to launch its four canvas-covered tanks. Nearby we saw other Sherman tanks being launched from an LCT and almost immediately sinking, and our commanding officer knew we had to move closer in.

10   The scene had already become chaotic and confused, and no one seemed to be where they should have been. Our group, with canvas screens up, hit the water some 250 yards from the low tide mark on the beach, ready to fire, but our screen would not collapse. The tank commander had to get out on the hull to break the struts holding the screen in place. Just at that moment the canvas fell, exposing him standing there in full view of the enemy. The gunners on the cliffs were firing rifles and machine guns through clouds of black smoke created by the off-shore naval bombardment. On our right an 88-millimeter cannon in a concrete pillbox was knocking out other tanks. The German beach defenses all seemed to be in place, for somehow the Air Force had missed the beach and dropped its bombs inland. All around, infantry and engineers were falling in the shallow water.

11   If the pillbox had not been silenced, our own group of tanks would undoubtedly have been next. The Navy saved us and many others when destroyers supporting the beach assault moved in so close that it seemed they were about to go aground. Each time we fired a burst of tracers at a target, the ships poured shells on it, knocking it out. Meanwhile we fired our turret gun, providing cover for men in the water as German artillery and mortars inundated the area with high explosives.

12   For us the old expression "the tide has turned" only meant disaster as the water rushing toward the beach threatened to drown the wounded and even swamp the tanks. We had to move forward, yet risked running over helpless GIs we still could not see from inside the tank. The saddest relic of that advance

was an almost entire pair of army issue long johns that remained entangled for days in one of our tank's tracks.

13   A disaster seemed imminent. Most of the engineer units that were supposed to destroy the ten-foot-thick concrete wall blocking the road off the beach had been killed or wounded, and we soon realized the timetable for the day's advance no longer meant anything. Luckily for our morale, we also did not know that an entire German division, the 352nd infantry, had moved into the cliffs over Omaha Beach for further training just before the attack.

14   Strangely, none of the four of us in the tank believed we wouldn't get off that terrible strip of sand or that the landings would fail; but as the hours passed, the mere fact of surviving unwounded seemed miraculous and wonderful, beyond mere luck. On the sixteenth hour of D-Day, the 743rd Tank Battalion finally moved off the beach to bivouac in a pasture near Vierville-sur-Mer for the night. We learned later that twenty-one of the fifty-one tanks in our battalion had not survived the landings. (Of the 4,649 casualties among the 55,000 Americans put ashore that day, 2,000 died at Omaha Beach.)

15   In the deadly atmosphere of the fighting that followed in the hedgerows of Normandy's pastoral landscape, the same feelings we had on D-Day recurred. Once again, the experts seemed confounded. No one had apparently regarded the steeply banked hedgerows as an offensive nightmare for tanks, but each field was like a jungle in which German troops could lie hidden and spring a surprise. The longstanding plans for coordinating tanks with the infantry were scrapped and new tactics had to be improvised on the spot. And before the battle for St. Lô, Allied aircraft twice bombed short of the target that the 743rd was poised to attack.

16   In reminiscences of combat different perspectives emerge gradually as the events deepen in memory, above all the memory of those whose lives ended in the sand. For me at least, the near catastrophe of June 6 diminished forever the credibility of the concepts of strategic planning and of tactical order; it provided me instead with a sense of chaos, random disaster, and vulnerability. But having come near death also induced a desire, which I would not otherwise have imagined, to live life to the fullest.

❧

Discussion Questions

1.   When he first heard that a way had been found to float and move a 32-ton Sherman tank, Preston's reaction was, "The idea seemed about as plausible as going to sea in a bathtub." Explain.

2.   After training, however, how did Preston's reaction to the idea change?

*3. Preston describes (paragraph 7) receiving a letter from a "favorite" uncle known for his "black humor": the uncle wrote that he hoped that Preston's outfit would "take the Germans the way Custer took the Indians," and added a postscript, "See you under a little white cross." Explain the "black humor" in the uncle's remarks.

4. What error does Preston describe in paragraph 8 as the "first hint of trouble" in the landing plans?

5. Explain what went wrong in the landing—with the landing screens, with the plan for the air force to knock out the German beach defenses, with the navy destroyers meant to support the beach assault, and with the engineer units meant to destroy the concrete wall blocking the road off the beach.

*6. After the tank battalion moved off the beach on to pasture land with its steep hedgerows, what happened to the "long-standing plans for coordinating tanks with the infantry"? Explain.

Writing Topics

1. At the end of the essay, Preston writes, "But having come near death also induced a desire, which I would not otherwise have imagined, to live life to the fullest." In an analytical essay, show from Preston's narrative why you think he came to this conclusion and would remember it fifty years later. In the process, indicate what you think "fullest" means, and whether you approve of this way of living life.

2. In paragraph 16, Preston writes, "For me at least, the near catastrophe of June 6 diminished forever the credibility of the concepts of strategic planning and of tactical order; it provided me instead with a sense of chaos, random disaster, and vulnerability." Do you believe that Preston reached a profound or superficial "truth"? In a brief essay, present your assessment of Preston's insight, and show how your own experience has shaped for you a similar or different insight.

Thirty years later, the WASP's were still trying to earn a legitimate place in history. While the House Veterans Affairs Committee was awarding rights to Polish men who fought on the Allied side, we were being denied them because we were women."

THE WOMEN WHO FLEW—
BUT KEPT SILENT

Ann Darr

Ann Darr was born in 1920 and took a B.A. from the University of Iowa in 1941. She teaches at American University in Washington, D.C., and at the Writer's Center in Bethesda, Maryland. Her volumes of poetry include St. Ann's Gut (1971), The Myth of a Woman's Fist (1973), Cleared for Landing (1978), and Riding with the Fireworks (1981). "The Women Who Flew—But Kept Silent" appeared in The New York Times Magazine on May 7, 1995, and is based on her service in the U.S. Army's Women's Air Force Service as a pilot during World War II.

1   That day in 1940 when I found out Civilian Pilot Training courses were starting at Shaw Airport outside of Iowa City, I skipped my university classes to sign up. Lucky me—one woman to each class of 10, and I made the cut. I was a prairie child. We didn't have the mountains, the sea; what we had was *sky*. And the yearning to take to the air was whetted by living history; Lindbergh had given the world a new dimension. I took lessons before my 8 o'clock classes. Later I learned the C.P.T. courses were intended to help provide the pilots we would desperately need if we entered the war.

2   From 1942 to 1944, the Army Air Forces trained 1,830 WASP's—Women Airforce Service Pilots—culled from 25,000 applicants. Only 1,074 earned wings. We were civilians, temporarily Civil Service, till the promised military status came through. Jacqueline Cochran, who became the first woman to break the sound barrier, was our director. At Gen. Hap Arnold's suggestion, she had gone to England to observe the Air Transport Auxiliary before setting

up a training school here. We would ferry planes and tow gunnery targets in all kinds of weather to free men for combat overseas. By the time we were disbanded on Dec. 20, 1944, 38 of us had died in airplane crashes.

3   Over the entrance to Avenger Field (named for British cadets who trained there) in Sweetwater, Tex., flew the gremlin the Walt Disney studio had designed for us—Fifinella, the yellow-helmeted, red-shirted guardian in her blue-rimmed goggles, red boots and spread blue wings. She was the insignia we wore on our flying jackets to protect us from storms and sabotage.

4   I often meet people who lived through the war and never knew we existed, people who thought Rosie the Riveter was the sole example of women's contribution to the war effort. Even the Air Force forgot us. In the 1970's it announced that women were being taught to fly military planes for the first time. Untrue. WASP's were flying every kind of plane the Army Air Forces owned in 1942, 1943 and 1944. We flew 60 million miles in various aircraft, from small primary trainers up to the B-29 Super Fortress. That first B-29 flight by WASP's was to show men who balked at flying it that this was a plane "even women could fly." My own class of 44-W-3 (third class of women in 1944) served as guinea pigs, too. We went directly from flying primary trainer planes to AT-6's, to see if it could be done. Once it was proved we could handle it, the leap was made official in the male cadet courses.

5   **October 1943–April 1944.** From reveille to taps, we practiced in ground school and the flight line and the exercise field. The 400 hours of ground school was comparable to a degree in aeronautics. We had hands-on experience with engines, communications, theory of flight, weather, history of aviation, law and lifesaving. We did daily calisthenics and practiced flying in a Link trainer (a flight simulator). And parachute landings. We trained by running as fast as we could and throwing ourselves onto the ground, learning to land on our backs instead of breaking the fall with hand or foot and risk breaking an arm or leg. Later we jumped from a high platform, or swung down on a pulley apparatus, all in preparation for an accident.

6   Texas weather runs the gamut, from prostrating heat to winds that blow rain horizontally and pepper the barracks with sand. One wind-savage morning the call went out: you're needed on the flight line immediately. We dropped our ground-school books and ran. We arrived in time to see a PT-19 primary trainer that was coming in for a landing get caught by a wind gust that warped the approach just as the plane reached the ground, very nearly toppling it. The pilot gunned the engine and swung the plane back into the air before the wing hit the ground. We saw what we had to do. We lined up on both sides of the runway so that as each plane came in we grabbed the wings and kept it steady as we ran alongside it. I think we saved all the trainers who landed that day.

7   I flew a B-17 bomber only once. I wanted to know how it felt to pilot a Flying Fortress full of student gunners instead of the TB-26, a modified trainer

bomber that towed the target, a monstrous windsock. A female pilot's height determined the kind of plane she would be assigned after flight school: 5 foot 6 and over, she went to bombers; under 5 foot 6, to fighters (pursuits).

8   The gunners trained first with cameras, shooting film as fighter planes whirled around them. Next, they were given automatic machine guns with clips of live ammunition that had been dipped in colored wax to identify their strikes: red for nose gunner, blue for tail gunner, green and yellow for side gunners. After a target was evaluated, it was ours. We used this holey cloth for curtains, bedspreads, slipcovers, dividers, sunning mats, table-cloths—even skirts, if we were desperate.

9   There was always the risk of being shot down, though it was not very likely. Bullet holes turned up in some of the tow planes flown by women at Camp Davis in South Carolina during ground-to-air gunnery practice. Many of the planes were in no condition to fly: altimeters that didn't work, inaccurate compasses, 500 hours' flying time since the last engine maintenance check. I'd heard of the poor conditions from a friend who was stationed there. But I was not prepared for the startling phrase I later read in "Those Wonderful Women in Their Flying Machines" by Sally Van Wagenen Keil: "sugar in the gas tank."

10   Cochran, our director, had flown down from Washington to investigate and flew back without revealing what she had learned. Apparently the traces of sugar were not to be discussed publicly; such knowledge might wreck the WASP program. But sugar cannot get into a gas tank accidentally. Sabotage was the only answer. But toward whom it was directed, or by whom, was never established.

11   In another incident, a WASP in training at Sweetwater was flying a BT-13 basic trainer when it went into an inverted spin. She survived the jump. An examination of the wreckage showed that the cable to the rudder had been cut, leaving just enough for a pilot to get off the ground.

12   Sabotage was a constant worry. A member of the first WASP class in Houston tells of ferrying P-47's, single-engine fighters, from Republic Field on Long Island and having to give the tower a false destination because a nearby shortwave radio was giving information to enemy submarines lurking in the Atlantic. Members of that first WASP class masked its activities by saying they were a basketball team. One was told the WASP's had to be a secret because the military didn't want Hitler to know America was so desperate for pilots.

13   When a utility plane crashed in the mountains near Las Vegas, killing all aboard, the body of the pilot was sent home with honors. And the female co-pilot? The Army said it was not responsible; the Civil Service said it was not responsible. We took up a collection to send her body home. Her family was not allowed to display a gold star in their window, which was at least some consolation for a family that lost a son.

14   **October 1944. Las Vegas.** We'd been assured our stay under Civil Service was temporary: if the militarization bill passed Congress, WASP's would take officer training. Then we'd have benefits accorded officers, like insurance and medical care. We already traveled under military orders and were expected to behave as officers would. One WASP whose husband visited her was not allowed to bring him to the officers' club to eat, the only dining facility on the base. He was only a sergeant.

15   The debate was heated. The WASP program was called a "blunder" and a "racket." Some military units and columnists like Drew Pearson fanned the hostility. A magazine article decrying "Jackie Cochran's glamor girls" jeered: "How about some of these 35-hour female wonders swapping their flying togs for nurses' uniforms? But that would be down-right rub-and-scrub work—no glamor there."

16   We, on the other hand, were ordered to remain silent, and though we were Civil Service, we followed orders. We were not to write or phone our Congressmen. We kept silent when we should have spoken up.

17   In October, the official letters arrived. We crossed our fingers. It didn't help. They read: We are sorry to announce, etc. We praise the work you have done, etc. The first was from Cochran, the second from General Arnold. The date was set: Dec. 20, all WASP's go home.

18   But the war wasn't over, and we had not finished our job. There was still a need for us at base after base, doing the aerial dishwashery that male pilots scorned. And we had not failed. We had proved that women could fly as well as men—in some cases, better. We had been pioneers in setting standards for proficiency. We felt discarded and depressed only because no one had said publicly, "Well done."

19   Thirty years later, the WASP's were still trying to earn a legitimate place in history. While the House Veterans Affairs Committee was awarding rights to Polish men who fought on the Allied side, we were being denied them because we were women. When the head of the committee told one of our witnesses he had no intention of letting our bill reach the House floor, we were stunned. "But sir," we said, "all we wanted to do was fly." I have never seen a face so contorted with rage: "That was the trouble! You wanted to *fly*."

20   When it turned out that one WASP's discharge papers were identical to those of a committee member, objections crumpled: "I'll be danged," he drawled, "her discharge papers read just like mine!"

21   The bill was signed into law on Thanksgiving Eve, 1977, in the White House. No WASP's were present.

♨

Discussion Questions

1. In paragraph 2, Darr describes the purpose for which the WASPs were brought into being and immediately after indicates that thirty-eight of the WASPs died in plane crashes. What was the purpose initially of the WASPs, and what was Darr's rhetorical purpose in linking information about purpose and the number of WASP deaths in plane crashes?
*2. Why is it, according to Darr, that so few people know that the WASPs ever existed?
3. According to paragraph 7, how was it decided to assign WASPs to bombers or to fighters?
4. How were WASPs trained to shoot automatic machine guns? Explain.
5. What was the "sugar in the gas tank" scare, and why was it of concern?
6. What happened when there was a crash near Las Vegas of a utility plane flown by a male pilot and a female pilot, both killed? Explain.
7. What kind of criticism was made against the WASPs and where did it come from?
*8. How and when did the WASPs finally gain the recognition they so well deserved?

Writing Topics

1. Write a brief essay showing the prejudices against women as revealed in Darr's account of the WASPs and of her experience as a pilot. Then reflect on your own experience and explore whether these prejudices have endured or changed.
2. Obtain copies of Darr's poems and explore her poetry for any allusions to her flying experience. Then write an essay in which you set forth your findings, indicating whether you believe her flying had any influence on her poetry and, if so, to what degree.

My own family, after three years of mess hall living, collapsed as an integrated unit. Whatever dignity or feeling of filial strength we may have known before December 1941 was lost. . . ."

A FAMILY DISRUPTED

Jeanne Wakatsuki Houston and James D. Houston

After Japan bombed the American fleet in Pearl Harbor in Hawaii on December 7, 1941, and entered the war as an ally of Germany, spurring U.S. entry into the war, there was great concern that the many Japanese-Americans living in the United States would prove more loyal to their old country than to their new one: strong loyalty to the Japanese Emperor Hirohito seemed to Americans a universal Japanese trait. As a result, the U.S. government rounded up some 100,000 Japanese Americans and placed them in hastily built "detention camps" resembling (as revealed in the essay below) the barracks, toilets, and mess halls that were the standard facilities for the GIs being mobilized to fight World War II. This move by the government, largely inspired by war-fever and the sneak attack on Pearl Harbor, turned out to be a major blunder as well as a violation of basic human rights.

Jeanne Wakatsuki Houston was born in California in 1934. She was a young girl when her family was moved to a detention camp, the Manzanar War Relocation Center, near Lone Pine, California. In spite of the hardships of this "disruption," she went on to earn a B.A. from the University of San Jose in 1956, briefly attended classes at the Sorbonne in Paris, and married James D. Houston in 1957. In 1973, she published (together with her husband) *Farewell to Manzanar: A True Story of Japanese American Experience during and after the World War II Internment*, from which "A Family Disrupted" is taken. The essay shows how the three-year experience tended to change permanently, and for the worse, the lives of what can only be called the "victims," primarily by under-mining traditional family ties. In 1985, her work *Beyond Manzanar and Other Views of Asian-American Womanhood* ap-peared in a volume with James D. Houston's *One Can Think about Life after Fish: In the Canoe and Other Coastal Sketches*.

1   The shacks were built of one thickness of pine planking covered with tarpaper. They sat on concrete footings, with about two feet of open space between the floorboards and the ground. Gaps showed between the planks, and as the weeks passed and the green wood dried out, the gaps widened. Knotholes gaped in the uncovered floor.

2   Each barracks was divided into six units, sixteen by twenty feet, about the size of a living room, with one bare bulb hanging from the ceiling and an oil stove for heat. We were assigned two of these for the twelve people in our family group; and our official family "number" was enlarged by three digits—16 plus the number of this barracks. We were issued steel army cots, two brown army blankets each, and some mattress covers, which my brothers stuffed with straw. . . .

3   The people who had it hardest during the first few months were young couples, . . . many of whom had married just before the evacuation began, in order not to be separated and sent to different camps. Our two rooms were crowded, but at least it was all in the family. My oldest sister and her husband were shoved into one of those sixteen-by-twenty-foot compartments with six people they had never seen before—two other couples, one recently married like themselves, the other with two teenage boys. Partitioning off a room like that wasn't easy. It was bitter cold when we arrived, and the wind did not abate. All they had to use for room dividers were those army blankets, two of which were barely enough to keep one person warm. They argued over whose blanket should be sacrificed and later argued about noise at night—the parents wanted their boys asleep by 9:00 P.M.—and they continued arguing over matters like that for six months, until my sister and her husband left to harvest sugar beets in Idaho. It was grueling work up there, and wages were pitiful, but when the call came through camp for workers to alleviate the wartime labor shortage, it sounded better than their life at Manzanar. They knew they'd have, if nothing else, a room, perhaps a cabin of their own. . . .

4   Months went by, in fact, before our "home" changed much at all from what it was the day we moved in—bare floors, blanket partitions, one bulb in each compartment dangling from a roof beam, and open ceilings overhead so that mischievous boys like Ray and Kiyo could climb up into the rafters and peek into anyone's life. . . .

5   I was sick continually, with stomach cramps and diarrhea. At first it was from the shots they gave us for typhoid, in very heavy doses and in assembly-line fashion: swab, jab, swab, *Move along now*, swab, jab, swab, *Keep it moving*.

That knocked all of us younger kids down at once, with fevers and vomiting. Later, it was the food that made us sick, young and old alike. The kitchens were too small and badly ventilated. Food would spoil from being left out too long. That summer, when the heat got fierce, it would spoil faster. The refrigeration kept breaking down. The cooks, in many cases, had never cooked before. Each block had to provide its own volunteers. Some were lucky and had a professional or two in their midst. But the first chef in our block had been a gardener all his life and suddenly found himself preparing three meals a day for 250 people.

6   "The Manzanar runs" became a condition of life, and you only hoped that when you rushed to the latrine, one would be in working order.

7   That first morning, on our way to the chow line, Mama and I tried to use the women's latrine in our block. The smell of it spoiled what little appetite we had. Outside, men were working in an open trench, up to their knees in muck — a common sight in the months to come. Inside, the floor was covered with excrement, and all twelve bowls were erupting like a row of tiny volcanoes.

8   Mama stopped a kimono-wrapped woman stepping past us with her sleeve pushed up against her nose and asked, "What do you do?"

9   "Try Block Twelve," the woman said, grimacing. "They have just finished repairing the pipes."

10   It was about two city blocks away. We followed her over there and found a line of women waiting in the wind outside the latrine. We had no choice but to join the line and wait with them. . . .

11   It was an open room, over a concrete slab. The sink was a long metal trough against one wall, with a row of spigots for hot and cold water. Down the center of the room twelve toilet bowls were arranged in six pairs, back to back, with no partitions. My mother was a very modest person, and this was going to be agony for her, sitting down in public, among strangers.

12   One old woman had already solved the problem for herself by dragging in a large cardboard carton. She set it up around one of the bowls, like a three-sided screen. . . . Mama happened to be at the head of the line now. As she approached the vacant bowl, she and the old woman bowed to each other from the waist. Mama then moved to help her with the carton, and the old woman said very graciously, in Japanese, "Would you like to use it?"

13   Happily, gratefully, Mama bowed again and said, "*Arigato*" (Thank you). . . .

14   Those big cartons were a common sight in the spring of 1942. Eventually sturdier partitions appeared, one or two at a time. . . .

15   Like so many of the women there, Mama never did get used to the latrines. It was a humiliation she just learned to endure: *shikata ga nai*, this cannot be helped. She would quickly subordinate her own desires to those of the family or the community, because she knew cooperation was the only way to survive. At the same time she placed a high premium on personal privacy, respected it in others and insisted upon it for herself. Almost everyone at Manzanar had inherited this pair of traits from the generations before them who had learned

to live in a small, crowded country like Japan. Because of the first they were able to take a desolate stretch of wasteland and gradually make it livable. But the entire situation there, especially in the beginning—the packed sleeping quarters, the communal mess halls, the open toilets—all this was an open insult to that other, private self, a slap in the face you were powerless to challenge.

16   At seven I was too young to be insulted. The camp worked on me in a much different way. I wasn't aware of this at the time, of course. No one was, except maybe Mama, and there was little she could have done to change what happened.

17   It began in the mess hall. Before Manzanar, mealtime had always been the center of our family scene. In camp, and afterward, I would often recall with deep yearning the old round wooden table in our dining room in Ocean Park, the biggest piece of furniture we owned, large enough to seat twelve or thirteen of us at once. A tall row of elegant, lathe-turned spindles separated this table from the kitchen, allowing talk to pass from one room to the other. Dinners were always noisy, and they were always abundant with great pots of boiled rice, platters of home-grown vegetables, fish Papa caught.

18   He would sit at the head of this table, with Mama next to him serving and the rest of us arranged around the edges according to age, down to where Kiyo and I sat, so far away from our parents, it seemed at the time, we had our own enclosed nook inside this world. The grownups would be talking down at their end, while we two played our secret games, making eyes at each other when Papa gave the order to begin to eat, racing with chopsticks to scrape the last grain from our rice bowls, eyeing Papa to see if he had noticed who won.

19   Now, in the mess halls, after a few weeks had passed, we stopped eating as a family. Mama tried to hold us together for a while, but it was hopeless. Granny was too feeble to walk across the block three times a day, especially during heavy weather, so May brought food to her in the barracks. My older brothers and sisters, meanwhile, began eating with their friends, or eating somewhere blocks away in the hope of finding better food. The word would get around that the cook over in Block 22, say, really knew his stuff, and they would eat a few meals over there, to test the rumor. Camp authorities frowned on mess hall hopping and tried to stop it, but the good cooks liked it. They liked to see long lines outside their kitchens and would work overtime to attract a crowd.

20   Younger boys, like Ray, would make a game of seeing how many mess halls they could hit in one meal period—be the first in line at Block 16, gobble down your food, run to 17 by the middle of the dinner hour, gulp another helping, and hurry to 18 to make the end of that chow line and stuff in the third meal of the evening. They didn't need to do that. No matter how bad the food might be, you could always eat till you were full.

21   Kiyo and I were too young to run around, but often we would eat in gangs with other kids, while the grownups sat at another table. I confess I enjoyed this part of it at the time. We all did. A couple of years after the camps opened,

sociologists studying the life noticed what had happened to the families. They made some recommendations, and edicts went out that families *must* start eating together again. Most people resented this; they griped and grumbled. They were in the habit of eating with their friends. And until the mess hall system itself could be changed, not much could really be done. It was too late.

22   My own family, after three years of mess hall living, collapsed as an integrated unit. Whatever dignity or feeling of filial strength we may have known before December 1941 was lost, and we did not recover it until many years after the war, not until after Papa died and we began to come together, trying to fill the vacuum his passing left in all our lives.

23   The closing of the camps, in the fall of 1945, only aggravated what had begun inside. Papa had no money then and could not get work. Half of our family had already moved to the east coast, where jobs had opened up for them. The rest of us were relocated into a former defense workers' housing project in Long Beach. In that small apartment there never was enough room for all of us to sit down for a meal. We ate in shifts, and I yearned all the more for our huge round table in Ocean Park.

24   Soon after we were released I wrote a paper for a seventh-grade journalism class, describing how we used to hunt grunion before the war. The whole family would go down to Ocean Park Beach after dark, when the grunion were running, and build a big fire on the sand. I would watch Papa and my older brothers splash through the moonlit surf to scoop out the fish, then we'd rush back to the house where Mama would fry them up and set the sizzling pan on the table, with soy sauce and horseradish, for a midnight meal. I ended the paper with this sentence: "The reason I want to remember this is because I know we'll never be able to do it again."

?●

Discussion Questions

1. Houston says in paragraph 3, "The people who had it hardest during the first few months were young couples." Explain.
2. Houston also notes in paragraph 3, "They continued arguing over matters like that for six months, until my sister and her husband left to harvest sugar beets in Idaho." Explore the implications of "matters like that" and the decision made by the sister and her spouse to "harvest sugar beets in Idaho."
3. What were "the Manzanar runs" (paragraph 6) and what caused them?
4. Paragraphs 7–15 are devoted to the latrines (military term for toilets). Describe the impact of the latrines on the people living in the camps.
*5. In paragraph 15, Houston writes, "Almost everyone at Manzanar had inherited this pair of traits from the generations before them

who had learned to live in a small, crowded country like Japan."
Explain the several references in this sentence, beginning with "this
pair of traits."

6. In paragraphs 16–22, Houston describes the way her family used to
eat their meals and contrasts this way with the family's new habits
of eating meals developed in the camp. What were the differences?
How did the new ways of eating meals affect her family and others?

7. As described in paragraph 23, what happened to the Wakatsuki
family after leaving the detention camp, especially in the way they
ate their meals? Explain.

*8. In the last paragraph, Houston recalls a paper she wrote for her
seventh-grade class, which she concluded, "The reason I want to
remember this is because I know we'll never be able to do it again."
What does "this" refer to, and what is the effect of ending her account of life in the detention camp with this paragraph?

Writing Topics

1. Write an analytical essay in which you support with relevant examples from the text that the two traits attributed to the Japanese—
cooperation and privacy—really were important to them. Does there
seem to have been a difference between the older and younger
generations? In your conclusion, indicate how important you believe these traits to be to Americans.

2. Write an essay in which you compare and contrast your family's
meals with those of the Wakatsuki family. In your conclusion, assess
how important—and why—mealtime experiences are to you and
your family, using the Wakatsuki essay as a point of reference.

The best man in my section was blown to pieces,
and the slime of his viscera enveloped me.
His body had cushioned the blow, saving my life;
I still carry a piece of his shinbone in my chest.
But I collapsed, and was left for dead."

OKINAWA:
THE BLOODIEST BATTLE OF ALL

William Manchester

William Manchester was born in Massachusetts in 1922 and, after his service in the Marine Corps in World War II (1942–1945), he took his B.A. from the University of Massachusetts in 1946 and his M.A. from the University of Missouri in 1947. After some experience in journalism (*The Daily Oklahoman*, *The Baltimore Sun*), Manchester filled a number of positions (writer-in-residence, professor of history) at Wesleyan University, Middletown, Connecticut, before retiring in 1992. He is the author of numerous books, among them biographies of H. L. Mencken, the Rockefellers, the Krupps, John F. Kennedy, and Winston Churchill. His novels include *The City of Anger* (1953), *Shadow of the Monsoon* (1953), *Beard the Lion* (1958), and *The Long Gainer* (1961). He is perhaps best known for his critical biography *American Caesar: Douglas MacArthur* (1978) and his reminiscence *Goodbye Darkness: A Memoir of the Pacific* (1980). "Okinawa: The Bloodiest Battle of All" first appeared in *The New York Times Magazine* in 1987 and is excerpted here. The invasion of Okinawa, lasting from April 1 to June 21, 1945, resulted in 12,500 Americans killed and 36,600 wounded.

1   Okinawa lies 330 miles southwest of the southernmost Japanese island of Kyushu; before the war, it was Japanese soil. Had there been no atom bombs — and at that time the most powerful Americans, in Washington and at the Pentagon, doubted that the device would work — the invasion of the Nipponese

homeland would have been staged from Okinawa, beginning with a landing on Kyushu to take place November 1. The six Marine divisions, storming ashore abreast, would lead the way. President Truman asked General Douglas MacArthur, whose estimates of casualties on the eve of battles had proved uncannily accurate, about Kyushu. The general predicted a million Americans would die in that first phase.

2   Given the assumption that nuclear weapons would contribute nothing to victory, the battle of Okinawa had to be fought. No one doubted the need to bring Japan to its knees. But some Americans came to hate the things we had to do, even when convinced that doing them was absolutely necessary; they had never understood the bestial, monstrous and vile means required to reach the objective—an unconditional Japanese surrender. As for me, I could not reconcile the romanticized view of war that runs like a red streak through our literature—and the glowing aura of selfless patriotism that had led us to put our lives at forfeit—with the wet, green hell from which I had barely escaped. Today, I understand. I was there, and was twice wounded. This is the story of what I knew and when I knew it.

3   To our astonishment, the Marine landing on April 1 was uncontested. The enemy had set a trap. Japanese strategy called first for kamikazes to destroy our fleet, cutting us off from supply ships; then Japanese troops would methodically annihilate the men stranded ashore using the trench-warfare tactics of World War I—cutting the Americans down as they charged heavily fortified positions. One hundred and ten thousand Japanese troops were waiting on the southern tip of the island. Intricate entrenchments, connected by tunnels, formed the enemy's defense line, which ran across the waist of Okinawa from the Pacific Ocean to the East China Sea.

4   By May 8, after more than five weeks of fighting, it became clear that the anchor of this line was a knoll of coral and volcanic ash, which the Marines christened Sugar Loaf Hill. My role in mastering it—the crest changed hands more than eleven times—was the central experience of my youth, and of all the military bric-a-brac that I put away after the war, I cherish most the Commendation from General Lemuel C. Shepherd, Jr., U.S.M.C., our splendid division commander, citing me for "gallantry in action and extraordinary achievement," adding, "Your courage was a constant source of inspiration . . . and your conduct throughout was in keeping with the highest tradition of the United States Naval Service."

5   The struggle for Sugar Loaf lasted ten days; we fought under the worst possible conditions—a driving rain that never seemed to slacken, day or night. (I remember wondering, in an idiotic moment—no man in combat is really sane—whether the battle could be called off, or at least postponed, because of bad weather.)

6   *Newsweek* called Sugar Loaf "the most critical local battle of the war." *Time* described a company of Marines — 270 men — assaulting the hill. They failed; fewer than 30 returned. Fletcher Pratt, the military historian, wrote that the battle was unmatched in the Pacific war for "closeness and desperation." Casualties were almost unbelievable. In the 22d and 29th Marine regiments, two out of every three men fell. The struggle for the dominance of Sugar Loaf was probably the costliest engagement in the history of the Marine Corps. But by early evening on May 18, as night thickened over the embattled armies, the 29th Marines had taken Sugar Loaf, this time for keeps. . . .

7   It may be said that the history of war is one of men packed together, getting closer and closer to the ground and then deeper and deeper into it. In the densest combat of World War I, battalion frontage — the length of the line into which the 1,000-odd men were squeezed — had been 800 yards. On Okinawa, on the Japanese fortified line, it was less than 600 yards — about 18 inches per man. We were there and deadlocked for more than a week in the relentless rain. During those weeks we lost nearly 4,000 men.

8   And now it is time to set down what this modern battlefield was like.

9   All greenery had vanished; as far as one could see, heavy shellfire had denuded the scene of shrubbery. What was left resembled a cratered moonscape. But the craters were vanishing, because the rain had transformed the earth into a thin porridge — too thin even to dig foxholes. At night you lay on a poncho as a precaution against drowning during the barrages. All night, every night, shells erupted close enough to shake the mud beneath you at the rate of five or six a minute. You could hear the cries of the dying but could do nothing. Japanese infiltration was always imminent, so the order was to stay put. Any man who stood up was cut in half by machine guns manned by fellow Marines.

10   By day, the mud was hip deep; no vehicles could reach us. As you moved up the slope of the hill, artillery and mortar shells were bursting all around you, and, if you were fortunate enough to reach the top, you encountered the Japanese defenders, almost face to face, a few feet away. To me, they looked like badly wrapped brown paper parcels someone had soaked in a tub. Their eyes seemed glazed. So, I suppose, did ours.

11   Japanese bayonets were fixed; ours weren't. We used the knives, or, in my case, a .45 revolver and M1 carbine. The mud beneath our feet was deeply veined with blood. It was slippery. Blood is very slippery. So you skidded around, in deep shock, fighting as best you could until one side outnumbered the other. The outnumbered side would withdraw for reinforcements and then counterattack.

12   During those ten days I ate half a candy bar. I couldn't keep anything down. Everyone had dysentery, and this brings up an aspect of war even Robert Graves, Siegfried Sassoon, Edmund Blunden and Ernest Hemingway avoided. If you put more than a quarter million men in a line for three weeks, with

no facilities for the disposal of human waste, you are going to confront a disgusting problem. We were fighting and sleeping in one vast cesspool. Mingled with that stench was another—the corrupt and corrupting odor of rotting human flesh.

13   My luck ran out on June 5, more than two weeks after we had taken Sugar Loaf Hill and killed the seven thousand Japanese soldiers defending it. I had suffered a slight gunshot wound above the right knee on June 2, and had rejoined my regiment to make an amphibious landing on Oroku Peninsula behind enemy lines. The next morning several of us were standing in a stone enclosure outside some Okinawan tombs when a six-inch rocket mortar shell landed among us.

14   The best man in my section was blown to pieces, and the slime of his viscera enveloped me. His body had cushioned the blow, saving my life; I still carry a piece of his shinbone in my chest. But I collapsed, and was left for dead. Hours later corpsmen found me still breathing, though blind and deaf, with my back and chest a junkyard of iron fragments—including, besides the piece of shinbone, four pieces of shrapnel too close to the heart to be removed. (They were not dangerous, a Navy surgeon assured me, but they still set off the metal detector at the Buffalo airport.)

15   Between June and November I underwent four major operations and was discharged as 100 percent disabled. But the young have strong recuperative powers. The blindness was caused by shock, and my vision returned. I grew new eardrums. In three years I was physically fit. The invisible wounds remain.

16   Most of those who were closest to me in the early 1940s had left New England campuses to join the Marines, knowing it was the most dangerous branch of the service. I remember them as bright, physically strong and inspired by an idealism and love of country they would have been too embarrassed to acknowledge. All of us despised the pompousness and pretentiousness of senior officers. It helped that, almost without exception, we admired and respected our commander in chief. But despite our enormous pride in being Marines, we saw through the scam that had lured so many of us to recruiting stations.

17   Once we polled a rifle company, asking each man why he had joined the Marines. A majority cited *To the Shores of Tripoli*, a marshmallow of a movie starring John Payne, Randolph Scott and Maureen O'Hara. Throughout the film the uniform of the day was dress blues; requests for liberty were always granted. The implication was that combat would be a lark, and when you returned, spangled with decorations, a Navy nurse like Maureen O'Hara would be waiting in your sack. It was peacetime again when John Wayne appeared on the silver screen as Sergeant Stryker in *Sands of Iwo Jima*, but that film underscores the point; I went to see it with another ex-Marine, and we were asked to leave the theater because we couldn't stop laughing.

18   After my evacuation from Okinawa, I had the enormous pleasure of seeing Wayne humiliated in person at Aiea Heights Naval Hospital in Hawaii. Only the most gravely wounded, the litter cases, were sent there. The hospital was packed, the halls lined with beds. Between Iwo Jima and Okinawa, the Marine Corps was being bled white.

19   Each evening, Navy corpsmen would carry litters down to the hospital theater so the men could watch a movie. One night they had a surprise for us. Before the film the curtains parted and out stepped John Wayne, wearing a cowboy outfit—ten-gallon hat, bandanna, checkered shirt, two pistols, chaps, boots and spurs. He grinned his aw-shucks grin, passed a hand over his face and said, "Hi ya, guys!" He was greeted by a stony silence. Then somebody booed. Suddenly everyone was booing.

20   This man was a symbol of the fake machismo we had come to hate, and we weren't going to listen to him. He tried and tried to make himself heard, but we drowned him out, and eventually he quit and left. If you liked *Sands of Iwo Jima*, I suggest you be careful. Don't tell it to the Marines.

21   And so we weren't macho. Yet we never doubted the justice of our cause. If we had failed—if we had lost Guadalcanal, and the Navy's pilots had lost the Battle of Midway—the Japanese would have invaded Australia and Hawaii, and California would have been in grave danger. In 1942 the possibility of an Axis victory was very real. It is possible for me to loathe war—and with reason—yet still honor the brave men, many of them boys, really, who fought with me and died beside me. I have been haunted by their loss these forty-two years, and I shall mourn them until my own death releases me. It does not seem too much to ask that they be remembered on one day each year. After all, they sacrificed their futures that you might have yours. . . .

&

Discussion Questions

1. We learn in paragraph 1 that General MacArthur, commander of the U.S. forces in the Pacific, "whose estimates of casualties . . . had proved uncannily accurate," was asked by President Truman for an estimate for the battle to take Japan itself. The general replied that "a million Americans would die in [the] first phase." How might this estimate prove relevant to the recent debate over the dropping of the atomic bombs on August 6 and 9, 1945, on Japan?

2. Paragraph 2 opens, "Given the assumption that nuclear weapons would contribute nothing to victory, the battle of Okinawa had to be fought." Given what did happen in August 1945, what irony might lurk in the thrust of this statement? Discuss.

3. What was the trap set by the Japanese for the Americans invading Okinawa?

4. In paragraphs 4–6, Manchester describes the taking of Sugar Loaf Hill. What was its importance, and what role did he play in the battle for it? What effect did the experience have on him?

*5. Why does Manchester limit paragraph 8 to one sentence? Explain.

6. How does the battlefield experience, as described in paragraphs 9–15, shape Manchester's feelings about such movies as *To the Shores of Tripoli* and *Sands of Iwo Jima*, as described in paragraph 17? Explain.

*7. When Manchester, left for dead, was discovered and hospitalized, what was his condition, and what changes in his physical condition occurred in three years? What does he mean when he says (paragraph 15), "The invisible wounds remain"?

*8. Why did Manchester take "enormous pleasure" in seeing John Wayne humiliated when Wayne visited the hospital in Hawaii where Manchester lay with his wounds?

9. Explain Manchester's meaning when he says in paragraph 21, "And so we weren't macho. Yet we never doubted the justice of our cause."

Writing Topics

1. Write a brief analytical essay in which you examine paragraphs 8–15 in detail to discover the sources—in the words, phrases, and sentences—of the vividness of Manchester's descriptive prose. In your conclusion, venture whatever generalizations about Manchester's method of writing you think appropriate.

2. Manchester writes in paragraph 12, "Everyone had dysentery, and this brings up an aspect of war even Robert Graves, Siegfried Sassoon, Edmund Blunden and Ernest Hemingway avoided." Determine what Manchester means by his statement, and then explore the work of one of the writers named or another "war writer" of your choice. After obtaining an impression of the author's descriptions of battlefield experience, write a comparison/contrast essay examining the work alongside Manchester's in light of his remark. Other writers to consider are John Dos Passos, Joseph Heller, Kurt Vonnegut, and Robert Stone.

❧ "*Scattered through the ruins are cash registers,*
typewriters, bicycles, safes,
all oxidized beyond recognition by the heat.
Many bottles had been partially melted and
twisted into fantastic forms."

EYEWITNESS: HIROSHIMA

Osborn Elliott

Born in New York City in 1924, Osborn Elliott served as a lieutenant junior grade in the U.S. Navy during World War II. He was on a ship headed for Japan on August 6, 1945, when a U.S. Air Force plane dropped the atomic bomb on Hiroshima. His firsthand account comes from a letter he wrote home after touring Hiroshima only a few weeks after the bomb was dropped. The selection comes from the July 24,1995, issue of *Newsweek*, which he served in various capacities from 1955 to 1976, ending as editor-in-chief. Elliott earned a B.A. at Harvard in 1946 and began his career as a journalist at *Time* magazine. In 1979, he joined the faculty of the Graduate School of Journalism at Columbia University, serving as dean from 1976 to 1986 and as a professor until his retirement in 1994. He is the author of two books, *Men at the Top* (1959), a work about businessmen, and *The World of Oz* (1979), a memoir of his life as an editor at *Newsweek*. In 1964, he edited *The Negro Revolution in America*.

1   When the news came, I was on the heavy cruiser Boston, steaming with the rest of the U.S. Third Fleet toward the coast of Japan. The shipboard radio crackled: some huge new bomb had just incinerated a place called Hiroshima. Like every other vessel in the sprawling armada, my ship erupted with whoops and shouts of joy. A few days earlier we had been bombarding the Japanese mainland, and the war seemed a long way from being over. But now all that had changed. And when some of us officers from the cruiser toured Hiroshima not many weeks later, we could see — and the ship's photographer recorded — just how persuasive the atomic bomb had been. Excerpts from my letter home:

2 "The city is/was situated in a valley—on one side the mountains, on the other the sea. As you stand in the middle of town, for miles on every side nothing rises above the level of your knees except for the shell of a building or the grotesque skeleton of a tree or perhaps a mound where the rubble has been pushed into a pile.

3 "We saw a fire station that seemed in relatively good condition. But inside, the two fire trucks were caricatures of twisted metal. Scattered through the ruins are cash registers, typewriters, bicycles, safes, all oxidized beyond recognition by the heat. Many bottles had been partially melted and twisted into fantastic forms.

4 "A couple of miles from Ground Zero, two trolleys lay on their sides, along with some cars that had been hurled off the street. Small concrete buildings were swollen out of shape—including a church whose walls bulged outwards and whose bell tower formed an S curve. In a residential district, someone's clothes dangled from a blackened tree branch. By contrast, a nearby shrine appeared untouched by the blast.

5 "One big building near the center of town once [had] a large dome. The building was a shell, and nothing was left of the dome except the curved metal frames.

6 "How anybody was left alive, I do not know. But here and there, women and children were sitting on the rubble that was once their homes. We didn't see many wounded—just a few on crutches or with bandages on their heads. Many people had sores on their faces. We stared at them, and they gazed blankly back at us."

7 On that day half a century ago, we felt pity but no remorse. In our view, the atom bomb had saved many thousands of lives—quite possibly including our own.

❧

Discussion Questions

1. According to paragraph 1, what was the reaction of Elliott and others aboard the cruiser *Boston* to the news of the bombing of Hiroshima? Explain.

2. Out of the five paragraphs that Elliott quotes from his letter home, what is the main difference in focus between the first four and the last? What might be the reason (or reasons) for this difference?

3. What appears to be the implication when Elliott says in the penultimate paragraph, "We didn't see many wounded"?

*4. Explore the effect of the last sentence of paragraph 6, "We stared at them, and they gazed blankly back at us."

Writing Topics

1. Assume that a reader has expressed shock that the sailors "erupted . . . with shouts of joy" on hearing that Hiroshima had been "incinerated" by a "huge new bomb"—considering such a response "inhumane." Write a brief essay showing why you agree or disagree with this reader's reaction.

2. In the last paragraph, Elliott writes, "On that day half a century ago, we felt pity but no remorse." Write a brief essay exploring the meaning (or meanings) of this statement, and conclude with your view as to whether the U.S. sailors should or should not have felt *remorse* as well as *pity*.

❧"Soon he found a good-sized pleasure punt drawn up
on the bank, but in and around it was an awful
tableau —five dead men, nearly naked, badly burned,
who must have expired more or less all at once, for they
were in attitudes which suggested that they had been
working together to push the boat down into the river."

THE DAY THE BOMB FELL

John Hersey

John Hersey (1914–1993) was born in China of missionary
parents, took a B.A. at Yale in 1936, and attended classes at
Clare College, Cambridge, England. He became a war correspondent early in World War II, and his early books grew
out of that experience: Men on Bataan (1942) and Into the
Valley (1943). He was a prolific writer, winning a Pulitzer
Prize in 1944 for his novel A Bell for Adano. His Holocaust
novel, The Wall (1950), and his journalistic account of an
American race riot, The Algiers Motel Incident (1968), attracted
much attention; but no other work by him has had the
impact on the American imagination as has "Hiroshima,"
which appeared in The New Yorker on August 31, 1946, filling
the entire magazine. The article stunned its readers. No
such account had been given the American people, portray-
ing so vividly the result of the dropping of the atomic bomb
on the people of the city. The text in its entirety was read on
the American Broadcasting Company radio network (television had not yet come into its own). To write the piece,
Hersey went to Hiroshima and interviewed numerous individuals, deciding ultimately to write in detail about the
disrupted lives of six survivors from the moment of the explosion at 8:15 A.M. on August 6, 1945, until his arrival the
following spring. His account covered what they saw, what
they felt, and what they did, surrounded as they were by the
dead and dying, the hopelessly maimed and scarred, a city
in ashes. The six individuals included a housewife with

three children (Mrs. Nakamura), a German priest (Father Kleinsorge), a Japanese Methodist minister (Mr. Tanimoto), two doctors (Dr. Fujii and Dr. Sasaki), and an office worker (Miss Sasaki). In observation of the fiftieth anniversary of the dropping of the bomb, *The New Yorker* published an excerpt, "The Day the Bomb Fell," included here. Only the first three of the survivors listed above appear in the selection.

1   All day, people poured into Asano Park. This private estate was far enough away from the explosion so that its bamboos, pines, laurel, and maples were still alive, and the green place invited refugees—partly because they believed that if the Americans came back, they would bomb only buildings; partly because the foliage seemed a center of coolness and life, and the estate's exquisitely precise rock gardens, with their quiet pools and arching bridges, were very Japanese, normal, secure; and also partly (according to some who were there) because of an irresistible, atavistic urge to hide under leaves. Mrs. Nakamura and her children were among the first to arrive, and they settled in the bamboo grove near the river. They all felt terribly thirsty, and they drank from the river. At once they were nauseated and began vomiting, and they retched the whole day. Others were also nauseated; they all thought (probably because of the strong odor of ionization, an "electric smell" given off by the bomb's fission) that they were sick from a gas the Americans had dropped. When Father Kleinsorge and the other priests came into the park, nodding to their friends as they passed, the Nakamuras were all sick and prostrate. A woman named Iwasaki, who lived in the neighborhood of the mission and who was sitting near the Nakamuras, got up and asked the priests if she should stay where she was or go with them. Father Kleinsorge said, "I hardly know where the safest place is." She stayed there, and later in the day, though she had no visible wounds or burns, she died. The priests went farther along the river and settled down in some underbrush. Father LaSalle lay down and went right to sleep. The theological student, who was wearing slippers, had carried with him a bundle of clothes, in which he had packed two pairs of leather shoes. When he sat down with the others, he found that the bundle had broken open and a couple of shoes had fallen out and now he had only two lefts. He retraced his steps and found one right. When he rejoined the priests, he said, "It's funny, but things don't matter anymore. Yesterday, my shoes were my most important possessions. Today, I don't care. One pair is enough."

2   Father Cieslik said, "I know. I started to bring my books along, and then I thought, 'This is no time for books.' "

3   When Mr. Tanimoto reached the park, it was very crowded, and to distinguish the living from the dead was not easy, for most of the people lay still, with their eyes open. To Father Kleinsorge, an Occidental, the silence in the grove by the river, where hundreds of gruesomely wounded suffered together,

was one of the most dreadful and awesome phenomena of his whole experience. The hurt ones were quiet; no one wept, much less screamed in pain; no one complained; none of the many who died did so noisily; not even the children cried; very few people even spoke. And when Father Kleinsorge gave water to some whose faces had been almost blotted out by flash burns, they took their share and then raised themselves a little and bowed to him, in thanks.

4   Mr. Tanimoto greeted the priests and then looked around for other friends. He saw Mrs. Matsumoto, wife of the director of the Methodist School, and asked her if she was thirsty. She was, so he went to one of the pools in the Asanos' rock gardens and got water for her. Then he decided to try to get back to his church. He went into Nobori-cho by the way the priests had taken as they escaped, but he did not get far; the fire along the streets was so fierce that he had to turn back. He walked to the riverbank and began to look for a boat in which he might carry some of the most severely injured across the river from Asano Park and away from the spreading fire. Soon he found a good-sized pleasure punt drawn up on the bank, but in and around it was an awful tableau—five dead men, nearly naked, badly burned, who must have expired more or less all at once, for they were in attitudes which suggested that they had been working together to push the boat down into the river. Mr. Tanimoto lifted them away from the boat, and as he did so, he experienced such horror at disturbing the dead—preventing them, he momentarily felt, from launching their craft and going on their ghostly way—that he said out loud, "Please forgive me for taking this boat. I must use it for others, who are alive." The punt was heavy, but he managed to slide it into the water. There were no oars, and all he could find for propulsion was a thick bamboo pole. He worked the boat upstream to the most crowded part of the park and began to ferry the wounded. He could pack ten or twelve into the boat for each crossing, but as the river was too deep in the center to pole his way across, he had to paddle with the bamboo, and consequently each trip took a very long time. He worked several hours that way.

5   Early in the afternoon, the fire swept into the woods of Asano Park. The first Mr. Tanimoto knew of it was when, returning in his boat, he saw that a great number of people had moved toward the riverside. On touching the bank, he went up to investigate, and when he saw the fire, he shouted, "All the young men who are not badly hurt come with me!" Father Kleinsorge moved Father Schiffer and Father LaSalle close to the edge of the river and asked people there to get them across if the fire came too near, and then joined Tanimoto's volunteers. Mr. Tanimoto sent some to look for buckets and basins and told others to beat the burning underbrush with their clothes; when utensils were at hand, he formed a bucket chain from one of the pools in the rock gardens. The team fought the fire for more than two hours, and gradually defeated the flames. As Mr. Tanimoto's men worked, the frightened people in the park pressed closer and closer to the river, and finally the mob began to force some of the unfortunates who were on the very bank into the water. Among those

driven into the river and drowned were Mrs. Matsumoto, of the Methodist School, and her daughter.

6   When Father Kleinsorge got back after fighting the fire, he found Father Schiffer still bleeding and terribly pale. Some Japanese stood around and stared at him, and Father Schiffer whispered, with a weak smile, "It is as if I were already dead." "Not yet," Father Kleinsorge said. He had brought Dr. Fujii's first-aid kit with him, and he had noticed Dr. Kanda in the crowd, so he sought him out and asked him if he would dress Father Schiffer's bad cuts. Dr. Kanda had seen his wife and daughter dead in the ruins of his hospital; he sat now with his head in his hands. "I can't do anything," he said. Father Kleinsorge bound more bandage around Father Schiffer's head, moved him to a steep place, and settled him so that his head was high, and soon the bleeding diminished.

7   The roar of approaching planes was heard about this time. Someone in the crowd near the Nakamura family shouted, "It's some Grummans coming to strafe us!" A baker named Nakashima stood up and commanded, "Everyone who is wearing anything white, take it off." Mrs. Nakamura took the blouses off her children, and opened her umbrella and made them get under it. A great number of people, even badly burned ones, crawled into bushes and stayed there until the hum, evidently of a reconnaissance or weather run, died away.

8   It began to rain. Mrs. Nakamura kept her children under the umbrella. The drops grew abnormally large, and someone shouted, "The Americans are dropping gasoline. They're going to set fire to us!" (This alarm stemmed from one of the theories being passed through the park as to why so much of Hiroshima had burned: it was that a single plane had sprayed gasoline on the city and then somehow set fire to it in one flashing moment.) But the drops were palpably water, and as they fell, the wind grew stronger and stronger, and suddenly—probably because of the tremendous convection set up by the blazing city—a whirlwind ripped through the park. Huge trees crashed down; small ones were uprooted and flew into the air. Higher, a wild array of flat things revolved in the twisting funnel—pieces of iron roofing, papers, doors, strips of matting. Father Kleinsorge put a piece of cloth over Father Schiffer's eyes, so that the feeble man would not think he was going crazy. The gale blew Mrs. Murata, the mission housekeeper, who was sitting close by the river, down the embankment at a shallow, rocky place, and she came out with her bare feet bloody. The vortex moved out onto the river, where it sucked up a waterspout and eventually spent itself.

9   After the storm, Mr. Tanimoto began ferrying people again, and Father Kleinsorge asked the theological student to go across and make his way out to the Jesuit Novitiate at Nagatsuka, about three miles from the center of town, and to request the priests there to come with help for Fathers Schiffer and LaSalle. The student got into Mr. Tanimoto's boat and went off with him. Father Kleinsorge asked Mrs. Nakamura if she would like to go out to Nagatsuka with the priests when they came. She said she had some luggage and her children were sick—they were still vomiting from time to time, and so, for that

matter, was she—and therefore she feared she could not. He said he thought the fathers from the Novitiate could come back the next day with a pushcart to get her.

10   Late in the afternoon, when he went ashore for a while, Mr. Tanimoto, upon whose energy and initiative many had come to depend, heard people begging for food. He consulted Father Kleinsorge, and they decided to go back into town to get some rice from Mr. Tanimoto's Neighborhood Association shelter and from the mission shelter. Father Cieslik and two or three others went with them. At first, when they got among the rows of prostrate houses, they did not know where they were; the change was too sudden, from a busy city of two hundred and forty-five thousand that morning to a mere pattern of residue in the afternoon. The asphalt of the streets was still so soft and hot from the fires that walking was uncomfortable. They encountered only one person, a woman, who said to them as they passed, "My husband is in those ashes." At the mission, where Mr. Tanimoto left the party, Father Kleinsorge was dismayed to see the building razed. In the garden, on the way to the shelter, he noticed a pumpkin roasted on the vine. He and Father Cieslik tasted it and it was good. They were surprised at their hunger, and they ate quite a bit. They got out several bags of rice and gathered up several other cooked pumpkins and dug up some potatoes that were nicely baked under the ground, and started back. Mr. Tanimoto rejoined them on the way. One of the people with him had some cooking utensils. In the park, Mr. Tanimoto organized the lightly wounded women of his neighborhood to cook. Father Kleinsorge offered the Nakamura family some pumpkin, and they tried it, but they could not keep it on their stomachs. Altogether, the rice was enough to feed nearly a hundred people.

11   Just before dark, Mr. Tanimoto came across a twenty-year-old girl, Mrs. Kamai, the Tanimotos' next-door neighbor. She was crouching on the ground with the body of her infant daughter in her arms. The baby had evidently been dead all day. Mrs. Kamai jumped up when she saw Mr. Tanimoto and said, "Would you please try to locate my husband?"

12   Mr. Tanimoto knew that her husband had been inducted into the Army just the day before; he and Mrs. Tanimoto had entertained Mrs. Kamai in the afternoon, to make her forget. Kamai had reported to the Chugoku Regional Army Headquarters—near the ancient castle in the middle of town—where some four thousand troops were stationed. Judging by the many maimed soldiers Mr. Tanimoto had seen during the day, he surmised that the barracks had been badly damaged by whatever it was that had hit Hiroshima. He knew he hadn't a chance of finding Mrs. Kamai's husband, even if he searched, but he wanted to humor her. "I'll try," he said.

13   "You've got to find him," she said. "He loved our baby so much. I want him to see her once more."

❧

Discussion Questions

1. What did Asano Park contain that attracted bomb-blast survivors like Mrs. Nakamura to gather there for protection? What was the condition of Mrs. Nakamura and her children?
2. Explain the theological student's statement (paragraph 1), "Yesterday, my shoes were my most important possessions. Today, I don't care."
3. When Mr. Tanimoto arrived in the park (paragraph 3), he found it difficult to "distinguish the living from the dead," and he found the silence in the bamboo grove by the river, filled with hundreds of wounded, "one of the most dreadful and awesome phenomena of his whole experience." Explain.
4. Paragraphs 4–5 describe the danger of the fire raging through Hiroshima toward the park. What did Mr. Tanimoto do to deal with the danger threatening to destroy Asano Park?
5. Other dangers threatened, including a rainstorm/whirlwind (paragraph 8). What was the rumor about the rain that alarmed those in the park? What caused the tornadolike "funnel"?
6. Later in the afternoon, as the people became hungry, Mr. Tanimoto and Father Kleinsorge set out to find food. What was the result of their mission?
7. The excerpt ends with the episode (paragraphs 11–13) in which Mr. Tanimoto encountered a young woman holding a dead baby. What did she request of Mr. Tanimoto, and what was his reaction? Explain.

Writing Topics

1. Note in paragraph 1 the brief appearance and fate of the woman named Iwasaki who asked Father Kleinsorge whether she should stay put or go elsewhere: "She stayed there, and later in the day, though she had no visible wounds or burns, she died." Write a brief essay analyzing Hersey's narrative in which you explore the extent to which the cumulative effect of horror is achieved by such terse and cryptic vignettes.
2. Obtain and read carefully a copy of the whole of Hersey's *Hiroshima* and then consider the following statement: "Although John Hersey's *Hiroshima* withholds moral judgment, it is subtextually a powerful condemnation of the United States for dropping the atomic bomb, destroying the lives of so many innocent people." Write an essay showing why you agree or disagree with this statement, bolstering your position with specific references to Hersey's work.

"Fire was runnin' all up my fatigues.
Somethin' just kept tellin' me, Pull your leg out.
Pull your leg out. My left leg. I was steady diggin' and
steady tryin' to get it out, and I finally got it out.
I just nearly tore my right hand off."

I DIDN'T COME HOME THE WAY I WENT

Robert L. Daniels (as told to Wallace Terry)

Robert L. Daniels was nineteen years old when he enlisted in the army during the Vietnam War (1964–1975). After three months of training, he went directly to Vietnam. He served as Radio Wireman, Howitzer Gunner, 4th Infantry Division, from September to November 1967, and with the 52nd Artillery Group, U.S. Army, from November 1967 to November 1968. Severely wounded by a land mine and hospitalized for over a year, he went through several operations for skin-grafting but lost a hand. He was discharged on May 6, 1969. His oral history was taken from Wallace Terry's *Bloods: An Oral History of the Vietnam War by Black Veterans* (1984). The journalist Wallace Terry was born in 1938 in New York City and earned a B.A. from Brown University in 1959. While serving as a correspondent for *Time* in Vietnam from 1965 to 1967, he also produced documentary films on African American Marines for the United States Marine Corps. Recently he has worked as a commentator for CBS, *The Washington Post*, *Newsweek*, and other news organizations.

1   I never been away from home when I joined the Army. I never been on a train before I went to Fort Campbell, Kentucky, for basic training. I never was in a plane before they took me to Fort Sill in Oklahoma. That was AIT. Seems like we would have gone somewhere for a few months or so. But we went straight from there to Vietnam. Three months after I got in.

2   Flying over all that water, I was scared to death. I thought we would never get there, and I didn't know whether I was coming back.

3   When we landed in Cam Ranh Bay, it was like I had never seen anything like it before. Just open land. A lot of sand. Grass. Water. I was in a strange land.

4   I was scared to death.

5   We came up poor on the South Side of Chicago.

6   I don't even remember my childhood. I don't even remember a birthday cake. I don't remember a birthday party. I don't remember my father takin' me to places like parks and to the movies.

7   The only thing I remember is my grandmother always put up a tree every Christmas, and she always gave us something.

8   My mother left my father when I was three. I remember that they used to argue all the time. They got married too young, I think. They was seventeen. They didn't finish high school, and there wasn't no money. I didn't know where my father was. I knew my mother was working, and she lived somewhere else. My grandmother raised me.

9   My grandmother took care of her kids and her kid's kids. They were livin' on and off with her and my grandfather, about 15 of us brothers, sisters, and cousins altogether. There was always five of us in my bedroom.

10   My grandmother always told us to try to go to school, and we all graduated from high school. But I wasn't too interested in school, because I never had anything to wear. I only had one pair of shoes at a time. Tennis shoes. We always had a coat. But no nice clothes, like a suit or a tie. They couldn't afford to buy me them. So I didn't go to the dances and benefits at school. I was too ashamed. I was a timid person.

11   I sometimes think the way I came up and didn't be no dope addict is a surprise, because I had to learn so much from the streets. But one thing my grandparents instilled into me was staying away from the wrong crowd. When I found out they was the wrong crowd, smokin' dope or messin' with people, I would just go off to myself. I was a loner.

12   Before I went into the service I worked at the post office in Skokie as a sub for about a year. I decided to enlist 'cause it didn't seem like I was gettin' anywhere. And I felt it was gon' make me sort of like grown up. I didn't have anybody to sort of rear me into becomin' a man. And I thought the GI benefits would help me go to college since I didn't have no money for college.

13   When my mother realized I was gettin' ready to go away into the service, she gave me a birthday party. It was my first birthday party. I was nineteen years old.

14   All we did the first days in Pleiku was fill sandbags. Then they taught me about the switchboard. But I spent most of my time on the 105 howitzers. There was six guys around it. Each guy has a different job. One guy tilts the artillery. One guy might be on the telephone runnin' from one gun to another. My job was either cleanin' it or help loadin' it.

15   It seems like at first they was always shellin' us, and we would run to the bunkers. I use to wonder sometimes why we would run to them. The way they were built, if a shell would hit it direct, it wouldn't do no good anyway. It was only made with a whole lot of sandbags on top. It ain't nothin' like a house.

Maybe it was just to keep you from gettin' some scrap metal if the round hit near it.

16   One night we was goin' to sleep. I was just wearin' them green things they give you, like shorts. I thought I heard things comin' in. I jumped up, got my rifle, and put my belt on. I was runnin' out the back way, tryin' to get to the bunker. The sergeant told me to go back to sleep, because it wasn't what I thought it was. Everybody laughed 'cause I had all these guns and just my shorts.

17   When I went on guard duty, you hear noises. You shoot, because it be so dark out there. But I didn't never see anybody. All I know, I was scared.

18   Before I went to Vietnam I was told they were helpin' the people from communism, so they could try to be a free country. The communism didn't let the people control their own rights. But it looked like we were fightin' 'em altogether. You didn't know who was who. One Vietnamese look like he be on your side, and then at night he might be VC.

19   When I see the Vietnamese comin' in to clean the barracks, they didn't say nothin' to me. I didn't say nothin' to them. I didn't know who was who. I didn't trust 'em.

20   Sometimes we had to drive trucks from one place to another. Guys'll stop on the road, and the Vietnamese be sellin' beer or something. I never did stop. I was too scared.

21   One time I was goin' to pick some sandbags up to bring 'em back to my base. I was drivin' a five-ton, and I had two flats on one side. The other three trucks that was with me, they had just left me 2 miles down the road all by myself. I didn't stop, but I was goin' so slow. And I didn't have a shotgun at the time. Charlie could've just picked me off. Now that scared me.

22   When there was nothin' to do, I stayed in the barracks and read the *Jet*, or just wrote letters.

23   It took me six or seven months to walk down to Pleiku village. I was too scared at first. You might just get shot just walkin' around.

24   My friend and I went to this little place that made trick pictures, like you holdin' yourself in your hand. They had warned us before we left not to be active over there with the women sexually in case you catch something. I was too scared anyway, because I didn't know who the women was.

25   In November '68 I had about a month left. When I think about it now, I should've been gone since I was out there 14 months already. They were tellin' me to go to the field. I told 'em I didn't wanna go.

26   They told me they didn't have any sergeants out there, and they needed one to drive out this amtrac. They said you gotta go 'cause you the only one.

27   It was dangerous out there, and I didn't know what might happen. I didn't know where I was goin'. I never been out there. And it was almost time for me to go home.

28   I had a shotgunner, but it wasn't like no company or battalion goin' together.

29   We spent the first night in the field in some tents. Got up that next morning. We had a long way to go. Up to Kontum.

30   We was way out in the boonies like, and they kept saying we was almost there. They said they was hookin' me up with somebody else. Somebody I don't even know. I didn't even get a chance to see 'em.

31   It wasn't no main road. It was like a old dirt trail.

32   There was a minesweeper in front of us. Then a couple of tanks. We was fourth in line, the last vehicle.

33   We hit this mine. Got blew up. Blew the track straight up in the air.

34   I thought it was all over.

35   When that thing blew up, I never heard nothin' like that before in my life. That was the loudest sound I ever heard in my life.

36   It blew us right out of the track.

37   When I came down, the track fell on my leg.

38   We didn't have the cover on it you put over the top if it rains. If that would've been on, we would've got trapped in there.

39   I don't know whether the shotgunner got killed or not. He was on the other side with his machine gun.

40   I was just burnin' up. I was burnin' everywhere.

41   It ain't no gas stations in the field. You run out of gas, you just run out of gas. It no tellin' when somebody might come by and bring you some. So we had these gas cans with us. They must've exploded, too.

42   Fire was runnin' all up my fatigues.

43   Somethin' just kept tellin' me, Pull your leg out. Pull your leg out. My left leg. I was steady diggin' and steady tryin' to get it out, and I finally got it out. I just nearly tore my right hand off.

44   I was never taught to roll over when you on fire, and I start runnin'. And that's what I did wrong.

45   It felt like I was in hell.

46   I just was screamin' and screamin'.

47   So the guy that was in the tank in front of me told me to lie down, and he put it out with the stuff they carry.

48   So they had me sittin' on the side of the road waitin' for the helicopter. It must have took 20 minutes. They gave me something. Maybe morphine, and I sort of passed out.

49   I had third-degree burns everywhere. The skin was just hangin' off my left arm. My right arm was burned completely to the bone. My face was all burnt up. It was white.

50   I remember in the hospital in Japan I kept tellin' 'em I was cold. I couldn't get covered up, because I was burnt all up. They kept puttin' some white stuff all over my body. And they kept puttin' me in a tub and takin' the dead skin off.

51   In the hospitals back here they took skin grafts off my leg and put 'em on top on my head, on my forehead, and on my arm.

52   I caught gangrene in my right hand, and they took the thumb off. The hand just kept getting bigger and bigger. Finally my doctor told me that he had to take it off, because gangrene was gettin' ready to go all through my body. Well, I didn't want to die. So they cut it off.

53   They had to take veins out of my legs, too. I have a little limp now. I figure it's just poor circulation.

54   They wanted to do some plastic surgery on my ear to make it look like the other one. I didn't go back. I was just tired of hospitals. I don't know how many operations they did on me. They said I had somethin' they call severe trauma.

55   Two Christmases had gone by me in the hospital.

56   That doctor say if I wasn't a young man, I wouldn't have made it.

57   I got my discharge papers May 6, 1969.

58   I came home and stayed with my mother.

59   I didn't come home the way I went. I went a tall, slim, healthy fella. You could look at me now and tell something had happened. I was either born like that, or I was in the war. I'm scarred all over. It ain't no way you can hide it.

60   After six months, I started goin' to school at Northwestern Business College. Using the GI benefits. I got a associate arts degree in accounting, and they sent me all over lookin' for a job.

61   I tried maybe 40 places in two years. But I never did get hired.

62   They would say I didn't have experience. Or they would make excuses like, "You think not having that hand would interfere with your doing this kind of work?" I thought, How would that interfere sittin' there at a desk? Or they would tell me they would let me know, but nobody never did call me back.

63   I got discouraged. I guess I just gave up, because I kept gettin' turned down. Nobody never really wanted to give me a break. I was black. A amputee. And it was an unpopular war. Maybe they didn't like the idea nobody from Vietnam workin' in they profession.

64   That was in 1975. I stopped lookin' for a job. I've been livin' on disability and Social Security.

65   I stay home most of the time. Just readin'. I'll walk my daughter sometimes. But as far as goin' out to plays or out to dinner, I don't do that. I wouldn't know how you s'posed to carry yourself. Like in a nice restaurant, I couldn't cut my own meat. And I'm gonna be stared at anyway.

66   In 1981 Social Security stopped sending me checks. So I have been havin' trouble with this house note. And somebody stole my car. The Social Security wrote me this, "We realize that your condition prevents you from doing any of your past jobs as a foot soldier, but does not prevent you from doing . . . various unskilled, light one-armed jobs." But it was Social Security that told me I was disabled and could have the money when I was discharged.

67   This lady, she said, "What do you expect, Mr. Daniels? To receive Social Security for the rest of your life?"

68   I started to tell her, "Yeah. My hand is gonna be missin' for the rest of my life." But I didn't say anything. Maybe Social Security thinks I've lived too long.

69   It's funny. When I see the Vietnamese who came over here, I just wonder how they start so fast. Get businesses and stuff. Somebody helpin' 'em. But the ones that fought for they country, been livin' here all along, we get treated like dirt.

70   I know you gotta help yourself, but you can't do everything. I can't hire me.

71   Sometimes I feel I'm worth more to my wife and daughter if I wasn't around because I got the insurance. Like you don't get your insurance until you die, right? Sometimes that what I think. Sometimes.

72   When I was nineteen, I know I didn't know too much about what's goin' on. Except you s'posed to fight for your country. And you come home. But where is my country when I come home?

73   And now I read where the people in Vietnam still havin' the same problems they had before the United States went over there. I read they say they wasn't no war. Well what the hell they sent us over there for? I read the Americans lost. It was nothin'. Nothin'.

74   But I wish I—I would've—I would've came back the way, you know, I went.

75   I might have realized which way my life would've went.

76   All I did was lost part of my body. And that's the end of me.

❧

Discussion Questions

1.   What can we tell about Daniels from the first four paragraphs?

2.   In paragraphs 5–13, Daniels summarizes his life up to the time he enlisted. He describes himself as a "timid person" and a "loner," and he gives as one reason for his enlisting, "I didn't have anybody to sort of rear me into becomin' a man." From the details of his life that he sets forth, are his self-characterizations apt and his motives for enlisting persuasive? Explain.

3.   In paragraphs 15–24, Daniels describes his life as a soldier in Vietnam in general, telling about various incidents to suggest the way it was—his running to the bunker during a shelling, his waking up and running out in his shorts with his gun, his difficulties in telling the difference between enemy and friendly Vietnamese, his being scared while driving his truck on the road, and his way of spending his time when there was nothing to do. What do these revelations tell us about Daniels? Explain.

*4. In paragraphs 27–49, Daniels describes the episode in which he was wounded. Does Daniels seem justified in saying at one point, "I thought it was all over," and at another point, "I felt like I was in hell"? Explain.

5. Describe the various operations Daniels went through in the hospital. What was the operation that the doctors wanted to do when he decided he didn't want any more operations?

6. What happened when Daniels protested because he was cut off from Social Security benefits? Explain.

*7. Daniels learned from his doctors that he suffered "severe trauma" from his war wounds. How would you describe the suffering he seems to be going through at the end of his account? Explain.

Writing Topics

1. Daniels's life, judging by his account of it, appears to have moved from one defeat or disaster to another, until at the end he appears to be bitter if not desperate. In an essay exploring his various misfortunes, assess how much he, or society, or chance was responsible for his plight. In your conclusion, consider what remedy for such cases as his you would propose.

2. Social Security wrote a letter to Daniels saying, "We realize that your condition prevents you from doing any of your past jobs as a foot soldier, but does not prevent you from doing . . . various unskilled, light one-armed jobs." Write a letter to both Social Security and the Veterans Administration in support of Daniels's application for continued help by detailing relevant information contained in his oral autobiography. You might conclude by saying that he is even willing to take any of the "various unskilled, light one-armed jobs," of which there must be plenty, in the vast bureaucracies of the Social Security Administration and the Veterans Administration.

Summary Writing Topics

1. "The U.S. government's treatment of the Indians in the nineteenth century may bear some superficial resemblance to Germany's treatment of the Jews during World War II, but in the end there are radical differences between the two." In an argumentative essay, set forth your agreement or disagreement with this statement, supporting your point of view with ideas from the essays of Black Elk and Elise Radell and your own experience.

2. From what you have learned in reading Jeanne Wakatsuki Houston's "A Family Disrupted," write an essay focusing on U.S. treatment of the Japanese Americans in World War II, but also include comparisons with U.S. treatment of the Indians as portrayed in Black Elk's essay and with Germany's treatment of the Jews as related in Elise Radell's essay. In your conclusion, summarize any important differences.

3. William Preston, Jr. ("On Omaha Beach") and William Manchester ("Okinawa: The Bloodiest Battle of Them All") describe their combat experiences in World War II, one in Europe, the other in the Pacific. Write an essay focusing on similarities in their experiences and/or in their feelings about their experiences.

4. In an essay, compare and contrast Robert Daniels's experience in Vietnam and his feelings about that experience with the experiences and feelings of William Preston, Jr. and William Manchester. In your conclusion, consider how much of whatever difference you find might be attributed to the differences in attitudes of the United States toward World War II and the Vietnam War.

5. Write a short story in which you must make a choice of landing on Omaha Beach, invading Okinawa, or driving vehicles on the dirt roads of Vietnam. Describe your choice and how you found your way to it.

6. Write an essay on Ann Darr's experience as described in "The Women Who Flew—But Kept Silent," showing how many if not all the difficulties the WASPs had in coming into being and in lasting until disbanded in 1944 may simply be attributed to prejudice against women. In your conclusion, indicate how far you think the United States has come in diminishing that prejudice.

7. Two selections in Cluster 12 are accounts of the results of the dropping of the atomic bomb on Hiroshima in 1945: "Eyewitness: Hiroshima" by Osborn Elliott and "The Day the Bomb Fell" by John Hersey. Write a comparison/contrast essay exploring the impact on the reader of these two essays. In your conclusion, summarize and assess the explicit or implicit "moral position" of the two authors. If you conclude that either or both of the authors take no moral position, explore the possible reasons for such notable "silence."

8. In William Preston's essay, "On Omaha Beach," he writes, "For me at least, the near catastrophe of June 6 diminished forever the credibility of the concepts of strategic planning and of tactical order; it provided me instead with a sense of chaos, random disaster, and vulnerability." Select an essay describing a similar experience of "near catastrophe" (Manchester's or Daniels's, for example), and write an essay showing the ways in which the experience was similar and how the author did or did not reach a conclusion—or philosophy—like Preston's.

9. In Jeanne Wakatsuki Houston's "A Family Disrupted," she describes two traits exhibited by the Japanese—cooperation and personal privacy—as traditional Japanese traits attributable to the Japanese experience of learning to live in a "small, crowded country like Japan." Consider your own experience in the United States and write an essay in which you describe one or more traits, positive or negative, that you believe to be American. Show why you believe them to be American and indicate what you believe to be their source.

10. Since the United States is a large country and not nearly so crowded as Japan, we might speculate, in accordance with Houston's theory in "A Family Disrupted," that Americans are likely to be uncooperative and open or sociable. Write an argumentative essay confirming or attacking this notion.

11. The essays in "Disruptions and Disasters" contain descriptions of many violent acts, some of them outrageous. Assume that a committee of parents from your community complains about their children being exposed to so much violence. The committee is holding a hearing and has invited you to testify. Prepare your written testimony, or opening statement, in which you condemn or approve the committee's position.

Cluster 13

Nature Unfolding, Nature Unbridled

The United States is the only country that defines *frontier* not as an established dividing line between two countries but as the shifting line separating the settled, cultivated lands and the unsettled, virgin territories—always west. After the 1890 census found the U.S. population density (people per square mile) at a sufficiently high level, the American frontier was declared officially closed. But myth derives its energy not from official but unofficial—and primal—authority: the American imagination remains deeply engaged with the frontier as past but not really extinct.

There is no wonder, then, that nature figures so importantly in American literature. And the ambiguity that nature poses runs through all the descriptions of it. Foreigners visiting the United States are almost always surprised by its size and awed by its natural monuments—Niagara Falls, the Grand Canyon, the clockwork-like Yellowstone geysers, the giant redwood forests, the overarching prairie skies, the vast stretches of desert. But the awe felt in viewing these and other natural phenomena is comprised of both wonder and dread, attraction and fear.

Thus the title of this cluster of selections—"Nature Unfolding, Nature Unbridled." Nature seems benevolent, for example, in the abundance it brings to humankind, with the sun and rain that grow the crops for the food we eat. And in the movement of the days, seasons, and years, natural beauty refreshes the spirit and inspires the fancy. But nature appears malevolent in the guise of hurricanes, tornadoes, earthquakes, floods, erupting volcanoes, runaway forest fires, all leaving random death and destruction in their wake. There are those, however, who believe that nature is neither benevolent nor malevolent but simply indifferent. Such indifference, if it is that, has not cheered those naturalists who invented it, for it suggests a universe without plan or transcendent presence.

Whatever we may conclude about nature, there is no way it will allow us to turn away and ignore it. Since encounter is inevitable, it should prove helpful to find out how others have fared in venturing up close to nature, gathering and recording their impressions. The right balance between sentimental worshipping and pointless protestation might just be a healthy ambivalence. If you go out on a summer day to enjoy the beauty of a cloudy sky, it might be wise to carry an umbrella.

"This morning one of the boys said that this was a God-forsaken country. I told him that the whole of Cass County was covered with No. 1 hard wheat, and the wayside was all abloom with goldenrod and asters which proves that God has not forsaken it."

HOMESTEADING IN THE DAKOTA TERRITORY

Mary Dodge Woodward

Mary Dodge Woodward (1826–1890), finding herself a widow at the age of fifty-six, left her Wisconsin home with three of her grown-up children to go to the Dakota Territory to establish a farm on former government land. Her diary provides a vivid account of both the daily hardships and the uncommon rewards of creating a farm out of virgin land. The diary was published in 1937 as *The Checkered Years: A Bonanza Farm Diary, 1884–1888*; it was reissued in 1989, edited by Mary Boynton Cowdrey.

[1885]

MAY 31, SUNDAY

1   The wheat is rising out of the ground. The day is very beautiful and I have been out nearly all of it picking posies. The air is soft and cool. I think there is something fascinating about gathering wild flowers, strolling along, not knowing what you will find. It gives one a childish delight. There is a bright yellow flower in bloom now which looks like a Montana verbena, except in color, and is as fragrant; and there are violets in great numbers, some of them nearly pink. Katie says that down at the Sheyenne the air is fragrant with blossoms. Yet I should not like to live there, for the storms follow the river and the mosquitoes are troublesome.

2   The river woods are looking green. I stand at the east chamber window—which is my observatory —with the spyglass every day and look at them. They seem as near as Vince's woods at home. There is only a narrow strip, but they are dense and filled with a thicket of underbrush, all tangled together. This has been cleared out in several places and farm houses stand close to the river. Hundreds of pounds of hops, growing wild, are gathered there by the settlers every year. Hops possess the qualities of yeast-making in a high degree. I think this is rightly called the land of bread—the wheat, the yeast, the water, and the coal—the very "staff of life."

June 3

3   It is hard to cook without vegetables, but I have learned to make use of dried fruits. I put in just enough water to swell the berries, then cool them before putting in the sugar, and they swell to their full size. I make all the bread myself. We like good bread and butter at every meal. I have made all the pies since we came here with the exception of lemon pies which Katie makes better than I.

4   Walter is painting the sitting room floor. It is useless to try to keep a carpet here. I never believed in making a parlor out of a sitting room where members of the family should feel free to come and go as they please.

5   I have cut out the dress which Nellie sent me so as to finish it before Daniel arrives. Were I farther west, I should not dare to make it "Mother Hubbard" as the paper says that in Pendleton, Oregon, that type of costume is prohibited unless worn belted. Bills to that effect have been posted in the town, ladies who violate the ordinance being fined heavily. The alleged reason is that such garments "scare horses, cause accidents, and ruin business."

June 7, Sunday

6   There was a terrific thunder and wind storm last night. The boys said the roof of the granary fairly wiggled, and the plows were positively blown out of the furrows. The wind tore my lovely pansies all to pieces, and the leaves on the trees hang in ribbons. Afterward, there was a hard frost which left the ground white. At half past nine this morning the ice was not all out of the watering troughs. The peonies froze so hard that the buds hung limp—what few had not been cut off. . . .

July 30

7   We had a fearful storm this morning at seven o' clock. The sky was black as ink. Then came the rain, wind, thunder, and lightening with terrible force. The wind laid flat everything in the garden, lodged the grain, and blew things around generally. It moved the machine house about an inch. A brood of chickens that I had taken a great deal of pains with was killed. The hen was out about two rods from the barn, too far to get in. She took the chicks under her wing, but she was blown off against the barn.

8   It seems strange to have Cousin Daniel here. He hitched up Gumbo, and he and Roxy and I rode around the quarter-section after supper. The daisies are blossoming in the sloughs, hundreds in one bunch: pink, purple, and white. They are about the size of a nickel. The fallen wheat and oats and vegetables have lifted. The wheat begins to have a ripe, yellow look.

AUGUST 11

9   Harvest has started. Now there will be no rest for man, woman, or beast until frost which comes, thank heaven, early here. I was nearly beside myself getting dinner for thirteen men, besides carpenters and tinners, with Katie sick in bed and Elsie washing. I baked seventeen loaves of bread today, making seventy-four loaves since last Sunday, not to mention twenty-one pies, and puddings, cakes, and doughnuts.

10   The men cut one hundred acres today. All four of our harvesters are being used as well as three which were hired to cut by the acre. Things look like business with seven self-binders at work on this home section. The twine to bind our grain will cost three hundred dollars this year.

11   One of the farm hands broke the thermometer. Now if we are ever so warm we will not know it. I shall send for one as soon as possible.

AUGUST 16

12   How beautiful the wheat fields look, long avenues between the shocks, just as straight, one mile in length! The whole country is covered with shocks, heavy ones too. Any time during the past week we could see a hundred reapers with the attendant shockers—six to four reapers. Daniel has been flying here, there, and everywhere. Everybody is rustling, which is what I like.

13   The boys have gone to the Sheyenne to see if there are any plums. Last year there were great quantities of them, very large for wild ones; and grapes, large ones too. The feathery plumes of the goldenrod are beautiful, growing everywhere. They remind me of home. This morning one of the boys said that this was a God-forsaken country. I told him that the whole of Cass County was covered with No. 1 hard wheat, and the wayside was all abloom with goldenrod and asters which proves that God has not forsaken it. . . .

NOVEMBER 26

14   Thanksgiving Day. This used to be a day of unusual gladness, for on this day Walter was born, and he has proved a great blessing to me. We used to try, after the fashion of New Englanders, to be all at home on Thanksgiving if it were possible. I have been very happy with my family around the table many years—how happy, I did not realize until that sad day on which the father was taken from us and I was left alone with the children. Never since then have all the children been with me on this day. It is our fourth Thanksgiving in Dakota. The turkey is roasted and eaten, and the day has gone; I am thankful. . . .

❧

Discussion Questions

1. How did Woodward spend May 31, 1885 (paragraph 1), and what was her feeling about that day?

*2. Paragraph 2 seems to demonstrate that Woodward was a serious and keen observer of nature. Cite details in the paragraph to support this statement.

3. In paragraphs 3–5, Woodward's observations touch on the necessities of life: food, shelter, and clothing. What were her concerns? Explain.

4. What damage was done during the two storms described in paragraphs 6–7? By the details she reported, what seem to have been Woodward's main worries?

5. Describe Woodward's contribution during the harvest (paragraphs 9–11). What do her remarks reveal about her overall responsibility and concern for the success of the farm?

*6. As indicated by the last paragraph, what role did Thanksgiving Day play in Woodward's life? How did she feel about the particular Thanksgiving Day that she writes about in this paragraph? Explain.

Writing Topics

1. Flowers, both wild and cultivated, seem to have played an important part in Woodward's life. Write an essay in which you demonstrate by examples the validity of this observation, and in your conclusion give your judgment of why flowers meant so much to her.

2. One poet has written, "Twixt optimist and pessimist / The difference is droll; / The optimist sees the doughnut, / The pessimist, the hole." Using this or any other reliable distinction between optimist and pessimist, write a brief essay in which you show how Woodward is one or the other. You might reveal your own opinion about these opposed approaches to life, perhaps in a conclusion venturing a judgment of Woodward's character.

The river was empty, the other shore just a thick green wall. At my back, beyond the little tent, stretched the limitless tundra, mile upon mile, clear to the Arctic Ocean. Somehow that day I was very conscious of that infinite quiet space."

BY MAIN STRENGTH

Margaret E. Murie

Margaret E. Murie, born in Seattle in 1902, grew up in Alaska from the age of nine. She attended Reed College in Portland, Oregon and Simmons College in Boston, Massachusetts. She was the first woman to graduate from the University of Alaska—in June 1924, with a major in business. Her marriage to Olaus Murie, a distinguished biologist and conservationist, initiated a unique partenship, involving frequent trips to the Alaska wilderness. The two of them collaborated on works about Alaska, including *Wapiti Wilderness* (1965). She also served as the editor of works by her husband, including *Journeys to the Far North* (1973) and *The Alaskan Bird Sketches of Olaus J. Murie* (1979). But she wrote *Two in the Far North* (1962) in her own voice, and it is the source of "By Main Strength." The essay relates a trip they took up the Porcupine and Old Crow Rivers to Arctic Alaska to band geese (to determine flight migration patterns). They were accompanied by their baby son and the guide they hired— along with his motorboat. Murie is currently at work, at age ninety-three in 1996, on *The Girl from Alaska: The Margaret Murie Story*. (When she attended Simmons College, she was called "that girl from Alaska.")

Asked to comment on "learning to write," Murie responded that she never had any courses in writing, aside from one course at Simmons in which the students had to write essays on the subjects they were studying. She relied, she said, on "her observations, her diaries, and her ability to tell stories, honed over many years of adventure and work on behalf of conservation."

1   On June 28 we camped at Black Fox Creek, three tumble-down cabins atop a high grassy bank in a thick stand of spruces. No one was there of course. If another human being had appeared anywhere on this river we would have thought we were seeing things, for we were to be the only people in the Old Crow Basin that summer. ("Even the natives stay out of there.") But sometime long ago someone had had a winter camp here. We knew we were getting close to the end of timber.

2   Next morning, hot and fair, we were purring along as usual, the folding canvas canoe set up now and being towed behind us, every eye looking out for geese. "There's a slough coming in up ahead. Might be geese on that beach." Olaus reached for his glasses.

3   Suddenly we heard a "clank, clank"—not a loud noise, but ominous; then silence. The engine had stopped. "What the Sam Hill!" Jess exclaimed, and began jigging this and that and muttering to himself. Finally he said: "Well, guess we'll have to pole over to shore till I see what it is. It might . . . but I'm afraid it's the crankshaft."

4   The moment the motor died the mosquitoes attacked. It was a great relief to get into the tent which Olaus quickly set up in the thick moss on top of the cut bank. I lay there playing with the baby. He was the one perfectly serene member of the party. I heard metallic sounds from below, but no explosions from Jess; this was a bad sign. Pretty soon I heard him say in a strangely quiet voice: "Well, we might as well go up and tell Mardy."

5   They both came crawling through the netting. Olaus was smiling at me. "Well, Mardy, our days of mechanized travel are over. Do you mind?"

6   The crankshaft. I'd never known there were such things. Now I found out how important they were. Jess had brought along practically a whole second engine. In the bottom of the boat lay a spare propeller shaft; stored away in the lockers were dozens of spark plugs, three extra wheels, all kinds of repair parts. But none of these things broke. Only the one most expensive, vital part that breaks only once in a million times!

7   We were just reaching the waterfowl grounds; the work for which we had come had just begun. They had banded twelve geese so far.

8   Quite a long time they sat there, discussing what had happened. My mind was leaping on to "What next?" but Olaus had not said anything about that yet and I suddenly remembered the government contract signed in Fairbanks. Jess and his motorboat had been hired together. He was under no obligation to go any farther. Twelve geese banded so far.

9   Jess was sitting cross-legged, tossing a bolt or nut and catching it as he talked. Suddenly the piece of iron went sailing against the tent wall and Jess said: "Well, by Jesus, we don't need to be stuck! We came up here to band geese and by Criminy we're *going* to band geese. I'm ready to go on if you are."

10   Olaus heaved a big sigh, and a big smile appeared on his face. "By golly, Jess, do you really mean that? Of course I want to; I've never been stuck on an assignment yet; only, I hate to ask you . . ."

11   Jess went right on. "Hell, of course we can. We'll take that boat back down to Black Fox Creek and tie her up; there's a good bank there. We'll put all the stuff we need in the scow and pull her and pole her on up—they said it was sluggish water all the way to the head of the river. Must be about two hundred and fifty miles, I guess. But if there's geese anywhere in the country we'll find 'em, even without an engine!"

12   Three hours later the motorboat, with the canvas canoe trailing behind, was disappearing round the bend downstream, two paddles dipping in rhythm, both raised in a reassuring salute as they slid from view. I climbed the ten-foot bank above the wet sand beach and knelt at the tent door, holding the netting close to my face so I could see inside. Martin was sound asleep on our bed, clad only in a diaper, arms flung out wide. It was a hot day and the tent was warm. How safe, how defenseless! I rose and went back down to the beach. Except for the incessant din of the mosquitoes, the world was quiet and still. Across the brown stream a white-crowned sparrow sang a lazy midday song; there was no other sound in this green world under the warm blue sky. The river was empty, the other shore just a thick green wall. At my back, beyond the little tent, stretched the limitless tundra, mile upon mile, clear to the Arctic Ocean. Somehow that day I was very conscious of that infinite quiet space.

13   But it was better to get busy. They had left me a pile of firewood. In a flour sack lay two geese, skinned the day before for specimens. I built up a fire. I would make rice stuffing for the geese. Where was the rice? Ah, that was a question! Here along the beach, in a heap measuring about ten by twenty feet, were piled all our possessions, everything but the cases of gas and oil and the tools for the engine. These were on their way downstream to Black Fox Creek. I began poking and peering and climbing about over the pile of boxes and waterproofed bags. It took quite a while to find and assemble the food needed for the next day's cooking, but eventually the two geese were simmering in the Dutch oven, and the baby cereal and dried fruit were on the grate. By the time those three thick chunks of wood burned down, they would be cooked. I drew the tarp back over the pile of goods, looked again at the line running from the precious scow to be sure it was securely tied, took a bowl of cooked mixed vegetables for the baby, and climbed up to the tent.

14   Before going in, I looked out over the tundra once more. Wavering, hummocky, softly green, it stretched to the sky, here and there a stunted spruce, a small feathery birch, tussocks of white Labrador tea in bloom. A white-crowned sparrow flipped into a nearby birch, and on the tip of a small spruce a tree sparrow was singing blithely. There was no other visible life. I crawled into the tent, pulled off my hat and veil and gloves, and unlaced my high leather boots.

15   There the baby and I stayed, all that day and the following night—night in which the sunlight was only slightly less intense. I played with the baby when he was awake, tossing the red rubber lamb back and forth for a long time, playing peek-a-boo behind his box—all the little games I could think of.

16   When he lay quiet with his bottle, or slept, it was still again. Almost afraid to look, I gave the river a quick glance—empty; then out over the tundra— nothing moving, every little tree in its place—good. And nothing moved across the river on the green grass either. Just the wilderness itself, friendly, and normal. My eyes were looking, not for any life, but for a reassuring lack of it. If I had spied a human form coming across the tundra, I would have been terrified; a bear or a wolf would have seemed excitingly normal.

17   So every little while, all that day and night, I had to go out and be reassured by looking all about, reassured that the baby and I were still safely alone. At two in the morning I banked some coals around the Dutch oven and lay down fully dressed beside the sleeping baby.

18   Someone was in the tent! Then the nicest voice in the world. "Hello, darlin', it's four in the morning and pretty cold, and the skeeters are gone for a while, and Jess and I are awfully hungry!"

19   Bill Mason had told us about Timber Creek and the cabin he had built there; how they had whipsawed spruce for the floor and roof and set in two windows they had brought from Fort Yukon. Old Crow had been a great spring muskrat region then; they had taken the muskrats and left the country on the first water, ahead of the mosquitoes!

20   On the morning of July 4, with Olaus pulling and Jess poling, the scow and canoe arrived at Timber Creek. The creek came in on the right side, from the north, and strangely enough, just where it emptied into the river there was the last stand of timber, and well back from the high bank, close to the spruces and tall cottonwoods, was the cabin, still sturdy and solid. Last timber, last cabin. From here on we would really be in the Arctic.

21   Jess loved to make things out of nothing. In five minutes we had a broom made of brush, the cabin was swept out, and Olaus had tacked netting over the windows.

22   Moving into this old cabin was our Fourth of July, and it was a real celebration. The day was bright and hot, just as Fourths should be. There was a wonderful breeze, so rare in this valley. We pulled off our heavy shirts, nets, and gloves, and hurried back and forth like small children playing house. This was a change, an excitement. In the vast quiet wilderness every little event was sharpened into thrilling poignancy.

23   Chattering incessantly, we were soon moved in; the floor was swept, a smudge built outside the door, the inside "Buhached," our gear in place. There were two built-in bunks, a table, shelves, stools—all waiting for us. Olaus spread a clean tarp on the floor in the back corner and tethered Martin to a bunk post. Here he crawled about, enjoying his new situation and all that space. And that very evening his daddy brought him great excitement. Olaus walked into the cabin with two golden-yellow downy goslings which he had caught and brought to the cabin to show Martin and me. He set them down at

the edge of the tarp where Martin sat; they ran cheeping right toward him. The baby reached out his hands, gurgled "Oh, oh, oh," and bounced up and down in a frenzy of excitement. When one gosling came very close, Martin reached out to grab it. Olaus, kneeling there, said quietly: "Easy now, easy—go easy."

24 And the baby seemed to sense that there was something different, to be touched gently. He stretched out one fat finger and touched the soft downy thing, looked up at his daddy, and laughed aloud. The two little goslings gave him an exciting interlude, and perhaps his first sense of handling wild creatures with gentleness. When the baby had fallen asleep, Olaus took the little goslings back to the riverbank and turned them loose to grow up.

25 To keep the cabin cool, we cooked outside. But we ate inside, and can you imagine the joy of sitting at a table, on a chair, without head net or gloves? All this we savored, along with the roast goose, the last of our fresh potatoes, hot biscuits, chocolate pudding. Martin sat on his daddy's lap and chewed on a goose bone and then shared in the opening of our Fourth of July package.

26 Back in Fairbanks, when the outfit had been loaded, Eddie Clausen, manager of the Northern Commerical Company, had handed us a package carefully wrapped and tied. "This is for your Fourth of July, wherever you are."

27 Martin watched the unwrapping, squealing and reaching out with his hands. Sure enough, in among the jars and bars of candy, nuts, dates, and chewing gum, was a box of Arrowroot biscuits for him! That was a real celebration. When it was over, Jess grabbed his rifle, strode out to the edge of the bank, and fired three shots into the air. ("Hello, all you big and little creatures of the Arctic. We have arrived among you. Don't let us disturb you too much—we aren't very important, but we're proud of ourselves today for having got here!")

28 So for six days. From the diary: "We thought we were taking a holiday, but we have all been going at our various duties every minute. It is nice to be settled and making a little home even for a few days and we enjoy it. We have more leisurely meals, and enjoy the evenings and other times when we are all in the cabin working and visting. Olaus has kept a mouse trapline going, done a little painting, explored about, collected birds. He and Jess have unloaded and sorted our gear, made repairs, developed films, kept smudge and fire going, carried water. A mammoth washing took us all of a day. Miraculously, there are a small tub and a homemade washboard here. I blessed whatever trapper made that board.

29 "I went out with Olaus the other night to set traps. We hiked back on a little birch-clad knoll, then down through the tundra. From the knoll we saw short mountain ranges here and there all around this flat timbered basin. The Old Crow Mountains looked dim blue. We found a new flower, a butterwort like a microscopic violet. The skeeters are unbelievable, vociferous, indescribable — you keep moving just to drown the noise a bit."

30 On one of those evenings at Timber Creek, Jess and I decided to take the canoe and go across the river to explore a bit. In the beautiful hot days the

water had been dropping, and below the muck and mud and clay of the banks, we could see a broad layer of gravelly soil coming to view. We landed on this and started wandering along. Suddenly Jess said: "You know, Olaus has been talking about maybe finding prehistoric stuff, if the river ever dropped down to the gravel level; he said he thought any bones or such would be in the gravel — remember? Be a heck of a note if we could find something right here and take it back to him, wouldn't it?"

31   He stooped and began scrutinizing the gravel more carefully, and so did I. A basic human urge, somehow — wanting to *find* something! "By gosh, Mardy, look here!"

32   Jess held out a brown object to me. It looked like part of a huge tooth. Neither of us could guess what it was, but we really began looking then, and our excitement mounted, for we did find things, many of them — pieces of bones and teeth. Finally Jess and I both pounced on something at the very edge of the water. "Look! It's just like a beaver tooth, only three times as big!"

33   By this time we had a sizable pile of bones at one end of the strip of beach. "You stay right here," said Jess. "I'm going back to the scow and get a gunny sack, quietly. We're going to surprise Olaus!"

34   A few minutes later Jess and I stomped into the cabin, where Olaus was at the table busily writing notes. Olaus didn't look up. Jess dropped the sack of fossilized bones on the floor at Olaus's feet with a great clank. "Well, you've been talking about wanting to find some bones. Here they are!"

35   What excitement then, as Olaus spread them all out and began trying to identify them — prehistoric horse, parts of mammoth teeth, and yes, that *was* a giant beaver tooth, the best specimen of the lot. How keen the sensations of a little adventure when you are far in the wilderness with nothing to dilute them! What a divine thing, enthusiasm, and Jess had it. We chattered and laughed over those bones, and related over and over to Olaus every detail of our discoveries. Aside from all that, they really were interesting finds, and later found their way to scientists who were happy to use them as data for their studies.

      ❧

Discussion Questions

1. Why did Murie insert the parenthetical statement in paragraph 1, "Even the natives stay out of there"?
2. Who was the "one perfectly serene member of the party" (paragraph 4) when it was discovered that the crankshaft had broken? Explain.
3. Explain the last sentence of paragraph 6, "Only the one most expensive, vital part that breaks only once in a million times!"
4. What plan was improvised for continuing the expedition, and who suggested it? What had to be done before the expedition could move on? Explain.

5. What caused Murie to exclaim, in paragraph 12, "How safe, how defenseless"?
6. Paragraph 13 begins, "But it was better to get busy." What is the reversal suggested by the word *but*? What did Murie "get busy" doing, and why did she consider the activity "better"?
7. What did Murie do "all that day and night" while the men were gone taking care of the motorboat? Explain.
*8. Describe and explain the effect of paragraph 18, beginning, "Someone was in the tent!"
9. What part does the Fourth of July play in the second half of the essay (paragraphs 19–27)?
10. In the last paragraph, Murie says, "What a divine thing, enthusiasm, and Jess had it." What prompts her remark and what does it mean?

Writing Topics

1. In a brief essay, explore the possible meanings of the title, "By Main Strength." In your conclusion, explain why you think it a strong or weak title. You might consider other possible titles, such as "Banding Geese," "The Barren Tundra," "Goose with Rice Stuffing."
2. Recall incidents in your past in which you have felt genuine fear. Write a brief narrative essay about the most vividly remembered of these incidents: tell how you got into the situation, how you felt and behaved in response to it, what if anything you did to allay your fear, and how the episode finally ended. In your conclusion, consider why this particular incident has stuck with you.

*"Night is very beautiful on this great beach.
It is the true other half of the day's tremendous wheel;
no lights without meaning stab or trouble it;
it is beauty, it is fulfillment, it is rest."*

NIGHT ON THE GREAT BEACH

Henry Beston

Born in Quincy, Massachusetts, Henry Beston (1888–1968)
graduated from Harvard and began a teaching career that
was interrupted by his service in the armed forces during
World War I. He moved in the mid-1920s to a cottage on
Nauset Beach, Cape Cod, Massachusetts, where he lived
alone observing the life of, in, and around the Atlantic
Ocean. In 1928, he published his first book based on his
experience there, *The Outermost House: A Year of Life on the Great
Beach of Cape Cod*, from which "Night on the Great Beach" is
taken. His style is remarkably lyrical and in its moments of
intensity seems to penetrate and communicate the deepest
mysteries of nature. In the latter part of his life, Beston
settled, with his wife, the writer Elizabeth Coatsworth, in
Nobleboro, Maine. In addition to other works, Beston edited *American Memory: Being a Mirror of the Stirring and Picturesque
Past of Americans and the American Nation* (1937), and he wrote
two books shaped by his Maine experience, *Northern Farm*
(1972) and *Cape Cod to the St. Lawrence* (1976).

1   Our fantastic civilization has fallen out of touch with many aspects of
nature, and with none more completely than with night. Primitive folk, gathered
at a cave mouth round a fire, do not fear night; they fear, rather, the energies
and creatures to whom night gives power; we of the age of the machines,
having delivered ourselves of nocturnal enemies, now have a dislike of night
itself. With lights and ever more lights, we drive the holiness and beauty of
night back to the forests and the sea; the little villages, the crossroads even, will
have none of it. Are modern folk, perhaps, afraid of night? Do they fear that
vast serenity, the mystery of infinite space, the austerity of stars? Having made
themselves at home in a civilization obsessed with power, which explains its

whole world in terms of energy, do they fear at night for their dull acquiescence and the pattern of their beliefs? Be the answer what it will, to-day's civilization is full of people who have not the slightest notion of the character or the poetry of night, who have never even seen night. Yet to live thus, to know only artificial night, is as absurd and evil as to know only artificial day.

2   Night is very beautiful on this great beach. It is the true other half of the day's tremendous wheel; no lights without meaning stab or trouble it; it is beauty, it is fulfillment, it is rest. Thin clouds float in these heavens, islands of obscurity in a splendour of space and stars: the Milky Way bridges earth and ocean; the beach resolves itself into a unity of form, its summer lagoons, its slopes and uplands merging; against the western sky and the falling bow of sun rise the silent and superb undulations of the dunes.

3   My nights are at their darkest when a dense fog streams in from the sea under a black, unbroken floor of cloud. Such nights are rare, but are most to be expected when fog gathers off the coast in early summer; this last Wednesday night was the darkest I have known. Between ten o'clock and two in the morning three vessels stranded on the outer beach—a fisherman, a four-masted schooner, and a beam trawler. The fisherman and the schooner have been towed off, but the trawler, they say, is still ashore.

4   I went down to the beach that night just after ten o'clock. So utterly black, pitch dark it was, and so thick with moisture and trailing showers, that there was no sign whatever of the beam of Nauset; the sea was only a sound, and when I reached the edge of the surf the dunes themselves had disappeared behind. I stood as isolate in that immensity of rain and night as I might have stood in interplanetary space. The sea was troubled and noisy, and when I opened the darkness with an outlined cone of light from my electric torch I saw that the waves were washing up green coils of sea grass, all coldly wet and bright in the motionless and unnatural radiance. Far off a single ship was groaning its way along the shoals. The fog was compact of the finest moisture; passing by, it spun itself into my lens of light like a kind of strange, aërial, and liquid silk. Effin Chalke, the new coast guard, passed me going north, and told me that he had had news at the halfway house of the schooner at Cahoon's.

5   It was dark, pitch dark to my eye, yet complete darkness, I imagine, is exceedingly rare, perhaps unknown in outer nature. The nearest natural approximation to it is probably the gloom of forest country buried in night and cloud. Dark as the night was here, there was still light on the surface of the planet. Standing on the shelving beach, with the surf breaking at my feet, I could see the endless wild uprush, slide, and withdrawal of the sea's white rim of foam. The men at Nauset tell me that on such nights they follow along this vague crawl of whiteness, trusting to habit and a sixth sense to warn them of their approach to the halfway house.

6   Animals descend by starlight to the beach, North, beyond the dunes, muskrats forsake the cliff and nose about in the driftwood and weed, leaving

intricate trails and figure eights to be obliterated by the day; the lesser folk—the mice, the occasional small sand-coloured toads, the burrowing moles—keep to the upper beach and leave their tiny footprints under the overhanging wall. In autumn skunks, beset by a shrinking larder, go beach combing early in the night. The animal is by preference a clean feeder and turns up his nose at rankness. I almost stepped on a big fellow one night as I was walking north to meet the first man south from Nauset. There was a scamper, and the creature ran up the beach from under my feet; alarmed he certainly was, yet was he contained and continent. Deer are frequently seen, especially north of the light. I find their tracks upon the summer dunes.

7 Years ago, while camping on this beach north of Nauset, I went for a stroll along the top of the cliff at break of dawn. Though the path followed close enough along the edge, the beach below was often hidden, and I looked directly, from the height to the flush of sunrise at sea. Presently the path, turning, approached the brink of the earth precipice, and on the beach below, in the cool, wet rosiness of dawn, I saw three deer playing. They frolicked, rose on their hind legs, scampered off, and returned again, and were merry. Just before sunrise they trotted off north together down the beach toward a hollow in the cliff and the path that climbs it.

8 Occasionally a sea creature visits the shore at night. Lone coast guardsmen, trudging the sand at some deserted hour, have been startled by seals. One man fell flat on a creature's back, and it drew away from under him, flippering toward the sea, with a sound "halfway between a squeal and a bark." I myself once had rather a start. It was long after sundown, the light dying and uncertain, and I was walking home on the top level of the beach and close along the slope descending to the ebbing tide. A little more than halfway to the Fo'castle a huge unexpected something suddenly writhed horribly in the darkness under my bare foot. I had stepped on a skate left stranded by some recent crest of surf, and my weight had momentarily annoyed it back to life.

9 Facing north, the beam of Nauset becomes part of the dune night. As I walk toward it, I see the lantern, now as a star of light which waxes and wanes three mathematical times, now as a lovely pale flare of light behind the rounded summits of the dunes. The changes in the atmosphere change the colour of the beam; it is now whitish, now flame golden, now golden red; it changes its form as well, from a star to a blare of light, from a blare of light to a cone of radiance sweeping a circumference of fog. To the west of Nauset I often see the apocalyptic flash of the great light at the Highland reflected on the clouds or even on the moisture in the starlit air, and, seeing it, I often think of the pleasant hours I have spent there when George and Mary Smith were at the light and I had the good fortune to visit as their guest. Instead of going to sleep in the room under the eaves, I would lie awake, looking out of a window to the great spokes of light revolving as solemnly as a part of the universe.

10   All night long the lights of coastwise vessels pass at sea, green lights going south, red lights moving north. Fishing schooners and flounder draggers anchor two or three miles out, and keep a bright riding light burning on the mast. I see them come to anchor at sundown, but I rarely see them go, for they are off at dawn. When busy at night, these fishermen illumine their decks with a scatter of oil flares. From shore, the ships might be thought afire. I have watched the scene through a night glass. I could see no smoke, only the waving flares, the reddish radiance on sail and rigging, an edge of reflection overside, and the enormous night and sea beyond.

11   One July night, as I returned at three o'clock from an expedition north, the whole night, in one strange, burning instant, turned into a phantom day. I stopped and, questioning, stared about. An enormous meteor, the largest I have ever seen, was consuming itself in an effulgence of light west of the zenith. Beach and dune and ocean appeared out of nothing, shadowless and motion-less, a landscape whose every tremor and vibration were stilled, a landscape in a dream.

12   The beach at night has a voice all its own, a sound in fullest harmony with its spirit and mood—with its little, dry noise of sand forever moving, with its solemn, overspilling, rhythmic seas, with its eternity of stars that sometimes seem to hang down like lamps from the high heavens—and that sound the pip-ing of a bird. As I walk the beach in early summer my solitary coming disturbs it on its nest, and it flies away, troubled, invisible, piping its sweet, plaintive cry. The bird I write of is the piping plover, *Charadrius melodus*, sometimes called the beach plover or the mourning bird. Its note is a whistled syllable, the loveliest musical note, I think, sounded by any North Atlantic bird.

13   Now that summer is here I often cook myself a camp supper on the beach. Beyond the crackling, salt-yellow driftwood flame, over the pyramid of barrel staves, broken boards, and old sticks all atwist with climbing fire, the unseen ocean thunders and booms, the breaker sounding hollow as it falls. The wall of the sand cliff behind, with its rim of grass and withering roots, its sandy crum-blings and erosions, stands gilded with flame; wind cries over it; a covey of sandpipers pass between the ocean and the fire. There are stars, and to the south Scorpio hangs curving down the sky with ringed Saturn shining in his claw.

14   Learn to reverence night and to put away the vulgar fear of it, for, with the banishment of night from the experience of man, there vanishes as well a reli-gious emotion, a poetic mood, which gives depth to the adventure of humanity. By day, space is one with the earth and with man—it is his sun that is shining, his clouds that are floating past; at night, space is his no more. When the great earth, abandoning day, rolls up the deeps of the heavens and the universe, a new door opens for the human spirit, and there are few so clownish that some awareness of the mystery of being does not touch them as they gaze. For a moment of night we have a glimpse of ourselves and of our world islanded in its stream of stars—pilgrims of mortality, voyaging between horizons across

eternal seas of space and time. Fugitive though the instant be, the spirit of man is, during it, ennobled by a genuine moment of emotional dignity, and poetry makes its own both the human spirit and experience.

❧

Discussion Questions

*1.   At the end of paragraph 1, Beston writes that today's "civilization is full of people who have not the slightest notion of the character or the poetry of night, who have never even seen night." Explore as deeply as you can Beston's possible meanings here, examining carefully the paragraphs that follow (paragraphs 2–5).

2.   In paragraphs 6–8, Beston describes the creatures that came on to the beach at night from both the land and the sea. What were the creatures and how did Beston interact with them?

3.   What kind of lights does Beston describe in paragraphs 9–11 as at times part of the mysterious beauty of night on the beach? Explain the effect of these "lights."

4.   Describe the sounds (and identify their sources) heard on the beach (paragraphs 12–13). What effect do they contribute to the whole "poetry of night" that Beston wishes to convey?

*5.   Beston writes in his last paragraph, "For a moment of night we have a glimpse of ourselves and of our world islanded in its stream of stars—pilgrims of mortality, voyaging between horizons across eternal seas of space and time. Fugitive though the instant be, the spirit of man is, during it, ennobled by a genuine moment of emotional dignity, and poetry makes its own the human spirit and experience." Such words as *moment, glimpse, fugitive,* and *instant* seem to indicate that the experience was short, temporary, or passing. How does the passage as a whole seem designed to reassure readers that such fleeting feelings can indeed be deep and religiously meaningful? Explain.

Writing Topics

1.   Beston asks in paragraph 1, "Are modern folk, perhaps, afraid of night? Do they fear that vast serenity, the mystery of infinite space, the austerity of stars? Having made themselves at home in a civilization obsessed with power, which explains its whole world in terms of energy, do they fear at night for their dull acquiescence and the pattern of their beliefs?" A critic might write, "In this atomic age, after we have probed the secrecy of the energy of the light of all the suns and stars in the universe, it is difficult not to take Beston with

a grain of salt. He is a romantic in love with mystery, and since he finds more mystery at night than in daylight, he has fallen hopelessly in love with night." In an argumentative essay, show why you agree or disagree with the critic.

2. Beston opens his last paragraph thus, "Learn to reverence night and to put away the vulgar fear of it, for with the banishment of night from the experience of man, there vanishes as well a religious emotion, a poetic mood, which gives depth to the adventure of humanity." Reviewing your own experience, consider whether the "religious emotion" or "poetic mood" Beston values as giving "depth to the adventure of humanity" may be—or has been—attained in other experiences at variance with his. Write an essay in which you narrate/describe such an experience, your own or someone else's.

The moon and stars, shining brilliantly as they do only on clear, cold nights, turned the meadow into a lake of glass. We built our fire at the top of a slight incline. The ice reflected us, and the leaping flames danced in the ice."

OUR NIGHT OF MAGIC

Charlotte Carpenter

Charlotte Carpenter's "Our Night of Magic" comes from *Legacies: Stories of Courage, Humor, and Resilience, of Love, Loss, and Life-Changing Encounters, by New Writers Sixty and Over* (1993), edited by Maury Leibovitz and Linda Solomon. A biographical note reveals, "Charlotte Carpenter, seventy-four, has lived on a farm all her life and has been married to a farmer for fifty-two years. They have five children, eight grandchildren, and three great-grandchildren. With the talent God gave her, she has been able to write hundreds of poems and articles, many of them published."

1   A slow but steady rain came down all that wintry morning and froze where it fell—on the ground, the trees, the buildings. By midafternoon the rain had stopped and we looked on a crystal world.

2   We were accustomed to the white hoarfrost of winter, but this was something else—a hard, clear coating of solid ice. Our five children, ages five to sixteen, returned from school exclaiming about how good the sledding would be on the steep hill in our pasture.

3   They took out at once, but they never reached their destination, for between home and hill lay a gently rolling, treeless meadow. Here they found that their sleds would speed over the ice from fence to fence with only the weight of their bodies to keep them going. What fun they had. When they came home to chores and supper, they were so excited. "Mom and Dad, you've got to come with us down to the pasture tonight," they said. They had never seen ice so slippery that they didn't need a hill for coasting on their sleds.

4   Why should fortyish parents risk life and limb going out on a dangerously slick night? They begged until we simply could not refuse them.

5   Gingerly we made our way to the meadow. Even with rubber footgear, we found it hard to walk. The sleds we pulled kept sliding into the backs of our legs. It was very cold, and Father, the practical one, carried an armload of wood to build a fire.

6   We will never forget the unbelievably beautiful sight that met our eyes when we reached the meadow. The moon and stars, shining brilliantly as they do only on clear, cold nights, turned the meadow into a lake of glass. We built our fire at the top of a slight incline. The ice reflected us, and the leaping flames danced in the ice.

7   Again and again the children and sleds flew over the ground. If two rode together the sled went faster, so fast the riders could barely turn in time to avoid crashing into the fence. The littlest ones rode back to the starting point, easily pulled by older brothers. We parents envied them—the hardest part for us was walking back after the ride. We left most of the sledding to our children and stayed near the fire, absorbed in the dreamlike magic of this night.

8   We all felt so good as we started back that we hardly noticed our cold feet and tired bodies. "Will the ice still be here tomorrow?" one of the children asked. "Probably not, if the sun shines," I answered. And sure enough, by mid-morning the ice was gone, leaving only an expanse of brown grass.

9   To this day, when we're in the meadow, whether it's covered with the luxuriant green of summer or the white snow of winter, we remember that night's wonder. I harbor a brief doubt, in spite of six other witnesses, for the experience seems like something we must have imagined.

10   My husband and I learned something that night—to enjoy an interlude of joy when it comes, not to put our children off when they find something wonderful, so unusual that it may never happen again, not to say, "We're too busy now, it will have to wait." We go with them to glimpse the moment—a new calf, a robin on the lawn, a butterfly or bug. We share their excitement over a ballgame, a school play, or graduation. For now we know this:

11   Refuse to take the time and you miss something precious to hold in memory, perhaps just the meaning of the mind. A magical sledding on glass in the starlight may happen only once in an entire lifetime.

❧

Discussion Questions

1. How, according to Carpenter, was the morning she is recalling different—"something else"—from that of other wintry mornings?
2. What differences did the children find when they went out sledding after school?
3. Why were Carpenter and her husband reluctant to go out with the children after supper? Explain.

4. Why did Carpenter call her husband the practical one when the family went out together for the sledding?
5. What part did the parents play in the sledding? Explain.
*6. According to Carpenter, what did she and her husband learn from the evening's experience?

Writing Topics

1. Review your past to find a "magic" moment similar to that which the Carpenters experienced. Write a narrative essay relating the experience and indicating what "lesson" you learned from it.
2. A critic might observe, "The Carpenter family behaves like a model family—too much like a model family. Reality tells us that things could not have gone so smoothly as described. There is, honestly, a touch of sentimentality running throughout." Write an argumentative essay in which you agree or disagree with the critic. Or try your hand at retelling the story with a comic effect, describing how everything went wrong: when the father spilled all the wood, slid down the slope on his belly, and got up with a bleeding nose; when Carpenter stood admiring the moon and stars, her feet slid out from under her, and she saw stars of a different kind; when two children on a sled hit a post and went sprawling in the path of an oncoming sled; and so on.

There are four abandoned tires,
any number of broken beer bottles,
fourteen shoes and a single sneaker, and a visible layer,
all over the surface, of that grayish-green film that
settles on all New York surfaces."

PONDS

Lewis Thomas

Lewis Thomas (1913–1993) was born in Flushing, New York, and took a B.S. at Princeton in 1933 and an M.D. at Harvard in 1937. As a doctor, scholar, professor, and administrator, he was associated with a long line of academic institutions— Johns Hopkins, Tulane, New York University, Yale, Memorial Sloan-Kettering Cancer Center in New York, and Cornell. His collections of essays include *The Lives of a Cell: Notes of a Biology Watcher* (1974, winner of the National Book Award), *Late Night Thoughts on Listening to Mahler's Ninth Symphony* (1984), *Etcetera, Etcetera* (1990), and *The Fragile Species* (1992). The essay below, "Ponds," comes from *The Medusa and the Snail: More Notes of a Biology Watcher* (1979), which won the American Book Award for science in 1981. In 1989, Thomas won the Albert Lasker Public Service Award for his writings, which, according to the citation, "converted many countless non-scientists into appreciative spectators and supporters of biomedical research."

1   Large areas of Manhattan are afloat. I remember when the new Bellevue Hospital was being built, fifteen years ago; the first stage was the most spectacular and satisfying, an enormous square lake. It was there for the two years, named Lake Bellevue, while the disconsolate Budget Bureau went looking for cash to build the next stage. It was fenced about and visible only from the upper windows of the old hospital, but pretty to look at, cool and blue in midsummer, frozen gleaming as Vermont in January. The fence, like all city fences, was always broken, and we could have gone down to the lake and used it, but it was known to be an upwelling of the East River. At Bellevue there were printed rules

about the East River: if anyone fell in, it was an emergency for the Infectious-Disease Service, and the first measures, after resuscitation, were massive doses of whatever antibiotics the hospital pharmacy could provide.

2   But if you cleaned the East River you could have ponds all over town, up and down the East Side of Manhattan anyway. If you lifted out the Empire State Building and the high structures nearby, you would have, instantly, an inland sea. A few holes bored in the right places would let water into the subways, and you'd have lovely underground canals all across to the Hudson, uptown to the Harlem River, downtown to the Battery, a Venice underground, without pigeons.

3   It wouldn't work, though, unless you could find a way to keep out the fish. New Yorkers cannot put up with live fish out in the open. I cannot explain this, but it is so.

4   There is a new pond, much smaller than Lake Bellevue, on First Avenue between Seventieth and Seventy-first, on the east side of the street. It emerged sometime last year, soon after a row of old flats had been torn down and the hole dug for a new apartment building. By now it is about average size for Manhattan, a city block long and about forty feet across, maybe eight feet deep at the center, more or less kidney-shaped, rather like an outsized suburban swimming pool except for the things floating, and now the goldfish.

5   With the goldfish, it is almost detestable. There are, clearly visible from the sidewalk, hundreds of them. The neighborhood people do not walk by and stare into it through the broken fence, as would be normal for any other Manhattan pond. They tend to cross the street, looking away.

6   Now there are complaints against the pond, really against the goldfish. How could people do such a thing? Bad enough for pet dogs and cats to be abandoned, but who could be so unfeeling as to abandon goldfish? They must have come down late at night, carrying their bowls, and simply dumped them in. How could they?

7   The ASPCA was called, and came one afternoon with a rowboat. Nets were used, and fish taken away in new custodial bowls, some to Central Park, others to ASPCA headquarters, to the fish pound. But the goldfish have multiplied, or maybe those people with their bowls keep coming down late at night for their furtive, unfeeling dumping. Anyway, there are too many fish for the ASPCA, for which this seems to be a new kind of problem. An official stated for the press that the owners of the property would be asked to drain the pond by pumping, and then the ASPCA would come back with nets to catch them all.

8   You'd think they were rats or roaches, the way people began to talk. Get those goldfish out of that pond, I don't care how you do it. Dynamite, if necessary. But get rid of them. Winter is coming, someone said, and it is deep enough so that they'll be swimming around underneath the ice. Get them out.

9   It is this knowledge of the East River, deep in the minds of all Manhattan residents, more than the goldfish themselves, I think. Goldfish in a glass bowl are harmless to the human mind, maybe even helpful to minds casting about for something, anything, to think about. But goldfish let loose, propagating themselves, worst of all *surviving* in what has to be a sessile eddy of the East River, somehow threaten us all. We do not like to think that life is possible under some conditions, especially the conditions of a Manhattan pond. There are four abandoned tires, any number of broken beer bottles, fourteen shoes and a single sneaker, and a visible layer, all over the surface, of that grayish-green film that settles on all New York surfaces. The mud at the banks of the pond is not proper country mud but reconstituted Manhattan landfill, ancient garbage, fossilized coffee grounds and grapefruit rind, the defecation of a city. For goldfish to be swimming in such water, streaking back and forth mysteriously in small schools, feeding, obviously feeding, looking as healthy and well-off as goldfish in the costliest kind of window-box aquarium, means something is wrong with our standards. It is, in some deep sense beyond words, insulting.

10   I thought I noticed a peculiar sort of fin on the undersurface of two of the fish. Perhaps, it occurs to me now in a rush of exultation, in such a pond as this, with all its chemical possibilities, there are contained some mutagens, and soon there will be schools of mutant goldfish. Give them just a little more time, I thought. And then, with the most typically Manhattan thought I've ever thought, I thought: The ASPCA will come again, next month, with their rowboat and their nets. The proprietor will begin pumping out the pond. The nets will flail, the rowboat will settle, and then the ASPCA officials will give a sudden shout of great dismay. And with a certain amount of splashing and grayish-greenish spray, at all the edges of the pond, up all the banks of ancient New York landfill mud, crawling on their new little feet, out onto the sidewalks, up and down and across the street, into doorways and up the fire escapes, some of them with little suckers on their little feet, up the sides of buildings and into open windows, looking for something, will come the goldfish.

11   It won't last, of course. Nothing like this ever does. The mayor will come and condemn it in person. The Health Department will come and recommend the purchase of cats from out of town because of the constitutional boredom of city cats. The NIH will send up teams of professionals from Washington with a new kind of antifish spray, which will be recalled four days later because of toxicity to cats.

12   After a few weeks it will be finished anyway, like a lot of New York events. The goldfish will dive deep and vanish, the pond will fill up with sneakers, workmen will come and pour concrete over everything, and by next year the new building will be up and occupied by people all unaware of their special environmental impact. But what a time it was.

᷾ᵁᷬ

Discussion Questions

1. Was there really a "Lake Bellevue," mentioned in paragraph 1? Explain.

2. Paragraph 1 ends, "At Bellevue there were printed rules about the East River: if anyone fell in, it was an emergency for the Infectious-Disease Service, and the first measures, after resuscitation, were massive doses of whatever antibiotics the hospital pharmacy could provide." Why are we given such information about the East River? Do you detect a "tongue in cheek" tone in this sentence? Explain.

3. What does Thomas mean in paragraph 2 when he refers to the creation in New York of an "inland sea" and a "Venice underground, without pigeons"? What is his tone of voice? Explain.

4. What caused the formation of the "pond" described in paragraphs 4–6, and why were complaints made about it?

5. Was the account of the ASPCA's attempt to deal with the goldfish problem (paragraph 7) true or a fantasy? (ASPCA is the American Society for the Prevention of Cruelty to Animals.)

*6. Explain Thomas's meaning when he says in paragraph 10, "Perhaps, it occurs to me now in a rush of exultation, in such a pond as this, with all its chemical possibilities, there are contained some mutagens, and soon there will be schools of mutant goldfish." What did Thomas imagine about these "mutant goldfish"?

*7. Explore the meaning and implications of the "prediction" in paragraph 11, "The NIH [National Institute of Health] will send up teams of professionals from Washington with a new kind of antifish spray, which will be recalled four days later because of toxicity to cats."

Writing Topics

1. Satire has been defined as the use of irony or humor to ridicule some vice or folly. Examine "Ponds" carefully and write an analytical essay demonstrating that it is a satire aimed at particular social attitudes and customs.

2. Assume the truth of Thomas's fantasy about the mutant goldfish and write a fantasy in which you imagine them surviving in the subways and sewers of New York City and becoming monstrosities even beyond those imagined by Thomas. Perhaps there could be a climactic scene in which police and firefighters wage a desperate battle against the fish in Times Square during a rainstorm.

3. Write an article for your local paper giving an account of the mutant goldfish showing up in your part of the country—in ponds, swimming pools, garbage dumps, or the water supply.

❧The Great Plains which I cross in my sleep are bigger than any name people give them. They are enormous, bountiful, unfenced, empty of buildings, full of names and stories. They extend beyond the frame of the photograph."

LONG DRIVES ON THE PLAINS

Ian Frazier

Ian Frazier was born in 1951 in Cleveland, Ohio, and earned a B.A. from Harvard in 1973. Early in his career, he became a staff writer for the *The New Yorker*, and his first books, *Dating Your Mom* (1986) and *Nobody Better, Better Than Nobody* (1987), were collections of his *New Yorker* pieces. In 1982, he moved from New York to Montana and, like an explorer coming upon new land, discovered a vast area of the United States that dazzled—and challenged—his imagination. His varied experiences there led to the writing of *Great Plains* (1989), the source of the essay below.

1   When I went for long drives on the plains, I might be on the road for weeks at a time. I could afford to stay in motels only every third or fourth night, so the others I spent in my van. I slept beneath the mercury lights of highway rest areas where my lone car was visible for six miles in any direction and the inside of the men's room looked as if it had been sandblasted with tiny insects, and on the streets of small towns where the lawn sprinklers ran all night, and next to dammed-up waters of the Missouri River where the white top branches of drowned trees rose above the waves. My van had so many pinholes from rust that it created a planetarium effect on the ground when I turned on the interior light. After a day of driving there was usually a lot of dust on the bed, and maybe a stunned grasshopper that had come through the open window.

2   One night I tried to sleep at a picnic area at the Double Mountain Fork of the Brazos River in Texas, on U.S. Highway 83. Highway 83 runs from Mexico to Canada and is like the Main Street of the Great Plains. Cars went by only occasionally, which somehow made them scarier. The moon was full, and the

wind was blowing harder than during the day. I got up and walked around. By moonlight I read a historic marker in the picnic area which said that in 1871 hunters brought more than a million buffalo hides to a trading post near this spot. When I lay down again, the unquiet spirits of a million buffalo were abroad in the windy night. My head kept falling through the pillow. The moon shone, the stars blinked, the trees tossed back and forth, the shadows waited under the picnic kiosks. I got up again and drove until dawn.

3   In New Mexico I slept well in front of a shuttered vegetable stand on the outskirts of a town. I woke in the morning to blue sky and the sound of small animals playing under my car and scurrying across the roof. On the vegetable stand I saw a sign posted. I went over to see what it said. It said:

> *PLAGUE*
> *is passed to man by*
> *WILD RODENTS, Rabbits,*
> *and by their FLEAS*
> *. . . DO NOT*
> *Pitch tents or lay*
> *Bedrolls on or near*
> *nests or burrows.*
> *Plague is CURABLE*
> *WHEN TREATED IN TIME.*

4   The best places to sleep were truck stops. At two-thirty in the morning a truck-stop parking lot full of trucks is the capital of sleep. The trucks park in close rows, as if for warmth. The drivers sleep with purposeful intent. The big engines idle; together, the trucks snore. Hinged moisture caps on top of the diesel stacks bounce in the exhaust with a pinging noise. I tried to park as close as I could without being presumptuous. Unlike tourists in rest stops, truck drivers seem careful about slamming doors and gunning engines late at night. Sometimes the truck I had gone to sleep next to would quietly leave and another would quietly pull in. One morning when I woke up a semi-trailer full of pickup-truck camper tops had been replaced by a stock truck. On the truck's door, in big letters, a poem:

> *Buck Hummer*
> *Hog Hauler*

5   In Colorado, Highways 71 and 36 make a big cross on the map when they intersect at the town of Last Chance. Sixty miles to the west, the prairie ends and greater Denver begins, and the uplands are barnacled with houses for a hundred miles along the Rocky Mountain front. Fewer than seventy people live in Last Chance. The wheat fields are eroding, the oil wells are running dry,

the only store in town burned down. "However, hope springs eternally in the breasts of our decreasing high school enrollment," a citizen of Last Chance wrote recently. On a night of many thunderstorms, I pulled over to sleep at that intersection. The wind made the streetlight sway, and made its shadows sway inside my van. A full cattle truck came sighing down the road and then squeaked to a stop at the blinking red light. I could hear the animals shifting and bumping inside. They were very likely on their way to one of the largest feedlots in the world, sixty miles north of Denver, where they would stand around with a hundred thousand other cows and eat until they were fat enough to slaughter. The truck sat for a moment. Then the driver revved the engine and found first gear, and the full load of cattle braced themselves for the start. In step, they set their many feet all at once, like a dance revue.

6   Now, when I have trouble getting to sleep, I sometimes imagine that my bed is on the back of a flatbed pickup truck driving across the Great Plains. I ignore the shouts on the sidewalk and the bass vibrations from the reggae club across the street. The back of this truck has sides but no top. I can see the stars. The air is cool. The truck will go nonstop for nine hours through the night. At first the road is as straight as a laser — State Highway 8, in North Dakota say — where nothing seems to move except the wheels under me and the smell of run-over skunks fading in and out in my nose. Then the road twists to follow a river valley, and cottonwood leaves pass above, and someone has been cutting hay, and the air is like the inside of a spice cabinet. Then suddenly the wheels rumble on the wooden planks of a one-lane bridge across the River That Scolds at All the Others. Ever since the Great Plains were first called a desert, people have gone a long way toward turning them into one. The Great Plains which I cross in my sleep are bigger than any name people give them. They are enormous, bountiful, unfenced, empty of buildings, full of names and stories. They extend beyond the frame of the photograph. Their hills are hipped, like a woman asleep under a sheet. Their rivers rhyme. Their rows of grain strum past. Their draws hold springwater and wood and game and grass like sugar in the hollow of a hand. They are the place where Crazy Horse will always remain uncaptured. They are the lodge of Crazy Horse.

❧

Discussion Questions

1. Where were the places that Frazier found to stay overnight when driving on the Great Plains?
2. As related in paragraph 2, what troubled his dreams, and what did he do as a result?

*3. Upon waking up outside a town in New Mexico, what noises did he hear under and on top of his van, and what was the warning on the sign he saw? Explain.

4. In paragraph 4, Frazier says that "the best places to sleep were truck stops." Explain.

5. In paragraph 5, what do we learn about Last Chance, Colorado, from Frazier's overnight stop there? From his stay there, what event did he choose to report? Explain.

*6. In the middle of paragraph 6, Frazier writes, "Then suddenly the wheels rumble on the wooden planks of a one-lane bridge across the River That Scolds at All the Others." Where was he, what was he doing there, and where was he going? Explain.

Writing Topics

1. In the closing sentences of his essay, Frazier remarks of the Great Plains, "They are the place where Crazy Horse will always remain uncaptured. They are the lodge of Crazy Horse." Do a bit of research on Crazy Horse, beginning with the essay by Black Elk in Cluster 12, "Walking the Black Road and the Killing of Crazy Horse." Then write a brief essay explaining the implications of Frazier ending his essay—and book—the way he does. (If you can find a copy of Frazier's *Great Plains*, you will find that Chapter 6 is devoted to Crazy Horse's life and death.)

2. Frazier names the states of the Great Plains early in his book: Montana, Wyoming, Colorado, New Mexico, North Dakota, South Dakota, Nebraska, Kansas, Oklahoma, and Texas. Many Americans have grown up in a Great Plains state and many more have some familiarity with or idea about this part of the United States. Write a short essay in which you compare and contrast your impressions of the Great Plains with Frazier's. If you wish to write a longer essay, you should obtain a copy of Frazier's book and absorb the full picture he gives.

"No matter where my head and feet may go,

my heart and my entrails stay behind,

here on the clean, true, comfortable rock,

under the black sun of God's forsaken country."

THE GREAT AMERICAN DESERT

Edward Abbey

Edward Abbey (1927–1989) was born in the Appalachian area of Pennsylvania and, at the age of seventeen, hitch-hiked to the vast stretches of the American Southwest, where he fell in love with the desert. He obtained two degrees from the University of New Mexico, a B.A. in 1951 and an M.A. in 1956. He spent some fifteen years as a park ranger and fire spotter in the Southwest (from 1956 to 1971), developing a jealous love for the area's arid and for-bidding lands. He wrote several works of fiction, including the novels *Black Sun* (1971), *The Monkey Wrench Gang* (1975), and *The Fool's Progress* (1988). His nonfiction works include *Desert Solitaire* (1968), *Appalachian Wilderness: The Great Smoky Mountains* (1970), *Abbey's Road: Take the Other* (1979), and *One Life at a Time, Please* (1988). *The Journey Home: Some Words in Defense of the American West* was published in 1977 and is the source of "The Great American Desert."

1   In my case it was love at first sight. This desert, all deserts, any desert. No matter where my head and feet may go, my heart and my entrails stay behind, here on the clean, true, comfortable rock, under the black sun of God's forsaken country. When I take on my next incarnation, my bones will remain bleaching nicely in a stone gulch under the rim of some faraway plateau, way out there in the back of beyond. An unrequited and excessive love, inhuman no doubt but painful anyhow, especially when I see my desert under attack. "The one death I cannot bear," said the Sonoran-Arizonan poet Richard Shelton. The kind of love that makes a man selfish, possessive, irritable. If you're thinking of a visit, my natural reaction is like a rattlesnake's—to warn you off. What I want to say goes something like this.

2   Survival Hint # 1: Stay out of there. Don't go. Stay home and read a good book, this one for example. The Great American Desert is an awful place.

People get hurt, get sick, get lost out there. Even if you survive, which is not certain, you will have a miserable time. The desert is for movies and God-intoxicated mystics, not for family recreation.

3   Let me enumerate the hazards. First the Walapai tiger, also known as conenose kissing bug. *Triatoma protracta* is a true bug, black as sin, and it flies through the night quiet as an assassin. It does not attack directly like a mosquito or deerfly, but alights at a discreet distance, undetected, and creeps upon you, its hairy little feet making not the slightest noise. The kissing bug is fond of warmth and like Dracula requires mammalian blood for sustenance. When it reaches you the bug crawls onto your skin so gently, so softly that unless your senses are hyperacute you feel nothing. Selecting a tender point, the bug slips its conical proboscis into your flesh, injecting a poisonous anesthetic. If you are asleep you will feel nothing. If you happen to be awake you may notice the faintest of pinpricks, hardly more than a brief ticklish sensation, which you will probably disregard. But the bug is already at work. Having numbed the nerves near the point of entry the bug proceeds (with a sigh of satisfaction, no doubt) to withdraw blood. When its belly is filled, it pulls out, backs off, and waddles away, so drunk and gorged it cannot fly.

4   At about this time the victim awakes, scratching at a furious itch. If you recognize the symptoms at once, you can sometimes find the bug in your vicinity and destroy it. But revenge will be your only satisfaction. Your night is ruined. If you are of average sensitivity to a kissing bug's poison, your entire body breaks out in hives, skin aflame from head to toe. Some people become seriously ill, in many cases requiring hospitalization. Others recover fully after five or six hours except for a hard and itchy swelling, which may endure for a week.

5   After the kissing bug, you should beware of rattlesnakes; we have half a dozen species, all offensive and dangerous, plus centipedes, millipedes, taran-tulas, black widows, brown recluses, Gila monsters, the deadly poisonous coral snakes, and giant hairy desert scorpions. Plus an immense variety and near-infinite number of ants, midges, gnats, bloodsucking flies, and blood-guzzling mosquitoes. (You might think the desert would be spared at least mosquitoes? Not so. Peer in any water hole by day: swarming with mosquito larvae. Venture out on a summer's eve: The air vibrates with their mournful keening.) Finally, where the desert meets the sea, as on the coasts of Sonora and Baja California, we have the usual assortment of obnoxious marine life: sandflies, ghost crabs, stingrays, electric jellyfish, spiny sea urchins, maneating sharks, and other creatures so distasteful one prefers not even to name them.

6   It has been said, and truly, that everything in the desert either stings, stabs, stinks, or sticks. You will find the flora here as venomous, hooked, barbed, thorny, prickly, needled, saw-toothed, hairy, stickered, mean, bitter, sharp, wiry, and fierce as the animals. Something about the desert inclines all living things to harshness and acerbity. The soft evolve out. Except for sleek and oily growths like the poison ivy—oh yes, indeed—that flourish in sinister profusion on the

dank walls above the quicksand down in those corridors of gloom and labyrinthine monotony that men call canyons.

7   We come now to the third major hazard, which is sunshine. Too much of a good thing can be fatal. Sunstroke, heatstroke, and dehydration are common misfortunes in the bright American Southwest. If you can avoid the insects, reptiles, and arachnids, the cactus and the ivy, the smog of the southwestern cities, and the lung fungus of the desert valleys (carried by dust in the air), you cannot escape the desert sun. Too much exposure to it eventually causes, quite literally, not merely sunburn but skin cancer.

8   Much sun, little rain also means an arid climate. Compared with the high humidity of more hospitable regions, the dry heat of the desert seems at first not terribly uncomfortable—sometimes even pleasant. But that sensation of comfort is false, a deception, and therefore all the more dangerous, for it induces overexertion and an insufficient consumption of water, even when water is available. This leads to various internal complications, some immediate—sunstroke, for example—and some not apparent until much later. Mild but prolonged dehydration, continued over a span of months or years, leads to the crystallization of mineral solutions in the urinary tract, that is, to what urologists call urinary calculi or kidney stones. A disability common in all the world's arid regions. Kidney stones, in case you haven't met one, come in many shapes and sizes, from pellets smooth as BB shot to highly irregular calcifications resembling asteroids, Vietcong shrapnel, and crown-of-thorns starfish. Some of these objects may be "passed" naturally; others can be removed only by means of the Davis stone basket or by surgery. Me—I was lucky; I passed mine with only a groan, my forehead pressed against the wall of a pissoir in the rear of a Tucson bar that I cannot recommend.

9   You may be getting the impression by now that the desert is not the most suitable of environments for human habitation. Correct. Of all the Earth's climatic zones, excepting only the Antarctic, the deserts are the least inhabited, the least "developed," for reasons that should now be clear.

10   You may wish to ask, Yes, okay, but among North American deserts which is the *worst?* A good question—and I am happy to attempt to answer.

11   Geographers generally divide the North American desert—what was once termed "the Great American Desert"—into four distinct regions or subdeserts. These are the Sonoran Desert, which comprises southern Arizona, Baja California, and the state of Sonora in Mexico; the Chihuahuan Desert, which includes west Texas, southern New Mexico, and the states of Chihuahua and Coahuila in Mexico; the Mojave Desert, which includes southeastern California and small portions of Nevada, Utah, and Arizona; and the Great Basin Desert, which includes most of Utah and Nevada, northern Arizona, northwestern New Mexico, and much of Idaho and eastern Oregon.

12   Privately, I prefer my own categories. Up north in Utah somewhere is the canyon country—places like Zeke's Hole, Death Hollow, Pucker Pass,

Buckskin Gulch, Nausea Crick, Wolf Hole, Mollie's Nipple, Dirty Devil River, Horse Canyon, Horseshoe Canyon, Lost Horse Canyon, Horsethief Canyon, and Horseshit Canyon, to name only the more classic places. Down in Arizona and Sonora there's the cactus country; if you have nothing better to do, you might take a look at High Tanks, Salome Creek, Tortilla Flat, Esperero ("Hoper") Canyon, Holy Joe Peak, Depression Canyon, Painted Cave, Hell Hole Canyon, Hell's Half Acre, Iceberg Canyon, Tiburon (Shark) Island, Pinacate Peak, Infernal Valley, Sykes Crater, Montezuma's Head, Gu Oidak, Kuakatch, Pisinimo, and Baboquivari Mountain, for example.

13   Then there's The Canyon. *The* Canyon. The Grand. That's one world. And North Rim—that's another. And Death Valley, still another, where I lived one winter near Furnace Creek and climbed the Funeral Mountains, tasted Badwater, looked into the Devil's Hole, hollered up Echo Canyon, searched for and never did find Seldom Seen Slim. Looked for *satori* near Vane, Nevada, and found a ghost town named Bonnie Claire. Never made it to Winnemucca. Drove through the Smoke Creek Desert and down through Big Pine and Lone Pine and home across the Panamints to Death Valley again—home sweet home that winter.

14   And which of these deserts is the worst? I find it hard to judge. They're all bad—not half bad but all bad. In the Sonoran Desert, Phoenix will get you if the sun, snakes, bugs, and arthropods don't. In the Mojave Desert, it's Las Vegas, more sickening by far than the Glauber's salt in the Death Valley sinkholes. Go to Chihauhua and you're liable to get busted in El Paso and sandbagged in Ciudad Juárez—where all old whores go to die. Up north in the Great Basin Desert, on the Plateau Province, in the canyon country, your heart will break, seeing the strip mines open up and the power plants rise where only cowboys and Indians and J. Wesley Powell ever roamed before.

15   Nevertheless, all is not lost; much remains, and I welcome the prospect of an army of lug-soled hiker's boots on the desert trails. To save what wilderness is left in the American Southwest—and in the American Southwest only the wilderness is worth saving—we are going to need all the recruits we can get. All the hands, heads, bodies, time, money, effort we can find. Presumably—and the Sierra Club, the Wilderness Society, the Friends of the Earth, the Audubon Society, the Defenders of Wildlife operate on this theory—those who learn to love what is spare, rough, wild, undeveloped, and unbroken will be willing to fight for it, will help resist the strip miners, highway builders, land developers, weapons testers, power producers, tree chainers, clear cutters, oil drillers, dam beavers, subdividers—the list goes on and on—before that zinc-hearted, termite-brained, squint-eyed, nearsighted, greedy crew succeeds in completely californicating what still survives of the Great American Desert.

16   So much for the Good Cause. Now what about desert hiking itself, you may ask. I'm glad you asked that question. I firmly believe that one should never— I repeat *never*—go out into that formidable wasteland of cactus, heat, serpents,

rock, scrub, and thorn without careful planning, thorough and cautious preparation, and complete—never mind the expense!—*complete* equipment. My motto is: Be Prepared.

17   That is my belief and that is my motto. My practice, however, is a little different. I tend to go off in a more or less random direction myself, half-baked, half-assed, half-cocked, and half-ripped. Why? Well, because I have an indolent and melancholy nature and don't care to be bothered getting all those *things* together—all that bloody *gear*—maps, compass, binoculars, poncho, pup tent, shoes, first-aid kit, rope, flashlight, inspirational poetry, water, food—and because anyhow I approach nature with a certain surly ill-will, daring Her to make trouble. Later when I'm deep into Natural Bridges National Moneymint or Zion National Parkinglot or say General Shithead National Forest Land of Many Abuses why then, of course, when it's a bit late, then I may wish I had packed that something extra: matches perhaps, to mention one useful item, or maybe a spoon to eat my gruel with.

18   If I hike with another person it's usually the same; most of my friends have indolent and melancholy natures too. A cursed lot, all of them. I think of my comrade John De Puy, for example, sloping along for mile after mile like a goddamned camel—indefatigable—with those J. C. Penny hightops on his feet and that plastic pack on his back he got with five books of Green Stamps and nothing inside it but a sketchbook, some homemade jerky and a few cans of green chiles. Or Douglas Peacock, ex-Green Beret, just the opposite. Built like a buffalo, he loads a ninety-pound canvas pannier on his back at trailhead, loaded with guns, ammunition, bayonet, pitons and carabiners, cameras, field books, a 150-foot rope, geologist's sledge, rock samples, assay kit, field glasses, two gallons of water in steel canteens, jungle boots, a case of C-rations, rope hammock, pharmaceuticals in a pig-iron box, raincoat, overcoat, two-man mountain tent, Dutch oven, hibachi, shovel, ax, inflatable boat, and near the top of the load and distributed through side and back pockets, easily accessible, a case of beer. Not because he enjoys or needs all that weight—he may never get to the bottom of that cargo on a ten-day outing—but simply because Douglas uses his packbag for general storage both at home and on the trail and perfers not to have to rearrange everything from time to time merely for the purposes of a hike. Thus my friends De Puy and Peacock; you may wish to avoid such extremes.

19   A few tips on desert etiquette:

1.   Carry a cooking stove, if you must cook. Do not burn desert wood, which is rare and beautiful and required ages for its creation (an ironwood tree lives for over 1,000 years and juniper almost as long).

2.   If you must, out of need, build a fire, then for God's sake allow it to burn itself out before you leave—do not bury it, as Boy Scouts and Campfire Girls do, under a heap of mud or sand. Scatter the ashes;

replace any rocks you may have used in constructing a fireplace; do all you can to obliterate the evidence that you camped here. (The Search & Rescue Team may be looking for you.)

3. Do not bury garbage—the wildlife will only dig it up again. Burn what will burn and pack out the rest. The same goes for toilet paper: Don't bury it, *burn it*.

4. Do not bathe in desert pools, natural tanks, *tinajas*, potholes. Drink what water you need, take what you need, and leave the rest for the next hiker and more important for the bees, birds, and animals— bighorn sheep, coyotes, lions, foxes, badgers, deer, wild pigs, wild horses—whose *lives* depend on that water.

5. Always remove and destroy survey stakes, flagging, advertising signboards, mining claim markers, animal traps, poisoned bait, seismic exploration geophones, and other such artifacts of industrialism. The men who put those things there are up to no good and it is our duty to confound them. Keep America Beautiful. Grow a Beard. Take a Bath. Burn a Billboard.

20 Anyway—why go into the desert? Really, why do it? That sun, roaring at you all day long. The fetid, tepid, vapid little water holes slowly evaporating under a scum of grease, full of cannibal beetles, spotted toads, horsehair worms, liver flukes, and down at the bottom, inevitably, the pale cadaver of a ten-inch centipede. Those pink rattlesnakes down in The Canyon, those diamondback monsters thick as a truck driver's wrist that lurk in shady places along the trail, those unpleasant solpugids and unnecessary Jerusalem crickets that scurry on dirty claws across your face at night. Why? The rain that comes down like lead shot and wrecks the trail, those sudden rockfalls of obscure origin that crash like thunder ten feet behind you in the heart of a dead-still afternoon. The ubiquitous buzzard, so patient—but only so patient. The sullen and hostile Indians, all on welfare. The ragweed, the tumbleweed, the Jimson weed, the snakeweed. The scorpion in your shoe at dawn. The dreary wind that blows all spring, the psychedelic Joshua trees waving their arms at you on moonlight nights. Sand in the soup de jour. Halazone tablets in your canteen. The barren hills that always go up, which is bad, or down, which is worse. Those canyons like catacombs with quicksand lapping at your crotch. Hollow, mummified horses with forelegs casually crossed, dead for ten years, leaning against the corner of a barbed-wire fence. Packhorses at night, iron-shod, clattering over the slickrock through your camp. The last tin of tuna, two flat tires, not enough water and a forty-mile trek to Tule Well. An osprey on a cardón cactus, snatch- ing the head off a living fish—always the best part first. The hawk sailing by at 200 feet, a squirming snake in its talons. Salt in the drinking water. Salt, selenium, arsenic, radon and radium in the water, in the gravel, in your bones. Water so hard it bends light, drills holes in rock and chokes up your radia-

tor. Why go there? Those places with the hardcase names: Starvation Creek, Poverty Knoll, Hungry Valley, Bitter Springs, Last Chance Canyon, Dungeon Canyon, Whipsaw Flat, Dead Horse Point, Scorpion Flat, Dead Man Draw, Stinking Spring, Camino del Diablo, Jornado del Muerto . . . Death Valley.

21   Well then, why indeed go walking into the desert, that grim ground, that bleak and lonesome land where, as Genghis Khan said of India, "the heat is bad and the water makes men sick"?

22   Why the desert, when you could be strolling along the golden beaches of California? Camping by a stream of pure Rocky Mountain spring water in colorful Colorado? Loafing through a laurel slick in the misty hills of North Carolina? Or getting your head mashed in the greasy alley behind the Elysium Bar and Grill in Hoboken, New Jersey? Why the desert, given a world of such splendor and variety?

23   A friend and I took a walk around the base of a mountain up beyond Coconino County, Arizona. This was a mountain we'd been planning to cir-cumambulate for years. Finally we put on our walking shoes and did it. About halfway around this mountain, on the third or fourth day, we paused for a while—two days—by the side of a stream, which the Navajos call Nasja because of the amber color of the water. (Caused perhaps by juniper roots— the water seems safe enough to drink.) On our second day there I walked down the stream, alone, to look at the canyon beyond. I entered the canyon and followed it for half the afternoon, for three or four miles, maybe, until it became a gorge so deep, narrow and dark, full of water and the inevitable quagmires of quicksand, that I turned around and looked for a way out. A route other than the way I'd come, which was crooked and uncomfortable and buried—I wanted to see what was up on top of this world. I found a sort of chimney flue on the east wall, which looked plausible, and sweated and cursed my way up through that until I reached a point where I could walk upright, like a human being. Another 300 feet of scrambling brought me to the rim of the canyon. No one, I felt certain, had ever before departed Nasja Canyon by that route.

24   But someone had. Near the summit I found an arrow sign, three feet long, formed of stones and pointing off into the north toward those same old purple vistas, so grand, immense, and mysterious, of more canyons, more mesas and plateaus, more mountains, more cloud-dappled sun-spangled leagues of desert sand and desert rock, under the same old wide and aching sky.

25   The arrow pointed into the north. But what was it pointing *at?* I looked at the sign closely and saw that those dark, desert-varnished stones had been in place for a long, long, time; they rested in compacted dust. They must have been there for a century at least. I followed the direction indicated and came promptly to the rim of another canyon and a drop-off straight down of a good 500 feet. Not that way, surely. Across this canyon was nothing of any unusual interest that I could see—only the familiar sun-blasted sandstone, a few scrubby clumps of blackbrush and prickly pear, a few acres of nothing where only a lizard could graze, surrounded by a few square miles of more nothingness

interesting chiefly to horned toads. I returned to the arrow and checked again, this time with field glasses, looking away for as far as my aided eyes could see toward the north, for ten, twenty, forty miles into the distance. I studied the scene with care, looking for an ancient Indian ruin, a significant cairn, perhaps an abandoned mine, a hidden treasure of some inconceivable wealth, the mother of all mother lodes. . . .

26   But there was nothing out there. Nothing at all. Nothing but the desert. Nothing but the silent world.

27   *That's why.*

❧

Discussion Questions

1. What does Abbey list as "survival hint #1" for those planning to explore the desert?

2. What are the three major hazards of the desert that Abbey discusses in paragraphs 3–8? What do they all have in common?

*3. What is the question Abbey sets out to answer in paragraphs 10–14? How does he answer the question?

4. How did Phoenix, Las Vegas, El Paso, Ciudad Juárez, strip mines, and power plants figure in Abbey's search for the answer to the question he poses in paragraph 10?

5. According to paragraph 15, what sorts of individuals did Abbey welcome to the desert, and what sorts did he wish to keep out?

6. In paragraph 16, Abbey announces his motto (also that of the Boy Scouts), "Be Prepared." What do we find out he means by this motto as described in paragraphs 7–18?

7. What in effect is "desert etiquette" as governed by the rules in paragraph 19?

*8. In paragraphs 20–22, Abbey returns to an earlier theme. Explain.

*9. What purpose does the narrative that ends the essay serve (paragraphs 23–27)?

Writing Topics

1. Write a brief essay after a fresh reading of "The Great American Desert," revealing whether you would like—or dislike—visiting the desert, citing from the essay the passages that shaped your opinion. Show *how* they affected you.

2. Write a brief analysis of the closing narrative of "The Great American Desert" (paragraphs 23–27), showing why you think it is a good—or bad—conclusion to the essay. You should begin by figuring out, as fully as possible, what it means—particularly the closing two paragraphs.

"While I was lying there, I thought,
'If this is it, then this is it.' I'm not a quitter,
but I knew that we were on our own and that nobody
in the whole area could do anything for us."

A LITTLE SPARK FROM
A GUY FLYING HIS KITE

California Firefighter

The only thing we know about the author of this essay is what is told to us: The author was at the time of the incident written about in this essay about near the end of his or her training as a firefighter and was preparing to take a "six-month probationary test." The essay is taken from *Firefighters: Their Lives in Their Own Words* (1988), edited by Dennis Smith. (For background on Dennis Smith, see his "Report from Engine Co. 82" in Cluster 11.)

1 In California we have what we call the Santa Ana winds, usually in August and September, where the winds come off the desert and bring a real dry heat all the way across to the coast. I had my six-month probationary test coming up, and I was studying all the time. I was with Engine 4 in the north part of the city.

2 This particular afternoon a young guy was flying a kite southeast of town and the kite caught on some high wires, causing an arc that jumped to the heavy brush and started a fire. So they dispatched the Forest Service and every nearby unit, leaving us to protect our part of the city. We looked out our back door and watched the fire grow, we listened to the radio traffic, and finally we were dispatched.

3 On the way to the fire, I was sitting in the jump seat behind the driver. Going down Foothill Road, I noticed our exhaust was shooting sparks out into the brush. I let the captain know, and thought, "Wouldn't it be ironic if our fire truck started a fire."

4 The fire was in a hilly area, with roads winding around and up and down the hills, an awkward place to fight a fire. Our assignment was to go up this narrow little road called Sycamore Vista. The second house on the left was on fire. A policeman lived there with his wife and two children. We couldn't do

much about the house. All we could do was make sure they got out. We did that. Then we went up to the next house. There were houses all over the place beginning to burn.

5   With some difficulty we backed into the driveway next door. I was with Captain Jim Embersby and Engineer Dave Stanley. There was a Chevy pickup in the driveway and a great big eucalyptus tree in the back. We pulled off a 150-foot preconnect and went to fight the fire. The house was on the side of a bank. The lower part of the bank was covered with brush, and that was all burning. The upper part of the bank was also covered with brush, and it was burning, and the big eucalyptus tree was on fire. I noticed the house was preheating, and white smoke was beginning to pump out of it. There wasn't really any fire yet, but I knew it was about to burst.

6   A very unusual thing happened to me at that point. I had been in forest fires before, and you normally have 21 percent oxygen in the air. But here the fire was so widespread around us that it was consuming the oxygen in the air and we couldn't breathe. We had bandannas on our faces, but they were just filtering the smoke, not giving us oxygen. The captain and Dave Stanley went across the lawn toward the house, and I lost track of them. I went back to the rig and grabbed a Scott air pack, and just about at that time the engine sucked an ember down the air intake, which burned the engine out, killed the pump, and prevented us from having any water. The hose in back of the truck was totally burned out, and I think the tires were, too.

7   The three of us were in an open air oven. We had fire above us, below us and to the sides. We were in a little spot right in the middle of the backyard. I figured there were other people in the same situation or worse, and that we were basically on our own. Funny, but my main concern during this whole time was passing my probationary test. I was dedicated!

8   So after I rejoined the other two, we all got into our fire tents. I think it was a miracle that we happened to be in a spot where there was a pocket of breathable air. I believe the Lord sent an angel down to protect us. There was so much fire around us. We shared the Scott pack, but it really wasn't that important. One of the things that helped me was something I learned in the Forest Service, which is, always carry some chewing gum with you. It helps keep some of the moisture in your mouth, otherwise you get real dry, then you get smoke and embers in your eyes and it's real uncomfortable.

9   We lay beneath our tents then for about forty minutes and listened to the fire popping all around us. We also listened to the radio traffic to see if anybody had any emergencies as bad as we had, and in fact they didn't. So we called for some help, for someone to come up to us. And Engine 1 and Squad 1 did try to come up to us. The driver of the engine got out, but the fire was so hot that he had to get right back in the engine. It was impossible for them to come through with hose lines and rescue us, because there was just too much fire and heat.

10   Usually brush fires pass over fairly quickly, but there was a lot of heavy brush which burned for a longer while, and, of course, there were all the buildings on fire around us. I noticed afterwards that the windshield of the pickup truck was just a clump of glass. It had melted.

11   While we were lying in our tents, we communicated with each other. We had the option of either staying where we were or taking a chance on running out through the brush and getting away. The captain convinced us that our best bet was to stay there, and so we did. There were other fire companies in similar situations, but their engines hadn't burned out, so that when they opened up the nozzle and water came out, they could put their faces close to the nozzle and breathe the cooler air with oxygen in it.

12   I kept lifting my tent and looking around. The heat only twenty feet from us was probably about 900 degrees, but to me the heat wasn't the problem, it was the lack of oxygen. It was difficult to breathe. And then there was the house. I remember looking at the house one time, and then, about twenty minutes later, the entire house was gone. All that was left was the chimney. It was like jumping from one scene to another in a movie. It was amazing.

13   While I was lying there, I thought, "If this is it, then this is it." I'm not a quitter, but I knew that we were on our own and that nobody in the whole area could do anything for us. I figured there were probably people in worse situations than we were. I prayed. I have a strong faith, and I believe that the Lord provided a little pocket of oxygen for us to breathe, because the fire consumed everything else. I knew that death was potentially nearby, as it is in a lot of the situations that we see. But I do appreciate life, and we all have a great concern for safety.

14   Finally, after forty minutes or so, the fire had passed over and settled down a little bit. The guys from the bottom made another attempt to get to us, and they got the pump going, but they were still not able to reach us. The ones who did finally reach us came over the top from the other side of the hill. They knew we were still alive, because we had kept in radio contact and given them updates of our situation.

15   When we got out, the fire was still going on. I would have stayed and gone through the whole thing, but during this time I had somehow cut my left eye. I don't know how, but I had scratched the cornea pretty good, and it got to the point where it bothered me so bad, I couldn't concentrate, and I couldn't do anything to get relief for it.

16   So they took me to the hospital, where they cleaned out my eyes, put in some medicine, and packed both of them. Actually they were more concerned about the black in my lungs. I had inhaled some smoke, which is common. So they cleared out the black stuff.

17   I didn't get to finish the whole fire. It stopped burning a couple of hours later, and that was it. History.

18   And to think that it all started from a little spark from a guy flying his kite! In all, that fire consumed 270 homes, and I don't think any lives were lost!

❧

Discussion Questions

1. What do we learn (paragraphs 1–2) was the cause of the fire? How did "nature" contribute?
*2. Why did the narrator think (paragraph 3), "Wouldn't it be ironic if our fire truck started a fire"?
3. As the fires surrounding the firefighters grew in intensity (paragraph 6), what did the narrator notice was happening? When the narrator went to the truck for a "Scott air pack," what happened to the truck's engine? Explain.
4. How did the three firefighters survive in their fire tents in the midst of the fire? Explain.
5. How were the firefighters finally rescued? At the end, what happened to the narrator?

Writing Topics

1. The narrator writes in paragraph 7, "Funny, but my main concern during this whole time was passing my probationary test." Assume that it is universally agreed that "experience is the best teacher." Write a letter to the firefighter's supervisor, setting forth why you think that the knowledge gained by the firefighter in the incident is far more useful than any book or manual knowledge.
2. Think over your own experience, recalling any occasion when you had to learn in the doing—in the heat of the moment—or suffer the consequences. Write a narrative essay describing the critical moment, how you behaved, and what your thoughts were then and afterward. Suggested topics include: The Day I Got Lost in a City [Department Store, Shopping Mall], The Night I Was Chased [Mugged, Robbed, Hit, Insulted, Taunted], The Time I Became Sick from Overeating [Drinking, Smoking, Overworking, Running].

*"By six o'clock, everything was done,
and everything outside was quiet. Inside,
there was the TV—the news programs full of alarms,
and charts showing the storm coming, and pictures of
people hauling in their boats and leaving their homes."*

HURRICANE THOUGHTS

Faith McNulty

Faith McNulty (born in 1918) assumed her position as staff writer for *The New Yorker* magazine in 1952. She is the author of many books, including *Wholly Cats* (1962), *The Great Whales* (1974), and over a dozen children's books, including *Mouse and Tim* (1978) and *How to Dig a Hole to the Other Side of the World* (1979). The letter below appeared in "The Talk of the Town" section of *The New Yorker* on August 23, 1976. It was introduced by the following comment: "We've received a letter, written on the night of last week's hurricane, from a friend of ours who lives on a small farm a few miles outside Wakefield, Rhode Island. Happily, as things turned out, Wakefield, like many other places on the northeast coast, was not hit as hard as had been anticipated. The electrical system was knocked out, and there was a certain amount of mild damage, but an ash tree that our friend was particularly concerned about was spared. Her letter follows."

1   I am writing this before the hurricane, on an electric typewriter. After the storm, this typewriter won't work. It is 9:30 P.M., and the six-o'clock news said the storm was coming straight at us. My husband and I have spent all day on the storm. By about six o'clock, we had done everything we could, and were very tired. In the morning, when we first heard that the storm was coming our way, we thought about food and light and fuel, but without any sense of real urgency. Then we drove to town around noon and found that our gas station had a queue of cars stretching out into the highway. In an instant, the psychology of shortage beset us. We drew up at the end of the line, wondering if the gas would hold out until we got to it. It did. We drove on, and found, to our surprise, that the hardware store was open, though today is a legal holiday

here—V-J Day. Al Damon, the proprietor, had opened the store because of the storm, and was alone behind the counter in semidarkness. We joined a huddle of people waiting to ask for hurricane lanterns, fuel, charcoal, candles. Damon handed out the supplies on his shelves and then went down into the basement and brought up all he had. With his permission, we telephoned a couple of friends and told them of the opportunity. When our turn came, we asked for four lanterns—the extra lanterns were for our friends. Next, we picked up the mail, and I was struck by how faithfully we performed this habitual errand, which could not possibly have anything to do with the coming night—the night the big ash tree might fall.

2   The big ash tree. That is at the heart of my foreboding. From the moment I remembered the tree—while we waited for our loot of lamps and charcoal—I have been aware of how terrible it will be if the ash tree falls. The ash tree is about ninety feet tall and about ninety feet wide. A tree man came by once and said that it must be at least two hundred years old. It is so big you can't see how big it is until you get right up to the trunk and imagine climbing into the lowest branches. They are as high above you as the second story of a house. They are as big around as ordinary tree trunks. A few years ago, one branch fell. It was just a small part of the tree, but it lay spread out on the ground like a dead whale. My husband spent days cutting it up. The ash tree is between our house and our barn. If it falls westward, it will crush our roof. If it falls toward the northeast, it could crash into the barn. But these dire possibilities do not bother me. It is the thought that it might fall at all that I cannot bear.

3   We made a list of things to do. Draw water in bathtubs, fill gallon jugs with drinking water, check window latches, and so on. A dreary round. Our sins of omission have all been uncovered—the unfixed leaks, the unhinged screens. All day long, I have been conscious of using things that most probably will not be here, or usable, tomorrow. Hot water from the faucet. The electric stove, on which I boiled a dozen eggs. The electric clock. I stifled an impulse to vacuum the floors—for me, an unprecedented desire. When the kitchen was tidy, we worked outdoors, dragging in the porch furniture, picking up every odd tool or object that might hurtle through a window. Most of the day, rain fell straight down—warm and needle-fine or warm and in fat streams, as though from an adjustable shower head. I often looked at the sky, where I supposed the sword of Damocles hung concealed in the wads of dark-gray cloud folded over us. There was almost no wind—strangely little wind for such a lot of rain. Between showers, a great many swallows came out and swooped and dived and rose again, as though very excited.

4   The pleasantest thing I did all day was to prepare our two horses for the night ahead. I cleaned the stalls, brought in fresh bedding and buckets of clean water, and filled the racks with hay. The horses were probably amazed, because in summer I don't usually do anything like this for them but leave them out to

take care of themselves. They were very wet, and entered the stalls willingly and ate the hay with a look of gratification. When I closed the doors of their stable, the small dwelling looked quite secure. It was the only thing I had done all day that I felt might really turn out all right.

5   By six o'clock, everything was done, and everything outside was quiet. Inside, there was the TV—the news programs full of alarms, and charts showing the storm coming, and pictures of people hauling in their boats and leaving their homes. A sudden lonesomeness assailed me. Earlier in the day, I had made one or two essential phone calls, but I hadn't had time for anything else. Now I began to call friends. A number of lines were busy. We were all establishing communication. Tomorrow, phoning will be impossible. Like us, several friends live at the end of long, tree-lined roads and very likely may not get their cars out for days, until the debris of fallen trees is cleared. We decided to leave our car out on the highway, a quarter of a mile from the house. I called three friends and arranged to go by tomorrow morning and look in their mailboxes, which are on the highway, so that if they have needs or messages for the outside world they can walk down their driveways and leave me a note. I was quite pleased at having thought of this simple way to survive the loss of the telephone. We exchanged hurricane lore. The heavy rain, we agree, increases the danger that trees will fall, because their roots can be more easily wrenched out of the softened earth. We discussed our nerves. We all hate waiting. "Are you nervous?" someone asks. "I've been nervous as a cat all day."

6   Just before dark, I went out and picked all the flowers—begonias, nicotiana, zinnias, well washed but still intact. I gathered an armful, in profusion. I looked at my dozens of green tomatoes and wondered if they would survive. There was still no wind.

7   Now we're battened down. There is no one else to call. We've had supper. The TV news says the storm is coming, but here inside the lighted house there is no sign of anything unusual, except the sound of leaves. A few minutes ago, I stepped outside and found that it was still warm—seventy-two degrees on the porch thermometer. The air was very soft, but there was no rain. The wind felt gentle and smelled sweet and tropical, alien to New England. Whereas all day we'd had the sound of dripping rain, now we had the sound of leaves stirring. The vanguard of the storm has arrived. I looked up into the branches of the monumental ash tree. They were moving restlessly, as though the tree were coming to life to meet the imminent struggle. It must have lived through many hurricanes, but now, in its great age, it is more vulnerable than ever before. There was nothing else I could do for it, so I pronounced a blessing on it, as though it were going into a battle. Its multitude of leaves reminded me of a medieval host. Its lashing arms seemed full of life and strength, and I returned to the house with new hope that the great ash tree would be there in the morning.

❧

Discussion Questions

*1. The "big ash tree" figures in the letter near the beginning and at the end. What were McNulty's concern for and feelings about the tree? Explain.

2. How did their attitude toward the approaching storm change when McNulty and her husband drove to the gas station? What did they then do?

3. What were the "sins of omission" mentioned in paragraph 3?

4. How did horses figure in McNulty's preparation for the storm? The telephone? Their automobile? The flowers blooming in the yard?

Writing Topics

1. Write a character sketch of McNulty based on the behavior she describes in her letter. Set forth what you would call her principal traits and then cite passages from her letter to illustrate them. In your conclusion, venture an overall assessment of her character.

2. Most people have lived through an approaching danger—a hurricane, a flood, a tornado, a heat wave, an ice storm, and the like. Write a narrative essay describing the preparations you and your family took, what actually happened, and the consequences afterwards. In your conclusion, consider how useful the preparations were (or dangerous the lack of preparations) in light of what happened. In short, what did you and your family learn from the experience?

❧ ❝The eruption cloud is very solid-looking, like sculptured marble, a beautiful blue in the deep relief of baroque curls, sworls, curled-cloud-shapes — darkening towards the top — a wonderful color.❞

A VERY WARM MOUNTAIN

Ursula K. Le Guin

Ursula K. Le Guin was born in California in 1929 and went to Radcliffe College (B.A., 1951) and Columbia University (M.A., 1952). She is renowned for her science fiction, which critics assert rises above the limitations of the form. Among her most popular novels are A *Wizard of Earthsea* (1968), *The Left Hand of Darkness* (1969), and *The Dispossessed*: *An Ambiguous Utopia* (1974). Among her multitude of published books are those labeled "Juveniles" (*Catwings*, 1988), "Poems" (*Wild Oats and Fireweed*, 1988) and "Other," a category that includes volumes of essays such as *Dreams Must Explain Themselves* (1975) and *Dancing on the Edge of the World: Thoughts on Words, Women, Places* (1989). Le Guin observed the eruption of the volcano Mount St. Helens (in the state of Washington) from the window of her home in Portland, Oregon. The first blast occurred on May 18, 1980, and shot the mountain's crown into the air, demolishing its familiar peak; other eruptions followed. Twenty-five people were confirmed dead, with some forty "missing." Economic loss was estimated at around three billion dollars. Le Guin published "A Very Warm Mountain" in *Parabola* in 1980.

An enormous region extending from north-central Washington to northeastern California and including most of Oregon east of the Cascades is covered by basalt lava flows. . . . The unending cliffs of basalt along the Columbia River . . . 74 volcanoes in the Portland area . . . A blanket of pumice that averages about 50 feet thick . . .
—*Roadside Geology of Oregon*
Alt and Hyndman, 1978.

1   Everybody takes it personally. Some get mad. Damn stupid mountain went and dumped all that dirty gritty glassy gray ash that flies like flour and lies like cement all over their roofs, roads, and rhododendrons. Now they have to clean it up. And the scientists are a real big help, all they'll say is we don't know, we can't tell, she might dump another load of ash on you just when you've got it all cleaned up. It's an outrage.

2   Some take it ethically. She lay and watched her forests being cut and her elk being hunted and her lakes being fished and fouled and her ecology being tampered with and the smoky, snarling suburbs creeping closer to her skirts, until she saw it was time to teach the White Man's Children a lesson. And she did. In the process of the lesson, she blew her forests to matchsticks, fried her elk, boiled her fish, wrecked her ecosystem, and did very little damage to the cities: so that the lesson taught to the White Man's Children would seem, at best, equivocal.

3   But everybody takes it personally. We try to reduce it to human scale. To make a molehill out of the mountain.

4   Some got very anxious, especially during the dreary white weather that hung around the area after May 18 (the first great eruption, when she blew 1300 feet of her summit all over Washington, Idaho, and points east) and May 25 (the first considerable ashfall in the thickly populated Portland area west of the mountain). Farmers in Washington State who had the real fallout, six inches of ash smothering their crops, answered the reporters' questions with polite stoicism; but in town a lot of people were cross and dull and jumpy. Some erratic behavior, some really weird driving. "Everybody on my bus coming to work these days talks to everybody else, they never used to." "Everybody on my bus coming to work sits there like a stone instead of talking to each other like they used to." Some welcomed the mild sense of urgency and emergency as bringing people together in mutual support. Some — the old, the ill — were terrified beyond reassurance. Psychologists reported that psychotics had promptly incorporated the volcano into their private systems; some thought they were controlling her, and some thought she was controlling them. Businessmen, whom we know from the Dow Jones Reports to be an almost ethereally timid and emotional breed, read the scare stories in Eastern newspapers and cancelled all their conventions here; Portland hotels are having a long cool summer. A Chinese Cultural Attaché, evidently preferring earthquakes, wouldn't come farther north than San Francisco. But many natives were irrationally exhilarated, secretly, heartlessly welcoming every steam-blast and earth-tremor: Go it, mountain!

5   Everybody read in the newspapers everywhere that the May 18 eruption was "five hundred times greater than the bomb dropped on Hiroshima." Some reflected that we have bombs much more than five hundred times more powerful than the 1945 bombs. But these are never mentioned in the comparisons. Perhaps it would upset people in Moscow, Idaho or Missoula, Montana, who

got a lot of volcanic ash dumped on them, and don't want to have to think, what if that stuff had been radioactive? It really isn't nice to talk about, is it? I mean, what if something went off in New Jersey, say, and *was* radioactive—Oh, stop it. That volcano's way out west there somewhere anyhow.

6   Everybody takes it personally.

7   I had to go into hospital for some surgery in April, while the mountain was in her early phase—she jumped and rumbled, like the Uncles in *A Child's Christmas in Wales*, but she hadn't done anything spectacular. I was hoping she wouldn't perform while I couldn't watch. She obliged and held off for a month. On May 18 I was home, lying around with the cats, with a ringside view: bedroom and study look straight north about forty-five miles to the mountain.

8   I kept the radio tuned to a good country western station and listened to the reports as they came in, and wrote down some of the things they said. For the first couple of hours there was a lot of confusion and contradiction, but no panic, then or later. Late in the morning a man who had been about twenty miles from the blast described it: "Pumice-balls and mud-balls began falling for about a quarter of an hour, then the stuff got smaller, and by nine it was completely and totally black dark. You couldn't see ten feet in front of you!" He spoke with energy and admiration. Falling mud-balls, what next? The main West Coast artery, I-5, was soon closed because of the mud and wreckage rushing down the Toutle River towards the highway bridges. Walla Walla, 160 miles east, reported in to say their street lights had come on automatically at about ten in the morning. The Spokane–Seattle highway, far to the north, was closed, said an official expressionless voice, "on account of darkness."

9   At one-thirty that afternoon, I wrote:

> *It has been warm with a white high haze all morning, since six A.M., when I saw the top of the mountain floating dark against yellow-rose sunrise sky above the haze.*

That was, of course, the last time I saw or will ever see that peak.

> *Now we can see the mountain from the base to near the summit. The mountain itself is whitish in the haze. All morning there has been this long, cobalt-bluish drift to the east from where the summit would be. And about ten o'clock there began to be visible clots, like cottage cheese curds, above the summit. Now the eruption cloud is visible from the summit of the mountain till obscured by a cloud layer at about twice the height of the mountain, i.e., 25–30,000 feet. The eruption cloud is very solid-looking, like sculptured marble, a beautiful blue in the deep relief of baroque curls, sworls, curled-cloud-shapes—darkening towards the top—a wonderful color. One is aware of motion, but (being shaky, and looking through shaky*

binoculars) I don't actually see the carven-blue-sworl-shapes move. Like the shadow on a sundial. It is enormous. Forty-five miles away. It is so much bigger than the mountain itself. It is silent, from this distance. Enormous, silent. It looks not like anything earthy, from the earth, but it does not look like anything atmospheric, a natural cloud, either. The blue of it is stormcloud blue but the shapes are far more delicate, complex, and immense than stormcloud shapes, and it has this solid look; a weightiness, like the capital of some unimaginable column — which in a way indeed it is, the pillar of fire being underground.

At four in the afternoon a reporter said cautiously, "Earthquakes are being felt in the metropolitan area," to which I added, with feeling, "I'll say they are!" I had decided not to panic unless the cats did. Animals are supposed to know about earthquakes, aren't they? I don't know what our cats know; they lay asleep in various restful and decorative poses on the swaying floor and the jiggling bed, and paid no attention to anything except dinner time. I was not allowed to panic.

10   At four-thirty a meteorologist, explaining the height of that massive, storm-blue pillar of cloud, said charmingly, "You must understand that the mountain is very warm. Warm enough to lift the air over it to 75,000 feet."

11   And a reporter: "Heavy mud flow on Shoestring Glacier, with continuous lightning." I tried to imagine that scene. I went to the television, and there it was. The radio and television coverage, right through, was splendid. One forgets the joyful courage of reporters and cameramen when there is something worth reporting, a real Watergate, a real volcano.

12   On the 19th, I wrote down from the radio, "A helicopter picked the logger up while he was sitting on a log surrounded by a mud flow." This rescue was filmed and shown on television: the tiny figure crouching hopeless in the huge abomination of ash and mud. I don't know if this man was one of the loggers who later died in the Emanuel Hospital burn center, or if he survived. They were already beginning to talk about the "killer eruption," as if the mountain had murdered with intent. Taking it personally . . . Of course she killed. Or did they kill themselves? Old Harry who wouldn't leave his lodge and his whiskey and his eighteen cats at Spirit Lake, and quite right too, at eighty-three; and the young cameraman and the young geologist, both up there on the north side on the job of their lives; and the loggers who went back to work because logging was their living; and the tourists who thought a volcano is like Channel Six, if you don't like the show you turn it off, and took their RVs and their kids up past the roadblocks and the reasonable warnings and the weary county sheriffs sick of arguing: they were all there to keep the appointment. Who made the appointment?

13   A firefighter pilot that day said to the radio interviewer, "We do what the mountain says. It's not ready for us to go in."

14   On the 21st I wrote:

> *Last night a long, strange, glowing twilight; but no ash has yet fallen west of the mountain. Today, fine, gray, mild, dense Oregon rain. Yesterday afternoon we could see her vaguely through the glasses. Looking appallingly lessened — short, flat — That is painful. She was so beautiful. She hurled her beauty in dust clear to the Atlantic shore, she made sunsets and sunrises of it, she gave it to the western wind. I hope she erupts magma and begins to build herself again. But I guess she is still unbuilding. The Pres. of the U.S. came today to see her. I wonder if he thinks he is on her level. Of course he could destroy much more than she has destroyed if he took a mind to.*

15   On June 4 I wrote:

> *Could see her through the glasses for the first time in two weeks or so. It's been dreary white weather with a couple of hours sun in the afternoons. —Not the new summit, yet; that's always in the roil of cloud/plume. But both her long lovely flanks. A good deal of new snow has fallen on her (while we had rain), and her SW face is white, black, and gray, much seamed, in unfamiliar patterns.*
>
> *"As changeless as the hills —"*
>
> *Part of the glory of it is being included in an event on the geologic scale. Being enlarged. "I shall lift up mine eyes unto the hills," yes: "whence cometh my help."*

16   In all the Indian legends dug out by newspaper writers for the occasion, the mountain is female. Told in the Dick-and-Jane style considered appropriate for popular reportage of Indian myth, with all the syllables hyphenated, the stories seem even more naive and trivial than myths out of context generally do. But the theme of the mountain as woman — first ugly, then beautiful, but always a woman — is consistent. The mapmaking whites of course named the peak after a man, an Englishman who took his title, Baron St. Helens, from a town in the North Country: but the name is obstinately feminine. The Baron is forgotten, Helen remains. The whites who lived on and near the mountain called it The Lady. Called her The Lady. It seems impossible not to take her personally. In twenty years of living through a window from her I guess I have never really thought of her as "it."

17   She made weather, like all single peaks. She put on hats of cloud, and took them off again, and tried a different shape, and sent them all skimming off across

the sky. She wore veils: around the neck, across the breast: white, silver, silver-gray, gray-blue. Her taste was impeccable. She knew the weathers that became her, and how to wear the snow.

18 Dr. William Hamilton of Portland State University wrote a lovely piece for the college paper about "volcano anxiety," suggesting that the silver cone of St. Helens had been in human eyes a breast, and saying:

> *St. Helens' real damage to us is not . . . that we have witnessed a denial of the trustworthiness of God (such denials are our familiar friends). It is the perfection of the mother that has been spoiled, for part of her breast has been removed. Our metaphor has had a mastectomy.*
>
> *At some deep level, the eruption of Mt. St. Helens has become a new metaphor for the very opposite of stability —for that greatest of twentieth-century fears —cancer. Our uneasiness may well rest on more elusive levels than dirty windshields.*

19 This comes far closer to home than anything else I've read about the "meaning" of the eruption, and yet for me it doesn't work. Maybe it would work better for men. The trouble is, I never saw St. Helens as a breast. Some mountains, yes: Twin Peaks in San Francisco, of course, and other round, sweet California hills —breasts, bellies, eggs, anything maternal, bounteous, yielding. But St. Helens in my eyes was never part of a woman; she is a woman. And not a mother but a sister.

20 These emotional perceptions and responses sound quite foolish when written out in rational prose, but the fact is that, to me, the eruption was all mixed up with the women's movement. It may be silly but there it is; along the same lines, do you know any woman who wasn't rooting for Genuine Risk to take the Triple Crown? Part of my satisfaction and exultation at each eruption was unmistakably feminist solidarity. You men think you're the only ones can make a really nasty mess? You think you got all the firepower, and God's on your side? You think you run things? Watch this, gents. Watch the Lady act like a woman.

21 For that's what she did. The well-behaved, quiet, pretty, serene, domestic creature peaceably yielding herself to the uses of man all of a sudden said NO. And she spat dirt and smoke and steam. She blackened half her face, in those first March days, like an angry brat. She fouled herself like a mad old harridan. She swore and belched and farted, threatened and shook and swelled, and then she spoke. They heard her voice two hundred miles away. Here I go, she said. I'm doing my thing now. Old Nobodaddy you better JUMP!

22 Her thing turns out to be more like childbirth than anything else, to my way of thinking. But not on our scale, not in our terms. Why should she speak in our terms or stoop to our scale? Why should she bear any birth that we can

recognize? To us it is cataclysm and destruction and deformity. To her—well, for the language for it one must go to the scientists or to the poets. To the geologists. St. Helens is doing exactly what she "ought" to do—playing her part in the great pattern of events perceived by that noble discipline. Geology provides the only time-scale large enough to include the behavior of a volcano without deforming it. Geology, or poetry, which can see a mountain and a cloud as, after all, very similar phenomena. Shelley's cloud can speak for St. Helens:

> *I silently laugh*
> *At my own cenotaph . . .*
> *And arise, and unbuild it again.*

23   So many mornings waking I have seen her from the window before any other thing: dark against red daybreak, silvery in summer light, faint above river-valley fog. So many times I have watched her at evening, the faintest outline in mist, immense, remote, serene: the center, the central stone. A self across the air, a sister self, a stone. "The stone is at the center," I wrote in a poem about her years ago. But the poem is impertinent. All I can say is impertinent.

24   When I was writing the first draft of this essay in California, on July 23, she erupted again, sending her plume to 60,000 feet. Yesterday, August 7, as I was typing the words "the 'meaning' of the eruption," I checked out the study window and there it was, the towering blue cloud against the quiet northern sky—the fifth major eruption. How long may her labor be? A year, ten years, ten thousand? We cannot predict what she may or might or will do, now, or next, or for the rest of our lives, or ever. A threat: a terror: a fulfillment. This is what serenity is built on. This unmakes the metaphors. This is beyond us, and we must take it personally. This is the ground we walk on.

⮞

Discussion Questions

1.   Why did Le Guin call her essay "A Very Warm Mountain"? Explain. (Note particularly paragraph 10.)

*2.   Explain the meaning in context of the sentence that ends paragraph 4, "But many natives were irrationally exhilarated, secretly, heartlessly welcoming every steam-blast and earth-tremor: Go it, mountain!"

3.   In the middle of paragraph 12, Le Guin says, "Of course she [St. Helens] killed. Or did they kill themselves?" What examples does she cite following this sentence, and what is Le Guin's implicit answer to her question?

*4.   In paragraph 15, Le Guin writes, "Part of the glory of it [experiencing the erupting volcano] is being included in an event on the geologic scale. Being enlarged. 'I shall lift up mine eyes unto the hills,' yes: 'whence cometh my help.' " The quotation comes from Psalms 121: 1. Explain both the explicit and implicit meaning.

5.   Explore the ramifications of meaning in the last sentences of paragraph 21, "Here I go, she [St. Helens] said. I'm doing my thing now. Old Nobodaddy, you better JUMP!" Note: William Blake's "To Nobodaddy": "Why art thou silent & invisible/Father of jealousy/ Why dost thou hide thyself in clouds/From every searching Eye// Why darkness & obscurity/In all thy words & laws/That none dare eat the fruit but from/The wily serpents jaws/Or is it because Secrecy/gains females loud applause."

*6.   Explore the ramifications of meaning in the opening sentences of paragraph 22, "Her thing turns out to be more like childbirth than anything else, to my way of thinking. But not on our scale, not in our terms."

7.   What does Le Guin mean in paragraph 22 when she says that "Shelley's cloud can speak for St. Helens"? Here is the complete last stanza of Percy Bysshe Shelley's "The Cloud" (the Cloud speaks):

> I am the daughter of Earth and Water,
>   And the nursling of the Sky;
> I pass through the pores, of the ocean and shores;
>   I change, but I cannot die—
> For after the rain, when with never a stain
>   The pavilion of Heaven is bare,
> And the winds and sunbeams, with their convex gleams,
>   Build up the blue dome of air—
> I silently laugh at my own cenotaph,
>   And out of the caverns of rain,
> Like a child from the womb, like a ghost from the tomb,
>   I arise, and unbuild it again.—

Writing Topics

1.   Le Guin opens her essay, "Everybody takes it personally." She returns to this idea throughout the essay, and it appears again at the very end. Write an analytical essay in which you explore the ways in which this concept is woven throughout the essay, considering whether it expands or contracts—or subtly changes—in meaning. In your conclusion, concentrate on its full or overarching meaning at the end.

2. In paragraphs 18–23, Le Guin begins by reporting Dr. William Hamilton's theory about the psychological reaction to Mount St. Helens and its eruption: the mountain represents a woman's breast and the blast represents a mastectomy. Le Guin disagrees and says that to her Mount St. Helens "is a woman" and "the eruption was all mixed up with the women's movement." In an essay, present your response to these views, indicating which you find more persuasive and why—or present your own, different view.

Summary Writing Topics

1. Write a comparison/contrast essay detailing the frightening aspects of nature as they appear in the essays by Mary Dodge Woodward and Margaret E. Murie. What similarities do you find and what differences? In your conclusion, consider which essay is more successful in evoking those aspects of nature and why.

2. In an analytical essay, compare and contrast the affirmative experiences with nature described in the essays by Henry Beston and Charlotte Carpenter. What difference does it make that one involves a single individual's experience, while the other involves an entire family?

3. Ian Frazier says in "Long Drives on the Plains," "Ever since the Great Plains were first called a desert, people have gone a long way toward turning them into one." In an essay, compare and contrast this concept of the desert with that of Edward Abbey in "The Great American Desert." Both writers seem to be in favor of preserving for the future what they have experienced in their own lives. Explore the ambiguities and complications that arise when the two essays are read side by side. In your conclusion, indicate which "world" you would most like to see firsthand—that described by Frazier or that by Abbey.

4. One reader of "A Little Spark from a Guy Flying His Kite" was heard to remark, "Why, this essay doesn't belong in Cluster 13, 'Nature Unfolding, Nature Unbridled,' but rather in 'Everyday Realities' or 'Disruptions and Disasters.'" Write a letter to the editors of this book, explaining why you agree or disagree with this comment, supporting your point of view with specific references to the text.

5. Both Lewis Thomas ("Ponds") and Edward Abbey ("The Great American Desert") share concerns about their environments—one the city, the other the desert. In an essay, compare what you take to be Thomas's "city etiquette" with Abbey's "desert etiquette." Show in your conclusion your own reaction to their rules of etiquette.

6. Thomas and Abbey both use wit and humor in their essays to make their serious points. Compare and contrast their methods and devices of humor and then, in a conclusion, indicate which one you find more interesting and why.

7. Both Abbey in "The Great American Desert" and Ursula Le Guin in "A Very Warm Mountain" deal with aspects of nature that seem, on the surface, hostile to humankind, yet both writers seem drawn to and fascinated by their subjects. Write an essay comparing how Abbey's awe/fear for the desert and Le Guin's awe/fear for Mount St. Helens become manifest in their essays. In your conclusion, consider how their ambivalence toward their subjects strengthens or weakens their essays.

8. In "A Very Warm Mountain," Ursula Le Guin deals with a great tragedy that involves many deaths, family upheavals, and enormous damage to property and products. In dealing with such subjects, it is difficult to avoid sentimentality. In an analytical essay on "A Very Warm Mountain," set forth your view as to the degree of sentimentality in the essay and support your view by citing and exploring passages from the text.

9. Assume a critic has indicated to the editors of this book that floods are important examples of "nature unbridled," yet the book includes no personal accounts of floods. Find such an account (or write one yourself) and send it to the editors with a letter pointing out why it should be included in the next edition.

10. Assume that another critic has said that a walk or a jog through a suburb early in the morning, around sunrise, constitutes an extraordinary experience, a kind of communion with nature. Find such an account (or write one yourself) and send it to the editors recommending it for the next edition.

Cluster 14

Sounding for Truths, Reaching for Verities

A dictionary definition of a *verity* is that it has that quality or state of being eternally or necessarily true and not merely true as a matter of fact. We tend to distinguish such transcendent truths (if we ever encounter them) by calling them *eternal verities*. The words are, of course, often used interchangeably. No matter. Truths and verities are so fragile, so elusive, that it is best to have more than one word to contemplate when we pursue them or undertake exploration of them.

Sounding, as in "sounding for depth," and *reaching*, as in "reaching for the stars," signal two different directions for discovery—one down in the waters to the earth below, the other up to the stars and the heavens beyond. The assumption is that we are surrounded by mysteries waiting to be probed, not by the instruments of science but by the imaginations of curious essayists.

We live in a time when many espouse antimetaphysical, antitranscendental views, often ridiculing "universal values" and proclaiming all judgments relative. Yet the very people who most earnestly assert these beliefs are the first to insist on their "universal" human rights. Belief in such rights is embedded in America's founding document, the Declaration of Independence, which ringingly declares, "We hold these truths to be self-evident, that all men are created equal, that they are endowed by their Creator with certain unalienable Rights, that among these are Life, Liberty and the pursuit of Happiness." It is from the United States that the world has adopted the concept of universal human rights, which no country should be able to violate with impunity.

This cluster brings together essays that explore, affirm, or tentatively put forward some aspect of one truth or another; that re-create moments at which the writers glimpsed a truth—or saw into the realm of eternal verities. Three of the essayists are professional scientists who have devoted their lives to the pursuit of "universal" scientific truths (like DNA and black holes), yet who seem bent on pursuing some kind of ultimate truth below or beyond. Implicit in all these essays is that we are all searchers after truth and that much of life's meaning is to be found in the search itself, as well as in the occasional sighting that whets our appetite to see, and know, and comprehend more.

What have we been doing all these centuries but trying to call God back to the mountain, or, failing that, raise a peep out of anything that isn't us? What is the difference between a cathedral and a physics lab? Are not they both saying: Hello?"

TEACHING A STONE TO TALK

Annie Dillard

Annie Dillard was born in Pittsburgh, Pennsylvania, in 1945 and attended Hollins College, obtaining a B.A. in 1967 and an M.A. in 1968. In 1974, she published two books: a collection of poems, *Tickets for a Prayer Wheel*, and an autobiographical/ meditative work, *Pilgrim at Tinker Creek*, which won the Pulitzer Prize for nonfiction in 1975. Her many other books include a critical work on literature, *Living by Fiction* (1982); a memoir, *An American Childhood* (1987); a book on her profession, *The Writing Life* (1989); and a novel, *The Living* (1992). In 1982, she published *Teaching a Stone to Talk: Expeditions and Encounters*, from which the following essay was taken. For more biographical information on Dillard, see page 325.

I

1   The island where I live is peopled with cranks like myself. In a cedar-shake shack on a cliff—but we all live like this—is a man in his thirties who lives alone with a stone he is trying to teach to talk.

2   Wisecracks on this topic abound, as you might expect, but they are made as it were perfunctorily, and mostly by the young. For in fact, almost everyone here respects what Larry is doing, as do I, which is why I am protecting his (or her) privacy, and confusing for you the details. It could be, for instance, a pinch of sand he is teaching to talk, or a prolonged northerly, or any one of a number of waves. But it is, in fact, I assure you, a stone. It is—for I have seen it—a palm-sized oval beach cobble whose dark gray is cut by a band of white which runs around and, presumably, through it; such stones we call "wishing stones," for reasons obscure but not, I think, unimaginable.

3   He keeps it on a shelf. Usually the stone lies protected by a square of untanned leather, like a canary asleep under its cloth. Larry removes the cover for the stone's lessons, or more accurately, I should say, for the ritual or rituals which they perform together several times a day.

4   No one knows what goes on at these sessions, least of all myself, for I know Larry but slightly, and that owing only to a mix-up in our mail. I assume that like any other meaningful effort, the ritual involves sacrifice, the suppression of self-consciousness, and a certain precise tilt of the will, so that the will becomes transparent and hollow, a channel for the work. I wish him well. It is a noble work, and beats, from any angle, selling shoes.

5   Reports differ on precisely what he expects or wants the stone to say. I do not think he expects the stone to speak as we do, and describe for us its long life and many, or few, sensations. I think instead that he is trying to teach it to say a single word, such as "cup," or "uncle." For this purpose he has not, as some have seriously suggested, carved the stone a little mouth, or furnished it in any way with a pocket of air which it might then expel. Rather—and I think he is wise in this—he plans to initiate his son, who is now an infant living with Larry's estranged wife, into the work, so that it may continue and bear fruit after his death.

II

6   Nature's silence is its one remark, and every flake of world is a chip off that old mute and immutable block. The Chinese say that we live in the world of the ten thousand things. Each of the ten thousand things cries out to us precisely nothing.

7   God used to rage at the Israelites for frequenting sacred groves. I wish I could find one. Martin Buber says: "The crisis of all primitive mankind comes with the discovery of that which is fundamentally not-holy, the a-sacramental, which withstands the methods, and which has no 'hour,' a province which steadily enlarges itself." Now we are no longer primitive; now the whole world seems not-holy. We have drained the light from the boughs in the sacred grove and snuffed it in the high places and along the banks of sacred streams. We as a people have moved from pantheism to pan-atheism. Silence is not our heritage but our destiny; we live where we want to live.

8   The soul may ask God for anything, and never fail. You may ask God for his presence, or for wisdom, and receive each at his hands. Or you may ask God, in the words of the shopkeeper's little gag sign, that he not go away mad, but just go away. Once, in Israel, an extended family of nomads did just that. They heard God's speech and found it too loud. The wilderness generation was at Sinai; it witnessed there the thick darkness where God was: "and all the people saw the thunderings, and the lightnings, and the noise of the trumpet, and the mountain smoking." It scared them witless. Then they asked Moses to

beg God, please, never speak to them directly again. "Let not God speak with us, lest we die." Moses took the message. And God, pitying their self-consciousness, agreed. He agreed not to speak to the people anymore. And he added to Moses, "Go say to them, Get into your tents again."

III

9 It is difficult to undo our own damage, and to recall to our presence that which we have asked to leave. It is hard to desecrate a grove and change your mind. The very holy mountains are keeping mum. We doused the burning bush and cannot rekindle it; we are lighting matches in vain under every green tree. Did the wind use to cry, and the hills shout forth praise? Now speech has perished from among the lifeless things of earth, and living things say very little to very few. Birds may crank out sweet gibberish and monkeys howl; horses neigh and pigs say, as you recall, oink oink. But so do cobbles rumble when a wave recedes, and thunders break the air in lightning storms. I call these noises silence. It could be that wherever there is motion there is noise, as when a whale breaches and smacks the water—and wherever there is stillness there is the still small voice, God's speaking from the whirlwind, nature's old song and dance, the show we drove from town. At any rate, now it is all we can do, and among our best efforts, to try to teach a given human language, English, to chimpanzees.

10 In the forties an American psychologist and his wife tried to teach a chimp actually to speak. At the end of three years the creature could pronounce, in a hoarse whisper, the words "mama," "papa," and "cup.".After another three years of training she could whisper, with difficulty, still only "mama," "papa," and "cup." The more recent successes at teaching chimpanzees American Sign Language are well known. Just the other day a chimp told us, if we can believe that we truly share a vocabulary, that she had been sad in the morning. I'm sorry we asked.

11 What have we been doing all these centuries but trying to call God back to the mountain, or, failing that, raise a peep out of anything that isn't us? What is the difference between a cathedral and a physics lab? Are not they both saying: Hello? We spy on whales and on interstellar radio objects; we starve ourselves and pray till we're blue.

IV

12 I have been reading comparative cosmology. At this time most cosmologists favor the picture of the evolving universe described by Lemaître and Gamow. But I prefer a suggestion made years ago by Valéry—Paul Valéry. He set forth the notion that the universe might be "headshaped."

13 The mountains are great stone bells; they clang together like nuns. Who shushed the stars? There are a thousand million galaxies easily seen in the

Palomar reflector; collisions between and among them do, of course, occur. But these collisions are very long and silent slides. Billions of stars sift among each other untouched, too distant even to be moved, heedless as always, hushed. The sea pronounces something, over and over, in a hoarse whisper; I cannot quite make it out. But God knows I have tried.

14   At a certain point you say to the woods, to the sea, to the mountains, the world, Now I am ready. Now I will stop and be wholly attentive. You empty yourself and wait, listening. After a time you hear it: there is nothing there. There is nothing but those things only, those created objects, discrete, growing or holding, or swaying, being rained on or raining, held, flooding or ebbing, standing, or spread. You feel the world's word as a tension, a hum, a single chorused note everywhere the same. This is it: this hum is the silence. Nature does utter a peep—just this one. The birds and insects, the meadows and swamps and rivers and stones and mountains and clouds: they all do it; they all don't do it. There is a vibrancy to the silence, a suppression, as if someone were gagging the world. But you wait, you give your life's length to listening, and nothing happens. The ice rolls up, the ice rolls back, and still that single note obtains. The tension, or lack of it, is intolerable. The silence is not actually suppression; instead, it is all there is.

V

15   We are here to witness. There is nothing else to do with those mute materials we do not need. Until Larry teaches his stone to talk, until God changes his mind, or until the pagan gods slip back to their hilltop groves, all we can do with the whole inhuman array is watch it. We can stage our own act on the planet—build our cities on its plains, dam its rivers, plant its topsoils—but our meaningful activity scarcely covers the terrain. We do not use the songbirds, for instance. We do not eat many of them; we cannot befriend them; we cannot persuade them to eat more mosquitoes or plant fewer weed seeds. We can only witness them—whoever they are. If we were not here, they would be songbirds falling in the forest. If we were not here, material events like the passage of seasons would lack even the meager meanings we are able to muster for them. The show would play to an empty house, as do all those falling stars which fall in the daytime. That is why I take walks: to keep an eye on things. And that is why I went to the Galápagos islands.

16   All this becomes especially clear on the Galápagos islands. The Galápagos islands are just plain here—and little else. They blew up out of the ocean, some plants blew in on them, some animals drifted aboard and evolved weird forms— and there they all are, whoever they are, in full swing. You can go there and watch it happen, and try to figure it out. The Galápagos are a kind of metaphysics laboratory, almost wholly uncluttered by human culture or history.

Whatever happens on those bare volcanic rocks happens in full view, whether anyone is watching or not.

17   What happens there is this, and precious little it is: clouds come and go, and the round of similar seasons; a pig eats a tortoise or doesn't eat a tortoise; Pacific waves fall up and slide back; a lichen expands; night follows day; an albatross dies and dries on a cliff; a cool current upwells from the ocean floor; fishes multiply, flies swarm, stars rise and fall, and diving birds dive. The news, in other words, breaks on the beaches. And taking it all in are the trees. The *palo santo* trees crowd the hillsides like any outdoor audience; they face the lagoons, the lava lowlands, and the shores.

18   I have some experience of these *palo santo* trees. They interest me as emblems of the muteness of the human stance in relation to all that is not human. I see us all as *palo santo* trees, holy sticks, together watching all that we watch, and growing in silence.

19   In the Galápagos, it took me a long time to notice the *palo santo* trees. Like everyone else, I specialized in sea lions. My shipmates and I liked the sea lions, and envied their lives. Their joy seemed conscious. They were engaged in full-time play. They were all either fat or dead; there was no halfway. By day they played in the shallows, alone or together, greeting each other and us with great noises of joy, or they took a turn offshore and body-surfed in the breakers, exultant. By night on the sand they lay in each other's flippers and slept. Everyone joked, often, that when he "came back," he would just as soon do it all over again as a sea lion. I concurred. The sea lion game looked unbeatable.

20   But a year and a half later, I returned to those unpeopled islands. In the interval my attachment to them had shifted, and my memories of them had altered, the way memories do, like particolored pebbles rolled back and forth over a grating, so that after a time those hard bright ones, the ones you thought you would never lose, have vanished, passed through the grating, and only a few big, unexpected ones remain, no longer unnoticed but now selected out for some meaning, large and unknown.

21   Such were the *palo santo* trees. Before, I had never given them a thought. They were just miles of half-dead trees on the red lava sea cliffs of some deserted islands. They were only a name in a notebook: "*Palo santo* — those strange white trees." Look at the sea lions! Look at the flightless cormorants, the penguins, the iguanas, the sunset! But after eighteen months the wonderful cormorants, penguins, iguanas, sunsets, and even the sea lions, had dropped from my holey heart. I returned to the Galápagos to see the *palo santo* trees.

22   They are thin, pale, wispy trees. You walk among them on the lowland deserts, where they grow beside the prickly pear. You see them from the water on the steeps that face the sea, hundreds together, small and thin and spread, and so much more pale than their red soils that any black-and-white photograph of them looks like a negative. Their stands look like blasted orchards. At every season they all look newly dead, pale and bare as birches drowned in a beaver

pond—for at every season they look leafless, paralyzed, and mute. But in fact, if you look closely, you can see during the rainy months a few meager deciduous leaves here and there on their brittle twigs. And hundreds of lichens always grow on their bark in mute, overlapping explosions which barely enlarge in the course of the decade, lichens pink and orange, lavender, yellow, and green. The *palo santo* trees bear the lichens effortlessly, unconsciously, the way they bear everything. Their multitudes, transparent as line drawings, crowd the cliff-sides like whirling dancers, like empty groves, and look out over cliff-wrecked breakers toward more unpeopled islands, with their freakish lizards and birds, toward the grieving lagoons and the bays where the sea lions wander, and beyond to the clamoring seas.

23   Now I no longer concurred with my shipmates' joke; I no longer wanted to "come back" as a sea lion. For I thought, and I still think, that if I came back to life in the sunlight where everything changes, I would like to come back as a *palo santo* tree, one of thousands on a cliffside on those godforsaken islands, where a million events occur among the witless, where a splash of rain may drop on a yellow iguana the size of a dachshund, and ten minutes later the iguana may blink. I would like to come back as a *palo santo* tree on the weather side of an island, so that I could be, myself, a perfect witness, and look, mute, and wave my arms.

VI

24 The silence is all there is. It is the alpha and the omega. It is God's brooding over the face of the waters; it is the blended note of the ten thousand things, the whine of wings. You take a step in the right direction to pray to this silence, and even to address the prayer to "World." Distinctions blur. Quit your tents. Pray without ceasing.

ﻉ

Discussion Questions

1. Although Dillard identifies Larry as a fellow "crank," she takes his attempts to teach a stone to talk seriously and says (paragraph 4) of his effort, "I assume that like any other meaningful effort, the ritual involves sacrifice, the suppression of self-consciousness, and a certain precise tilt of the will, so that the will becomes transparent and hollow, a channel for the work." Explain her meaning, both denotative and connotative.

2. In section II, Dillard refers to "the sacred groves" (paragraph 7) and Moses and the "wilderness generation" at Sinai (paragraph 8). Explain how these references play into her line of thought. (See the Bible, Exodus 34:13, in which the Lord commands Moses to destroy

the false idols the Israelites have raised in their "sacred" groves; see also Exodus 19:17–25 and 20:18–21, in which the terrified Israelites ask that God not speak to them lest they die.)

3. Dillard writes in paragraph 9, "We doused the burning bush and cannot rekindle it." Explain her meaning and explore how it relates to the thrust of section III. (See the Bible, Exodus 3:2.)

*4. In paragraph 14, Dillard writes, "You feel the world's word as a tension, a hum, a single choursed note everywhere the same. This is it: this hum is the silence." Explain Dillard's meaning in context. And then relate the meaning to the close of section IV, "The tension, or lack of it, is intolerable. The silence is not actually suppression; instead, it is all there is."

5. Section V opens, "We are here to witness." Explain the meaning of this sentence in the context of the passages that follow it.

*6. In paragraphs 16–23, Dillard describes her trip to the Galápagos Islands and how she and her fellow tourists, after observing the carefree life of the sea lions, decided that when they "came back" in a future life, they hoped to be sea lions. As Dillard reconsidered her wish, while writing this essay, she decided she would rather "come back" as a *palo santo* (holy wood) tree. Explore the reasons for and implications of her changing her mind.

Writing Topics

1. "The closing paragraph of 'Teaching a Stone to Talk' begins ambiguously with, 'The silence is all there is.' This may sound like despair. But the following sentences (beginning 'It is God's brooding over the face of the waters') assume the mysterious unseen presence of God in the silence. Therefore the last words become affirmative, especially with the advice, 'You take a step in the right direction to pray to this silence, and even to address the prayer to "World."' God *is* World!" Write an essay in which you agree or disagree with this statement, reexamining closely the entire essay to bolster your belief.

2. Some readers are frustrated because the title of Dillard's essay arouses curiosity that is never really satisfied. In fact, these readers say, the title figures in an anecdote introduced at the beginning of the essay and then is largely forgotten about for the remainder and not even mentioned in the conclusion. In an essay, agree or disagree with this "reading" of Dillard's essay. Support your position by citing passages from the text.

It seems to me that in both science and art we are trying desperately to connect with something — this is how we achieve universality. In art, that something is people, their experiences and sensitivities. In science, that something is nature, the physical world and physical laws."

I = V/R

Alan P. Lightman

Alan P. Lightman was born in Memphis, Tennessee, in 1948 and earned a B.A. at Princeton University in 1970 and a Ph.D. at the California Institute of Technology in 1974. He taught astronomy and physics at Harvard from 1976 to 1989 and moved to the Massachusetts Institute of Technology in 1989. His books have appealed to both the science specialist and to the general reader. He has published a number of books, including A Modern Day Yankee in a Connecticut Court, and Other Essays on Science (1986), Origins: The Lives and Worlds of Modern Cosmologists (with Roberta Brawer, 1990), Ancient Light: Our Changing View of the Universe (1991), Time for the Stars: Astronomy in the 1990s (1992), and Einstein's Dreams (1993). His Time Travel and Papa Joe's Pipe appeared in 1984 and is the source for the essay "I = V/R." For more biographical information on Lightman, see page 320.

1   I was somewhat embarrassed not so long ago when I opened a year-old physics journal and read that two Japanese fellows had attacked the same problem I was currently finishing up, obtaining an identical solution. The problem, not so consequential now as I reflect stoically on my preempted calculations, concerned the spatial distribution that would eventually be achieved by a group of particles of different masses interacting with each other by gravity.

2   The underlying theories of gravity and of thermodynamics necessary for solving such a problem are certainly well established, so I suppose I should not have been surprised to find that someone else had arrived at similar results.

Still, my pulse raced as I sat with my notebook and checked off each digit of their answers, in exact agreement with mine to four decimal places.

3   After doing science for a number of years, one has the overwhelming feeling that there exists some objective reality outside ourselves, that various discoveries are waiting fully formed, like plums to be picked. If one scientist doesn't pick a certain plum, the next one will. It is an eerie sensation.

4   This objective aspect of science is a pillar of strength and, at the same time, somewhat dehumanizing. The very usefulness of science is that individual accomplishments become calibrated, dry-cleaned, and standardized. Experimental results are considered valid only if they are reproducible; theoretical ideas are powerful only if they can be generalized and distilled into abstract, disembodied equations.

5   That there are often several different routes to a particular result is taken as an indication of the correctness of the result, rather than of the capacity for individual expression in science. And always there is the continual synthesis, the blending of successive results and ideas, in which individual contributions dissolve into the whole. Such strength is awesome and reassuring; it would be a tricky business to land a man on the moon if the space ship's trajectory depended on the mood of the astronauts, or if the moon were always hurrying off to unknown appointments.

6   For these same reasons, however, science offers little comfort to anyone who aches to leave behind a personal message in his work, his own little poem or haunting sonata. Einstein is attributed with the statement that even had Newton or Leibniz never lived, the world would have had the calculus, but if Beethoven had not lived, we would never have had the C-minor Symphony.

7   A typical example of scientific development lies in the work of the German physicist Georg Simon Ohm (1789–1854). Ohm was no Einstein or Newton, but he did some good, solid work in the theory of electricity. Coming from a poor family, Ohm eagerly learned mathematics, physics, and philosophy from his father. Most of Ohm's important research was done in the period 1823–1827, while he worked grudgingly as a high school teacher in Cologne. Fortunately, the school had a well-equipped physics laboratory. In 1820 Hans Christian Oersted had discovered that an electric current in a wire could affect a magnetic compass needle, and this development impassioned Ohm to begin work in the subject. In those days electrical equipment was clumsy and primitive. Chemical batteries, invented in 1800 by Alessandro Volta and known as voltaic piles, were messy affairs, consisting of ten or more pairs of sliver or copper and zinc disks separated by layers of moist cardboard. Ohm connected a wire to each pole of a voltaic pile and suspended above one of the wires a magnetic needle on a torsion spring. This was a crude device, operating on Oersted's principles, which could measure the current flowing through a wire. Ohm then completed the circuit by inserting test wires of various thicknesses and lengths between the two battery leads, measuring how the current changed and depended on the properties, or "resistance," of each test wire.

8   This initial work was done inductively, by the seat of the pants. Ohm published his results in a semiempirical form, smacking of the flavor of the laboratory. Some of the quantitative expressions of experimental data in the first paper in 1825 are actually slightly incorrect. This was soon to be rectified, however, for Ohm was enamored of the elegant and mathematical work of Jean Fourier on heat conduction and recognized some striking similarities to current flows. Under this influence, Ohm further developed and recast his results into more general mathematical expressions, not exactly matching his data but cleaving to the analogies with Fourier's work, a creative and crucial step.

9   The final results, stating in part that the current is directly proportional to voltage and inversely proportional to resistance (now universally known as Ohm's Law), were codified in an abstract and well-manicured paper published in 1827, very distant from those late nights with jumbles of wires and repeated exhortations to the voltaic pile to hold steady on the voltage.

10   When the complete theory of electromagnetism was assembled by James Clerk Maxwell in 1864, Ohm's work was deftly stitched in, like a portion of a giant tapestry. In 1900 Paul Drude published the first microscopic theory of resistance in metals, giving at last a satisfying theoretical understanding of Ohm's Law. Today we use Ohm's Law routinely in designing electrical circuits, in calculating how deep a radio wave will penetrate into the ocean, and so on. But there is little of Ohm in the abstract statement $I = V/R$ (Current equals voltage divided by resistance).

11   Max Delbrück, the physicist-turned-biologist, said in his Nobel Prize address, "A scientist's message is not devoid of universality, but its universality is disembodied and anonymous. While the artist's communication is linked forever with its original form, that of the scientist is modified, amplified, fused with the ideas and results of others and melts into the stream of knowledge and ideas which forms our culture." Perhaps if Georg Ohm had been a painter or a poet, we would now be celebrating his leaky voltaic pile, his uncalibrated galvanometer, his exact arrangement of odd wires and mercury bowls, or reliving the loneliness of his bachelor nights, his emotions and thoughts during the experiments.

12   It seems to me that in both science and art we are trying desperately to connect with something—this is how we achieve universality. In art, that something is people, their experiences and sensitivities. In science, that something is nature, the physical world and physical laws. Sometimes we dial the wrong phone number and are later found out. Ptolemy's theory of the solar system, in which the sun and planets revolve about the Earth in cycles and cycles within cycles, is imaginative, ingenious, and even beautiful—but physically wrong. Virtually unquestioned for centuries, it was ungracefully detonated like a condemned building as soon as Copernicus came along.

13   Very well. Scientists will forever have to live with the fact that their product is, in the end, impersonal. But scientists want to be understood as people.

Go to any of the numerous scientific conferences each year in biology or chemistry or physics, and you will see a wonderful community of people chit-chatting in the hallways, holding forth delightedly at the blackboard, or loudly interrupting each other during lectures with relevant and irrelevant remarks. It can hardly be argued that such in-the-flesh gatherings are necessary for communication of scientific knowledge these days, with the asphyxiating crush of academic journals and the push-button ease of telephone calls.

14   The frantic attendance at scientific conferences has been referred to as a defense of scientific territoriality, a dead giveaway to our earthy construction. I think it is this and more. It is here, and not in equations, however correct, that we scientists can express our personalities to our colleagues, relish an appreciative smile, speculate on the amount of Carl Sagan's latest royalty advance, and exchange names of favorite restaurants. Sometimes I enjoy this as much as the science.

                              ❧

Discussion Questions

    1. How do what Lightman calls his "preempted calculations" (paragraph 1) figure into the subject of this essay?

    2. Explain Lightman's meaning when he says at the opening of paragraph 4, "This objective aspect of science is a pillar of strength and, at the same time, somewhat dehumanizing. The very usefulness of science is that individual accomplishments become calibrated, dry-cleaned, and standardized. "

    3. Why does Lightman conclude paragraph 5, "It would be a tricky business to land a man on the moon if the space ship's trajectory depended on the mood of the astronauts, or if the moon were always hurrying off to unknown appointments"? Explain.

  *4. Paragraphs 7–10 present the example of Georg Simon Ohm and his discovery of Ohm's law, "Current equals voltage divided by resistance." What did Ohm's case demonstrate for Lightman, and why did he use I = V/R for his title?

  *5. In paragraph 12, Lightman says, "Sometimes we dial the wrong phone number and are later found out." How does Lightman relate Ptolemy and Copernicus to this statement?

    6. Explain the first sentence of paragraph 14, "The frantic attendance at scientific conferences has been referred to as a defense of scientific territoriality, a dead giveaway to our earthy construction." What is given away in this "dead giveaway"? What does "our earthy construction" refer to?

Writing Topics

1. Lightman remarks in paragraph 6, "Science offers little comfort to anyone who aches to leave behind a personal message in his work, his own little poem or haunting sonata. Einstein is attributed with the statement that even had Newton or Leibniz never lived, the world would have had the calculus, but if Beethoven had not lived, we would never have had the C-minor Symphony." In a brief essay, indicate whether you agree or disagree with this statement, or whether you find your position somewhere in-between, seeing the statement in its implications as perhaps oversimplified in its assumptions about the nature of creativity in the arts?

2. At the beginning of paragraph 12, Lightman writes, "It seems to me that in both science and art we are trying desperately to connect with something—this is how we achieve universality. In art, that something is people, their experiences and sensitivities. In science, that something is nature, the physical world and physical laws." A critic might say, "Yet products of art do not, like the products of science, 'melt' into the stream of knowledge—or, in effect, become obsolete. Homer, Shakespeare, Melville endure. Literary works live largely in their particularity, detail by detail. The local is the only source for the 'universal.' That 'universal' can be comprehended only by *experiencing* the work of art." Write an essay in which you agree with either Lightman or his critic—or show how Lightman might respond to his critic. Incorporate into the essay your own beliefs about the nature of art and science, their likenesses and differences.

I have come to believe that it is the flesh alone that counts. The rest is that with which we distract ourselves when we are not hungry or cold, in pain or ecstasy. In the recesses of the body I search for the philosophers' stone."

THE EXACT LOCATION OF THE SOUL

Richard Selzer

Richard Selzer was born in Troy, New York, in 1928 and took a B.S. from Union College in Schenectady, New York, in 1948 and an M.D. from Albany Medical College in 1953. After a stint in the U.S. Army (1955–1957), he spent his career combining a private practice as a surgeon with teaching surgery at Yale Medical School. Upon his recent retirement from his practice and teaching, he began devoting his full time to writing and lecturing. His books include *Rituals of Surgery* (short stories, 1974), *Confessions of a Knife* (essays, 1979), *Letters to a Young Doctor* (essays and fiction, 1982), *Taking in the World for Repairs* (essays, 1986), and *Down from Troy: A Doctor Comes of Age* (autobiography, 1992). "The Exact Location of the Soul" is taken from *Mortal Lessons: Notes on the Art of Surgery* (1976).

1   Someone asked me why a surgeon would write. Why, when the shelves are already too full? They sag under the deadweight of books. To add a single adverb is to risk exceeding the strength of the boards. A surgeon should abstain. A surgeon, whose fingers are more at home in the steamy gullies of the body than they are tapping the dry keys of a typewriter. A surgeon, who feels the slow slide of intestines against the back of his hand and is no more alarmed than were a family of snakes taking their comfort from such an indolent rubbing. A surgeon, who palms the human heart as though it were some captured bird.

2   Why should he write? Is it vanity that urges him? There is glory enough in the knife. Is it for money? One can make too much money. No. It is to search for some meaning in the ritual of surgery, which is at once murderous, painful, healing, and full of love. It is a devilish hard thing to transmit—to find, even.

Perhaps if one were to cut out a heart, a lobe of the liver, a single convolution of the brain, and paste it to a page, it would speak with more eloquence than all the words of Balzac. Such a piece would need no literary style, no mass of erudition or history, but in its very shape and feel would tell all the frailty and strength, the despair and nobility of man. What? Publish a heart? A little piece of bone? Preposterous. Still I fear that is what it may require to reveal the truth that lies hidden in the body. Not all the undressings of Rabelais, Chekhov, or even William Carlos Williams have wrested it free, although God knows each one of those doctors made a heroic assault upon it.

3   I have come to believe that it is the flesh alone that counts. The rest is that with which we distract ourselves when we are not hungry or cold, in pain or ecstasy. In the recesses of the body I search for the philosophers' stone. I know it is there, hidden in the deepest, dampest cul-de-sac. It awaits discovery. To find it would be like the harnessing of fire. It would illuminate the world. Such a quest is not without pain. Who can gaze on so much misery and feel no hurt? Emerson has written that the poet is the only true doctor. I believe him, for the poet, lacking the impediment of speech with which the rest of us are afflicted, gazes, records, diagnoses, and prophesies.

4   I invited a young diabetic woman to the operating room to amputate her leg. She could not see the great shaggy black ulcer upon her foot and ankle that threatened to encroach upon the rest of her body, for she was blind as well. There upon her foot was a Mississippi Delta brimming with corruption, sending its raw tributaries down between her toes. Gone were all the little web spaces that when fresh and whole are such a delight to loving men. She could not see her wound, but she could feel it. There is no pain like that of the bloodless limb turned rotten and festering. There is neither unguent nor anodyne to kill such a pain yet leave intact the body.

5   For over a year I trimmed away the putrid flesh, cleansed, anointed, and dressed the foot, staving off, delaying. Three times each week, in her darkness, she sat upon my table, rocking back and forth, holding her extended leg by the thigh, gripping it as though it were a rocket that must be steadied lest it explode and scatter her toes about the room. And I would cut away a bit here, a bit there, of the swollen blue leather that was her tissue.

6   At last we gave up, she and I. We could no longer run ahead of the gangrene. We had not the legs for it. There must be an amputation in order that she might live—and I as well. It was to heal us both that I must take up knife and saw, and cut the leg off. And when I could feel it drop from her body to the table, see the blessed *space* appear between her and that leg, I too would be well.

7   Now it is the day of the operation. I stand by while the anesthetist administers the drugs, watch as the tense familiar body relaxes into narcosis. I turn then to uncover the leg. There, upon her kneecap, she has drawn, blindly, upside down for me to see, a face; just a circle with two ears, two eyes, a nose, and a

smiling upturned mouth. Under it she has printed SMILE, DOCTOR. Minutes later I listen to the sound of the saw, until a little crack at the end tells me it is done.

8   So, I have learned that man is not ugly, but that he is Beauty itself. There is no other his equal. Are we not all dying, none faster or more slowly than any other? I have become receptive to the possibilities of love (for it is love, this thing that happens in the operating room), and each day I wait, trembling in the busy air. Perhaps today it will come. Perhaps today I will find it, take part in it, this love that blooms in the stoniest desert.

9   All through literature the doctor is portrayed as a figure of fun. Shaw was splenetic about him; Molière delighted in pricking his pompous medicine men, and well they deserved it. The doctor is ripe for caricature. But I believe that the truly great writing about doctors has not yet been done. I think it must be done *by* a doctor, one who is through with the love affair with his technique, who recognizes that he has played Narcissus, raining kisses on a mirror, and who now, out of the impacted masses of his guilt, has expanded into self-doubt, and finally into the high state of wonderment. Perhaps he will be a nonbeliever who, after a lifetime of grand gestures and mighty deeds, comes upon the knowledge that he has done no more than meddle in the lives of his fellows, and that he has done at least as much harm as good. Yet he may continue to pretend, at least, that there is nothing to fear, that death will not come, so long as people depend on his authority. Later, after his patients have left, he may closet himself in his darkened office, sweating and afraid.

10   There is a story by Unamuno in which a priest, living in a small Spanish village, is adored by all the people for his piety, kindness, and the majesty with which he celebrates the Mass each Sunday. To them he is already a saint. It is a foregone conclusion, and they speak of him as Saint Immanuel. He helps them with their plowing and planting, tends them when they are sick, confesses them, comforts them in death, and every Sunday, in his rich, thrilling voice, transports them to paradise with his chanting. The fact is that Don Immanuel is not so much a saint as a martyr. Long ago his own faith left him. He is an atheist, a good man doomed to suffer the life of a hypocrite, pretending to a faith he does not have. As he raises the chalice of wine, his hands tremble, and a cold sweat pours from him. He cannot stop for he knows that the people need this of him, that their need is greater than his sacrifice. Still . . . still . . . could it be that Don Immanuel's whole life is a kind of prayer, a paean to God?

11   A writing doctor would treat men and women with equal reverence, for what is the "liberation" of either sex to him who knows the diagrams, the inner geographies of each? I love the solid heft of men as much as I adore the heated capaciousness of women — women in whose penetralia is found the repository of existence. I would have them glory in that. Women are physics and chemistry. They are matter. It is their bodies that tell of the frailty of men. Men have not their cellular, enzymatic wisdom. Man is albuminoid, proteinaceous, laked

pearl; woman is yolky, ovoid, rich. Both are exuberant bloody growths. I would use the defects and deformities of each for my sacred purpose of writing, for I know that it is the marred and scarred and faulty that are subject to grace. I would seek the soul in the facts of animal economy and profligacy. Yes, it is the exact location of the soul that I am after. The smell of it is in my nostrils. I have caught glimpses of it in the body diseased. If only I could tell it. Is there no mathematical equation that can guide me? So much pain and pus equals so much truth? It is elusive as the whippoorwill that one hears calling incessantly from out the night window, but which, nesting as it does low in the brush, no one sees. No one but the poet, for he sees what no one else can. He was born with the eye for it.

12   Once I thought I had it: Ten o'clock one night, the end room off a long corridor in a college infirmary, my last patient of the day, degree of exhaustion suitable for the appearance of a vision, some manifestation. The patient is a young man recently returned from Guatemala, from the excavation of Mayan ruins. His left upper arm wears a gauze dressing which, when removed, reveals a clean punched-out hole the size of a dime. The tissues about the opening are swollen and tense. A thin brownish fluid lips the edge, and now and then a lazy drop of the overflow spills down the arm. An abscess, inadequately drained. I will enlarge the opening to allow better egress of the pus. Nurse, will you get me a scalpel and some . . . ?

13   What happens next is enough to lay Francis Drake avomit in his cabin. No explorer ever stared in wilder surmise than I into that crater from which there now emerges a narrow gray head whose sole distinguishing feature is a pair of black pincers. The head sits atop a longish flexible neck arching now this way, now that, testing the air. Alternately it folds back upon itself, then advances in new boldness. And all the while, with dreadful rhythmicity, the unspeakable pincers open and close. Abscess? Pus? Never. Here is the lair of a beast at whose malignant purpose I could but guess. A Mayan devil, I think, that would soon burst free to fly about the room, with horrid blanket-wings and iridescent scales, raking, pinching, injecting God knows what acid juice. And even now the irony does not escape me, the irony of my patient as excavator excavated.

14   With all the ritual deliberation of a high priest I advance a surgical clamp toward the hole. The surgeon's heart is become a bat hanging upside down from his rib cage. The rim achieved — now thrust — and the ratchets of the clamp close upon the empty air. The devil has retracted. Evil mocking laughter bangs back and forth in the brain. More stealth. Lying in wait. One must skulk. Minutes pass, perhaps an hour. . . . A faint disturbance in the lake, and once again the thing upraises, farther and farther, hovering. Acrouch, strung, the surgeon is one with his instrument; there is no longer any boundary between its metal and his flesh. They are joined in a single perfect tool of extirpation. It is just for this that he was born. Now — thrust — and clamp — and *yes*. Got him!

15   Transmitted to the fingers comes the wild thrashing of the creature. Pinned and wriggling, he is mine. I hear the dry brittle scream of the dragon, and a hatred seizes me, but such a detestation as would make of Iago a drooling sucktit. It is the demented hatred of the victor for the vanquished, the warden for his prisoner. It is the hatred of fear. Within the jaws of my hemostat is the whole of the evil of the world, the dark concentrate itself, and I shall kill it. For mankind. And, in so doing, will open the way into a thousand years of perfect peace. Here is Surgeon as Savior indeed.

16   Tight grip now . . . steady, relentless pull. How it scrabbles to keep its tentacle-hold. With an abrupt moist plop the extraction is complete. There, writhing in the teeth of the clamp, is a dirty gray body, the size and shape of an English walnut. He is hung everywhere with tiny black hooklets. Quickly . . . into the specimen jar of saline . . . the lid screwed tight. Crazily he swims round and round, wiping his slimy head against the glass, then slowly sinks to the bottom, the mass of hooks in frantic agonal wave.

17   "You are going to be all right," I say to my patient. "We are all going to be *all* right from now on."

18   The next day I take the jar to the medical school. "That's the larva of the botfly," says a pathologist. "The fly usually bites a cow and deposits its eggs beneath the skin. There, the egg develops into the larval form which, when ready, burrows its way to the outside through the hide and falls to the ground. In time it matures into a full-grown botfly. This one happened to bite a man. It was about to come out on its own, and, of course, it would have died."

19   The words *imposter, sorehead, servant of Satan* spring to my lips. But now he has been joined by other scientists. They nod in agreement. I gaze from one gray eminence to another, and know the mallet-blow of glory pulverized. I tried to save the world, but it didn't work out.

20   No, it is not the surgeon who is God's darling. He is the victim of vanity. It is the poet who heals with his words, stanches the flow of blood, stills the rattling breath, applies poultice to the scalded flesh.

21   Did you ask me why a surgeon writes? I think it is because I wish to be a doctor.

ॐ

Discussion Questions

1. How does Selzer answer the question as to why he writes? Explain.

2. In paragraph 3, Selzer writes, "Emerson has written that the poet is the only true doctor. I believe him, for the poet, lacking the impediment of speech with which the rest of us are afflicted, gazes, records, diagnoses, and prophesies." How is this passage related to the conclusion of the essay, "Did you ask me why a surgeon writes? I think it is because I wish to be a doctor." Explain.

3. Paragraphs 4–7 describe the case of the blind woman with the gangrenous leg. What happened on the day of her operation? How does the episode relate to the comments in paragraph 8, such as, "I have become receptive to the possibilities of love (for it is love, this thing that happens in the operating room), and each day I wait, trembling in the busy air"?

4. In paragraph 10, Selzer concludes his story of Unamuno's non-believing priest, "He cannot stop for he knows that the people need this of him, that their need is greater than his sacrifice. Still . . . still . . . could it be that Don Immanuel's whole life is a kind of prayer, a paean to God?" What relevance does the story have to the questions raised in Selzer's essay? Explain.

*5. Selzer says in paragraph 11, "Yes, it is the exact location of the soul I am after. The smell of it is in my nostrils. I have caught glimpses of it in the body diseased. . . . It is elusive as the whippoorwill that one hears calling incessantly from out the night window, but which, nesting as it does low in the brush, no one sees. No one but the poet, for he sees what no one else can." Explain, sorting through the imagery to disentangle direct statement and metaphor.

6. Paragraphs 12–19 describe the case of the young man who had recently returned from excavating in the Mayan ruins of Guatemala; Selzer extracted from the abscess in his arm a creature that seemed to be a "Mayan devil"—that seemed for the moment indeed to be the "whole of the evil of the world." Selzer learned the next day that the creature was the larva of a botfly, which usually bites a cow but this time bit a man. What was Selzer's reaction to the scientific truth? Explain.

Writing Topics

1. In paragraph 20, Selzer writes, "No, it is not the surgeon who is God's darling. He is the victim of vanity. It is the poet who heals with his words, stanches the flow of blood, stills the rattling breath, applies poultice to the scalded flesh." In a brief essay, explain this seemingly paradoxical statement in light of what you find most relevant in the foregoing paragraphs of the essay. You might want to consider, too, the possibility that, in addition to being a surgeon, Selzer himself is no mean poet in his essays.

2. What adventurous encounters have you had with members of the healing profession? Write a narrative essay in which you set forth the details, painful or blissful, of your encounter with a doctor, surgeon, dentist, ophthalmologist, or other specialist. You may aim for comedy or tragedy, but keep in mind that you need to hold your reader's interest.

❧"If the man in the water gave a lifeline to the people gasping for survival, he was likewise giving a lifeline to those who observed him."

THE MAN IN THE WATER

Roger Rosenblatt

Roger Rosenblatt, born in New York City in 1940, took a B.A. at New York University (1962) and both an M.A. (1963) and a Ph.D. (1968) at Harvard. He taught American literature at Harvard from 1963 to 1973. After a brief appointment at the National Endowment for the Humanities (1973–1975), he began his journalistic career at *The New Republic*. He held positions with the *Washington Post*, *Time*, and *U.S. News and World Report* and has been a regular contributor to *The Atlantic Monthly* and *Modern Maturity*. His books include *Black Fiction* (1974), *The Children of War* (1983), *Witness: The World Since Hiroshima* (1985), and *Life Itself: Abortion in the American Mind* (1991). He is one of the television essayists on *The News Hour with Jim Lehrer* on PBS. His most recent book, *The Man in the Water: Essays and Stories* (1994), is the source for the essay below. It first appeared in *Time* on January 25, 1982.

1   As disasters go, this one was terrible, but not unique, certainly not among the worst on the roster of U.S. air crashes. There was the unusual element of the bridge, of course, and the fact that the plane clipped it at a moment of high traffic, one routine thus intersecting another and disrupting both. Then, too, there was the location of the event. Washington, the city of form and regulations, turned chaotic, deregulated, by a blast of real winter and a single slap of metal on metal. The jets from Washington National Airport that normally swoop around the presidential monuments like famished gulls are, for the moment, emblemized by the one that fell; so there is that detail. And there was the aesthetic clash as well—blue-and-green Air Florida, the name a flying garden, sunk down among gray chunks in a black river. All that was worth noticing, to be sure. Still, there was nothing very special in any of it, except death, which, while always special, does not necessarily bring millions to tears or to attention. Why, then, the shock here?

2   Perhaps because the nation saw in this disaster something more than a mechanical failure. Perhaps because people saw in it no failure at all, but rather something successful about their makeup. Here, after all, were two forms of nature in collision: the elements and human character. Last Wednesday, the elements, indifferent as ever, brought down Flight 90. And on that same afternoon, human nature — groping and flailing in mysteries of its own — rose to the occasion.

3   Of the four acknowledged heroes of the event, three are able to account for their behavior. Donald Usher and Eugene Windsor, a park police helicopter team, risked their lives every time they dipped the skids into the water to pick up survivors. On television, side by side in bright blue jumpsuits, they described their courage as all in the line of duty. Lenny Skutnik, a twenty-eight-year-old employee of the Congressional Budget Office, said: "It's something I never thought I would do" — referring to his jumping into the water to drag an injured woman to shore. Skutnik added that "somebody had to go in the water," delivering every hero's line that is no less admirable for its repetitions. In fact, nobody had to go into the water. That somebody actually did so is part of the reason this particular tragedy sticks in the mind.

4   But the person most responsible for the emotional impact of the disaster is the one known at first simply as "the man in the water." (Balding, probably in his fifties, an extravagant mustache.) He was seen clinging with five other survivors to the tail section of the airplane. This man was described by Usher and Windsor as appearing alert and in control. Every time they lowered a lifeline and flotation ring to him, he passed it on to another of the passengers. "In a mass casualty, you'll find people like him," said Windsor. "But I've never seen one with that commitment." When the helicopter came back for him, the man had gone under. His selflessness was one reason the story held national attention; his anonymity another. The fact that he went unidentified invested him with a universal character. For a while he was Everyman, and thus proof (as if one needed it) that no man is ordinary.

5   Still, he could never have imagined such a capacity in himself. Only minutes before his character was tested, he was sitting in the ordinary plane among the ordinary passengers, dutifully listening to the stewardess telling him to fasten his seat belt and saying something about the "no smoking sign." So our man relaxed with the others, some of whom would owe their lives to him. Perhaps he started to read, or to doze, or to regret some harsh remark made in the office that morning. Then suddenly he knew that the trip would not be ordinary. Like every other person on that flight, he was desperate to live, which makes his final act so stunning.

6   For at some moment in the water he must have realized that he would not live if he continued to hand over the rope and ring to others. He *had* to know it, no matter how gradual the effect of the cold. In his judgment he had no choice. When the helicopter took off with what was to be the last survivor, he watched everything in the world move away from him, and he deliberately let it happen.

7   Yet there was something else about the man that kept our thoughts on him, and which keeps our thoughts on him still. He was *there*, in the essential, classic circumstance. Man in nature. The man in the water. For its part, nature cared nothing about the five passengers. Our man, on the other hand, cared totally. So the timeless battle commenced in the Potomac. For as long as that man could last, they went at each other, nature and man: the one making no distinctions of good and evil, acting on no principles, offering no lifelines; the other acting wholly on distinctions, principles, and, one supposes, on faith.

8   Since it was he who lost the fight, we ought to come again to the conclusion that people are powerless in the world. In reality, we believe the reverse, and it takes the act of the man in the water to remind us of our true feelings in this matter. It is not to say that everyone would have acted as he did, or as Usher, Windsor, and Skutnik. Yet whatever moved these men to challenge death on behalf of their fellows is not peculiar to them. Everyone feels the possibility in himself. That is the abiding wonder of the story. That is why we would not let go of it. If the man in the water gave a lifeline to the people gasping for survival, he was likewise giving a lifeline to those who observed him.

9   The odd thing is that we do not even really believe that the man in the water lost his fight. "Everything in Nature contains all the powers of Nature," said Emerson. Exactly. So the man in the water had his own natural powers. He could not make ice storms, or freeze the water until it froze the blood. But he could hand life over to a stranger, and that is a power of nature too. The man in the water pitted himself against an implacable, impersonal enemy; he fought it with charity; and he held it to a standoff. He was the best we can do.

❧

Discussion Questions

1. In paragraph 1, describing the plane crash in the Potomac, Rosenblatt observes, "And there was the aesthetic clash as well— blue-and-green Air Florida, the name a flying garden, sunk down among gray chunks in a black river." Explain both the position and meaning of this sentence.

2. What are the "two forms of nature in collision" that Rosenblatt names in paragraph 2? How are they described?

3. In paragraph 3, Rosenblatt says there were four heroes in the moments after the crash. Why does he name only three, and what did the three do to become "heroes"?

4. What do we find out about the fourth hero in paragraphs 4–6, and what did he do to become a hero?

*5. What is the relevance of the Emerson quotation in paragraph 9, "Everything in Nature contains all the powers of Nature"? Explain.

Writing Topics

1. Rosenblatt opens paragraph 8 with what appears to be a contradictory statement, "Since it was he who lost the fight, we ought to come again to the conclusion that people are powerless in the world. In reality, we believe the reverse, and it takes the act of the man in the water to remind us of our true feelings in this matter." Write a brief argumentative essay in which you agree or disagree with Rosenblatt, using not only the incident he describes but whatever material your own experience or observation can supply.

2. In paragraph 7, Rosenblatt says that there was something special in the incident that causes us to keep our thoughts on the fourth hero, "He was *there*, in the essential, classic circumstance. Man in nature. The man in the water. For its part, nature cared nothing about the five passengers. Our man, on the other hand, cared totally. So the timeless battle commenced in the Potomac." Write an essay in which you explain Rosenblatt's meaning here and then summon other examples of such "timeless battles" from your own experience or your reading—in literature, newspapers, or magazines. Disasters—airplane crashes, terrorist bombings, floods, hurricanes—are reported daily on the front pages of newspapers.

"He had had a wife, a young woman properly paid for, and she had deserted him. He wanted either her or the bride price back . . . two sheep, a pirogue, and ten chickens, including a laying hen."

I SAY THIS

Emily Hahn

Born in St. Louis in 1905, Emily Hahn earned a B.S. at the University of Wisconsin in 1926 and did graduate work at Columbia University (1928) and at Oxford University (1934–1935). She has spent her career as a free-lance writer and traveled widely in Africa and Asia, at one time serving as a correspondent for *The New Yorker*. She has published numerous volumes of essays, journalistic accounts, travel books, biographies, autobiographies, fiction, and children's books. A sampling of her titles suggests her range: *Congo Solo: Misadventures Two Degrees North* (1933), *China to Me: A Paradoxical Autobiography* (1944), *Love Conquers Nothing: A Glandular History of Civilization* (1952), *Spousery* (1956), *Diamond: The Spectacular Story of Earth's Rarest Treasure and Man's Greatest Greed* (1956), *Romantic Rebels: An Informal History of Bohemianism* (1967), and *The Cooking of China* (1968). "I Say This" appeared in the July 31, 1995, issue of *The New Yorker*; it is based on her experience working for the Red Cross in the Belgian Congo (now Zaire) in 1930 and 1931.

1   It was a long time ago.

2   Most of my anecdotes, it occurs to me now, start with that sentence, and usually it is superfluous. Who cares, after all, at what time in my life it happened? The tale's the thing. Still, for some anecdotes, like this one, the time matters: many things that were true in the Belgian Congo then are not true now. For one thing, it isn't Belgian anymore, nor is it even the Congo, that name having been adopted by another, smaller country. What was my Congo has been renamed, by her own people, Zaire. Also, the status I am remembering, of the women of the Congo—or, rather, Zaire—may well have changed completely, though somehow I doubt it. Changing the name of a country is simpler than

changing the way its women are treated. In the old days, if I had said to a Congolese woman that she might be able to improve her lot she would have replied with the Kingwana word denoting skepticism: "*Wapi!*"—which in English would be "Sez you!" And very likely she would have gone on with whatever I had interrupted, scrubbing something, her back bent whether or not she was carrying a baby. Incidentally, those women carry and nurse their babies much longer than we do. At the stage when we are promoting our young from pram to stroller, they are still slinging their babies from back to hip and letting them suckle from Mother's skinny, pendulous breast.

3   In that far-off time, I was taking a long trip on foot toward the east coast, because that was the way one had to travel in the forest. There were no roads yet through the trees; there was just a system of pathways that were—at least, half of them—elephant tracks. Apart from my head boy, Shabani, I needed a guide to figure them out. Mine was a Pygmy, whose people, of course, knew all the ways of elephants. You could always rely on a Pygmy.

4   I was heading for the coast of Tanganyika, on my way back home to either England or America: because of the Depression, I was unsure which. But what was certain was that I still had a long way to go. Ten bearers, as they were called, carried my belongings, which were carefully limited, considered, and spaced out, because, according to local law, each bearer carried at the most thirty pounds. For food we had plantains, rice when we could get it, tea leaves, and sugar. We bought chickens (*kuku*, as they were called) on the way when-ever we could. The men carried them live but upside down until they were needed, and I had long got over being squeamish about it. On earlier trips, I had added to this Spartan diet canned goods such as butter and meat. But the cans were heavy and costly, and once they were opened the stuff inside quickly spoiled, so I did without such refinements. In camping, I practiced a similar frugality, ignoring the ordinary white man's example of carrying a tent for the night's shelter, a bathtub, and a metal cot. Instead, I had a light bamboo-frame bed and no bathtub. What, I asked myself, are rivers for? Rivers without croco-diles, naturally. As for shelter, the bearers and I planned each day's walk so that we would arrive, at more or less the right time of day, at a village where I could rent a hut for the night for a few francs, and the bearers would share a fire with village friends. Underfoot, a hut was not always clean, but an impor-tant piece of my luggage was a roll of native mats, to keep my feet safe from chiggers. With the addition of a bowl and a pail, I felt as well outfitted as I would have been in a rest house. There were no rest houses in the forest anyway.

5   Our arrival at a village followed a pattern set by travelling government officials. The party approached, to the music of the bearers, who always chanted, claiming that their work seemed easier if they sang; they made up the words as they went along. At the head marched the official, in his sun helmet and khaki shorts and shirt. According to the rules of etiquette, he was to be met

by the village headman—or, as he was called, the *capita*—who would make polite noises and tell the official's head boy where to pitch his tent and so on. My party's arrival was not much different when it came to marching in, with me at the head, but then the *capita* always hesitated, looked around, and asked, "Where is your master, Madamu?" I should explain that in Kingwana the word for "master" is the same as that for "husband," and, as things went in that society, it was a logical connection. But I never got used to it; it always irritated me. Still, I replied as politely as I could, "I have no husband"—or, truthfully, within the limits of the language, "I have no master." As usual, then, the *capita* and I looked at the huts and selected a likely one, and the bearers found their friends and inquired where they would be sitting around the fire after chaffering for chickens. At the fire, they would talk late into the night before rolling up in their blankets to sleep.

6   We had walked for four or five days before we reached this particular village, and we were unusually tired, because our way had not been the customary one—through trees along damp, slippery paths. Instead, we had soon had to climb a lot, and the first couple of days of easy travel had spoiled us. So I was more sensitive than usual when the *capita* asked the inevitable question about my master, and my tetchy reaction possibly dismayed the poor innocent man. However, for a while things went along according to schedule, with the bearers bringing my belongings into the hut and everybody settling down. Soon afterward, though, I noticed something unusual going on near the hut. It had a path of well-trodden earth in front of it, with shade supplied by a bit of roofing sticking out in front. But not until local men brought out a table and set it down on the trodden patch did I realize the truth, that the village was getting ready for a *baraza*. I was appalled. A *baraza* (the etymology of the word is obscure: could it be derived from "bazaar"?) was a calling together of people—male, of course—for disputation and, if possible, settlement of some knotty affair. It was a sort of colloquy of all those who mattered, and it was held whenever the people could get hold of a personage of authority to head the proceedings.

7   Everyone I met in the Congo was great on disputation—the men, I mean. I can still call up in memory the sound of those beautiful voices raised in public argument—flowing, expressive, often passionate. Women's voices were not heard among them, though the women had plenty to say on their own topics. They would complain among themselves, discussing children and such matters, but the sound was more ordinary, neither glib nor musical. They just didn't have the time to orate.

8   No, this *baraza* was almost certain to be a man's affair—except, I feared, for me. A hasty conversation with Shabani confirmed my fears. Meanwhile, the *capita* had ordered a chair to be brought and set up behind the table, obviously to serve as a judgment seat. It was my own fault, I realized, for travelling without a master. I had unsexed myself. Because I was a white woman travelling alone, of course I was fit to chair a *baraza*. Besides, so Shabani had told me, the

village badly needed a *baraza* to settle some sort of woman trouble, which he did not understand very well. So, just at the right time, here I was, having arrived with a retinue and all that pomp. I defy any white woman to have chickened out and refused to take that chair, which the *capita* was now holding politely, inflexibly. I sat down in it. What the hell? It was only a bad dream, after all.

9   All around the chair and me stood the village men, bright-eyed and ready for the excitement. The two leaders of the argument were easy to place. They seemed about the same age—mid-thirties, perhaps—and both were eager, like dogs straining at the leash. Well, no, they weren't, either: dogs don't pout, and these men certainly did. At least, each had a sombre look, as if musing on his own grievance—a normal sort of emotion, I supposed, in the circumstances.

10   Shabani stood next to me, ready to translate any hard parts. The proceedings were opened by another man—a sort of stage manager, I thought. He called on the aggrieved husband to say his piece, and in the meantime I looked around for the woman who was the cause of all this. I didn't see her, however.

11   The husband (plaintiff?) started with the usual sentence, which I understood; it meant "I say this." What he had to say—in a great outpouring, flowery and aggrieved—was this: He had had a wife, a young woman properly paid for, and she had deserted him. He wanted either her or the bride price back. This, though not put as starkly as I have rendered it, was the burden of his complaint, and I felt that the sentiment of the crowd was with him. Certainly Shabani was. I paid more attention to the bride price, which the deserted husband carefully itemized: two sheep, a pirogue, and ten chickens, including a laying hen. It did sound rather a lot, I had to admit. Shabani thought so, too. I thought for a minute that he would whistle, but that's not a Kingwana gesture. Well, naturally the bridegroom wanted that fortune back, but it seemed that the bride's father couldn't see things that way. If a man couldn't keep a woman, he said, that was his bad management, his bad luck.

12   The argument went on and on, the bride's father taking her side, the groom's family making snide remarks to encourage him. It became, finally, unpleasantly noisy. But I found myself taking sides. I was curious, too. Where was she, this Helen of the Congo woodlands? After a bit more haranguing, I remembered that I had certain powers.

13   "Tell them to bring out the woman," I directed Shabani. He did so, and she appeared—young, shrinking slightly at the publicity, but defiant.

14   I asked, for I knew that much Kingwana, "Why did you run away?"

15   "I don't like him," she replied.

16   I suppose I was the only person to whom this seemed a rational argument. At least, everybody else looked puzzled, but that look didn't last long. After all, they seemed to conclude, it figured: though white, I, too, was a woman.

17   I realized that I had lost my public's sympathy, so I turned to the bride's father and asked, "Is it true that he gave you all that wealth?"

18   Well, yes, he admitted, but it wasn't his fault if the man couldn't hold on to his woman. To pay him back was impossible. Hadn't he kept his side of the bargain?

19   The bargain, the wife, stood there, silent but still rebellious. In fact, everybody stood there, waiting.

20   Then I had an inspiration, which lent power to my tongue. I found enough words to say to the husband, "I say this. What good is this woman to you? Get her back and she will only run away again, isn't it true?"

21   "Yes," said the husband and, after him, the crowd. "Yes, it's true," they buzzed, as if it were a new and surprising thought.

22   "So I say this," I went on. "Make friends again with her father, and he will try as time goes on to pay you back. Won't you?" I added to the father.

23   "I'll try, Madamu," the father said.

24   "Then talk it over between you, and settle something now," I directed.

25   Wonder of wonders, they accepted the judgment. I heard them haggling as I went into the hut, and I heard the bearers and their friends talking after I went to bed. However, I didn't really sleep well. I kept thinking of that defiant girl: I had done the best I could for her, but it wasn't enough.

26   Sometime during the troubled night, I remembered a Swahili maxim: "Woman is wealth, and wealth is woman."

27   I thought of being able to tell the girl to take heart. "Someday, you will find things easier," I might say. "Someday, you will have power to decide for yourself about everything."

28   But in my imagination she replied only "*Wapi.*"

❧

Discussion Questions

1.   Why does Hahn say, in the middle of paragraph 2, "Changing the name of a country is simpler than changing the way its women are treated"?

2.   In paragraphs 3–4, Hahn refers to her method of travel, to the time of her trip, and to her possible destination, and she describes in some detail what she carried along. What purpose does this background information serve? Hahn also points out how her practice differed from that of "the ordinary white man's example." Explain.

3.   Whenever Hahn arrived in a village, she was asked in Kingwana (a Bantu dialect) where her husband was. Why did this question irritate Hahn?

*4.   In paragraphs 6–8, Hahn describes the arrival of her party in a "particular village" where the activity of the evening aroused her suspicions that there was going to be a *baraza*. Explain. What does Hahn mean when she says, "It was my own fault, I realized, for travelling without a master. I had unsexed myself. Because I was a white woman travelling alone, of course I was fit to chair a *baraza*"?

*5.   In paragraph 12, Hahn writes, "But I found myself taking sides. I was curious, too. Where was she, this Helen of the Congo woodlands?" Explain.

*6.   When, in paragraphs 13–16, the young bride was summoned and asked by Hahn why she had run away from her husband, what did the bride reply? And what was Hahn's reaction to her answer?

*7.   What motivated Hahn to impose a settlement, and what was the nature of the settlement she announced?

8.   What was the reaction to the terms of Hahn's settlement by the principals involved and the other natives assembled?

Writing Topics

1.   Some readers say that Hahn was wrong to impose the settlement she did and think she should have expressed her honest opinion that the young bride had the right to run away because she disliked the husband who had purchased her. In a short essay, agree or disagree with this opinion. Make clear your position and the reasons for taking that position.

2.   It is often said that we have no right to apply our standards and values in judging other cultures. Cultural anthropologists pride themselves on nonjudgmental observation of other cultures and societies. Relativists say that there are no universals—and therefore no universal human rights. Consider the situation in the Congo as described by Hahn and assess her behavior in criticizing the "mistreatment" of women she observed. Indicate whether you believe her right or wrong in the judgments she passed on the incidents she observed.

3.   Hahn writes about the situation of women in the Congo (now Zaire) during the time of the Great Depression (the 1930s). Do some research on life in modern Zaire and write an essay setting forth how much has changed and how much has not in the position of women in Zaire society. A brief updated account of contemporary Zaire can be found in the most recent *World Almanac and Book of Facts*.

A common denominator emerged:
The source of continuing aliveness was to
find your passion and pursue it with whole heart
and single mind."

THE PURSUIT OF PASSION: LESSONS FROM THE WORLD OF THE WISEWOMEN

Gail Sheehy

Gail Sheehy was born in 1937 in Mamaroneck, New York, and took a B.S. from the University of Vermont in 1958. She has spent her career as a journalist and free-lance writer and is the author of a number of books. These include *Lovesounds* (a novel, 1970), *Hustling: Prostitution in Our Wide Open Society* (1973), *Passages: Predictable Crises of Adult Life* (1976), *The Man Who Changed the World: Mikhail S. Gorbachev* (1990), and *The Silent Passage: Menopause* (1992). Her essays have appeared in many magazines, including *Cosmopolitan, Good Housekeeping,* and *The New York Times* Magazine. "The Pursuit of Passion" comes from *Modern Maturity,* July/August 1995, which excerpted it from Sheehy's *New Passages: Mapping Your Life across Time* (1995).

1   I was in for some surprises when I accepted an invitation to the premier conference on "The New Older Woman" held at the Esalen Institute in the summer of 1991. A small group of prominent American women from diverse backgrounds came together to share viewpoints on what it's like to be energetic, ambitious, optimistic and over 50 in today's America. The participants agreed that there had come a point, sometime in their 50s, when they had to let go of — or at least stop trying to hang on to — their youthful image, and move on. Although painful at the time, they had all found a source of new vitality and exhilaration — a "kicker." For some the kicker was a large-scale social mission like AIDS activism or a political goal like teaching women how to use power. For others it was a more private challenge: writing a book, or pursuing knowledge in a special field for the pure pleasure of knowing.

2　　A common denominator emerged: The source of continuing aliveness was to find your passion and pursue it with whole heart and single mind.

3　　As peppy and provocative as were the discussions, it was sharing a room with my 84-year-old roommate that dissolved barriers in my thinking about "the older woman." When I first encountered Mildred Mathias she was doubled over, brushing her hair. A botanist, she had just come in from her daily brisk walk, excitedly displaying a handful of pungent herbs and grasses. What was the secret of her zest, I wondered?

4　　It turns out that Mildred had retired from her prestigious teaching position in the University of California system at age 70. She languished for a while, developing ailments and boredom, thinking her life was just about over. A few years later she had an opportunity to take her first field trip down the Amazon River to collect scarce plants with medicinal uses. She dared to step off the precipice. The experience was thrilling. And she felt useful again. She had repeated the trip every year with a commitment bordering on the sacred. "Each trip down the Amazon, I'm convinced, peels back ten years of my life," Mildred Mathias told me.

5　　Her story brought to mind other women I've known or interviewed who had joined the walking dead, almost dropping out of life for some years, but who revived themselves later by plunging into some new adventure that held both risk and meaning for them. We can learn so much from vital older women. It should be a conscious exercise to pick out those who live their passions with purpose and direction and let them suggest possibilities and guiding principles for our own future selves. These are the transformative figures I call Wisewomen.

A Wisewoman model, age 60

6　　I met a very down-to-earth Wisewoman model, a school principal from St. Louis, who was approaching her 60th birthday. Here is a woman who had never taken hormones, but who had come through menopause, hysterectomy, microscopic breast cancer, and widowhood. I'll call her Elise.

7　　The way she comes through the door tells a story in itself. She doesn't walk in, she *enters*, with laughter, her tall limber body an exclamation point on a life fought for and twice saved. No sooner had Elise recovered from a hysterectomy than her husband, desperately ill with cancer, slipped into a ghastly morphine twilight. "Having gone through the menopause thing, and now having lost my uterus, I kept thinking that my life was going to be over along with my husband's," she remembers. She was 55; she felt buried alive.

8　　Except for the horniness. As she tended her husband in a long, laboring death, these anomalous surges became more and more obvious to her, perhaps because she couldn't fulfill them. When she now looks back, she realizes it probably wasn't a total accident that she crossed paths again with a high-school sweetheart struggling through a divorce. Over dinner, he looked across the candlelight and said, "You know, you're the girl I wanted to marry but was afraid to ask. I'm not afraid of you anymore."

9   It wasn't a hot flash that inflamed her cheeks. It was an old-fashioned girlish blush. In no time they were in bed. She was astonished to find that everything still worked. Elise had crossed the dreaded divide of menopause, and guess what? "It's not only okay, but it's better than I thought it would be. Vanity is involved, too. You've heard for so many years that you won't be able to find an orgasm, you're going to be bitchy, sweaty and dried up—and you're not! You're still a woman."

10   It was an affair of need. It took some negotiating with her guilt, but she decided that at some point the living have to cut loose from the dying. "Making a connection with a man at that lowest point was probably the most important thing that's happened to me in the last ten years."

11   During the mourning period after her husband's death, Elise made an effort to take care of herself for the first time. She invested in a trainer and embarked on a strict exercise program. A complete lifestyle change to a diet of vegetables and fruit and varied exercise left her feeling exhilarated. For sustenance of the spirit she found a small retreat near water where she could escape for long weekends and sleep for ten hours at a stretch if she needed it.

12   "Mom, you look younger than you did ten years ago!" her children marveled. They were right. People look at her now as an expert in education, and she feels tremendous respect from her community. "I suppose I've reached a different level of self-confidence," she said. Rather than the need for a primary relationship, an exclusive source of emotional nourishment, as before, this radiant woman finds herself needing, and offering, an ever-expanding *connectedness*.

13   "My own vocabulary of intimacy has extended—it's like a root system spreading out. It's much more expansive. I've had this intense feeling of being available to many people—women and men—as friends and acquaintances. I'm not willing to let a day go by where my life hasn't been touched, or I haven't touched someone else's life."

Congratulations, you're a new grandmother!

14   Traditionally, the wisdom of the older woman has been concentrated (or confined) in the role of grandmother. It is one of the prerogatives and pleasures most women can look forward to. But the sudden mutation can also be a jolt, challenging our personal identity and our sense of time and future. The anthropologist Margaret Mead described to me her own ambivalence: "Grandparenthood is one life transition over which you have no control. It's done *to* you."

15   But from the way even the most blasé businesswomen describe the impact of seeing the first new sapling born from their own generational tree, it is still a profoundly soul-shaking, even transforming, experience. Kay Delaney, a media executive nearing 60, couldn't stop talking about it between sets of her Saturday morning tennis game.

16   A few weeks before, her daughter had produced the first grandchild. "It took me four times of seeing the baby before I could do anything but cry," she said. "I was just overwhelmed by so many emotions." It wasn't easy for her to untangle the jumble of those emotions. "I could see in that little face the whole family—my parents, my aunts and uncles going all the way back to my grandmother, my ex-husband and his family. I kept thinking, 'This child is a continuation of all these people. He's part and parcel of them. And me, *he's part of me.*'"

17   A rush of immortality overwhelmed her. There is a continuum and now she was an integral part of it, "because when I die, part of me will still be alive. I never felt that with my own children. But with a grandchild I definitely felt it, and it's an incredible experience."

18   For Kay, the new babe brings forth all the feelings of that young, scared, divorced mother with three little children to feed who had to take on the world before she was 35. But by now she can allow these feelings; she doesn't have to suppress her tenderest instincts to forge an image of herself as a fearless businesswoman. With her own kids, a working mom longs to be there so *they* don't miss out. With the grandchild, she wants to be there so *she* doesn't miss out.

19   "I am going through this whole questioning thing about changing my life," Kay disclosed. "I'm really getting a sense of my own chronological time frame, which I never had before. Sure, I'm in good health, vital, all the rest of it, but I have a sense that I want to be there as part of this new life. How can I be if I'm running off on planes all the time?"

20   The question is not really the job, she has decided. "The issue is, 'Who do I want to be *now?*'"

Love and life beyond loss

21   On the day her husband died, Genevieve Burke had an experience of profound collapse. "The sensation was so strong I clutched my center to hold myself together," she says. "It left me feeling weak and empty." For almost the whole decade of her 50s, she had made it her job to keep her husband alive. Now, having "failed," she felt she had nothing to live for.

22   The life that doesn't have a sense of responsibility to something broader than oneself is not much of a life. But to practice it intelligently, we need to understand that we can only be responsible in matters open to our control— our own choices and actions, no one else's.

23   Women like Genevieve, who suspend their own lives indefinitely in order to nurse a spouse or relative, may unconsciously be tying themselves up so they don't have to face making the next passage themselves.

24   The reality was, Genevieve had to support herself now. She didn't have much time for reeducation. But one doesn't always have to spend years in graduate school to prepare for finding a new dream. Many older women don't

realize how valuable their life skills, equanimity and dependability can be to an employer.

25   Genevieve was dubious that anyone would hire a 60-year-old woman; nevertheless she applied for a secretarial position at the state university. "Somehow I found an assertive streak in me," she says, "and within a few days I was hired and began my new life." The shock of being in the working world quickly galvanized Genevieve into realizing that her real responsibility was to find out who she was, not merely as an extension of her husband or her children.

26   She found herself by degrees. Along with working two part-time jobs, she is now a columnist for a new local magazine and is exhilarated by learning to express herself in prose at the age of 72. Her sense of time is altered utterly. She loves being with friends and family, but also cherishes being alone. She is not afraid of dying; rather, she finds it imperative to *live* life.

27   "Today, although I'm the same person, I feel more integrated," she says. "I know *why* I was the way I was, and now I feel like strutting my stuff!"

Caretakers of the world

28   More and more older females are putting themselves in training as Wisewomen by expanding their knowledge base. Over [1,900] women ages 50 to 64 are presently studying in the United States for their first professional degree, seriously applying themselves to law, dentistry, pharmacy, social psychology, or, increasingly, coming out of divinity schools. These highly trained women, with the "sense of mission" that so often solidifies in their 60s, become almost venerated when they return to work in their communities. This is especially true of minority older women.

29   Generativity—feeling a voluntary obligation to care for others in the broadest sense—was a brand-new notion to Ella Ivey. She remembers reading about it in *Passages* when she first started back to college, a little abashed about being in her 50s. As a black woman raised in Blenheim, South Carolina, rather than settle for segregated schools, she had made her way to New York City and finished public high school there. She was the first in her family to have finished college. In her 50s she began looking for a way to defeat stagnation in later life. This notion of generativity gave her a goal.

30   "I wanted to do more [than a college degree would permit]," she told me, "I wanted to teach instead of being a school secretary." At 59, Ella had a master's in education from Fordham University. And then the best part of the journey began.

31   Swinging down the street with a book bag on her back, in jeans and sandals, with metal-framed glasses and salt-and-pepper hair, this tall determined lady of 60 cut a wide swath through her Bronx neighborhood. She was out to class by ten in the morning and often not home from the library until ten at night, studying for a Master of Divinity degree at New York Theological Seminary.

Having reflected on the joy she took from counseling young people in her Sunday school classes, she finally understood that she wanted to be an ordained minister.

32 "I found younger people who would act as my mentors," she says, "some the ages of my children!"

33 This is a pleasant twist on the generativity concept. The older person isn't confined only to the role of teacher, counselor, guru, always dipping into the experience bank to give out; he or she can also feel cared for and cared about by others who, although much younger, may be more experienced in cutting-edge methods and technology.

34 Ella found strengths in herself she never had when she was younger.

35 "Sticktoitiveness is the big one," she says. She was also surprised how much easier it was to conceptualize at her age, an observation confirmed by studies of people educated at late ages. They have also been found to be especially creative in thinking through social problems. The greatest benefit of becoming a scholar in her 60s, says Ella Ivey, was having to write her credo, a thesis of belief required to graduate from the seminary.

36 "It forced me to understand what I had done to get to that point," Ella says. "I now had a context in which to place my journey."

37 That journey has paid off. She earned her Master of Divinity degree at 63 and works as an ordained minister and a college professor.

Looking ahead

38 It is useful to look to the most vital women of age and see how they have met the challenges of later-life passages. Cecelia Hurwich, one of the participants in the Esalen conference, had done a study over time on women in their 70s, 80s and 90s for her doctorate at the Center for Psychological Studies in Albany, California. The women selected had remained active and creative through un-usually productive Second Adulthoods and well into old age.

39 What were their secrets?

40 They had mastered the art of "letting go" of their egos gracefully so they could concentrate on a few fine-tuned priorities. They continued to live in their own homes but involved themselves in community or worldly projects of con-suming interest. Close contact with nature was important to them as was maintaining a multigenerational network of friends.

41 And as they grew older they found themselves concerned more with feed-ing the soul than the ego.

42 Wisdom, or the collective practical knowledge of the culture that we call common sense, has been associated from the time of premodern female healers with older women. Those of us eager to be Wisewomen in training have scarcely begun to tap the wisdom of those old enough to understand life backward.

❧

Discussion Questions

1. When Sheehy attended the 1991 conference on "The New Older Woman," what did she learn about the new source of vitality found by the prominent women over fifty as they "let go" of their "youthful image"?

2. At the conference, her roommate turned out to be an eighty-four-year-old botanist. What did Sheehy learn about how the botanist pulled herself out of her languishing state after her retirement at age seventy? In what way did the botanist's story turn out to provide Sheehy with a pattern? Explain.

3. What incident pulled the school principal out of her feelings of being "buried alive" after her husband's death (paragraphs 6–13)? Explain how it turned her life around.

4. What effect did becoming a grandparent—as different from becoming a parent—have on Kay Delaney (paragraphs 14–20)? How did her grandchildren affect her attitude toward her job—as compared to the effect her children had? Explain.

5. After almost a decade of "failing" to nurse her sick husband back to health (paragraphs 21–28), how did Genevieve Burke feel on the day of his death? What happened to her to turn her life around?

*6. What is *generativity* and how did it figure in revitalizing Ella Ivey's life when she reached her fifties (paragraphs 29–38)? What is *sticktoitiveness* and what part did it play in her education?

*7. Sheehy writes in "Looking ahead" (paragraphs 39–42), "And as they [the women discussed earlier] grew older they found themselves concerned more with feeding the soul than the ego." Explain—or explore—the meaning of this statement.

Writing Topics

1. "The Pursuit of Passion" presents full portraits of four different women who have found their lives renewed after their fifties. Choose one among them that you would like to have as a friend, and in an essay write about the qualities that have led you to select her over the others.

2. You all have had the experience of knowing older women, perhaps relatives and friends, or relatives of friends. Write a character sketch of one who strikes you as having much in common with one or more of the women portrayed in Sheehy's essay. In preparation, you might want to interview the person you have chosen.

"This is what travelers discover:
that when you sever the links of normality and its claims,
when you break off from the quotidian,
it is the teapots that truly shock."

THE SHOCK OF TEAPOTS

Cynthia Ozick

Born in New York City in 1928, Cynthia Ozick earned a B.A. at New York University in 1949 and an M.A. from Ohio State University in 1950. As a free-lance writer, she has contributed both essays and fiction to numerous magazines and books and has published a number of volumes of her own. Her works of fiction include the novels *Trust* (1966), *The Cannibal Galaxy* (1983), and *Messiah of Stockholm* (1987) and the collections *Bloodshed and Three Novellas* (1976) and *Levitation: Five Fictions* (1981). Her volumes of essays include *Art and Ardor: Essays* (1983), *Metaphor and Memory: Essays* (1989), and *What Henry James Knew and Other Essays* (1993). "The Shock of Teapots" was first published under the title "Enchantments at First Encounter" in *The New York Times Magazine, Part II: The Sophisticated Traveler*, on March 17, 1985, and was reprinted under the present title in *Metaphor & Memory*. For more biographical information on Ozick, see page 42.

1   One morning in Stockholm, after rain and just before November, a mysteriously translucent shadow began to paint itself across the top of the city. It skimmed high over people's heads, a gauzy brass net, keeping well above the streets, skirting everything fabricated by human arts—though one or two steeples were allowed to dip into it, like pens filling their nibs with palest ink. It made a sort of watermark over Stockholm, as if a faintly luminous river ran overhead, yet with no more weight or gravity than a vapor.

2   This glorious strangeness—a kind of crystalline wash—was the sunlight of a Swedish autumn. The sun looked *new*: it had a lucidity, a texture, a tincture, a position across the sky that my New York gape had never before taken in. The horizontal ladder of light hung high up, higher than any sunlight I had ever seen, and the quality of its glow seemed thinner, wanner, more tentatively

morning-brushed; or else like gold leaf beaten gossamer as tissue—a lambent skin laid over the spired marrow of the town.

3   "Ah yes, the sun *does* look a bit different this time of year," say the Stockholmers in their perfect English (English as a second first language), but with a touch of ennui. Whereas I, under the electrified rays of my whitening hair, stand drawn upward to the startling sky, restored to the clarity of childhood. The Swedes have known a Swedish autumn before; I have not.

4   Travel returns us in just this way to sharpness of notice; and to be saturated in the sight of what is entirely new—the sun at an unaccustomed slope, stretched across the northland, separate from the infiltrating dusk that always seems about to fall through clear gray Stockholm—is to revisit the enigmatically lit puppet-stage outlines of childhood: those mental photographs and dreaming woodcuts or engravings that we retain from our earliest years. What we remember from childhood we remember forever—permanent ghosts, stamped, imprinted, eternally seen. Travelers regain this ghost-seizing brightness, eeriness, firstness.

5   They regain it because they have cut themselves loose from their own society, from every society; they are, for a while, floating vagabonds, like astronauts out for a space walk on a long free line. They are subject to preternatural exhilarations, absurd horizons, unexpected forms and transmutations: the matter-of-fact (a battered old stoop, say, or the shape of a door) appears beautiful; or a stone that at home would not merit the blink of your eye here arrests you with its absolute particularity—just because it is what your hand already intimately knows. You think: a stone, a stone! They have stones here too! And you think: how uncannily the planet is girdled, as stone-speckled in Sweden as in New York. For the vagabond-voyeur (and for travelers voyeurism is irresistible), nothing is not for notice, nothing is banal, nothing is ordinary: not a rock, not the shoulder of a passerby, not a teapot.

6   Plenitude assaults; replication invades. Everything known has its spooky shadow and Doppelgänger. On my first trip anywhere—it was 1957 and I landed in Edinburgh with the roaring of the plane's four mammoth propellers for days afterward embedded in my ears—I rode in a red airport bus to the middle of the city, out of which ascended its great castle. It is a fairy-book castle, dreamlike, Arthurian, secured in the long-ago. But the shuddery red bus— hadn't I been bounced along in an old bus before, perhaps not so terrifically red as this one?—the red bus was not within reach of plain sense. Every inch of its interior streamed with unearthliness, with an undivulged and consummate witchery. It put me in the grip of a wild Elsewhere. This unexceptional vehicle, with its bright forward snout, was all at once eclipsed by a rush of the abnormal, the unfathomably Martian. It was the bus, not the phantasmagorical castle, that clouded over and bewildered our reasoned humanity. The red bus was what I intimately knew: only I had never seen it before. A reflected flicker of the actual. A looking-glass bus. A Scottish ghost.

7   This is what travelers discover: that when you sever the links of normality and its claims, when you break off from the quotidian, it is the teapots that truly shock. Nothing is so awesomely unfamiliar as the familiar that discloses itself at the end of a journey. Nothing shakes the heart so much as meeting—far, far away—what you last met at home. Some say that travelers are informal anthropologists. But it is ontology—the investigation of the nature of being—that travelers do. Call it the flooding-in of the real.

8   There is, besides, the flooding-in of character. Here one enters not landscapes or streetlit night scenes, but fragments of drama: splinters of euphoria that catch you up when you are least deserving. Sometimes it is a jump into a pop-up book, as when a cockney cabdriver, of whom you have asked directions while leaning out from the curb, gives his native wink of blithe goodwill. Sometimes it is a mazy stroll into a toy theater, as when, in a museum, you suddenly come on the intense little band following the lecturer on Mesopotamia, or the lecturer on genre painting, and the muse of civilization alights on these rapt few. What you are struck with then—one of those mental photographs that go on sticking to the retina—is not what lies somnolently in the glass case or hangs romantically on the wall, but the enchantment of a minutely idiosyncratic face shot into your vision with indelible singularity, delivered over forever by your own fertile gaze. When travelers stare at heads and ears and necks and beads and mustaches, they are—in the encapsuled force of the selection—making art: portraits, voice sonatinas, the quick haiku of a strictly triangular nostril.

9   Traveling is seeing; it is the implicit that we travel by. Travelers are fantasists, conjurers, seers—and what they finally discover is that every round object everywhere is a crystal ball: stone, teapot, the marvelous globe of the human eye.

ॐ

Discussion Questions

1. In paragraphs 1–3, Ozick concludes her description of the Stockholm "crystalline wash" sky thus, "Whereas I, under the electrified rays of my whitening hair, stand drawn upward to the startling sky, restored to the clarity of childhood. The Swedes have known a Swedish autumn before; I have not." What point does Ozick make here, and how does it relate to the rest of her essay?

2. Paragraph 5 concludes, "For the vagabond-voyeur (and for travelers voyeurism is irresistible), nothing is not for notice, nothing is banal, nothing is ordinary: not a rock, not the shoulder of a passerby, not a teapot." Explain the meaning of this sentence and its relation, along with that of the first sentence of paragraph 9, to the title of the essay.

3. Why did the red airport bus (paragraph 6) make a deeper, more complex impression on Ozick than the "phantasmagorical castle"? Explain.

*4. In paragraph 7, Ozick answers the question of what travelers discover or do by saying finally that they investigate the "nature of being" which may be called "the flooding-in of the real." And in paragraph 8 she adds to the "flooding-in of the real" the "flooding-in of character." Explore as deeply as you can what Ozick means by these phrases.

Writing Topics

1. Ozick says in paragraph 4, "What we remember from childhood we remember forever—permanent ghosts, stamped, imprinted, eternally seen. Travelers regain this ghost-seizing brightness, eeriness, firstness." In a brief essay, agree or disagree with Ozick's generalization, drawing on your own experience with memory and in traveling. In your essay, explore your reaction to what you saw that startled you (or failed to startle you) in the way the Stockholm sky startled Ozick.

2. When "The Shock of Teapots" first appeared in *The New York Times Magazine*, it was entitled "Enchantments at First Encounter." Write an essay showing which title in your view is best for the essay and set forth your reasons, based on the meaning of the essay, as persuasively as possible.

"I was transfixed at Lourdes because through those imprisoning bodies, some entangled yet separate will to continue living had glinted out with shocking immediacy—the same I had witnessed elsewhere in travels to other pilgrimage sites."

ON THE PILGRIM'S PATH TO LOURDES

Eleanor Munro

Eleanor Munro was born in Brooklyn, New York, in 1928 and took a B.A. at Smith College in 1949 and an M.A. at Columbia University in 1965. She studied for a time at the Sorbonne in Paris, France, and then began her career as writer and lecturer, primarily on art. She is the author of a number of books and essays, among them *Originals: American Women Artists* (1979), *On Glory Roads: A Pilgrim's Book about Pilgrimage* (1986), *Memoir of a Modernist's Daughter* (1988), and *Art in America: Essays by Contemporary Soviet and American Writers* (1990). "On the Pilgrim's Path to Lourdes" was first published in the *San Francisco Examiner and Chronicle* in 1987 and was selected to appear in *The Best American Essays, 1988*, edited by Annie Dillard.

1   Among sacred pilgrimage sites of the world—far-off snowy peaks on which gods are thought to dance, thronged temples by the Ganges, gold-domed cathedrals or humble country altars—the French shrine of Lourdes in its gloomy mountain setting may be one of the most instructive.

2   That is to say, if you look beyond the blatant commercialism of the new town and steep yourself instead in the geography, architecture and massed population of the sacred precinct, you may gain an inkling of the meaning of this ancient and universal human practice. For pilgrimage is an enterprise of deep antiquity and powerful psychological appeal, and its associated rites are much the same across all religions, and the same today as in the past.

3   When a pilgrim arrives at his destination (it can as well be a natural feature, rock, tree or riverbank as a man-made church or temple), he invariably can be seen walking a circular path around or in it, often following the clockwise

course of the sun. If by night, he will carry a candle or torch, which, multiplied many times in many hands, becomes a galaxy of stars turning slowly in darkness. The metaphor holds. In these circumambulations, the pilgrim imitates the flight of the stars and planets, which orbit the celestial pole, disappearing and reappearing in a harmonic order we on earth find both beautiful and eternal. So the pilgrim enacts the answer to his longing for immortality.

4   Indeed, the folklore that has grown up around Lourdes describes its location at "the confluence of seven valleys"—seven being one of those immemorial mystical numbers in scripture and myth referring to the visible planets, the outermost travelers of the solar system. Mystical Lourdes thus is identified as its axis.

5   Legend in this case enhances geography. Actual Lourdes lies betwixt gorges and bare cliffs, where icy torrents off the high slopes collide in a perpetual tumult of white water, ethereal rainbows and ghostly low-hanging clouds.

6   A hundred years ago, when its modern history began, Lourdes was no more than a scatter of wretched stone huts wedged along a couple of crooked climbing streets. Perched on an overhanging rock stood the town jail. In one of those freezing dwellings lived a poor miller, sometimes resident in the jail, and his wife and children, all of them suffering from hunger and ill health.

7   It was a bitter February day in 1858 when Bernadette, the eldest child, went with her sister to the riverbank to gather kindling. And there, as she later recalled with the help of her confessor and other priests of the region, "I heard a noise like a gust of wind. I saw the trees were not swaying. I heard the same noise again. As I lifted my head and looked at the grotto, I saw a lady in white. Fear took hold of me. My hand shook."

8   What she reported seeing in an "aureole of sunlight" was a woman who much resembled a statue of the Madonna in a church nearby, save that instead of treading on a snake as the plaster woman did, the Beautiful Lady wore on each foot a yellow rose.

9   Not till her third visit did the Lady explain who she was, adding, "I cannot promise to make you happy in this world, but in *the other*." A skeptic may suppose Bernadette's life history shaped her visions, for she had twice been sent as a boarder to another village, once in infancy and later as a hired shepherdess, where she enjoyed milk and bread in abundance offered by a warm-hearted foster mother. In any case, at her ninth appearance, the Lady spoke words both motherly and rural: "Go drink and wash at the fountain. Eat the grass you will find there."

10   So strange a suggestion led Bernadette to tear hungrily at the grass by the cliff and so to widen the opening over an underground spring which today, some 125 years later, is the most famous water source in the Western world. Over four million pilgrims visit it each summer, and it has become the nexus of a vast ecclesiastical, touristic and economic bureaucracy.

11   For the Beautiful Lady, who in the end identified herself in terms Bernadette said she had never heard before—"I am the Immaculate Conception"—asked that a chapel be built by the spring and pilgrims attend it "in procession." And so it was done, and so they do, but not by miracle alone.

12   Four years before the visions, in 1854, the Pope, against stiff opposition from within the church but in response to a centuries-long groundswell of popular faith, had announced the dogma of the Immaculate Conception of the Virgin. Bernadette's visions, tailored and broadcast by her confessors, brought that arcane dogma down to earth and gave it sentimental color.

13   She herself died at thirty-six, a reclusive nun, leaving only a modest disclaimer: "The Blessed Lady used me. I am nothing without her." In 1925, she was beatified and, eight years later, on the Feast Day of the Immaculate Conception, canonized. The Vatican still maintains a stiffish attitude toward the occasional reported cures at the place, but pastors from all over Europe shepherd their charges there, often in special railroad cars fitted out as hospitals. Even if the cures are dubious or short-lasting, the patients return home, sometimes to institutions that are their lifelong homes, lifted in mind and heart by the experience.

14   The modern commercial town of Lourdes offers hotels and boarding houses great and small—some four hundred of them—wax museums, audio-visual instructional parlors and shops where you can pick up a cuckoo clock, pine candy, a skein of Pyrenees wool, a set of cowbells, color prints of the Angelus and all sizes of plastic Virgin-shaped water bottles.

15   Near the sacred precinct stands the Hospice of Our Lady of Seven Sorrows, where bedridden pilgrims are tenderly housed and fed before and after their ritual visit to the shrine. The order was started four years after the visions were officially accepted, by Marie St. Frai, a mountain woman with a mission toward the terminally ill. Her nuns still wear black in bereavement. But the rule of the order is *allegresse*, lightness of heart, and so these sisters' spirit seems to be.

16   I asked one of them, Sister Stanislaw, a dainty young person with dancing eyes, how she came to the order. She grew up in a secular, bourgeois home, in which she danced and partied and wore pretty clothes. But, she said, "I loved the poor and I followed the thread to the end. When I came into the order, I shut the door behind me. And ever since, it's as if I were in heaven."

17   The mystical center or axis of heavenly Lourdes is the place by the riverbank where Bernadette knelt to tear at the grass. There bubbles the famous spring, its open mouth protected by plate glass. Its waters are piped off into twice-seven tubs in as many little cold bathrooms where volunteer attendants convey the suffering hopeful. Alternately, in the open air is a row of bright copper taps, through which water is constantly drawn off into gallon tanks, thermoses and bottles to be carried to Christian homes around the world.

18   Behind that place of holy power, the ground rises sharply toward the cliff top, where great trees fill with mountain wind, bending half-over under the scudding clouds. At the axial summit stands the basilica, a neo-Gothic concoction like a Disneyland castle. In the sanctuary's mosaic-adorned dome, a smiling teenage Bernadette in a golden crown holds out thin arms to her petitioners.

19   At four each afternoon and again at eight in the evening, a procession takes place in Lourdes. The pilgrims form rows, six abreast, some walking but most wheeled by attendants in chairs or litters.

20   The lines, also guided by ecclesiastics in full regalia, move gravely, in perfect order, along the base of the cliff beside the spring and the water taps, then out along a wide, tree-shaded alley leading toward the commercial town, where they turn as if in orbit to return toward the basilica and begin again.

21   I stood there one afternoon watching and asking myself what the meaning was of what I saw.

22   I was standing as if on a shore while toward me flowed faces by the six, by the twelve, by the hundred—peasant faces and faces suggestive of high station, such a host of sufferers I couldn't have imagined without being there. I even wished for the power of a Homer to help me describe that tremendous host—thick fingers twisted in blankets or splayed upon them, wasted flesh gray as cement, cheeks and noses sharp as cut stone, black brows bristling over sunken eyes; polio-afflicted children in their mothers' arms; a handsome woman whose well-combed hair framed frantic, maniacal eyes; men with barrel chests and legs like rolled towels, stretching anguished faces back toward the spring even after their litters had been wheeled on past.

23   *Look*, these shapes on their beds seemed to be saying to the clouds—Look on us: *your handiwork*.

24   There were still more painful cases to come, reaching with hands flailing like flags run off their pulleys, crossing themselves with the heels of those flapping hands. There were beings without legs or arms at all, with swollen heads too heavy to lift, or shaped like turnips.

25   The procession moved to amplified music, minor-keyed folk songs, plaintive chants, wistful children's choirs, until at last, inevitably, came the cry from loudspeakers all along the way: *Lord . . . heal us*.

26   That evening I stood on the balcony of my hotel looking down on thousands of little lights turning in rainy darkness, asking myself whether it was morbidity that had kept me fixed to the sight of so many individuals there in extremes of deformity and fear. But I thought it was not.

27   I was transfixed at Lourdes because through those imprisoning bodies, some entangled yet separate *will* to continue living had glinted out with shocking immediacy—the same I had witnessed elsewhere in travels to other pilgrimage sites.

28   In India, you see human suffering in the open, unapologetically displayed, considered an inevitable feature of the material world. Hindu religious practice helps you overlook immediate pain and dwell instead on vast metaphysical abstractions. Western religious thought focuses on the narrower, more piercing mystery of human consciousness in an inhuman world. And every single person who walked or was rolled before my eyes at Lourdes was like a plumb-weight pulling the cords of a whole belief system into alignment.

29   I went down to the shrine where the lights were still turning among the trees and took a flame from a taper in the hand of a country woman with averted eyes and heavy facial hair who, when I thanked her, replied in the deep stoic timbre of a hermaphrodite.

30   There came into my mind then the well-known words *Eppur si muove*: And still it moves. That there exists some natural law or force that binds such pilgrims into their passionate faith and labor seems to me as unarguable — yet still as mysterious — as was, to Galileo, the turning of the earth around the sun.

ै&

Discussion Questions

1.   In paragraphs 1–3, Munro describes pilgrimages in general, noting in paragraph 3 that at night the pilgrims usually form a procession moving clockwise around the shrine, "a natural feature, rock, tree, or riverbank" or "a man-made church or temple," carrying candles and torches that become "a galaxy of stars turning slowly in darkness." Munro adds, "The metaphor holds. In these circumambulations, the pilgrim imitates the flight of the stars and planets, which orbit the celestial pole, disappearing and reappearing in a harmonic order we on earth find both beautiful and eternal." Explore both the denotative and connotative meanings of this passage in context.

2.   In paragraphs 6–13, Munro sketches briefly the origin of Lourdes as a shrine. Summarize the important details of the narrative, explaining particularly the relation that developed between the appearance in 1858 of the Madonna to Bernadette and the church's dogma of the Immaculate Conception. What was the attitude of the Vatican toward the "reported cures" at Lourdes?

3.   Munro paints (paragraphs 14–18) with quick, brisk strokes the modern Lourdes, ranging from the cheap commercialization of the town to the "mystical center or axis of heavenly Lourdes." What is the ultimate effect? Explain.

*4.   Munro remarks in paragraph 21, "I stood there [in Lourdes at the hour of the procession] one afternoon watching and asking myself what the meaning was of what I saw." How did Munro answer the question she asked herself? Explain.

5. Munro says at the end of paragraph 28, "And every single person who walked or was rolled before my eyes at Lourdes was like a plumb-weight pulling the cords of a whole belief system into alignment." Explore the meaning and implication of this statement.

*6. Munro ends the essay by describing her lighting a taper and joining in the Lourdes procession. Why did she move from observer to participant, and what is the effect?

Writing Topics

1. Munro says in her last paragraph, "There came into my mind then the well-known words *Eppur si muove*: And still it moves. That there exists some natural law or force that binds such pilgrims into their passionate faith and labor seems to me as unarguable—yet still as mysterious—as was, to Galileo, the turning of the earth around the sun." Galileo was threatened with imprisonment for supporting the then-revolutionary discovery by Copernicus that the sun did not move around the earth as formerly believed but, rather, the earth moved around the sun. Galileo, recanting his belief in Copernicus to avoid incarceration, was reported to have muttered, "Nevertheless it moves." In an essay, explore the meaning of these closing lines in the context of the whole of "On the Pilgrim's Path to Lourdes" and the circumstances of Galileo's remark quoted in the last paragraph.

2. Have you ever had an experience that made a difference in the way that you looked at the world? Such experiences may or may not be religious, but they usually revolve around some mystery that is either "solved" or resolved into a deeper context with its own unresolvable but tolerable ambiguity. Such experiences usually leave an indelible impression of the time, place, and the insight or state of mind bestowed. Write a narrative essay in which you describe the what, where, how, and why of the experience—and conclude with the enduring consequences. (You may, if you wish, try your hand at a narrative of an imagined experience or of a real experience that seemed promising but somehow self-destructed. Feel free to roam the territory.)

"I see it then—the trunk that stretches monstrously behind him. It winds out of the door, down dark and obscure corridors to the cellar, and vanishes into the floor. It writhes, it crawls, it barks and snuffles and roars, and the odor of the swamp exhales from it. That pale young scholar's face is the last bloom on a curious animal extrusion through time."

A FAINT CRACK INTO THE ABSOLUTE

Loren Eiseley

Loren Eiseley (1907–1977) was born in Nebraska and took his B.A. from the University of Nebraska in 1933 and both an M.A. (1935) and a Ph.D. (1937) at the University of Pennsylvania. He spent his career as a professor of anthropology at the University of Pennsylvania, but his fame rests on a series of books written in a lucid, lyrical style about the mysteries of the universe and of human existence. His books include The Immense Journey (1957), Darwin's Century: Evolution and the Men Who Discovered It (1958), The Unexpected Universe (1969), and The Night Country (1971). His poetry appears in Notes of an Alchemist (1972), The Innocent Assassins (1973), Another Kind of Autumn (1977), and All the Night Wings (published posthumously in 1979). And in 1975 he brought out his autobiography, All the Strange Hours: The Excavation of a Life. "A Faint Crack into the Absolute" comes from "How Natural Is Natural?" one of six lectures published as The Firmament of Time in 1960. For more biographical information on Eiseley, see page 331.

1   We who are engaged in the life of thought are likely to assume that the key to an understanding of the world is knowledge, both of the past and of the future—that if we had that knowledge we would also have wisdom. It is not my intention here to decry learning. It is only to say that we must come to understand that learning is endless and that nowhere does it lead us behind the existent world. It may reduce the prejudices of ignorance, set our bones, build our cities. In itself it will never make us ethical men. Yet because ours, we conceive, is an age of progress, and because we know more about time and history than any men before us, we fallaciously equate ethical advance with scientific progress in a point-to-point relationship. Thus as society improves physically, we assume the improvement of the individual, and are all the more horrified at those mass movements of terror which have so typified the first half of this century.

2   On the morning of which I want to speak, I was surfeited with the smell of mortality and tired of the years I had spent in archaeological dustbins. I rode out of a camp and across a mountain. I would never have believed, before it happened, that one could ride into the past on horseback. It is true I rode with a purpose, but that purpose was to settle an argument within myself.

3   It was time, I thought, to face up to what was in my mind—to the dust and the broken teeth and the spilled chemicals of life seeping away into the sand. It was time I admitted that life was of the earth, earthy, and could be turned into a piece of wretched tar. It was time I consented to the proposition that man had as little to do with his fate as a seed blown against a grating. It was time I looked upon the world without spectacles and saw love and pride and beauty dissolve into effervescing juices. I could be an empiricist with the best of them. I would be deceived by no more music. I had entered a black cloud of merciless thought, but the horse, as it chanced, worked his own way over that mountain.

4   I could hear the sudden ring of his hooves as we came cautiously treading over a tilted table of granite, past the winds that blow on the high places of the world. There were stones there so polished that they shone from the long ages that the storms had rushed across them. We crossed the divide then, picking our way in places scoured by ancient ice action, through boulder fields where nothing moved, and yet where one could feel time like an enemy hidden behind each stone.

5   If there was life on those heights, it was the thin life of mountain spiders who caught nothing in their webs, or of small gray birds that slipped soundlessly among the stones. The wind in the pass caught me head on and blew whatever thoughts I had into a raveling stream behind me, until they were all gone and there was only myself and the horse, moving in an eternal dangerous present, free of the encumbrances of the past.

6   We crossed a wind that smelled of ice from still higher snowfields, we cantered with a breeze that came from somewhere among cedars, we passed a gust like Hell's breath that had risen straight up from the desert floor. They

were winds and they did not stay with us. Presently we descended out of their domain, and it was curious to see, as we dropped farther through gloomy woods and canyons, how the cleansed and scoured mind I had brought over the mountain began, like the water in those rumbling gorges, to talk in a variety of voices, to debate, to argue, to push at stones, or curve subtly around obstacles. Sometimes I wonder whether we are only endlessly repeating in our heads an argument that is going on in the world's foundations among crashing stones and recalcitrant roots.

7   "Fall, fall, fall," cried the roaring water and the grinding pebbles in the torrent. "Let go, come with us, come home to the place without light." But the roots clung and climbed and the trees pushed up, impeding the water, and forests filled even the wind with their sighing and grasped after the sun. It is so in the mind. One can hear the rattle of falling stones in the night, and the thoughts like trees holding their place. Sometimes one can shut the noise away by turning over on the other ear, sometimes the sounds are as dreadful as a storm in the mountains, and one lies awake, holding, like the roots that wait for daylight. It was after such a night that I came over the mountain, but it was the descent on the other side that suddenly struck me as a journey into the eons of the past.

8   I came down across stones dotted with pink and gray lichens—a barren land dreaming life's last dreams in the thin air of a cold and future world.

9   I passed a meadow and a meadow mouse in a little shower of petals struck from mountain flowers. I dismissed it—it was almost my own time—a pleasant golden hour in the age of mammals, lost before the human coming. I rode heavily toward an old age far backward in the reptilian dark.

10   I was below timber line and sinking deeper and deeper into the pine woods, whose fallen needles lay thick and springy over the ungrassed slopes. The brown needles and the fallen cones, the stiff, endless green forests were a mark that placed me in the Age of Dinosaurs. I moved in silence now, waiting a sign. I saw it finally, a green lizard on a stone. We were far back, far back. He bobbed his head uncertainly at me, and I reined in with the nostalgic intent, for a moment, to call him father, but I saw soon enough that I was a ghost who troubled him and that he would wish me, though he had not the voice to speak, to ride on. A man who comes down the road of time should not expect to converse—even with his own kin. I made a brief, uncertain sign of recognition, to which he did not respond, and passed by. Things grew more lonely. I was coming out upon the barren ridges of an old sea beach that rose along the desert floor. Life was small and grubby now. The hot, warning scarlet of peculiar desert ants occasionally flashed among the stones. I had lost all trace of myself and thought regretfully of the lizard who might have directed me.

11   A turned-up stone yielded only a scorpion who curled his tail in a kind of evil malice. I surveyed him reproachfully. He was old enough to know the secret of my origin, but once more an ancient, bitter animus drawn from that

poisoned soil possessed him and he raised his tail. I turned away. An enormous emptiness by degrees possessed me. I was back almost, in a different way, to the thin air over the mountain, to the end of all things in the cold starlight of space.

12   I passed some indefinable bones and shells in the salt-crusted wall of a dry arroyo. As I reined up, only sand dunes rose like waves before me and if life was there it was no longer visible. It was like coming down to the end—to the place of fires where we began. I turned about then and let my gaze go up, tier after tier, height after height, from crawling desert bush to towering pine on the great slopes far above me.

13   In the same way animal life had gone up that road from these dry, envenomed things to the deer nuzzling a fawn in the meadows far above. I had come down the whole way into a place where one could lift sand and ask in a hollow, dust-shrouded whisper, "Life, what is it? Why am I here? Why am I here?"

14   And my mind went up that figurative ladder of the ages, bone by bone, skull by skull, seeking an answer. There was none, except that in all that downrush of wild energy that I had passed in the canyons there was this other strange organized stream that marched upward, gaining a foothold here, tossing there a pine cone a little farther upward into a crevice in the rock.

15   And again one asked, not of the past this time, but of the future, there where the winds howled through open space and the last lichens clung to the naked rock, "Why did we live?" There was no answer I could hear. The living river flowed out of nowhere into nothing. No one knew its source or its departing. It was an apparition. If one did not see it there was no way to prove that it was real.

16   No way, that is, except within the mind itself. And the mind, in some strange manner so involved with time, moving against the cutting edge of it like the wind I had faced on the mountain, has yet its own small skull-borne image of eternity. It is not alone that I can reach out and receive within my head a handsbreadth replica of the far fields of the universe. It is not because I can touch a trilobite and know the fall of light in ages before my birth. Rather, it lies in the fact that the human mind can transcend time, even though trapped, to all appearances, within that medium. As from some remote place, I see myself as child and young man, watch with a certain dispassionate objectivity the violence and tears of a remote youth who was once I, shaping his character, for good or ill, toward the creature he is today. Shrinking, I see him teeter at the edge of abysses he never saw. With pain I acknowledge acts undone that might have saved and led him into some serene and noble pathway. I move about him like a ghost, that vanished youth. I exhort, I plead. He does not hear me. Indeed, he too is already a ghost. He has become me. I am what I am. Yet the point is, we are not wholly given over to time—if we were, such acts, such leaps through that gray medium, would be impossible. Perhaps God himself may rove in similar pain up the dark roads of his universe. Only how would it be, I wonder, to contain at once both the beginning and the end, and to hear, in helplessness perhaps, the fall of worlds in the night?

17   This is what the mind of man is just beginning to achieve—a little micro-cosm, a replica of whatever it is that, from some unimaginable "outside," con-tains the universe and all the fractured bits of seeing which the world's creatures see. It is not necessary to ride over a mountain range to experience historical infinity. It can descend upon one in the lecture room.

18   I find it is really in daylight that the sensation I am about to describe is apt to come most clearly upon me, and for some reason I associate it extensively with crowds. It is not, you understand, an hallucination. It is a reality. It is, I can only say with difficulty, a chink torn in a dimension life was never intended to look through. It connotes a sense beyond the eye, though the twenty years' impressions are visual. Man, it is said, is a time-binding animal, but he was never intended for this. Here is the way it comes.

19   I mount the lecturer's rostrum to address a class. Like any work-worn professor fond of his subject, I fumble among my skulls and papers, shuffle to the blackboard and back again, begin the patient translation of three billion years of time into chalk scrawls and uncertain words ventured timidly to a sea of young, impatient faces. Time does not frighten them, I think enviously. They have, most of them, never lain awake and grasped the sides of a cot, staring upward into the dark while the slow clock strokes begin.

20   "Doctor." A voice diverts me. I stare out near-sightedly over the class. A hand from the back row gesticulates. "Doctor, do you believe there is a direction to evolution? Do you believe, Doctor . . . Doctor, do you believe? . . ." Instead of the words, I hear a faint piping, and see an eager scholar's face squeezed and dissolving on the body of a chest-thumping ape. "Doctor, is there a direction?"

21   I see it then—the trunk that stretches monstrously behind him. It winds out of the door, down dark and obscure corridors to the cellar, and vanishes into the floor. It writhes, it crawls, it barks and snuffles and roars, and the odor of the swamp exhales from it. That pale young scholar's face is the last bloom on a curious animal extrusion through time. And who among us, under the cold persuasion of the archaeological eye, can perceive which of his many shapes is real, or if, perhaps, the entire shape in time is not a greater and more curious animal than its single appearance?

22   I too am aware of the trunk that stretches loathsomely back of me along the floor. I too am a many-visaged thing that has climbed upward out of the dark of endless leaf falls, and has slunk, furred, through the glitter of blue glacial nights. I, the professor, trembling absurdly on the platform with my book and spectacles, am the single philosophical animal. I am the unfolding worm, and mud fish, the weird tree of Igdrasil shaping itself endlessly out of darkness toward the light.

23   I have said this is not an illusion. It is when one sees in this manner, or a sense of strangeness halts one on a busy street to verify the appearance of one's fellows, that one knows a terrible new sense has opened a faint crack into the Absolute. It is in this way alone that one comes to grips with a great mystery,

that life and time bear some curious relationship to each other that is not shared by inanimate things.

24   It is in the brain that this world opens. To our descendants it may become a commonplace, but me, and others like me, it has made a castaway. I have no refuge in time, as others do who troop homeward at nightfall. As a result, I am one of those who linger furtively over coffee in the kitchen at bedtime or haunt the all-night restaurants. Nevertheless, I shall say without regret: there are hazards in all professions.

❧

Discussion Questions

1.   What distinction does Eiseley draw, in paragraph 1, between knowledge and wisdom?

2.   In paragraph 2, Eiseley begins the description of a journey he made on horseback "across a mountain" in order to "settle an argument" within himself. What was the argument?

3.   In paragraphs 4–6, Eiseley describes crossing the "divide" on the heights and encountering the wind in the "pass" to the other side of the mountain. What did the wind do to his thoughts? When he began his descent, his mind seemed "cleansed and scoured" and began "to talk in a variety of voices, to debate, to argue, to push at stones. . . ." Explain.

4.   In paragraph 10, Eiseley says, "I saw it finally, a green lizard on a stone. We were far back, far back. He bobbed his head uncertainly at me, and I reined in with the nostalgic intent, for a moment, to call him father. . . ." Explain this passage and explore its suggestiveness.

5.   As Eiseley emerged on a desert floor, he saw a scorpion "who curled his tail in a kind of evil malice" (paragraph 11). How did Eiseley respond to the scorpion's threat?

*6.   Eiseley appears to have had a kind of evolutionary vision (paragraphs 12–14) of the movement of life from "envenomed things" on the desert floor to the deer in the meadows above, climbing a "figurative ladder of the ages." How is this vision related to his questions in paragraph 13, "Life, what is it? Why am I here?" and in paragraph 15, "Why did we live?" Explain Eiseley's meaning and trace the implications as far as you are able.

7.   In paragraph 17, Eiseley says, "It is not necessary to ride over a mountain range to experience historical infinity. It can descend upon one in the lecture room." Describe the incident to which Eiseley refers and show how it resulted in an "experience of historical infinity."

*8. In paragraph 22, Eiseley refers to the tree of Igdrasil (usually spelled Yggdrasil), the tree of divine life of Norse or Scandinavian mythology, with its three great roots reaching to the three realms of energy, one to the physical realm of lower nature, another to the mental or intellectual realm, and the third to the spiritual or moral realm of the gods. In the boughs of the tree sits the eagle, at the roots are the serpents, and on the trunk is a squirrel running back and forth. How does Eiseley's use of this myth help shape the meaning of the vision Eiseley experienced when he was asked a question by a student in his class? Explain.

9. In paragraph 23, Eiseley writes, "It is in this way alone [through knowledge that a "terrible new sense has opened a faint crack into the Absolute"] that one comes to grips with a great mystery, that life and time bear some curious relationship to each other that is not shared by inanimate things." Explore the meaning of this "conclusion" in all its ramifications.

Writing Topics

1. In paragraph 15, Eiseley writes, "'Why did we live?' There was no answer I could hear. The living river flowed out of nowhere into nothing. No one knew its source or its departure. It was an apparition. If one did not see it there was no way to prove that it was real." In paragraph 16, Eiseley immediately reverses himself: "No way, that is, except within the mind itself." The secret is that "the human mind can transcend time." Write an essay explaining Eiseley's meaning within the context of the whole of his piece. Did his mind succeed or fail in his attempt to "transcend time"? In your conclusion, show why you are persuaded or unpersuaded by Eiseley's line of reasoning.

2. Rarely has anyone lived for very long without finding it necessary to withdraw to a retreat in order to "think things over" or "sort things out"—usually about the "big" questions of life of the kind Eiseley posed to himself in "A Faint Crack into the Absolute": "Life, what is it? Why am I here?" and "Why did we live?" You can no doubt come up with similar questions, such as: "Who am I?" "What does life mean?" "Is there life after death?" Write an essay in which you tell the story of such a withdrawal in your life—what led up to it, what was it like, what were the consequences? Or if you know someone who has gone through such an experience and who is willing to share the details with you, conduct an interview and report the results.

Summary Writing Topics

1. The Galápagos Islands are famous because they were one of the important stopping places of Charles Darwin when, as a young man, he sailed to the southern islands (1831–1836). He found much material there that would be used later in On *the Origin of Species by Means of Natural Selection*, published in 1859, which set forth his "theory of evolution" and began immediately to undermine religious beliefs in the divinity of human beings as created by God. Do a bit of library research on Darwin and his theory of evolution. Then write an essay focusing on Annie Dillard's essay as shaped in some way by Darwin's thoughts and influence. Note especially section III, in which Dillard cites the modern psychology experiment attempting to teach chimpanzees to speak (Darwin posited humankind's remote kinship with the apes), and consider also the following question from section III, "What is the difference between a cathedral and a physics lab? Are not they both saying: Hello?"

2. Assume you are planning to become a physicist. Would reading Alan P. Lightman's essay "I = V/R" confirm your decision or cause you to change your mind—or have no effect either way? Write an essay taking one of the positions and explaining your reasons, showing how specific passages in the essay affected your decision.

3. If you were considering becoming a surgeon, would Richard Selzer's "The Exact Location of the Soul" inspire you to go ahead with your plans, or would it turn you off the profession? Write an essay taking one position or the other, referring to relevant passages in the essay in explanation of your position.

4. Gail Sheehy, in "The Pursuit of Passion," says that she learned in attending the conference on "The New Older Woman" in 1991 that many of the older women had found within themselves resources of renewed energy. She writes, "A common denominator emerged: The source of continuing aliveness was to find your passion and pursue it with whole heart and single mind." Write an essay in which you test this advice for people of all ages—for yourself, as an example. Consider whether the "pursuit of passion" in life is not better than the pursuit of money, fame, pleasure, thrills, and the like.

5. Henry David Thoreau wrote in his journal (February 4, 1851) the following entry, which may be called "Seeing Beyond Understanding":

> We shall see but little way if we require to understand what we see. How few things can a man measure with the tape of his understanding! How many greater things might he be seeing in the meantime!

One afternoon in the fall, November 21st, I saw Fair Haven Pond with its island and meadow; between the island and the shore, a strip of perfectly smooth water in the lee of the island; and two hawks sailing over it; and something more I saw which cannot easily be described, which made me say to myself that the landscape could not be improved. I did not see how it could be improved. Yet I do not know what these things can be; I begin to see such objects only when I leave off understanding them, and afterwards remember that I did not appreciate them before. But I get no further than this. How adapted these forms and colors to our eyes, a meadow and its islands! What are these things? Yet the hawks and the ducks keep so aloof, and nature is so reserved! We are made to love the river and the meadow, as the wind to ripple the water.

In an essay, compare and contrast Thoreau's notions about "seeing" with those of Cynthia Ozick in "The Shock of Teapots." Thoreau considered his life a journey, and he found in this passage the "unfamiliar" in the "familiar," as did Ozick's traveler (paragraph 7). May not his concern also have been like Ozick's ontology—"the investigation of the nature of being"? Ozick's essay ends, "Traveling is seeing; it is the implicit that we travel by."

6. After reading the quotation from Thoreau in question 5 and rereading Loren Eiseley's "A Faint Crack into the Absolute," write an essay in which you assess Eiseley's "seeing" by the measure of Thoreau. It is perhaps instructive that Thoreau says in *Walden* ("Where I Lived and What I Lived For"), "Time is but the stream I go a-fishing in," whereas Eiseley says in his last paragraph, "I have no refuge in time, as others do who troop homeward at nightfall."

7. Annie Dillard in "Teaching a Stone to Talk" and Eleanor Munro in "On the Pilgrim's Path to Lourdes" seem to have gone through experiences that helped them to sift through their thoughts and feelings to some kind of answer to their deepest beliefs. Both evoke scientific figures who in their time were perceived as attacking the foundations of religious beliefs—Galileo in the seventeenth century, with his support of Copernicus's view that the earth revolved around the sun, and Darwin in the nineteenth century, with his theory of the evolution of human beings from previous life forms. Have you ever had or wanted to have such a revelation? Write a narrative essay of a real or imagined experience that bestowed some kind of clarification where before there was a muddle. Use the essays men-

tioned above as models, but don't feel bound by their order or form.

8. Three scientists have essays in this cluster: Alan P. Lightman, a physicist; Richard Selzer, a surgeon; and Loren Eiseley, an anthropologist. After reviewing their essays, determine whose essay held your interest most. Write a letter to the scientist you have chosen, explaining what you found most attractive in the essay and posing some questions about matters related to the essay that you would like to know more about.

9. In the essays of both Annie Dillard and Loren Eiseley, the Darwinian theory of evolution figures either directly or indirectly. Write an essay comparing and contrasting their references to Darwin and his ideas. In your final paragraphs, indicate which essay you find more persuasive in its ultimate conclusion.

10. Refresh your memory of the essays by Emily Hahn and Cynthia Ozick, both of which relate tales about traveling. Write a letter to the author whose essay you found more compelling, either in narrative or ideas. Describe what you found most appealing about the essay and raise any questions you believe might enhance your understanding.

11. Many of you may remember occasions when, on a city street lined with apartments, an assaulted or mugged individual cried out for help but to no avail, because people did not "want to become involved." Such an incident paints a negative picture of people, one that is radically different from that presented in Roger Rosenblatt's "The Man in the Water." Write an essay in which you adopt one of these views of human nature and show why, drawing on your experience or the experiences of people you know, you think as you do.

Acknowledgments

Abbey, Edward. "The Great American Desert," from *The Journey Home* by Edward Abbey. Copyright © 1977 by Edward Abbey. Used by permission of Dutton Signet, a division of Penguin Books USA Inc.

Agee, James. "Knoxville: Summer 1915" by James Agee, reprinted by permission of Grosset & Dunlap, Inc. from *A Death in the Family*, copyright © 1957 by The James Agee Trust, copyright renewed © 1985 by Mia Agee.

Baker, Russell. Reprinted from *Growing Up* by Russell Baker, © 1982. Used with permission of Congdon and Weed, Inc. and Contemporary Books, Chicago.

Ballou, Sullivan. Letter to Sarah Ballou. Courtesy of Adin Ballou Papers, Illinois State Historical Library, Springfield, Illinois.

Barth, John. "Teacher." Copyright © 1986 by John Barth, first published in *Harper's Magazine*, reprinted with the permission of Wylie, Aitken & Stone, Inc.

Baskin, John. Reprinted from *New Burlington: The Life and Death of an American Village*, by John Baskin, with the permission of W. W. Norton & Company, Inc. Copyright © 1976 by John Baskin.

Bernstein, David. "Mixed Like Me" by David Bernstein, copyright © 1994 by David Bernstein. Reprinted by permission of W. W. Norton & Company, Inc.

Beston, Henry. From *The Outermost House* by Henry Beston. Copyright 1928, 1949, © 1956 by Henry Beston. Copyright © 1977 by Elizabeth C. Beston. Reprinted by permission of Henry Holt and Co., Inc.

Bly, Carol. "Getting Tired" from *Letters from the Country*. Copyright © 1981 by Carol Bly. Reprinted by permission of Georges Borchardt, Inc. for the author.

Brodsky, Joseph. "In Praise of Boredom" from *On Grief and Reason: Essays* by Joseph Brodsky. Copyright © 1995 by Joseph Brodsky. Reprinted by permission of Farrar, Straus & Giroux, Inc.

Capote, Truman. "A Christmas Memory." From *Breakfast at Tiffany's* by Truman Capote. Copyright © 1956 by Truman Capote. Reprinted by permission of Random House, Inc.

Chase, Mary Ellen. Reprinted with the permission of Simon & Schuster from *A Goodly Fellowship* by Mary Ellen Chase. Copyright © 1939 by Mary Ellen Chase, renewed 1967 by Mary Ellen Chase.

Colon, Jesus. "Kipling and I." From *Puerto Rican in New York* by Jesus Colon. Reprinted by permission of International Publishers Co., Inc.

Conroy, Frank. "The Coldness of Public Places," from *Stop-Time* by Frank Conroy. Copyright © 1965, 1966, 1967 by Frank Conroy. Used by permission of Viking Penguin, a division of Penguin Books USA Inc.

Cowdry, Mary Boynton. From *The Checkered Years* by Mary Boynton Cowdry. The Caxton Printers, Ltd., Caldwell, Idaho. Reprinted by permission.

Cowles, Elizabeth B. "Where Is My Everything" from *Legacies* by Maury Leibovitz and Linda Solomon. Copyright © 1993 by The Jewish Association for Services for the Aged. Reprinted by permission of HarperCollins Publishers, Inc.

Dabney, Virginia Bell. "My Father the Stranger." © 1990 by Virginia Bell Dabney. From *Once There Was a Farm*, available in paperback, Ballantine Books. Reprinted by permission.

Dabney, Virginia Bell. "The Way It Was." From *Once There Was a Farm* by Virginia Bell Dabney. Copyright © 1990 by Virginia Bell Dabney. Reprinted by permission of Random House, Inc.

Darr, Ann. "The Women Who Flew—but Kept Silent." Copyright 1995 by Ann Darr. Reprinted from *The New York Times Magazine* by permission of the author.

Davis, Marilyn P. From *Mexican Voices/American Dreams*. Copyright © 1990 by Marilyn P. Davis. Reprinted by permission of Henry Holt and Co., Inc.

de Vinck, Christopher. "Father Time," *The Wall Street Journal*, June 17, 1994. Reprinted with permission of The Wall Street Journal. © 1994 Dow Jones & Company, Inc. All rights reserved.

Didion, Joan. "On the Morning After the Sixties" from *The White Album* by Joan Didion. Copyright © 1979 by Joan Didion. Reprinted by permission of Farrar, Straus, & Giroux, Inc.

Dillard, Annie. Excerpt from *An American Childhood* by Annie Dillard. Copyright © 1987 by Annie Dillard. Reprinted by permission of Harper-Collins Publishers, Inc.

Dillard, Annie. "Teaching a Stone a Talk" from *Teaching a Stone to Talk* by Annie Dillard. Copyright © 1982 by Annie Dillard. Reprinted by permission of HarperCollins Publishers, Inc.

Downing, Lucia B. "Teaching in the Little Red Schoolhouse," *Vermont Quarterly, A Magazine of History*, Vol. XIX, No. 4, October 1951. Reprinted by permission of the Vermont Historical Society.

Early, Gerald. From *Daughters: On Family and Fatherhood*, © 1994 by Gerald Early. Reprinted by permission of Addison-Wesley Publishing Company, Inc.

Eighner, Lars. "On Dumpster Diving" from *Travels with Lizbeth* by Lars Eighner. Copyright © 1993 by Lars Eighner. Reprinted by permission of St. Martin's Press, Inc. New York, NY.

Eiseley, Loren. "One Night's Dying." Reprinted with the permission of Scribner, a Division of Simon & Schuster, Inc. from *The Night Country* by Loren Eiseley. Copyright © 1971 Loren Eiseley.

Eiseley, Loren. Reprinted with the permission of Scribner, a Division of Simon & Schuster from *The Firmament of Time* by Loren Eiseley. Copyright © 1960 by Loren Eiseley, renewed 1988.

Elliott, Osborn. "Eyewitness" by Osborn Elliott as appeared in *Newsweek*, July 24, 1995. Reprinted by permission of the author.

Ellison, Ralph. From *Shadow and Act* by Ralph Ellison. Copyright © 1953, 1964 by Ralph Ellison. Reprinted by permission of Random House, Inc.

Franklin, Penelope. From "The Diary of Yvonne Blue" in *Private Pages, Diaries of American Women, 1830s–1970s*, edited by Penelope Franklin. (Ballantine Books, 1986). Reprinted by permission of the author.

Frazier, Ian. Excerpt from *Great Plains* by Ian Frazier. Copyright © 1989 by Ian Frazier. Reprinted by permission of Farrar, Straus & Giroux, Inc.

Gartner, Michael. "My Son, a gentle giant, dies" as appeared in USA *Today*, July 5, 1994. © 1994 Michael Gartner, used by permission.

Gates, Jr., Henry Louis. "Change of Life." From *Colored People* by Henry Louis Gates, Jr. Copyright © 1994 by Henry Louis Gates, Jr. Reprinted by permission of Alfred A. Knopf, Inc.

Glasgow, Ellen. Excerpts from *The Woman Within* by Ellen Glasgow, copyright 1954 and renewed 1982 by Harcourt Brace & Company, reprinted by permission of the publisher.

Hahn, Emily. "I Say This" from *The New Yorker*, July 31, 1995. Reprinted by permission; © 1995 Emily Hahn. Originally in *The New Yorker*. All rights reserved.

Hersey, John. From *Hiroshima* by John Hersey. Copyright 1946 and renewed 1974 by John Hersey. Reprinted by permission of Alfred A. Knopf, Inc. Originally appeared in *The New Yorker*.

Hirsch, James. "The Grammarian Who Lost a War of Words," *The Wall Street Journal*, December 29, 1994. Reprinted with permission of The Wall Street Journal. © 1995 Dow Jones & Company, Inc. All rights reserved.

Horgan, Paul. "L'Après-midi de Mary Garden" from *Encounters*, edited by Kai Erikson. Copyright © 1989 by Yale University. Reprinted by permission of Yale University Press.

Houston, Jeanne Wakatsuki and James D. Houston. Excerpts from *Farewell to Manzanar* by James D. Houston and Jeanne Wakatsuki Houston. Copyright © 1973 by James D. Houston. Reprinted by permission of Houghton Mifflin Co. All rights reserved.

Hurmence, Belinda. Excerpted from *My Folks Don't Want Me to Talk About Slavery* edited by Belinda Hurmence, published by John F. Blair, Publisher. Reprinted by permission.

Marshall, Kathryn. "Mary Stout." From *In the Combat Zone: Vivid Personal Recollections of the Vietnam War from the Women Who Served There* by Kathryn Marshall. Copyright © 1987 by Kathryn Marshall. By permission Little, Brown and Company.

McClane, Kenneth A. "A Death in the Family." Copyright © 1985 by the Antioch Review, Inc. First appeared in the *Antioch Review*, Vol. 43, No. 2 (Spring, 1985). Reprinted by permission of the Editors.

McInerney, Jay. "Raymond Carver, Mentor" originally titled "Raymond Carver: A Still, Small Voice" from *The New York Times*, August 6, 1989. Copyright © 1989 by The New York Times Company. Reprinted by permission.

McNulty, Faith. "Hurricane Thoughts" from *The Wildlife Stories of Faith McNulty* (Doubleday). © 1976 Faith McNulty. Originally in *The New Yorker*. All rights reserved. Reprinted by permission.

Mehta, Ved. "A Donkey in a World of Horses" by Ved Mehta. Copyright © 1978 by Ved Mehta, from *Face to Face* (Oxford University Press), reprinted with the permission of Wylie, Aitken & Stone, Inc.

Moody, Anne. From *Coming of Age in Mississippi* by Anne Moody. Copyright © 1968 by Anne Moody. Used by permission of Doubleday, a division of Bantam Doubleday Dell Publishing Group, Inc.

Morrison, Joan and Charlotte Fox Zabusky. "Elise Radell from Germany" from *American Mosaic* by Joan Morrison and Charlotte Fox Zabusky. Copyright © 1980, Joan Morrison and Charlotte Fox Zabusky. Currently available from the University of Pittsburgh Press. Reprinted by permission.

Morrison, Joan and Charlotte Fox Zabusky. "Katherine O'Hara from Ireland, 1930" from *American Mosaic*. Copyright © 1980, Joan Morrison and Charlotte Fox Zabusky. Currently available from the University of Pittsburgh Press. Reprinted by permission.

Munro, Eleanor. "On the Pilgrim's Path to Lourdes." Copyright © 1987 by Eleanor Munro. Reprinted by permission of Georges Borchardt, Inc. for the author.

Murie, Margaret E. "By Main Strength" from *Two in the Far North* by Margaret E. Murie. Reprinted by permission of Alaska Northwest Books.

Neihardt, John G. Reprinted from *Black Elk Speaks*, by John G. Neihardt, by permission of the University of Nebraska Press. Copyright 1932, 1959, 1972, by John G. Neihardt. Copyright © 1961 by the John G. Neihardt Trust.

O'Connor, Flannery. "The Total Effect and the Eighth Grade" from *Mystery and Manners* by Flannery O'Connor. Copyright © 1969 by the Estate of Mary Flannery O'Connor. Reprinted by permission of Farrar, Straus & Giroux, Inc.

Ozick, Cynthia. "The Seam of the Snail." From *Metaphor and Memory* by Cynthia Ozick. Copyright © 1989 by Cynthia Ozick. Reprinted by permission of Alfred A. Knopf, Inc.

Author-Title Index